AF844221

Gerard Brennan's Articles and Speeches

Maintaining the Law's Skeleton of Principle

VOLUME 2

Law in Accord with Justice

Father Frank Brennan SJ

EDITOR

Connor Court Publishing Pty Ltd

Published in 2025 by Connor Court Publishing Pty Ltd

Copyright © Fr Frank Brennan SJ

ALL RIGHTS RESERVED. This book contains material protected under International and Federal Copyright Laws and Treaties. Any unauthorised reprint or use of this material is prohibited. No part of this book may be reproduced or transmitted in any form or by any means, electronic or mechanical, including photocopying, recording, or by any information storage and retrieval system without express written permission from the publisher.

Connor Court Publishing Pty Ltd
PO Box 7257
Redland Bay QLD 4165
sales@connorcourt.com
www.connorcourt.com

NATIONAL LIBRARY OF AUSTRALIA

A catalogue record for this book is available from the National Library of Australia

ISBN: 9781923224698 (vol 1)
ISBN: 9781923224704 (vol 2)

Cover Design by Maria Giordano
Cover image: Gerard Brennan, Australian Catholic University Graduation, 2017.

Printed in Australia

Contents

15. Tributes to Gerard Brennan

Chapter 8

Enduring Community Values

8.1 Law, Ethics and Medicine

Editor's note

This is an extract from Brennan's 1977 Langford Oration delivered at the Annual Meeting of the College of Medical Administrators in Brisbane in October 1977.[1]

In the vortex of specialization, there is risk of forgetting that the layman whom each profession seeks to serve is not a loosely connected series of specialist interests, but an entirety. He will be served adequately only if the professions perceive that each specialty satisfies a part of the needs of man, but none satisfies the whole.

The divisions of knowledge and experience which are the domains of the respective professions are not bounded by lines drawn with a sharp precision. Each division shades into others, affecting them and being affected by them. The aggregate of professional skills and professional art is, as its human objectives dictate, an organic whole, and the effective functioning of its parts depends upon the synaptic reactions between them.

The notion of interdisciplinary studies and cooperation is not novel to the medical administrator. Modern medical teams bear testimony to the ability of one medical discipline to learn from, and work with the disciplines of, another. However, you may have to bear with us in other professions while we acquire the humility which is demanded when one profession learns from the science of another.

Recently, as a member of the Australian Law Reform Commission, I had the benefit of interdisciplinary consultations in the preparation of the Report on Human Tissue Transplants when difficult questions were raised: Was it necessary for the Attorney-General to refer the matter to the Commission? Why not leave well alone? Why should the law be concerned with transplants? These are perhaps the easiest of the questions which were raised. Others were more difficult: At what point in the continuum of degenerative change does death occur? Should an infant be allowed to donate non-regenerative tissue to a sibling? Should a parent be entitled to consent to the donation of non-regenerative tissue on behalf of an infant or a mentally defective child? The report lists other topics which are, or are about to be, thrown up for consideration: in-vitro fertilization of human ova, embryo transplants, transplants of fallopian tubes and ovaries, artificial insemination, transplants of foetal tissue, euthanasia and active assistance to die. And there are cognate problems of grave importance: the issue of criminal sanctions for abortion remains in controversy; the maintenance of bio-emporiums where the tissues of the dead may be harvested for use by the living has been canvassed; sterilization of the mentally retarded, and the surgical or chemical alteration of human personality are questions of controversial difficulty. Difficult though all of these questions may be, and worthy of discussion as they are, I do not attempt here a solution of any of them. I am concerned to inquire not what the answers should be, but rather how the answers should be sought. We are in common need of a methodology, and none is readily to hand.

The first observation that may be made about each of these questions is that the subject involves intervention by the medical profession. The second observation is that controversy or doubt exists whether the medical procedures which are involved ought to be performed; and that is a problem of legal concern or of ethical concern, or of legal and ethical concern.

The controversial questions would not have arisen, of course, if technology had not opened the way to novel procedures; nor if the community had a consensus as to the values which should be reflected in a common ethic or enforced by a universal law. But technology has burst upon the community when it lacks an adequate ethical matrix in which to receive it, and when the establishing of an ethical and legal consensus is far from achievement. How do we as a community find an answer to these questions?

If we adopt the usual patterns of problem-solving, we shall choose one of three models: we shall refer the questions to a Law Reform Commission, because the questions are thought possibly to require an answer in law; or we shall, without adequate prior inquiry, submit the questions to Parliament to debate and resolve; or we shall leave the questions to the consciences of the individual medical practitioners aided by the uncoordinated advice proffered from time to time by professional associations and, occasionally, by the churches.

The solution of the Law Reform Commission

A lawyer is ordinarily concerned with the application of the law to concrete cases. Frequently, since the law is one of the tools of his trade, the public attributes to the lawyer a function of making or reforming the law. Sometimes, the lawyer is at risk of overreaching himself by assuming a function to reform any law, irrespective of the subject matter with which the law deals. True, there are some areas of the law where the technical skills of the lawyer are sufficient to dictate the amendments which should be made to improve the law's operation. There are other areas of the law where the skills of the lawyer are not required, except to express in legal terms the judgment which is made by the community or is approved by its Parliament as to what the law should be. In areas of vital concern to the community, law reform, as has often been said, is too important to be left to lawyers.

We are here concerned with questions to the solution of which the professional skills of the lawyer make no contribution. The lawyer possesses no deeper knowledge of the technology involved, or of the values which should be adopted, than most other members of the medical profession's laity. He does have a view to contribute as to whether, if a particular procedure is rejected as wrong or inappropriate, it should be proscribed by law.

There are, and there will continue to be, many shades of professional legal opinion as to the extent to which the law should go in seeking to enforce the tenets of a moral code, but there would be general agreement that the law should extend to protecting a person who would otherwise suffer harm. The difficulty about applying this general principle arises because one must decide when a person comes into and goes out of existence, and one must decide what is the kind of harm against which a person should be protected. These are not issues to be' remitted to a lawyer's decision. They are issues for a wider wisdom and a deeper experience than a lawyer is required to muster.

Although lawyers or Law Reform Commissions usefully lend legal skills to the reform of laws of social importance, I suggest it is inappropriate, if not worse, to require them to expound solutions to questions which lie outside their technical competence. They are not, and are not trained to be, the ethical conscience of the community. There are occasions when lawyers may foster discussion on a subject which is ripe for reform, and may invite the periti in a discipline to expound their special knowledge. The Australian Law Reform Commission has, I think, been especially useful in this kind of interdisciplinary seminar. But at the end, the Commission has no special competence to make ethical judgments of the kind which we are now considering.

The solution of Parliament

Confidence in the parliamentary process is essential to the ordering of the economic and political welfare of society; but the parliamentary process is not designed to examine problems of the complexity we are now considering, to elicit the facts, and to arrive at a decision after quiet and deep consideration. The Parliament is entitled to look to the community and to the professions for guidance in the exercise of its legislative powers. Parliament is entitled to have guidance not only as to the ethical judgments which should be made but also as to the desirability of translating any of those judgments into law. If the community should arrive at a consensus with respect to these questions, and if it should be thought desirable to entrench that consensus in law, the interposition of parliament is, of course, essential. But parliamentary debate and majority vote is not the way to establish an informed consensus on these questions, much less to give an assurance of right moral judgment.

The solution of individual conscience

A comparison between law and ethics may tempt one to say that law is coercive, and ethics are a matter of choice. In truth, the reality is the other way round. Both are concerned with human conduct. Law seeks to mould human conduct to its precepts by providing a system of sanctions. It wears the aspect of coercion. But it succeeds only to the extent to which men decide for themselves to conform to the legal precepts. In an ultimate sense, it is the individual human conscience which dictates whether a law is breached or not. Law is variable in effectiveness; conscience has a much more predictable outcome. The forming of conscience is far more influential in determining the quality of the community's life than the laying down of law. Indeed, the declaration of the law and its subsequent enforcement are but some of the influences which go to mould the attitudes and the consciences of the community.

The questions with which we are concerned involve moral judgments of the most fundamental kind-when human personality begins and how life may be brought into existence, the balancing of the interests of one life against the interests of another, the measures to prolong or to shorten life, when life ends and the use of the body after death. There are no more fundamental moral questions than these.

To characterize these questions as moral questions is to say, of course, that they are the concern of conscience. But they are more than a matter for the conscience of an individual. In the context of the medical team, there is a need to ensure that the consciences of the members of the team are satisfied with the morality of the procedure. The surgeon or team leader may be the medical director of the team, but he may not demand the loyalty of another's genuinely anguished conscience. Let me take an example. The Australian Law Reform Commission recommendations would hold a person to be dead if there is an irreversible cessation of the functions of the brain, whether or not the ventilator is still switched on. The body may be breathing and the heart may be beating, but the person is to be treated as dead, and his kidneys (subject to the conditions applicable to cadaver donations) are available for transplant. Are the nurses in the donor's ward satisfied in conscience to take the donor to the theatre and attend his ventilated body in order to assist the transplant team? Or to vary the example, is the transplant team obliged to respect the conscience of one who insists that the ventilator should be disconnected and the donor's heart should stop before the kidneys are removed?

In cases where team work is involved, the medical administrator cannot avoid the need for achieving a consensus; he cannot avoid the questions by leaving the answers to the conscience of the individual. In the medical team, the team conscience will form and will be formed by the consciences of the members. Each will contribute the wisdom of his judgment, and a consensus will be the precondition of successful team therapy.

Nor can one avoid the need to provide institutional policies in response to these questions. Patients and their relatives are entitled to know whether the institution has a policy with reference to the treatment in which they have an interest. Such a policy is not defined by the several. and possibly diverse, opinions of the individual staff members.

Nor can one avoid the need to seek a community consensus upon the answers to these questions. The questions have wide ramifications: the laws of inheritance, assault, negligence, and homicide may require adjustment according to the answers given; the funding of research programs, the support of institutions, the payment for health care, and for pathology services are involved. But, most importantly, these basic ethical questions affect the community's appreciation of its own role in relation to the life of its members and its future generations. Without a consensus upon the answers, the division of the community, a division not merely in belief, but in the action that implements belief tends to its own destruction.

There is no present unanimity with respect to the answers to these questions. The existing law-making institutions are not appropriate to devise the answers. Indeed, to provide laws in advance of the moral judgments which the laws should reflect is to build an edifice on shifting sands.

The solution to the problem of methodology is not easy to devise, but whatever solution is chosen it must satisfy two criteria. First, as the questions are fundamental ones which affect life itself, the solving of them is not the narrow concern of any one profession or, indeed, of the professions alone. They are so fundamental that only a broad community consensus will provide the kind of solutions with which the community can be satisfied. Second, as they are so fundamental, the knowledge and wisdom which is sought for their solution should be evoked from the many disciplines which can contribute.

Though the process be long, unstructured, and unproductive of early results, it may be that the establishment of groups, which I would call Life Ethics Groups, to study and discuss and disseminate ideas upon these questions may ultimately provide the only kind of answer which will be useful and, it is to be hoped, right. The groups should, I suggest, be sponsored by those upon whom the problems raised by the questions bite most deeply- the medical administrators.

Though sponsored by the administrators, the active and equal contributions of other professions must be obtained: the theologians and the lawyers, the psychologists and social workers and counsellors, the nurses and the medical scientists of all these and any others who have knowledge to contribute or interest to stimulate. The answers will require a combination of spiritual insight, of human understanding, of technical competence, of legal analysis, of sociological judgment and, not least, of community acceptance. No method other than the slow growth of a widely based consensus is possible; no other method will suffice. We may, in the process, not merely learn from one another, but we may learn more of the objects of our service – man and the community in which he lives. We may make a single contribution to the understanding of issues that without consensus will tend to disrupt the basic order of our society.

These are tasks fit for the modern professional people who pride themselves on responding to the awesome challenges of our time.

---

1. This extract was first published in (1978) 2 (13) *Medical Journal of Australia*, 577.

8.2 Law and Professional Standards

Editor's note

Brennan delivered this address to the ACT Branch of the Australian Medical Association on 13 July 1981.

I speak to you tonight about the standards of your profession with qualifications that may seem to be derived from others: I am honoured to be the son in law, husband, the father and the father in law of medical practitioners, but I confess that I should be quite unlikely to identify a femur if it were separated from a complete skeleton, and I tend to associate ganglia with invaders from outer space. Let me say however that, true to the traditions of my profession, I have in my day exchanged medical profundities with eminent specialists – witnesses who were giving the courts the benefit of their immense knowledge and experience, while my instant expertise was hurriedly gleaned from a textbook on the night before. I pass over the outcome of these unequal contests!

But I do not presume to speak about matters of medical technique. Rather I wish to reflect in general terms upon how the law affects the medical profession, and in particular whether it may serve to determine the profession's standards and to assure the profession's standing. It is a paradox that law is powerful to affect a profession in some respects, yet it is powerless in others. This is not due to a need to reform the positive law (though there is room for change in that; it is due to the essential difference between law and professional standards, and to the inability of law to infuse the members of a profession with attitudes which earn respect for an entire profession.

Sometimes we speak – that is, doctors, lawyers, engineers, scientists, and the rest – we speak of our respective professions as though membership of a profession were to be likened to membership of an exclusive and commodious club. In truth, a profession is quite different. Its essence was stated by Sir Owen Dixon, perhaps the greatest Australian jurist and a former Chief Justice of the High Court of Australia. He said: 'It is the essence of a profession that its members master and practise an art. The art must depend on a special branch of organized knowledge and be indispensable to the progress or maintenance of society, and the skill and knowledge of the profession must be available to the service of the state or the community.'[1]

Sir Owen's statement focusses upon three matters: knowledge, an art which is necessary for society, and service to the state or the community. How aptly it describes the medical profession! The orientation of the statement is outwards, for society's need for expertise, and the availability of that expertise to the state or the community, are essential to confer the character of a profession. And here one may perceive the limits of the laws power.

How can a law define the standards of professional expertise which ought to be manifested in answer to society's needs? How can a law measure the service which ought to be given by a profession to the state or the community? All that law can do is to prescribe the consequences of failure, to manifest some minimum standard of expertise, and to require some minimum standard of service in exchange for the remuneration or other benefit which is allowed to members of the profession. The legal threshold standards are not sufficient to earn the status and title of a profession. A profession earns its status by adopting and adhering to standards of its own devising, and the mere observance of legal requirements is insufficient for the purpose. The reason is not hard to perceive.

The service of others is an essential aspect of every profession, and the status of a profession is accorded by the judgment of its laity. The profession is responsible to the laity which it serves. It is they who judge how well or ill we perform: whether we are mere tradesmen or whether we strive to do better in their interest; whether we seek membership of a profession for the returns we can obtain therefrom or whether we are moved primarily to give service. And over the years the laity judge wisely. They give little credit to a profession which does no more than its legal duty; which barely meets the threshold standards of skill and knowledge, and which makes its services available only to those who are legally entitled to them and only to the extent of that legal entitlement. A laity expects more of a profession than the discharge of a legal duty. The status of a profession, and the respect accorded to its members, depend largely upon the extent to which professional standards exceed the legal minima.

Law is an important but blunt tool which we use in fashioning the society we desire. True, it provides a system of incentives and disincentives for conduct and it prescribes rules to govern rights to property, but its remedies in these fields of the law are restricted typically to the payment of money, the transfer of property or, in extreme cases, the loss of liberty. A relationship between one person and another which can be formed or rectified by these means is no more than a business or commercial connection, falling far short of the relationship of a doctor with his patient. It is that relationship, I suggest, and not the law which ought to determine the standards of the profession as a caring profession. I shall mention later the standards of the profession when it is engaged in assessing the rights of others -the judicial function of the medical profession but that function has been engrafted on to a profession which sees itself and is seen to be a caring profession. The central feature of the caring profession is its relationship with the patient.

The doctor-patient relationship is not, of course, the only milieu of medical service or patient care, but it is the paradigm and it governs the profession's other aspects and activities. That relationship is largely beyond the reach of legal control, and so it must remain. At its best, that relationship has elements of devotion to the patient's needs, high art and skill, and respect for the dignity of the patient on the one hand; trust, co-operation, and respect for the expertise of the doctor on the other; and a mutual personal regard which frequently leads on to friendship and affection. It is a rich and often complex relationship, and it would be wrong to suppose that the law could, much less should, form or regulate such a relationship.

Consider briefly these elements. First, the doctor's devotion to the patient's needs. To the extent to which an individual doctor is able to answer that need, so will his professional reputation grow; to the extent to which the profession answers those needs, so will its status be enhanced. I would not suggest, much less endeavour to define, the function of the medical profession or of any branch of it in participating in the particular systems of health care which are introduced from time to time. What I am concerned to say is that the laws which govern the extent of a doctor's duty to render service, or which regulate his remuneration or other entitlements for doing so, do not define the necessary or desirable limits of a doctor's service. His service is evoked more by the need of the patient or the community than by the legal definition of a doctor's obligation. The standards of devotion to a patient's needs are imposed by professional tradition and by the opinion of a doctor's peers.

Similarly, the legal minimum of skill, knowledge and attention which is demanded by the law of negligence is wholly insufficient to satisfy a doctor's self-esteem, much less to satisfy the expectations of patient or community. The concern of the professional bodies with post-graduate training, in-service training and the sponsoring of lectures by eminent scientists and practitioners has been a commendable feature of medical life in this country. Those programs would not be maintained if it were not for a widespread desire to improve standards of patient care by the exercise of the skills and arts of medicine at a level beyond the legally exacted minimum. I wonder, however, whether your profession is impeded – as our profession sometimes is – by too great a separation between town and gown, between the practitioners on the one hand and the academic and research workers on the other. All have the same objective: the care of the patient, and the closest co-operation can only be in the patient's interest. The patient, let it be remembered, is the *raison d'etre* of the profession. May I, in passing, confess to a respectful astonishment at the ability of doctors to profit from the enormous volume of glossy literature with which medical suppliers fill the letter boxes of the profession.

The third element is respect for the dignity of the patient. A patient is not a loosely connected series of specialist interests, but an entirety. Each of us can best serve another by recognizing that we cannot serve all his needs, but only those which lie within our special area of expertise. And if we employ all our professional skills and arts, we shall serve only part of the person in our care. This sense of perspective seems to me to be important in a variety of ways.

It suggests that communication should be fostered between doctor and patient, as it should be between other professions and their clients, in order to assure the patient that he is not a mere object upon which medical skills are being employed, but a person to whom medical service is being rendered. No doubt the extent of the communication varies from case to case, but in principle communication should be encouraged. It is not merely a matter of allaying a patient's fear by explaining to him the details of the treatment or procedures to be undertaken. It is a matter of allowing the patient access to the information which he needs to have in order that he can adjust his life, outlook and affairs to the treatment or procedures proposed and, particularly in the terminal stages, to put his eternal as well as his temporal affairs in order. Of course, every profession tends to see its patient or client as a manifestation of the particular problem with which he presents. It is a useful shorthand for your profession to speak of a patient as a fractured tibia or an appendectomy, and for my profession to speak of a break and enter or a breach of trust. But the shorthand should not be allowed to obscure the reality of the person who is the object of our professional concern and who has a variety of interests and outlooks, and for whom the particular professional problem is but one of the elements in the complex of his life.

At one time, the notion of respect for the dignity of the patient was simply understood, and it governed the kind and extent of treatment which was administered. It is no longer a simple concept. Basically, the notion of a patient's dignity reflects the notion we have of the importance of human life, the solutions to human suffering, the adjustment of the interests of one person with those of another. In short, it reflects our philosophy or, if you will, our morality. And that is clouded in uncertainty.

What treatment or procedure is to be adopted, what research is to be done to develop new treatments and procedures, and what funding should be made available to carry them out are questions which are important to a caring profession; and the answers to some of these questions are now uncertain because there is uncertainty as to the meaning of the dignity of the patient.

When I was a member of the Law Reform Commission, we grappled with the problems of organ and tissue transplants, and we touched upon some problems which it was not then necessary to resolve: euthanasia, genetic engineering, in vitro fertilization and foetal tissue transplants. We heard of suggestions of bio-emporia where bodies could be maintained from which tissue could be harvested as needed. The Report showed a divergence of opinion about allowing infants to donate non-regenerative tissue to a sibling.[2] We encountered problems which require the wisdom of many disciplines for their solution. Ultimately, perhaps, it may prove possible to define a consensus in terms of a positive law, if the theologians and medical scientists, lawyers and psychologists, social workers, nurses and administrators, all who have insights to contribute, are able to reach a consensus and have it accepted by the community.

These problems are not merely medical problems, nor are they merely ethical problems. They are problems which concern a much wider area of a patient's interests than a particular medical condition and the community as a whole may have a concern in the solution adopted.

The difficulty for the medical profession is that they presently bear the responsibility for treatment, and they are administering treatment according to differing notions of what the dignity of the patient demands, and they are without the assurance and support either of positive law or of community consensus. For my part, I should hope that the healing hand of medicine does not try to remake creation, or to eliminate immediate suffering at the cost of consequences which cannot be foreseen or evaluated. I came recently upon a quotation from C S Lewis:

> We must get rid of (organic life). By little and little, of course; slowly we learn how. Learn to make our brains live with less and less body: learn to build our bodies directly with chemicals, no longer have to stuff them full of dead brutes and weeds. Learn how to reproduce ourselves without copulation...
>
> You would understand if you were peasants. Who would try to work with stallions and bulls? No, no; we want geldings and oxen. There will never be peace and order and discipline so long as there is sex. When man has thrown it away, then he will become finally governable.[3]

Some disorder is of the nature of human existence, whether we speak of medical conditions, the organization of society, or the seasons. Perhaps there is a deeper order which underlies it all, but we do not see it. However that may be, the caring profession is currently without legal guidance as to its discretion in many areas of new expertise, and it will have to fix its standards in these areas in consultation with other disciplines.

The final element of the doctor patient relationship to which I would refer is the friendship. It is not necessary to dwell on the friendships which so frequently develop between doctor and patient. These must be some of the great rewards of medical practice. But they are more. They assure the profession of its status, which depends not upon the law but upon the esteem of those whom it serves. Absent that esteem, and legal support will prove of little comfort. Upon that esteem, and not upon compliance with legal duties, the standing and reputation of the caring profession depends.

Now I should like to add a little upon the judicial aspect of the medical profession. Because the medical profession has insisted upon its independence and because of the great esteem in which its members are held, it has been understandable that governments have reposed in qualified medical practitioners functions of certification which partake of judicial functions rather than medical. The administration of a complex of legislative provisions – workers compensation, accident compensation, superannuation and pensions – has relied upon the medical profession to say whether a person should or should not have the benefits for which this legislation provides. In some ways the burden has been unfairly placed. In one of A P Herbert's *Misleading Cases* he wrote –

> The doctor, so far as I know, is not better qualified to exercise judicial functions than the banker, the business man, the civil servant, landowner, soldier, sailor, or schoolmaster. Indeed, a priori, much as I admire the medical profession, there are good reasons for thinking the contrary.
>
> Once my dear doctor has pronounced that I have mumps or whooping-cough I have mumps or whooping-cough. A 'second opinion' may ultimately show that I have, in fact, some glandular affection or tropical disease. But the taking of a 'second opinion', as you know, is a rare proceeding, only consented to in cases of exceptional doubt or difficulty. This apparent self-confidence is without doubt a valuable part of the technique of the medical world, where the patient's belief in the infallibility of his adviser is often an essential contributor to his recovery.
>
> But in the legal profession we do not pretend to be quite so clever. The splendid pyramid of our appeal tribunals has been erected upon the generous assumption that the judge and the lawyer are as liable to error as those whom they advise or condemn.[4]

In practical terms, one can readily understand why the doctor is being asked to certify and why his certificate is brought under challenge on review. But when these new functions of the welfare state fall to be discharged by doctors it is desirable that our two professions should move in harness together. The lawyers, for their part, must respect the opinions of the doctors honestly expressed; and the doctors, for their part, must appreciate that thoroughness of examination and integrity of judgment is an entire safeguard against embarrassment.

The frequent and increasing contact between our two professions will remove, I hope, both the apprehension and the misunderstanding of the judicial process, though it is clear that a composition of methodologies is essential. The inductive, sometimes intuitive, method of the medical profession is suspected by the lawyer – not, I think, because lawyers have found doctors to be inefficient but because we find that the intuitive method in legal research has led us often and disastrously to error and confusion.

---

1. Sir Owen Dixon, 'The Profession of Accountancy' in *Jesting Pilate*, 3rd edition, The Federation Press, 2019, 279.
2. Australian Law Reform Commission, Report No 7, *Human Tissue Transplants*, AGPS, November 1977.
3. C.S. Lewis, *That Hideous Strength,* The Bodley Head, London, 1945, p. 211.
4. A P Herbert, '*Tristram v the Moon Life Assurance Company*', *Uncommon Law*, Methuen & Co, London, 6th edition, 1948, 261 at 262-3.

8.3 Evil in Man

Editor's note

Brennan presented this address at the 4th Austral-Asian Pacific Forensic Sciences Congress on 'Evil in Man', organised by the Australian Academy of Forensic Sciences and the World Psychiatric Association (WPA). Brennan delivered the address at the Sydney Opera House on 26 August 1982.[1]

The papers to be delivered at this Conference address a number of aspects of evil. No doubt some definitions of evil will be offered. However, I suspect that no definition is universally satisfying. Even if it were possible to devise a definition of evil upon which all men might agree, there would be no universal agreement as to the 'phenomena of life' which would fall within its terms. Yet evil is one of the constant and common ideas of all men in all ages.

How is evil to be recognized if no universal denotation, valid for all men in all circumstances, can be stated? For those who believe in God, evil and sin may be coterminous; for those who do not share that belief, evil is identified in some other way. But whether evil be identified by religious faith or by another illumination, the basic notion of what is evil is deeply personal: evil is recognized, experienced, avoided or diminished by each of us in his own way. Our several ideas of what is evil owe much, of course, to the culture in which we live, to the media and to those individuals whose ideas form our cultural ambience: family, peer group, associates, teachers, clergy, authors, artists and the rest.

There are times in history when there is a wide and firm consensus as to what is evil and what is good; and other times when the consensus is less general and less sure. The consensus of earlier times has now ceased to command general assent. I do not pause to examine the reasons why. I wish rather to ascertain the significance of 'the frailty of such consensus as remains for the law and its administration. The change from consensus to uncertainty in moral values has left many floundering in their own thoughts, unresolved as to the path which they should follow. Indeed, what was once widely regarded as evil now sometimes appears to many to be good—a wicked masquerading of evil, in the view of the earlier majority; a revelation of truth, in the view of the modern cognoscenti. Dietrich Bonhoeffer wrote in 1942 in an environment where moral values seemed to be turned upside down: 'The great masquerade of evil has played havoc with all our ethical concepts. For evil to appear disguised as light, charity, historical necessity, or social justice is quite bewildering to anyone brought up on our traditional ethical concepts, while for the Christian who bases his life on the Bible it merely confirms the fundamental wickedness of evil .'[2]

When values are turned upside down in a short time, there are important implications for the community: the generation gap becomes wider and family life more stressful, institutions lose popular support, political and religious adherences fall away or shift, and human relationships more frequently evoke tolerance rather than trust. There is no purpose to be served by shutting one's eyes to the shifts which have taken place, and which are still taking place, in moral values. As those values shift, evil is perceived in altered ways and the law must change to cope with new perceptions. But how should it change? The question evokes consideration of the relationship between evil and the law. But not every kind of evil, for there are some kinds of evils which man is powerless to affect. We are concerned here with those kinds of evils which are amenable to influence by law, more particularly by the criminal law.

Evil. And the Law. Two subjects which, in conjunction, take on the appearance of a compound of negatives – a denial of good and a sanction for wrongdoing. We shan't get very far forward by considering negative conceptions. Let us start, then, by considering the purpose which these conceptions may serve. I suggest that the purpose is the well-being or, if you will, the welfare of mankind. That is the purpose to which both morality and law are directed. I do not suggest, of course, that mankind is the measure of all moral systems, so that evil has only an anthropomorphitic significance. But it is generally true to say that systems of morality are oriented to identifying and achieving the well-being of mankind. The law has the same orientation. A system of law in a democratic society cannot be supported unless one of its chief purposes is the maintaining and perhaps the improving of the well-being of mankind.

There is no conflict in purpose between morality and law. Both operate in a social milieu, both affect relationships among members of a society, both must take account of human nature, and, in the long run, both must accord with the well-being of mankind. What tends to achieve that well-being is good; it ought not to be forbidden by law. What tends to deny that well-being is evil; it ought not to be encouraged by law. A law is bad which forbids what is good or encourages what is evil. Yet it does not follow that the law should encourage what is good or forbid what is evil. Law should not oppose morality, for they share a common purpose, yet it does not follow that law should enforce every moral precept.

The ways in which law and morality achieve the well-being of mankind are different, even where there is no opposition between the content of the law and accepted morality. The law's encouragement or prohibition consists in the awarding of benefits or penalties by the state's coercive powers. Criminal law, which takes evil as its especial concern, imposes punishment on those whom it characterises as evil-doers. Punishment is not, of course, a matter for voluntary acceptance; it is immaterial that the offender does not acknowledge his liability to be punished. Morality, on the other hand, is a matter of conscience.[3] Though morality has no immediate sanctions save those we impose upon ourselves, morality is more efficient than law in the moulding of human conduct, more ennobling of the human spirit, more demanding in its precepts.

A moral imperative operates with no sanction other than its acceptance by conscience, yet it is effective to govern conduct and the actor conforms with the moral principle accepted by him. In a contest between conscience and the law, conscience will seldom yield.[4] In a settled society, contests between conscience and the law are few, and so the law is observed not so much because it is efficiently enforced, but because it corresponds with the moral sense of the community. In such a society, law does not seek to override conscience; it is the auxiliary of conscience.

Morality is more ennobling of the human spirit than law, for law is put in motion by those who would compel another to conform to its tenets and external compulsion is placed upon the party liable to perform; morality acts upon the consciences of those who accept obligations binding on them. Morality is not primarily concerned with the enforcement of one's own rights, but with the discharge of one's own obligations, of which others may be the beneficiaries. A person seeking to enforce his right's or to impose a penalty on another does something less ennobling than discharging an obligation resting on himself. From society's viewpoint, legal proceedings to enforce the fasciculus of rights to which each of us is entitled are inefficient; if our rights were put to the test in every case, the lawsuits would be legion. Social relationships within the framework of the law are maintained chiefly because our shared morality leads each of us to discharge our obligations to others, and legal proceedings in occasional cases merely reinforce that shared morality. The virtue of doing our duty, including our legal duty, is the true lubricant of social relationships.

When morality and law cover the same kind of conduct, morality is more demanding than the law. We acknowledge moral obligations—of honour, of courtesy, of friendship, of love—which far transcend the legal obligations which bind us. The honouring of obligations thus goes further than the performance of legal obligations in advancing the well-being of our fellow-men.

It is both inevitable and desirable that the precepts of the criminal law should fall short of the precepts of morality. There is necessarily an area of moral precept upon which that law ought not to enter, even if it were practicable to do so. The area upon which criminal law does not enter is the area of a society's freedom. Freedom, essential alike to the flowering of the human spirit and to the practice of virtue, must be respected by the law: unduly to limit freedom is to deny what is essential to the well-being of men. But it would be a mistake so to extend the area of freedom and so to confine the operation of the law that the cohesion of society, its culture and its commitment to an irreducible minimum of common values are put in jeopardy.[5]

Law is essential to maintain the cohesion of a society. Morality without law does not suffice. Without law, anarchy would make short work of a society's culture and common values. The pressures of lawlessness on the part of the minority would make it impossible for the majority to live together in the harmony of common understanding. To the extent to which the law is enforced, it affords the cohesion which society requires, assuring each member of that society that he may build his relationships with others upon the understanding that their conduct will conform to the legal norm.[6] A society is stable when there is a common and realized expectation that the law will be observed by others, and there is a minimum level of expectation below which society becomes fragmented or dissolves.

The law, binding together the disparate elements in a society, has another role to perform. Giving its protection equally to all, the law is especially important to those who have no other protection, to those whose infirmity—whether by reason of years, health, poverty, race, sex or creed—exposes them to the risk of being overborne. By giving equal protection to all, law defines and limits the power of one man to his interests at the expense of another.

There is an inevitable tension between the desirability of leaving an extensive area of legal freedom and the desirability of buttressing the stability of society and the protection of its members. What areas of activity should be governed by law and what should be left free is necessarily a matter of imprecision and dispute. For present purposes it is sufficient to note that large areas of activity must be governed, and effectively governed, by law to preserve the stability of society and the protection of its members.

To govern effectively, however, law requires the support of a moral consensus, a coincidence between the legal precept and an accepted moral value to which it gives expression, between a moral precept and its legal analogue: 'Thou shalt not kill' and the crime of murder, for example. By applying a moral precept, evil is recognized; by applying the law, the power of the state is lent to the suppression of that evil. It is hard to overstate the importance of the recognition of evil to the maintenance of the rule of law. Indeed, without the recognition of evil, the maintenance of the rule of law would be dubious, and the enforcement of the rule of law would be adventitious.

Law and the recognition of evil

Sometimes it is said that law exceeds its function if it seeks to enforce morals. This statement is made usually in reference to what is called private morality, particularly the morality of sexual relations. Of course, morality comprehends a much wider area of human conduct, and it is plainly wrong to say that law should not seek to enforce any norms which moral judgment holds to be good or virtuous. Law cannot provide stability to a society or protection to its members unless a commonly or widely shared morality supports the chief precepts of the law. The maintenance of the rule of law depends upon the moral sense of the society in condemning as evil what the law and its agencies of enforcement set out to suppress.

The consternation excited by evil is a most powerful aid in the apprehension and prosecution of a malefactor, sometimes so powerful as to make difficult the securing of a fair trial. A kidnapper or a rapist of a frail and lonely woman can expect little comfort in his flight from apprehension and little mercy from a jury when he is brought to book. It is necessary to take care to ensure that a blackmailer or a big-time heroin pusher, whose crime is revolting to the common sense of decency, is fairly tried. Law enforcement agencies depend upon the community's sense of evil, for the support given to law enforcement is proportionate to the strength of the community's moral condemnation of the malefactor. Absent the condemnation of evil, and law enforcement has neither sympathy nor support; indeed, law enforcement then tends to alienate the members of society from the agencies of enforcement and to make more difficult the prosecution of offenders whose only offence is to break the mere husk of the law — a law emptied of the kernel of recognition of evil.

Let me take an old and uncontroversial example. In this country, we are familiar with the stories of prosecutions for 'poddy dodging': the offence of stealing unbranded calves or yearlings. It is notorious that in many country circuits jurors would not convict even in the clearest cases. No evil was seen in taking another's cattle when fences were often down or herds which suffered depredation belonged to those who were thought well able to bear the loss.

Take a more recent example which has enlivened public comment. There has been a remarkable recognition by the community of the evil of tax evasion. It was not always so. Not very long ago, the tax evader was perceived to be a kind of Robin Hood whom it would be almost churlish – and certainly unsporting – to pursue. Perhaps it was the realization that the Sherwood Forest of tax evasion was over-populated which led to the now widespread condemnation of the practice. The enforcement of the law in this area of financial activity has been facilitated by the development of a general recognition of the evil of tax evasion.

The recognition of evil is essential also to the judicial process. A judge who is required to exercise a discretion in imposing a sentence is guided by his assessment of evil – a moral judgment – rather than by a legal precept.[7] If the relevant legal precepts define merely the maximum sentence which the judge may impose and the salient factors which he must consider (prevalence of the offence, age of the offender, etc), the way in which he quantifies the punishment to be imposed depends upon his appreciation of the moral standards of the community and the community's view as to the gravity of the conduct to be punished.[8]

It makes nonsense of the administration of criminal justice to say that the law should not enforce morals; that is what the criminal law is about. It is about the suppression of what is recognized as evil. The legitimate area of controversy is not whether the law should enforce morals; the legitimate area of controversy is as to the morals to be enforced.[9] The effective enforcement of the criminal law requires the recognition of the evil it sets out to suppress. There are, however, some cases where the evil is ascertainable by the majority of the community only by reference to the law itself, as distinct from those cases where the law expresses a particular concrete standard by reference to which specific conduct may be judged.[10]

Law as a definition of evil

In some cases, the only general moral consensus is that some law is needed to regulate a particular matter, in order to eliminate unacceptable confusion. A simple instance is provided by the rules of the road. The driver who fails to yield right of way to another driver is likely to excite the latter into a fervent condemnation of his conduct, of himself and even of his parentage. Yet if the give way rule had not been promulgated, neither driver would have been morally guilty merely by proceeding.

Apart from laws which are merely regulatory, there are some laws where the moral precept to which effect is given is not perceived except as inhering in the law itself. An illustration is provided by laws regulating some kinds of financial transactions. A wide moral consensus about some kinds of financial transactions is not possible – they are too complex and, when corporations are involved, the transactions may take on the artificiality of the person involved. The laws which regulate those transactions take on the character of a moral precept – in default of any other. Thus, s 129 of the *Companies Act 1981* (Cth) which, speaking generally, prohibits a company from giving financial assistance in connection with the purchase of its own shares may be conducive to financial probity, but at least some familiarity with corporate financing is required in order to appreciate the moral value to which the section is intended to give effect.[11]

To equate morality with lawfulness is to leave the law without antecedent support; and also to damage morality. If a particular act is permitted by such a law, it is assumed to be morally good; whereas evil is to be recognized only by a final judgment pronounced by a Court of Appeal after litigation. Where there is no antecedent recognition of evil, and the law itself becomes the only recognised criterion of what is good and what is bad, moral judgments become an exercise in legal interpretation. The lawyer becomes the moral counsellor, and takes away from his client the responsibility for forming a moral judgment. Moral accountability is diminished and the standard of conduct is unlikely to be improved beyond the point fixed by the law-maker and effectively enforced by appropriate agencies. Law, which does not aspire to induce moral perfection, sees its standard taken for the ideal. There is no need or occasion to aspire to any higher morality.

The need to make new laws to fill a gap in a moral consensus must nevertheless be acknowledged, albeit sparingly. It is desirable only when the content of the proposed law is morally indifferent – a right of way rule, for example – and the law is needed merely to bring order into what would otherwise be unacceptable confusion. But it is regrettable if a law which is not morally indifferent is introduced to regulate conduct upon which no moral consensus has developed where the development of a consensus is possible. Not only will the law tend to stultify the development of a consensus; when the law comes into force it commands no support of moral opinion and its enforcement depends rather upon the diligence of supervising agencies than upon the conscientious adherence of those who are bound to obey it. Coercion by the State, not assent to its terms, is the means and measure of its operation.

A law which begins its work without support from a moral consensus is unlikely to command general assent if it relates to a topic upon which the ordinary man and woman is equipped to form an opinion; and if it were able to command general assent, that assent would be likely to be at so rudimentary a level that it would debase, not elevate, the ultimate moral consensus.

Law is an ineffective means of forming a moral consensus, but it is a powerful means of maintaining a consensus once formed. That is not merely because the coercive power of the State is directed to suppressing what the existing consensus recognizes as evil; it is because a sense of obligation to obey the law is added to the law's expression of the values of society, so that an individual who contemplates contravention of the law knows that he must either put himself at odds with the rest of society or take an initiative to persuade society that the value expressed by the law should be changed. Of course, if the consensus upon the values expressed by the law changes, so ultimately must the law change – though it is a question as to how far it may lag behind. It is precisely because a new idea, however valid, does not overthrow a law before there is a consensus for change that the law functions as an agent of social cohesion. A law which suppresses an evil acknowledged as such today, will continue to suppress that evil tomorrow though the supporting moral precept may be under revision, and it will continue to suppress it, with decreasing efficiency, as the moral precept is revised until what was once acknowledged as an evil is no longer so regarded. And then the law is spent.

The recognition of evil is an essential condition for the making of a new law for its suppression, and the derecognition of evil is an essential condition for the repealing of an old law when suppression is no longer appropriate. But law is not itself an appropriate or desirable means of defining evil; law is itself dependent upon society's recognition of the evil it seeks to suppress. To rely on law as the means of identifying a moral precept is to acknowledge that society either does not have the information or lacks the moral sense to define a moral precept governing the issue in hand. The priority both in time and in importance of moral over legal precepts has some profound implications for a rapidly changing society.

When a society undergoes a radical alteration in its moral values in a short time, the law too must change, but the rate of change and the criteria for change become questions of central importance. There is a limit to a society's tolerance both of anachronistic laws and of rapid institutional change. When a new law is called for, there is a need to ensure that, if the existing enforcement agencies – whose authority is generally recognized – are appropriate agencies to enforce the new law, their personnel are trained for their new duties, or, if a new enforcement agency is required, that the administrative steps are taken for its creation. Administrative considerations, as well as the definition of new precepts, affect the rate of institutional change effected by new laws. Old laws can be repealed so soon as the supporting consensus requires. But administrative considerations are of minor significance. The major question is the ascertainment of the criteria for change, and they must be ascertained according to whether the problem under consideration is a new problem which is thought to require legal suppression or regulation or whether it is a problem which is already the subject of legal suppression or regulation.

The distinction is of some significance at present when new technology has thrown up novel moral problems and perhaps new problems for the law.

We are currently experiencing the pain, not to say the tragedy, of gaps in our moral consensus upon issues of transcendental importance relating to the beginning of human life, to the creation of future generations. Developments in technology have given rise to problems upon which no moral consensus has been formed and upon which no full moral consensus is likely to be formed for some time to come: sperm and ova banks, in vitro fertilization, surrogate motherhood, genetic engineering, human cloning, and the transplantation of foetal material and organs harvested from cadavers maintained on respirators. These are new problems upon which, sooner or later, society generally will and must make moral judgments. At the moment, these are problems which divide moral opinion and about which information has been lacking. So long as technology bounds ahead of the community's ability or willingness to form a moral judgment, there will be an increasing number of critical moral issues upon which no consensus is reached. Some will see the developments to be evil; by other eyes, they will be seen to be good. What is to be done?

To form an adequate moral opinion upon any of these great issues we need to know the relevant facts and their significant implications. A judgment which condemns them as evil without this knowledge is itself erroneous; equally a judgment which affirms their moral goodness. We, as a society, know something of the state of technology which throws up these problems, though we know little as to the implications of that technology or the direction in which that technology is advancing. We, as a laity, should not remit to those who know more than we do the function of defining a moral precept to be generally accepted. On issues of such grave importance for the well-being of future generations, we cannot leave only to those with a special knowledge, and perhaps with a special interest, the function of deciding what the moral and the legal precepts should be.

Somehow we have failed to ensure that we know what our scientists are doing, and we have given little attention to the moral implications of scientific research. The mere acquisition of knowledge or the mere development of new techniques has been isolated from the moral implications of applying that knowledge or using that technique.

It is of the first importance that the public be informed of what research scientists are doing and what the foreseeable implications of their work may be. I wonder whether it would be practicable to seek scientific impact statements. Would they impermissibly infringe scientific freedom, or would they be an appropriate means of ensuring that the first person to consider the moral implications of a piece of research is the scientist who is engaged in it?

I confess that I am concerned by the suggestions of some scientists engaged in these fields, and others besides, who look to the law to provide guidelines for the application of new reproductive technology beyond the point of a moral consensus. I wonder whether the limits of efficacy of the law are realized: the law's dependence upon an antecedent moral consensus, its need to have the assent of those who are governed (not merely guided) by its precepts, the provision for its enforcement by external and impartial agencies. Of course, consensus may grow piecemeal and thus provide a foundation for laws affecting a part of the field which is expected to be covered by legal regulation at some future time. There may even be a consensus to maintain the status quo temporarily until new problems are explored. Whether the law should remain silent awaiting the development of a consensus, with all the risks of aberrancy which that may entail, or whether it should seek to prohibit conduct which gives rise to the problem until a further consensus develops is a matter for prudent choice. The law cannot, even if it would, stop the dynamics of change (I forbear from using pejorative terms such as 'progress' or 'the widening of knowledge' which, assuming what the moral consensus will be, relegate the law to the role of Mother Grundy, looking askance at every novel development).

But take surrogate motherhood, for example. Is it best for the time being to leave existing laws unamended in the expectation that the rights and obligations of a woman who accepts the fertilized ovum of another can be governed by the terms of a contract made before she became pregnant? Is it desired that the ordinary principles of a contract law should be made effective to bind her to give up the child whom she has sustained during the period of gestation when it is born? Or should a court, in the exercise of jurisdiction over infants, decide Who should have custody of the baby? Or is a new law needed which would affirm the rights of the surrogate mother and deny to the donors of the fertilized ovum possession of a child whose life they first created? Or, again, is the prospect of tragedy and anguish so apparent that at this stage the practice should be forbidden?

Each new moral problem requires separate analysis. Blanket decisions on all new questions of bioethics cannot be made. Developments in a moral consensus on a particular problem may support a law as to that problem, but the law may need to be amended from time to time to reflect the changes in consensus as more knowledge is acquired or more implications perceived.

Only when there is a moral consensus upon a problem should a decision be made as to whether there should be a law and as to What it should be. That is not a decision to be taken according to the opinions only of concerned scientists, professional technicians or of Law Reform Commissions. Why? Because the basic question is not what law would be thought by experts to be beneficial, but what is the moral consensus? To answer that question, the informed opinions of many disciplines must be sought, and each professional group must be stimulated into discussion of the issues: theologians and moral philosophers, social workers and psychologists, lawyers and administrators and that handful of invaluable thinkers who are effective in stimulating us, as a community, to think about the consequences of our actions and attitudes. All of those, in short, who are able to recognize good and evil in a technological setting. Of course, scientists, technicians and Law Reform Commissions may provide the stimulus for discussion but they cannot limit the time which the community may take to develop a consensus.

Not all our moral problems are the consequences of new technology. Some arise because the traditional identification of evil is being questioned or denied by a proportion of society. The clearest example is euthanasia; it is thought by some no longer to be a moral evil. Again, what is the law to do? Leave the existing prohibition intact, modify it or remove it? Here we are concerned not only with the cohesive purpose of the law, but with its protective function also. The termination of human life raises issues which are not present in problems concerning its beginning. When a society identifies as evil the causing or accelerating of another's death and invokes a law to suppress it, the suppression of the evil binds all within that society, and the society is presumptively committed to preserve the law, not only to protect the aged or sick who may be better protected by it, but to preserve the society's estimate of the worth of human life. To preserve, if you wish, a moral precept of society which is regarded as important to its cultural unity. It is only when a new consensus has emerged and the once-recognized evil suppressed by the law is no longer generally regarded as evil that repeal is warranted.[12] The thesis is simple and consistent: law should follow the recognition or derecognition of evil; only in that way can the law perform its function of providing coherence to a society. If the law precedes the development of a moral consensus – whether in respect of the recognition or derecognition of evil – it prejudges and perhaps stultifies the growth of the developing consensus, and the law may then be a focal point of division within, and not the cement of, society.

The reference to euthanasia invites reference to the distinction between suffering and evil; between the fact or phenomenon of suffering, and the responsibility for another's suffering or one's reaction to it. Law cannot suppress suffering – it would be a mistake to regard law as having a capacity to do so – but it can suppress evil. Suffering is a part of the human condition – sometimes it can be, or appear to be, destructive; sometimes it gives birth to joy, to love, to strength and courage, to fellowship and holiness. Law is irrelevant to the alleviation of one's own suffering, unless one chooses to alleviate it by inflicting suffering on another. What the law is concerned to do is to affect the conduct bearing upon the suffering of another. The law is at one with morality in condemning an act done in order to cause suffering to another and, in some cases, in condemning an omission to act to prevent or alleviate the suffering of another.

The legal duty to alleviate suffering is limited, however, to certain relationships and to certain measures. There is no legal duty imposed upon all members of society to succour the poor, to nurture the sick, to clothe the naked, to feed the hungry, to visit prisoners, to befriend the lonely, to love one's neighbour. The alleviation of suffering depends more on the discharge of moral obligations than the observance of the law. In so far as evil consists in a failure to respond to suffering, the law makes only modest efforts to suppress it. But the law stands fast in rejecting one solution to human suffering. It prohibits the elimination of suffering by eliminating the sufferer. To take the life of a person suffering keeps us free from the sight of his suffering and relieves us of responsibility to help the suffered, but it could not be justified without proof that the sufferer would be better off dead. Upon what grounds could such a judgment be made? Man knows nothing of what death means to the dead, of 'the undiscovered country from whose bourn no traveller returns'.[13] Though the law forbids the elimination of the sufferer, it makes few demands upon individuals to alleviate suffering. Caring institutions are created, but the law is not able to alleviate much of the suffering we see, particularly the suffering of a man alone and isolated.

Law can take us only so far along the road to a warm and humane society. In part, the law must stop before it reaches the end of the road because some members of society will not make the journey any further, and law must stop when society would otherwise break up. So far as we will go together, the law binds us, but for the rest of the journey those who would make it are on their own, voluntarily improving the well-being of mankind: the neighbours who chat over the back fence, the voluntary welfare societies, the churches, the trusted professionals and the countless people who find a fulfilment of themselves in caring for others. Love, the true alleviation of suffering, is not amenable to the prescript of the law.

Instead, we place our trust oftentimes in the creation of new legal rights as though the law's recognition of those rights will necessarily improve the well-being of mankind. The movement towards enhancing rights is valid only so long as the corresponding liabilities are acceptable and accepted – not only by others, but by ourselves. The contemporary rhetoric of rights is of limited use unless the corresponding obligations are accepted: not only imposed, but accepted. Their imposition is the function of law, but the acceptance of obligations is the stuff of morality.

I have wandered away from evil to speak about the role of the law in alleviating suffering, that is, in doing good. But it is all of a piece. The well-being of mankind depends upon the moral consensus of the society in which man lives: assured where the moral consensus is good, damaged where the moral consensus is evil. Given a good moral consensus, legal and moral obligations will be discharged to the benefit of all, society will be stable, evil will be recognized and law will be effective to suppress it. If the good moral consensus abates, evil will be less clearly recognized and the law will be less effective in suppressing it for, in the long run, law cannot exceed in ambit the fundamental moral consensus of society. The utility of the law in the suppression of evil, in cementing society and protecting its members is thus a function of the society's moral consensus.

Evil will prosper, uninhibited by law, so long as there is no common recognition of it; it will be suppressed by common sentiment to which the law may lend its potent aid. The well-being of mankind depends in the last analysis not on the law but on a morality common to their society. The notion is well stated by Lord Devlin in these terms:

> . . . without shared ideas on politics, morals, and ethics no society can exist. Each one of us has ideas about what is good and what is evil; they cannot be kept private from the society in which we live. If men and women try to create a society in which there is no fundamental agreement about good and evil they will fail; if, having based it on common agreement, the agreement goes, the society will disintegrate. For society is not something that is kept together physically; it is held by the invisible bonds of common thought. If the bonds were too far relaxed the members would drift apart. A common morality is part of the bondage. The bondage is part of the price of society; and mankind, which needs society, must pay its price.[14]

---

1. This address was published in (1982) 15 (1) *Australian Journal of Forensic Sciences* 4-16.
2. Cited by R C Zaehner, 'The Wickedness of Evil' (1974) (42) *Encounter* 50.
3. Cf Norman St John-Stevas, *Life, Death and the Law* (Eyre & Spottiswoode, 1961) 14.

4. See R Dworkin, 'Taking Rights Seriously' in AWB Simpson (ed), *Oxford Essays in Jurisprudence, Second Series* (Clarendon Press, 1973) 205.
5. See Peter Stein and John Shand, *Legal Values in Western Society* (Edinburgh University Press, 1974) Chapter 6: 'Personal Freedom'.
6. See AM Honore, 'Groups. Laws, and Obedience' in AWB Simpson (ed), *Oxford Essays in Jurisprudence, Second Series* (Clarendon Press, 1973)
7. But see Professor HLA Hart's discussion in *Punishment and Responsibility* (Clarendon Press, 1968) 169 of Sir James Fitzjames Stephen's dictum that 'the sentence of the law is to the moral sentiment of the public what a seal is to hot wax'.
8. Though the 'tariff' is a moderating influence: see David Thomas and Sir Leon Radzinowicz, *Principles of Sentencing* (Heineman Educational, 2nd ed, 1979) 8.
9. The famous controversy between Lord Devlin and Professor Hart: see Lord Devlin, *The Enforcement of Morals* (Oxford University Press, 1965), and HLA Hart, *Law, Liberty and Morality* (Oxford University Press, 1963). For commentaries, see Dr John Bray, 'Law, Liberty and Morality' (1971) 45 *Australian Law Journal* 452; Basil Mitchell, *Law, Morality, and Religion in a Secular Society* (Oxford University Press, London, 1970).
10. As to the latter function of law, see J Raz, 'On the Functions of Law' in AWB Simpson (ed), *Oxford Essays in Jurisprudence, Second Series* (Clarendon Press, 1973) 281.
11. See *Re VGM Holdings Ltd.* [1942] Ch 235, 239.
12. This approach maximises the law's cohesive power. In the divisions appropriate to the Devlin-Hart controversy, I suspect it is an approach which would commend itself more to the 'conservatives' whose 'favourite freefloating evil is drastic cultural change as such', according to Joel Feinberg, 'Legal Moralism and Freefloating Evils'. (1980) 61 *Pacific Philosophical Quarterly*, 122, 153.
13. See *McKay v. Essex Area Health Authority* (1982) 2 WLR 890, the 'Wrongful Life Case per (Stephenson LJ, 903), (Ackner LJ, 910), (Griffith LJ, 913).
14. Devlin, *The Enforcement of Morals* (Oxford University Press, 1965) 10.

8.4 Commercial Law and Morality

Editor's note

Brennan delivered this address at the dinner at the conclusion of a seminar on Commercial Law and Morality convened by Professor Michael Crommelin at the University of Melbourne on 10 November 1988.[1]

When Professor Crommelin did me the honour of inviting me to attend this dinner at the end of a seminar on 'Commercial Law and Morality', I accepted with alacrity. I thought that it would be a comforting experience to be among those professional colleagues whose presence testified to their commitment to morality. In the event, the experience has been far more rewarding. It has furnished a stimulating review of the proper role of law and of lawyers in commercial transactions. For me, Professor Finn's paper was an additional bonus. He illuminated what has been going on around me for eight years past! It is the role of the academic profession to be, in a sense, a final court of appeal – to examine the principles which judges state or imply, to identify other relevant principles and to evaluate critically the solutions adopted by the court. That is a demanding role which calls for familiarity with the literature in foreign as well as domestic jurisdictions, incisive and dispassionate analysis and an ability to place the law in its social context. We are indebted to Professor Finn for the stimulus of a paper of great intellectual sweep and vigour which, standing back from the workface of individual cases, essayed a description of the paths of legal development. If I do not agree with all that Professor Finn has said, I respectfully acknowledge the force of the argument he presents.

I have come to repent my joyful acceptance of Professor Crommelin's invitation. At the time, the juxtaposition of the topics 'commercial law' and 'morality' had the charm of novelty but as the need to say something about their connection approached, the complexity of the problems inherent in the joint topics has become more manifest and the prospect of propounding a solution has become more elusive. At the outset, let me confess my remoteness from the topic. I last practised at the Bar in commercial law matters in 1976, and the intervening decade has seen not only a growth in commercial law but a transformation in the way in which it is practised. In the intervening years, the glimpses of the real world to be had from a judicial Arcady have been fleeting and fragmentary. As to morality, no doubt each of us treasures his or her own visions of the moral imperatives binding on everyone else whilst, for ourselves, we earnestly pray the prayer which St Augustine prayed in resisting conversion from the profligate life: 'Not yet, 0 Lord, not yet!' Without propounding a precise theory of morality for application to commercial law, I do not doubt that there is a moral standard to be observed. It would be too cynical to accept the truth of George Essex Evans' 'Ode to the Philistines':

> Six days shalt thou swindle and lie!
> On the seventh – tho it soundeth odd –
> In the odour of sanctity
> Thou shalt offer the Lord, thy God,
> A threepenny bit, a doze, a start, and an unctuous smile,
> And a hurried prayer to prosper another six days of guile.

I must undertake the task assigned, attributing to commercial law and to morality such content as my imperfect understanding will permit.

In many areas, law and morality work in a symbiotic relationship. This is especially true of the general criminal law, which would hardly be enforceable if the common moral values of the community were at odds with the law's proscriptions. In tort also, a close relationship of law and morality can be perceived. As Professor Finn observed, 'Moral values. . . can and manifestly do inform the law'. I respectfully agree, though it is desirable that the dichotomy between law and morals be borne steadily in mind in determining the content of each. Law which is the subject of our professional concern does not mirror all the tenets of morality. Nor should it try to do so. The coercive power of the State must be reserved to the enforcement of those moral principles which, by a broad community consensus, enjoy recognition and acceptance and which need to be expressed as universal binding rules in order to facilitate a peaceful, ordered, just but free society.

The stimulus which moral values provide in the development of legal principle is hard to overstate, though the importance of the moral matrix to the development of judge-made law is seldom acknowledged. Sometimes the impact of the moral matrix is obvious, as when notions of unconscionability determine a case. More often the influence of common moral values goes unremarked. But whence does the law derive its concepts of reasonable care, of a duty to speak, of the scope of constructive trusts – to name but a few examples – save from moral values translated into legal precepts? How often do we see the construction of a statute turn on an intention of the legislature imputed by reference to a moral value?

There is room for debate about the method of legal development at the hands of the judges. The role of precedent, the need for certainty, the desirability of judicial reform by piecemeal development in cases arising almost adventitiously, candid recognition of the role of policy in legal development, simplification of legal principle – these are the heady topics about which the tide of debate rises and eddies under the influence of moral values pressing for legal recognition. The call for judge-made law increases as Parliamentary inclination to keep the law in good condition diminishes. There are some areas of the law which will never be swept by the statutory broom, and judicial refurbishment offers the only prospect for keeping these areas in a satisfactory condition.

As legal transactions become more complex, the input of morality – or policy, for in this context the terms are interchangeable – will increase inevitably, for morality furnishes the reference points for legal development. There are manifest dangers, of course, and I would mention two:

1. The danger that a judge might mistake his or her own moral predilections for the moral imperatives which, by broad consensus, enjoy recognition and acceptance; and
2. The danger that orderly legal development will be imperilled by the piecemeal dismantling of old principles without substitution of a new coherent body of doctrine.

Acknowledging the dangers, the development of legal rules is nevertheless a necessity. There are but three possible sources of any proposition which is employed to determine a case once the facts are found: legal rules, morality or idiosyncrasy. If legal principle is not sufficiently precise to determine the result, morality or idiosyncrasy will make up the deficit. Better that new and precise legal rules be informed by morality than that morality and idiosyncrasy vie for supremacy in a succession of ad hoc contests. Whether the development of the law is in the direction of new legal rules or of broadening and loosening existing rules, morality has a part to play.

Before morality can be employed by judges to inform legal principle, the particular moral imperative must exhibit certain characteristics. I have already mentioned one characteristic: a broad consensus for recognition and acceptance. Such an imperative is easily translated into a legal precept for it represents a common community value. Law, the binding cement of society, simply adds the coercive powers of the State to the value which the community has accepted. And thus, the crimes which stir the community to moral outrage become the more heinous crimes in the calendar. At the discretionary level, we may note that the heaviest penalties are imposed when the moral sense of the community is most deeply offended.

The second characteristic of moral imperatives which inform the law is that they relate – for the most part – to personal morality. By that I mean the kind of ethical standards by which people live in their personal, as distinct from their public, lives. These are familiar standards. We do not deliberately set out to inflict physical harm on our neighbour or to damage his land or his possessions; when we foresee that harm or damage might happen, we take care to avoid causing it; we do not try to deceive or defraud people with whom we deal; we do not engage in calumny or detraction of another. These ethical standards are the stuff of the law of torts. Equally with the criminal law: murder, rape, offences against the person, larceny. There are few crimes which have what might be called a public element in them. The chief exceptions, I suppose, would be treason, sedition, perversion of the course of justice and conspiracy to corrupt public morals (if *Shaw* v *Director of Public Prosecutions*[2] is good law in this country). By referring to standards of personal morality, I do not mean to imply that personal morality is, or ought to be seen as, private morality in which the public can have no interest. Perhaps there is no area of morality more personal than that which affects consensual sexual relations, yet the public interest in the health consequences of sexual activity is manifest. In one sense, I suppose all morality is a matter of profound public interest for the strength of a nation cannot survive the moral decadence of its people. But the point of present relevance is that public interest is seldom an element in the immediate circumstances which give rise to the moral standards which are translated into law.

The moral standards of personal life apply, generally speaking, to situations where the consequences of their non-observance are immediate or are clearly foreseeable by the person who engages in the forbidden conduct. This is reflected in judge-made law. Liability will be imposed on a landholder who allows water to escape onto and damage his neighbour's land, but the law is much slower in devising a remedy for farmers at the mouth of a river whose irrigation supply is contaminated by the use by upstream farmers of agricultural chemicals.

In the general law which is informed by moral imperatives those imperatives can be identified: general recognition and acceptance, applicability of the standard to one's own conduct in personal living and immediacy or foreseeability of the consequences of non-observance. These three characteristics facilitate the translation of a moral imperative into legal precept. Absent any of these characteristics and the difficulties of translation are increased. Commercial law, particularly the law relating to corporations, is not able to draw to the same extent as some other branches of law upon the support of moral imperatives which exhibit these characteristics. This is not a defect of commercial law; rather it is a lacuna in the development of moral imperatives. Why is this? Many problems of commercial law relate to the exercise of intangible legal rights. There is not, and perhaps there cannot be, a broad consensus on the morality of acquiring or exercising intangible legal rights. Their variety and the differing circumstances in which they arise and in which they operate preclude reliance on any generally accepted standard to govern their creation or their exercise. Similarly, there is no relevant moral imperative relating to the use of financial power. Since the mediaeval abhorrence of usury has been replaced by a search for maximal return on investment, there is no general moral objection to a person laying out his own money in whatever way he chooses. Yet much of the law of commerce has to do with the acquisition and exercise of abstract legal rights and of financial strength.

Next, the morality of many commercial activities depends on considerations much more complex than those which govern personal morality. The rules about a company giving assistance in the purchase of its own shares which in my day used to be found in s 67 but which I now find in s 129 of the *Companies Code* in a more complex and qualified form, do not reflect a canon of personal morality. Indeed, for those who never lift, pierce or rend the corporate veil, the rules may appear to run counter to the company's moral freedom to spend its money on whatever it chooses. Perhaps sub-s (10) reflects the appropriate limits of moral freedom. Of course, if laissez faire or deregulation were the overwhelming philosophy of commercial law, it would not be necessary to retain the mass of positive laws which have become familiar to commercial lawyers of modem times. That is a consummation which, I understand, Mr Morgan holds to be desirable. Yet, as Mr Walsh reminded us, some laws have been found to be necessary in order to protect interests which might be overreached by those for whom the call of morality is but distantly heard. Presumably the reason why statutory commercial law has become so voluminous and complex is because commercial relationships are so complex that proper regulation is impossible if it be left to simple drafting expanded by judicial invocation of recognized and accepted moral standards. Section 52 of the *Trade Practices Act 1974* (Cth) is an obvious exception.

In company law, the interests of company, company officers and employees, directors, shareholders, creditors, suppliers and customers are often interdependent and there may be little or no connection between the person whose conduct is regulated or prohibited and the class of persons whose interests are to be protected. It is difficult in such a situation for those who are not familiar with the consequences of the conduct to perceive the moral value which underlies the statute. Generally accepted moral values cannot hope to equal in sophistication, much less to inform, the complex of modem commercial laws. There is a great shortfall between the furthest point to which generally accepted personal morality goes and the ultimate reach of commercial law, and that shortfall raises problems of unique difficulty for the practitioner of commercial law. The law abhors a moral vacuum, not only because society treats with indifference the enforcement of laws which have no recognizable moral purpose but also because the reference points for statutory construction are missing. The natural inclination of mind is to find a moral purpose for the law to fulfil – a moral end or policy of the law – and to predicate of Parliament an intention to achieve that purpose.

In a mass of regulatory provisions, the obstacles in a search for the law's moral purpose resemble those encountered in a maze. Contradictory signposts are seen on the way, theories which lead promisingly in one direction will be blocked by the intransigence of an unsuspected subsection. Yet the search must yield a solution and the moral purpose must be revealed for acceptance by those who practise in that field. In other words, although the complexity of much commercial law hides the underlying moral purpose so that that purpose is not immediately revealed by reference to the community's general set of personal moral values, the commercial lawyer must search for the moral purpose by ascertaining the operation of the law he or she practises.

It is not a light burden. Study is required to gain an insight of the purpose which the law is intended to serve. Let me remind those of you to whom the provisions of the *Companies (Acquisition of Shares) Code* have become thoroughly familiar that, on first reading, the purpose of the several provisions of the Code were – and to me still are – far from self-evident. Once the operation of a law is ascertained, the discovery of its moral purpose depends ultimately on perceiving the moral value which the operation is apt to serve. Candour, equitable treatment of a class, the securing to a class of the benefit of assets which in justice belong to them may be seen to be the moral purpose of the law - values which are not found in the words of the statute but which, to the professional eye, explain and inform the statutory text.

The hidden morality of much of the commercial law and the traditional role of the lawyer as the adviser on law alone raises peculiar difficulties for the commercial lawyer.

Because the moral purpose of much commercial law is known to or ascertainable by commercial lawyers alone, the commercial lawyer becomes by default the moral as well as the legal adviser of the client. There is nobody else to be the moral adviser. The role sits somewhat uneasily on a lawyer's shoulders. Yet it must be accepted if professional advice is to avoid the reproach of being the solvent of the client's moral responsibility.

How often does one hear the financial journalist who, seeking to embarrass a captain of commerce, is met with the disarming response: 'We took the best advice and what we did is entirely lawful'. Yet legality and morality are not interchangeable terms and both are appropriate fields for advice by the well-furnished commercial lawyer. Take as an example, the debt defeasance transactions to which Mr Justice Marks referred. If the client is advised merely that such a transaction is legally valid, he may fail to consider whether it is morally objectionable.

In a case where the underlying moral purpose of the law on which advice is sought is not and perhaps cannot be perceived by the client unless the lawyer tells him, the commercial lawyer's duty cannot be restricted to legal advice, for then the moral decision – what ought to be done as distinct from what can lawfully be done – will not be addressed. If the lawyer alone knows the moral dimension of the decision to be made, it is morally unacceptable for him to be silent. If he perceives that it is within the client's legal power to impair the rights of a third party whom the legislature has ineffectually tried to protect or to exercise that legal power in a way which is unjust, surely the moral dimension must be pointed out. But the moral decision is not for the lawyer to make: that decision is for the client. But what if the client chooses to disregard the moral dimension? Is the lawyer under an obligation to carry the decision into execution? This is a question which must be left to the ethics committees of the professional associations to answer but it is a fundamental ethical problem: should a lawyer do for a client what he would not do as a person? It seems to me that the problem does not admit of a simple solution and that much depends on the nature of the transaction, the extent of the lawyer's participation and the moral issue involved. But there are some relevant propositions about which there can be little doubt.

There is a temptation for a lawyer advising in a commercial transaction, as there is for lawyers in other fields, to identify closely with the interests of the client. This temptation is enhanced, of course, by the offer of services additional to the strictly legal services of advice, documentation and representation in legal proceedings. If the lawyer offers commercial or accounting advice or undertakes the negotiation of the transaction, he not only steps outside the bounds of strictly legal professional duty; he also tends to identify himself with the interests his client is pursuing. This has two consequences. One, the lawyer bridges that remoteness from the client which is the safeguard of independence. It is difficult enough to advise a client about the legal and moral implications of a transaction in order that the client may make an informed decision. It is more difficult to assure the client of independence when additional services are offered and where the acceptance of the offer redounds to the financial advantage of the lawyer. Next, if the transaction may disadvantage third parties and its morality (as distinct from its legality) is open to question, can it be right for the lawyer to participate beyond the giving of legal and moral advice and the rendering of strictly professional services? A good case can be made for the duty of a lawyer to render strictly professional services to a client who seeks to take full advantage of the law. It is strongly arguable – I need not conclude – that a lawyer should not discharge himself from his retainer merely because his client refuses to take his moral advice. But if the client insists on extra-professional services, perhaps because they have usually been provided, what justification can the lawyer offer to himself for rendering those services in a cause of questionable morality?

If there be one thing more important than another in the conduct of any branch of the legal profession it is preservation by the lawyer of his self-esteem. A lawyer who leaves the moral decisions to the client but then seeks to justify extra-professional activity as though he were simply performing his legal professional obligation will lose his self-esteem. Losing that, he loses not only his capacity to render a professional service of the quality to which his clients are entitled; he forfeits his own entitlement to membership of an honourable profession.

The practice of commercial law offers a great challenge to lawyers of ability and integrity. An understanding of commercial law requires technical skills of a high order and a sensitivity to the subtle influence of morality on the interpretation and development of that law. A duty of moral advice is often added to the duty of providing legal services, and ethical questions of nicety must be addressed. So long as the commercial branch of the profession sees itself as independent, competent and acting with a moral integrity that will not be compromised, it will continue to contribute greatly to the commercial life of this country. This Seminar is splendid evidence of a profession – academic, practising and judicial – which is alive to its responsibilities and which has resolved to discharge them. We are all indebted to the Melbourne University Law School Foundation for assembling us to consider the purpose of morality and the purpose of law in commercial transactions. The purpose of one is justice; the purpose of the other is justice according to law. The purposes are not coincident, but they are not opposed.

---

1. The address is published in the *Melbourne University Law Review*: Sir Gerard Brennan, 'Commercial Law and Morality' (1989) 17 (1) *Melbourne University Law Review* 100.
2. [1962] AC 220.

8.5 A Critique of Criticism

Editor's note

Brennan delivered this address at the annual dinner of the Monash University Law Review on 30 August 1992.[1]

Now that the last formal links with the Privy Council have been severed and we perceive more clearly the distinctive character of Australian law, we are conscious that Australian parliaments and courts bear the responsibility for its development. You who are entering the legal profession come to it at a critical stage in the development of Australian law. You face the challenge and the excitement of moulding a legal system to serve a free and diverse Australian community. A University Law Review can perform a significant role in that development.

Tonight, I should like to say something about the role of a University Law Review in the judicial development of the law. But, in order to do that, I must first say something about the judicial method of legal development. Some years ago, the accepted rhetoric of judicial method was based on Sir Owen Dixon's 'strict and complete legalism'. The method, as he explained it, proceeded 'upon the assumption that the law provides a body of doctrine which governs the decision of a given case'.[2] Sir Owen Dixon accepted the development of the law from a base of long-accepted legal principle but not the rejection of an accepted rule which was unjust in its operation. The assumption of a universally available body of legal doctrine buttressed the authority of the courts, for their judgments were taken to be the articulation by judicial oracles of principles which were already in existence though awaiting formal declaration. The assumption served the courts well. Respect for the law, as Lord Radcliffe pointed out, is 'the greater, the more imperceptible its development'.[3] But the assumption could not be sustained. Lord Reid said it was a fairytale that courts do not make law but only declare it.[4] The demonstrable fact was that there were cases where the existing body of legal principle provided ,little or no guidance to the solution of a justiciable issue.[5] And there were many other cases where the governing principle was ascertained by an uncertain analogy or treated as obsolete in order to avoid injustice. The rhetoric based on strict and complete legalism masked the truth of the judicial method.

Once the assumption of a universally available body of legal principle was abandoned, the very existence of a disciplined judicial method came into question. Superficiality and cynicism, those twin purveyors of popular fallacies, combined to assert an even more unlikely theory than strict and complete legalism. They propounded the theory that judges applied their private values idiosyncratically, disguising them with a patina of legal reasoning. Law, far from being a normative guide to decision-making, was treated as a collection of empty formulae – shibboleths to be invoked by a judiciary bent on the implementation of their private value systems.

The truth is different. In ascertaining the rule by which to decide a case, a judge must start with the existing body of law. There is no other starting point. The existing body of law is the intellectual matrix in which judges have lived their professional lives. Their work in courts structured hierarchically requires the acceptance of the doctrine of precedent. Precedent shapes judicial thinking: it prescribes the frames of reference. It is nonsensical to speak of legal argument without reference to the existing body of law and it is by reference to that body of law that decisions must be not only made but justified. It would be impossible for a judge to implement private value systems while paying consistent lip-service, but no real obedience, to the existing body of law.

But that is not to say that, in the higher appellate courts, there is no room for choice of the relevant legal rule. The existing body of law may yield no relevant legal rule or, in rare cases, may yield a legal rule which is offensive to basic contemporary conceptions of justice. Then the existing body of law must be examined to discover the principles that underlie particular rules and, ultimately, the enduring community values that underlie the principles. This is no idiosyncratic exercise. Scholarship and experience must be employed in order to identify the principles and purpose of the law and the values which it implements. If an existing rule is to be modified or a new rule declared, analogy derived from existing principles is the primary source. Moreover, the modified or new rule must be articulated as an integer of the existing body of law, interlocking with related rules. The consistency of the law is achieved by developing rules consistent with the existing body of legal principles and, except in rare cases, with the values that underlie them. There is room for divergence of opinion in this exercise, but not for unstructured idiosyncrasy. Divergence of opinion may come in the identification of the principles and purpose of the law and, infrequently, in the identification of enduring community values. If the judicial method were idiosyncratic, ephemeral political, social and economic values would predominate – as they do in the political branches of government – and legal development would depend on its pragmatic acceptability to the majority. Judges do not approach their function in that way.

The judicial method is rigorous and, with the acknowledgment that the courts make law, I venture to suggest that it has become more patently rigorous. The reasons for judgment in the higher appellate courts increasingly look behind the legal rule to discover the informing legal principle and behind the informing legal principle to discover the basic value. Legal development then proceeds in the reverse order: provided the basic value is consistent with the enduring values of the contemporary community, the informing legal principle is stated in terms which are consistent with other legal principles and the legal rule is stated in terms interlocking with related legal rules. If you ask, from what does a judge discover the enduring values of the contemporary community, the answer, given by Justice Cardozo, is 'from experience and study and reflection; in brief, from life itself'.[6] But the judge's legislative power is hedged about with restrictions. In modifying a rule or declaring a new rule, the judge is not free to innovate at pleasure. Cardozo said, in a well known description of the judicial method, that the judge is 'to exercise a discretion informed by tradition, methodized by analogy, disciplined by system, and subordinated to "the primordial necessity of order in the social life". Wide enough in all conscience is the field of discretion that remains.'[7]

It is the function of the academic profession and, in particular, of University Law Reviews to supervise the modern development of Australian law. But that must be done with an understanding of what is involved in judicial development of the law.

In the first place, the reviewer must put a newly propounded legal rule in its context. As judicial development of the law would fail if novel rules were derived simply from a judge's private set of social values, the reviewer must enquire whether a particular legal development is an organic growth, deriving its sustaining sap from the vine of existing law to which it must be grafted. Attached to that vine, a new growth in the law can be developed and sustained; detached from that vine, a new growth has no support save the opinion of the judge who called it forth. And so the first evaluation of a novel legal development calls for an appreciation of the way in which it fits into the existing body of the law and reacts with other legal rules.

Next, the newly propounded legal rule must be assessed for its utility or convenience. How does it operate? Is it generally conducive to justice and efficiency in the cases to which it is expressed to be applicable? This enquiry admits of differing answers if the underlying principle is controversial. Regrettably, this criterion of assessment is frequently misunderstood. A new legal rule is often assessed simply according to the reviewer's opinion of the merits of the case. The result of a case is of critical importance to the litigants but, to the reviewer, it is the legal rule, stated in universal terms, that is the proper focus of attention. The question must be whether that rule has the tendency to do justice and to do it efficiently. Of course, the result in the particular case is one illustration of the operation of the rule, but it is the operation of the rule, not the merits of the particular case, which is of importance to the legal critic. A review which fails to identify the ratio decidendi but criticises the merits is not worthy of consideration.

A third criterion of assessment is whether the newly propounded legal rule has been so articulated that it can be applied without unduly invoking a judicial discretion. Freedom under the law is maximized by legal rules which reduce judicial discretion to a minimum. Of course there is room for judicial discretion in some instances but, to the extent that the application of a rule depends on judicial discretion, power is reposed in the judge to determine the rights and liabilities of the parties. Where there is a choice between enforceable rights and discretionary relief, the former is generally to be preferred.

If University Law Reviews, in their published analyses of judgments and their articles propounding new legal rules for consideration, subject their material to the rigour of the judicial method, their influence on the judicial development of Australian law will be substantial. One of the chief reasons why judges write judgments is to give a public account of the manner in which they exercise their enormous powers. Criticism, informed and impartial, of those judgments and the scholarly propounding of new rules suitable for the Australian community will provide powerful stimuli for the work of the higher appellate courts. As the *Monash University Law Review* provides that kind of stimulus, it gives me great pleasure to be with you this evening as you celebrate your efforts.

---

1. The address was first published in the *Monash University Law Review*: Gerard Brennan, 'A Critique of Criticism' (1993) 19 (2) *Monash University Law Review* 213.
2. 'Concerning Judicial Method', address delivered at Yale University, 1955, reproduced in Sir Owen Dixon, *Jesting Pilate,* (ed Judge Woinarski) (Law Book Co, 1965) 152, 155.
3. Lord Radcliffe, *The Law and its Compass*, 1960 Rosenthal Lectures, (Faber & Faber, 1961) 39.
4. 'The Judge as Law Maker' (1972) 12 *Journal of the Society of Public Teachers of Law* 22, 22. See also Lord Diplock, 'The Courts as Legislators' (1965), published in Brian Harvey (ed) *The Lawyer and Justice* (Sweet & Maxwell, 1978) 265, 266.
5. For stark modem examples, see the difficult bioethical cases *Secretary, Department of Health and Community Services v JWB and SMB [Marion's Case]* (1992) 175 CLR 218; and *Airedale NHS Trust v Bland* [1993] 2 WLR 316.
6. Benjamin N Cardozo, *The Nature of the Judicial Process* (Yale University Press, 1921) 113-114.
7. Ibid 141.

8.6 Law in Search of a Principle

Editor's note

Brennan delivered his dissenting judgment in *Marion's Case* on 6 May 1992.[1] The argument in the case had been heard one year previously over three days (30 April 1991 – 2 May 1991). The case related to the legal authorisation of non-therapeutic sterilisation of a child with disabilities. Brennan was the sole dissentient. He wrote: 'The law will protect equally the dignity of the hale and hearty and the dignity of the weak and lame; of the frail baby and of the frail aged; of the intellectually able and of the intellectually disabled.... Our law admits of no discrimination against the weak and disadvantaged in their human dignity. Intellectual disability justifies no impairment of human dignity, no invasion of the right to personal integrity. Although the law's respect for the unique dignity of every person is the same, the protection of physical integrity which is required to preserve the dignity of one person may change from time to time and it may differ from the protection of physical integrity required to preserve the dignity of another. Differing measures of protection are required according to the physical and mental capacities of individuals at particular times: the baby whose dignity is respected by being carried and cared for by his or her parents grows into a man or woman whose dignity would be offended by such treatment; a donation of blood by a person of full age and understanding may enhance dignity, while the extraction of blood from a person who is incapable of consenting is an invasion of that person's physical integrity. Human dignity requires that the whole personality be respected: the right to physical integrity is a condition of human dignity but the gravity of any invasion of physical integrity depends on its effect not only on the body but also upon the mind and on self-perception. In assessing the significance of sterilization of a female child, it is erroneous to have regard only to the physical acts of the anaesthetist and surgeon (even when major surgery is performed involving the removal of the uterus and ovaries) and to the physiological consequences. Regard must also be had to the disturbance of the child's mind and the emotional aftermath of the sterilization and a comparison must be made between her self-perception when sterilized and the perception she would have had of herself if she had been permitted to live with her natural functions intact.'[2] This paper was the fruit of his deliberations over the year he spent pondering bioethical issues generally before formulating this significant judgment described by Sir Anthony Mason as 'the best exposition in Australian law of the common law right to integrity of the person.'[3]

In a liberal democracy, the law derives its force from acceptance by the people. Its acceptance depends to no small extent on the way in which it is applied by the courts and tribunals charged with its enforcement. If the law, in its day to day application, corresponds with and buttresses the values of society, the law finds ready acceptance. If the law is at odds with the values of society, the law falls into disrepute and loses the force it needs to ensure conformity with its precepts. Law and the values of society live in a symbiotic relationship. Law by itself is a friable mortar with which to bind a society together; law needs the cement of common values to give it strength. Conversely, the values of a society that are not reinforced at strategic points by law are powerless to protect society from the unscrupulous.

The development of law calls for a consensus by the informed community as to the values to which the law should give effect. If old laws are to be repealed, there should be a consensus that the old values are no longer accepted. If new laws are to be created, there should be a consensus upon the values to which the law is to give effect. I have stated that law itself can be a powerful influence on the values which a society adopts and can sometimes be in advance of the values which it helps to form and which then underpin it. But in general the law lags a little, changing when a change in value demands. The law does not change because of some ephemeral shift of political or social opinion: Values have a more fundamental and enduring significance than opinions of that kind. Thus law operates as a force for conserving society, following its basic trends without forcing changes.

The values of society find their expression in legal principles manifested in particular rules of law. Legal principle provides the *raison d'etre* of legal rules; it guides the interpretation of statutes which express the law. It is the growth point of rules devised by judges in deciding concrete cases. Principle has a unifying function, providing the law with its internal consistency and dictating consistency in the decision of particular cases. If consistency is lacking, the law will not command acceptance by society. Principle is the life-blood of the law; without it, law becomes a mere charter of power. A principle must at once reflect a consensus value and be capable of articulation as a normative proposition from which it is possible to reason logically and analogically.

These truisms have an especial relevance to laws which govern or are proposed to govern medical research and practice affecting the beginning and the end of human life. A need for new laws or for the refinement of old laws has arisen because modern technology has developed procedures – embryo experimentation and the mechanical maintenance of life, to take two familiar examples, which demand from the community an answer to the question: How does the law value human life? Unless an answer to that question can be given with the support of a tolerable social consensus, the law will be problematic. But there is no consensus among the informed community about the value to be accorded by the law to human life. Yet the law, which is pressed into service to solve concrete cases, needs a unifying principle, and a unifying principle needs a supporting consensus as to the value to which effect is to be given. Absent such a consensus, any legal regime, whether created by legislative enactments, judicial declarations or academic treatises, will lack the cogency to command general obedience.

The legal problem is that, if it is impossible to state a basic principle which informs the law affecting the beginning and the end of human life, we have no starting point from which to reason to a legal solution of particular problems. Lord Browne-Wilkinson expressed his concern in the difficult case of Anthony Bland:

> Where a case raises wholly new moral and social issues, in my judgment it is not for the judges to seek to develop new, all embracing, principles of law in a way which reflects the individual judges' moral stance when society as a whole is substantially divided on the relevant moral issues. Moreover, it is not legitimate for a judge[,] in reaching a view as to what is for the benefit of the one individual whose life is in issue[,] to take into account the wider practical issues as to allocation of limited financial resources or the impact on third parties of altering the time at which death occurs.... If Parliament fails to act, then judge-made law will of necessity through a gradual and uncertain process provide a legal answer to each new question as it arises. But in my judgment that is not the best way to proceed.[4]

Among the values which have gained some acceptance by a proportion of those who have an interest in these problems, we can identify three which lead to widely differing principles. In endeavouring to state them, there is a risk of oversimplification and misplaced emphasis. Accepting that risk, it seems that the first value can be stated as follows: All human life is of equal value and its integrity is not to be subordinated to the interests of society or of another life without consent freely given. This view owes much to the natural law and to the Judeo-Christian tradition. A second body of informed opinion espouses another value, namely, that the value of human life is variable and its integrity can be subordinated to the interests of society or of another human life without consent when the benefit of society or to the other life exceeds the benefit of respecting the integrity of the human life in question. This view owes much to the doctrines of utilitarianism and legal positivism.[5] The third value to be mentioned is that the value of human life is variable and its integrity can be subordinated to other interests, including the interests of other forms of life, without consent, when the benefit to those other interests exceeds question. This view depends upon the notion that the universe contains many forms of life which are of graduated importance and that the importance of each life is not to be gauged merely by reference to the species to which the life belongs.[6]

The first view focuses its attention on human life as a subject intrinsically worthy of legal protection; I shall call it the 'human life' value. The second view focuses attention on the quality of human life; I shall call it the 'quality of life' value. The third view focuses attention on the comparative value of the life of all living beings. The third view is very much a minority view at the moment. Partly for that reason, but chiefly because the legal problems raised by the third view are similar in nature – though much more extensive than the problems raised by the second view, I shall refer only to the first two views and the implications that they hold for laws that are founded on principles supported by those views.

There are, of course, some situations of bioethical interest where the human life and quality of life values lead to a common solution. Experimentation on normal people is one such area. In the aftermath of the Nazi experiments, the Nuremberg Code laid down a set of ethical rules about human experimentation.[7] It was expanded by the Declaration of Helsinki, adopted by the Eighteenth World Medical Assembly in 1964, and revised by the Twentieth World Medical Assembly in Tokyo in 1975.[8] These codes accepted that, while research is essential to the relief of suffering, the personal integrity of the individual subject could not be subordinated to the benefits of research. Thus the Declaration stated: 'Concern for the interests of the subject must always prevail over the interest of science and society .... The right of the research subject to safeguard his or her integrity must always be respected.'[9] The Australian National Health and Medical Research Council issued a Statement on Human Experimentation in 1982, to the same effect: 'In the conduct of research, the investigator must at all times respect the personality, rights, wishes, beliefs, consent and freedom of the individual subject.'[10] So jealous was the Council of the integrity of the subject that, in the case of nontherapeutic research on children, it stated that: 'The risk to the child should be so minimal as to be little more than the risks run in everyday life.'[11] The primacy of personal integrity over the acquisition of knowledge by human experimentation has been generally acknowledged. The two views are in harmony on this point because the quality of life view sees the life of a normal person more worthy of protection that other interests.

In embryo experimentation, on the other hand, a substantial body of informed opinion would accord primacy to the interests of society at large, or of other individuals over the integrity of the embryo. The difference in approach is lucidly explained by Baroness Dame Mary Warnock, who chaired the 1984 British Commission on Human Fertilization and Embryology.[12]

Seeing 'the crucial question' to be the equality of the value of human life,[13] she stated the alternative view as thus:

> Those who propose that the human embryo should be given limited but not total protection under the law (limited, that is, in that the early embryo may be used but only for certain purposes, and only up to a fixed number of days, before it is destroyed), presuppose that, though the embryo is undoubtedly human and alive, it represents a kind of human life which is not so worthy of protection as other kinds, (for example, the lives of children, adults or fetuses.) Those who oppose any research whatever do so on the ground that all human life is equally valuable, equally worthy of the full protection of the law.[14]

As the human life and quality of life values lead to differing results in the area of embryo experimentation, a choice must be made between them in order to frame a law. If the human life value prevails, the law would prohibit acts done to prejudice the integrity of an embryo. If the quality of life value prevails, the law might prohibit acts done to prejudice the life of an embryo after a fixed number of days from fertilization, or it might leave each case to be determined according to its unique circumstances.

Birth is a clear and objective criterion which might be used to discriminate between laws protecting human life and laws which permit interference with or termination of human life. The common law of murder and manslaughter protected only persons born alive. Statutory law was enacted to protect the fetus. Should post-natal protection be based on the human life value and pre-natal protection be based on the quality of life value? The division is not so simple. Some principle must be found to determine whether protection should be afforded to defective neonates, especially anencephalic neonates, by the laws of murder and manslaughter. Those are the chief laws which protect post-natal life. An aspect of the problem of defective neonates, namely, the availability of organs for donation, was addressed by the Australian Law Reform Commission, under the chairmanship of Justice Michael Kirby, early in its corporate existence.[15]

The problem of organ and tissue transplants was stimulated, of course, by the development of new transplant technology. Transplant teams were seeking suitable well-perfused organs from donors and the need was being met in part by organs removed from the bodies of donors who, having been traumatically and fatally injured, were placed on life support machines. The patient awaiting a transplant organ, that patient's relatives and the transplant team all had an interest in acquiring the desired organ from the donor in optimal condition. The donor was in a position of comparative weakness and, unless her or his life was to be terminated or put at risk of premature termination by removal of the wanted organ, it was necessary to prohibit ante-mortem removal. The prohibition was seen to be not only in the donor's interest but in the interests of the donor's relatives and the donor's medical and nursing staff. The view was taken, in the case of live donors, 'that persons lacking legal capacity for reasons other than minority whether adult or not, should under no circumstances be subjected to tissue removal. It should not be lawful to take tissue from the mentally incompetent.'[16] The Commission's recommendations accorded with the view taken about human experimentation in the Nuremberg Code and the Helsinki Declaration. The recommendations declined to subordinate the interests of a living though mortally injured donor to the interests of the transplant recipient. The consideration that the recipient had the prospect of a better quality of life if he received the donation of an organ or tissue than the donor would have held if he were to retain it did not prevail over the integrity of the life of the potential donor. The law was framed on the simple principle that both lives were of equal and unique value and one was not to be subordinated to the interests of the other. The recommendations accorded primacy to the value of human life. Once a potential donor dies, of course, there is no human life at risk, and so the cadaver was regarded as a source from which organs or tissues might be taken for transplanting into another, subject to certain conditions.

That conclusion then focused attention on the definition of death. Death was defined as occurring when a person suffers irreversible cessation of all function of the brain, even though breathing and circulation are artificially maintained. Pursuant to that definition, a general regime of control over cadaver donation of organs and tissue was prescribed. A less stringent definition would accord primacy to a different view. It has been suggested that 'cerebral death' may be regarded as tantamount to brain death.[17] But that definition has not been an accepted criterion for permitting the removal of organs and tissue when some function of the brain stem and cerebellum is retained. By shifting the criterion for removal of organs and tissue to cerebral death, living anencephalic infants would be an available source of supply for suitable organs for paediatric recipients. Dr McCullagh notes an abrupt increase in renal and cardiac transplantation from anencephalic donors[18] and recites a letter to the editor of the *New England Journal of Medicine* in 1987:

> As with many other very important principles, the total brain death definition may have to be modified for a special 'borderline' situation. ... It may be that a majority of the community would give a higher priority to the life of persons needing transplants than to symbolic commitments that do not directly protect other persons.

> As far as the total brain death definition and anencephalic infants are concerned, we think that one can treasure the principle and at the same time argue for a morally acceptable exception. In view of the severe shortage of organs for transplantation, kidneys from anencephalic donors can give recipients who otherwise might die a chance to live full lives, and help the parents of such infants feel that some good has come of a shocking and tragic experience.[19]

Anencephalic infants, says Dr McCullagh, 'are incapable of cognition but are likely to be sentient and to exhibit responses that can be mediated by brain stem activity.'[20] The anencephalic infant may be borne alive and thus within the prima facie protection of the laws protecting post-natal life, although total brain death may follow rapidly. To remove the organs or tissue of such an infant before total brain death would be to subordinate the life of the donor to the interests of the recipient. It follows that, if anencephalic infants were to be a 'morally acceptable exception' standing outside the laws which protect post-natal life, those lives would require a comparison to be made between the quality of life of the donor and the quality of life of the recipient. So the problems occurring in ante-natal situations. The differences trouble us in defining the laws affecting every stage of human existence. Nor are the problems confined to cases where trauma or physical abnormality affect the quality of a life. Perhaps the most acute areas of controversy at present relate to the laws relating to abortion and active euthanasia, actions which may terminate a normal life at its beginning or at its end.

Professor Singer of the Monash Centre for Bioethics, in an article entitled 'Sanctity of Life or Quality of Life?', has noted that '[t]he first major blow to the sanctity of life view was the spreading acceptance of abortion throughout the Western world.'[21] When an abortion is contemplated, the possibilities confronting the fetus are stark: The life it has whatever be its quality – or death; from the viewpoint of the mother, father or family, a choice might be made between the life of the fetus and the quality of the other lives involved. Leaving aside those instances, now mercifully rare, where a choice must be made between the life of the mother and the life of the fetus,[22] a law which permits abortion calls for a comparison of the value of the life of the fetus with the value of the life of the mother, father or others whose interests may be affected by allowing the fetal life to continue. If the value of the fetal life is held to be less than the value of the quality of the lives of those whose interests may be affected, the fetal life may be terminated. In this area, those who would give the law's protection to fetal life – of whatever quality – over the quality of the other lives involved espouse the same view as those who would reject embryo experimentation, namely that all human life is equally valuable. Those who would make the alternative choice must give primacy to the quality of the more mature human life or lives over the fetal life.

The difference between the human life value and the quality of life value, which lies at the heart of the controversy about abortion, has not always been clearly perceived. In *The King* v *Bourne*,[23] which, though only a ruling by a single judge during a criminal trial, has had a significant influence on the statement of abortion law in Australia,[24] Mr Justice MacNaghten arguably transformed a statutory value of life test into a quality of life test. His Lordship gave the jury a direction which extended the phrase 'for the purpose of preserving the life of the mother' to cover the termination of a pregnancy which would probably 'make the woman a physical or mental wreck.'[25] Once the quality of the mother's life, including her psychological state, became a criterion justifying the termination of a pregnancy, the legal protection of the fetus under the statute was diminished. In practice, and in some jurisdictions, in law the quality of life value has prevailed.

By contrast, the human life value appears to remain in the ascendancy in its influence on the law governing the termination of life, as the case of Anthony Bland shows. Anthony has been in a persistent vegetative state for three years after being crushed at the Hillsborough Football ground in 1989. The courts of England declared that his artificial feeding through a nasogastric tube, together with other medical treatment which had helped sustain his life, could be lawfully discontinued though the known and intended result would be his death by lack of nutrition if not by some supervening infection.[26] Some of the judgments expressly rejected the proposition that the decision to leave Anthony to die could be justified on the ground that Anthony, having no cerebral function, had such a diminished quality of life that it was not worth preserving.[27] Their Lordships' decision turned on the scope of the duty to provide medical treatment for Anthony. The existence of a duty was essential if there were to be a sheeting home of responsibility for the death which was intended to follow the cessation of nutrition. To determine the scope of the duty to provide treatment for an unconscious patient, their Lordships held it was necessary to ascertain his 'best interests.' Unless it were in Anthony's best interests to be provided with medical treatment, there was no duty to provide it. Absent a duty of that kind, there could be no liability, criminal or civil, for a failure to perform it. Their Lordships held that there was no duty to provide medical treatment. In reaching this conclusion, two steps were necessary: First, that feeding through the nasogastric tube was medical treatment and, second that artificial feeding was not in his best interests. Accordingly, it was held that there was no duty to leave the nasogastric tube in place and to continue to feed Anthony through it.

In deciding that artificial feeding was not in Anthony's best interests, their Lordships made an evaluation of the quality of his life. But this evaluation was not made for the purposes of a possible subordination of Anthony's life to the quality of the life of his family, friends, or carers, nor for the purpose of considering whether the National Health Service should bear the financial burden of his care. The evaluation was made in order to determine whether Anthony would derive some benefit from continuation of the treatment he had been receiving.

Lord Keith of Kinkel said that, although in some cases it is possible to compare the effect of giving or withholding medical treatment on the quality of a patient's life, '[i]n the case of a permanently insensate being, who if continuing to live would never experience the slightest actual discomfort, it is difficult, if not impossible, to make any relevant comparison be- tween continued existence and the absence of it. It is, however, perhaps permissible to say that to an individual with no cognitive capacity whatever, and no prospect of ever recovering any such capacity in this world, it must be a matter of complete indifference whether he lives or dies.'[28]

Lord Goff of Chieveley, in reference to cases where 'treatment is of no benefit to [the living patient] because he is totally unconscious and there is no prospect of any improvement in his condition,'[29] said that 'there is in reality no weighing operation to be performed. Here the condition of the patient, who is totally unconscious and in whose condition there is no prospect of any improvement, is such that life-prolonging treatment is properly regarded as being, in medical terms, useless.'[30] Lord Browne-Wilkinson said '[w] hether he lives or dies he will feel no pain or distress. All the purely physical considerations indicate that it is pointless to continue life support.'[31] Lord Mustill refused to accept any argument that it was in the best interests of Anthony that his life should be brought to an end.[32] An argument in those terms would 'serve to legitimate a termination by much more direct means.'[33] But his Lordship was prepared to accept the argument that 'his best interests in being kept alive have also disappeared'[34] and that the duty to provide medical treatment disappeared accordingly.

It was one thing to hold that, if treatment was of no benefit to Anthony, there was no duty to provide it. It would have been an entirely different thing to hold that Anthony's life was of so minimal a quality that it was no longer within the protection of the law. The principle to be derived from the Bland case is that human life of whatever quality is protected by the law and is not subordinated to the interests of other lives or of society, but the duty to sustain human life depends on whether the treatment available to sustain it is beneficial to the life in question.

Their Lordships were careful to point out that their decision in Anthony's case was not necessarily a guide to the decision that should be made in other cases. Clearly enough, while artificial feeding of Anthony through a nasogastric tube was, in the circumstances of his overall condition and management, held not to be beneficial treatment to him, artificial feeding might well be held to be beneficial for a patient in slightly different circumstances for example, a partially anencephalic infant. The facts in Bland were extremely difficult to evaluate. Such facts are notoriously difficult to evaluate, and the evaluation of facts may be influenced by the standards of contemporary medical treatment. This evaluation has attracted and will attract some criticism. But the law, searching for a general principle, cannot determine the facts to which it is to apply: The law's concern is to identify an applicable principle supported by a community consensus.

All of this serves to emphasize the difficulty of the problems that new medical technology raises for determination. The importance of being able to identify principles which might inform a legal regime to govern the beginning and the end of life is manifest. It is unsatisfactory to adopt one principle to apply to some forms of human life and another to apply to other forms of human life. The division of the continuum of human life into segments to be governed by different regimes denies the possibility of consistency in the way in which the law regards human life. But if a legal regime is to be based on one value or another, it is desirable to recognize the problems to which each of the possible regimes may give rise.

If a legal regime is based on the human life value, laws can be framed so that their operation depends to a large extent on objective criteria: Is the patient dead? Will the treatment or the procedure preserve or prejudice the maintenance of life? Is a treatment or procedure beneficial to the patient having regard to the patient's condition and standards of contemporary medical practice? Is the purpose of treatment to relieve suffering or to cause death? These are questions of fact. In answering some of these questions, medical opinion will be decisive. In answering others, regard must be had to the patient's wishes and the position and wishes of family and carers. A regime based on the human life value seeks to protect any human life whatever its quality against any act that might be done to destroy it, and imposes a duty to provide reasonable care and treatment where that care and treatment are for the benefit of the life in question. A criticism made of this approach is that it appears not to provide for the relief of suffering that may be prolonged by maintaining life. The criticism is unwarranted so far as it related to palliative care. The general duty is to provide care and treatment for the benefit of the patient and, unless the patient consciously and lucidly refuses to accept it, that care and treatment included palliative care designed to alleviate suffering. It may be administered for that purpose though it may incidentally hasten death. The criticism, if criticism it be, that the human life value does not permit the deliberate hastening of death in order to prevent further suffering is valid. A legal regime based on the human life value alleviates suffering, but not by causing the death of the sufferer.

A regime which gives effect to the quality of life value is much more difficult to construct. It requires some definition of what constitutes quality of life and some calculus for comparing the quality of life of A with the quality of life of B or, when the termination of a human life is in question, how the quality of that life can be compared with its death. The problem in making comparisons between the quality of human lives was highlighted by Dame Mary Warnock when she sought to apply utilitarian principles to solve the problem of embryo experimentation. The attempt failed 'since the balance of benefit over harm is intended by utilitarianism to apply only to human persons. The question about which there is no agreement in this case is precisely whether or not to count early human embryos among that class, whether their benefits and harms should or need not enter into the felicific calculus.'[35]

Moreover, in the balancing of benefit and harm, there is no clear understanding of what is to count as harm. 'There is no doubt that the infertile, and children who might be born with fatal or damaging inherited diseases and many others will ultimately benefit from the research; the embryos themselves will not. How are we to weigh up the benefits and harms?'[36] And if suffering may be relieved by terminating the life of the sufferer in some circumstances, how is a decision to be made between the life in question and death? That is a decision which is incapable of control by legal means. As Lord Justice Griffiths has pointed out 'The court ... has to compare the state of the plaintiff with non-existence, of which the court can know nothing; this I regard as an impossible task.'[37]

If it is impossible legally to evaluate either the comparative quality of human lives at least when one of them is an ante-natal life or to compare a human life of whatever quality with death, can a law be construed which prescribes legal criteria governing the choice for or against the human life in question? The choice would have to be made according to the discretion of the person in whom the power to choose is vested. In whom should such a power be vested? The pregnant mother in the case of the fetus, the parents in the case of the embryo or the defective neonate, and the parents, children or next-of-kin in the case of the incurably or terminally ill are the logical candidates in whom the power to choose might be vested. Yet each of them has an interest which may be in conflict with the interest of the life in question. Usually a power to affect the interests of one party is not vested in a party whose interests are in conflict. Nor would it be characteristic of a legal regime to vest a discretionary power in a party who has an interest in the manner of its exercise.

An objection often times advances against a regime of laws based on the quality of life value is that is places the law on a slippery slope, there being no objective criterion which serves to protect a life in jeopardy. If quality of life is to be judged by reference simply to intellectual capacity, human life is not intrinsically worthy of any protection. Professor Singer makes this point:

> If we compare a severely defective human infant with a nonhuman animal, a dog or a pig, for example, we will often find the nonhuman to have superior capacities, both actual and potential, for rationality, self-consciousness, communication, and anything else that can plausibly be considered morally significant. Only the fact that the defective infant is a member of the species Homo sapiens leads it to be treated differently from the dog or pig. Species membership alone, however, is not morally relevant.
>
> .....
>
> If we can put aside the obsolete and erroneous notion of the sanctity of all human life, we may start to look at human life as it really is: at the quality of life that each human being has or can achieve. Then it will be possible to approach these difficult questions of life and death with the ethical sensitivity that each case demands.[38]

As far as one can see, it is unlikely that the divergent views held by members of the informed community are likely to coalesce. It may be that, despite the absence of a unifying principle, regimes based on differing values will govern the several stages of human life and the several conditions in which human beings exist. The regimes may be based not on a general consensus of values but on a majority view about the value which is to prevail in respect of this stage of life or that, this condition or that.

In that event, lawyers must concentrate on the text and scope of the particular rules. Legal analysis and criticism will be impeded by the absence of an informing principle. Although much ink may be split in discussing the problems and apparent inconsistencies in court decisions or in theories advanced by learned commentators, the discussions themselves will be flawed by the absence of a principled intellectual foundation. Unless the competent constitutional authorities settle the rules to be followed, the courts will perforce be engaged in making new laws to fill the legal vacuums created by technological advances. Controversy will be unavoidable.

Yet scholarship and discussion have never had a more important role to play. As the genius of the human mind encompasses more of the majestic mysteries of life and examines its origins and the manner of its existence more deeply, the societies in which men and women strive to live in harmony will need laws reasonable to the new learning and attuned to the intuitive aspirations of the human spirit which lie beyond the ken of science. In the devising of these laws, scholarship and compassion, insight and humility of mind will be in rare demand.

---

1. See *Department of Health & Community Services* v *JWB & SMB ('Marion's Case')* (1992) 175 CLR 218
2. See *Marion's Case* (n 1) 266.
3. This paper was first published in (1993) 9 *Journal of Contemporary Health Law and Policy 259.*
4. See *Airedale NHS.Trust* v *Bland* (1993) 2 WLR 316, 382.
5. See, for example, Baroness Mary Warnock, 'Mortality and the Law: Some Problems', (1987) 18 Cambrian Law Review 14. This was the third Lord Morris of Borth-y-Gest Memorial Lecture.
6. This view denies any special importance to human life as such. It is a particular but extreme example of the more widely held view which gives respect to all forms of life. The more widely held view has great implications, of course, for animal experimentation and the morality of animal killing.
7. Nuremberg Code, 19 August 1974, Articles 5-6, reprinted in A S Duncan et al (eds) *Dictionary of Medical Ethics* (Darton, Longman and Todd, New Rev Ed, 1981) 130 -132.
8. Declaration of Helsinki: recommendations guiding medical doctors in biomedical research involving human subjects, 1964, revised in 1975, reprinted in A S Duncan et al (eds) *Dictionary of Medical Ethics* (Darton, Longman and Todd, New Rev Ed, 1981) 132 – 135.
9. Ibid 134, Article 1, paras 5-6.
10. Australian National Health & Medical Research Council, Statement on Human Experimentation, Medical *Journal of Australia* (1982).
11. Ibid 8.
12. See Warnock, 'Mortality and the Law' (n 5) 14-24.
13. Ibid 23.
14. Ibid 22. For a discussion of the human life value in experimentation, see Reverend Graham Hardy, 'Shall We Be as Gods? A Theological Assessment of Experimentation with Life' (1985) 17 *Australian Journal of Forensic Science* 119, and Reverend. Francis Harman, 'A Christian Philosophy on Experimenting with Life' (1985) 17 *Australian Journal of Forensic Science* 131.Human Tissue Transplant, Law Reform Commission Report No 7, (1977).
15. Human Tissue Transplant, Law Reform Commission Report No. 7, (1977).
16. Ibid 51, para 113.
17. Peter McCullagh, 'Experimental and Clinical Transplantation: Implications for Regulation of Medicine', in Hiram Caton (ed) *Trends in Biomedical Regulation* (Butterworths, 1990)

128, 132 (citing Julius Korein, 'The Problem of Brain Death Development and History', (1978) 19 Annals of New York Academy of Science 315).

18. McCullagh, 'Experimental and Clinical Transplantation: Implications for Regulation of Medicine' (n 17) 135.
19. W Holzgreve & F K Belier, *Letter to the Editor*, (1987) 317 *New England Journal of Medicine* 916.
20. McCullagh, 'Experimental and Clinical Transplantation: Implications for Regulation of Medicine' (n 17) 135
21. Peter Singer, 'Sanctity of Life or Quality of Life?' (1983) 72 *Pediatrics* 128.
22. The loss or taking of one life to preserve another raises a distinct area of moral decision-making, embracing capital punishment, pacificism and self-defence, as well as therapeutic abortion.
23. See *R* v *Bourne* [1939] 1 KB 687.
24. See, for example, *R v Davidson* [1969] VR 667. Cf *R v Ross* [1955] St R Qd 48.
25. See *Bourne* (n 23) 694.
26. See *Airedale NHS v Bland* [1993] 2 WLR 316.
27. Ibid (334 Sir Thomas Bingham MR); (395 Lord Mustill); Cf (354-355 LJ Hoffmann), (387 Lord Browne Wilkinson).
28. See *Airedale NHS v Bland* [1993] 2 WLR 316.
29. Ibid 371.
30. Ibid 372.
31. Ibid 386.
32. Ibid 397-98.
33. Ibid 398.
34. Ibid
35. Warnock, 'Mortality and the Law' (n 5) 19.
36. Ibid 22.
37. See *McKay* v *Essex Area Health Authority* [1982] 1 QB 1166, 1192-93. See also *Udale* v Bloomsbury *Health Authority.*, [1983] 1 WLR 1098, 1108-9 ; *Airedale NHS* v *Bland* [1983] 2 WLR 316, 398 (Lord Mustill).
38. Singer, 'Sanctity of Life or Quality of Life?' (n 21) 129.

8.7 Profession or Service Industry: The Choice

Editor's note

This was Brennan's opening address at the Australian Bar Association Conference held in San Francisco on 18 August 1996.

It is a great satisfaction for me to open this Conference of the Australian Bar Association, particularly as the conference has the support of another Bar which shares many of the ideals and aspirations of the Australian Bar Association. My satisfaction stems largely from recollections of and gratitude for a life at the Bar, replete with its triumphs and its tragedies, its wins and its losses, the friendships forged and the battles fought, the long nights of reading and the flashes of inspiration that sometimes fail in their application. The Bar captures the mind and governs the life of those who join it. Its rewards are sometimes financially generous, sometimes financially parsimonious. It is a profession to be entered only by those who have a passionate desire to be a barrister. But that is the best of all reasons. For those, the experience of practice does not disappoint.

I hope that that sense of satisfaction remains in the Australian Bar today, though there are signs of strain and sometimes of disaffection. Chief Justice Rehnquist has noted something of a change in sentiment in the United States. He said: 'I think successful lawyers today, on average, earn more than did successful lawyers in my day, even after adjustments for inflation. I think successful lawyers today put a good deal more time into the practice of their profession than did successful lawyers in my day. And I think, though this is the riskiest generalization, that the lawyers among whom I practiced enjoyed the practice of law more than do lawyers today.'

He attributed much of the disenchantment to the pressures of a successful practice. He said this: 'The fact that the work is enjoyable makes it easier than it otherwise would be to succumb to the subtle pressures to put more and more time in on the job. These subtle pressures are often the result of successful performance, which means an increasing demand for your services that is both flattering and financially rewarding. Without realizing it, you can slide imperceptibly into a mode where demands the job makes are automatically accorded priority over other demands.'

His Honour is surely right and I hope that, in this Conference, you may all have an opportunity to enjoy some of the friendships and stimuli that are offered by others who share the same professional interests.

In reading what Chief Justice Rehnquist had to say, I thought back to the time when I came to the Bar and mused about the changes that have occurred. Some of those changes have had an effect on public appreciation of the Bar. Even if financial prospects of practice may have increased, I doubt whether public confidence in and respect for the profession has been maintained. And I wondered why.

Nearly 45 years ago, eleven or twelve of us (I don't now remember), recent graduates of the Law School, were admitted to practice by the Supreme Court of Queensland 'as barristers of this Honourable Court.' I practised as such for 25 years – 14 as a junior; 11 as a silk. The numerical strength of the practising Queensland Bar when I joined it was slightly more than 80; it was, I think, about 130 when I left for the bench. The new barristers found a corner in the chambers of more senior members. That wasn't particularly difficult, because the rooms were large and sparsely furnished, the rents were low, the secretaries were shared and financial expectations were not exalted. For those of us who were awaiting briefs, and for those fortunate enough to have a chamber application with or against a senior counsel near the top of the list at 10 am, there was a general exodus for coffee and conversation at 11. The state of the nation, the idiosyncrasies of judges, judicial aspirations and the prospects for next Saturday were discussed with great authority. When the briefs came, they were diverse. Committal proceedings, minor collision cases, landlord and tenant, assaults, maintenance cases, undefended divorces, motions for probate and an occasional reduction of capital provided a varied diet. There was no legal aid work unless you were already briefed to go on circuit and the Public Defender had a matter in the list for which he offered a small fee sufficient to pay for an extra day at the country hotel. 'Smithy', the bibulous and beloved salesman for the Law Book Company, determined when we should buy books and how we should pay for them. The fledgling barrister, with few overheads, was anxious to do any brief for the sake of experience. If there were a fee as well, so much the better. There was no talk of anti-competitive rules in that environment. My first lesson in competition policy came when I asked Bob Andrews (as he then was) how much I should charge for a paying brief I had just done. 'How much were you thinking of?' he asked. 'Eight guineas,' said I. 'Well,' said Bob, 'I would charge 10. And if I were a solicitor and I could have you for 8 or me for 10, I'd take me every time!' It was good advice. Now I understand that the experience of coming to the Bar has changed.

A smaller proportion of barristers come to the Bar direct from Law School; many already have family responsibilities; they must take Chambers in expensive buildings in the central business district; they have heavy overheads to meet and, if they buy their chambers, many have substantial interest bills; they specialize from an early stage in order to establish a niche in the work area of their choice; they do not have the freedom to be without paying work for long. For some, legal aid is a financial lifeline. For others, survival at the Bar depends upon briefs to appear for corporate, industrial or government bodies that have the funds to pay counsel's fee. The proportion of briefs to appear on behalf of individuals in big cases has diminished. When a *pro bono* brief is accepted, the motivation is likely to be solely altruistic rather than the acquiring of experience. Fees are necessarily higher than they used to be and litigants who can afford to pay them now probably represent a smaller segment of society than in earlier days. The pattern of litigation has changed; the volume of litigation has increased; the jurisdictions of the lower courts have been extended. Alternative dispute resolution and mediation have become a familiar feature of the litigation landscape. Lay clients are now more knowledgeable about the services rendered by the Bar. Solicitors are under great pressure to conduct their practices as commercial enterprises, even to the extent of joining in multi-disciplinary partnerships. Some firms provide and others would wish to provide advocacy services by in-house counsel, albeit few of those counsel venture into the higher courts.

Now, all of these factors have produced a profession that is necessarily different from the profession which I first entered. In some respects, we may be justifiably nostalgic about 'the good old days' – the days of the long lunch when the case was settled, of the idle chatter in one another's chambers and the innumerable stories that were built around the Bar's characters. The Bar's ethics were enforced almost always without a complaint procedure – usually by peer group pressure or, in graver cases, by a caution administered by a Senior whose authority was undoubted. But nostalgia does not solve the problems of today's profession. Some of the changes are worth a comment not only to identify them but also to note their effect on the profession.

First, specialisation is more commonplace than it used to be. In an age of ever-increasing legal complexity, a barrister who purports to offer a high level of service in advice and advocacy encounters real difficulty in acquiring the necessary fund of knowledge in diverse areas of practice, especially in those years when the briefs relate to problems arising from the minutiae of the law rather than from broad principle. So, specialisation, at least to some degree, is inevitable. But specialization comes at a price.

Lawyers are the engineers who operate the legal machinery that maintains social relationships and orders social activity. The lawyer who confines his or her attention to a particular piece of machinery fails to appreciate the social significance of the law he or she practises. Such a lawyer is more like a trained repairer of domestic appliances than a professional engineer. But a lawyer who sees his or her piece of legal machinery as part of an institutional force that both expresses the values of, and governs, society has a more profound understanding of the contribution which his or her piece of legal machinery makes to the welfare of society.

From the viewpoint of the Bar as a whole, narrow specialisation brings the risk of transformation from a profession to a business. If specialist barristers were to lose the consciousness of the law as an entirety, the Bar would be a loose federation of specialist interest groups. Institutional cohesion would be weakened. Then the barrister practising in a speciality would find it increasingly difficult to resist being subsumed into a multi-disciplinary service organization. Professional status would be exchanged for a place on the business letterhead. There are some indicia of strain between sections of the Bar, especially between those who practise in the criminal jurisdictions and those who practise the civil law. In Sydney the divergence seems to be accentuated by the distance between the chambers of these two categories of counsel. I venture to suggest that the practitioner in the Family Court needs to see the working of the equity jurisdiction; the practitioner in trade practices would do well to appreciate the dynamics of a jury trial.

Another trend in practice, associated with specialisation, is the narrowing of the client base. The litigation in which barristers are briefed today seems to be more confined than in earlier times. Perhaps I am too far removed from the coalface of practice to know the true extent of the areas of work now performed by the Bar, but I suspect that cost and specialisation have combined to restrict briefing to the more remunerative areas of litigation. If this be right, the public goodwill of the Bar has been diminished. Is the barrister seen more as a gun for hire by the powerful than a cab for hire by anybody?

Whatever the truth may be, media references seldom acknowledge the Bar to be the protectors of the oppressed or the champions of the righteous. Rather the emphasis seems to be that the Bar is the institution that frustrates the doing of justice and the visiting of the powerful unrighteous with their just deserts. Such a portrayal can be reversed only if the Bar is and is seen to be available to serve the interests of clients across the range of areas in which advice and advocacy are required. I imagine that might require a significant increase in work accepted on an unremunerative or pro bono basis in areas in which the Bar's services have not been often sought.

The cab-rank rule, so often and so rightly advanced as a cornerstone of the profession's ethical standards, can be easily negatived in practice. The rule, as you know, has two limbs: the obligation to accept a brief exists only in respect of briefs in an area in which counsel ordinarily practises and for which a reasonable fee is offered. If counsel confines the area of practice too narrowly, or if the notion of reasonableness in relation to fees is not properly applied, the cab-rank rule becomes a cloak for a failure in professional standards. Then the Bar is seen to be oriented more towards commerce than it is to the service of the public. Yet it is the hallmark of a profession that its services answer a social need.

Sir Anthony Mason has written:

> The professional ideal is not the pursuit of wealth but public service. That is the vital difference between professionalism and commercialism. It is timely to repeat what O'Connor J (with whom Rehnquist CJ and Scalia J agreed) said in *Shapero v. Kentucky Bar Association*:[1]
>
> 'One distinguishing feature of any profession, unlike other occupations that may be equally respectable, is that membership entails an ethical obligation to temper one's selfish pursuit of economic success by adhering to standards of conduct that could not be enforced either by legal fiat or through the discipline of the market. There are sound reasons to continue pursuing the goal that is implicit in the traditional view of professional life. Both the special privileges incident to membership in the profession and the advantages those privileges give in the necessary task of earning a living are means to a goal that transcends the accumulation of wealth.'[2]

Sir Anthony adds the comment: 'Unless the Bar dedicates itself to the ideal of public service, it forfeits its claim to treatment as a profession in the true sense of the term. Dedication to public service demands not only attainment of a high standard of professional skill but also faithful performance of duty to client and court and a willingness to make the professional service available to the public.'

Of course, the Bar cannot be expected to provide an across-the-board social service to represent litigants in every class of litigation. The Bar's function is to provide that service so far as it is reasonable for the collective strength of the Bar to do so. By performing this function, the Bar earns the respect and goodwill of the community.

Practices must be carried on so as to return a reasonable income and in that respect the barrister is in business as well as in a profession. But, with due respect, those who would seek to regulate the Bar as though it were a service industry profoundly misunderstand the purpose of the Bar's existence. Perhaps barristers themselves sometimes fail to appreciate the social importance of what they do, especially in the conduct of litigation. Barristers are not mere agents of the client seeking to employ their skill and knowledge to gain whatever benefit the client desires: they are involved in the administration of justice according to law, a function on which a free and democratic society depends. In *Giannarelli v Wraith,* Mason CJ said (and I omit a part of the quotation):

> The peculiar feature of counsel's responsibility is that he owes a duty to the court as well as to his client. His duty to his client is subject to his overriding duty to the court. In the performance of that overriding duty there is a strong element of public interest. So, in *Swinfen v Lord Chelmsford*, Pollock CB, after speaking of the discharge of counsel's duty as one in which the court and the public, as well as the client, had an interest said: 'The conduct and control of the cause are necessarily left to counsel....'[3]
>
> The performance by counsel of his paramount duty to the court will require him to act in a variety of ways to the possible disadvantage of his client. Counsel must not mislead the court, cast unjustifiable aspersions on any party or witness or withhold documents and authorities which detract from his client's case. And, if he notes an irregularity in the conduct of a criminal trial, he must take the point so that it can be remedied, instead of keeping the point up his sleeve and using it as a ground for appeal.[4]

In the same case, I quoted Lord Eldon:

> He lends his exertions to all, himself to none. The result of the cause is to him a matter of indifference. It is for the court to decide. It is for him to argue. He is, however he may be represented by those who understand not his true situation, merely an officer assisting in the administration of justice, and acting under the impression, that truth is best discovered by powerful statements on both sides of the question.[5]

And I added 'By a paradox which is obvious to any who have experience in our courts, the client is best served by a counsel who is manifestly independent.'

Absent an independent Bar, how would the voice of the oppressed be heard? Where would one find an effective champion of an unpopular cause? How would the courts be able to function without the distillation of issues by skilled and independent minds? And how would any tendency to judicial tyranny be restrained? The point was well made by Chief Justice McEachern of British Columbia: 'I believe an independent bar and an independent judiciary are sentries posted by the constitution to guard our people of their danger. A re-born Erskine would remind us that our greatest threat is not from insurrection, but rather from earnest, misguided, well-intentioned philosophies that suggest some combination of Jeffersonian democracy and Harvard Business School efficiency could organize the legal system better, if troublesome judges and lawyers would just get out of the way.'[6]

The independence of the Bar is as valuable to the client as it is to the public welfare. To the client, it gives an assurance of such accuracy as knowledge and skill can contribute; to the community, it gives the service of applying the law in the manner in which the law is intended to act. It is independence that makes the barrister essential to the administration of justice according to law. Independence that cannot be bought in a market; independence that will not be bartered for money, or for privilege, status or favour or even for a momentary success. This is the characteristic that, more than any other, stamps the Bar as a profession and not a service industry. Competition policy assumes that profit is the governing motive of commercial conduct; that is an assumption which, if it were ever to be true of the Bar, would transform it from a profession to a service industry. That is the quality which, above all, must be preserved not only in the interests of clients and of the courts but in the interests of the community as a whole.

Independence is preserved by the sole practice rule. It would be sapped by a need to give loyalty to partners, or to lay clients on whose patronage a barrister depended for income, or to sources of power or patronage. Independence is the mother of candour and candour is the ally of advocacy. Thus, independence is the quality exhibited by all leaders in the profession. And any compromise with expediency is quickly sensed by the peer group and reflected in a loss of the respect which is essential to professional eminence.

In the years that lie ahead, there will be enormous pressure on the Bar to alter its rules and practices to conform more closely to some commercial template. Of course, there will be changes – and so there should be. Mediation and alternative dispute resolution will evoke skill in the negotiation of settlements rather than in the adversarial battles of the court room. Problem solving will become as important a function as the set joust of litigation. Technology will alter in a variety of unforeseen ways the conduct of counsel's practice. We are familiar with the word processor and, to an extent, with the document scanner, with video connections to distant places and with the keeping of records electronically. The methods and even the nature of legal research is changing with the development of data bases and of CD-Roms that direct the user to relevant research material. Technology will place new demands on the advocate, challenging him or her to produce submissions of such cogency and precision that they might be downloaded with minor editing into a judgment. The pressure of cases will require ever more pithy written submissions and the utilisation of advocacy time to advance arguments that do not ramble aimlessly or tendentiously around the point for decision.

Nation-wide eligibility to practise cannot now be far distant. We shall see the emergence of what can be described with complete accuracy as an Australian Bar. And from that Australian Bar, there will in time grow an Australian Judiciary familiar with the legal systems of all parts of the Commonwealth and preserving the characteristics which develop from a lifetime of independent thought. A competent and independent Bar is the vital training ground for judges in the modern age who must possess experience in litigation and a fair and robust mind to stand against the buffeting that many decisions attract. An Australian Bar will not be created, I hope, merely as a supplier of services in what some economic regulators choose to call a national legal services market. The Bar has far more extensive duties to perform than the provision of services to so-called 'consumers'. If the Bar were to see itself simply as such a supplier, our national court system would have to be reconstructed with features and safeguards that are presently unnecessary. The survival of the Bar as a separate and independent institution may make little sense to an economist who does not appreciate its social utility and does not foresee the consequences of its destruction. But the possibility that the Bar will not survive is minimal provided the Bar has a sufficient conceit of its function in the maintenance of a free democracy and, to that end, retains its competence and its independence. It must reject the notion that it is concerned with the marketing of expertise rather than with the use of skill and knowledge in the service of the client and the community. That was the message which Sir Daryl Dawson delivered in his significant paper '*The Legal Services Market*' which he delivered to the 29th Australian Legal Convention. The Bar must change with the times, but it must cling to its ideals of independence and competence in the service of justice according to law. These are the ideals that, for those who have practised at the Bar, make it a true home for mind and spirit. These are the ideals of which Judge Cardozo spoke when addressing the lawyers of New York County 'The tradition, the ennobling tradition, though it be myth as well as verity, that surrounds as with an aura the profession of the law, is the bond between its members and one of the great concerns of man – the cause of justice upon earth.'

That is the tradition in which we meet, and I am glad to be part of it.

---

1. 486 US 466 (1988), 488-489.
2. See *The Independence of the Bench* (1993) 10 *Australian Bar Review* 1, 9.
3. (1860) 5 H & N 890, 921;157 ER 1436,1449.
4. (1988) 165 CLR 543, 555-556.
5. Ibid 579.
6. Chief Justice McEachern, 'The changing face of the Judiciary and Legal Profession' (1995) 29 (1) *Law Society Gazette of Upper Canada* 1,5.

8.8 The Third Branch and The Fourth Estate

Editor's note

Brennan delivered the second lecture in the series 'Broadcasting, Society and the Law' at the Faculty of Law, University College Dublin on 22 April 1997.[1]

When I was invited to deliver this second lecture in the series on 'Broadcasting, Society and the Law', I had some misgiving about speaking from the viewpoint of an Australian judge. My visits to Ireland have been too few to grasp the dynamics of modern Irish life and my knowledge of Irish law is too fragmentary to appreciate the wellsprings of forensic thought in this country. In the anticipation of visiting again the home of my forebears, I put the misgiving aside. And, I rationalised, the similarity in the democratic ideals of our societies, in the institutions which safeguard our freedoms, in the legal traditions and judicial methodology which we value and, perhaps, in that insouciant lack of respect for pomp and authority (which we in Australia owe substantially to the influence of the Irish), gives sufficient warrant for an Australian judge to speak to an Irish audience on a subject of common concern: the role of the courts and the media in securing the rule of law.

The rule of law is like the air we breathe: so long as it is there – undiluted and freely flowing – we are not ordinarily conscious of its presence. But let the rule of law be polluted or impeded and we choke under the excesses of raw power. Fundamental to both our societies is freedom under the law, that is to say, our peoples are ruled by laws which leave individuals free to think as they please, to act without restraints that are unnecessary to achieve the common good and to be secure in their person and their property. Both countries boast a government of laws and not of men, a government under which the legal rights of minorities, of the powerless, of the poor are protected equally with the legal rights of majorities, of the powerful and the affluent.

In a democracy, the rule of law is not achieved by raw power but by public acceptance of the law and by public confidence in the institutions which promulgate and administer it. This is not the occasion to speak of the content of the law except to say this: if the law works or tolerates injustice, the injustice will compound with every generation until, finally, disaffection with the law becomes so general and so deeply felt that the rule of law breaks down. But that is not my topic. I would focus not on the law itself but on the institutions – particularly the courts – that administer the law. Public confidence in those institutions has to be built on their due performance of function and the public perception of that performance. One is the reality; the other is the perception.

The political branches of government make the news of the day. They affect great issues of policy that concern large sections of the community. The legislature and executive are under continual scrutiny by the media. Politicians continually enliven political debate. The members of the political branches of government and the media necessarily live in a symbiotic relationship. The media need the political stories, the pictures, the background and the insights to weld together a presentation – whatever the medium may be – which informs, intrigues and perhaps entertains the public. Political figures need to publicise their policies and personalities and to ensure that both are presented in a favourable light. Public discussion of political issues is alive and well. And that is to be expected not only in the homeland of the Irish people, but in countries where the Irish diaspora has contributed to the national character.

The courts, the apolitical branch of government, seem dull and pedestrian by comparison. They are focused on the individual, not on great questions of policy; they are slow, costly, deliberate to the point of tediousness, sometimes quite out of sympathy with popular sentiment, punctilious about publication of the grounds on which they exercise their power but reticent in the usual modes of public relations. Judges do not comment on their judgments or seek to vindicate their judicial pronouncements. There are no background briefings, no titillating leaks, few photo opportunities, no exposition of the implications of judgments. Yet it is the judicial branch that bears the primary responsibility for maintaining the rule of law, for safeguarding the freedom of individuals, for regulating the very institutions of State power, for imposing condign punishment on those who contravene the law and for preventing the centres from overreaching the rights of those less powerful. It has no agenda of its own devising, no armoury other than that provided by the executive; it can procure no favours and its own interests are unaffected by the exercise of any of its powers. 200 years ago, Alexander Hamilton called it 'the least dangerous branch'.[2] He noted that -

> The executive not only dispenses the honors, but holds the sword of the community. The legislature not only commands the purse, but prescribes the rules by which the duties and rights of every citizen are to be regulated. The judiciary, on the contrary, has no influence over either sword or the purse; no direction either of the strength or of the wealth of the society, and can take no active resolution whatever. It may truly be said to have neither FORCE nor WILL, but merely judgment; and must ultimately depend upon the aid of the executive arm even for the efficacy of its judgments.

Having no power but the power of judgment, the judiciary has no power base but public confidence in its integrity and competence in performing the functions assigned to it. There must be such a degree of public confidence in the courts' application of the law that neither power nor riches, nor political office nor numerical superiority can stand against the weight of the court's authority. If that confidence is eroded, there is nothing to redress injustice or to prevent abuses of raw power. If the law is to rule, there must be an arbiter whose authority is accepted by the powerful and the weak, rich and poor, government and governed, majority and minority. And there's the rub. The public knows little of the functions and methodology of the courts. Without adequate explanation or technical knowledge, the public may not know how it is that the judiciary maintains a free society under the law. Even the most familiar of curial functions, the sentencing of offenders, is often attended by misunderstanding of sentencing principles.

Of course, a sophisticated blend of legal and journalistic skills is needed to translate to the public the technical language of the law, the differing functions of judge and jury, the significance of precedent, the social significance of a judgment and its impact on future legal development. In earlier days there was a class of barrister-journalists, now sadly diminished in Australia. In this country, the tradition may still be maintained. There were some eminent practitioners of these fused professions. Charles Gavan Duffy, who established *The Nation* in 1842 was one of them. After serving both in prison and the House of Commons, he left for Australia where he became Premier of Victoria. His second wife bore Frank, who became Chief Justice of the High Court of Australia; his third wife bore George, who became President of the High Court of Ireland. Serjeant Sullivan QC followed Gavan Duffy as editor and proprietor of *The Nation* when the latter left for Australia. Even in his advanced years, the Serjeant exhibited a capacity for evocative descriptions of courts and judges. He remembered a Chief Justice of Common Pleas before whom, he said, 'no case was certain and no case was hopeless'.[3] But I digress, and I must return to my theme.

In the modern world, public understanding of any institution is conveyed largely by the media. The influence of those who work in the media led to their description, over 150 years ago, as the Fourth Estate. In 1840, Thomas Carlyle attributed the term to Edmund Burke. 'Burke' he wrote 'said there were Three Estates in Parliament; but, in the Reporters' Gallery yonder, there sat a *Fourth Estate* more important far than they all. It is not a figure of speech, or a witty saying; it is a literal fact, – very momentous to us in these times. ... Whoever can speak, speaking now to the whole nation, becomes a power, a branch of government, with inalienable weight in law-making, in all acts of authority.'[4]

Carlyle himself had used the term on an earlier occasion, speaking of 'A

Fourth Estate of Able Editors'.[5] In both references Carlyle treats the Fourth Estate as 'Men of Letters'. Today he would have to expand his references to the men and women versed in the art and technology of radio, television and the Internet.

The popular media are more familiar to us than the street in which we live, more pervasive than the aromas of the kitchen, more influential with many than the Sunday sermon. They inform, they entertain, they prescribe fashion, they form tastes, they mould attitudes and values. They present the three branches of Government to the people. The Fourth Estate is not a fourth branch of Government but, in the life of a free and democratic society, it has great power and influence. Its power and influence will be expanded by new technology.

It is tempting to say that the third branch – the judiciary – and the Fourth Estate – the media -share a responsibility to create or maintain confidence in the work of the courts. But that would cast the media in the role of apologists for the courts and thus undermine the independence of the media and their proper relationship with the public. The media's function is quite different from the court's. The court's function, entrenched in public expectation, is to decide cases and, in doing so, to apply the law competently and impartially. The media's function is to report and critically to analyse the work of the courts. So, we are speaking in the present context of disparate but interlocking functions which, if properly performed by both institutions, should produce public confidence in the maintenance of the rule of law by the courts.

There are several factors relating to the constitution of the courts and their procedure that affect public confidence in the rule of law. First, the courts must be constituted by competent judges: these are men and women who, by study and practice, have become learned in the law, resolute in character, beyond suspicion of partiality, possessed of a worldly wisdom and with a passion for justice. Where, you might ask, does one find such paragons of virtue? They may come from various avocations, but they are identified most clearly by their peers in the legal profession who have seen them at work in weak cases and in strong, in complex issues and in run of the mill work, retained for the deserving and the undeserving. How are such judges to be identified? In neither of our countries have we opted for either of the American systems: popular election or confirmation after public inquiry. Ireland's Constitution Review Group has given sound reasons for rejecting the public inquiry model, including their observation that 'the intense public scrutiny [of a candidate] is likely to deter the sort of people who would be suitable appointees'.[6] Judicial qualities are best vouched for by confidential report appraised by a few selectors, leaving the responsibility for the ultimate choice with a government that is accountable to the public. Governments that make patently inappropriate judicial appointments pay a political price. And, apart from more obvious considerations, they have to bear in mind that the recruitment of future judges of quality is linked to professional assessment of the quality of their predecessors. The Irish solution to the problem of judicial selection is *The Courts and Courts Officers Act 1995* which provides, as you know, for a Judicial Appointments Advisory Board to advise Government on the selection of judges.

Once appointed, the judge must avoid not only the reality but also the appearance of partiality. Lord Devlin commented that 'The Judge who does not appear impartial is as useless to the process as an umpire who allows the trial by battle to be fouled or an augurer who tampers with the entrails.'[7]

Want of impartiality poisons the stream of justice at its source; an appearance of partiality dries it up. That is why the courts have adopted the rule[8] that a challenge to a decision on the ground of bias will succeed if 'in all the circumstances the parties or the public might entertain a reasonable apprehension that the judge might not bring an impartial and unprejudiced mind to the resolution of the matter before him'.[9] That is the Australian test. The same test of reasonably apprehended bias has been expressed in the Supreme Court of Ireland. That is not surprising for, as Mr Justice O'Flaherty observed, Lord Hewart's maxim that 'justice should not only be done, but should manifestly and undoubtedly be seen to be done'[10] is 'probably a concept as old as the common law itself and it is in perfect harmony with our constitutional situation.'[11] In *Dublin Wellwoman Centre Ltd v Ireland*, Mrs Justice Denham, speaking for the Supreme Court, said 'It has long been a practice of the judiciary in this State not to act as a judge in a case where they have an interest, or where there are grounds on which a reasonable person might fear that in respect of the issues involved he would not get an independent hearing.'[12]

It is not enough to have judges who are competent and impartial. To ensure public confidence, they must sit publicly and in open view. 'Publicity', said Bentham, 'is the very soul of justice. It is the keenest spur to exertion and the surest of all guards against improbity. It keeps the judge himself while trying on trial.' The judge receives and hears in public whatever is to affect the decision to be made. No representation is received by a judge in the privacy of his chambers. No telephone calls are accepted from parties or their protagonists. Secrecy does not cloak the exercise of judicial power unless privacy is necessary for reasons of physical or national security, or to protect the identity of children or some victims of crime or the protection of trade secrets. 'The public administration of justice' said an Australian judge[13] 'tends to maintain confidence in the integrity and independence of the courts. The fact that courts of law are held openly and not in secret ... distinguishes their activities from those of administrative officials, for "publicity is the authentic hall-mark of judicial as distinct from administrative procedure"'.[14] The Constitution of Ireland provides: 'Justice shall be administered in Courts established by law by Judges appointed in the manner provided by this Constitution, and, save in such special and limited cases as may be prescribed by law, shall be administered in public.'[15]

However, I understand that the effect of this provision on the contemporary broadcasting of proceedings is in question in pending litigation. Therefore, I shall refrain from further comment.

After trial comes the judgment and perhaps an appeal. The reasons for judgment, whether at first instance or on appeal must also be in the public domain. If the steps in the reasoning to judgment are exposed, they are amenable to correction on appeal except, of course, in the court of final appeal. And there, in particular, the steps in the reasoning must be available to the public and open to public criticism. As Sir Frank Kitto pointed out: 'The process of reasoning which has decided the case must itself be exposed to the light of day, so that all concerned may understand what principles and practice of law and logic are guiding the courts, and so that full publicity may be achieved which provides, on the one hand, a powerful protection against any tendency to judicial autocracy and against any erroneous suspicion of judicial wrongdoing and, on the other hand, an effective stimulant to judicial high performance.'[16]

By sitting in public and by publishing their reasons for judgment, the judges give an account of the exercise of their judicial powers.

Court critics sometimes complain that judges are unaccountable. To whom should they be accountable and for what? In charging a jury, judges expose their conception of the law to be applied. In reasons for judgment, they give a full and public account of the facts they find and the law as they hold it to be. How otherwise are they to give an account of the exercise of their powers? Should the judge be accountable to the government of the day? Certainly not. Should the judge be accountable in some way to an interest group or to the public? The rule of law would be hostage to public relations campaigns or majoritarian interests. Should a judgment be fashioned to satisfy popular sentiment? That would be the antithesis of the rule of law.

The rule of law does not ensure that the decision in a particular case will be pleasing to an interest group, to a government or to the public. Take, for example, the case of a garda officer who, following established procedure, obtains a warrant from a peace commissioner to enter premises and search for controlled drugs. Drugs are found on the premises and a person is charged and convicted of being in possession of them. It turns out that the procedure for obtaining the warrant is defective and the warrant is invalid. Although the gardai acted in good faith, a majority of the Supreme Court held that the constitutionally protected personal rights of the citizen[17] demand the exclusion of the evidence obtained under the warrant and the consequential acquittal of the suspected drug dealer.[18] Now a report of this case could be: 'Suspect freed on a technicality'. But the real significance of the case is that priority is given to the rule of law over the punishment of an alleged offender. Except in extraordinarily excusing circumstances, personal constitutional rights are held to prevail over law enforcement practices which are mistakenly believed to be valid. That betokens a cohesive society confident of its freedom but it does not mean that the rule of law is skewed in favour of defendants. And so, while the Supreme Court has acknowledged a right to silence, the right is seen as correlative to the right to freedom of expression and thus to be subject to legislative encroachment in the interests of public order and morality. [19] Again the Constitution is upheld.

The rule of law is vindicated not in the result of a case but in the process of reaching the result. The law and the facts are the premisses in the judicial syllogism[20] qualified on occasions by a judicial discretion. If the law when applied to the facts leads to an unpalatable result, it is beside the point to criticize the result. Unless judges are to reach decisions that are socially acceptable, or popular, or beneficial to the majority whatever effect they may have on a minority, it is useless to look at the result and not the process. Indeed, the fact that a decision is unpalatable may be an indicium that the judge has applied the rule of law.

Hard cases, they say, make bad law. Conversely, good law may not work well in hard cases. The cases which test the law, which take it to the limit, which attract attention, are often the hard cases. These cases may evoke a development of the law within the constraints of the judicial method and the result may then attract criticism. But, as Sir Frank Kitto warned: 'Every Judge worthy of the name recognises that he must take each man's censure; he knows full well that as a Judge he is born to censure as the sparks fly upwards; but neither in preparing a judgment nor in retrospect may it weigh with him that the harvest he gleans is praise or blame, approval or scorn. He will reply to neither; he will defend himself not at all.'[21]

If a judge is to be unaffected by praise or approval or unmoved by blame or scorn, the judge must be protected by a commitment to the rule of law. The law is the shield of the judiciary for it is the protection against allegations of the arbitrary exercise of power. Absent a commitment to the rule of law, a judge would be beset by the concerns to which a German judge recently pointed: 'There is only one major issue in this context not usually taken into account, the well established "fourth power" – not separated, not controlled but endangering the system of checks and balances – the power of the mass media. The extreme importance of this fourth power for the judicial system begins with the question inherent covertly or overtly in the daily work of a judge. "What will the newspapers say if I decide this case in that way?"'[22]

This is not a new problem. An American judge of a century ago is reported to have made the bitter comment that the press 'have combined to bring the courts and the administration of justice under their control, by their appeals to popular prejudice, accompanied by the usual amount of lying.' Justice Ruth Bader Ginsburg, who reported the comment, doubted whether any of her colleagues would make that comment today.[23] No modern judge, committed to the rule of law, would contemplate yielding to populist pressure. And, for their part, even if the media make the most trenchant criticism of a case, they would not wish judges to bow to populist demand. The law is rightly expected to protect the critics of the court's work as well as those who support it.

It is one thing to point to the manner in which courts must be constituted and the procedures which must be followed in order to maintain public confidence in the rule of law. It is another to identify the perceptions which create that confidence. So I turn to the problems of communicating what happens in the courts to the public.

It is in the reasons for judgment rather than in the formal judgment or order of the court that one must search to find what the court is doing. Sometimes, when the judgment has a political significance or the case or a litigant has a high public profile, the judgment itself attracts public attention rather than the reasons given. That may be justified in some cases, but in others the reasons for judgment should also be publicized.

Take, for example, *Crotty v An Taoiseach.*[24] In that case, the Supreme Court by majority held that the *Constitution* precluded ratification of Title III of the Single European Act. The decision, so it was reported, was welcomed by some interest groups and disappointed others.[25] The decision had significant political consequences, both domestic and European. And those consequences had to be addressed by the Irish people in the ensuing referendum which amended Art. 29.4.3° of the *Constitution*. No less significant than the judgment were the principles by which the Court reached its conclusion. First, it was held that the Court had jurisdiction, at the instance of an individual citizen[26] who, like every other citizen, would be affected by the Single European Act, to intervene to prevent the Government from acting without constitutional authority. That question, said Chief Justice Finlay, was 'an issue of a fundamental nature, the importance of which ... transcends by far the significance of the provisions of the SEA'. The issue was fundamental because it concerned the subjection of government to the *Constitution* and the authority of the Court to enforce the *Constitution*. Secondly, a majority of the Court, construing Title III of the SEA, found that it would impermissibly constrict the exercise of the Government's constitutionally vested power – and responsibility -to formulate foreign policy. Mr Justice Walsh said: 'The foreign policy organ of the State cannot, within the terms of the Constitution, agree to impose upon itself, the State or upon the people the contemplated restrictions upon freedom of action.'

Citing Article 6, he held that 'In the last analysis it is the people themselves who are the guardians of the Constitution. In my view, the assent of the people is a necessary prerequisite to the ratification of so much of the Single European Act as consists of title III thereof.'

The people gave their assent. The Supreme Court gave judgment on 9 April 1987; the referendum which carried the amendment approving Ireland's accession to the SEA was held on 25 May in the same year. But the enduring importance of the principles embraced in *Crotty* is that the *Constitution* governs all branches of government, even in matters of foreign affairs and that the Courts' jurisdiction can be invoked to ensure that no organ of government acts without the authority that the people, through the *Constitution,* have conferred. As the preamble to the *Constitution* states, it was adopted and enacted by the people of Eire and given to themselves. In Ireland, as now in Australia, sovereignty is vested in the people. And the people should know that the courts give practical effect to that doctrine.

Both Ireland and Australia are governed by written Constitutions, but the Irish *Constitution* contains many provisions which protect the rights and freedoms of individuals while the Australian *Constitution* contains few provisions of that kind. It was created chiefly to apportion powers between the Commonwealth which it created and the States which are reincarnations of the antecedent Colonies. It follows that, although similar problems can arise in both countries and similar conclusions be reached, the legal rules applied in reaching those conclusions may be different. Thus, when the extent of confidentiality of Cabinet communications arose before the Supreme Court of Ireland in *Attorney-General v Hamilton (No 1)*[27] and before the High Court of Australia in the *Commonwealth v Northern Land Council*,[28] both Courts concluded that Cabinet confidentiality could not ordinarily be breached. But the judgments in Ireland turned largely on the provisions of the *Constitution* and the judgments in Australia turned on what were seen as principles of the common law. Of course, the same values may inform the interpretation of a term in a Constitution and the definition of a rule of the common law. Some years ago, Peter Wright, an erstwhile member of the British Security Service wrote *Spycatcher*. The Attorney-General of the United Kingdom unsuccessfully sought an injunction against its publication in Australia.[29] Two years earlier, a similar application was heard in the High Court of Ireland[30] with respect to another book written by a deceased member of the same Service. That application was also unsuccessful. The reasons in the two cases were similar, but they proceeded from different starting points. In both cases, the plaintiff's interests were identified as those of a foreign government and, on that account, distinguished from the interests of a private litigant. The starting point of the Irish case was the *Constitution*. Mrs Justice Carroll said: 'Any consideration of the question of preventing publication of material of public interest must be viewed in the light of the Constitution. Article 40.6.1° guarantees liberty for the exercise of the right of citizens to express freely their convictions and opinions subject to public order and morality.'

By contrast, the Australian case proceeded on the general principles of equity and the common law. Conversely, different results may be reached when similar constitutional provisions are construed. The constitutional requirement that 'no person shall be tried on any criminal charge without a jury'[31] permits majority verdicts in Ireland[32] but, in Australia, the requirement that trial on indictment for federal offences be 'by jury'[33] has been held to prescribe an unanimous verdict.[34]

Constitutional cases lend themselves to reporting from the viewpoint of their political significance. This is inevitable and, indeed, desirable – especially when there is a readiness, as there is in Ireland, to submit the question decided to a referendum for constitutional change.

The *Constitution* of Ireland may be amended with the approval of a simple majority of those voting at a referendum to approve the amending Bill.[35] The *Constitution* of the Commonwealth of Australia, on the other hand, can be amended only if the amending Bill is passed by an absolute majority of both Houses of the Parliament and approved at a referendum by a majority of voters in a majority of States and by a majority of all voters throughout Australia.[36] In Australia, few referenda for constitutional amendment have been carried. While the reasons for judgment in a constitutional case may be the subject of public discussion in the conduct of a referendum in Ireland, the reasons for judgment in a constitutional case in Australia may not command so much public attention although the reasons become a relatively immutable addition to the constitutional text. There, the judgment itself often seems more significant to the media than the reasons for judgment since the judgment sets the parameters within which political debate is conducted.

In both countries, the people are entitled to be informed not only of a judgment which affects their constitutional destiny but also of the faithful and impartial application of the rule of law by their delegates, the Courts, in coming to judgment. As Mrs Justice Denham said in the *Dublin Wellwoman case:* 'With the development of the modern communications media and an increasingly educated and enquiring society the public perception of the impartiality of the courts is a cornerstone of the administration of justice in our constitutional democracy.' [37]

The problem, as Justice Ruth Bader Ginsburg has noted is that 'It is indeed hard, under the pressure of publication deadlines, to describe judicial opinions with entire accuracy.[38] And, to describe court actions accurately ... is, in many cases, to describe them boringly.' [39]

Of course, the rehearsing of facts, the recitation of constitutional or statutory texts, the invocation of precedent and the expression of concise legal reasoning, are hardly the stuff to be digested with breakfast or to entertain on the evening television screen. True it is that the reporting of some cases would be tedious and technical. Yet legal rules are laden with values. They contain the ethos of the society they serve and, to the eye of the trained observer, the curial acceptance or rejection of a legal proposition can sometimes be seen as a dramatic signpost to the way in which society is heading. The bio-ethical cases, which are the inevitable concomitant of advancing medical technology, provide some examples.

In the cases arising under Article 40.3 of the *Constitution*, difficult and controversial questions have fallen for determination. The constitutional right to life of the unborn[40] and the right to life of the terminally ill[41] have evoked instructive judgments on the nature and priority of those rights.[42] In one of these cases,[43] the Supreme Court recognized the *Constitution* as the fundamental and supreme law of the State representing the will of the people and not inferior to the natural law. However, in interpreting the *Constitution*, the Court adopted a judgment of Mr Justice Walsh espousing the interpretation of constitutional rights in the light of the preamble to the *Constitution* so that the judges must 'as best they can from their training and their experience interpret these rights in accordance with their ideas of prudence, justice and charity.' [44] Reasons for judgment can be expected to reveal contemporary judicial notions of these virtues. Although these virtues do not displace the text, judicial notions of them inform the provisions of Ireland's *Constitution.*

In cases of notoriety, the public and the media are immediately interested in the outcome. But what can be done to ensure that the public is aware of, and justifiably confident in, the integrity of the system? The answer depends on the role that the media choose for themselves in reporting and analysing the work of the courts. In a recent article which sketched the obstacles in the way of adequate reporting of the work of the Supreme Court of the United States, the Court correspondent for the *New York Times* observed: 'Especially in an era when the political system has ceded to the courts many of society's most difficult questions, it is sobering to acknowledge the extent to which the courts and the country depend on the press for the public understanding that is necessary for the health and, ultimately, the legitimacy of any institution in a democratic society.'[45]

The author reports[46] the criticism by a Judge of the Constitutional Court of South Africa of press coverage of that Court's first and significant decision which struck down the death penalty.[47] His Lordship complained that the reporters 'had not thought it necessary to tell the public what the court's reasons for the decision actually were.' He wondered whether effective constitutional government could exist if the press did not enlighten the public about the reasoning behind the court's decisions. In 1990, the Canadian Judicial Council, acknowledging the need for 'accurate, balanced and complete report of the hearing and disposition of specific cases' accepted that the Judiciary, Court Officials and the Bar 'have a responsibility appropriate to their roles to assist the media in the provision of such coverage'.[48] The Council urged enhanced media access to court proceedings and, more contentiously, suggested that the media representatives should be provided with legal information and assistance. I respectfully agree that the courts should facilitate media access to whatever is on public record or in the public domain. But it is another question whether the court should act as an interpreter of its own decisions or should seek to explain the reasons why a decision was reached.

Accurate reporting and critical analysis of the work of the courts require some legal skills and experience. Who should provide them? Public confidence in the rule of law is not to be won by the issuing of media statements nor by background briefings that might be suspect as putting a favourable spin on the work of the courts. The media would abandon their responsibility if they were to publish uncritically summaries of cases or other media releases issued with the authority of the courts. The media must themselves probe and analyse the reasons for judgments of public importance. The basic justification for freedom of the press is the employment of an informed and critical faculty and the employment of that faculty is a source of pride to the competent journalist. If the courts were to furnish digests of information for the media to publish, they would abandon the independence which both must assert and defend in the public interest. Better by far that the media should sense that there are stories of vital public interest in the dramas of a trial, in the tensions between the organs of government, in the priorities of constitutional rights or immunities, in the interplay of legal rules and in the exposition of principles under which society lives.

I venture to suggest that the journalist who is familiar with the jargon, the procedure, the statutes and the precedents will find much to report and comment upon in the work of the courts and their fidelity to the rule of law, including the legitimacy of the techniques which the courts employ in interpreting and developing the law. The well-furnished legal journalist who perceives the principle underlying a rule appearing in reasons for judgment and who perceives the community value that underlies the principle is well placed to offer insightful criticism and, however indirectly, to play a part in the development of the law. The journalist who cannot or does not bring that critical faculty to bear upon what emerges from the courts is at risk of misleading the public about the work of the institution on which our freedom under the law largely depends. The priceless heritage of the rule of law depends not on a supine acceptance by the public of what the courts are doing nor on misinformation that leads to disaffection but on an informed and critical insistence that the courts should apply the law competently and impartially and be seen to be doing so.

The courts and the media each have a distinct part to play. And so there is truth in the conclusion reached by Linda Greenhouse when she says: 'despite our divergent interests – the press corps' interest in accessibility and information, the Court's in protecting the integrity of its decisional process – I am naive enough ... to think of these two institutions as, to some degree, partners in a mutual democratic enterprise to which both must acknowledge responsibility.'[49]

The authorities that broadcast and the courts that administer the law both seek to serve society and, in that sense, are partners in a democratic enterprise but the pride which each has in its professional standards and the independence which they boast offer the surest guarantee that the enterprise will succeed.

---

1. This article is a revised version of the lecture, and it was first published in *The Irish Jurist:* see Sir Gerard Brennan, 'The Third Branch and the Fourth Estate' (1997) 32 *The Irish Jurist* (NS) 62-76.
2. Hamilton, *The Federalist Papers* (No 78), (New American Library, New York, 1961) 465, first published in 1787.

3. A M Sullivan, 'The Last Forty Years of the Irish Bar' (1927-1929) 3 *Cambridge Law Journal* 365.
4. 'The Hero as Man of Letters' published in Thomas Carlyle, *On Heroes, Hero-Worship and the Heroic in History* (Oxford University Press, 1904) 219, first published in 1840.
5. See *A History of the French Revolution,* (Chapman and Hall, 1910) 186, originally published in 1837.
6. See *Report of the Constitution Review Group (*Stationery Office, 1996) 181.
7. Lord Devlin, 'Judges and Lawmakers'(1976) 39 (1) *Modern Law Review* 1, 4.
8. The rule does not apply when, of necessity, a particular judge must sit on a case.
9. See *Grassby v The Queen* (1989) 168 CLR 1, 20 per Dawson J citing *Livesey v New South Wales Bar Association* (1983) 151 CLR 288 and *R v Watson; Ex parte Armstrong* (1976) 136 CLR 248.
10. See *R v Sussex Justices, ex parte McCarthy* [1924] 1 KB 256, 259.
11. See *O'Reilly v Cassidy* [1995] 1 ILRM 306, 310.
12. [1995] 1 ILRM 408, 421-422.
13. See *Russell v Russell* (1976) 134 CLR 495, 520 (Gibbs J).
14. See *McPherson v McPherson* [1936] AC 177, 200.
15. Article 34.1.
16. 'Why Write Judgments?', a paper presented in 1973 to a Convention of Judges of the High Court of Australia and the Supreme Courts of the States and Territories and published: Sir Frank Kitto, 'Why Write Judgments' (1992) 66 *Australian Law Journal* 787, 790.
17. Article 40.3.1°.
18. See *The People (Director of Public Prosecutions) v Kenny* [1990] 2 IR 110; [1990] ILRM 569.
19. See *Heaney v McGuinness v Ireland and the Attorney-General* (unreported (247/94), 23 July 1996).
20. See *R v Trade Practices Tribunal; Ex parte Tasmanian Breweries Pty Ltd* (1970) 123 CLR 361, 374.
21. Kitto, 'Why Write Judgments?' (n 16) 790.
22. Judge Schomburg, 'Position and Role of the Judiciary within the Context of Separation of the Legislative, Executive and Judicial Powers', a paper presented to the 10th Annual Meeting of the Society for the Reform of Criminal Law, Whistler; British Columbia, Canada, (August 1996) 20-24.
23. Ruth Bader Ginsburg, 'Communicating and Commenting on the Court's Work' (1995) 83 *Georgetown Law Journal* 2119, 2123.
24. [1987] IR 713.
25. See *Irish Times,* 10 April 1987.
26. See also *Society for the Protection of Unborn Children (Ire) Ltd v Coogan* [1989] IR 734 and *McGimpsey v. Ireland* [1990] 1 IR 110, 123-124 (McCarthy J).
27. [1993] 2 IR 250; [1993] ILRM 81.
28. (1993) 176 CLR 604.
29. See *Attorney-General (United Kingdom) v Heinemann Publishers Australia Pty Ltd* (1988) 165 CLR 30.
30. See *Attorney General for England and Wales v Brandon Book Publishers Ltd* [1987] ILRM 135.

31. Article 38.5.
32. See *O'Callaghan v Attorney General and the Director of Public Prosecutions* [1993] 2 IR 17.
33. Constitution, s 80.
34. See *Cheatle v The Queen* (1993) 177 CLR 541.
35. Article 47.1.
36. Section 128.
37. [1995] ILRM 408 at 422.
38. See *Virginia Pharmacy Bd v Virginia Citizens Consumer Council* 425 US 748 at 777 (1976) per Stewart J.
39. Ginsburg, 'Communicating and Commenting on the Court's Work' (n 23) 2128.
40. Article 40.3.3°.
41. Article 40.3.2°.
42. See *Attorney-General (at the relation of SPUC) v Open Door Counselling Ltd* [1988] IR 593; *Attorney-General v X* [1992] IR 1; *In the Matter of a Ward of Court* [1995] 2 ILRM 401.
43. See *Information (Termination of Pregnancies) Bill* 1995 [1995] 1 IR 1.
44. See *McGee v The Attorney-General* [1974] IR 284, 319.
45. Greenhouse, 'Telling the Court's Story: Justice and Journalism at the Supreme Court' (1996) 105 *Yale Law Journal* 1537, 1538.
46. Linda Greenhouse, Telling the Court's Story: Justice and Journalism at the Supreme Court' (1996) 105 *Yale Law Journal* 1537, 1552.
47. See *State v Makwanyane* 1995 (3) SA 391 (Const Ct)
48. Canadian Judicial Council, *Principles Governing Relations between the Judiciary and the News Media", Canadian Judicial Council Annual Report* (1990-1991), 21-22.
49. (1996) 105 *Yale Law Journal* 1537, 1561.

8.9 Human Rights, Disability and Education

Editor's note

As Chancellor of the University of Technology, Sydney, Brennan was invited to deliver the opening address at a conference of the Social Relations of Disability Research Network and the Australian Human Rights Centre on 17 September 1999. UTS was a founding member of this research network in 1995. This was the network's vision: 'Driven by people with lived experience, disability research can enable evidence-based change to improve and benefit society. Inclusive, high-quality research can positively influence the broader context of life for people with disability. They have a right to participate equally in society, accessing the same opportunities as others in the areas of education, employment, housing, social relationships and access to justice.' As Chancellor, Brennan was delighted to support such an academic initiative.

In a society which lauds achievement and envies material success, the physically or mentally disabled suffer a double disadvantage. To the extent that their disability makes them less competitive, they are disadvantaged in achieving the goals which society places before them. But the more significant disadvantage is the devaluation of the disabled by some members of the society to the detriment of self-image and self-respect.

Those of you who work with the disabled have long since discarded the superficial assessment of a person by reference to his or her appearance; you have come to know, to respect and to appreciate the personality of those with whom you work; you know them to have the same emotions, to be possessed of the same aspirations, to be capable of love, hate and frustration as other members of the community. But the superficial response of many in our society to the appearance of disability carries a threat to the human rights of the disabled and demands protective measures on the one hand and education of the community on the other. I should say something about each of those requirements.

First, protective measures. Protective measures must satisfy two criteria: they must secure a benefit responsive to, and (so far as practicable) proportionate to, the disability and they must not patronise or otherwise undermine self-image and self-respect. The pre-eminent protective measure is education. Education as the term implies, draws out to the maximum the abilities of the individual. Education confers on the individual the inestimable benefit of personal fulfilment, of self-confidence, of achievement, of understanding of the society in which we live. And it enhances the prospects of gainful employment. For many disabled people, education provides the opportunity not only to command respect as a member of the community but also to develop to the full the latent capacities of body, mind and spirit which may otherwise have been depressed by the disability. Thus, this Conference is of great importance. In your discussions, you will further develop the skill and art of delivering the most effective educational services to those who are affected by a variety of disabilities, each calling for individual evaluation.

For many, the emphasis must be on physical education or the provision of physical assistance. For others, the learning of knowledge and the development of intellectual abilities will be uppermost. What is important is the recognition of the unique needs, dignity and worth of the individual and the tailoring of educational services to suit the individual's requirements. Our general system of education is tailored to the differing requirements of the mass of the community – some streams leading to high academic achievement, some to the development of important manual skills and some streams lie between the two. Just as the several streams of the general educational system are tailored to meet the requirements of people with different aptitudes and interests, so the system of education for the disabled should be tailored to meet their different requirements.

This is not always easy to achieve. Special arrangements may have to be made, additional funds may have to be committed, particular access may have to be provided, higher staffing levels and more intensive work may have to be done. Sufficient resources to satisfy the educational human rights of the disabled may be hard to come by when the educational budget is under serious strain, yet a civilized community's responsibility for the disabled requires that there be equality of opportunity for the abled and the disabled, so far as the capacities of each person permit.

When severe disability makes an individual dependent on the care of another, the need for protective measures increases correspondingly. This is especially true in the case of severe mental disability when the individual's capacity for autonomous decision-making is diminished, sometimes completely. Then legal measures are required not merely to safeguard the person and property of the disabled but to supervise the decisions which are made on the disabled person's behalf. In recent years, there have been a number of cases in which the courts have had to grapple with these problems. In *Marion's Case*[1] and in its sequel *P* v *P*,[2] the High Court was concerned with the sterilization of mentally disabled young women. In the former case, the majority of the Court held that the decision to sterilize a minor severely disabled in intellect 'falls outside the scope of parental powers' and must be made by a court in possession of the material facts. But, it was said, sterilization is a step of last resort and can be authorized only when 'other procedures or treatments are or have proved inadequate, in the sense that they have failed or will not alleviate the situation so that the child can lead a life in keeping with his or her needs and capacities.' In England in the *Anthony Bland Case,*[3] the Court of Appeal and the House of Lords had to make the anguishing decision whether to authorize the withdrawal of tube feeding and ventilation from a young man whose brain damage had reduced him to a permanent vegetative state. In these cases, the courts have been left to develop principles – hopefully in accordance with contemporary community standards – to determine cases which, 20 years ago, would not have been thought to be soluble by litigation.

The reasons for the emergence of bioethical litigation are not hard to find. The advance of life-saving medical skills have preserved many lives that would have been lost in earlier times, albeit the injured are often left with massive disabilities. When the disabilities have been caused in circumstances which attract compensation, litigation is inevitable. Then there are some decisions which, having an ethical dimension, might have been solved in earlier times by reference to commonly agreed religious and/or moral precepts but which must now be solved, in default of a uniform morality, by the courts. If you will pardon me for quoting from a judgment of my own, I said in *Marion's Case:*

> The questions raised by this case starkly demonstrate the quandary of the law when it is invoked to settle an issue which is a subject of ethical controversy and there are no applicable or analogous cases of binding authority. Although the issues in this case relate to the law's protection of the physical integrity of a person suffering from an intellectual disability, there is no clear community consensus on these issues which the courts or the legislature can translate into law. Nevertheless, concrete and poignant cases – Marion's among them – arise for decision.[4]

Here is a fertile field for the development of the jurisprudence of human rights. The jurisprudence of human rights has the purpose of securing the dignity of every person and it may be enlisted in aid of disabled people who stand in need of legal protection to secure their dignity. To give effective legal teeth to human rights, however, it is necessary for lawyers to translate the broad and rhetorical terms in which human rights are necessarily cast into precise legal propositions capable of curial enforcement. When a legal proposition giving effect to a human right is formulated, it can be incorporated into the general body of the law either by judicial declaration (as occurred in *Marion's Case)* or by legislative action.

If the relevant human right is a right to educational services, it must be given effect according to the condition of the individual whose right is to be vindicated. It is impossible to articulate in detail and with precision the content of the educational rights of every disabled person. Non-discrimination may not be an adequate statutory safeguard. What is needed is a statutory statement of the principle by reference to which the sufficiency of educational services can be judged. Such a statement would be useful not so much as a foundation for court orders as a definition of the standards to be observed by educational authorities. There is much to be said for a Charter of Educational Rights for the Disabled provided it is formulated with sufficient particularity to admit of its application in concrete circumstances.

Of course, a broad and rhetorical enunciation of human rights ordinarily operates upon the values of the respective communities who assent to its application. It helps to mould community standards and in that indirect way it helps in the formulation of laws of concrete application. In other words, it is a valuable educational tool. The community which embraces the concept of human rights and seriously desires to implement them is a compassionate community which respects the dignity of each of its members. The human rights movement can do much to enhance community attitude to the disabled so as to ensure that they are respected as contributing members of society, each with an individual worth and dignity comparable with the worth and dignity of everybody else.

That is a truth to which those who work with the disabled will testify. It seems that those who work most closely with the most seriously disabled will testify also to the contribution which the disabled make to their own growth and joy. One of the notable examples of this is Jean Vanier, the Founder of L'Arche, the movement which brings the mentally disabled and their helpers together in small households marked by mutual respect and affection. In his 1988 Lectures to the Harvard Divinity School, now published in one of his many books, he said:

> it is my belief that in our mad world where there is so much pain, rivalry, hatred, violence, inequality and oppression, it is people who are weak, rejected, marginalized, counted as useless, who can become a source of life and of salvation for us as individuals as well as for our world. And it's my hope that each one of you may experience the incredible gift of the friendship of people who are poor and weak, that you too may receive life from them. For they call us to love, to communion, to compassion and to community.[5]

Those are the observations of a deeply religious man speaking to a Divinity School. They may not resonate with the same power in every audience, but they sufficiently indicate that disability is not always a negative, diminishing tragedy. With understanding and compassion, it may return to those who render service a reward greater than the service given.

I wish you success in the conduct of this brief seminar. It will not solve all the problems, satisfy all the demands or remove all the obstacles in the way of progressing the disabled. But if it be right to say that the measure of a civilization is the manner in which it treats its minorities, your enlisting of the ideals of human rights in support of the disabled minority will enhance the quality of our nation. And for that you deserve our nation's thanks.

---

1. See *Department of Health & Community Services v JWB & SMB* (*Marion's Case'*) (1992) 175 CLR 218.
2. See *P v P* (1994) 181 CLR 583.
3. See *Airedale NHS Trust v Bland* [1993] AC 789.
4. See *Marion's Case* (n 1) 264.
5. 'From Brokenness to Community', The 1988 Harold M Wit Lectures to the Harvard University Divinity School, 9-10.

8.10 Law and Ethics for Members of Parliament

Editor's note

Professor Gerard Carney from Bond University had been Brennan's Executive Associate when Brennan was Chief Justice. This was Brennan's speech at the launch of Carney's 2000 book: Members of Parliament: Law and Ethics (Prospect Media, 2000).

In a democracy, political institutions depend ultimately on public confidence in their efficiency and integrity. Confidence in these institutions is not maintained solely by the ballot box. The discipline of the party system, control over the selection of candidates and the ephemeral nature of electoral issues and promises place a limit on the effective accountability of political institutions to the general public.

The efficiency and integrity of political institutions are functions of the qualifications and character of those in whom political power is reposed and of the manner in which that power is exercised. The public expects that certain standards will be maintained and, provided those standards are maintained, accepts and peacefully submits to the exercise of political power. The maintenance of proper standards underpins the peace, order and good government of society. This book is about the maintenance of those standards. It is also about the means of protecting democratic debate inside and outside the Parliament.

The standards of political conduct are defined and buttressed by a number of institutional mechanisms which themselves command public support, albeit their content is not fully known to the public, nor fully appreciated by those who are expected to observe the relevant standards. Constitutions, laws, conventions, guidelines and practices all have an effect – sometimes coercive, sometimes persuasive, sometimes by providing a touchstone of desirable propriety. These are the subject of Professor Carney's treatise.

The author has covered the standards applicable to practically every aspect of public conduct on the part of those vested with political authority. But the value of this treatise lies not so much in its breadth as in its depth, insights and accuracy. Parliamentary history and contemporary practice, constitutional imperatives and speakers' rulings, statute and the common law, promulgated guidelines, committee reports and the lessons of notorious 'affairs' are examined and expounded to show the way in which political power should be exercised on behalf of the community which entrusts that power to their political representatives.

The book is not a mere anthology of ethical *desiderata.* This is a practical handbook for those engaged in politics and for their advisers and an authoritative textbook for lawyers and public administrators. It is at once a work of scholarship and a lucid roadmap of political propriety. When an issue has not hitherto been clarified by law or practice, the author says so. When existing law or practice is arguably defective, the author proposes reform.

The book contains a long overdue exposition of the relationship between, on the one hand, constitutional imperatives, the general law (including the relevant principles of tort and equity) and the law and custom of Parliament, and on the other, the ethics, practices and problems of parliamentary and political life. The division of this book into three Parts – Qualifications and Disqualifications, Parliamentary Privilege and Freedom of Speech, and Standards of Conduct helpfully focus on elements of a general subject few parts of which can be considered in isolation.

Erskine May's *Treatise on the Law, Privileges, Proceedings and Usage of Parliament* and the Practice Books of the Australian Senate and House of Representatives do not provide the same depth of analysis covering the field of law and ethics affecting members of Parliament. Yet there are some issues – including the difficult topic of Article 9 of the Bill of Rights 1689 and disclosure of Parliamentary proceedings in court – which require not only an examination of diverse authorities but the skill of precise legal analysis.

By the publication of this book, Professor Carney has made a considerable contribution to public law and public administration in Australia. The scholarship with which for a time he assisted me in the judicial branch of government is now directed to a wider audience and to the service of Parliaments of the Commonwealth – the institutions which are at the heart of our democracy.

8.11 Donald Horne's *Australian Compact*

Editor's note

After the failed referendum on the republic, the New South Wales Centenary of Federation Committee invited Brennan to launch Donald Horne's *An Australian compact?: what are the core values that all Australians might respect?* in the Dixon Room at the State Library of New South Wales on 20 March 2002. In the four years since his retirement from the High Court, Brennan had been wondering how one would determine the enduring community values at a time of rapid change – the values which would inform the principles from which one could then derive the rules of common law and good governance.

The Centenary of Federation should have ushered in a joyous second century of national life. We should be starting this century sure of our identity, proud of our institutions, confident of our future, respected by our neighbours and with unqualified pride in being Australian. The sufferings and the triumphs, the innovations and the achievements of the last century and of the antecedent years leading to Federation warrant such a celebration. Yet we find today an Australia of diminished national spirit, the sureness of our identity sapped by an uncertain commitment to reconciliation and multiculturalism; pride in our institutions eroded by concerns about the conduct and character of office holders and by an unseemly pettiness in political debate; confidence in our future undermined by a lack of resources for our public educational system and for research; the respect of our neighbours risked by policies of self-interest; pride in being Australian tarnished by our fear and our treatment of asylum seekers whose terrible stories and lives of despair are hidden in remote places. Our vision seems to have narrowed to material success. To borrow Xavier Herbert's phrase 'Poor Fella my country'. What do we celebrate in today's Australia? Sportspeople and film stars. Donald Horne, as ever reading the national mood correctly, invites us to adopt an Australian Compact as a mechanism which will help us to lift our spirits and rekindle our confidence in ourselves and our nation.

He rightly perceives that there is no 'typical Australia'. Each of us conceives of this country and of our relationship to it and its people according to his or her own experience and beliefs. But the corollary is that, desiring to live together in peace, order and self-respect, each must be accorded the freedom and the social and political opportunities which are essential to his or her unique dignity. The term currently used to describe that freedom and those opportunities is 'human rights'. The implications are enormous. No government may infringe its people's human rights; on the contrary, it must defend and advance them. A society in which all are accorded their human rights flourishes, for its people are secure and its government stable. A Compact expressing the values we all respect would be a bastion of our human rights, an important political and social instrument embodying the determination of the Australian people to live in peaceful co-existence in a stable society.

The values which Donald Horne articulates are not derived from a treatise on political philosophy, though a liberal philosopher would commend them. They are derived from Australian history and an observation of contemporary Australian life.

We are not, nor have Australians ever been, entirely homogeneous. The laws and customs of the Aboriginal peoples were various; so were the laws and customs (as well as the ethnic origins) of the early European settlers. The waves of migration in the last two centuries have introduced peoples from different parts of the globe bringing with them diverse customs, religions and cultures. As Donald Horne points out, we have known divisions based on religion and class and today we see differences in the regions in which we live, the work we do, the beliefs we hold, the incomes we earn and the property we own. How then, as a people, are we to advance together? By making a compact about our shared and basic values.

At a bare minimum, we must agree on the rule of law – the binding effect of known rules operating equally on the governors and the governed, on the rich and poor, on the powerful and the weak, impartially and openly administered by independent courts and tribunals to which all have equal access. There will be shortcomings in the implementing of the rule of law, but so long as we agree on its value there will be pressure to remedy its defects and to strive for its improvement. On the rule of law, all else depends: our freedom to think, to be and to do; political, social and economic order; family life and relationships; the protection of the environment.

How should the laws be made? Not by a dictator but by the people through their representatives. We shall abide by the laws, even if we do not agree with them, provided the process which makes them is a process owned by us, the people. And so, we should want a system of government that truly represents us: a representative democracy. To be truly representative of a people who are different in a variety of ways, the political opinion of each must be given equal value. So, our democracy must be based on universal adult suffrage.

But the mainstream, the majority, may not always protect the human rights of the marginalised and the minorities. Unless we all agree on the way in which power is to be exercised, power and the laws which confer power can become the instruments of tyranny. We know that the laws and practices which denied the human rights of Aboriginal Australians in earlier times were not then opposed by a majority of the electorate. And why was that? Not because of some conscious antipathy but certainly because the majority did not then recognize the dignity of Aboriginal Australians equal to the dignity of every other Australian. Yet Aboriginal Australians were not even counted in the census, much less given access to the ballot box.

To accord to each his or her human rights means that the laws and institutions of the nation must treat each person equally. To achieve that result, three conditions must be satisfied: tolerance of difference, conventions of respect and institutions to maintain our human rights. Donald Horne points out that tolerance of difference does not mean that we must like those who are different or yield to opinions or standards that are different from our own. Our own integrity is not infringed by accepting the right of others to their integrity – their freedom to pursue their own beliefs and their own ways so long as they do not harm others.

Conventions are needed, at least in the absence of laws to achieve the same result, to ensure that some basic freedoms are not infringed. Donald Horne lists the freedoms which he sees as 'some of the hallmarks of a liberal representative democracy':

- free expression of opinion
- freedom of information
- freedom of assembly
- freedom to demonstrate
- freedom of association.

The list is not exhaustive. More extensive lists can be found in a number of international instruments dealing with human rights. But the list itself is not important. What is important is the spirit of the people – a spirit which acknowledges that every person is entitled to be treated with respect, a spirit that accepts that every person has an equal right to reach an informed opinion and to participate freely in public affairs without fear of penalty – that is, without fear that dissent will be visited with disfavour, disadvantage or neglect. And, in case the spirit of tolerance and the conventions of respect should fail, there must always be an independent system of courts and tribunals to ensure at least the minimal protection of human rights that are essential in a liberal democracy.

Donald Horne raises two other important issues. First, 'respect and care for the land we share' and next 'the unique status of the Indigenous people'.

These issues are not unrelated. David Malouf has noted that the crops and animals that were imported by European settlement were alien to the Australian landscape and that 'the very industry that gives us a hold on the earth has no roots in the land itself, no history, no past.' So most Australians, though they love this wide brown land, must be careful to ensure that our economy and our culture do not destroy it. For Aboriginal Australians, on the other hand, land 'meant hearth, home, the source and locus of life and everlastingness of spirit' – moving words which WEH Stanner used in trying to describe the significance of land to Aboriginal people. These two great issues – land care and respect for Aboriginal Australians, their homeland and their culture – face Australia today and we will be severely diminished as a nation unless we appreciate the dimensions of these issues and resolve them with clear and open minds.

Australians have much to be proud of. We have a Constitution which has seen us through a century, political institutions which are largely responsive to majority opinion, courts whose integrity and competence is undoubted, a substantial tradition of tolerance (albeit mere inertia sometimes masquerades as tolerance), a general acceptance of the equality of individuals and liberation from ancient and rigid societies which allows us to be creative and courageous. But we retreat when we fear what we do not know or understand. Thus, when we think of constitutional change, we might cling to the idea that 'if it ain't broke, don't fix it'. If, as Donald Horne points out, political leaders are not vigilant to ensure that fear of the unknown does not lead to prejudice, our tolerance vanishes and our respect for human dignity disappears. If illustration be necessary, contemplate for a moment our treatment of those people who come in boats risking their lives to reach our shores from strange countries with strange customs practising strange religions and in numbers which we mistakenly think are more than Australia can accept.

If Australia has anything to fear from the future, it is (to borrow from Churchill) fear itself. Once we understand, we do not fear. Once we do not fear, our tolerance, our respect for others, our initiative and our courage emerge. We become what we all aspire to be: proud citizens of a free and confident nation.

Donald Horne has given us a blueprint for a more hopeful future. We are again in his debt. It gives me much pleasure, for I am greatly honoured, to launch his *Australian Compact.*

8.12 Australian Values and the Australian Social Conscience

Editor's note

The first Jesuits to arrive in Australia landed by boat on 8 December 1848. Marking 150 years in Australia, the Jesuits organised a series of seminars in Melbourne and Sydney during Lent 1999. The first seminar in Melbourne was held on Ash Wednesday, 19 February 1999. The Governor-General, Sir William Deane introduced the series. Brennan was the first speaker. The second speaker was Morag Fraser. Respondents included Professor Peter Steele SJ, Professor Dorothy Lee, Susan Crennan QC (later a High Court Justice), Professor Max Charlesworth, Sir Gustav Nossal, Hugh Mackay, Professor Martin Krygier, and Professor Bettina Cass. These were Brennan's opening remarks.[1]

Values are broad articles of faith, of belief in what is good or useful. Some of our individual values come from, or are verified by, practical experience; some come from beliefs we have taken from others and, with or without qualifications, have made our own. As the good and the useful can depend on circumstances, no value can be stated in terms that are universal and absolute. Liberty and equality are estimable values, but absolute liberty can be the enemy of equality and absolute equality would demand the curtailing of liberty.

Values are expressed in broad terms, without the qualifications necessary to define the precise moral or legal precepts which they indicate. Although their content is imprecise, they are powerful influences on thought and conduct. Values continually contribute to the formation of our attitudes to specific issues or problems.[2] We may not always form our attitudes or act in harmony with our values, but we assume that they tell us what is good or useful. Values give us our character, affect our conduct, inform our relationships, and mould our future. They define our identities.

So, it is with a society whose members generally embrace a set of values. Values give a society its character, they determine (mediately or immediately) its laws and institutions,[3] they inform the society's relationships with other societies and – significantly – they are the charter of the society's future. National values define the identity of the people. National values are derived from the religious and philosophical beliefs of the people, from their history and from the physical environment. It may not be possible to list exhaustively the values of a society or to express them in terms susceptible of application to provide the solution to specific cases.[4] As values are expressed in broad terms and are derived from sources having a diverse impact on individuals, they have a greater currency in flowery political rhetoric than they do in deductive or legal reasoning. However, there can be no doubt about the close relationship and the need for accord between a society's values and its laws and institutions.[5] The invocation of values in rhetoric demonstrates their talismanic power.

In speaking of Australian values, we are speaking of the values of a pluralist and ethnically diverse nation. So, the question must be asked whether there *is* a set of Australian values. To answer the question, we must start at the beginning with the Aboriginal inhabitants of this country.

Professor Stanner, that sensitive observer of the Aboriginal peoples, noted that their societies were immensely old, virtually completely isolated, and existed in a fairly constant environment with an unprogressive material culture.[6] Unchanging order, enduring through a continuing present, was at the heart of Aboriginal values. Theirs was a self-regulating society, dependent on the complementary functions of clans and moieties. '[T]here [were] no great conflicts over power, no great contests for place or office'.[7] They were nomads, for whom possessions would have been an encumbrance and for whom the significance of their country and everything that was in it was spiritual rather than material. To the Aboriginal, land meant 'hearth, home, the source and locus of life, and everlastingness of spirit'.[8] The Aboriginal belonged to the land; it was not an item in the market economy. 'The things of the Market', says Stanner, 'money, prices, exchange values, saving, the maintenance and building of capital – which so sharply characterise our civilisation, are precisely those which the Aborigines are least able to grasp and handle.'[9] Aboriginal society had 'a general design or plan of life at the opposite pole to our own'.[10]

By contrast, we Australians of European ancestry placed our trust in continual change to improve our way of life; we placed reliance on possessions and the market economy. We may have cherished the land we owned, but we did not belong to it or take our identity from it. David Malouf has noted that – 'We came as immigrants and brought our culture with us - not just a language and the many forms of social organisation, but the crops and animals we needed to feed us and from which, through effort and industry, our economy has grown. …So there … is, at the centre of our lives here, a deep irony: that the very industry that gives us a hold on the earth has no roots in the land itself, no history, no past. …'[11]

We maintained order by the exercise of hierarchies of power and we were familiar with competitions to acquire power. We emphasised individual rights and responsibilities, rather than the rights of groups. Our relationships with people outside our nuclear families seldom involved greater responsibilities than the avoiding of harm. Our society embraced Christian values, but they took root only in the shallow soil of a society marked by materialism and antipathies between the different Christian affiliations.

Immigration from non-European sources introduced further variations in the patterns of life of the Australian community. Value systems based in non-Christian religions accompanied an increasing diversity in the ethnic composition of the Australian community. We became more familiar with the cultures of Asia and the Middle East, we observed stronger ties among extended families and groups than were customary in Euro-Australian society, and we witnessed that intense industriousness and passion for education which are characteristic of every wave of migrants.

Of course, the strands of Australian society have been interwoven and each set of values has affected the values of other sets. But, because of the comparative numerical, political and economic strength of Euro-Australians, their values have had the greatest influence on the values of the Australian nation. Our history and topography have shaped the pre-eminent Australian value: egalitarianism.[12] Aboriginal society knew no kings or chiefs; mutual reliance, especially in ceremony, was a feature of nomadic life. Among early European settlers, the shared hardships of the bush did not eliminate class distinction but they made it suspect; the waves of immigrants from non-British countries denied the prospect of an Australian Ascendancy; and a proposal for a Bunyip aristocracy was quickly scotched. The shared hardship of diggers, first in the mining boom,[13] later in the trenches,[14] created a tradition of mateship which crossed every line of social demarcation. The universal suffrage (though completed only in 1967) was both the product of and the producer of an egalitarian ethos.

Egalitarianism must cope with differences: differences in colour and ethnic origin, in religion and culture, in natural gifts and acquired characteristics or incidents. Egalitarianism bespeaks tolerance and it must be sustained by tolerance. Without tolerance, differences would produce divisions that would tear the social fabric. In Australia, tolerance is expressed by the aspiration of a '*fair go*' for everyone.[15] Although Australia has known sectarian bitterness, no Australian colony was settled as the fiefdom of a religious group. We have had no established religion and ideologies have excited few passions. Australians are less morally judgmental than Americans, perhaps because convicts were more disposed to tolerance than Puritans.[16] Tolerance was not strained in earlier times by gross disparities in material wealth and, when the economy was in reasonable repair, there was enough to go around. A relaxed life-style was generally enjoyed and Jack's opinions were as good as his master's. Tolerance attributed an equal dignity to all, to the weak as well as the powerful, the poor as well as the rich, the fringe-dwellers as well as the mainstream. It is an enduring Australian value that entitles each of us to equal respect in our personal relations and to equality of opportunity to attain our own potential and to share in society's benefits.

Egalitarianism and tolerance underwrite the peace and order of a pluralist, multicultural society. Of course, peace and order can be enhanced by laws that prohibit unjustified discrimination, but laws do not automatically create values nor can laws command obedience if they are opposed to the enduring values of a society. Legal coercion is always a remedy of last resort. Despite the convict beginnings of European settlement in Australia, its mainstream society developed in times and in places where the law's writ did not always run. There is a larrikin streak in the Australian character that dislikes the exercise of authority by one person over another,[17] although the law itself is seen as a necessary safeguard of peace and order. When something bad happens, it is agreed that 'there should be a law against it'. But Law is one thing; uncontrolled power is another. Both Aboriginal[18] and Euro-Australian societies exist under a system of '*government of laws and not by men*'. In an egalitarian and tolerant society, only minimal legal coercion is needed to maintain social cohesion, peace and order. Australians do not support laws or powers that unnecessarily interfere with the freedom to do, to be and to think whatever the individual chooses to be, to do or to think – especially to think, for that is the paradigm freedom.[19] This country has been and is a haven of freedom for all who come to its shores.

Egalitarianism, tolerance, and freedom in combination can be identified as the most fundamental and characteristic Australian values. These are the values which have facilitated the development, and are now necessary to the maintenance, of a multi-cultural society. They are values which encourage initiatives unfettered by history or class or ethnic origin. They are values which foster and are fostered by a vigorous democracy.

But there is a downside. Whom do the egalitarian Australians treat as equals? Geography and history made us remote from other places and peoples, and our immigration laws were designed to maintain an Anglo-Celtic enclave in the South Pacific. For generations, mainstream Australians did not admit Aborigines to their hallowed circle, nor did first generation migrants easily achieve that status. Egalitarianism assumed a sameness of ethnic and social structure.[20] Indeed, the White Australia policy was justified by the view that it was the necessary protection of equality in working conditions. Egalitarianism, confined by fear, promoted intolerance.[21] It can still do so, if differences that ought not give rise to distinctions are permitted to do so. Fortunately, for most Australians ethnic differences now have significance only if the ethnic group isolates itself from intercourse with the general community. We have become a more confident nation. Of course, there are still some Australians who feel secure only in a homogeneous society, isolated from the rest of the world and separate from those people who are seen as different. For them, equality, tolerance and freedom stop short where their fear begins.

A confident society is imperilled by fear. Fear turns us inwards, away from our fellow men and women; fear destroys the confidence that a nation must have in itself if it is to prosper and play its part in the community of nations.

Paradoxically, economic freedom risks another fear. It is a fear that grows from the disparity in wealth between the haves and the have nots. The haves fear a loss of possessions; the have nots fear oppression and exploitation. The haves resent interference with economic power; the have nots retreat into alienation and antipathy to social order. Generally speaking, State power has been exercised in Australia to foster equality, not to perpetuate privilege.[22] Perhaps the pendulum has swung too far in deregulating some elements of the economy if equality is now at risk. The Governor-General has recently testified to experience that 'the gap between the haves and the have nots in our affluent Australia is actually widening.'[23] Whatever economic rationalists may proclaim in defence of economic freedom, great disparity in wealth erodes and ultimately undermines a society.

I have spoken thus far about Australia as a pluralist, multi-cultural society. The absence of an established religion in any of the Australian colonies, the easy-going, materialist lifestyle that has been possible for many and the inability of most of the principal Churches to inspire their congregations have blunted the interest of many Australians in the spiritual life. We are a secular society, albeit religious belief is respected and, in a rather vague way, Christian values are esteemed.

The preamble to our *Constitution* declares that the people of the Colonies relied 'on the blessing of Almighty God', and that relationship of the people with their Creator affords a transcendental justification for the three values we have been discussing: egalitarianism, tolerance and freedom. Speaking of human rights, the Pope said recently: 'Every person, created in the image and likeness of God and therefore radically oriented towards the Creator, is constantly in relationship with those possessed of the same dignity.'[24]

We have the dignity of children of God,[25] each equally precious in His eyes.[26] We are bound to one another by an obligation of mutual love;[27] none is to be judgmental of another;[28] and all are blessed with that freedom[29] without which virtue would be impossible.[30] If we have lost that understanding of ourselves and our values, we do not fully celebrate our own humanity and the lodestar of our future is dimmed. But let those values be infused by the spirit of the Gospels and they become the dynamic to produce a vibrant, inclusive and confident people.

The working document for the Oceania Synod declared that witnessing to Christianity 'is inspired by charity and justice, by solidarity with the poor, the marginalised, the oppressed, in short, the less fortunate of this world.'[31]

If this were the way in which we understood egalitarianism and tolerance, our society would be marked by social justice, cohesiveness and peace. We would lose the fears, and the antipathy, that gross disparity in wealth engenders; we would be a stronger and more confident member of the family of nations.

The freedom, especially the freedom of conscience, that we enjoy in Australia facilitates obedience to Divine Law. It was Newman who defined conscience as the law of God 'as apprehended in the minds of individual men' – which 'though it may suffer refraction in passing into the intellectual medium of each … is not therefore so affected as to lose its character of being the Divine Law, but still has, as such, the prerogative of commanding obedience.'[32]

Pope John Paul, following Vatican II,[33] asserted the importance of freedom of conscience: 'Religious freedom .. constitutes the very heart of human rights.... People are obliged to follow their conscience in all circumstances and cannot be forced to act against it.'[34]

In the light of this clear statement of principle, it is sad to note the different tone and message in the report of the 'Statement of Conclusions' of the meeting between some Australian Bishops and the Roman Curia before the Oceania Synod. The prelates are troubled by 'a concept of conscience that elevates the individual conscience to the level of an absolute, thus raising the subjective criterion above all objective factors and having no point of reference beyond itself.'[35]

The prelates are concerned that 'The tolerance characteristic of Australian society naturally affects the Church also. While it has many positive elements, tolerance of and openness to all opinions and perspectives on the truth can lead to indifference, to the acceptance of any opinion or activity as long as it does not impact adversely on other people.'

But an honestly formed conscience is surely absolute for the individual and, as Newman points out: 'conscience is not a judgment upon … any abstract doctrine … but bears immediately on something to be done or not done.'[36]

No doubt the prelates are seeking to confirm the teaching authority of the Church as a repository of spiritual truth which is not to be discounted by merely private reflection. And, as Professor Zubrzycki has pointed out, freedom of conscience is consistent with the acceptance of the 'defined and narrow' authority of popes and bishops which has 'authenticity only with respect to its proper and central objects: faith and morals.'[37] But the Statement uses the language of command, ecclesiastical government and discipline. *The Tablet* says the Statement is intended to guide the Australian Bishops so that they may 'affirm, admonish and correct' their people.[38]

Is faith the product of submission under coercion? Or is it the acceptance of a Divine gift by an informed and reflective mind? Is truth so fragile that it cannot be openly examined and debated? Fear of dissent, fear of disobedience, fear of loss of control are self-fulfilling fears for they mistake the authority of the Church to teach for a power to compel belief. There need be no concern about the acceptance of truth in the minds and hearts of men and women of goodwill provided the truth is clearly, rationally and fearlessly proclaimed – a proviso which raises a substantial question for the Australian Church today. It would be a mistake to think that, in today's Australia, an episcopal *ipse dixit* is sufficient by itself to produce that assent of the mind and will from which a steadfast faith will grow.

Arguably, the Church in Australia has been too insistent on the incidents of hierarchical authority, too concerned with the fabric and conduct of our institutions, too timid in challenging us, the laity, with the radical requirements of the Gospel. And we, the laity, anxious not to be distinguished from our fellows, fearful of the loss of status or possessions, have found the Church a safe haven for our complacency.

The Australian Church is our Church, our responsibility, our beloved home. In that context, egalitarianism means that, while Bishops, Priests and People have different functions to perform, each has an equal responsibility for, and an equal right to, performance of those functions. Tolerance requires that we understand that the Church, Divine in origin, depends on humans to perform their several functions and we must accept the failures and the shortcomings of ourselves and others, keeping our minds and hearts on Him who is our end and purpose. And freedom empowers us to follow our conscience and, hopefully, to choose to bear the burdens of the Christian life and to rejoice in the love, divine and human, which they bring.

Australian values pose no threat to the Christian life, but neither do they absolve us from the burdens of following in the way of the Cross. Therein lies our greatest challenge: Are we, am I, ready to abandon the prayer of St Augustine – 'Not yet, O Lord, not yet'?

---

1. The proceedings were published in *Discerning the Australian Social onscience*, (Jesuit Publications, 1999). For Brennan's paper see 9-17.
2. See Milton Rokeach, *Beliefs, Attitudes and Values*, Jossey-Bass Inc., U.S., 1968, 159-161.
3. See *Onus v Alcoa of Australia Ltd* (1981) 149 CLR 27, 42; Mabo *v Queensland [No 2]* (1991) 175 CLR 1, 29, 30, 42; *Dietrich v The Queen* (1992) 177 CLR 292, 328, 364.
4. Klaus A Ziegert 'Judicial Decision-Making, Community and Consented Values' (1995) 17(3) *Sydney Law Review* 373, 383.
5. John Braithwaite, 'Community Values and Australian Jurisprudence' (1995) 17(3) *Sydney Law Review* 351 and John Braithwaite, 'A Reply: Broadening Disciplines that Dull as well as Sharpen' (1975) 17 (3) *Sydney Law Review* 397.
6. W E H Stanner, *White Man Got No Dreaming: Essays, 1938 – 1973* (Australian National University Press, 1979) 37-38.
7. Ibid 39.
8. Ibid 230.
9. Ibid 58.
10. Ibid 59.
11. David Malouf, 'Putting ourselves on the map', *The Age* (Melbourne), 23 January 1988, Bicentenary Extra, p. 1.
12. See Elaine Thompson, *Fair Enough – Egalitarianism in Australia* (UNSW Press, 1994); Craig McGregor, *Profile of Australia* (Penguin, 1968), 49-50.
13. Thompson (n 12) 8 – 10.
14. Donald Horne *The Lucky Country* (Angus & Robertson, 1964) 17.
15. Ibid 14-15.
16. Ibid 18-19.
17. McGregor, (n 12) 44-45.
18. See *Milirrpum v Nabalco Pty Ltd. [The Gove Land Rights case]* (1971) 17 FLR 141, 267 (Blackburn J).
19. See *Church of The New Faith v Commissioner of Pay-roll Tax (Vict)*(1983) 154 CLR 120, 130.
20. William K Hancock, *Australia* (Jacaranda Press, 1961) 57.
21. Thompson (n 12) 250-251.
22. Thompson (n 12) 250.
23. Address to Australia Day Council of NSW, 22 January 1999.
24. Message for World Peace Day, 1 January 1999: see *The Tablet*, (2 January 1999) 32.
25. Romans 8:15; Galatians 4:6; 1 John 3:1-2.
26. Matthew 6:29-30; Luke 12:7,25,28.

27. Matthew 19:19; Mark 12:31; John 13:34; 15:12; Romans 13:9-10; 1 John 4:7,11.
28. Matthew 7:15; Luke 6:36,37.
29. See *Gaudium et Spes* Ch II Art 62; *Lumen Gentium* Ch IV Art 37.
30. See *Dignitatis Humanae* Ch I Arts 2,3.
31. See *Instrumentum Laboris,* par 3.
32. Letter to the Duke of Norfolk, quoted by Ian Ker *John Henry Newman* (Oxford University Press, 1988) 688.
33. Second Vatican Ecumenical Council, Declaration on Religious Freedom *Dignitatis Humanae*, 3.
34. Pope John Paul II, Message for World Day of Peace, 1 January 1999.
35. Interdicasterial Meeting with a Representation of the Australian Bishops and the Roman Curia.
36. Ker (n 32) 689.
37. Jerzy Zubrzycki, 'Authority and Freedom can coexist' *The Australian*, (28 December 1998) 11.
38. See *The Tablet, (*2 January 1999) 23

8.13 Australian Values and *The Australian Quarterly*

Editor's note

Brennan was invited to launch the 75th Anniversary edition of *The Australian Quarterly* at Parliament House, Canberra on 18 June 2007.

Thank you for your kind invitation to speak at the launch of the 'Values' edition of *The Australian Quarterly*. Looking at the contents and the contributors and conscious of the profession of many of those here this evening, I doubt the wisdom of saying anything about Australian values. Perhaps it is the privilege of longevity which allows me to reflect on some changes and the honour of judicial service which emboldens me to say something about Australian values and the law.

There is a paradox about values. They are vague and imprecise, incapable of prescribing a specific course of conduct, a particular rule of law or a precise criterion of action. Yet they have an enormous, often determinative, effect on the way we act, the way we think, the laws we embrace and the policies we approve. They are at the heart of our culture and our identity. Some of our values are shared by other peoples, other nations, yet they have an indigenous flavour and they find expression in ways that are distinctively Australian. It was nearly 70 years ago, when I read 'Inky' Stephensen's *Foundations of Culture in Australia*, that I first became conscious of the uniqueness of Australian values, though a recent glance at that book was a stark reminder of the changes that have occurred since its publication in 1936.

Perhaps the most distinctly Australian value is egalitarianism. It is part of our history. Aboriginal society was not socially or economically stratified. Early European settlers had no claims to social pre-eminence. We rejected a Bunyip aristocracy. Australians shared the rigours of the environment and diggers shared the campaigns of the mines and later of the battlefields. Equality was expressed in a streak of larrikinism and it allowed that easy familiarity when strangers look you in the eye, smile and say 'g'day!'. Today, that familiarity remains in the country but is largely lost in the anonymity of the cities and the self-imposed isolation of the iPod, though the ideal of egalitarianism remains. On examination, however, Australian egalitarianism was far from fully realized.

As a child, I remember the proud men of the depression who hawked bundles of clothes props on their shoulders or who 'jumped the rattler' to get another issue of rations and domestic servants who were pleased to earn a pittance with half a day off a week. The war, soldier settlement, the post-war training schemes, enhanced educational facilities, the expansion in resources and agriculture and a sometimes faltering development of manufacturing industry has created a large economic middle class.

The Second World War forced on Australia the realization that we belonged to a world society. We were no longer a colonial island. The proclamation by Prime Minister Menzies in 1939 that 'Great Britain has declared war upon [Germany] and that, as a result, Australia is also at war' had less resonance with Australians in 1945. Gradually, very gradually, we asserted our national independence and opened up to the world around us. We could no longer ignore the region in which we were placed and the great movements that were sweeping through the international community. But there were many who were not included in the circle blessed by equality.

It took almost a further three decades before the White Australia policy was abandoned and people of Asian or African ethnicity could become the beneficiaries of Australian egalitarianism. And the original Australians were not even counted in reckoning the numbers of the people of the Commonwealth before the 1967 referendum. That referendum did not destroy the legislation that kept Aborigines under bureaucratic controls, nor did it undo the common law rule which had deprived them of the land which was, to quote Professor WEH Stanner, the Aborigines' 'hearth, home, the source and locus of life, and everlastingness of spirit.[1]

These exclusions were symptomatic of a negative Australian value: fear of the other, the different, the unfamiliar. I suppose much of this fear is the product of geographical and cultural isolation which was conducive to an inward-looking self-sufficiency. The quelling of much of this fear ushered in a richer society. We recognized the importance of Aboriginal culture, the role which land plays in that culture, the depth of Aboriginal spirituality and the need to remedy the scandal of Aboriginal health and to provide the dignity of employment. We successfully integrated the waves of post-war migrants from Europe and, after our immigration policy was transformed by the abolition of the White Australia Policy and liberalized to receive the persecuted of many nations, we came to possess a vibrant multicultural society.

Of course, a multi-ethnic, multi-cultural society must cope with differences in colour, in religion, in acquired characteristics or incidents. Egalitarianism must be sustained by the practice of another virtue: tolerance. Without tolerance, differences would produce divisions that would not only tear the social fabric but return Australia to the ghetto mentality of earlier times. Tolerance is a value that gives everyone a '*fair go*'[2] and respects divergent life styles and beliefs. The coincidence of Pope John XXIII, John F Kennedy, Adenauer and de Gaulle offered the western world the prospect of permanent peace through tolerance. Although Australia had known sectarian bitterness, no Australian colony was settled as the fiefdom of a religious group. We had no established religion and our Constitution forbids it. For other reasons, however, we have diminished the influence of the spiritual while we pursue material interests. Australians are less morally judgmental than Americans, perhaps because convicts were more disposed to tolerance than Puritans.[3] Tolerance was not strained in earlier times by gross disparities in material wealth, but there are emerging signs of economic intolerance today. We need to heed these signs, for egalitarianism and tolerance underwrite the peace and order of a pluralist society.

Tolerance is strained by those who choose to be intolerant of others, especially if that intolerance leads to insult or violence. Intolerance invites response and becomes a self-fulfilling prophecy. We saw the ugly face of intolerance in the Cronulla riots and we have seen the benefits of tolerance in the active steps of reconciliation that have since been taken on both sides. Hanging over us today, there is an apprehension of violence by Islamic extremists which is damaging Australia – not only by facilitating intolerance towards peace-loving Muslim citizens but by engendering the fear which erodes two other fundamental Australian values: personal freedom and the rule of law. Many Australians, believing that there must be sacrifices made in the so-called war on terror and that they will not personally be affected, are willing to accept incursions on personal freedom and even some restriction on legal remedies which protect our freedom.

The need for laws infringing personal freedom is, of course, to be assessed by the Parliament. The courts respect the will of the legislature expressed in statute but, as freedom is central to the rule of law, the courts will always interpret such statutes narrowly. Fifty years ago, Justice Fullagar noted that the right to personal liberty is 'the most elementary and important of all common law rights'.[4] The courts remember the centuries old wisdom of Blackstone who warned that: 'if once it were left in the power of any, the highest, magistrate to imprison arbitrarily whomever he or his officers thought proper there would soon be an end of all other rights and immunities.'[5]

Personal liberty and other relatively permanent values have a role to play in interpreting statutes, reviewing executive action and in moulding the common law. Sir Anthony Mason has said that 'personal liberty, freedom of expression, no imprisonment without trial, procedural fairness are commonly identified by judges as values which inform legal principle and require an unambiguous expression of statutory intention to override them. This emphasis on values protected by the common law is in one sense an instance of institutional values or morality. ... it may be that [judges] tend to treat those values as absolute or near absolutes.'[6]

Nevertheless, as I once wrote, 'the court cannot deny the validity of an exercise of a legislative power ...merely on the ground that the law abrogates human rights and fundamental freedoms or trenches upon political rights which, in the court's opinion, should be preserved'.[7]

There was a time when some thought that judges were moulding the law in accordance with their idiosyncratic values. *Mabo*[8] seemed to frighten some of the horses and, after the *Wik*[9] decision, Mr Tim Fischer thought there was a need to call for 'Capital C Conservatives' to join the ranks of the High Court. *Mabo* was a contemporary application of the legal principle of non-discrimination and *Wik* turned on the interpretation of a Queensland statute. I should be concerned to think that the courts, especially the High Court, might forsake the function of playing their part in ensuring that the common law is kept in conformity with the relatively permanent (or enduring) values of the Australian community.[10] However, the restraints of precedent, the desirability of legal certainty and predictability, the necessity for integration with the general body of the law and professional experience limit the occasions when values might have some effect on a judgment. In truth, the enduring values of which a court might take account are quite unremarkable. Freedom, the rule of law, human dignity, procedural fairness, reasonableness in the exercise of discretionary power – few would quarrel with these values.

The peace and order of society depend on the acceptance of the law and its impartial and competent application by independent courts. On the rule of law, all else ultimately depends: our freedom to think, to express, to be and to do; political, economic and social order; family life and relationships. We have had our *Constitution* for over 100 years – one of the longest-surviving Constitutions of any nation. We have had controversies over legislation or judicial decisions but never have we had a general rejection of our constitutional distribution of power, of the binding effect of the law or the authority of the courts. The rule of law is the underlying and underpinning value of our society. The implication is that we should be respectful of the work of the Parliament, we should be jealous of the independence and competence of the courts and of the integrity of their jurisdiction and we should rejoice in the public accountability of the executive government except when public review is seriously destructive of national security.

For the future, we must ask ourselves the question which Sir Ivor Richardson posed in New Zealand: '. . . what kind of society are we and what kind of society do we want to be? The question recognizes that present realities may not match our aspirations. We may want to change our objectives. We need to articulate and give effect to what we see as our underlying values.'[11]

We still have this negative value of fear of the other. It has a powerful influence. We heard it in the speech of Pauline Hanson and the controversy that followed, we hear and read it in the criticisms of our peaceful Muslim citizens, we saw it in action in the way we dealt with boat-borne refugees, the Tampa affair and the 'Pacific Solution' and in our silent acceptance of the terrible injustice and the squalid politics that Leigh Sales has exposed in her description of the treatment of *Detainee 002.* Fear destroys our confidence. By contrast, it is the tolerance of difference that leads to the building of a cohesive and confident society, allowing a nation to prosper and play its part in the community of nations. Laws should impose condign punishment on those who destroy peace and order, but should be careful not to trespass upon the freedom of others who, sensing intolerance or worse, may make common cause with the malefactor so that the last state is worse than the first.

Let our laws and policies treat equally all who live in this land, accepting difference and fostering tolerance. Let there be respect for the rule of law and the jurisdiction of our courts to administer it. Those are guarantees of Australian values. Thus, we may be united, as we were in war, in repelling threats to our peace and security. Then, blessed by the gifts which nature has bestowed, we may celebrate our character as a free and confident nation.

---

1. WEH Stanner, *White Man Got No Dreaming* (Australian National University Press, 1979), 230.
2. Donald Horne, *The Lucky Country* (Agnes & Robertson, 1964) 14-15.
3. Ibid 18-19.
4. See *Trobridge v Hardy* (1955) 94 CLR 147, 152.
5. See *Commentaries on the Laws of England* (Oxford, 1765), Book 1, 120-121,130-131 cited in *Williams v The Queen* (1986) 161 CLR 278, 292.
6. See 'Reshaping Australian Institutions', ANU Public Lecture 3, 13 August 1996; (1997) *Australian International Law Journal* 1.
7. See *Nationwide News Pty Limited v Wills* (1992) 177 CLR 1.
8. See *Mabo v Queensland [No 2]* (1992 175 CLR 1.
9. See *Wik Peoples v Queensland* (1996) 187 CLR 1.
10. See *Dietrich v The Queen* (1992) 177 CLR 292, 319.
11. 'The Courts and the Public' (1995) *New Zealand Law Journal* 11.

8.14 Raymond Gaita's Common Good

Editor's note

Professor Raymond Gaita delivered the opening lecture in a series of lectures on the common good. The series was organised by the Aquinas Academy. Brennan was invited to make some opening remarks at the first lecture held in the Dixson Room at the State Library of New South Wales on 5 March 2008.

This evening, we are assembled to hear Mr Raymond Gaita, distinguished philosopher, author, screen writer and public figure, deliver the opening lecture of a series devoted to the Common Good.

The term 'Common Good' may sound like a term of warm-feeling, something with which all reasonable people are in agreement and which offers no area for controversy or further thought. Nothing could be further from the truth. We live in a society in which the prime value is our individual material interests, whatever may be the effect of those interests on the interests of others. The common good speaks of different values.

The common good takes each individual as a member of society, deriving his or her identity and status from that membership and attributing both rights and responsibilities by reason of that social membership. There are, however, two elements in this conception: one is the individual, the other is society. The dignity of the individual is not to be impaired by action which is justified merely by an intention to confer a benefit on a majority of society. The utilitarian calculus has no place in the notion of the common good. The common good seeks to advance individual dignity; but it does not do so at the expense of the dignity of others.

In a pluralist, secular democracy such as ours, the common good implies that all members of society are free to form respectful relationships with others, to have an opportunity to develop capacities and to contribute usefully to society. It implies a duty to do what can reasonably be done to see that others enjoy these social benefits. Those benefits include not only monetary and material benefits but equality under the law, freedom of religious belief and practice, freedom from the exercise of arbitrary power, freedom from discrimination on the basis of sex, race or ethnicity, an opportunity to obtain an education and a means of livelihood, an opportunity to found a family and an opportunity to employ one's capacities gainfully.

To achieve such a society, there must be a consensus that this is the way in which we should define our policies and practices – a common cast of mind which rejects a crude majoritarian materialism and gives real meaning to the notion of a fair go for all. Christianity provides a spiritual basis for this conception, but the value system which satisfies Christ's injunction to love your neighbour as yourself can be, and is, consistent with a secular humanism based on respect for every person as a member of the human family. Whatever basis appeals to each of us, we need thinkers to lead us to an understanding of what we must be and do in order to achieve a social order which observes and implements the common good. We are indebted to the Aquinas Academy, its Director Fr Michael Whelan and his assistants Professor Paul Redmond and Mr François Kunc for taking the initiative in organizing this series of lectures and for having invited Raymond Gaita to open it. I am honoured and delighted formally to launch the Common Good Lectures.

8.15 Scrutiny's role in the Rule of Law

Editor's note

This was Brennan's address to the Australia-New Zealand Scrutiny of Legislation Conference held in Brisbane from 26-28 July 2011.

The rule of law finds frequent expression in the rhetoric of lawyers and members of the political branches of government. The term connotes a free and peaceful society, in which the powers of the State are limited and are exercised fairly and reasonably, in which the law applies equally to all and disputes – whether the parties be the State, corporations or individuals – can be settled by impartial adjudication. Thus, the community can live in peace, secure in person and in property and free of arbitrary interference by State authority.

The principle of the rule of law originated in mediaeval times. In the 13th century, Bracton, in common with other mediaeval lawyers and political philosophers, declared that the law both gave the King his estate and vast royal power and provided that the King, like all his subjects, is ruled by the law.[1] On the Continent, the rule of law was also acknowledged as a general principle, but there the reality of dominant royal power prevailed over the restraining influence of the moral principle. In England, however, the principle gathered force and acquired its distinctive character with the rise of the power of Parliament. The development of the doctrine was interrupted by the Stuarts' assertion of the divine right of Kings but was reasserted after the Bill of Rights in 1689 asserted the supremacy of Parliament. Holdsworth, in his mammoth *History of English Law* says that the 'doctrine of the supremacy of the law becomes a far more practically workable principle by reason of its connection with Parliament...at the close of the Middle Ages it was coming to mean the supremacy of a law which Parliament could change and modify; and because the lawyers worked in alliance with Parliament they rarely showed any desire to question the power of Parliament to make, change or modify the law.'[2]

Parliament possessed 'sovereign and uncontrolled authority' over the law,[3] and the ruling law was seen as the common law with additions and modifications enacted by the Parliament. Three centuries ago, when the Bill of Rights reined in executive power and the *Act of Settlement* established the security of judicial tenure and remuneration, the two institutions which underpinned the rule of law – Parliament and the Courts – were secured in their respective roles. Parliament had the authority to enact law and the courts had authority to define and apply the law. Even in the time of the Stuarts, Lord Coke famously rejected[4] James I's pretensions to assume the functions of the judge because 'His Majesty was not learned in the laws of his realm of England'.[5] In the 19th century, the noted English constitutional author, A V Dicey was able to give this as the primary meaning of the rule of law: – 'the absolute supremacy or predominance of regular law as opposed to the influence of arbitrary power... Englishmen are ruled by the law, and by the law alone; a man may with us be punished for a breach of law, but he can be punished for nothing else. It means, again, equality before the law or the equal subjection of all classes to the ordinary law of the land administered by the ordinary law courts; the "rule of law" in this sense excludes the idea of any exemption of officials or others from the duty of obedience to the law which governs other citizens or from the jurisdiction of the ordinary tribunals.'[6]

The complementary labours of the Parliament and the courts have given us the rule of law as we know it today – a society governed by the laws enacted by the Parliament and the doctrines of the common law developed by the courts. Each institution developed separately and the separation was found to be conducive to the good of the community. Blackstone, in his *Commentaries on the Laws of England,* observed that 'In [the] distinct and separate existence of the judicial power in a peculiar body of men, nominated indeed, but not removable at pleasure, by the crown, consists our main preservation of the public liberty; which cannot subsist long in any state, unless the administration of common justice be in some degree separated from both the legislative and also from the executive power.'[7]

We have accepted the familiar words of Chief Justice Marshall in *Marbury v Madison,*[8] 'It is emphatically the province and duty of the judicial department to say what the law is'. More recently, Lord Bingham pointed out that 'the function of independent judges charged to interpret and apply the law is universally recognised as a cardinal feature of the modern democratic state, a cornerstone of the rule of law itself.'[9]

If the courts are needed to declare and administer the law, the rule of law requires that their ordinary jurisdiction should not be truncated. Sometimes, there may seem to be good grounds for limiting the prospect of litigation by withdrawing the jurisdiction of a court. That may have considerable attraction for an executive and even for a Parliament but, when courts are stripped of their jurisdiction over a particular subject matter, the subject matter is without legal control and becomes an area of unbridled power. That is incompatible with the rule of law. The Founding Fathers of our Constitution foresaw that risk and entrenched a provision designed to ensure that all Commonwealth officers, including judges, should exercise their powers in accordance with law. Section 75(v) of the *Constitution* entrenches the jurisdiction of the High Court to judicially review decisions by officers of the Commonwealth.[10] And recently, when a New South Wales statute provided that a decision of the State Industrial Court should be exempt from judicial review for jurisdictional error, the High Court held that, under the *Constitution*, it was beyond power to deny that authority to the State's Supreme Court.[11] The plurality judgment observed 'To deprive a State Supreme Court of its supervisory jurisdiction enforcing the limits on the exercise of State executive and judicial power by persons and bodies other than that Court would be to create islands of power immune from supervision and restraint.'[12]

The preservation of the supervisory jurisdiction of the superior courts is essential to the maintenance of the rule of law in contemporary conditions. But, by itself, it does not guarantee the maintenance of the rule of law.

An unqualified application of laws which trample on a minority's human rights may be the very antithesis of the rule of law. Such laws can be maintained only by force. Some of Hitler's heinous policies were implemented in accordance with German law as it then was, but no one could regard the Holocaust as justified by the rule of law. There is a difference between the rule *of* law and rule *by* law. A recent British Attorney-General, Lord Goldsmith QC, said that the rule of law 'is not simply about rule by law. Such a proposition would be satisfied whatever the law and however unfair, unjust or contrary to fundamental principles, provided only that it was applied to all. Instead it seems to me clear that the rule of law comprehends some statement of values which are universal and ought to be respected as the basis of a free society.'[13]

In April 2011, the European Commission for Democracy through Law (known as the 'Venice Commission') published its *Report on the Rule of Law*. Acceptance of the rule of law is a condition of membership of the Council of Europe[14] and is regarded as one of its three pillars[15]. The Commission listed six elements of the rule of law,[16] the first of which is: 'Legality, including a transparent, accountable and democratic process for enacting law.'[17]

The Commission is concerned both with the process, which must be transparent, and with the enacting authority's accountability to the community. As Lord Steyn has pointed out, 'the rule of law enforces minimum standards of fairness, both substantive and procedural.'[18] Laws and practices which ignore or offend the community's sense of fairness stimulate rejection and a breakdown in the rule of law. The European Court of Human Rights has said that: 'pluralism, tolerance and broadmindedness are hallmarks of a "democratic society". Although individual interests must on occasion be subordinated to those of a group, democracy does not simply mean that the views of a majority must always prevail: a balance must be achieved which ensures the fair and proper treatment of minorities and avoids any abuse of a dominant position'.[19]

Here, then, is the role of the Parliament and of its Scrutiny Committees: to ensure that the enacted laws do not offend the values to which Lord Goldsmith referred as 'universal and ....the basis of a free society'. The rule of law implies that those who live under the law are living in a free and ordered society, in which individual dignity is respected and all enjoy immunity from the exercise of arbitrary power or unjust discrimination. Each branch of government must play its part to effect that result. Lord Goldsmith further commented – 'In my view all the organs of state – the executive, legislature and judiciary – have a shared responsibility for upholding the rule of law. This is not to down play the responsibility of the courts – they provide the critical long-stop guarantee – but the rule of law will only have real meaning in practical terms in a society in which all organs of the state are mindful of their obligations to respect it.'[20]

I should like to focus on the role of the legislature, for the legislature bears responsibility for the enacted law. But first we must understand the function of the other two branches of government in maintaining the rule of law. The executive performs the administrative functions that implement the law, including the enforcement of court judgments and, subject to appropriation, the allocation of the resources (whether financial or *in specie*) needed for the efficient operation of the Parliament and the courts, the law enforcement agencies and the police. The National Executive has important functions in defence and external affairs. In short, the executive must provide the mechanisms by which the law is enforced. If the Executive were to fail in enforcing the law, the rule of law would collapse. Indeed, an argument in favour of a Governor's or a Governor General's reserve power to dismiss a Premier or Prime Minister is the need to provide a drastic sanction if ever the executive were to fail substantially to enforce the law.

The executive does not possess any legislative power save that which the Parliament confers. When Parliament delegates to the executive, power to enact subordinate legislation, it is usually to facilitate the implementation of a policy adopted by the delegating statute. Bureaucratic devotion to that policy may create subordinate legislation conferring executive powers that are thought to be excessive or oppressive. To safeguard the fundamental rights and freedoms of individuals, most Australian Parliaments have appointed Subordinate Legislation Committees charged with the scrutiny of delegated legislation which is then subject to Parliamentary disallowance.[21] Exceptionally, a Parliament may enact legislation containing a Henry VIII clause, enabling an Act to be expressly or impliedly amended by subordinate legislation or executive action.[22] Scrutiny Committees and Law Reform Commissions[23] rightly view the use of Henry VIII clauses as generally objectionable. They erode the principle that legislation should have sufficient regard to the institution of Parliament;[24] they do not respect the need for a 'democratic process for enacting law'. Putting aside subordinate legislation promulgated under a Henry VIII clause, it is the Parliament and the courts which have the responsibility of ensuring that the provisions of enacted law are consonant with the requirements of the rule of law.

For their part, the courts define and apply the common law and interpret and apply enacted law. Statute operates in the matrix of the common law and the common law includes rules of statutory interpretation, subject to statutory override. The relevant starting point of the common law is that the individual is free to engage in conduct or to enjoy property to the full extent that falls outside the scope of any lawful restriction. Thus, in *Lange v Australian Broadcasting Commission,* the High Court said: 'Under a legal system based on the common law, "everybody is free to do anything, subject only to the provisions of the Law", so that one proceeds *"upon an* assumption of freedom of speech" and turns to the law "to discover the established exceptions to it"'.[25]

Freedom is not unqualified. Limitations must be imposed in the interests of the common good. The common law imposes limitations in order to protect the community or individuals against those who have the power to damage or oppress. Freedom of speech is limited by the torts of libel and slander in order to protect personal reputations; the freedom of an attacker is restrained by the common law's torts of assault and battery in order to protect physical integrity; the common law's invalidation of contractual clauses in unreasonable restraint of trade contributes (albeit to a limited extent) to both the strength of the economy and the freedom of the individual trader or artisan; the common law (or its colleague, equity) gives relief to those who have suffered from fraud or unconscionable conduct. To the extent that the common law is the source of legal rules prescribing the boundary between freedom and limitations on freedom, its methodology works well. Its provisions, especially the requirement that the law should apply equally to all, are the bastion of the rule of law. Freedom is restricted only to the extent necessary to preserve the rights of other individuals or to protect the common good. The policy of the common law accords with the principle set out in the *Universal Declaration of Human Rights:* 'In the exercise of his rights and freedoms, everyone shall be subject only to such limitations as are determined by law solely for the purpose of securing due recognition and respect for the rights and freedoms of others and of meeting the just requirements of morality, public order and the general welfare in a democratic society.'[26]

The limitations on freedom which the common law imposes do not infringe the rule of law. The common law takes a similar approach to the construction of statutes. In *Bropho v Western Australia*, the majority judgment explained the rationale. It

> … is to be found in the assumption that it is 'in the last degree improbable that the legislature would overthrow fundamental principles, infringe rights, or depart from the general system of law, without expressing its intention with irresistible clearness…'.[27] If such an assumption be shown to be or to have become ill-founded, the foundation upon which the particular presumption rests will necessarily be weakened or removed. Thus, if what was previously accepted as a fundamental principle or fundamental right ceases to be so regarded, the presumption that the legislature would not have intended to depart from that principle or to abolish or modify that right will necessarily be undermined and may well disappear.[28]

The common law assumes that Parliament, in order to maintain the rule of law, intends to leave intact three classes of overlapping interests: fundamental principles, for example, the principle that all persons are equal before the law and are equally bound by its provisions;[29] individual rights, for example, the right not to be compulsorily deprived of property without compensation;[30] and the general system of law, for example, the duty of the courts to exercise their jurisdiction when it is regularly invoked.[31] The assumption relates only to fundamental interests and the question whether an interest is fundamental is assessed according to the contemporary values of the community. Last year, French CJ in the *Finks Motor Cycle Club Case* observed that this principle is 'well known to the drafters of legislation' but it 'does not constrain legislative power'.[32] I had pointed out in *Nationwide News Pty Ltd v Wills* that 'A court …cannot deny the validity of an exercise of a legislative power expressly granted merely on the ground that the law abrogates human rights and fundamental freedoms or trenches upon political rights which, in the court's opinion, should be preserved.'[33]

Although the common law rule of interpretation does not restrict legislative power, yet it provides a continuing reminder that legislative interference with fundamental principles, individual rights and the general system of law – the very elements of the rule of law – requires 'clear an unequivocal language for which the Parliament may be accountable to the electorate.'[34] As the Parliament is accountable for both Acts of the Parliament and subordinate legislation, it is the role of the Parliament to ensure that enacted law does not infringe these interests without a compelling necessity to protect the common good. Thus, the Parliament has a crucial role to play in maintaining the rule of law.

The appointment of Scrutiny of Bills Committees and Subordinate Legislation Committees has been a necessary step in providing Parliaments with an opportunity to take account of the interests protected by the rule of law. A Committee's work is detailed, perhaps painstaking. It is assisted by professional expertise and is more efficiently discharged as experience develops. Professional expertise can inform a Committee about particular rules that the common law treats as 'fundamental principles', or about those rights, both procedural and substantive, which are jealously guarded by the law, or about the features of 'the general system of law'[35] which safeguard individuals and minorities against oppression and injustice. The operation of a proposed law on these matters can be assessed in committee better than in the course of partisan debate in the chambers of a Parliament. The proposed law's operation is not an issue for political controversy; its operation is simply the legal effect that flows or may flow from a particular statutory text. With experience, members of Scrutiny Committees no doubt find it easier to spot the kind of provision that needs consideration.

I am indebted to Mr Don Colagiuri, NSW Parliamentary Counsel, who provided me with references to parliamentary practice in several States and to Mr Stephen Argument for allowing me advance access to his paper *Legislative Scrutiny in Australia: Wisdom to Export?*.[36] This paper records, *inter alia,* the Australian development of Parliamentary Committees first, to scrutinize subordinate legislation and, later, to scrutinize Bills coming before the Parliament. Committees to scrutinize subordinate legislation and bills have now been established by the Parliaments of the Commonwealth,[37] Queensland,[38] New South Wales,[39] Victoria,[40] Western Australia[41] and the Australian Capital Territory.[42] The Parliaments of South Australia,[43] Tasmania[44] and the Northern Territory[45] have established Committees to scrutinize subordinate legislation.

The architects of the scrutiny system in Australia have developed a number of principles to guide the work of the Committees and those principles have reflected a lively awareness of parliamentary responsibility for maintaining the rule of law. In Queensland, the principles of scrutiny have been given statutory form by *the Legislative Standards Act 1992* (Qld).[46] That Act states that the legislative principles which a Committee is to consider are the principles 'that underlie a parliamentary democracy based on the rule of law' including 'principles ... requiring that legislation has sufficient regard to rights and liberties of individuals; and the institution of Parliament'. There is considerable similarity among the expressions used by several Australian Parliaments to identify the matters which a scrutiny Committee should take into account in considering the rights and liberties of individuals and the institution of Parliament. For example, the Senate provisions direct the Committee to consider, inter alia, whether Bills –

- trespass unduly on personal rights and liberties;
- make rights, liberties or obligations unduly dependent upon insufficiently defined administrative powers;
- make rights, liberties or obligations unduly dependent upon non-reviewable decisions;
- inappropriately delegate legislative powers; or
- insufficiently subject the exercise of legislative power to parliamentary scrutiny.[47]

Similar provisions are to be found in New South Wales, Victoria and Australian Capital Territory and are consistent with the Queensland provisions. One State lists the question whether a Bill authorizes an amendment of an Act otherwise than by another Act[48] – a clear caveat against Henry VIII clauses. Another State lists the question whether a Bill raises an issue as to the jurisdiction of the Supreme Court[49] – flagging access to judicial remedies as an issue for consideration. The listed matters, which extend beyond those mentioned here, are not intended to limit the matters to be considered. Some States do not list the matters to be taken into account, leaving its Committee to formulate its own criteria of review.

Recent Human Rights legislation in Victoria and the Australian Capital Territory has relied on scrutiny procedure to secure protection of statutory human rights. Victoria requires the Scrutiny Committees to report to the Parliament whether a Bill or Subordinate Legislation is incompatible with human rights.[50] Similarly, in the Australian Capital Territory,[51] the scrutiny Committee must report 'about human rights issues raised by bills presented to the Assembly'[52] but, curiously, the Act does not require the Committee to report about the same issues arising from subordinate legislation. Scrutiny for compliance with human rights that are enumerated in a statute may provide an additional protection of the elements of the rule of law, but those elements are deserving of protection irrespective of their statutory expression. However, by way of comparison with jurisdictions which have a lively experience of Human Rights litigation, I have appended to this paper a copy of the Venice Commission's check list of issues for evaluating a State's compliance with the rule of law.

The very existence of scrutiny Committees is designed to ensure that the Parliament – not the Government but the Parliament – is alerted to the effect of Bills or Subordinate Legislation on the elements of the rule of law. In the pressure of Parliamentary business and in the heat of political debate, the fundamental rights and freedoms of individuals might easily be overlooked and the ordinary procedures for applying the law may seem too cumbersome. But scrutiny Committees are accustomed to considering whether individual rights and freedoms are trespassed upon 'unduly', or whether they depend on 'insufficiently defined administrative powers' or 'non-reviewable decisions', or whether legislative powers have been inappropriately delegated or escape adequate Parliamentary scrutiny. These Committees, focusing not so much on the policy of a Bill or of Subordinate Legislation as upon its effect on fundamental principles, individual rights and the general system of law, provide a safeguard of the rule of law. Absent the work of a Scrutiny Committee, a provision of a Bill or a regulation may come into force and prove to be an intractable, but unnecessary, incursion on the interests which the rule of law seeks to protect.

Scrutiny Committees have not been primarily concerned by considerations of policy. Stephen Argument's paper recalls a passage from the 71st Report of the Senate Regulations and Ordinances Committee:

> As the principles indicate, the Committee has always been concerned to ensure that policy aspects of delegated legislation do not intrude upon its primary task of protecting the individual. To that end, the Committee's evaluation of delegated legislation has never touched upon the merits of parent legislation passed by the Parliament. The Committee's continuing concern, rather, is to achieve a balance between necessary executive functions, on the one hand, and the individual rights and liberties of citizens, on the other.[53]

The scrutiny of the policy of a Bill or of subordinate legislation is a question on which Stephen Argument and Dennis Pearce disagree.[54] Stephen Argument favours the traditional view and he cites the powerful observations of Senator Barney Cooney:

> Properly limited by its narrow remit, [the Committee] does not look for the political acceptability of the policy being pursued. That is the province of the Parliament itself. Rather the Committee looks for wisdom, fairness, justice and restraint in the regulatory procedures to be followed in achieving that policy. The Committee is concerned with the justice and propriety of ways and means.

> It is because of its avoidance of issues of policy that the Committee has traditionally been such a strong bipartisan force within the Senate. It is a backbench Committee whose members can temporarily set political differences to one side. The Committee's remit thus allows strongly held and shared principles of liberty and propriety to create and underpin the bipartisan spirit which is the source of the Committee's authority in the Chamber, and beyond that in the Government and the Public Service.

This approach leaves it to the Parliament to determine whether a particular provision should be retained in the relevant legislation. Parliamentary debate is informed by the work of the Committee and the possibility of unintended interference with fundamental principles, individual rights, or the general system of law is eliminated or, at least, reduced.

On the other hand, Dennis Pearce points to the increasing practice of remitting major policy matters to subordinate legislation. That development is inevitable having regard to the pressure on parliamentary time, the detailed and technical nature of much legislation and the desirability of providing more legislative flexibility in dealing with changing situations and emergencies. There is force in the observation that, if policy is remitted to subordinate legislation, it has to be considered by a Scrutiny Committee or the policy will pass without consideration by the Parliament or any committee of a House.

There is strength in both views, reflecting the pressures on a modern parliamentary democracy in the welfare state. A vital democracy requires not only powerful but peaceful debate on policy; it requires also an assurance that the individual, the minorities, the marginalized are not oppressed by majorities or by those who wield or influence political power. That is the hallmark of a civilized society under the rule of law. But it is not easily achieved by a busy Parliament. Must Parliament abdicate much of its responsibility to the executive, trusting to the bureaucracy's technical skills and wisdom, to the industry of Ministers and to their ultimate responsibility to the Parliament to produce subordinate laws needed for the regulation of a complex society? It may be that Lord Hailsham's description of a modern parliamentary democracy as 'an elective dictatorship, absolute in theory if hitherto thought tolerable in practice'[55] is fairly accurate. Nevertheless, Scrutiny Committees adequately resourced and constituted by members from both, or all, sides of the Parliamentary House committed to the protection of our traditional rights, freedoms and practices, provide a valuable mechanism for safeguarding the rule of law and maintaining respect for the institution of Parliament.

Scrutiny Committees have a constant and challenging function in ensuring that the laws do not go beyond what is necessary 'for the purpose of securing due recognition and respect for the rights and freedoms of others and of meeting the just requirements of morality, public order and the general welfare in a democratic society.' Thereby the rights and freedoms we enjoy allow us to be a free and confident nation. And we thank the members of Scrutiny Committees for their contribution to keeping it that way.

VENICE COMMISSION REPORT ON THE RULE OF LAW

Annex: Checklist for evaluating the state of the rule of law in single states

1. Legality (supremacy of the law)

a) Does the State act on the basis of, and in accordance with the law?

b) Is the process for enacting law transparent, accountable and democratic?

c) Is the exercise of power authorised by law?

d) To what extent is the law applied and enforced?

e) To what extent does the government operate without using law?

f) To what extent does the government use incidental measures instead of general rules?

g) Are there exception clauses in the law of the State, allowing for special measures?

h) Are there internal rules ensuring that the state abides by international law?

i) Does the *nulla poena sine lege* system apply?

2. Legal certainty

a) Are all the laws published?

b) If there is any unwritten law, is it accessible?

c) Are there limits to the legal discretion granted to the executive?

d) Are there many exception clauses in the laws?

e) Are the laws written in an intelligible language?

f) Is retroactivity of laws prohibited?

g) Is there a duty to maintain the law?

h) Are final judgments by domestic courts called into question?

i) Is the case-law of the courts coherent?

j) Is legislation generally implementable and implemented?

j) Are laws foreseeable as to their effects?

k) Is legislative evaluation practiced on a regular basis?

3. Prohibition of arbitrariness

a) Are there specific rules prohibiting arbitrariness?

b) Are there limits to discretionary power?

c) Is there a system of full publicity of government information?

d) Are reasons required for decisions?

4. Access to Justice before independent and impartial courts

a) Is the judiciary independent?

b) Is the department of public prosecution to some degree autonomous from the state apparatus? Does it act on the basis of the law and not of political expediency?

c) Are single judges subject to political influence or manipulation?

d) Is the judiciary impartial? What provisions ensure its impartiality on a case-by-case basis?

e) Do citizens have effective access to the judiciary, also for judicial review of governmental action?

f) Does the judiciary have sufficient remedial powers?

g) Is there a recognised, organised and independent legal profession?

h) Are judgments implemented?

i) Is respect of *res iudicata* ensured?

5. Respect for human rights

Are the following rights guaranteed (in practice)?

a) The right of access to justice: Do citizens have effective access to the judiciary?

b) The right to a legally competent judge

c) The right to be heard

d) *Ne bis in idem* (double jeopardy)

e) Non-retroactivity of measures

f) The right to an effective remedy

g) The presumption of innocence

h) The right to a fair trial

6. Non-discrimination and equality before the law

a) Are the laws applied generally and without discrimination?

b) Are there laws that discriminate against certain individuals or groups?

c) Are laws interpreted in a discriminatory way?

d) Are there individuals or groups with special legal privileges?

---

1. William Blackstone, *Commentaries on the Laws of England* (1765-1769) Book 1 Ch 6; William Holdsworth, *History of English Law* ii, 251-252; x 647-648.
2. Holdsworth (n 1) 441-442.
3. Blackstone (n.1) Book 1 Ch 2.
4. In the case of *Prohibitions Del Roy* (1607) 12 Co Rep 63 at 64-65 [77] ER 1342 at 1343].
5. The relevant passage reads: 'His Majesty was not learned in the laws of his realm of England, and causes which concern the life, or inheritance, or goods, or fortunes of his subjects, are not to be decided by natural reason but by the artificial reason and judgment of law, which law is an act which requires long study and experience, before that a man can attain to the cognizance of it: that the law was the golden met-wand and measure to try the causes of the subjects; and which protected His Majesty in safety and peace.'
6. A V Dicey, *Introduction to the study of the law of the Constitution* (Macmillan & Co, 10th ed, 1959) 202-203.
7. (1765-1769) Comm. i, 469; quoted x *HEL* 715.
8. (1803) 5 US (1 Cranch) 137, 177.
9. See *A v Secretary of State for the Home Department* [2005] 2 AC 68; [2004] UKHL 56, [42].
10. See *Chu Kheng Lim v Minister for Immigration* (1992) 176 CLR 1, 36; *Bodrudduza v MIMA* (2007) 228 CLR 651, 671.
11. See *Kirk v Industrial Court (NSW)* (2010) 239 CLR 531. More recently, in *Wainohu v New South Wales* [2011] HCA 24 para 44, the High Court has held that a court cannot be deprived of its essential characteristics including the reality and appearance of the court's independence and its impartiality, the application of procedural fairness, the adherence, as a general rule, to the open court principle and the giving of reasons for its decisions.
12. See *Kirk v Industrial Court (NSW)* (2010) 239 CLR 531,581.
13. 'Government and the Rule of Law in the Modern Age' in the LSE Law Department and Clifford Chance Lecture series on Rule of Law 22 February 2006.
14. See *Statute of the Council of Europe* (ETS No 001) Art.3.
15. See *Report on the Rule of Law,* par 1. The other pillars are democracy and human rights.
16. See *Report on the Rule of Law,* par 41.
17. The full list reads as follows:

    (1) Legality, including a transparent, accountable and democratic process for enacting law

    (2) Legal certainty

    (3) Prohibition of arbitrariness

(4) Access to justice before independent and impartial courts, including judicial review of administrative acts

(5) Respect for human rights

(6) Non-discrimination and equality before the law.

18. See *R v Secretary of State for Home Department; Ex parte Pierson* [1998] AC 539.
19. See *Chassagnou v France (29 April 1999).*
20. 'Government and the Rule of Law in the Modern Age' in the LSE Law Department and Clifford Chance Lecture series on Rule of Law 22 February 2006.
21. See, for example, the Senate Standing Committee's Report on ***Parliamentary control of delegated legislation.***
22. I have taken the definition of a Henry VIII clause from the Report of the Scrutiny of Legislation Committee of the Queensland Parliament on *The Use of 'Henry VIII' Clauses in Queensland Legislation,* January 1997, pars 3.20,5.5.
23. See Queensland Law Reform Commission, *Henry VIII Clauses*, (Report No 39, 29 June 1990).
24. See the definition of Legislative Standards in the *Legislative Standards Act 1992* (Qld), s 4.
25. (1997) 189 CLR 520,564.
26. Article 29(2).
27. See *Potter v Minahan* (1908) 7 CLR 277, 304, and see, also *Ex Parte Walsh and Johnson; In re Yates* (1925) 37 CLR 36, 93.
28. (1990) 171 CLR 1, 18 (Mason CJ, Deane, Dawson, Toohey, Gaudron & McHugh JJ).
29. See *R v Shrestha* (1991) 173 CLR 48, 60; *Leeth v The Commonwealth* (1992) 174 CLR 455, 485.
30. See *Attorney General v De Keyser's Royal Hotel Ltd* [1920] AC 508 and *Burmah Oil Co (Burma Trading) Ltd v Lord Advocate* [1965] AC 75.
31. See *Oceanic Sun Shipping Company Inc v Fay* (1988) 165 CLR 197, 239; *Jago v District Court (NSW)* (1989) 168 CLR 23, 76.
32. See *South Australia v Totani* (2010) 242 CLR 1, 29.
33. (1992) 177 CLR 1, 43.
34. See *South Australia v Totani* (2010) 242 CLR 1, 29 (French CJ).
35. See, for example, the matters referred to in the plurality judgment in *Wentworth v New South Wales Bar Association;* (1992) 176 CLR 239.
36. Stephen Argument, 'Legislative Scrutiny in Australia: Wisdom to Export? (2011) 32 (2) *Statute Law Review* 116.
37. Regulations and Ordinances Committee: Senate Standing Orders 23 (Subordinate legislation) and Scrutiny of Bills Committee: Senate Standing Orders 24 (Bills).
38. Section 93 of the *Parliament of Queensland Act 2001* (Qld) (as amended) places responsibility for both Bills and subordinate legislation on portfolio Committees of the Parliament. Previously that responsibility was placed by s 103 on the Scrutiny of Legislation Committee, a standing Committee of the Parliament.
39. Legislation Review Committee: Sections 8A (Bills) and 9 (Subordinate legislation) of the *Legislation Review Act 1987* (NSW).
40. Scrutiny of Acts and Regulations Committee: Section 17 of the *Parliamentary Committees Act 2003* (Vic) (Bills, Subordinate Legislation and Human Rights).

41. Legislation Committee: Legislative Council Standing Orders, Schedule 1 Clause 4 (Bills referred by the House or under Standing Order 125A); Uniform Legislation and Statutes Review Committee: Legislative Council Standing Orders, Schedule 1 Clause 8 (B) (Bills referred under Standing Order 230A, uniform law proposals); Legislative Council Standing Orders, Schedule 1 Clause 3: Joint Standing Committee on Delegated Legislation (Subsidiary Legislation and instruments subject to disallowance).
42. Standing Committee on Justice and Community Safety (when performing the duties of a Scrutiny of Bills and Subordinate Legislation Committee): Assembly resolution of appointment (Subordinate legislation and Bills).
43. Legislative Review Committee: *Parliamentary Committees Act 1991* (SA) and *Subordinate Legislation Act 1978* (SA) (Subordinate legislation and statutory sunset clauses).
44. Parliamentary Standing Committee on Subordinate Legislation: Section 8 of the *Subordinate Legislation Committee Act 1969* (Tas) (Subordinate legislation).
45. Standing Committee on Legislation and Publications: Section 20 of Standing Orders of the Legislative Assembly (Subordinate legislation).
46. Section 4.
47. These 5 scrutiny principles are repeated in the Senate Standing Committee for the Scrutiny of Bills, *Guidelines*, 2nd edition, July 2022, 6, 11, 14, 17, 21.
48. See *Queensland Legislative Standards Act 1992* (Qld), Section 4(4)(c).
49. Victorian *Parliamentary Committees Act 2003* (Vic), section 17(b)(i) and (iii).
50. Section 30 of the *Charter of Human Rights and Responsibilities Act 2006* (Vic); section 21 of the *Subordinate Legislation Act 1994* (Vic).
51. The *Human Rights Act 2004* (ACT).
52. The Standing Committee on Justice and Community Safety (performing the duties of a Scrutiny of Bills and Subordinate Legislation Committee).
53. March 1982.
54. Stephen Argument, 'Legislative Scrutiny in Australia: Wisdom to Export?' (2011) 32 (2) *Statute Law Review* 116.
55. Lord Hailsham, 'Elective Dictatorship', The Richard Dimbleby Lecture 1976 (British Broadcasting Corporation, 1976).

8.16 A Celebration of Scholarship

Editor's note

This is the text of an address delivered by Brennan on the occasion of the Monash University Law Faculty 'In Review' Celebration of Scholarship event held in Melbourne on 18 October 2011.[1]

This evening, we are gathered in celebration of years of scholarly endeavour, undertaken in one of our finest law schools. Tonight, Professor Bryan Horrigan will present the works which have been published during the last triennium and which testify to the vigour of the Monash research tradition. But first I must pay my respects and record my debt to the Law School of Monash University and to several of its graduates who, as my Associates, shepherded me through my judicial years. It was Louis Waller who, identifying students of ability and industry, recommended recent graduates for appointment. All of them proved to be not only brilliant and enthusiastic lawyers but men and women who became continuing friends and whose friendship grew out of lively discussion following long hours of research. As a consumer emeritus of the scholarly work of others, I have been given this opportunity to say something about the nature and purpose of legal research – research which finds a natural home in the Law Schools of our Universities although its benefits are not confined to the halls of Academe.

Research in any discipline is an antidote to atrophy. And so, it is with law. Law is a living collocation of concepts that together provide the rule of law in a changing world. And, as Chief Justice French pointed out: 'Like most infrastructure projects, the Rule of Law requires continual maintenance, upkeep and renovation'.[2] A continuing curiosity about the law and its operation is needed to maintain the skills and utility of a lawyer, whether judge or practitioner, academic or corporate executive, government adviser or social scientist. But legal research is different from research in the physical sciences. Research in the physical sciences is directed to the discovery or verification of new truths about phenomena, ascertained by the classical scientific method of observation, hypothesis formulation, experimentation and verification or falsification. The processes of phenomenological research are observable and the outcomes are often quantifiable. Legal research is of a different kind and we need a distinct taxonomy of legal research to describe its purpose, methodology and outcomes. This difference often works to the disadvantage of legal research and, indeed, of research in the social sciences generally, perhaps because legal research does not exhibit quantifiable criteria[3].

The sources of the common law, from which the contemporary law flows, owes little or nothing to statistical analysis. (I use the term 'common law' as a shorthand for judge-made law so, if I may be pardoned by the Chancery lawyers, I should like to use it to include equity and, as well, judicial interpretation of statues). History, philosophy, religion, culture, economic conditions and human experience have informed the concepts which are expressed in legal principles and rules. Phenomena belong to a different order. Normative concepts are not the stuff of databases. They belong to the realm of ideas that are not susceptible of sensory perception. Empirical research has a role to play in legal research but the role is limited[4].

Nevertheless, legal research always has the purpose of finding some new idea or some new way of expressing or presenting a legal concept. It may be a new refinement of expression, or a new account of the origin or development of a legal concept, or a new insight into its legal or social significance. A mere restatement in familiar terms of the existing law is not legal research. That is not to deny the utility of students' texts which state existing legal rules in bald terms that equip the student with a basic understanding of current legal concepts – the concepts with which the graduate will work in the quotidian tasks of the practising lawyer. A pedagogical skill is required to compile and present current legal concepts in a way that brings understanding to the minds of fledgling lawyers and pedagogical skill assumes a sophisticated insight into the relevant subject matter. That insight can be acquired only by research, though the production of basic texts may not itself be an example of legal research. If undergraduate law courses consisted of no more than instruction in current legal concepts, there would be a strong case for remitting the teaching of law to the professional bodies which undertook the task in earlier days. But universities have assumed the responsibility of legal education, which extends to legal and historical research, legal analysis and reasoning, legal theory and the influence of law on culture and social institutions. This wider ambit of undergraduate education is welcomed by the courts and the profession, for it provides a more profound understanding of the meaning and scope of current legal concepts than the meaning and scope to be derived merely from a bare contemporary text. Legal research is essential to the intellectual strength of a law school for a number of reasons, and the enhancing of teaching and learning is one of them.

Law consists of concepts – not phenomena. And the concepts have a history, they emerge from a culture, they are the product of human experience and wisdom which has organized them according to a broad logic, they are interrelated, they have been developed to regulate particular fields of human activity, they are both normative and adaptable, they reflect the society they serve and they are amenable to change as the society changes. The law is a complex, living body of concepts which define government and its functions and the relationships, the rights and the duties of corporations, entities and people in a living society. Research into this body of concepts is needed not only to obtain an accurate understanding of the law's provisions but also to assess the function of law in society. Many a lawyer has become enchanted by the sheer intellectual adventure of research.

Legal research is of different kinds. One important category has been called 'doctrinal research' – research that analyses existing legal rules and, by reference to factors other than their current expression, clarifies, expounds or criticizes their content and operation. This kind of research illuminates the meaning of legal rules by a variety of approaches, sometimes finding the origin and tracing the development of a legal rule, sometimes identifying the influences which have shaped it, sometimes noting the terms in which it has been expressed at different times and in different circumstances, sometimes reconciling it with other legal concepts. An example of this category of research appears, at the time of writing, in an article by Chief Justice Spigelman (as he then was) in the July 2011 issue of the *Australian Law Journal* on the extrinsic evidence rule in the interpretation of contracts[5]. Not all doctrinal research is directed to the common law. In an age when statute governs ever widening fields of activity, the meaning and operation of statute law constitute an important category of doctrinal research.

Doctrinal research is much appreciated by judges and the practising profession; it reveals the true meaning of the legal rule which is to be applied as the major premiss in the judicial syllogism – that is, the syllogism in which the minor premiss is the facts of the instant case and which yields the legal consequence of those facts as the conclusion. If a rule, thus illuminated, applies precisely to the facts, there is no occasion to consider a modification (much less a rejection) of the rule unless the consequence is demonstrably unjust or inefficient and, even then, only if it is a common law rule and the court's position in the hierarchy[6] and the doctrine of *stare decisis*[7] allow it to modify or reject the rule.

Doctrinal research and judicial decisions have a symbiotic relationship. Doctrinal research into any legal proposition must take account of the judicial decisions relevant to that proposition, for the common law grows out of judicial decisions and any proposal to modify the common law requires judicial approval. Whether research is directed to the past history of a proposition or its current content, judicial decisions are fundamental to the research. Conversely, the formation of a judgment proceeds from an accurate appreciation of the current state of the law, even where a judge proposes to reject a current rule or to apply a modified rule to the facts in the instant case. So, the judge draws on doctrinal research which shows the meaning and operation of the common law in its current state and the serviceability of that law for the regulation of contemporary society. In turn, that judgment is subject to critical analysis by those engaged in doctrinal research[8], though adverse criticism must relate not to the result of the judgment but to the process by which that result was reached. Doctrinal research comprehends all the factors that may affect the formation of a judgment. They are the factors by which the validity or orthodoxy of a judgment may be assessed or by which the future path of legal development may be charted. Those factors cannot be exhaustively defined, as Cardozo's well-known analysis of the judicial process shows:

> My analysis of the judicial process comes then to this, and little more: logic, and history, and custom, and utility, and the accepted standards of right conduct, are the forces which singly or in combination shape the progress of the law. Which of these forces shall dominate in any case must depend largely upon the comparative importance or value of the social interests that will be thereby promoted or impaired. One of the most fundamental social interests is that law shall be uniform and impartial. There must be nothing in its action that savors of prejudice or favor or even arbitrary whim or fitfulness. Therefore, in the main there shall be adherence to precedent.[9]

Some of the factors which contribute to an accurate and complete understanding of a legal concept are familiar, others are encountered less frequently. The history of a legal rule is often critical to an appreciation of its contemporary meaning, as Holdsworth's classic *History of English Law* continually reveals to the student. Oliver Wendell Holmes observed that –

> The law embodies the story of a nation's development through many centuries, and it cannot be dealt with as if it contained only the axioms and corollaries of a book of mathematics. In order to know what it is, we must know what it has been and what it tends to become. We must alternately consult history and existing theories of legislation.[10]

Philosophy and jurisprudence have played a vital, if often unacknowledged role, in legal development: witness Julius Stone's *Province and Function of Law*. And scholarly legal texts such as *Fleming's Law of Torts* and Law Journals such as the *Monash Law Review* have been considerable influences on legal developments.

The scholarly and sensitive legal researcher is interested not only in the scope and current operation of the law but also in the direction of its development. As a collection of norms affecting a changing society, the law itself must change to remain serviceable. In 1995, Sir Anthony Mason referred to his earlier criticism of some academic legal commentary. He said:

> Some 15 or more years ago I was critical of the quality of much academic legal commentary. It was, in my view, deficient both in analysis and in constructing a way forward. Too much of it was simply descriptive of what had been said and decided in particular cases. At the time I thought that academic lawyers, as well as professional lawyers, left the development of legal principle to the High Court, unlike United States academics who blazed a trail ahead of court decisions . . . [11]

Acknowledging some improvement, he nevertheless regretted that –

> The number of articles which have the potential to influence judicial legal thinking in a significant way is relatively few. In general, articles are not written with that end in view. Their purpose is limited to providing a summary of how the law stands in Australia, by reference to Australian, New Zealand and United Kingdom decisions.

He observed that '[d]octrinal research is of greater utility to judges, practitioners and law reform agencies when it is accompanied by identification and examination of relevant policy factors.'

To chart the way in which a legal proposition will, or should, move forward, it is necessary to bear in mind the restrictions of precedent and *stare decisis*. Those restrictions give judge-made law uniformity, consistency, certainty and continuity. These are qualities which contribute to public confidence in the curial process – an essential precondition to a society under the rule of law – but rigidity must yield to the necessity of keeping the common law in a serviceable condition.

The doctrine of precedent has sometimes been misunderstood, chiefly by those who proclaim themselves to be adherents to 'strict and complete legalism' – the judicial method of which Sir Owen Dixon spoke when he was sworn in as Chief Justice in 1952.[12] Some devotees are suspicious of judicial innovation, believing that the judicial function is limited to the application of the existing law, and does not extend to the development of new law. Research would be correspondingly confined.

In truth, Sir Owen Dixon accepted the judicial obligation to develop the law but the methodology on which he insisted limited the extent to which the law might respond to changed social conditions. Three years after he became Chief Justice, he observed in his celebrated paper 'Concerning Judicial

Method'[13] that courts 'proceed upon the assumption that the law provides a body of doctrine which governs the decision of a given case. It is taken for granted that the decision ... conforms with ascertained legal principles and applies them according to a standard of reasoning which is not personal to the judges themselves.'

Doctrinal researchers and the judiciary all aspire to identify and articulate the 'body of doctrine' available for application in the present day, yet sometimes that body of doctrine does not reveal a principle applicable to the facts of a given case. Sir Owen thought the courts might legitimately develop the law beyond its current content provided the development remained rooted in the existing body of doctrine. The courts would be acting within legitimate limits if they were[14] 'to extend the application of accepted principles to new cases or to reason from the more fundamental of settled legal principles to new conclusions or to decide that a category is not closed against unforseen instances which in reason might be subsumed thereunder.'

Perhaps Sir Owen gave a very generous interpretation to these techniques, illustrated by his paper's discussion of the development of estoppel. Nevertheless, by requiring the development to be rooted in the existing body of doctrine, Sir Owen imposed a restriction which could be accepted only in an age when social conditions and ways of thought were comparatively stable. In the modern age, new technology and radical changes in societal values have demanded development of principles and rules where there is no precedential body of doctrine or where the existing body of doctrine is based on values which have permanently changed. There were no ascertained legal principles available for application in cases of sterilisation of the mentally retarded[15] or the withdrawal of life support from the brain damaged victim[16], or pecuniary liability for the birth of a child following negligent medical treatment[17] but the jurisdiction of the courts was invoked and decisions had to be given. Proposals to develop the common law have been advanced to deal with cases arising from *in vitro* fertilisation.[18] internet 'piggybacking'[19] and phone hacking.[20] Changes in public morality may demand changes in common law rules based on the moral standards of an earlier time, for example, the equitable rights to property of same sex couples[21]. And the common law which reflected the strict sexual *mores* of an earlier age[22] is no longer applied[23].

Nevertheless, familiarity with the principles of the common law allows the researcher and the judge to extend 'the application of accepted principles to new cases'. Take, for example, the High Court's decision that the *locus* of the tort of defamation for material disseminated on the internet is where the material is downloaded[24]. And note the assertion by English courts in the *Datafin Case*[25] of a jurisdiction to judicially review some decisions of a non-statutory body. This was a new departure, but judicial familiarity with judicial review of the exercise of powers of a public nature led to the assertion of the new jurisdiction.[26] So far as I know the High Court has not ruled on the applicability of the *Datafin* principle to Australia[27], but it has been applied by other courts in the Australian hierarchy.[28]

Research can suggest when the time has come for generally accepted legal rules to be discarded or varied – namely, when they appear to be incompatible with contemporary standards or the efficient operation of the legal system. Precedent has not inhibited a reformulation of the law relating to the duty of care to trespassers,[29] or the rights of a defaulting purchaser under an instalment contract,[30] or the land rights of Aborigines and Torres Strait Islanders[31] or liability for the escape of fire[32] or liability for rape in marriage[33]. In recent times judges have been more open about the judicial technique employed in keeping the law in a serviceable condition[34]. Some years ago, at an Annual Dinner of the *Monash University Law Review,* I spoke[35] about the technique which is employed by the higher appellate courts in a time of rapid social change. I venture to repeat what I then said:

> The reasons for judgment in the higher appellate courts increasingly look behind the legal rule to discover the informing legal principle and behind the informing legal principle to discover the basic value. Legal development then proceeds in the reverse order: provided the basic value is consistent with the enduring values of the contemporary community, the informing legal principle is stated in terms which are consistent with other legal principles and the legal rule is stated in terms interlocking with related legal rules. If you ask, from what does a judge discover the enduring values of the contemporary community, the answer, given by Justice Cardozo, is 'from experience and study and reflection; in brief, from life itself'[36]. But the judge's legislative power is hedged about with restrictions. In modifying a rule or declaring a new rule, the judge is not free to innovate at pleasure. Cardozo said, in a well-known description of the judicial method, that the judge is 'to exercise a discretion informed by tradition, methodized by analogy, disciplined by system, and subordinated to "the primordial necessity of order in the social life". Wide enough in all conscience is the field of discretion that remains'.[37]

Two issues determine whether this methodology may authorize changes in the law that go beyond the Dixonian 'reason[ing] from the more fundamental of settled legal principles to new conclusions': efficiency of operation and changes in the enduring values of the community.

Sixty years ago,[38] Lord Denning recalled instances of where that had happened. He referred first to the doctrine of common employment which had originated in 1843 in the age of *laissez faire* but which was emptied of its content by a series of judicial decisions in the following century; then, he pointed out that a third party beneficiary of a contractual promise, who had been entitled to enforce the promise in an age when 'the Canon Law and the Christian ethic' bound a promisor to keep his promise, had lost that right when the notion of individual freedom was thought to restrict the liability of a promisor to the party with whom he had contracted. Modern examples of departure from settled legal principles can be found in the abandoning of the complex law of occupiers' liability,[39] the abolition of the rule in *Rylands v Fletcher*[40] and acceptance of rape in marriage.[41]

Such changes are rare but the law must change if it is to avoid injustice. That is why doctrinal research is so critical in a time of rapid social change. Research is needed to show what is the core of a legal principle, what are the values which underpinned its development and how it operates. Doctrinal research, ranging more widely than the mere text of an earlier judgment, is needed to ensure that the law is kept in a serviceable condition for the contemporary community.

The press of litigation and the tyranny of judgment writing are not conducive to reflective doctrinal research. Such research is the Academy's invaluable contribution to the judicial process. It is for that reason that it is sometimes said that the Academy should be the ultimate court of appeal in difficult areas of the law. The Academy's aspiration to acquire and expound knowledge for its own sake gives an assurance that the treatment of a legal concept will take account of the various influences that have contributed to the concept's development, its operation as an integer in the complex of related rules and its compatibility with the enduring values of the community. The research may point to the desirability of a modification of judge-made law or the need for statutory intervention.[42]

Apart from doctrinal research which is focussed on the elucidation of legal concepts, the Academy has another vital role in legal research. It must deal with the law as one of the chief normative influences on society and a reflection of societal values. There are no limits to the areas of social activity that can potentially be affected by law. Research is needed both to identify the role which the law plays in affecting social institutions, social customs, cultural values and relationships and to examine areas that may benefit by the introduction of governing law. As an example, the Australian Law Reform Commission's Report *'Multiculturalism and the Law'* observed:

> Multiculturalism as a social policy requires a systematic examination of Australian law to consider first, whether it creates barriers to the expression of cultural identity and secondly, whether it could play a more positive role in achieving the goals of multiculturalism by promoting effective equality before the law ... A further question is whether the law could be administered so that it does not have an unintended, discriminatory impact on the members of particular ethnic minority groups.[43]

Social research must embrace at least the other social sciences that affect the quality of social life. It is multi-disciplinary research, especially when law is proposed to regulate fields of technology. Thus, the National Health and Medical Research Council's *'Report ... on Facilities for Organ Transplantation and Renal Dialysis'* influenced the legal acceptance of death by cessation of brain function.[44] Modern technology has created new problems requiring consideration of legal regulation, for example, the patentability of genes.[45] As an example of significant multi-disciplinary research which drew on a number of allied disciplines, Justice Margaret Stone mentioned[46] Professor John Braithwaite's theory of 're-integrative shaming' which does not stigmatise an offender and disintegrate the moral bonds between the offender and the community but which strengthens those bonds and allows the offender to be re-integrated in the community. Or there may be a need for a modification of existing legal principle to respond to the practicalities of modern life, such as the imposition of a limit on an occupant's right to airspace above his land.[47]

In an interesting paper on 'The Taxonomy of Interdisciplinary Legal Research',[48] Professor Siems instanced a number of subjects which he assigned to interdisciplinary research, including the economics of contractual remedies, the comparative effects of the common law and civil law systems on capitalism, the role and utility of legal regulation in climate change, the correlation (if any) between the death penalty and the crime rate. Of course, the practising lawyer and the sitting judge have to accept the practical results flowing from the operation of existing law. Their concern is the due application of the existing law to the case in hand, whatever the consequences may be. They may well need to consider the law as it was in order properly to define the law as it is, but they may not be equipped to determine what it ought to be nor may they be at liberty to introduce an ameliorating change to the existing law. But society is concerned with the law as it ought to be, and scholarly research is needed to identify the possible directions of development and their respective merits or otherwise. That research may well involve other disciplines and techniques such as empirical research which is not in the usual armoury of legal skills. Social research may focus on law's impact on society, not on the validity or orthodoxy of the legal doctrines or rules which produce that impact.[49]

Legal expertise is essential to the work of an interdisciplinary research team but so is the lawyer's ability and willingness to learn from colleagues in other disciplines and to acquire a sufficient understanding of other relevant disciplines. The purpose of social research is not the same as the purpose of doctrinal research, but there may be common fields of enquiry. Thus both the doctrinal and the social researcher may need to consider the relationship between factors which have contributed to the development of the existing law in order to explain the origin and meaning of a legal rule (the objective of the doctrinal researcher) and the way in which a legal rule in turn affects or will affect corresponding factors in the contemporary milieu (an objective of the social researcher). Practising lawyers and sitting judges can participate in doctrinal research, but Law Reform Commissions and the Universities are the institutions to which we must look to find assessments of the law in the social context and proposals for enhancing law's social utility.

When Professor Horrigan was considering the Academy's relationship to law reform[50], he proposed that 'both …teaching and …research must be informed by a seven-pronged framework of levels of analysis that embraces the socio-ethical, jurisprudential, international/comparative, regulatory, doctrinal, practical and cross-disciplinary dimensions of law.'

When that research is done and when the research points to a need for changes in the law, research must chart the pathway. And that presents a further challenge. Professor Horrigan asks 'whether it is possible for any lawyer or judge to have a view on what would be good or bad development in the law without an overarching, or at least working, theory of law and legal reasoning, directed towards the objectives of law reform and social justice in particular legal systems …' He cites Professor Duncan Ivison's caveat that 'By not talking about social justice, by failing to connect it to Australia's challenges, we are left with the idea that justice is simply a mirage – as Hayek thought – or is whatever outcomes the market generates.'[51]

Social justice is surely an objective of law which treats all persons equally. The evaluation of a legal concept according to its compatibility with social justice is a necessary aspect of social research. The Academy accepts the obligation of social research to discharge a public function, namely, to enhance the function of law as a normative influence on social life and conduct. It would frustrate the purpose of social research and invalidate the academic undertaking if the research did not evaluate the social justice of a proposed reform. Law is more than an intellectual construct; it embodies the history and the values of a people and is their staff of support as they march towards the unattainable end of perfect justice.

The research output of the Monash Law School is found in the books and papers that are celebrated this evening. They bear testimony to a culture of deep scholarship and a concern with human rights and social justice. Those have been attributes of the Law School since its foundation in 1964, characteristics of the distinguished academics who have built the School's reputation. They are attributes that create a spirit in a Law School and inject vitality into the work of both Faculty and students. Tonight's celebration is therefore a celebration of the spirit and vitality of the Monash Law School and a tribute to those who have made it so. Apart from the present members of the Faculty, that honour role includes David Derham, Bob Williams, Enid Campbell, Bob Baxt and Judge Christie Weeramantry, to name some but not all. Their stimulus to research has borne fruit as we see this evening.

I offer my respectful congratulations to the authors and publishers of the books and papers we celebrate and my best wishes to the Law School as it enters on the next period of research and the next generation of researchers.

---

1. The address was first published in the *Monash University Law Review*: see (2011) 37 (3) *Monash University Law Review* 1.
2. Chief Justice Robert French, 'Swapping Ideas: The Academy, the Judiciary and the Profession' Speech, Australian Academy of Law 2008 Symposium Series, 1 December 2008.
3. See the discussion about funding models by Professor Jenny M Lewis and Dr Sandy Ross, 'What counts and what is valued? Research Policy across Disciplines and Countries' (Speech, APSA Conference, Macquarie University, 28-30 September 2009).
4. See the insightful comments of Professor Goldsworthy, 'Research Grant Mania' (2008) 50 (2) *Australian Universities' Review* 17.
5. Hon J J Spigelman, 'Contractual Interpretation: A Comparative Perspective' (2011) 85 (7) *Australian Law Journal* 412.
6. See the much-discussed case of *Farah Constructions Pty Ltd v Say-Dee Pty Ltd* (2007) 230 CLR 89.
7. See *John v Federal Commissioner of Taxation* (1989) 166 CLR 417.
8. Mark Tushnet, 'Academics as Law Makers?' (2010) 29 (1) *University of Queensland Law Journal* 19, 22.
9. B Cardozo, *The Nature of the Judicial Process* (Yale University Press, 1921) 112.
10. Oliver Wendell Holmes, *The Common Law* (Little Brown, 43rd printing, 1949) 1.
11. Geoffrey Lindell, *The Mason Papers: selected articles and speeches by Sir Anthony Mason* (The Federation Press, 2007) 345, 350-351.
12. Reproduced in Sir Owen Dixon, *Jesting Pilate* (Law Book Co, 1965) 245, 247.
13. Ibid 152, 155.

14. Ibid 152, 158.

15. See *Secretary, Department of Health and Community Services v JWB and SMB (Marion's Case)* [1992] 175 CLR 218.

16. See *Airedale NHS Trust v Bland* [1993] AC 789.

17. See *Cattanach v Melchior* [2003] 215 CLR 1.

18. In 1988, the New South Wales Law Commission reported (No 58) that – 'The application of traditional legal principles to [IVF] was likely to produce results that were unexpected and often unwanted. For example, common law principles for determining paternity, maternity and legal personality were formulated long before IVF technology was developed and based on assumptions about conception and parenting which are no longer valid.': New South Wales Law Reform Commission, *Artificial Conception: In Vitro Fertilization* (Report No 58, 1988) [2.1].

19. Rachel Anne Carter and David Makin have pleaded for an extension of the tort of conversion in order to 'recognise the importance of the Internet in modern society and the need to alter our existing legal system so that it acknowledges that technological advances are essential to the functionality of a modern world': Rachel Anne Carter and David Makin, *Piggyback Hunting – Browsing the Internet in Australia via Unsecured Wireless Networks: Virtual Theft or Acceptable Behaviour in an Online World?* (2009) 16 *James Cook University Law Review* 20, 39-40.

20. But in *Wainwright v The Home Office* [2004] 2 AC 206 Lord Hoffman noted that 'an attempt to create a tort of telephone harassment by a radical change in the basis of the action for private nuisance in *Khorasandjian v Bush* [1993] QB 727was held by the House of Lords in *Hunter v Canary Wharf Ltd* [1997] AC 655 to be a step too far. The gap was filled by the 1997 Act.'

21. Hon David Malcolm, 'Same Sex Couples: Equity's Response' [1996] 3 (3) *Murdoch University Electronic Journal of Law* 25

22. See *Pearce v Brooks* (1873) LR 1 Exch 213; *Upfill v Wright* [1911] 1 KB 506.

23. See *Magill v Magill* (2006) 226 CLR 551.

24. In *Dow Jones & Company Inc v Gutnick* (2002) 210 CLR 575, 607, Gleeson CJ, McHugh, Gummow and Hayne JJ said: 'In the case of material on the World Wide Web, it is not available in comprehensible form until downloaded on to the computer of a person who has used a web browser to pull the material from the web server. It is where that person downloads the material that the damage to reputation may be done. Ordinarily then, that will be the place where the tort of defamation is committed.'

25. See *R v Panel of Take-overs and Mergers; Ex parte Datafin plc (Norton Opax plc intervening)* [1987] QB 815.

26. In *R v Jockey Club; Ex parte Aga Khan* [1993] 2 All ER 853, 864, Bingham MR commented that the effect of the decision in *Datafin* was 'to extend judicial review to a body whose birth and constitution owed nothing to any exercise of governmental power but which had been woven into the fabric of public regulation in the field of take-overs and mergers.' And Mann LJ held in *R v Lautro; Ex parte Ross* [1992] 1 All ER 422, 431-432 that, where a non-statutory power may be exercised to affect the interests of a third party, an obligation to afford natural justice to the third party is a condition on a valid exercise of the power.

27. See *Neat Domestic Trading Pty Ltd v AWB Ltd* (2003) 216 CLR 277.

28. See the review by Kyrou J in *Ceca Institute Pty Ltd v Australian Council for Private Education and Training* [2010] 30 VR 555; [2010] VSC 552.

29. See *Hackshaw v Shaw* (1984) 155 CLR 614.

30. See *Legione v Hateley* (1983) 152 CLR 406.
31. See *Mabo v Queensland [No 2]* (1992) 175 CLR 1
32. See *Burnie Port Authority v General Jones Pty Ltd* (1994) 179 CLR 520.
33. See *R v L* (1991) 174 CLR 379.
34. See, for example, Sir Anthony Mason, 'Rights, Values and Legal Institutions' in Geoffrey Lindell, *The Mason Papers: selected articles and speeches by Sir Anthony Mason* (The Federation Press, 2007) 80.
35. Reported in Sir Gerard Brennan, 'A Critique of Criticism' (1993) 19 (2) *Monash University Law Review* 213.
36. Benajmin N Cardozo, *The Nature of the Judicial Process* (Yale University Press, 1921) 113-14.
37. Ibid 141.
38. Lord Denning, 'The Universities and Law Reform' (1949) *1 Journal of the Society of Public Teachers of Law* 258, 261.
39. See *Australian Safeway Stores Pty Ltd v Zaluzna* (1987) 162 CLR 479.
40. (1968) LR 3 HL 330, abolished by *Burnie Port Authority v General Jones Pty Ltd* (1994) 179 CLR 520.
41. See *R v L* (1991) 174 CLR 379.
42. See Sir Anthony Mason, 'Legislative and Judicial Law Making: Can we locate an identifiable boundary?' in Geoffrey Lindell, *The Mason Papers: selected articles and speeches by Sir Anthony Mason* (The Federation Press, 2007) 59.
43. Australian Law Reform Commission's Report, *Multiculturalism and the Law* (Report No 57, 1992) [1.17], 9.
44. See Australian Law Reform Commission, *Human Tissue Transplants* (Report No 7, 1992) para [120]. Similarly, the ALRC cited many learned scientific papers in its report on *Gene and Ingenuity: Gene Patenting and Human Health* (Report No 99, 2004).
45. Australian Law Reform Commission, *Genes and Ingenuity: Gene Patenting and Human Health* (Report No 99, 2004); Diane Nicol *On the Legality of Gene Patents* [2005] 29 (3) *Melbourne University Law Review* 809.
46. Margaret Stone 'The Academy's Contribution to the Development of Law" (2002) 25 (3) *UNSW Law Journal* 798.
47. See *Bernstein v Skyviews and General Ltd* [1978] QB 479; *Star Energy Weald Basin Ltd & Anor v Bocardo SA* [2011] 1 AC 380.
48. Mathias Siems, 'The Taxonomy of Interdisciplinary Legal Research : Finding the Way out of the Desert' (2009) 7 (1) *Journal of Commonwealth Law and Legal Education* 5.
49. See Jeremy Webber 'Legal Research, the Law Schools and the Profession' (2004) 26 (4) *Sydney Law Review* 565, 579.
50. Bryan Horrigan, 'Reforming Law Reform's engagement with the Academic Arm of the Legal Profession' [2008] 3 *Australasian Law Teachers Association Law Research Series*.
51. Ibid.

8.17 The Accountability Roundtable

Editor's note

The Accountability Roundtable (ART) is a company limited by guarantee with a board which includes retired judges, politicians and journalists. The objects of the company are 'to generate public debate about, and improve the standards of, accountability, honesty, probity, transparency, anti-corruption systems and measures and democratic practice in all parliaments and governments in Australia. In 2013, the ART selection committee chaired by retired Supreme Court judge, Tim Smith from Victoria gave 'integrity awards' to a range of public officials. The ceremony took place at Parliament House in Canberra on 11 December 2013. Brennan was invited to deliver the occasional address.

I join in the acknowledgement of the Traditional Owners, their Elders past and present, custodians of the land on which we meet and on which this Parliament House is built.

For those of you who work here day by day, familiarity may rob this building of its majesty and authority, but for those of us who come here on invitation or to inspect this symbol of Australian democracy, the building has a grandeur appropriate to an auditorium of the aspirations of the Australian people. I was honoured to attend here as the delegate of the Governor-General to open formally the Parliament that was summoned to meet after the 1996 General Election. On that occasion, I was conscious of the importance of the separation of powers and I believed – correctly, I think – that the practice of appointing a judicial officer to open the Parliament was born of a misunderstanding of British precedent. I was uneasy then about fulfilling that role and I have retained some unease about any involvement in the political process. Hence, I had some misgiving about an invitation to a former member of the judiciary to take part in a ceremony commending members of the political branches of government for what they have done in their political lives.

The separation of powers, a bastion of our freedoms, demands that a respectful reticence is maintained by the judicial branch of government about the conduct of the members of the political branches[1]. And a similar inhibition, albeit not so restrictive, applies to former judges. The public memory tends to attribute to former judges a set of values expressing legal rights and duties. Criticism of political conduct may be thought to be warranted by the law of the land, while commendation may be thought to be an endorsement of legal rectitude. There is another and more basic reason why judges or former judges should refrain from commenting on political conduct: they lack the lifetime experience needed to form a sound judgment of political conduct except in the more extreme cases. For these reasons I shall forego the opportunity to commend our Awardees or to compare their merits with the merits of other members of the Parliament. Determination of merit has been the prerogative of the Selection Committee established by the Accountability Round Table[2] whose experience and competence entitle them to make the difficult assessments that lead to these Awards.

But it does not follow that the judiciary is not interested in the celebration and re-affirmation of the qualities expressed in the Awards criteria. The laws of the Parliament must be applied by the courts and the courts must give effect to the valid acts of the Executive Government, so the work of the political branches of Government provide the courts with the rules to be observed in administering justice according to law. When the leading criterion for these awards is a candidate's 'outstanding commitment to the public interest', it is clear that the Awards are intended to celebrate a democracy under a rule of law which advances the public interest. That is the essential characteristic of the rule of law in a free democracy. When judges are satisfied that they are working under a rule of law in the public interest, the administration of justice according to law presents no difficulties but rather a sense of satisfaction. It is a privilege therefore for a former judge to present Awards to members of the political branches of government commending their commitment to the public interest.

This notion of the public interest is not merely a rhetorical device – a shibboleth to be proclaimed in a feel-good piece of oratory. It has a profound practical significance in proposals for political action and in any subsequent assessment. It is derived from the fiduciary nature of political office: a fundamental conception which underpins a free democracy.

It has long been established legal principle that a member of Parliament holds 'a fiduciary relation towards the public'[3] and 'undertakes and has imposed upon him a public duty and a public trust'.[4] The duties of a public trustee are not identical with the duties of a private trustee but there is an analogous limitation imposed on the conduct of the trustee in both categories. The limitation demands that all decisions and exercises of power be taken in the interests of the beneficiaries and that duty cannot be subordinated to, or qualified by the interests of the trustee. As Rich J said[5]: 'Members of Parliament are donees of certain powers and discretions entrusted to them on behalf of the community, and they must be free to exercise these powers and discretions in the interests of the public unfettered by considerations of personal gain or profit'.

Now how does this fit in with poll-driven politics, when actions are taken chiefly to ensure some electoral advantage? A case of this kind arose in England in 2001 concerning a local authority decision taken largely to gain an electoral advantage. The principle was explained by the senior Judge, Lord Bingham of Cornhill:

> Elected politicians of course wish to act in a manner which will commend them and their party… to the electorate. Such an ambition is the life blood of democracy and a potent spur to responsible decision-taking and administration. Councillors do not act improperly or unlawfully if, exercising public powers for a public purpose for which such powers were conferred, they hope that such exercise will earn the gratitude and support of the electorate and thus strengthen their electoral position. The law would indeed part company with the realities of party politics if it were to hold otherwise. But a public power is not exercised lawfully if it is exercised not for a public purpose for which the power was conferred but in order to promote the electoral advantage of a political party.[6]

Public fiduciary duties depend for their content on the circumstances in which power is to be exercised. The obligations cast on members of Parliament and officers of the Executive Government are many and varied and the law takes cognizance of the realities of political life, but asserts and, in interpreting statutes, assumes that the public interest is the paramount consideration in the exercise of all public powers. The many and varied demands made upon Parliamentarians – by constituents, by party, by lobbyists, by family and by friends – all call for a response. Fred Chaney spoke of these demands when he delivered the Inaugural Accountability Round Table Lecture at the Melbourne Law School in October 2011. He spoke of the compromises needed in government and the many claims on the loyalty of practising politicians. But he did not suggest that any of these claims should subvert consideration of the public interest. Whenever political action is to be taken, its morality – and, indeed, its legality – depends on whether the public interest is the paramount interest to be served.

True it is that the fiduciary duties of political officers are often impossible to enforce judicially[7] – the motivations for political action are often complex – but that does not negate the fiduciary nature of political duty. Power, whether legislative or executive, is reposed in members of the Parliament by the public for exercise in the interests of the public and not primarily for the interests of members or the parties to which they belong. The cry 'whatever it takes' is not consistent with the performance of fiduciary duty.

Fred Chaney sought to identify what he called 'the sea anchors' which would 'enable the electorate to discern the direction of travel' of a government or an alternative government, by which politicians could 'demonstrate … how they will judge where their duty lies' and by which 'we can see integrity in their actions.' But Fred Chaney insisted that politics 'must be much more than the technology of power' and he expressed a need 'to define our national purpose, to have a light on the hill', a need 'to re-engage the electors by giving them a story about Australia that they can believe in.' I respectfully and heartily agree.

The political realities of which Fred Chaney spoke are not likely to be correctly evaluated by those who are unfamiliar with the political process. For that reason, the Button and Missen Awards are determined by, and derive their authority and legitimacy from, the judgment made in exercise of the combined talents and experience of the members of the Accountability Round Table's Selection Committee. They are familiar with the varied moral demands made of those who throw their hats into the political ring. It would be impossible, or at least it would be inappropriate, for a judge to determine the recipients of these Awards.

The criteria for the Awards identify the issues on which the Accountability Round Table place an especial importance: transparency and accountability in government, good Parliamentary practice and the institution of Parliament, justifiable changes in political policies and practices and protection of political and civil rights. Eligibility for these awards is restricted to candidates who commit to these objectives with honesty and civility and who demonstrate their independence and/or political courage. These are qualities of political leadership that can command the confidence of the Australian people.

Generally speaking, political action must accord with popular opinion, but popular opinion does not always perceive where the public interest truly lies. Sometimes false or out of date information swamps popular opinion, sometimes popular opinion may fall short of the vision appropriate to a confident nation in a changing world. True political leadership is needed when such issues arise, leadership that can 're-engage the electors by giving them a story about Australia that they can believe in'.

A headline issue of the recent election illustrates the problem of determining political action in the public interest. Both major political parties proposed to quash the miserable trade of people smugglers by imposing hardship on refugees who have been smuggled. This is an excruciating problem, and it raises major issues which affect not only asylum seekers but the self-image of the Australian people. Can we justify inflicting injuries on the innocent in order to hurt the pockets of the guilty? Can we maintain our humanitarian quota of migrants or is it being destroyed by people smugglers? Are we really concerned by the risk of deaths at sea or is our principal concern the survival and arrival of un-visaed refugees? Is policy to be determined by a fear that an uncontrolled flood of foreigners will damage the comfortable order of our lives? These grave issues call for leaders who are noted for their honesty, civility and political courage and who articulate a vision for an honourable and confident nation. The nation will be served by leadership which formulates policies and decides on practical measures that take account of Australia's position as a wealthy Western country in the Asian hemisphere, retaining the rule of law and our traditional cultural links but bound to respond to the human crises affecting thousands of people in Iraq, Syria, Afghanistan, Sri Lanka and other countries where civilised living is destroyed by conflict.

These Awards celebrate the values that underpin leadership of high quality and standing and we are grateful to the Accountability Round Table for identifying such values and promoting their acceptance among those who serve this nation in the political branches of government.

And we congratulate those who are to receive these Awards this evening, thanking them for their service to our nation and for the example of outstanding commitment to the public interest and honesty, civility, independence and/or political courage that they have given.

---

1. My letter to Hon Tim Fischer 3 January 1997.
2. The decisions were made by the ART Selection committee comprising Lyn Allison (former leader of the Democrats, and Senator), The Hon Jim Carlton (former federal Liberal Party Minister), The Hon Dr. Ken Coghill, (former ALP member of and Speaker of the Victorian Legislative Assembly, Associate Professor, Business and Economics, Monash University), Harry Evans (Former Clerk of the Senate), Professor Charles Sampford (Director, The Institute for Ethics, Governance and Law) and Dr David Solomon, Queensland Integrity Commissioner. It was chaired by the Chair of the ART, Hon Tim Smith QC (retired Victorian Supreme Court judge and Adjunct Professor, Business and Economics Monash University).
3. See *R* v *Boston* (1923) 33 CLR 386, 412 (per Higgins J).
4. Ibid 408
5. See *Horne* v *Barber* (1920) 27 CLR 494, 501.
6. See *Porter* v *Magill* [2002] 2 AC 357, [2001] UKHL 67, para 21
7. The Courts will not invalidate a law of the Parliament for failure to secure the public interest: *Union Steamship Co of Australia Pty Ltd* v *King* (1988) 166 CLR 1,10.

8.18 A Letter in Support of Onshore Asylum Seekers

Editor's note

During 2021, there was considerable public controversy over the Morrison government's treatment of long-term onshore asylum seekers who had arrived by boat without visas. Some of these asylum seekers were on bridging visas being held in community detention, having given birth to children in Australia. One family attracted much media interest. This was the Nadesalingam family who were Tamils from Sri Lanka. They had been residing in the Queensland country town of Biloela for some time, having won the support of the local community. But as the parents' claim for a protection visa had been rejected, the government was adamant that they were to be removed from Australia. The government had the family removed to the detention facility on Christmas Island, with adequate medical care being available only in faraway Perth. By this time, Brennan was a resident in an aged care facility, having endured lockdowns on account of COVID. Brennan wrote this letter to major newspapers. The letter was published on 11 June 2021.[1] The letter was simply signed 'Gerard Brennan, Bronte'. The Albanese Labor government was elected on 21 May 2022, the day before Brennan's 94th birthday. He was hoping that the new government would grant him a birthday wish. Just before his death on 1 June 2022, he learnt that the family was to be released from detention and returned to Biloela. Two months later the family was issued with permanent visas.

Are other Australians ashamed, as I am? How can Australia, proud of our freedoms, respectful of all our peoples, and insistent on human dignity, inflict cruelty on Australian children as a means of achieving a goal of government policy? The cruelty suffered by Tharnicaa – Australian-born and now in a Perth hospital – is not an unintended consequence of a general policy; it is cruelty inflicted on a child deliberately as a warning to others not to come to Australia by boat without a visa. Tharnicaa has committed no offence; she presents no danger. Cruelty is being inflicted upon her to punish her parents who came by boat without a visa and thus to discourage others from breaching one of our immigration policies.

If we want to enforce a policy to stop people smuggling, we must do so by action taken against the people smugglers or the people being smuggled. It is a hard policy to implement, but if action is ineffective to prevent potential parents from settling in Australia, and the parents do settle and have children here, it is unconscionable to impose deliberate cruelty on those children to rectify the earlier failure to exclude the parents.

The family had settled in the small central Queensland town of Biloela which had welcomed and valued Tharnicaa and Kopika. It would be a cruelty obnoxious to Australian values to deprive those children of their parents and it is cruelty obnoxious to Australian values to isolate them with their parents to discourage future people smugglers. Basic and important Australian values are at stake. They must not be discarded by a show of heartlessness towards Australian children.

---

1. The letter was published in *The Sydney Morning Herald* and *The Age* on 11 June 2021. See https://www.smh.com.au/national/nsw/obnoxious-cruelty-towards-tamil-girls-is-un-australian-20210609-p57ziq.html

8.19 Keeping Government Honest

Editor's note

Brennan was one of 34 retired judges who wrote to Prime Minister Morrison in December 2018 expressing concerns about corruption. They wrote: 'Confidence and trust in government and public institutions is at an all-time low. When this confidence and trust is diminished, pessimism, divisiveness, and conflict increase; and social cohesiveness is harmed. As a result, the economy and the welfare of all Australians suffers. Ultimately, as international experience has shown, democracy itself is threatened and may be irreparably damaged. Governments ignore at their peril demands by citizens to combat corruption with vigour. A major cause of the current deterioration in trust is the suspicion that corruption permeates many governmental decisions and actions. Corruption, broadly understood in this context, occurs when those in public office place private interests over the public good.' One of the retired judges who organised the letter was Stephen Charles. When the Morrison government took no action, Charles joined with Catherine Williams in publishing 'Keeping Them Honest: the case for a genuine national integrity commission and other vital democratic reforms.' They asked Brennan to write the Foreword. The book was published in April 2022, two months before Brennan's death. He lived long enough to learn that the newly elected Albanese government was committed to legislation for a National Anti-Corruption Commission. This is the Foreword.[1] It was Brennan's last published piece.

This is a disturbing book. It is meant to be. The authors have listed a series of corrupt activities charting a decline in the integrity of Australian public and political life. Corruption has flourished. At the Commonwealth level, there is evidence that decisions involving the expenditure of large amounts of money have been made to secure political advantage without complying with the 'value for money' requirement of s 71 of the *Public Governance, Performance and Accountability Act 2013* (Cth). Sadly, the community has been rather tolerant of this decline. This book may enliven the community conscience and lead us to insist on integrity in public life.

In earlier times, when the community expected higher standards in public and political life, the political system itself provided some mechanism for controlling corruption. If some element of corruption was attributable to one political party, the opposing political party was eager to expose it. Exposure gave a political advantage, as it appealed to the community's sense of integrity. Integrity was a political strength; it commanded community support, and it was embraced by leading politicians and career public servants. There were occasional lapses, but, as a system, it served the community well.

But integrity has been sapped by political ambition and by the seeking of party and personal benefits. Private interests have increasingly influenced political and administrative action. Legality has taken the place of morality in defining the permissible limits of political and administrative action. The decline in standards opens the way to corruption, and the absence of a political mechanism for alerting the community to corrupt conduct facilitates the concealing of corrupt practice.

Corruption can be stemmed if the community is made aware that public assets are being acquired improperly by private interests, or that public duties are being performed to benefit private interests improperly. This book describes attempts that have been made and opportunities that have been neglected for creating mechanisms that might expose corruption, identify its participants, and offer some prospect of remedy. The creation of such a mechanism is not a simple exercise.

The authors are alive to the risk that reputational damage to the persons or institutions involved in an inquiry may be inflicted unjustly by public and privileged hearings. They are conscious that great care is needed in determining the terms of reference under which an inquiry must function.

Accordingly, the book reproduces the design principles for a national commission recommended by the National Integrity Committee (a group of retired judges).

In December 2018, 34 former judges wrote a letter to the prime minister expressing their support for the establishment of a national integrity commission with the power to hold public hearings. Regrettably, no legislative action has been taken. Instead, there has been a flow of political rhetoric aimed at securing success at the forthcoming poll — a result that would deny the prospect of any substantial Commonwealth reform.

Judges and former judges do not usually enter the public political arena. The judiciary does not have a political agenda. Its function is to resolve disputed facts and to apply the law to the facts as found, unaffected by political influence. Lest intervention on political issues might seem inconsistent with political independence, even former judges usually abstain from political comment. But corruption that erodes honest administration and the disregard of the rule of law in the pursuit of political power are not issues about which former judges must or should be silent. They are issues that affect the social health of the community.

The authors, a distinguished former appellate judge and the research director at the Centre for Public Integrity, have shown the extent of maladministration in our public affairs. We are indebted to them for a book that is a timely reminder of the community's need for higher moral standards and for more publicity, transparency, legitimacy, and integrity in the conduct of our public affairs.

---

1. The Foreword to Stephen Charles and Catherine Williams, *Keeping Them Honest: the case for a genuine national integrity commission and other vital democratic reforms* (Scribe Publications, 2022) vii-ix.

Chapter 9

Aboriginal Rights

9.1 Oral Submissions to the Woodward Royal Commission on Land Rights

Editor's note

Brennan was appointed as senior counsel for the Northern Land Council in the Aboriginal Land Rights Commission set up by the Whitlam Government and chaired by Mr Justice A E Woodward. Woodward had published an initial report on 19 July 1973. That week, Woodward was attending the Australian Legal Convention in Perth when he asked Brennan to accept the brief. Brennan then spent some months visiting Aboriginal communities in the north of the Northern Territory before putting detailed submissions to the Royal Commission in February-March 1974. Woodward presented his final report on 3 May 1974 noting that there were 'three important areas in which I do not feel able to recommend that the Aboriginal claims should be granted in full. These relate to the ownership of minerals, the extension of present reserve boundaries from the coastline to a distance of 12 miles out to sea and the traditional ownership of land now subject to pastoral leases.'[1] Brennan had advocated very strongly particularly in relation to the issues of mining rights and pastoral leases. In his autobiography, Woodward reflected that he was still able to make far-reaching recommendations in response to Brennan's submission that 'this is a report which will for all time mark the high-water mark of possible Aboriginal aspirations. Whatever Your Honour does not recommend in favour of Aborigines at this stage, will never be granted.'[2] Woodward's chief anthropologist, Nicolas Peterson later explained that the Northern Territory Land Rights Act's genius lay in the fact that it benefited 'the most tradition-oriented and poorest Aboriginal people, the great majority of whom were actually living on or near the land with which they had traditional connections. It was legislation concerned with the future rather than the past, and it was based substantially on the drafting instructions written by Brennan.'[3] Here are nine extracts from Brennan's advocacy before the Royal Commission.

The importance of cultural and spiritual aspects relating to land [4]

The reason why we would submit that it is essential to discover the nature of the land-holding unit is because the primary reason for the need to grant Aboriginal land rights is not so much economic, although it is very largely economic, but it is basically cultural or spiritual, and the deculturization, to use an awful word, of the Aborigines before separation from their traditional land is one of the most grievous wrongs that the people have suffered. The object of the scheme must therefore be, in our submission, to identify how that cultural relationship can be reconstructed with an identification of the relationship between a group and a particular tract of country.

The significance of sacred sites [5]

We have drawn a distinction between the recognition of traditional relationship of land and the satisfactional needs which would derive both from the traditional relationship of land and from other social, financial or tribal, matters and the only justification for the recognition of traditional rights to land, as we see it, is not what might be regarded as social need but cultural and spiritual affiliation. If those are factors of importance to the Aboriginal people, then the recognition of those factors leads to a recognition of traditional rights, and it is for those reasons that traditional rights are to be recognised and not for simply social or economic reasons.

We certainly see it as necessary that the right of access to sacred places, for example, should be strengthened as far as possible. That in itself is not easily to be accomplished either by regulation or by the publication of the names and places of the sites, so that whilst we are in sympathy with that approach, it has its own difficulties. But that is not to say that a public recognition of a relationship between the traditional owners of country and the country so far as our existing system permits does not give to its traditional owners a feeling of satisfaction and security that they would not otherwise have. But in the question of the acquisition of cattle stations, our answer is that cattle stations should be acquired privately because they will satisfy the aspirations of the Aboriginal people who will live there, if possible spiritually, culturally and materially, and that the policy ought to be inverted from what it is at the moment. One ought not to acquire a cattle station either because it is going cheap or because it can make money and give jobs. But to refer to the justification for Your Honour's basic question – recognition of traditional rights in the way in which we are suggesting, the reversionary concept is based upon a cultural and spiritual affinity to the land. If we disregard those things we come to a wider area of need in which those factors play a part.

......

It has been put to us in one of the comments we have had upon our submission that that is going to exclude far too many people but on discussions with our observer as to how wide the net should be cast, once you depart from the criteria of the spiritual and cultural tie and go beyond that, you come to a well-meaning sloppiness of thought.

The need to vest control in the traditional owners [6]

Your Honour is aware, of course, of the pressures for change in Aboriginal society and the pressures that any Aboriginal group of today is subject to in relation not only to their traditional way of life but in relation to the adoption, either superficially or profoundly, of the European lifestyle. It has been our understanding that there has been very little acceptance of the European lifestyle at anything beyond the superficial level, but this in turn raises a problem in which we find difficulty because for me to stand here and say that, is of no assistance to Your Honour at all. The submissions that we are putting here are based, understandably, upon our appreciation of a situation. Our appreciation of a situation may be wholly erroneous and we can give Your Honour no guarantee that it is not wholly erroneous. All we can say is so far as we appreciate, we have followed the instructions that have been given to us by the Northern Land Council and they conform to what we understand to be the situation from those who in turn have advised us.

……

[T]he problem of getting into individual Aboriginal hands the sorts of rights that land rights ought to give can be approached in this way. In a situation of social change, the Aboriginal land control system ought not to preclude the use of land in traditional ways. I think everybody agrees with that proposition. Next, in a situation where modern land usage may be required the lease is an appropriate land title, and that is the experience of the Northern Territory with respect to the whole of its land usage since the Second World War. Now, it follows, in our submission, that if ownership is vested in the clan, and by that I mean the power of control and I will delete the word 'owner', if the power of control of land usage is vested in the clan, in substance the clan can grant a lease or, using the machinery that is available, the clan can consent to the legal owner granting a lease, in effect the transition of the land from traditional use to modern use by the device of granting a lease. If the power of control is not vested in traditional owners, then the traditional owners can be given no title under our law to support traditional use. There is no prospect of a lease which will allow traditional use because the lease confers by definition the right of exclusive possession for a limited time and those concepts are alien to the traditional use. If the clan, however, in a given situation does not wish to grant a lease to somebody who wishes to use the land in the modern fashion, let us say for housing – then the question arises who should determine the way in which that piece of land should be used, he who wishes to use it in the modern fashion or he who has the traditional right to control it. It is the choice between those two sources of authority and a possible position of conflict that, in our submission, leads to the conclusion that the power must ultimately be vested in the clan. The clan then controls the pace of change and by the exercise of its power to allow the granting of a lease it can permit at a pace which suits it the transition from traditional land use to modern land use. The converse situation is impossible under our system of law. That situation is possible under our system of law.

It is these considerations that not only have led us but in a very real sense have driven us to the submissions that we now make. But none of this trespasses upon the question of who should be regarded as a suitable title holder in the machinery of producing this result. I rather had the impression that I was emphasising too much the concept of the Northern Land Council and the Central Land Council as being the bodies which controlled and if that was so then, as my friend says, they are much further removed from the local council and from the clan than any village council is and if they were exercising the ultimate power of control, that criticism would be unanswerable. I think it is right to say that the Northern Land Council must be responsive and they intend to be responsive to the views of the traditional owners of the land. Their function is simply to ensure that the traditional owners of the land are given access to the expertise which ensures that the traditional owners' true interests are protected in relation to rentals or in relation to mining deals or whatever it may be.

Traditional ownership in an era of change[7]

Your Honour will appreciate that the definition is one of 'traditional Aboriginal owners' in plural, so it is intended to describe, first of all, the unity of spiritual aspiration of a group of people and then to describe the group relationship to the sites, so that it is not essential that 'A' may establish his entitlement to be registered as a clan owner that he should have all the knowledge or all the association which others in the clan may have. Clearly some of the older men would have far more knowledge and far more intimate association than others. So that we would see the chain of proof, as it were, as a chain of proof which identified a given number of persons as members of a group and then on behalf of that group the establishment of evidence which would show a relationship of the kind there referred to, to the sites and to the country. Now, the question which Your Honour asks is if there should be a substantial dropping off of this traditional relationship at what point does it become impossible for people to fail to establish this claim. That can only be answered by saying that there is a question of degree involved here and if there is no longer any traditional association with the country then the claim which is based upon traditional ownership is one which is weak to the point of expiry. That is not to say that people who can say, 'This was my country', or 'This is my country', or 'I have been told certain things about it', may not be entitled to get possession of a large tract of their country because they need it and because they are separated from it, but if one is speaking in terms of a recognition of the traditional rights one has to define the traditional rights which are to be recognised, and we know of no way to identify traditional rights save by the definition which has been preferred.

So that we do reach here an area where there may be a change in traditional association with land of one group of Aborigines from another, and the terms of reference invite Your Honour to advise upon the recognition of traditional rights in areas off reserves. We therefore have endeavoured to define what the traditional association is and to suggest a way in which the right may be recognised. We know of no other way of defining the traditional right and we know of no other way in which it may now be recognised except, of course, by the process of acquisition of land and that, we suggest, is something which must be dealt with as a matter of priority with other needs of Aboriginal people.

Mineral rights [8]

This brings me to the terms of reference and again to the question of minerals in 5.2. The Terms of Reference which your Honour has, require your Honour to consider, amongst other things: 'Arrangements for vesting title to land in the Northern Territory of Australia now reserved for the use and benefit of the Aboriginal inhabitants of that territory, including rights in minerals and timber, in appropriate body or bodies'.

Two things may be observed with respect to this part of the Terms of Reference. The first is that it expressly relates to the Northern Territory and does not relate to other areas within Australia and one can appreciate why that may be, because of the fact that the crown's title to minerals in other parts of Australia are governed for the most part by a complex of sections to which I earlier referred, whereas the crown's title to minerals in the Northern Territory depends upon sections of South Australia or Commonwealth Acts or the Northern Territory Ordinances which regulate the disposition or the crown's interest in property.

The second thing that may be said is that it relates to rights in minerals, not rights with respect to minerals and not rights relating to minerals but rights in minerals, and that, we consider, is an invitation to Your Honour to advise upon the way in which arrangements for vesting proprietary rights in minerals ought to be taken. Not some other rights with respect to the extraction of minerals; not rights which depend upon the extraction of minerals such as royalties, or with respect to the mining of minerals such as leases, but these are rights in the minerals. This is rights of property. Indeed, that is the appropriate language to deal with property rights in minerals as appears from a passage in the judgment of Mr Justice Blackburn: 'It was not disputed that minerals, existing in the land in their natural state, are within the definition of "land" in all relevant statutory provisions.'

Therefore, when one speaks of rights in minerals one is speaking of rights in land and when one speaks of rights in land one is speaking of property and not of personal rights. So that in our submission in a very real sense the area of debate which is open on this part of the Terms of Reference is narrowed by the very terms themselves. We would therefore invite Your Honour to recommend the vesting of property rights in minerals corresponding with the vesting of proprietary rights of the land to be vested.

HIS HONOUR: I would not be recommending that, I would be expecting that was inevitable from your submission, that whatever was to happen to the land, the same thing had to happen to the mineral rights.

MR BRENNAN: If Your Honour thought it was necessary to recommend that if something should happen to the mineral rights giving those into Aboriginal ownership in a different way from the way in which the land is given to Aboriginal ownership, we suggest Your Honour should recommend that it be given in the same way as part of the same land. There is, of course, a particular reason why proprietary interest in the minerals, assuming our first argument not to be acceptable as a matter of construction, needs to be confirmed in the Aborigines.

In the case of mines, the objective is to restrain the urgent desire of mining companies to extract the minerals. A possessory interest in the land is liable to be defeated if a superior possessory right is conferred upon a mining company in respect of the same land. As possessory rights are crucial to the Aboriginal relationship with land, the proprietary right in minerals ought to follow the possessory right in land into Aboriginal ownership. Otherwise, the most important feature of the Aboriginal title, undisturbed possession, will be vulnerable to attack by those who wish to secure ownership of the minerals.

It is a possessory right which is crucial to Aboriginal enjoyment of the land and if possessory right is given to a mining company superior to the Aboriginal right of possession, there is inevitably a frustration of what might be conveniently termed Aboriginal land rights. I do not think it is necessary at this stage to further develop the mining argument.

HIS HONOUR: Coming back to the question of a right. In approaching the Terms of Reference to Royal commissions, my approach is that they ought not to be interpreted in the same strict way as in an Act of Parliament. It is much better for a Royal Commission to answer a question which was not asked rather than fail to answer a question which it was intended should be asked. Therefore, I feel one cannot, if there was an ambiguity, go wrong by applying a wider possible approach and answering the question which would then be asked. But if in fact you were not meant to do that, no harm was done.

MR BRENNAN: The question first of all, is what question was Your Honour asked and that is a matter of construction of language and that is a question that is common to Terms of Reference or statutes. Therefore, if Your Honour is asked, what is the way in which proprietary rights in minerals should be vested, we invite Your Honour to answer that question whether or not Your Honour goes along to answer another question, that is, should they be vested at all?

A veto over mining [9]

We suggest that the vesting of the title to minerals is essential to give substance to the right, that is the right to exclude miners. There is only the one language that one can be confident that all will respect, and that is the language of property. One might say that before 1964 the Aboriginals were safe on their reserves. One may say that by that time there was a complete embargo on the violation of their country within their reserves by miners but we see how easy it was by a local ordinance to strip down the protection they then had and to allow miners to have access to their country. This is a question of high policy and it is a question no doubt upon which views may legitimately vary and it depends, I suppose, upon the values which one ultimately espouses.

If one starts on the proposition that the most valuable thing that the Australian people have is their own respective dignity and their right to seek their own way of life in their own way, then the vesting of a title to minerals to Aborigines is essential to give substance to that value. One cannot be confident that in any other way the right of the Aboriginal to protect his country can be assured.

One can say, let there be written in a statutory right to protect them, to allow them to veto any proposal to mine. Statutes can pass as quickly and as easily as the 1964 statute passed. The one thing governments cannot do is to expropriate property once granted. At least they take a longer time to do it, and therefore, in our submission, the basic argument in favour of the title to minerals is the giving of substance to the right of protection of country and it is on that basic right that we raised our primary submission in relation to the title to minerals.

One cannot be confident, if one chooses to adopt as a point of principle at this stage in our nation's history that Aborigines are to have the right of benefits of associations with our country, one cannot be sure that that right will endure either towards performance or towards minority groups or anything else that is dealt with in the expediency of blocks.

We are well aware that this is one of the most sensitive areas on which Your Honour has been asked to report and we are well aware that the report that Your Honour may deliver in due time to His Excellency is a report which we would hope would have a practical chance of being implemented but of the greatest importance is this, that this is a report which will for all time mark the high water mark of possible Aboriginal aspirations. Whatever Your Honour does not recommend in favour of Aborigines at this stage, will never be granted.

It may be that whatever Your Honour recommends may not be granted in full, but whatever Your Honour does not recommend now will never be granted. More than that, Your Honour has been asked to make recommendations on matters of the most difficult and vexing kind and Your Honour should not, in our submission, underestimate the persuasive value of the report that you will deliver. That in itself has its own validity and we foresee that it would carry a great deal of weight simply because it is the report of this Commission.

We would not, therefore, invite Your Honour to place too great a weight upon the views of those who might, in the fullness of time, have cause to argue against proposals of the kind we are now submitting to Your Honour, if Your Honour feels convinced by the validity of the argument. In other words, the questions we invite Your Honour to address yourself to and make recommendations upon are these:

What are the values which this commission is entitled to implement? We submit they are the values of Aboriginal relationship to land.

How can those values best be implemented in relation to the question of minerals? If the answer to that is the title of minerals shall be granted, if Your Honour sees fit to make it, it may in the fullness of time run into difficulties. Let it, because the validity of the arguments Your Honour might accept and propound and the moral persuasion of Your Honour's report would have, in our submission, in the long run a much greater and more beneficial result than one which would take cognisance of the mass of feelings, as there may well be a mass of feeling, which may tend in the opposite direction. I cannot put it any higher than that.

Our concern, Your Honour, is that whatever might now be said should not, as it were, have a brake put upon it. It could never be achieved again in the future.

Common ground between the Northern Land Council and the Central Land Council[10]

Although there have been differences in approach between the Central Land Council and the Northern Land Council[11] there are certain fundamental similarities which ought not to be overlooked; for example, it is clear that both would desire to have full Aboriginal control of the land and that without interposition of control by other sources including the department.

Next, both see the necessity for some central body to provide the type of protection which local groups desire to have or feel in need of, especially in relation to complex activities such as mining. That is undoubtedly perhaps the most vital feature of the schemes which have been propounded to Your Honour.

The third is that both schemes acknowledge the necessity to pay respect to traditional values. How they are to be paid may be a matter of disagreement, but the traditional values are important as acknowledged in both schemes.

Finally, the concept of acknowledgment of traditional rights off reserves is a common feature of both.

In other words, the distinctions that Your Honour will have noted between the approaches of the Central and Northern Land Councils are matters of technique in achieving a result but there has emerged from discussions a basic similarity in the expression of land needs.

Countering the Mining Industry's claim that this would create two classes of people[12]

The point which Mr Fisher[13] stresses, of course, is the desirability of not developing two classes of people, and I gather the division suggested between those two classes are the 'haves' and 'have nots'. One may wonder, with great respect, whether there are not now two classes of people who may be divided in that way. If one looks at the debate on the 1964 *Mining Bill (number 2)* one can see the tenderness with which one of those classes of people has been dealt with by those who have exercised the powers of dealing with reserves within this Territory and opening them up to the authority to prospect mining which has been able to move in there in a much larger way than the previous permit holder. So, one cannot, with great respect, be sanguine about the understanding of the Aboriginal aspirations with respect to mining.

It is said that the vesting of the mineral rights in the Crown has worked out well and that if there was to be any change with respect to the vesting of the mineral rights there would be a risk of creating two classes of persons amongst the Aboriginals themselves.

I gather these two classes may be those that have and those that have not. For those of us who have not gained as much advantage as others as the result of the mineral boom in Australia over recent years that comes as a rather odd type of criticism of the scheme.

If one wants to look at the question of mining in Australia at the moment, there are those who are interested in mining and there are those who are not. There are those who have profited by it and those who have not, and one cannot really use that as any criteria of division between classes of people in the same group.

Your Honour, it is said that one cannot say that Aborigines are going to revert back to their original lifestyle. Leaving aside the question of the concept of reverting back, we would submit that what is important is that they might be given the opportunity to adopt a lifestyle. The reference to the areas which are open to them, the elbow room, scarcely takes into account the value of the Tanami Desert or the sandhills on five miles of which an Aboriginal might live.

The proposition that the economy is necessary to do anything, and this is what is done to look after people is an interesting proposition and no doubt it is a right proposition when one sees the way in which, for example, the pastoral leases throughout the whole of the Northern Territory have been inadequate to produce in the economy even the cost of their own collection. When one sees that the taxpayer in Australia has subsidised, in effect, the pastoral industry of the Northern Territory to enable it to remain on the land in the sense that they have not derived an economic rental and that the rentals for the unimproved value are less than the cost of collection.

And when one sees that by inter-action of the *Income Tax Assessment Act 1936*, section 45 of the *Crown Lands Ordinance 1939-1959* does ensure that the pastoralist should obtain a deduction of up to 47.5% in the case of a company in respect of investments on improvements in pastoral areas and is guaranteed 100% return by section 45 of the *Crown Lands Ordinance* at the expiration of his time, one can scarcely feel that the development which has been spoken of in the Northern Territory is one which has been even handed in respect of the various classes within it. So in our submission, what is necessary at this stage is a re-examination of the values that land use is to be put to in the Northern Territory.

Pastoral Leases[14]

Mention was made as to whether or not the national interests of Australia required that there be preserved from Aboriginal ownership a major portion, at all events, of the pastoral portion of the Northern Territory in order that its development may continue and its productivity be furthered in the light, among other things, of the protein shortage which faces the world today. Two questions may be asked: one is, who is going to eat the protein that is going to be so developed? And our concern would be, of course, that the protein should be available for consumption by Aboriginals in the first instance.

Is not the real question, which is raised by this observation, the question of whether cattle are more important than people? The sort of cry that one has heard so often from Aborigines in the Northern. Territory and in our submission, when one evaluates the importance of the land with, let it be assumed, a diminished productive capacity and places that against the prospect of Aboriginal isolation from the land and increased production capacity, the national and international submission is to be answered in only one way, in terms of Australia's international necessity. May we respectfully refer Your Honour to the concluding part of our written submission which suggests that in a very real sense Australia's international interest is to be served by demonstrating an understanding and compassionate concern for our Aboriginal people. In this area of the world, it may be said that every country up until now, with the exception of Australia, has dealt with the Aboriginal under-developed people by preserving to them a privileged position. One has in mind, for example, the provision in the Malaysian constitution with respect to the Malays; the position of non-alienability of Fijian land in the case of Fijians; the provision with respect to land in native ownership in the case of Papua-New Guinea; the rights with respect to Maori land in New Zealand. Australia alone until now with the exception of reserves, has given to its Aboriginal people no privileged position.

In our submission the time has now arrived in order to restore the sort of balance that is involved in a dual culture situation, to endeavour to equalise the imbalance which is born of a difference in training and a difference in cultural background. So that in our submission the very real international interest of Australia is to be served by demonstrating our capacity to deal with the problem which is such an acute one and may become more acute in the future.

---

1. A E Woodward, *Aboriginal Land Rights Commission (*Second Report, 1974) 3.
2. A E Woodward, *One Brief Interval: A Memoir* (Miegunyah Press, 2005) 141.
3. N Peterson, 'Common law, Statutory Law, and the Political Economy of the Recognition of Indigenous Australian Rights in Land' in Louis Knafla and Haija Westra (eds), *Aboriginal Title and Indigenous Peoples: Canada, Australia and New Zealand* (UBC Press, 2010) 177.
4. Aboriginal Land Rights Commission, The Honourable Mr Justice Woodward – Commissioner, *Transcript of Proceedings* (20 February 1974) 48.
5. Ibid., 20 February 1974, 118-9.
6. Aboriginal Land Rights Commission, The Honourable Mr Justice Woodward – Commissioner, *Transcript of Proceedings* (26 February 1974) 208 – 9.
7. Ibid 239-240.
8. Ibid 246-8.
9. Ibid 258-260.
10. Aboriginal Land Rights Commission, The Honourable Mr Justice Woodward – Commissioner, *Transcript of Proceedings* (27 February 1974) 290.
11. The differences between the submissions by counsel for the Central Land Council (Mr Elliott QC) and Brennan QC for the Northern Land Council were heightened when Elliott submitted: 'There has been so much mixture in Australia. It has been going on for so long that I think the definition under the South Australian *Aborigines Act* is the only one that should be used. It does not cut anybody out who has a touch of the tar brush, as they used to rashly say in the past.' See Aboriginal Land Rights Commission, The Honourable Mr Justice Woodward – Commissioner, *Transcript of Proceedings* (20 February 1974) 135.
12. Aboriginal Land Rights Commission, The Honourable Mr Justice Woodward – Commissioner, *Transcript of Proceedings* (1 March 1974) 425-426.
13. William Joseph Fisher was a miner and member of the Northern Territory Legislative Council who appeared before the Royal Commission to join issue with some of the matters raised by the land councils.
14. Aboriginal Land Rights Commission, The Honourable Mr Justice Woodward – Commissioner, *Transcript of Proceedings* (1 March 1974) 461-2.

9.2 The Case for Land Rights

Editor's note

The Whitlam government was dismissed on 11 November 1975 before its proposed Land Rights legislation could pass the Parliament. There was no guarantee that the newly elected Fraser government would honour the principles set down for the legislation in the Woodward Royal Commission. Having returned to full time practice at the Queensland Bar, Brennan was invited to join Patrick Dodson, then the first Aboriginal Catholic priest, addressing the annual meeting of the Queensland Conference of the Aboriginal and Islander Catholic Council in January 1976 at Yeppoon in central Queensland. Brennan gave two addresses. In this first address, he drew on his experience as counsel for the Woodward Royal Commission in the Northern Territory to set out the fundamental principles for workable and fair land rights legislation.

There are two things that I want to say before I start this talk. First, there is no sense in talking in English law terms about Aboriginals 'owning' land. An Aboriginal does not acquire possession. He does not hold land that can be sold when it suits. The Aboriginal is part of the land; he belongs to the land; not the land to him; but he to the land. Therefore, separate him from his land and you deprive him of his spiritual sustenance. You deprive him of his dignity as an individual and as a member of the clan and tribe. You deprive and depersonalise the Aboriginal by taking him away from that to which he belongs. Just as you might say take that big tree outside, take it out of its land and expect it to live. The notion of the Aboriginal relationship with land is as intimate and as imperishable as that.

The second thing I want to say is since this relationship is one of intimacy between the Aboriginal and his land, there is not much purpose in talking about the relationship between an Aboriginal and somebody else's land. We are not talking about Aboriginals through Australia being given 'patches of dirt' in various places of the Commonwealth. We are talking about the relationship of Aboriginal people to their country; to their parts of the country. The parts which form them, which give them life, of which they are a part. What I have to say is based upon a very limited experience of the kind of matters that Father Dodson has just spoken about. It is also restricted to the limit of that experience, which was in the Northern Territory. Now I'm going to develop something of the story of the land rights claims that were made before Mr Justice Woodward's Commission, how they came about and the kinds of claims that were made and the kinds of results that followed.

Let's take up the story back in 1963. There were people then living at

Yirrkala, which is a settlement as you know on the north eastern tip of Arnhem land. It was an area where a company wanted to mine for bauxite and install a refinery. The Aboriginal people were told that there was going to be mining on their country. They presented a petition in the Aboriginal language of the area to the Federal Parliament. And that rocked the Parliament.

The Parliament immediately appointed a standing committee to look into the condition of the Aboriginal people. That committee recommended within a short space of time, that for the next 10 years, there should be a standing committee of the House of Representatives to examine from time to time, the conditions of the Yirrkala people and the carrying out of this committee's recommendations which were designed to protect them.

Five years later the Ordinance known as the *Mining (Gove Peninsula Nabalco Agreement) Ordinance 1968* (NT) was passed by the Northern Territory legislative assembly. The rights which the people were trying to protect in their country at Yirrkala were destroyed by the equivalent of an Act of the Northern Territory Parliament. The committee was not then meeting. The people of Yirrkala then decided to challenge the validity of that Act in a court case, and there followed a long and important court case known as the *Gove Land Rights Case* or more formally *Milirrpum* (who was one of the Aboriginal plaintiffs) *and others* v *Nabalco Pty Ltd and another*.

In 1971 a decision was given in that case, and the decision had basic importance for the land rights question in Australia. The judge held that, even though the Aboriginal people belong to this area, they did not own it, as that term is understood in English law. Therefore, when the English Crown took possession of this area, all Aboriginal rights terminated under English law and the English Crown acquired the ownership of all the land.

From that point onwards if the Aboriginals were to have any use or occupation of the land, it was at the grace or at the gift of the government. Therefore, so the judge held, under English law, the Aboriginal people could have no complaint if the government decided to allow somebody to mine what was the government's land – even though the Aboriginal people had thought it was their land.

There followed the statement by the then Prime Minister, Mr McMahon, in January 1972 in which he expressed the new policy of the government. This is what he said, 'The government will consult with any Aboriginal communities who might be affected by such activities so that their welfare can be taken into account when applications for exploration and development rights are being considered. Exploration rights will be granted on the basis that development rights may be deferred if, in the government's view, they would be detrimental to the interests or wellbeing of an Aboriginal community in the area.'

It was going to be left to the government to decide but the government promised to consider Aboriginal interests.

In December 1972, Mr Whitlam, the then Prime Minister, announced the creation of a Judicial Commission of inquiry into Aboriginal land rights and in February of the following year, Mr Justice Woodward was appointed.

In the middle of 1973, Mr Justice Woodward produced his first interim report and he said, I want to have two Aboriginal land councils created in the Northern Territory drawn from settlements in the top (that's the northern end) and in the centre and they'll be called the Northern Land Council and the Central Land Council and I want the government to get lawyers to go and help these people to present their case to me. This is where I and others became involved in the exercise in going and meeting with the Northern Land Council and then going around the settlements one by one in the top end having meetings with the people and asking them what they wanted out of land rights.

In April 1974, Mr Justice Woodward produced his final report. But it was not until 16 October 1975 that the Aboriginal Land Northern Territory Bill was introduced into the parliament. That was then left to lie and there were some who wanted it to lie for a lengthy period because it was said the Aboriginal people hadn't had enough chance to consider it.

On 3 November of last year, the Northern Land Council at Bathurst Island in the absence of all European advisers passed this resolution, 'That the bill be sent and asked to be passed as soon as possible by telegram tomorrow morning'. That telegram was sent on the 4 November. On 11 November parliament was dissolved and there is no Aboriginal Land Bill in existence. So, that, shortly is the history so far, the modern history of the land rights movement in the Northern Territory. Hopefully, when the parliament is reassembled that bill or some bill of the same kind implementing Mr Justice Woodward's recommendations will be introduced.

Now what are Aboriginal land rights? We are concerned here not with rights as understood by Aboriginal people under Aboriginal law. The problem has arisen because English law has displaced Aboriginal ownership and English law is the law which is now effective. So, if we are to have Aboriginal land rights, we want rights which can be enforced under the present effective legal system and the problem therefore is to create rights which are enforceable in courts; not rights which depend on someone's say so; not rights which might be given if the government or Director or some administrative official think it appropriate. Land rights are rights which Aboriginal people themselves have got and which they can enforce by themselves and for themselves when they wish to do so. So, we are therefore speaking not of Aboriginal rights; we are speaking of rights which Aboriginal people may have under English law.

The problem that arose about land rights arose because the taking of possession of the country on behalf of the British crown and because the establishment of English law in Australia abolished the rights that we now want to have renewed.

Now what are these rights? First of all, they must be legal rights, that is, enforceable rights. Second, they must be perpetual and inalienable. Now what do these words mean? They mean they must last forever and nobody can sell them.

We hear a lot about compensation for the loss of land rights. There is no real compensation for the loss of land rights. No amount of money can pay for the deprivation of land, so, if we can acquire land for the Aboriginal people for the purposes we have been speaking about, that land, when acquired, must be held and not sold. It is needed not for this generation but for the next and the next and the next; and consequently, the sort of rights that are needed in respect of land rights which are perpetual and which cannot be sold or alienated.

The rights could possibly be of two kinds. They could be property rights where you own something under English law, or they could be statutory where the Act of Parliament says you shall be entitled to use the land or the property in such and such a way. The decision was taken in the Northern Territory that we weren't really interested in statutory rights; they last for only so long as the statute lasts. An Act of Parliament lasts only for as long as the government decides to keep it. But all governments under English law have a healthy respect for property and they don't take property back without paying for it and if they have to pay for it, they usually don't want to take it back. Therefore, the notion is that land rights should be rights of property. They should give the Aboriginals ownership, the ownership of the land which they seek.

Now let's look at the other term in 'land rights' and that is 'land'. There are a number of ways in which land could be claimed, and we journeyed into the Northern Territory to obtain the opinion of the Aboriginal people on these ways. In our journey throughout the Northern Territory, we never talked as a group to a group such as this today. We would not have talked to a group such as this for a number of reasons, but there are two reasons that are important. One is there is a number of women here today. We would not talk to women even in International Women's Year! And why? Because it was the old men we wanted to speak to. Those who had the authority; those whom the Aboriginal people respected as their spokesmen in matters of ceremony and policy. The second difference is that we would not speak ordinarily in the presence of any whites except ourselves, because we wanted to ensure that the views that were expressed were the views of the Aboriginal people and not the views which had been recommended to them by other people however well-meaning they maybe. Whether we succeeded, I don't know, but I think probably we did, because most of the Aboriginal people whom we have spoken to, either before the Woodward Commission, or since, have wanted the Woodward Commission recommendations implemented.

Now, as I say there are a number of kinds of claims that were made but the most important kind of claim is the traditional claim, the one which guarantees to the Aboriginal not only his food but his dignity, his religion and his spirit. That was the traditional claim which had already been acknowledged by the judge in that court case that I was speaking about. If I could read for a minute what he said about the Aboriginal's relationship with land. He said this, 'The fundamental truth about the Aboriginal's relationship with the land is that whatever else it is, it is religious relationship. This was not in dispute. It is a particular instance of the general proposition that the physical and spiritual universe are not felt as distinct. There is an unquestioned scheme of things in which the spirit ancestors, the people of the clan, particular land, everything that exists on and in it are parts of the one indissoluble whole.' That was acknowledged as a result of the evidence that was given before the judge in the case. It was acknowledged by Mr Justice Woodward in his recommendations. It has never been in dispute. This, then, was the basic claim that was made. Such a claim makes it necessary to find the traditional owners and to define the country which is the country those 'owners' obtain, under English law, and the maximum rights of control and ownership which English law can provide. In that way, one may hope to sustain the Aboriginal traditions which that country had for those people.

The areas that were available for this claim were the reserves. Now, why do I say that? The answer is that the rest of the Northern Territory is mainly pastoral properties on which pastoralists run their cattle, and on which there are fences, and on which bores have been erected and roads constructed and it was impossible to ensure that the Aboriginal people could use that land in the traditional way. If the Aboriginal people were going to be given complete control of their land, there was only one lot of land that was available for it – and that was the reserves. The reserves then were to be handed over to Aboriginal control and the rights that the Aboriginals were to have to use that land was to correspond exactly with the rights which they had under traditional Aboriginal law. Only on this occasion the Act of Parliament was to guarantee that the rights that they had were to be enforceable as English rights – English law rights – even though they were to be spelled out in accordance with Aboriginal law.

But the notion was to give back to the Aboriginal people, the land on the reserves and allow them to use it in the way in which they traditionally used that land. Whether for ceremony or for hunting or whatever other purpose they might have been entitled to use it under Aboriginal law.

Now there were of course a number of Aboriginal people who didn't live on the reserves, whose country wasn't on reserves and who oftentimes had lost a great deal of their traditional relationship. The old stories were not passed on. We found some places where the old men wouldn't pass on the stories because they said the young men hadn't earned the right to learn the stories and to know them. There was therefore a gradual diminution of the cultural ties of some Aborigines with their traditional land. Those Aborigines, nonetheless, had a need for land, not perhaps in the traditional sense but because they had other needs even if they were on pastoral properties, for example, they were at risk of being thrown off by the pastoralists. They had recently got the same wages as stockmen as white employees and the result of this was that a number of Aboriginal employees and their families were being encouraged to leave the pastoral properties. They were then finding their way into the towns or onto the reserves.

Now, in the case of these claims it was necessary to find pieces of land where people could sit down and to live where they had been accustomed to live for generations past. Therefore, sit down areas on pastoral properties had to be obtained. That by itself wouldn't give the people any employment, any jobs, anything to do. Therefore, it was necessary to get further pastoral properties; to buy pastoral properties and to hand them over to Aboriginal ownership so that the people could have something to do, could have some work to do, some employment which would be rewarding, so they could have their children educated at a local school and so they could have the facilities of a shop, medicine and so forth.

So, there are really two kinds of land rights which are involved. One is the traditional kind and one is a claim for land based upon the needs of the people. Here I want to say something about the notion of land rights in general. If we're talking about land rights for Aboriginal people, we need to know who the Aboriginal people are who need to have rights in respect of land. What is the land that they should have and why do they need it? We need to understand what it is that is lacking from that community's life that can be fixed up by a grant of land. It may be simply as Father Dodson was saying this morning that they've got no home to go to. They've got nowhere to live. They're fringe dwellers on a town. Maybe they wanted to go and live in a town so that their children could go to school, or so that the mother could come in and be close to the doctor when she's having a baby, or whatever. Maybe they're so far out of town, and the transport is so poor and their physical condition is so weak that they're at risk, living on the fringe. It's a scandal to think that there is no land in a town for the varying needs of the Aboriginal people.

Now, this is the second point. There is no good talking about giving land within a town for Aborigines, as though all Aborigines are the same. Aborigines are as different as any other group in the community. They have different aspirations, they have different needs. There are mothers with babies. There are people who are sick. There are people who are passing through towns. There are people who simply want to come in and spend the paycheck that they've got somewhere else. They've all got different needs. And one of the things that was discovered in Darwin was the reserve, which was there for any Aborigine who came in town, was an area where there were fights, trouble with grog, police being called, violence being done. Why? Because not all Aborigines wanted to live together in that one part.

Aborigines, when it comes to a question of land in towns, must be considered as people with individual or group needs. They're not one general mass of people who are to be given one compound and everybody is to go into it. Yet that has been the thinking for so long. It has been the thinking here in the case of reserves that everybody goes to this reserve or that reserve. It doesn't matter how many tribes you put in there, how much tension you build up, how much disagreement there might be, there's a reserve and everybody shall go to it.

That kind of thinking was to be abolished if Mr Justice Woodward's recommendations were accepted.

The same with regard to accommodation. Some Aborigines would want to live in European style houses. Some would want to live in a house which consisted perhaps of a bedroom, perhaps with a roof and perhaps with a community kitchen serving half a dozen houses. Some would want to live in even simpler shelter with only a lean-to with plenty of space around. It should never be thought, either by Aboriginal Housing Cooperatives or by anybody else, that there is some social scale in the kind of housing that any Aboriginal wants. Some want simple housing, some want European style housing and some want what is in between. It is necessary to provide for the varying kind of housing within the towns, and land needs to be acquired for each of these purposes.

A few more points. First, the term 'Aboriginal' was accepted by the people in the Northern Territory as including any person who is a descendant of an Aboriginal. They did not restrict it to full bloods and they did not restrict it to people who belong to that country. They wanted included within that term, for the purposes of land rates, any Aboriginal, part or full blood, from any part of the Commonwealth.

That was not to say that if people went there and were causing trouble, for example, that they would not then be thrown out. They reserved the power for old men in the reserves and for the community councils to exclude anybody who was causing trouble when they come there.

The other thing I want to say is something about the question of Aboriginal culture and its relationship with the land in general.

The traditional Aboriginal relationship with land gives the Aboriginal person dignity, motivation, religious spirit, food, shelter and family. Without that the Aboriginal person is a battler in white society. Therefore, if we are speaking about land rights other than the traditional land rights we really need to examine, not so much what land is available, but what is the land which can be given to an Aboriginal group in order to give them what the land traditionally gave them – dignity, motivation, religious spirit, food, shelter and family. Land can give these entitlements, but money cannot buy them.

We do not want to see an Aboriginal community which is marked by the European marks of acquisitiveness, aggression, individual motivation and a lack of peaceable nature. Yet we oftentimes hear that there ought to be some kind of handout given to Aborigines, as though the handing over of some money or something can restore to them the dignity which land gave them. There is no easy solution to the problem of land rights anywhere.

Bishop O'Loughlin gave us a lot of help with the land rights problem. When we gave him our paper and asked, 'Have you any comments on it?' He said it was very good but 'you and others will come and go but the Church will still be here to help the individual people who need help in ways which you will never have been able to help, in all the grand plans that you design'. There is no easy solution to the problems of individual human dignity.

Finally, one of the reasons why Aborigines lost their land was that they were never organised to fight, as with the American Indians or the Maoris of New Zealand. There is no hierarchical structure in Aboriginal society, indeed the notion of a spokesman or a chief is almost foreign to Aboriginal society. But what the Aborigines did have was an individual self-respect and dignity and that is what has been taken from them when the land has been taken away from them.

This seems to me to indicate that the Church has a particular role to play, in first by helping the Aborigines to fight for their land and secondly in encouraging the restoration of their dignity and self-respect. Not in encouraging acquisitiveness, aggression or individual motivation.

The unity of the Church and that the Aboriginal cause is manifest. The problem is to be answered by an anxious concern and understanding of the individual problems of Aboriginal communities or groups. Not by some general broad sweeping proposal that some government somewhere is to introduce. We need to understand what it is that Aboriginal community needs, how that need can be answered by the grant of land, and then to seek to get it. In this, the object of the Aboriginal cause and the leadership of the Church should be as one.

9.3 Queensland's Shortcomings on Land Rights

Editor's note

This was Brennan's second address to the Queensland Conference of the Aboriginal and Islander Catholic Council in January 1976. Having previously set out the principles for workable and fair Land Rights legislation and policy, he provided a critique of the existing Queensland provisions and challenged the Queensland churches to take a stand in support of Aboriginal rights.

The problem of mining on Aboriginal lands is probably one of the most important problems of land rights. To an Aboriginal, and particularly to traditional Aboriginals such as the people who have come down to us here from Aurukun, the desecration of land by mining is a desecration of land which is sacred to them. Justice Woodward wrote: 'I believe that to deny to Aborigines the right to prevent mining on their land is to deny the reality of their land rights. I find it quite impossible to inspect developments on Groote Eylendt or the Gove peninsula, or proposed works on uranium deposits in Arnhem Land and to say that such developments without consent could be consistent with traditional land rights for Aborigines'. Now what we have seen in the case of Aurukun, is a provision which takes away from traditional Aborigines their land rights without, as it seems, their consent. Their rights, in relation to mining, were taken away by a provision of the *Aurukun Associates Agreement Act 1975* (Qld), which was passed in December.

Their rights were taken away by a provision in the Act, (Part 3, clause 2, subclause iii) which simply says that the mining companies shall have the right to disturb those parts of the surface of the reserves included in the special bauxite mining lease to the extent necessary to enable them to exercise all the rights and powers granted to them pursuant to this Agreement Act.

The parliament of Queensland took away from the Aurukun Aborigines the substance of rights in respect of their own land. It went on, however, to say that this was subject to the terms of the agreement between the Director, as trustee of the reserve, and the companies. And that agreement was set out as part of the Act.

So, we might look to that agreement to see whether that protected the land rights of the Aurukun Aborigines. When we turn to it, we find that it didn't. Not only do we find that it didn't, but it appears that this agreement between the Director and the mining companies was signed on 4 December. Now that was the day when the bill for this Act was introduced into the parliament and before this Act was passed. It was two days after the visit to Aurukun of the

Minister and the Director, Mr Killoran who is the trustee for the Aborigines. He signed this agreement on 4 December, two days afterwards. Did the agreement between Mr Killoran and the companies protect the interests of the Aurukun people? It says in Clause 3 of that agreement that the Director, in his capacity as trustee of the reserve, 'hereby approves the proposed granting of the special bauxite mining lease'.

Were there any benefits and any protection provided in this agreement? There is a protection in relation to sacred sites but it is in these terms. The Director or the council will from time to time inform the companies of the location of all relics sacred sites etc. But who is going to tell the Director and who, in the council, will necessarily be prepared to tell the position of all the really sacred sites? And how is that information going to be given to the companies? There is no requirement here for the consultation with the elders, no method of arranging for the people who have the dreaming, who have the secret, who have the story, to go with the companies and to talk about them. That is the only provision with respect to the sacred sites.

There is a provision which says that the companies will employ employable Aborigines in positions and occupations which Aborigines are reasonably capable of filling. That's a provision which is very much like the provision that was in the Gove arrangement.

In the Gove arrangement there was a provision which was virtually in the same terms. This is in the language of the arrangement made in Gove – 'that the company will employ local residents of the Gove Peninsula so far as it is practicable, commensurate with the skill and training of personnel, so as to fit them for employment by the lessee'. At Gove two years ago, there was one Aboriginal on the staff!

Now, what other the benefits are to flow from this agreement which the Director made? The benefits, it seems, are those which are provided for in Clause 11 of the agreement.

The principal benefit is that there will be paid three percent of the net profits of the companies to the Director for the benefits of the Aborigines. Three percent OF THE NET PROFITS!! That's a different thing from royalties – a very different thing, because profit is the difference between what it is sold for and what it costs and there is nothing in here which guarantees what this material is going to be sold for. Nobody can check on how companies' profit is calculated and the agreement makes sure that nobody could ever check on it. This agreement provides the certificate of the companies auditors as to the amount of the net profits shall be final and conclusive

So nobody can look at the books. Nobody can see the contracts. Nobody can find the figures. BUT THREE PERCENT WILL BE PAID. Three percent of what? Yet this was evidently the principal consideration of the promises which moved the Director to consent to the grant of the bauxite mining lease!

Let's see what other provisions are contained in this document of protection. We are talking, it will be remembered, of traditional Aboriginals and their attachment to land, – not simply the soil, but all that goes with it, and in particular, the vegetation and the trees. There's a provision that the companies will not disturb any natural millable timber on a reserve without the prior approval of the Director of Forests!

And how are the companies to operate the mine? They are to be very considerate for the Aborigines, because they are to conduct their operation upon the reserve so as to cause as little inconvenience as practicable to the Aborigines. What is going to determine what is practicable in terms of this inconvenience that the Aborigines might feel? As an agreement which protects the interests of the Aurukun Aborigines, that gives them NOTHING!!

In terms of financial protection – departmental policy (from what we have just been told) is not to consider simply the interests of the Aurukun Aborigines, but all Aborigines in Queensland. Therefore, the agreement was thought to be for the benefit of all Queensland Aborigines, evidently by reason of the three percent of the profits which is to be paid. Well, one can only wonder whether the Aurukun people in those circumstances need to be considered at all, in the Director's mind, or whether he must only consider the question of whether there is some income which can be used for Aboriginal purposes throughout the state. If there is to be some income which can be used for Aboriginal purposes throughout the state, that relieves the claims of the Department of Aboriginal Advancement upon the Budget of the state from year to year. So, one is entitled to wonder whether the benefits to Aboriginals is really regarded as a benefit to the state Budget.

Let me just come back for a moment to the question of the consultation between mining companies, governments, and Aboriginals. I don't want to talk about the Northern Territory all the time but it does throw up some experiences that are relevant. The whole of the land rights scheme that was devised for Arnhem land in the Northern Territory in regard to mining, turned round this question of consultation with the local people. The scheme is this, the Northern Land Council consists entirely of Aboriginals, nobody else. They can have white advisors, but it is Aboriginal. They have Aboriginal field officers whose duty it is to go out to each area that might be affected by mining and sit down and talk to the people for days on end or weeks on end if necessary, to get the understanding of the people and their feelings. And to get approval, not simply of somebody who might be willing to advance himself as a spokesman, but of the old men of the clan and of the people as a whole.

Then they come back to the Northern Land Council and said 'yes the people are agreeable' or 'no the people aren't'. If the people aren't agreeable that is the end of it. If the people are agreeable then the Northern Land Council looks after all the arguments about money and so forth.

You can't have consultation with Aboriginal people, with great respect, by getting somebody down in October 1975 and sitting him down in a chair and saying: 'Do you agree that the Neely Letters are going to be the basis of the future arrangements?' If that is the department's understanding of what Aboriginal consultation is, then there is great room for improvement. Aboriginal consultation is not something which lasts for a day, or an hour, but something that goes on over a period of months, and there's talk and more talk and more consultation, amongst the people. It is clear that never happened – clear beyond argument, and clear upon the statement we've been given here today.

It is also clear, it seems to me, that the Presbyterian Church letters must have gone unanswered because the letters, copies of which are here, say: 'We agree to PROSPECTING, but we need to have further consultations if this should ever come to mining'. Then there is a copy of the letter sent by the Director to the mining companies, and the Presbyterian Church said: 'Look there's some misunderstanding here. You're talking about mining in your letter to the companies but so far as the Aurukun people are concerned they've been talking about PROSPECTING. We must have further consultation about mining. We don't want to have any misunderstanding about that. There must be further consultation if mining is to take place.' AND THOSE CONSULTATIONS HAVEN'T OCCURRED, according to the series of facts we've been given here this morning.

So, we have this situation: inadequate consultation with the Aurukun people; doubtful consent given by any of them, but certainly no full consent given by all of the people; a consent given by the Director to the desecration of the Aurukun land; and absence of protection for Aurukun rights – AND ALL OF IT HAS BEEN SANCTIONED AND BLESSED BY AN ACT OF THE QLD PARLIAMENT. This is a sad and sorry chapter in Queensland's history in its relationship with the Aboriginal people.

What I've said this morning – I would not like Mr Burless to think there's any reflection upon the task which he has devoted himself to at short notice in coming here – but I don't think that anything I've said is something which would be changed by longer consideration or deeper thought. We are talking after all about written facts which are in an Act of Parliament, and the agreement which is contained in the Act of Parliament. So, we're not really talking about anything Mr Burless could have expounded more fully; although I must say, for myself, I would dearly love to know more of the consultation which took place in October 1975 in Brisbane between the department and some persons who came from Aurukun.

But it seems to me that there is a problem here, which is a problem with a very real moral dimension for the nation, certainly for Queensland. We have a situation in which a people, their dignity, their lifestyle, is being affected, and I wonder whether this is not a feature which marks out the necessity for the churches support for the remedying of injustice.

I'm not suggesting that the Catholic Church should assume the responsibilities of administering the Aurukun mission. I think the Catholic Church's responsibility – and that's the responsibility of all of us, not just of the bishops – is a responsibility to see that justice is done by the Aboriginal people in the matter of land rights. In order to achieve this, however, there needs to be some focus, some central point from which submissions can go forward to governments from which statements can be made, which will inform the whole mass of the people. There is within the Catholic Church in Queensland, but one body that answers that description and that's the conference of Queensland bishops.

The need for something to be done, is manifest not only in the case of Aurukun but in the case of those who live within the cities, and who have nowhere to live within the cities; those who live in the towns, and have no security of tenure, those who live on settlements and have no title to their land. We have then, a landless Aboriginal people in Queensland. That situation should be changed.

As I said yesterday, however, I'm against the notion of, as it were land rights in the blank. The Aboriginal people who have the needs should be asked to state them. But I would suggest that having stated them, the need should then be channelled through an advisory committee, which can get expert advice, as need be, from educationists, lawyers, psychiatrists, doctors, whoever it might be, to formulate a policy which might then be put with confidence to the government and to the public.

I would like to suggest for consideration a resolution which runs along this line:

> *As the Aboriginal peoples in Queensland have no title to their land; as land is essential to the life and dignity of Aboriginal people; as Aboriginal people have frequently been removed from*

> *their land, and homes, without their consent; and Aboriginal people who wish to do so should be entitled to live in a traditional style, this conference asks the conference of Queensland bishops to support the granting to the Aboriginal people of rights to land to allow them to live with dignity, and security and to support the campaign to persuade governments of the crying need for these rights to land. This conference suggests that the bishops form a central advisory committee, which will obtain necessary expert advice as required and that subcommittees should be constituted to identify the precise land needs of Aboriginal people who live:*
>
> *(1) on the Palm Island, Cherbourg, Woorabinda or other similar settlements.*
>
> *(2) in a traditional style in the north of Queensland.*
>
> *(3) in all other urban or rural areas of the state.*

And the notion I would have is that the Aboriginal people in these various classifications, or perhaps others that occur to you, should be able to state for themselves what their needs are. Those could then be analysed and put together in one scheme by the central advisory committee, getting expert advice, if necessary and then the total plan should go to the bishops for their endorsement, commendation and promulgation. I think it would be appropriate, if the bishops thought so, to involve the other churches in the exercise of obtaining justice in the matter of land for the Aboriginal people. But I would suggest we need practical knowledge of the issue, we need to have expert advice upon them, and we need to have a focal point through which the views of the Aboriginal people and the views of the Church can be promulgated. The initiative in that sense needs to come from the conference of bishops.

9.4 Memorandum for the Minister of Aboriginal Affairs on the Land Rights Bill

Editor's note

After Justice Woodward submitted his second report to the Whitlam government, a draft Land Rights Bill was prepared. The dismissal of the Whitlam government on 11 November 1975 placed the future of the Bill in doubt. Brennan, having been senior counsel for the Northern Land Council, was asked to accompany some Aboriginal leaders to Canberra for meetings with the new Prime Minister Malcolm Fraser and the new Minister for Aboriginal Affairs, Ian Viner. In preparation for the meetings, Brennan prepared this memorandum on 27 April 1976. He and Viner worked very well together.

Re: The Second Report of the Aboriginal Land Rights Commission (Woodward J.)

A. THE ISSUES

These observations relate to three issues:

- the title which should be granted
- the right to veto mining
- the role of the Northern Land Council.

These issues are, of course, at the very centre of the Land Rights problem. The Woodward Report propounds inter-dependent solutions in respect of each of these issues. A significant variation from the Woodward recommendations in respect of any of these issues will require a radical revision of the other recommendations.

Thus, on the hypothesis that some new statutory title, unfamiliar to the common law were in contemplation, reconsideration of the following matters would be required: the persons who are to hold the title, the relationship between the title holder and the traditional owners (who cannot be the title holders), and the disposition of those rights which are incidental to a freehold title but which might be withheld in the hypothetical title. Should the miner seek approval for mining from the statutory title holder, the traditional owners (assuming he can identify them and their land), or the holders of the withheld rights?

In short, it is easier to propound a solution to a specific question than to alter a whole scheme, which propounds interdependent solutions. A jigsaw, patiently put together, is distorted if one removes a piece and attempts to force an unfitting and foreign piece in its place.

The Woodward recommendations followed upon the delivery of a written submission by the Northern Land Council (175 pages plus a book of annexures). That submission sets out the reasons why:

- a fee simple title was required to give effect to land rights;
- title to minerals was sought to protect the land (Woodward J agreeing that protection of the land was necessary but preferring the solution of the right of veto);
- the Northern Land Council was required to protect, and serve, the interests of the clan.

It should be stressed that the written submission of the Northern Land Council was circulated to interested parties some weeks before the public hearings before Woodward J. Aboriginals may well feel a sense of injustice when objections are raised two years later, when the opportunity to discuss the issues before the appointed Commissioner was not taken.

This observation does not apply to the pastoral interests (represented by Mr de Vos) and to general submissions made by the Australian Mining Industry Council. The Commissioner dealt with their submissions. Lesser submissions were evidently made by others, whose names are listed in the Commission's Report, 141, Appendix B and who include members of the Northern Territory Legislative Assembly.

It is not suggested that there is some kind of estoppel, but it is unfortunate that the opportunity for helpful debate was declined.

B. THE TITLE: FEE SIMPLE LEASEHOLD OR STATUTORY?

The essential feature of any title sufficient to satisfy Aboriginal cultural and spiritual needs, and the expressed aspirations of the Aboriginal people is perpetuity. The fee simple alone gives this title. There is no risk of a breach of covenant to pay rent or to perform some other duty which (as in the case of leasehold) can lead to a forfeiture of the vested interest.

Moreover, as the primary object of any land rights scheme should be the vesting, under Australian law, of rights corresponding with traditional Aboriginal rights, there should be no risk that the rights conferred may not be sufficient to cover traditional Aboriginal rights. Traditional rights, usufructuary in nature and perhaps involving legal 'waste' may be uncertainly covered by leasehold interests. Only the plenitude of rights conferred by the fee simple gives the security required.

As Aboriginal land is a likely target for compulsory acquisition, just compensation can best be assured by conferring a title with well-established incidents rather than some novel form of statutory title. The rights which such a title may confer lies only within the continuing gift of the legislature. Aboriginal land ought to find its security in rights recognized by the law of property, not in the continuing political favour of the legislature.

If, in the years to come, it is deemed desirable to withdraw the proposed legislative prohibition against alienation, the title holders will be enabled to pass a title with recognised incidents.

See generally paragraphs 4.1 to 4.27 of the Northern Land Council submission. It will be seen that the conclusions arrived at are not merely one of a number of options. The conclusions are the inevitable result of selecting the appropriate legal solution for a problem, the parameters of which are clearly defined.

C. THE RIGHT TO VETO MINING

The claim made to the Commission was for title to minerals 'in order to protect the religion, culture and life style of the Aborigines'. The claim in those terms was not accepted by the Commissioner. Nor did the Commissioner accept 'the main result contended for' by the mining industry (paragraph 568).

The Commission did accept, however, that a grant of land rights to Aborigines subject to an intrusive right to invade and disturb the land would be an illusory grant. As the report stated:

'I believe that to deny to Aborigines the right to prevent mining on their land is to deny the reality of their land rights'. (paragraph 568)

Whilst refusing proprietary rights as the method of protecting the land, the Commission recommended the creation of a statutory power of protection – the veto.

This power is unlikely to be used, it seems, in cases where the miner takes the time and the trouble to consult. The path of consultation may not always be favourable to the miner. But understanding, patience, protection of sacred sites, and compensation have produced consent – witness the Oenpelli/Queensland Mines and the recent Yirrkala/Nabalco discussions.

However, without the power of veto the Aboriginal negotiating position is hopeless and land rights, born out of the Yirrkala litigation, are seen to lack substance.

As to the problems of both the Aboriginal clan and the miner, see the Northern Land Council submission, paragraphs 7.1 to 7.30.

D. THE ROLE OF THE NORTHERN LAND COUNCIL

The role of the Northern Land Council is defined by four considerations –

1. the necessity in law to define the boundaries of the land to be vested;
2. the present uncertainty of the boundaries of the country of a land-holding aboriginal descent-group;
3. the wish of all communities that a 'big council' in Darwin should protect then;
4. the need of non-Aboriginals to deal with a title holder who can confer rights of access to the land.

The first two considerations exclude a clan-based system of vesting the Australian law title to land.

The last two considerations require a focal point of contact between Aboriginal and non-Aboriginal interests.

No system which will permit non-Aboriginal access to traditional Aboriginal lend can operate without a focal point. That point may in theory be either –

a) an Aboriginal institution; or

b) a Government department.

As an Aboriginal institution is necessarily the institution of choice, its responsibility must be to consult with the clan; its power must be to express the results of that consultation so as to bind the clan and the non-Aboriginal party.

The trustees 'hold the piece of paper' only – they have no power and no responsibility save in accordance with the Land Council direction.

<u>But</u> the Land Council is the servant of the clan, not the clan's master. Its role is consultative and advisory. But it bears a heavy administrative burden.

It has no interest in the land, save the theoretical residual interest after the traditional rights of the clan are exhausted (see paragraph 4.19).

As the Northern Land Council submission recognized, the Northern Land Council field officers are the pivot of the scheme. There is no satisfactory alternative to the idea of a central council which, by its officers –

i. identifies the clans and their country,
ii. consults with them,
iii. provides expert advice to the clans,
iv. carries out the clans wishes,
v. provides a contracting party to those seeking access to Aboriginal land.

The reasons which led to the notion of a Land Council are dealt with, inter alia, in paragraphs 6.7 to 6.17 of the Northern Land Council submission.

E. THE BALANCE

The balance of interests between Aborigines and others (especially miners) was adverted to in the Northern Laud Council submission. See paragraphs 14.1 to 14.5. The recommendation of the Commission as to where that balance should be struck is indicated above.

9.5 Aboriginal Land Claims: An Australian Perspective

Editor's note

Three years after the Mabo decision, Brennan was appointed by the Keating government as Chief Justice of Australia. As Chief Justice, he attended the 7th International Appellate Judges Conference in Ottawa, Canada. He delivered this address on 27 September 1995.

On 26 January 1788, the British flag was raised on land that is now part of the City of Sydney. The colony of New South Wales was established. Later, other colonies were formed in other parts of Australia or by separation of territory from New South Wales. The colonial boundaries included some offshore islands. Included within Queensland's maritime boundary are the Murray Islands, the largest of which is Murray Island or Mer, in the Torres Strait between Papua New Guinea and Australia. In 1982, Eddie Mabo and four other Murray Islanders instituted proceedings against the State of Queensland claiming ownership of parcels of land on Mer as the holders of native title. This litigation, bearing Mabo's name, defined the modern Australian law on native title.

In 1788, the territory that is now the Commonwealth of Australia was populated by Aboriginal hunters and food gatherers whose numbers are uncertain, probably between 300,000 and 500,000. The legal theory espoused by the Privy Council in the 19th and early 20th centuries regarded these peoples, and the peoples of at least some other settled colonies, as 'so low in the scale of social organization' that it was 'idle to impute to [them] some shadow of the rights known to our law and then to transmute it into the substance of transferable rights of property as we know them'.[1] The land in these colonies was treated as ownerless and thus available for acquisition by the European power which settled the territory. This doctrine was known inaccurately as *terra nullius*. It supported the proposition that, on settlement, the Crown acquired not only sovereignty but beneficial ownership of all land in the acquired territory. Universal ownership of land by the Crown allowed the adoption of the feudal doctrine of tenure – a basic doctrine of the common law of real property – whereby all private ownership of land was held to depend ultimately on a Crown grant.[2] As Aborigines had received no grant, they had no title to the land. When the self-governing Australian colonies were given control of the alienation of land within the colony, the theory was that the power of alienation was merely a political function transferred from the Government in Westminster to the Colonial Government,[3] but the Crown in right of the Colony had had the beneficial title to that land since the colony was acquired. Alienation of land has been governed by statute since the early days of colonization.

In each colony, land was reserved from alienation for public purposes including the provision of land for Aborigines. The reserves did not, however, give security of occupation, much less title. Then, in 1976, the Commonwealth Parliament enacted a law for the Northern Territory[4] under which Aborigines with a traditional connection with unalienated land could apply for a grant of an inalienable fee simple – a freehold title. This title allows Aborigines to use the land in accordance with Aboriginal tradition[5] except where a lease or licence of a particular parcel of land is granted or issued for specified purposes with the consent of the Aboriginal Land Council for the area and with the assent of the traditional owners of the land.[6] A refusal of consent can be overridden by the Government where a grant of a mining tenement is required in the national interest.[7] Some of the States, especially South Australia, subsequently enacted laws designed to give or to allow Aborigines to acquire a secure title or comparatively secure right to possession of land.[8]

Then the two cases that bear the name of Eddie Mabo were decided by the High Court. By this time, the authority of Privy Council decisions was no longer binding on the High Court[9] or, indeed, on any Australian Court.[10] The High Court, in the absence of any prior decision of its own or any prior decision of any appellate court in Australia, had to define the common law relating to native title for Australia.

When the plaintiffs claimed ownership of land on Mer by virtue of their native title, the Queensland Parliament countered with an Act[11] that declared that the Queensland coastal islands were vested in the Crown freed of all other rights or claims.[12] However, there stood – and there stands now – on the Commonwealth statute book the *Racial Discrimination Act 1975* (Cth) which gives effect in municipal law to the key provisions of the International Convention on the Elimination of All Forms of Racial Discrimination. In *Mabo [No 1]*[13] the High Court held that the Queensland Act discriminated against the people of the Murray Islands in the enjoyment of their right to own property, assuming that the traditional rights of ownership existed. On that assumption, the Queensland Act was inconsistent with the *Racial Discrimination Act 1975* (Cth). Under the Australian *Constitution*,[14] a State law that is inconsistent with a law of the Commonwealth is, to the extent of the inconsistency, invalid. The Queensland Act thus failed in its purpose.

That left for determination the critical question whether the common law of Australia recognized native title or whether native title had been extinguished and the Crown had become beneficial owner when the Crown acquired sovereignty. In *Mabo [No 2],*[15] the Court held that native title to the land on Mer, with the exception of a few parcels, is vested in the people of the Murray Islands as a communal title recognized by the common law, and that that title is protected by the *Racial Discrimination Act 1975* (Cth) from discriminatory extinction. The content of native title is ascertained by reference to Aboriginal laws and customs.[16]

The Court held the acquisition of sovereignty to be a non-justiciable question in a municipal court but the effect of the acquisition of sovereignty on native title to be a justiciable question.[17] The acquisition of sovereign power and the acquisition of beneficial ownership of land were not necessarily linked.[18] Rejecting the notion of *terra nullius*, native title was held to survive the acquisition of sovereignty.[19] Although sovereign power enabled the Crown to extinguish native title, any instrument purporting to exercise that power would be rigorously construed. No legislative or executive instrument would be taken to extinguish native title unless it revealed a clear and plain intention to do so.[20]

However, the sovereign power of the Crown included the power to make grants of land. As that power might be exercised to create a tenure of land in the grantee, it was tantamount to a radical title to the land.[21] Native title was ousted when the sovereign power had been exercised inconsistently with the continued enjoyment of native title, but otherwise native title survived. Crown grantees were secure in their titles but the holders of native title were unprotected at common law against an exercise of the power of alienation. By majority,[22] it was held that the expropriation of native title pursuant to any valid legislative authority is not compensable. But the holders of native title are now protected by the *Racial Discrimination Act 1975* (Cth) to the same extent as are the holders of other forms of title. They are therefore no longer amenable to expropriation without compensation.

The *Mabo* decisions gave rise to considerable controversy. After much public debate, in 1993 the Commonwealth Parliament enacted the *Native Title Act 1993* (Cth) which, adopting the common law as defined in *Mabo [No.2]*[23] prescribed a system for dealing with native title. The Act contemplates the enactment of complementary laws by the States and Territories.[24] The *Native Title Act* provided, inter alia, for determinations as to the existence or non-existence of native title to particular parcels of land. Access to native title land for mining or other non-Aboriginal purposes can be obtained[25] but there are extensive provisions relating to negotiation, arbitration and ministerial intervention in respect of proposals to grant access.[26] A National Native Title Tribunal,[27] presided over by a Judge of the Federal Court, has certain mediation and administrative functions and is presently dealing with the processing of claims. The Federal Court has jurisdiction[28] over issues calling for judicial determination, including appeals from the Tribunal on questions of law.

The State of Western Australia, in which 52% of the land is unalienated and which contains significant deposits of minerals, took serious objection to the *Native Title Act*. Its Parliament enacted a law to deal with native title[29] and mounted a challenge to the validity of the Commonwealth law. However, the High Court upheld the validity of the *Native Title Act* and held the Western Australian law to be invalid.[30]

The modern development of Australian law governing Aboriginal title to land is part of that post-colonial jurisprudence that has been developed in other countries to protect the relationship between the descendants of the indigenous inhabitants and their traditional lands. In other jurisdictions, although the paramount power of government has been accepted, there has been a recognition of some form of native title. The basis of title has been variously supported by reference to proclamations,[31] legislative acts,[32] treaties,[33] the fiduciary duty of the Crown,[34] use or possession[35] and the common law.[36] The post-colonial relationship of the indigenous population with their traditional land is not only, or even chiefly, a problem for the courts. But the courts, sensitive to the demands of justice for minorities and the disadvantaged in society, are likely to remain a forum in which indigenous peoples will seek to right what are now perceived to be historic wrongs.

---

1. See *In re Southern Rhodesia* [1919] AC 211, 233-234; see also *Cooper v Stuart* (1889) 14 App Cas 286.
2. See *Attorney-General v Brown* (1847) 1 Legge 312 at 316, 319 (NSW); *Randwick Corporation v Rutledge* (1959) 102 CLR 54, 71 (Windeyer J); *New South Wales v The Commonwealth* (1975) 135 CLR 337, 438-439 (Stephen J).
3. See *Williams v Attorney-General for New South Wales* (1913) 16 CLR 404, 453-454.
4. See *Aboriginal Land Rights (Northern Territory) Act* 1976 (Cth).
5. Ibid s 71.
6. Ibid s 19.
7. Ibid ss 40, 45, 46.
8. See *Pitjantjatjara Land Rights Act 1981* (SA); *Maralinga Tjarutja Land Rights Act 1984* (SA); *Aboriginal Land Rights Act 1983* (NSW); *Land Act (Aboriginal and Islander Land Grants) Amendment Act 1984* (Qld).
9. See *Viro v The Queen* (1978) 141 CLR 88; *Cook v Cook* (1986) 162 CLR 376; *Privy Council (Limitation of Appeals) Act 1968* (Cth); *Privy Council (Appeals from the High Court) Act 1975* (Cth).

10. The *Australia Act 1986* (identical Acts contemporaneously enacted by the Parliaments of the Commonwealth of Australia and the United Kingdom) whereby the last legal ties, other than monarchical succession, between Australia and the United Kingdom were severed.
11. See *The Queensland Coast Islands Declaratory Act 1985* (Qld).
12. Ibid s 3.
13. See *Mabo v Queensland* (1988) 166 CLR 186.
14. See *Constitution* s 109.
15. See *Mabo v Queensland [No2]* (1992) 175 CLR 1.
16. Ibid 58, 110.
17. Ibid 31-32, 81-82 and see also 129-130.
18. Ibid 57, 80-81, 180.
19. Ibid 57-58, 109, 180, 182, 192, 216.
20. Ibid 64, 110-111, 195-196.
21. Ibid 48.
22. Ibid 15; cf 111, 119, 195-196.
23. See *Native Title Act 1993* (Cth), ss 10 and 223.
24. See the *Native Title (New South Wales) Act 1994* (NSW); *Native Title (Queensland) Act 1993* (Qld); *Native Title (South Australia) Act 1994* (SA); *Validation of Titles and Actions Act 1994* (NT); *Land Titles Validation Act* 1993 *(Vic)*; *Native Title (Tasmania) Act* 1994 *(Tas)*.
25. See *Native Title Act 1993* (Cth), s 23.
26. Ibid Sub-division B of Div 3 of Pt 2.
27. Ibid Pt 6.
28. Ibid ss 81, 145, 169.
29. See *The Land (Titles and Traditional Usage) Act 1993* (WA).
30. See *Western Australia v The Commonwealth* (1995) 183 CLR 373; 69 ALJR 309; 128 ALR 1.
31. See *St Catherine's Milling and Lumber Co v The Queen* (1888) 14 App Cas 46, 54-55; *Calder v Attorney-General of British Columbia* (1973) 34 DLR (3d) 145, 151-152, 203; *Guerin v The Queen* (1984) 13 DLR (4th) 321, 335.
32. See *Tee-Hit-Ton Indians v United States* (1955) 348 US 272, 278-279.
33. See *Te Weehi v Regional Fisheries Officer* [1986] 1 NZLR 680, 686.
34. See *R v Sparrow* (1990) 70 DLR (4th) 385, 408; *Guerin v The Queen* (1984) 13 DLR (4th) 321, 334, 356-357; and see Toohey J in *Mabo [No 2]* (1992) 175 CLR 1, 203-205.
35. See *United States v Santa Fe Pacific Railway Co* (1941) 314 US 339, 345, 347; *Calder v Attorney-General of British Columbia* (1973) 34 DLR (3d) 145, 156, 200-201; *Guerin v The Queen* (1984) 13 DLR (4th) 321, 335; *Te Weehi v Regional Fisheries Officer* [1986] 1 NZLR 680, 690, 692.
36. See *Hamlet of Baker Lake v Minister of Indian Affairs* (1979) 107 DLR (3d) 513, 542-543.

9.6 Reconciliation

Editor's note

In 1999, the *University of New South Wales Law Journal* convened a forum on 'Requirements Of Justice: Legal Perspectives On Reconciliation'. Brennan having retired as Chief Justice the previous year accepted appointment as Scientia Professor at the university. He was invited to contribute to the forum. This was his reflection on reconciliation.[1]

Reconciliation is an obligation of justice, not a manifestation of benevolence. It is bilateral, healing the division created by past injustice. Past injustice would be compounded and divisions would be more entrenched by a continuing failure to reconcile and to be reconciled. As reconciliation is a matter for the heart as well as the head, the law cannot achieve reconciliation of and by itself. But it has an important role to play. Injustice is revealed by application of the law in particular cases and, as the law is a mirror of contemporary values, its application can highlight shortcomings in our community morality. Sometimes a development of, or a change in, the law can be fashioned to eliminate the cause of an injustice revealed in a particular case; sometimes the injustice is beyond legal remedy.

Even if the law identifies the cause of a past injustice, it cannot undo the hurt, the alienation, the loss of dignity, the self-abnegation which the injustice (and particularly institutionalised and repetitive injustice) has produced. The law does not provide, indeed cannot provide, remedies for every kind of injustice or for every aftermath of an injustice suffered. It provides remedies only for an infringement of a legal right and its remedies are too blunt to undo all the effects of past injustices. Although, in the absence of reconciliation, injustice festers with the passing of time, in that time there may be such a change in relationships and rights that a remedy for the first injustice would be productive of a later injustice. In such a situation, if a compromise of rights is impossible or inadequate, no legal remedy is available. There may be a moral claim on the State for some form of compensation in those cases.

To recognise the limited role which law can play in the reconciliation between Aboriginal and non-Aboriginal Australians is to avoid false expectations that resort to the courts will cure all past injustices. Disappointed expectations of that kind, like dishonoured political promises, are cruel impositions on the victims of injustice and a massive barrier to true reconciliation. The courts are the protectors of a minority's legal rights, and it would undermine public confidence in that role if it be thought that the courts have the power to achieve reconciliation by decree and alone bear the responsibility for doing so. What the courts can do and have done, when the cases raise the issue, is to identify the legal cause of a past injustice and, where it is within their jurisdiction to provide some remedy for the injustice, to do so provided the remedy does not infringe the legal rights of others. In recent years, in a series of cases in the High Court, past injustices suffered by Aboriginal Australians have been identified. Sometimes the law has provided some relief; sometimes it has not been able to do so.

The greatest detriment suffered by Aboriginal people as a result of legal injustice was their loss of homeland. This loss was described movingly by the late Professor W E H Stanner in *White Man Got No Dreaming*,[2] which I quoted in *R* v *Toohey; ex parte Meneling Station Pty Ltd*:

> When we took what we call 'land' we took what to them meant hearth, home, the source and locus of life, and everlastingness of spirit. At the same time it left each local band bereft of an essential constant that made their plan and code of living intelligible. Particular pieces of territory, each a homeland, formed part of a set of constants without which no affiliation of any person to any other person, no link in the whole network of relationships, no part of the complex structure of social groups any longer had all its co-ordinates. What I describe as 'homelessness', then, means that the Aborigines faced a kind of vertigo in living. They had no stable base of life; every personal affiliation was lamed; every group structure was put out of kilter; no social network had a point of fixture left.[3]

It is not surprising that land rights litigation has produced the most controversial judgments: the taking of land from Aborigines during two centuries was identified as a cause of grave injustice that cannot be remedied by restitution of all that had been taken. It led Deane and Gaudron JJ in *Mabo* v *Queensland [No 2]*[4] to speak of the early dispossession of Aboriginal peoples as a 'conflagration of oppression and conflict which was, over the following century, to spread across the continent to dispossess, degrade and devastate the Aboriginal peoples and leave a national legacy of unutterable shame.'

The supposed legal rule under which this injustice was perpetrated[5] was contemptuous of the Aboriginal peoples as:

> so low in the scale of social organization that their usages and conceptions of rights and duties are not to be reconciled with the institutions or the legal ideas of civilized society. Such a gulf

> cannot be bridged. It would be idle to impute to such people some shadow of the rights known to our law and then to transmute it into the substance of transferable rights of property as we know them.[6]

That approach, which underlay the doctrine of terra nullius, was firmly rejected and native title was recognized as a title which the common law would, subject to its infirmities, protect. But it was not possible to remedy the injustice of dispossession by restitution of land in which inconsistent legal interests had been acquired since 1788. Thus, native title was held to be extinguished over land alienated for an estate in fee simple.[7] Although native title could survive over land held under a pastoral lease in Queensland, the rights of the pastoralist were paramount.[8]

The disadvantages which Aboriginal peoples might labour under in securing legal protection for their native title was referred to in the joint judgment in *North Ganalanja Aboriginal Corporation and Another* v *The State of Queensland and Others*: 'The remoteness of many Aboriginal communities and their lack of familiarity with the legal criteria for determination of native title posed practical difficulties for many people who might be entitled to claim native title. Moreover, the task of tracing the tenure history of any parcel of land during the previous 200 years was likely to be beyond the resources of many would-be claimants.'[9]

The right to negotiate under the *Native Title Act 1993* (Cth) *('NTA')* was held to arise as soon as an application showing an arguable case for native title was lodged.

The policy of compulsorily separating some Aboriginal children from their parents was revealed in terrible particularity in the Report of a Commission of Inquiry. The Court acknowledged this awful truth – a truth which 'profoundly distressed the nation' in *Kruger* v *The Commonwealth*,[10] but the Court was unable to hold that the measures under which the separations had been carried out were invalid.

In *Onus* v *Alcoa*,[11] the Gurnditch-jmara people invoked a statute that was intended to preserve relics of Aboriginal significance for the cultural benefit of all people. It was recognised that the destruction or obliteration of the relics would be a distinctive detriment to the Gurnditch-jmara people. A challenge to their standing to sue was dismissed.

In *Walden* v *Hensler*, the Aboriginal appellant had been convicted of an offence under the *Fauna Conservation Act 1974* (Qld) which prohibits the taking or keeping of fauna without a permit. The appellant, in accordance with Aboriginal custom, killed a scrub turkey for his family's food. The High

Court confirmed that the killing of the turkey was in breach of the Act but set aside the punishment imposed in the courts below. I said:

> To deprive an Aboriginal without his knowledge of his traditional right to hunt for bush tucker for his family on his own country and then to convict and punish him for doing what Aborigines had previously been encouraged to do would be an intolerable injustice. It adds the insult of criminal conviction and punishment to the injustice of expropriation of traditional rights. It can and should be avoided by discharging the appellant absolutely under s 657A. [12]

These cases illustrate both occasions of legal injustice and the limited ability of the Court sometimes to award a remedy that will remove, at least in part, a cause of the injustice. But injustices which have been entrenched by law cannot be cured by merely changing the law. Over centuries, the self-confidence of Aboriginal people was eroded by or in the name of the law. That erosion produced frustration and, on some occasions, an outbreak of violence. *Neal* v *The Queen* was such a case, the appellant having been convicted and sentenced for an unpleasant attack on a government official managing an Aboriginal reserve. Murphy J graphically described the underlying cause of the appellant's conduct:

> Aboriginal sense of grievance has developed over the two hundred years of white settlement in Australia. Early in the nineteenth century Aborigines were 'being treated with arrogant superiority, often accompanied by considerable brutality'... The plight of the Aborigines was compounded by the introduction of European diseases and alcohol which, in addition to white colonisation, 'contributed to the fragmentation of Aboriginal society and helped to promote the apathetic attitudes erroneously attributed by the Europeans to inferior intellectual capacity'... Aborigines have complained bitterly about white paternalism robbing them of their dignity and right to direct their own lives. [13]

Frustration at Aboriginal powerlessness did not excuse the violence but was a factor relevant to the punishment to be imposed. This was but one of the many criminal cases in which contraventions – often serious contraventions – of the criminal law have been attributable to a diminished self-esteem, a want of self-confidence and a sense of frustration on the part of an Aboriginal offender. Aboriginal self-esteem, self-confidence and the power to cope with the modem world are not easily or quickly achieved. Reconciliation is needed to open the gate through which mutual respect and goodwill may pass.

Lawyers have played and will continue to play a part in effecting reconciliation. They must ascertain whether the state of the law is a cause of injustice and determine whether some remedy can eliminate, completely or partially, that cause. If the remedy lies in a variation of the common law, the lawyer must determine whether it is open to the court, consistently with the judicial function, to develop the law to provide the remedy. If such a development is possible, the lawyer must undertake substantial historical research, analyse precisely the authorities and select a suitable vehicle for raising the issue. If it is beyond the capacity of the court to provide the remedy, statutory intervention may be needed. That involves an engagement with the political branches of government, at least to the point of drawing to the attention of the relevant authorities the possibility of legislative remedy for the perceived injustice.

The significance of the impact of our legal system on Aboriginal life and culture is reflected in the terms of the Declaration for Reconciliation produced by the Council for Aboriginal Reconciliation. The second paragraph declares that 'We value the unique status of Aboriginal and Torres Strait Islander peoples as the original owners and custodians of traditional lands and waters.'

Leaving aside the words 'and waters', which have not been the subject of judicial decision, the balance of the paragraph corresponds with the decision in *Mabo [No 2]* – and corresponds, of course, with the undoubted historical facts. The original owners and custodians – the peoples, as distinct from the individual members of the peoples – were the only owners and custodians of the land before adverse titles came to be asserted by Colonial Governments or under Colonial authority.

The third and fifth paragraphs of the Declaration state that 'We respect and recognise continuing customary laws, beliefs and traditions' and 'We acknowledge this land was colonised without the consent of the original inhabitants.'

These paragraphs accord with the decisions in *Mabo [No 2]* and the *Wik People's Case* which acknowledge that the content of native title depends on Aboriginal laws and customs which were not obliterated by the establishment of Colonial regimes.

Other paragraphs of the Declaration find support in the adoption of laws prohibiting discrimination on racial and certain other grounds. There is an inadequate public understanding of the impact of law on Aboriginal life and culture. But lawyers are well fitted to explain the close relationship between law and the declared aspirations for reconciliation. When the explanation is accurate, many of the misunderstandings which undermine reconciliation can be dispelled. Lawyers can walk on the 'new journey' which the Council for Reconciliation asks us to begin: 'We must learn our shared history, walk together and grow together to enrich our understanding.'

---

1. This article was first published in (1999) 22 (2) *University of New South Wales Law Journal*, 595.
2. W E H Stanner, *White Man Got No Dreaming (*Australian National University Press, 1979) (1979).
3. (1982) 158 CLR 327, 354. Hereafter, '*Mabo [No 2]*'.
4. (1992) 175 CLR 1, 104.
5. Ibid 39.
6. See *In re Southern Rhodesia* (1919) AC 211, 233-4.
7. See *Fejo* v *Northern Territory of Australia* (1998) 195 CLR 96.
8. See *Wik Peoples* v *Queensland* (1996) 187 CLR 1. Hereafter, *Wik People's Case*.
9. (1996) 185 CLR 595, 614.
10. (1997) 190 CLR 1, 36.
11. (1981) 149 CLR 27.
12. (1987) 163 CLR 561, 578.
13. (1982) 149 CLR 305, 317-8.

9.7 Scholarship and the *Mabo* Case

Editor's note

Eddie Mabo had worked at James Cook University in Townsville for many years. Several academics at the University knew him well. In 2002, the *James Cook University Law Review* dedicated an issue to 'Native Title: A Decade after Mabo'. Having retired from the bench, Brennan was free to write the Foreword.[1]

The dispossession of indigenous Australians from their land can be traced back to the instructions given to Captain Arthur Phillip when he was appointed Governor in Chief over the Territory of New South Wales on 25 April 1787. King George III declared his –

> Will and Pleasure that you do immediately upon your landing after taking Measures for securing Yourself and the people who accompany you, as much as possible from any attacks or interruptions of the Natives of that Country, as well as for the preservation and safety of the Public Stores, proceed to the Cultivation of the land, distributing the Convicts for that purpose in such manner, and under such Inspectors or Overseers and under such Regulations as may appear to You to be necessary and best calculated for procuring Supplies of Grain and Ground Provisions

His Majesty added, however, that –

> You are to endeavour by every possible means to open an Intercourse with the Natives and to conciliate their affections, enjoining all Our Subjects to live in amity and kindness with them... You will endeavour to procure an account of the Numbers inhabiting the Neighbourhood of the intended settlement and report your opinion to one of our Secretaries of State in what manner Our Intercourse with these people may be turned to the advantage of this country.

So, the interests of the original inhabitants were to be subordinated to the interests of the colonisers and the colonial power. It is not surprising that, from this beginning, there developed a belief that Aborigines possessed no legal rights which might be recognized and enforced by the imported legal system, even though it was clear that the establishing of the colony was to be achieved by dispossession of 'the Natives' and by the use of force, if need be, to repel them.

In time, the injustice of the dispossession was realised, brought home by writers such as the late Professor W E H Stanner:

> No English words are good enough to give a sense of the links between an Aboriginal group and its homeland.... I have seen an Aboriginal embrace the earth he walked on... A different tradition leaves us tongueless and earless towards this other world of meaning and significance. When we took what we call 'land' we took what to them meant hearth, home, the source and locus of life, and everlastingness of spirit.[2]

The relationship of indigenous Australians with their traditional country was one of the foundations of Sir Edward Woodward's recommendations in his significant Report on Aboriginal Land Rights in 1975. That Report led to the enactment of the *Aboriginal Land Rights (Northern Territory) Act 1976* (Cth). The Act grafted native title onto the fee simple tenure of the common law. That device gave the security of the fee simple to successive generations of traditional Aborigines, but the fee simple and dependent native title waited on the making of a grant by the sovereign power. In *Mabo (No 2)* the High Court was required for the first time to determine the question whether native title is itself recognized by the common law. Earlier cases and judicial dicta had suggested a negative answer but the Courts' examination of the legal bases for this view showed that the view rested on propositions that could no longer command support. This change in legal thinking was but a first step in the jurisprudential exercise of accommodating native title within the framework of the common law. That task was to be worked out in the traditional common law way; that is to say, in a case by case resolution of issues thrown up by actual problems. And the methodology for developing the law would call for the 'strict logic and high technique' which, as properly understood, was espoused by Sir Owen Dixon. That methodology requires an understanding of the values which underlie the principles of the law which, in turn, inform its particular rules. Legal scholarship and critical analysis of judgments was required.

This issue of the Journal of the Law School of James Cook University essays that important task. It is not merely a thematic issue, but a critical review of the steps taken in development of the law and an identification of the issues awaiting authoritative resolution. Scholarship is evident in the critical examination of the relevant judgments. That criticism has avoided, for the most part, the academically false approach of comparing the orders of the court with the result expected or hoped for by the critic. Rather the criticism has sought to discover whether a coherent body of principle is emerging. Justice Cullinane has placed the development of native title doctrine in its historical context, both pre – and post – Mabo. Diana Henriss-Anderssen and Peter Poynton have analysed the important *Yorta Yorta Case* and M A

Stephenson has compared the rights and interests of Australian holders of native title with the rights and interests of those who hold an indigenous title under the laws of Canada. Andrea Olsen raises the issue of the effect of planning legislation and planning orders on native title.

Then Associate Professor Amankwah and Dr Ulla Secher contribute a magnum opus. The effects of both common law and statute on the rights of the holders of native title – community title and individual title – are identified. The rights are various: mineral rights, food gathering rights, water rights. The capacity of various statutes and various kinds of executive action to extinguish native title is examined, and the cases which have construed the statutes relied on to effect extinguishment are analysed. The authors discuss the concepts relevant to the proprietary rights to land beneath offshore territorial waters and to land beneath inland waters. They examine the consequences for native title of statutes which authorise the resumption of land, including compulsory acquisitions by the Commonwealth. In the latter context, they question the meaning of the judgments delivered in the 1923 case *Commonwealth* v *New South Wales*,[3] when considered in the light of the doctrine of native title accepted in *Mabo*. Finally, the authors review the complex provisions of the *Native Title Amendment Act 1998* (Cth) relating to the validation of non-native titles and the regime for future extinguishment of native title. Academics and practitioners who revisit these questions will find that the authors have been there already and offer shafts of illumination on many of the problems that are not already covered by settled law.

The journal would not be complete without some practical advice. Professor Geoff Clark takes the reader through the process of mediation of claims, alert to the legal structure, the cultural exigencies, the methodology of mediation, the operation of the Native Title Tribunal and the role of the Federal Court. All of this reminds us of the purpose in pursuing the theories and the intellectual challenges of native title. The pursuit is in order that, so far as practicable at this time, justice may be done to individuals – both natural and corporate – whose well-being depends on the interests they hold in the finite natural resources of our nation.

---

1. The Foreword is at (2002/2003) 9 *James Cook University Law Review* 6.
2. W E H Stanner, Boyer Lectures: 'After the Dreaming' delivered in 1968 and reproduced in the book of his essays, *White Man Got No Dreaming* (Australian National University Press, 1979) 230.
3. (1923) 33 CLR 1.

9.8 This Country: A Reconciled Republic?

Editor's note

Prime Minister Paul Keating had established a Republic Advisory Committee in 1993. It was chaired by Malcolm Turnbull. In February 1998, the Howard Government convened a Constitutional Convention which supported, in principle, Australia becoming a republic. The Convention resolved that 'a referendum for change to a republic or for the maintenance of the status quo be held in 1999'. The referendum was held on 6 November 1999. The proposal for a republic was defeated 45:55, and in all states. Those advocates seeking change went back to the drawing board. Professor Mark McKenna published 'This Country: A Reconciled Republic?'[1] in 2004. He invited Brennan to launch the book at Gleebooks in Sydney on 8 June 2004, five days after the 12th anniversary of the Mabo decision.

Mark has chosen an auspicious time for the launch of his latest book: *This Country: A Reconciled Republic?* The Canberra launch by Gatjil Djerrkura and this launch straddle 3 June. That date is significant for *This Country.* It was the date in 1769 which brought Captain Cook to the South Seas to observe the transit of Venus and to go on to claim this country – or at least the eastern coast – for the Crown of Great Britain and Ireland. It is a date that has some significance for a Republic, for it was on 3 June 1953 that, in this country, we received reports of the coronation of Queen Elizabeth II. Queen Elizabeth and her heirs and successors 'in the sovereignty of the United Kingdom' are, by force of the Imperial *Commonwealth of Australia Constitution Act,* the monarchs of this country. And 3 June is significant for Reconciliation, for it was on that date in 1992 that the judgment of the High Court in *Mabo v Queensland [No 2]* was published.

But the title of the book does more than draw attention to a date. It is an evocative title, challenging us to define our conceptions of the place where we are, the kind of people we aspire to be and the type of government we favour.

'Country' is a term which resonates with all Australians. It is, says Mark McKenna 'a word that goes deeper than nation.' Dorothea Mackellar proclaimed 'Core of my heart, my country!' and she wrote–

> I love a sunburnt country,
> A land of sweeping plains,
> Of ragged mountain ranges,
> Of droughts and flooding rains;
> I love her far horizons,

I love her jewel-sea,
Her beauty and her terror –
The wide brown land for me.

Do we love this land? Do we care for its survival as the inland rivers dry, the old growth forests are clear felled and salt rises as the water table sinks? Is sustainability the key word in our plans for development of energy supply, transport, housing and urbanisation? Country is a term that evokes warm sentiments in all Australians, but it does not always translate into action. It is a term which evokes a deeper meaning in the minds and hearts of Aboriginal Australians. It is the term which our indigenous citizens use to describe the land to which they belong – not land as an integer of commerce but land as a source of life. The significance of country to Aboriginal Australians was eloquently described by the late Professor Bill Stanner:

> When we took what we call 'land' we took what to them meant hearth, home, the source and locus of life, and everlastingness of spirit. At the same time it left each local band bereft of an essential constant that made their plan and code of living intelligible. Particular pieces of territory, each a homeland, formed part of a set of constants without which no affiliation of any person to any other person, no link in the whole network of relationships, no part of the complex structure of social groups any longer had all its co-ordinates. What I describe as 'homelessness', then, means that the Aborigines faced a kind of vertigo in living. They had no stable base of life; every personal affiliation was lamed; every group structure was put out of kilter; no social network had a point of fixture left. [2]

This is the legacy of European settlement. There are now only remote areas in which Aboriginal Australians can perform the ceremonies and discharge the duties they owe to their country, and even in those areas the pervasive culture of the west has eroded the traditions and impaired the transmission of the sacred stories of the Dreaming. We cannot contemplate a future without reconciliation between Australians of Aboriginal and Torres Strait Islander descent and other Australians. As Sir William Deane observed: 'Where there is no room for national pride or national shame about the past, there can be no national soul'.

At Federation and thereafter we boasted that we had a continent for a nation and a nation for a continent. We were unique. We shared no land boundaries; we had no divisions of the kind which marked Britain and Ireland. We achieved our national and constitutional identity and independence without rebellion or civil war. The people of the federating Colonies 'humbly relying on the blessing of Almighty God, agreed to unite in one indissoluble Federal Commonwealth under the Crown of Great Britain and Ireland'. We were the lucky country that enjoyed the blessing of Almighty God.

The rhetoric of the time saw Australians as a mono-cultural, mono-ethnic community, but the Aboriginal peoples of Australia were constitutionally ignored. We did not achieve our national and constitutional identity in unity with our indigenous people. When we moved to a national Federation, ss 25, 51(xxvi) and 127 of the *Constitution* removed Aboriginal Australians from the Constitutional radar screen. And so, it remained until 1967 when the enfranchised people of Australia voted to remove the reference to Aboriginal people in s 51(xxvi) and to delete s 127.

What explains this lengthy delay in recognition? Aboriginal society and culture were, and traditional Aboriginal society and culture are, so different from the society and the culture of the West that it is not surprising that it was not understood by European settlers and, indeed, is not well understood by most of us in the Western tradition today.

It was not understood that Aboriginal people could share their country but would never reduce it into exclusive private possession. In earlier times, if Aboriginal people tried to share country which had been granted to Europeans, the Europeans would treat the Aborigines as trespassers and the Aborigines would treat the Europeans as usurpers. Conflict was inevitable. Nor was it understood that Aborigines would allow others the right to forage over their country, so it is not surprising that they would forage for cattle or sheep that were regarded as the property of Europeans. Nomadic Aborigines were unlikely to understand the need for settlement of an agrarian society. Nor could an understanding of the social structure of the two societies be easily appreciated. A nomadic Aborigine had no concept of saving possessions; of necessity, each day was sufficient for itself and so the Aborigine appeared to be wasteful and incapable of joining our western society in a successful industrial and post-industrial age. Aboriginal people have never been restricted to a nuclear family; their obligation is to share what they have with members of a widely extended family. But Aboriginal society had the strength of a deep spirituality, and it has largely retained that characteristic while western society has drifted more into materialism and consumerism, forgetful of the spiritual and the transcendent. Western society could never understand the Aborigine who went walkabout to perform his spiritual duties and to join members of the extended family gathered for a ceremonial occasion.

Each culture had an intrinsic logic but the logic of each was the converse of the other. And so the policies of the Western society were formed, the laws enacted and the practices followed which were designed to bring about the mono-cultural community envisaged at Federation; policies to smooth the dying pillow of the expected-to-disappear Aboriginal race; policies to assimilate indigenous Australians into the European way of living and thinking; and policies to take children from their families so that they acquired Western and not Aboriginal values. Policies which were tragic failures because they failed to acknowledge not only the culture of the indigenous Australians but their very humanity.

In time the policy of compulsory abduction of children was abandoned and an appreciation of the intrinsic strength of the Aboriginal culture and tradition led to the realization that Aboriginal Australians would never be forcibly assimilated into the Western culture or mainstream. Gradually, when Mr Whitlam poured the soil into the hands of Vincent Lingiari and Sir Edward Woodward's report was implemented by Mr Viner and Mr Fraser and the High Court delivered its judgments in *Mabo* and *Wik* we came to recognise that unoccupied Crown land was not Crown land but Aboriginal land – held by a fragile title, it is true, but nonetheless Aboriginal land. Then there was the massive outpouring of compassion when people marched in their thousands to say 'Sorry'. We have seen some great steps taken towards reconciliation but a long distance is yet to be traversed.

Mark McKenna challenges us to take the journey as we move to a republican form of government. He shows how the movement towards reconciliation has been quieted – by political diversion, by 'the fear of cultural difference' and, he contends, by the timidity of a republican movement which treated reconciliation as a separate issue when it should have embraced constitutional recognition of Aboriginal people and their right to freedom from racial discrimination.

He proposes a new incentive and a new solution. Marry reconciliation with the Republic, each movement giving vitality to the other. Let reconciliation be an objective of the new Republic and let the Republic be sought as a means of achieving reconciliation. This is a heady challenge and it deserves careful consideration. But I wonder about the wisdom of the marriage of these two movements in the context of constitutional amendment. Two questions come to mind: one is practical, the other political.

First, the practical question. How can constitutional amendment advance reconciliation? One section to which objection is rightly taken is s 25. It is offensive and obsolete. It should go but it changes nothing. Another provision is s 51 (xxvi) which gives the Parliament power to make laws with respect to 'the people of any race for whom it is deemed necessary to make special laws'. Should it be removed? The *Constitution* does not contain a Bill of Rights; for the most part, it simply distributes power between the Commonwealth and the States and among the Parliament, the executive and the judiciary. If the *Constitution* were to deny the power to make laws for the people of a race and were to forbid racial discrimination, a law could not be made to benefit only one race. A Constitution endures indefinitely, so if we made an exception of beneficial laws for Aborigines or Torres Strait Islanders, what would we do if, in the years to come, we need to make special provision for Pacific Islanders whose homes are inundated by rising seas?

Of course, reconciliation would be advanced by the protection of indigenous rights but reference to the complexities of the statutes which currently protect Aboriginal land rights shows that, in a pluralist society, no individual right can be protected without qualification. Moreover, no broad statement of principle will suffice to achieve reconciliation. A variety of measures must be taken – some which prohibit conduct which is inimical to reconciliation, some which positively advance that objective. Take a current issue: what can be done to diminish the symptoms of despair – substance abuse and violence – that blight all our communities and especially some Aboriginal communities? Whatever be the answer to this problem, we cannot risk diminishing the power of any government to come to the assistance of those in despair.

But Mark McKenna does not seek to achieve reconciliation simply by substantive amendment of the *Constitution*. He would have indigenous rights and indigenous history recognized as an element in an eloquent preamble to a republican Constitution. He proposes a preamble which expresses three fundamental principles:

1. Constitutional recognition of Aboriginal people and freedom from racial discrimination;
2. The values and principles of Australian democracy;
3. A commitment to care for the land and the Australian environment.

This is a feasible proposal. It would acknowledge our history and identity, our basic political values and our respect for this country. As for reconciliation, a careful wording of the first principle would permit governments to work for reconciliation by taking steps according to the needs of particular communities. The preamble could affirm a commitment to this country as the 'core of my heart'.

Is all this an empty symbolism? I think not. True symbols are the expression of our deepest values and the guideposts to our actions. For too long in this country have we been fearful of acknowledging the grandeur of our environment, the cultural richness of our population, the vitality of our next generation, the splendour of our tradition of equality and tolerance. A new constitutional departure could celebrate all these characteristics and dismiss the narrow, fearful attitude that seems to rob us of our unity, our independence and our national pride. It could be a liberating stimulus to produce a free and confident nation. But the preamble would have to acknowledge not only the injustices of the past and our respect for Aboriginal tradition and culture; it would have to acknowledge our unity in the diversity of the many peoples who have enriched the Australia of today. Australia is no longer mono – or even duo- cultural, mono – or even duo- ethnic. The history and culture of modern Australia has roots not only in this country or in Great Britain and Ireland; it has roots in Europe and Asia and the islands of the Pacific. If we move to a Republic, it must be a Republic for all Australians, a Republic that celebrates our unity in diversity and the mutual respect of all sections of our multi-cultural, multi-ethnic, multi-religious community.

Now the second question: the politics. Many Australians have been made fearful of the future, troubled by change, clinging to what they see as the certainties of the past. They may be in the minority on one issue or another, but if two or more issues are joined, the combined minorities may be marshalled to make a majority. We witnessed an alliance between monarchists and direct electionists in the most recent vote on the Republic with a President elected by Parliament. So, if we wish to see changes in our *Constitution* – both a preamble and a Republic – let the issues be separated into separate pieces of legislation and permit each issue to be addressed by the electorate as it sees fit. That was the procedure favoured by the Constitutional Commission in 1988 when it drafted as many Bills as were needed to deal with the series of recommendations made for constitutional amendment. Else a coalition of the unwilling will defeat what would be a majority view on a discrete proposal.

For these reasons, I have some reservations about Mark's thesis but not about his objective. A Preamble which acknowledges the first peoples of our nation and their unique and resilient culture and their occupation and custodianship of the land, which celebrates our unity in the diversity of all who make Australia home, which reaffirms our commitment to the rule of law and the system of representative and responsible government and which is expressed to further the protection of our homeland would be a powerful statement of the character of our people and society. To achieve reconciliation among indigenous and non-indigenous Australians and to adopt a Constitution for an Australian Republic would be to see our nation achieve its full maturity and dignity. For those of us in the autumn of our lives (or later), our hope is that our children and our children's children will see such an Australia – an Australia reconciled, a republican Australia, a free and a confident nation.

---

1. Mark McKenna, *This Country: A Reconciled Republic?* (University of New South Wales Press, 2004).
2. Professor W E H.Stanner in his Boyer Lectures 'After the Dreaming' delivered in 1968 and reproduced in the book of his essays, *White Man Got No Dreaming : Essays 1938-1973* (Australian National University Press, 1979) 230.

9.9 The Indigenous Barristers' Trust

Editor's note

As Chancellor of the University of Technology, Sydney, Brennan was invited to launch the Indigenous Barristers' Trust at the University Law School on 2 December 2004.

The Indigenous Barristers' Trust is the practical outcome of a vision which sees Australians of Aboriginal descent taking their place as ministers of justice according to the laws of our society. For two centuries the Indigenous and non-Indigenous people of this country failed to communicate to each other the importance of the laws which expressed their respective cultures. To the Aborigine, white man's law seemed to be only a source of oppression and injustice. To Europeans, Aboriginal society lacked the institutions which were thought to be necessary to give law the normative force needed to maintain social order. In the dawn of the third century of living together in this country, we have discovered that these views were misconceived. The research of anthropologists and a change in the Australian mindset evident in the 1967 referendum opened the way to an acknowledgement of the spiritual and social significance of Aboriginal law and tradition. And so, in 1971 Justice Blackburn in *Milirrpum v Nabalco Pty Ltd* acknowledged that evidence of Aboriginal law and custom convinced him that 'if ever a system could be called "a government of laws and not of men" it is that shown in the evidence before me'.[1]

Then with the statutory and common law development of Native Title, the recognition of traditional customs and the enactment of laws proscribing racial discrimination, Aboriginal Australians came to see that white man's law could provide at least some measure of protection and dignity to Aboriginal citizens. Today's launch of the Indigenous Barristers' Trust is a significant milestone in the movement which not only reconciles peoples but marks the mutual respect which Aboriginal and non-Aboriginal citizens have for the laws and traditions of the other.

The Indigenous Barristers' Trust is not intended simply to provide money for Aborigines who choose to place their names on the Bar Roll. It is intended to address the commonly recognised difficulties of commencing practice at the Bar which, for a variety of reasons, impact particularly heavily on Indigenous entrants to the legal profession. It is not intended to provide soft options but rather to ensure that the exacting professional standards to which a competent barrister must attain will be maintained by all the beneficiaries of this scheme.

In different Australian jurisdictions Indigenous Australians have already left their mark and made a contribution. But representation of Indigenous Australians in the ranks of the practising Bar has remained low. This is anomalous for success at the Bar has always depended upon individual ability and high ethical standards, and not on wealth or patronage. So, any qualified Australian who is willing to apply himself or herself in a competitive profession with high standards should find a ready acceptance at the Bar. The competitive ethos of the profession demands that any disadvantages suffered by Indigenous Australians should be addressed to ensure that their entry into practice will give them a fair and equal opportunity of success. That is a noble vision that the practising Bar has formed. It is a practical step to assist those who have pursued and surmounted difficult educational goals to the point of tertiary graduation. It is a step which will not only be a help to the beneficiaries of the Trust; it is a step which will enrich the culture of the Bar.

I congratulate the Bar on taking this initiative. Indeed, I am proud to be associated with those who have implemented practical measures to ensure that the message of reconciliation in this country bears copious fruit.

---

1 (1971) 17 FLR 141 at 267.

9.10 Settling with Indigenous People

Editor's note

In 2006, Professor Marcia Langton and others published a collection of essays entitled 'Settling with Indigenous People: Modern treaty and agreement-making'.[1] Brennan was asked to write a Preface reflecting on Case Studies in Agreement Making from Australia, Canada and New Zealand.

In Australia, Canada and New Zealand, colonisation has produced similar effects on the Indigenous population. Dispossession of land and loss of autonomy led to a depreciation of culture, poverty, a loss of dignity and a sense of alienation and despair. The resurgence of Indigenous identity in the late 20th and early 21st centuries has been marked by movements to redress these disadvantages. At the forefront of these movements have been claims of land rights. Land has been sought not to secure economic benefits alone but also – and more importantly – to grow and sustain Indigenous culture and spiritual values.

The legal mechanisms by which land rights have been obtained have varied – sometimes by recognition of Aboriginal title under the common law, sometimes by reservation for Aboriginal purposes, sometimes by grant of a statutory or common law title. Whichever mechanism has been used, however, the legal system of the sovereign authority has necessarily been the underpinning of Indigenous interests in land. The same legal system has then underpinned the benefits which Indigenous groups have been able to secure in reliance on their interests in their land. But legal systems are limited in their capacity to fulfil all Indigenous aspirations.

This book documents a number of processes designed to achieve the agenda of particular Indigenous groups. It shows that less reliance is now placed on litigation than on negotiation to achieve the agenda. Attention is drawn to both the processes and the outcomes of negotiations in each of the jurisdictions. There are some interesting lessons to be learnt.

Apart from whatever leverage has been provided by interests in land, Indigenous negotiators have drawn on popular and governmental goodwill to strengthen Indigenous culture and to enhance the educational and training opportunities for Indigenous people. There has been no shortage of rhetoric extolling these objectives, but the rhetoric has not always produced practical results.

Practical results have followed when negotiators shared an understanding of local conditions: the social, cultural, spiritual and political realities, the legal system, the continuity of the relationship between Indigenous and non-Indigenous populations and the benefits which all parties may reasonably hope to obtain by reaching agreement. Successful negotiations have grown out of respect and trust among the negotiators. Respect and trust lead to consensus on terms of agreement and to support for its implementation.

But it would be a mistake to suppose that legally enforceable agreements can settle every issue. Relationships between community groups continue and change; finality in agreeing some aspects of their relationship may be unreal, if not undesirable. Nor can the written expression of an agreement guarantee its harmonious and effective implementation. That spirit grows only when all those who are responsible for, or affected by, an agreement come to know its terms and to own them. Only then can the agreement foster that mutual respect and sense of solidarity among the parties which are essential to achieve their human dignity. In the final analysis, it is not documents but inter-personal relationships which are the test of reconciliation between Indigenous and non-Indigenous people.

Leaders in reconciliation will find much to reflect on, and a considerable stimulation to research, in the pages which follow.

---

1. Marcia Langton et al (eds) *Settling with Indigenous People: modern treaty and agreement – making* (Federation Press, 2006).

9.11 Indigenous Australians and the Law

Editor's note

Brennan was invited to address the National Indigenous Lawyers Conference in the Common Room of the Bar Association of New South Wales on 22 September 2006. These were his remarks.

This Conference is a great occasion. It brings together indigenous lawyers and lawyers interested in indigenous affairs from every mainland State. At the end of this Conference, you will have made many personal contacts and you will have learnt a great deal about the issues which confront indigenous people in various parts of the Commonwealth. I confess that it gives me much joy to see so many involved in concerns about Australia's first peoples and to see so many of Australian's first peoples entering the legal profession. It was not always so, of course. But the transformation in the recognition of Aboriginal rights and dignity has been achieved, and will continue to be achieved, by law and by lawyers working within the law.

Earlier this year I had the pleasure of attending the Annual Dinner of the Victorian Bar. The guest speaker was Jeffrey Sher, QC, and he spoke about the challenge of representing the interests of indigenous Australians. The speech was well received and the fact that a leader of one of the great Australian Bars can speak at its dinner on such a subject with great enthusiasm is an indication of the extent to which the Bar – and perhaps the whole legal profession – has moved since the days when the interests and aspirations of indigenous Australians received little consideration in the laws of this country. I suppose the major change came with the Referendum in 1967 followed by the Whitlam Government's establishment of the Woodward Land Rights Commission for the Northern Territory and Gough Whitlam's pouring of the sand into the hands of Vincent Lingiari. I had the pleasure and the honour of appearing for the Northern Land Council which was summoned into existence by the interim report which Justice Woodward delivered. It was a rather inchoate body when it was first created and I well remember its first meeting which Eric Pratt and I, with our instructing solicitor Alec Rorrison, attended. A Chairman had to be elected. For me, that day was an education. Discussion had drifted on for most of the day when somebody said 'Silas, maybe you be the Chairman'. There was no formal nomination, no vote, but a clear consensus arrived at via a method familiar to the blackfella but completely novel to the balanda. The wisdom of the old men was manifest. Silas Roberts was an outstanding leader of the Northern Land Council though his office took a terrible toll on him and on Rose, his wife, as they struggled with the demands and cultures of two communities. Silas was living in Maningrida but he belonged to the Roper River Mob. One night after a corroboree staged for the benefit of the visiting Northern Land Council at Numbulwar, Silas spoke. He had been made a special magistrate by this time and he delivered a stern lecture to the young men, telling them to behave themselves and to obey the old men and learn their story. Then he warned them that if they misbehaved, he would exercise his powers as a special magistrate and put them in the slammer! Later the word was that the number of young men going bush for their initiation had increased dramatically.

I am pleased to be able to pay my tribute to Silas, a little known but great Australian, whose leadership of the Northern Land Council ensured the acceptance of the new regime of land ownership in the Northern Territory.

Moving around the Top End visiting large and small communities was a wonderful experience. It was an introduction to the wisdom, the gentleness and the humour of the peoples in those parts. It also illustrated the difficulty that may be experienced in getting adequate instructions about issues that have no resonance in traditional culture. Shortly after we had proposed that Aboriginal land titles should not be merely statutory but should consist in a common law estate in fee simple out of which the traditional Aboriginal rights and interests should be carved, we were in Maningrida holding a large meeting to get instructions. I tried to communicate to our clients some notion of a fee simple held in trust for beneficiaries, but to no avail. Eric Pratt, who had spent a lot of time in Papua New Guinea and had been Mayor of Port Moresby, then tried his hand. Not in English but in Pidgin. The people in Maningrida at that time had been accustomed to tuning their radios to Papua New Guinea and light immediately dawned in their eyes. Although it is difficult to communicate concepts and values in the common law system to those who have no experience of it, it is the common law that must be relied on to protect the interests of indigenous Australians. That is not to diminish the importance of the political process in remedying past injustices.

The political process is important in alleviating oppression and disadvantage, particularly if it produces a beneficial change in community opinion. But it is not sufficient by itself, for two reasons. First – and this is obvious – political support is unreliable as political leaders can conjure up majority support by disparaging a minority. Secondly, and this is not always obvious, alterations in law or policy that may be effected by the political process may fail to take account of the differing interests and aspirations of particular individuals or groups. Lawyers, on the other hand, bound by the instructions of individuals or particular groups, must represent their interests and aspirations whether or not they conform to those of the mainstream. It seems to me that this is of particular relevance to those who are representing indigenous Australians.

Of course, there are similarities of outlook or culture which can be found in every Australian indigenous community. There is that wonderful self-effacing and impish sense of humour which finds amusement in common place situations. I remember when we were getting instructions from the Oenpelli Community. After lunch we resumed a session sitting in a bush clearing and another Silas, husband to one of the owners of the Green Ant Dreaming, was holding forth about what he wanted to be done. Halfway through a sentence, he dozed off and fell off the log he was sitting on. This produced a roar of laughter, the loudest from the awakened Silas himself.

Another basic uniformity among traditional communities is the spiritual bond between the people and the land. Relationship with the land is at the heart of Aboriginal culture. There is no more eloquent description of this bond than the description given by Professor W E H Stanner which I have quoted in the past:

> No English words are good enough to give a sense of the links between an Aboriginal group and its homeland. Our word 'home', warm and suggestive though it be, does not match the Aboriginal word that may mean 'camp', 'hearth', 'country', 'everlasting home', 'totem place', 'life source', 'spirit centre' and much else all in one. Our word 'land' is too spare and meagre. We can now scarcely use it except with economic overtones unless we happen to be poets. The Aboriginal would speak of 'earth' and used the word in a richly symbolic way to mean his 'shoulder' or his 'side'. I have seen an Aboriginal embrace the earth he walked on. To put our words 'home' and 'land' together into 'homeland' is a little better but not much. A different tradition leaves us tongueless and earless towards this other world of meaning and significance. When we took what we call 'land' we took what to them meant hearth, home, the source and locus of life, and everlastingness of spirit. At the same time it left each local band bereft of an essential constant that made their plan and code of living intelligible. Particular pieces of territory, each a homeland, formed part of a set of constants without which no affiliation of any person to any other person, no link in the whole network of relationships, no part of the complex structure of social groups any longer had all its co-ordinates. What I describe as 'homelessness', then, means that the Aborigines faced a kind of vertigo in living. They had no stable base of life; every personal affiliation was lamed; every group structure was put out of kilter; no social network had a point of fixture left. [1]

It was this spiritual relationship with the land that Sir Edward Woodward incorporated in the definition of Aboriginal ownership. That definition was accepted by the Parliament when Ian Viner, QC, then Minister for Aboriginal Affairs, secured the passage of the *Aboriginal Land Rights (Northern Territory) Act 1976* (Cth).

Again, among traditional communities the values of the nomadic lifestyle can be detected. Possessions are available to be shared by all members of the extended family so that an accumulation of wealth to the exclusion of others is not acceptable. Nor is it necessary to save for the morrow, for possessions impede the movement of nomads, not their comfort or contentment.

But the memories and influences of nomadic life diminish and differences develop. Nowadays traditional values inform the life and culture of urban communities or communities that have long been separated from their country in varying degrees. The interests and aspirations of Aboriginal peoples have become diverse. Of course, it was always a mistake to speak of indigenous Australians as a homogeneous people. The differences in country to which particular clans belong, differences in social customs, cultural conditions and local stories and differences in skin groups distinguished one people from another. Now, varying degrees of contact and intermarriage with non-Aborigines, different employment opportunities from place to place, and vastly different health facilities and educational opportunities distinguish Aboriginal individuals or groups one from another. Those distinctions produce differences in interests and aspirations. These differences must be recognized and provided for.

They are significant for lawyers who must not assume that the services appropriate for one client will be appropriate for another simply because both are indigenous. That is obvious but it means that there is a need for a sufficient number of lawyers who are committed to serve the diverse interests and aspirations of Aboriginal Australians and who have an adequate understanding of the values and basic culture of their clients.

Next, these differences are significant in the political process for it should not be assumed that, in legislation and policy affecting Aborigines, one size fits all. It is good to see the emergence of indigenous leadership capable of participating effectively in public affairs but it is a cautionary consideration that traditionally there was no notion of political representation. No man, nor woman either, could speak for and bind another. So, one needs to be careful in assuming that a policy or opinion of one indigenous leader expresses the policy or opinion of all, or even a majority, of Aboriginal Australians. I wonder, for example, how general is the support for 2006 amendments to the *Aboriginal Land Rights (Northern Territory) Act* (Cth) which authorize the alienation of leasehold interests in Aboriginal land for longer periods and wider purposes than before.

When characteristics, qualifications and opportunities vary so widely from community to community, there is a need for community advocates in the public sphere to express the corresponding interests and aspirations of the people. Those with legal training are particularly suited to this role.

For these reasons it is good to see an increasing number of indigenous qualified lawyers and law students. And it is good to see that movements such as the Indigenous Barristers Trust Mum Shirl Fund of the New South Wales Bar are providing practical assistance to establish new indigenous lawyers as successful working members of the profession. Their advent to the ranks of active practitioners will be welcomed by more senior lawyers such as Mullenjaiwakka who have opened the ranks of the profession for those of later generations.

This National Conference which Chris Ronalds, Tony McAvoy and their helpers have made a reality and which you have attended in large numbers is a milestone in the progress of two groups. It is truly an historic event. It marks the progress of indigenous lawyers into active practice and it marks the progress of non-indigenous lawyers in their appreciation of Aboriginality and the debt which Australians and Australian culture owe to the indigenous members of our society. You are dealing with some vital topics relating to customary law: its integration into the legal system, its relevance to criminal justice and the environment and how it may affect a Bill of Rights and structures of Governance. I am sorry that another commitment will prevent me from hearing the Yolngu experience of conflict resolution. I recall a day spent with Roy Marika from Nhulunbuy and Silas Roberts dealing with conflict as we toured Canberra corridors of power seeking support for the Land Rights Bill. Silas and Roy were masters of conflict resolution. I wish you much instruction and satisfaction as you share your experiences and insights in this Conference.

---

1. Professor W E H Stanner in his Boyer Lectures 'After the Dreaming' delivered in 1968 and reproduced in the book of his essays, *White Man Got No Dreaming* (Australian National University Press 1979) 230.

9.12 Indigenous Lawyers Conference

Editor's note

On 14 September 2007, Brennan addressed the Indigenous Lawyers Conference convened in Brisbane. These were his opening remarks.

I acknowledge the traditional Indigenous owners of the country that we call Brisbane and I acknowledge the spirit of their ancestors. It is on this traditional land that this courtroom and this courthouse are constructed – a court in which white man's law is administered to both the descendants of the original Indigenous owners and to those who have come more recently to this land and to their descendants.

This reality spells out the importance of today's conference. This is the second conference which has gathered those who are, or are the descendants of, traditional owners of Australian country and who are engaged in, or who propose to become engaged in, the administration of the white man's law. You may ask: why does it matter that lawyers or future lawyers are of Indigenous descent? If the law applies equally to all, as the rule of law implies, does it matter whether the people involved in it are of any particular ethnic origin? The answer to these questions is both 'no' and 'yes'. 'No' because all legal rights and responsibilities are enforced by the courts, irrespective of the party who invokes the court's jurisdiction or resists the making of a court order and irrespective of the ethnic origin of the persons who are representing or assisting the parties to the litigation.

But that is not even half the answer. An Indigenous lawyer may have special insights which assist in articulating an Indigenous interest which is susceptible of enforcement in the courts. Or there may be an easy rapport between the Indigenous lawyer and an Indigenous client. The function of an Indigenous lawyer acting for a client is the same as the function of a non-Indigenous lawyer but the one may have better appreciation of the client's problems than the other. It is for lawyers to discover whether the state of the law is occasioning some injustice or whether some remedy is available to alleviate an injustice. If the remedy involves simply the invoking of settled law, the lawyer is well placed to assist in alleviating the injustice. Of course, some legal rights are recognized only after research and reflection or after the evidence is found to enliven them. A land claim under the *Aboriginal Land Rights (Northern Territory) Act 1976* (Cth), for example, calls for an understanding of the relevant criteria and identification of the evidence available to satisfy the criteria. Or a remedy for contravention of the *Racial*

Discrimination Act 1975 (Cth) may depend on an analysis of international law authorities and the availability of evidence precisely demonstrating the contravention. If an injustice can be remedied by some change in a legal rule, the lawyer must discover whether the change can be effected by a development of the common law within the confines of the judicial method or whether statutory modification is required. In either case, there is a need for research and reflection so that the argument in favour of the change can be clearly and logically presented. Where legislative or executive action is needed to remedy an injustice or a discriminatory disadvantage suffered by Indigenous people, the skills and insights of an Indigenous lawyer may be needed to achieve reform. So, there are many reasons why it matters to have Indigenous lawyers actively participating in the administration of the law.

Law is a noble profession. Its purpose is to ensure the peace and order of the community in which we live. It does this by providing the rules which regulate our relationships with one another and our relationship with the State. The rules govern property and inheritance, marriage and reputation, crime and punishment. We live in a complex society and we need competent lawyers to administer the complexity of the law. The law regulates the distribution and use of power – whether the power is the power of government, or wealth, or industrial bodies or the power of those who can otherwise affect our interests or our freedom. We need competent and fearless lawyers to defend the interests of those who are less powerful as well as those who seek advice about the limits of the power they may lawfully exercise. The law is intended to protect the legal interests of the minorities and the underprivileged, so lawyers are needed to ensure equality in the law's administration. And, most basically, the law exists for the resolution of disputes, so that those who might otherwise be tempted to engage in self-help or revenge, or who might be unjustifiably oppressed by others can have a remedy which maintains their dignity and the peace and order of society. Law provides the framework in which we can live peaceful and ordered lives, tolerant of others who are bound to respect our own entitlements.

The law is a profession of service. In practice, of course, the service is primarily rendered to the particular client pursuant to the particular retainer by which the lawyer is bound. The service may be rendered by the giving of advice, or the drafting of a document, or the obtaining of evidence or the securing of a witness, or the negotiation of a transaction, or the issuing or defending of court process. But also, since the law has a fundamental social function, it is a service to the community. And for those of you who will be engaged in the service of an Indigenous community or whose clientele will include a proportion of Indigenous people, there is an enormous challenge to protect the interests of those who are still among the most disadvantaged members of our society. I shall say something more about this later. For the moment, it is enough to see that this Conference gathers together some of those Indigenous lawyers who have been and some who will be engaged in protecting the Indigenous people who need protection. It is a gathering of those who have the noble ambition of furthering justice in a tangible way. They should meet to celebrate the emergence of a professional group that has grown exponentially during the last 40 years. We can pay tribute to the courage, the tenacity and the professional service of those few who, like Mullenjaiwakka, in earlier times carried the beacon which so many of you are following here today.

You will be encouraged by meeting with others of similar ambition and you may be inspired by the great American jurist, Justice Cardozo, who told the lawyers of New York County that – 'The tradition, the ennobling tradition, though it be myth as well as verity, that surrounds as with an aura the profession of the law, is the bond between its members and one of the great concerns of man, the cause of justice upon earth.'[1]

Justice and law are not synonymous but in a stable society the operation of the law must generally do justice. When the law unjustly discriminates against a particular group, however, there is a need for advocates who can protect the group by demonstrating the injustice and charting a course to remove it. Indigenous peoples have suffered injustices in this country but some remediation has taken place. The historic 1967 Referendum was a major step in the removal of an injustice arising from the *Constitution*. The Constitutional amendment was achieved by the effective advocacy of people like Faith Bandler and appealed to the Australian sense of fairness.

You are meeting 40 years after the 1967 Referendum. What a change has been observable in those 40 years. I do not remember many, indeed any, Indigenous Australians – or any claiming Indigenous ancestry – in the ranks of the legal profession 40 years ago. That was not then surprising. Aborigines resided in remote areas, or on distant cattle properties or in Aboriginal settlements under the control of the Director, or they were fringe-dwellers of the towns. There were few town-dwellers who proudly proclaimed their Aboriginal ancestry. They and the Torres Strait Islanders were not accorded the same respect and dignity as their fellow Australians. There were very few who had the opportunity to progress or progressed to secondary education. All were heartened by the hope which came with the 1967 Referendum.

Today we rejoice that so many Australians celebrate their Indigenous heritage and rightly find that heritage to be a source of pride. In the 1971 census, only 115,953 people identified themselves as being of Aboriginal or Torres Strait Islander heritage. By 1991, that number had increased to 265,492. The Bureau of Statistics reported that 'it is believed that a substantial proportion of the increases reflect a growing willingness of people to identify themselves as Aboriginals or Torres Strait Islanders.'[2] In 2001, the Bureau of Statistics produced a more accurate estimate of numbers – the Estimated Resident Population – which estimated that there were 458,500 Indigenous Australians, a number which jumped in 2006 to 517,200, an increase of 13%. Indigenous Australians are now 2.5% of the total population.

These numerical changes are significant for Indigenous lawyers. The number who now proudly acknowledge and are confident in their Indigenous ancestry are a category of clients who will seek advice and assistance from others who share that pride and confidence. Indigenous Australians are involved in activities of greater diversity than in earlier times, so the advice and assistance that they will seek will be in correspondingly more diverse fields of the law. Indigenous lawyers will need expertise in wider fields than those that have been of prime concern to the Indigenous community in the past – crime, social security and land rights. The changes in the level of secondary and tertiary education are also important. The educational level of Indigenous people has been raised dramatically in the last 40 years, although that level is still significantly below the level of the non-Indigenous population. Thus, the Bureau reported that in 2002, 3% of the Indigenous population had Bachelor degrees or above, an increase from 1% in 1994. In 2002 Dr Nelson, then the Minister for Education, Service and Training, wrote 'The essential despair that permeates many aspects of Aboriginal life can only be broken with determination led by Indigenous people. They need leadership qualities forged in the kind of education that can come only from Universities.'

No doubt there has been further progress but I understand that the 2006 figures are not presently available.[3]

As the numbers attending this Conference show, we can anticipate an expansion in the number of Indigenous lawyers whose services will be available not only for Indigenous but for non-Indigenous Australians. Indigenous lawyers have already taken their place in the mainstream professional bodies and have done so with distinction. When Judge Bob Bellear, the first Indigenous judge of the District Court of New South Wales, passed away, the Attorney-General of the State addressed the Legislative Assembly, saying: 'Earlier today a State funeral was held for Judge Bellear, and speaker after speaker described him as a man of compassion and learning, a warrior against injustice for his people, and a hardworking judge who strove to bring justice to all Australians...He was a man of high degree for all Australians.'

Ms Pat O'Shane AM was appointed to the bench of Magistrates after a time as a senior public servant, and later took her place with distinction as the Chancellor of the University of New England. During the years when I was Chancellor of the University of Technology, Sydney, I was delighted that the University appointed Larissa Behrendt as a Professor of Law and Director of the Jumbunna Indigenous House of Learning. These and others have earned their distinctions by their legal skills and experience, their industry and their devotion to the interests of all Australians and especially the Indigenous people. They are notable role models for aspiring Indigenous lawyers.

The changes have been not only statistical. Although, as Professor Behrendt has pointed out, 'the 1967 Referendum did not create the even playing field or the era of non-discrimination, it was a high-water mark for the relationship between Aboriginal and non-Aboriginal people.'[4] There has been a vast enhancement in the consciousness of Indigenous dignity, culture and rights. It was not always so. Recently I looked at one of Garth Nettheim's early books. It was called 'Outlawed – Queensland's Aborigines and Islanders and the Rule of Law'. In it, the author reviewed the 1971 Queensland *Aborigines Act 1971* (Qld) and *Torres Strait Islanders Act 1971* (Qld) and the regulations made under those Acts. This was in the age when the policy of both Commonwealth and State governments was assimilation and before the International Convention on the Elimination of All Forms of Racial Discrimination was enacted into Commonwealth law in 1975. Those Acts denied the dignity of Queensland's Indigenous peoples. Nettheim concluded that the Acts were open to criticism on three grounds: Lack of consultation with the people most directly affected, excessive delegation of power to the Administration without effective review, and a series of major and minor violations of fundamental human rights. Many non-Indigenous people have not known the condition of those who lived 'under the Act' and that chapter of history has been passed over or treated as presently irrelevant. In time, the Acts were repealed and land title was given in the form of deeds of grant in trust. That is not to say that all past injustices were wiped away – far from it. But, as the work of remedying by legal means many of the past injustices continues in current litigation, I should not comment on those issues.

Similarly, when we call to mind the frightening injustices which marked the case of Max Stuart who, in 1959, was convicted of the rape and murder of a 9-year-old girl in South Australia. Although Stuart was an Arrente man and an illiterate itinerant with a boxing troupe, the substantial evidence against him was a confession expressed in good English. He was sentenced to death at the age of 27. Appeals to the Full Court, the High Court and the Privy Council failed, and a Royal Commission presided over by a judge who had presided at the Full Court appeal concluded that the conviction was justified. But he had powerful defenders in Rupert Murdoch, then a young Adelaide newspaper owner, and Father Dixon, a gaol chaplain. His execution was stayed 7 times because of an upsurge in public concern before his sentence was commuted to life imprisonment. He served his sentence until paroled in 1973 – and then only after the chair of the Parole Board, who had been the prosecutor at his trial, stood aside. He was never pardoned. In 1985, Pat Dodson gave him a job with the Central Land Council. He became the chairman and welcomed the Queen to Alice Springs. The *Stuart Case* was notable as the case which not only caused an upheaval in the legal establishment of the time but also made a major contribution to the struggle for equal treatment of Australia's Indigenous people.

Then there were the years and destructive practices described in the report on the Stolen Generation. A challenge to the validity of the laws which were said to authorize those practices in the Northern Territory failed in *Kruger's* case.[5] Judged by contemporary community standards, those practices were disgraceful. But that is only to demonstrate the extent to which community standards have changed and the respect which the community has given to Indigenous family ties.

The events at Wave Hill culminating in Gough Whitlam's iconic action of pouring the soil into the hands of Vincent Lingiari, the *Milirrpum* judgment[6] of Blackburn J, the passage in Malcolm Fraser's time of the *Aboriginal Land Rights (Northern Territory) Act 1976* (Cth), the *Mabo*[7] and the *Wik*[8] cases in the High Court, and the passage of the *Native Title Act 1993* (Cth) in Paul Keating's time are significant events on the road to recognition of the importance of land to the culture and spirituality of Indigenous peoples. Some of these events were attended by controversy. In particular the *Mabo* cases,[9] raising the issue of land title on Murray Island in the Torres Strait, and the *Wik People's* Case,[10] relating to mainland pastoral leases, were the subject of much examination and some severe criticism. As I do not comment on the judgments of the High Court, especially on judgments to which I have been a party, I will not say anything about those cases, except to point out that the decisions were applications of the *Racial Discrimination Act 1975* (Cth). Nevertheless, these events have changed the climate in which any debate on Indigenous issues now takes place. No longer are Indigenous people denied their identity as full citizens of our nation albeit in some cases citizens whose standards of living, of health, wealth and housing fall short of the standards to which all citizens are entitled.

It has been a long and oftentimes frustrating struggle to achieve the legal reforms that have ensured a measure of dignity for Australia's Indigenous people. This was recognized in the tribute which Pope John Paul II paid to the Aborigines assembled in Alice Springs in 1986:

> Take heart from the fact that many of your languages are still spoken and that you still possess your ancient culture. You have kept your sense of brotherhood. If you stay closely united, you are like a tree standing in the middle of a bush-fire sweeping through the timber. The leaves are scorched and the tough bark is scarred and burned; but inside the tree the sap is still flowing, and under the ground the roots are still strong. Like that tree you have endured the flames, and you still have the power to be reborn.

There have been heroes in the struggle for Indigenous dignity whose names are public property and others whose contributions have not been widely recognized. Last year, I spoke about one whom I knew and greatly respected – Silas Roberts, first chairman of the Northern Land Council. I am delighted to think that that body has just opened its new premises in Darwin with festivities to celebrate the 30 years that have passed since the Commonwealth Parliament passed the *Aboriginal Land Rights (Northern Territory) Act 1976* (Cth). That Act[11] followed substantially the recommendations of Sir Edward Woodward who had effectively created the Land Council structure and consulted widely with them and the communities they represented. The Act provided for the establishment of Aboriginal Land Trusts to hold title to Aboriginal Land 'for the benefit of Aboriginals entitled by Aboriginal tradition to the use or occupation of the land concerned' subject to compliance with the directions of the local Land Council whose functions were declared to be, inter alia –

> (a) to ascertain and express the wishes and the opinion of Aboriginals living in the area of the Land Council as to the management of Aboriginal land in that area and as to appropriate legislation concerning that land;
>
> (b) to protect the interests of traditional Aboriginal owners of, and other Aboriginals interested in, Aboriginal land in the area of the Land Council.[12]

The Hon Ian Viner, QC, the Minister who introduced the Bill for that Act said in his Second Reading Speech 'This Bill is a major step forward for Aborigines in the Northern Territory not only for this generation but also for future generations who will benefit from it. They will have a land base that will be preserved in perpetuity.'

In the light of the *Northern Territory National Emergency Response Act 2007* (Cth) and its associated Acts, Mr Viner's step forward may now be moving into reverse and the Northern Land Council's festivities may not have taken full account of recent developments. The recent legislation, while it is proclaimed to be a 'special measure' within the meaning of that term in the *Racial Discrimination Act 1975* (Cth), nevertheless excludes the operation of that Act – a course which the Law Council deemed 'utterly unacceptable'. The Human Rights and Equal Opportunity Commission ('HREOC') was concerned by the absence of consultation with the Aboriginal people who would be affected by the legislation and by the negative impact which the legislation would have. HREOC made a submission to the Senate Legal and Constitutional Committee which I quote:

> 5. ... HREOC does not support the [Response Act] measures being exempt from the RDA. [13]
>
> 6. These laws clearly have a number of significant actual and potential negative impacts upon the rights of Indigenous people which are discriminatory. The laws generally must therefore be justifiable as a 'special measure' taken for the advancement of Indigenous people to be consistent with human rights principles.[14] If the [Response Act] measures are not 'special measures', they should not be enacted.
>
> 7. HREOC submits that a fundamental feature of 'special measures' is that they are done following effective consultation with the intended beneficiaries and generally with their consent. The absence of effective consultation with Indigenous people concerning the [Response Act] measures is therefore a matter of serious concern.
>
> 8. HREOC accepts the need for urgent action. However the success of that action both immediately and in the long term will depend upon effective consultation. And such consultation is fundamental to respecting the human rights of Indigenous people.
>
> 9. More broadly, HREOC is concerned that the [Response Act] measures are likely to produce unintended negative consequences that adversely impact upon the rights of Indigenous people."

The 'Response Act' was introduced as a response to the revelation of the sexual abuse of some Aboriginal children and serious deficiencies in some areas of Aboriginal health. These are issues which the broadly-based Indigenous People's Organization, speaking through Denese Griffin, addressed in the Fifth Session of the UNESCO Permanent Forum on Indigenous Issues in May 2006. Ms Griffin presented a paper in her capacity as the Coordinator of the national Network of Indigenous Women's Legal

Services Inc of Australia. This is the peak body of Indigenous women's legal services in Australia and the Family Violence Prevention Legal Units. Its vision is to create a just society that respects, upholds and protects the rights of Indigenous women, children and families, including our men. She noted that 'As we meet here in New York, there are distressing debates taking place in the national media in Australia about family violence and abuse in Australian communities. This debate is of great concern to each of the Indigenous organisations participating in this session.'

She spoke about inadequate housing and services and recommended to the Forum that, inter alia 'It re-iterate the importance of adopting a human rights based approach to addressing Indigenous disadvantage and discrimination, including the right to health, and in particular that experienced by Indigenous children, youth and women; and that this includes ensuring the full and effective participation of Indigenous women in all levels of decision making and in the design and implementation of all policies and programs. '

Whatever view is taken of the 'Response Act', it is clear that any special interests of the Indigenous people – or at least the special interests of mainland Aborigines – will not necessarily be negotiated with the 'full and effective participation of Indigenous women'. When the actions of government do not meet with the approval of those affected, the dispute is often to be resolved by legal means. It is reasonable to assume that there will be many issues between governments and Indigenous Australians which will require the services of lawyers, Indigenous as well as non-Indigenous. Understanding, as well as sheer professional skill, will be called for in the resolution of such disputes.

The history of Indigenous advancement in the last 40 years has often shown the importance of identifying and changing laws or legal preconceptions which have oppressed or discriminated against Indigenous people. Based on that history, we can see that the skills, experience and insights of Indigenous lawyers will be an important weapon in the armoury of any movement to defend and advance Indigenous interests.

I venture to suggest that there are two distinct but related roles for Indigenous lawyers to perform. The first is the classical professional role of advice and advocacy. The disadvantages still encountered by Indigenous people and the discrimination which both results from and causes disadvantage will continue to provide a massive case load for competent Indigenous lawyers. It will be an enormous service to the Indigenous communities and to the Australian nation to bear that case load and to articulate and defend the interests of Indigenous people.

The second role may be even more challenging. It is the role of public Indigenous leadership. This is necessarily a difficult role for Aboriginal Australians. Traditional Aboriginal society has no notion of representation. No person can speak for or bind another in the public forum. That was both a weakness and a strength in the survival of traditional Aboriginal culture. But in our modern society, spokespeople are needed to express and advocate the interests of a group. Another difficulty flows from the fact that there are no single homogeneous Aboriginal people: there are many Aboriginal peoples and they differ in country, in culture and in interest. This suggests that what is needed is not a single Aboriginal voice but as many voices as there are interests – combined, however, to express a unity in that diversity. There may be a united voice to achieve a common goal when the benefits of the goal can be shared without disadvantage but unless there be prior agreement on the goal, there can be no assumption that one voice speaks for all. Redfern is not Cape York, is not Nhulunbuy, is not Yuendumu, is not Turkey Creek, is not the Pitjantjatjara lands of South Australia. Yet the challenge of public advocacy remains and perhaps the challenge of crafting a body in which all voices can be heard and some decisions reached in unison will be a worthy legal contribution to the reconciliation of Indigenous and non-Indigenous Australians. Lawyers can be leaders in the building of reconciliation, remembering with Sir William Deane[15] that 'until true reconciliation with its Indigenous peoples is reached, Australia is a diminished nation'.

I wish you well in your Conference. I respect your competence and courage in your professional lives.

---

1. Benjamin Cardozo, New York County Lawyers Address, in Margaret E Hall (ed) *Selected Writings Of Benjamin Nathan Cardozo: The Choice of Tycho Brahe,* (Fallon Publications, 1947) 104.
2. Australian Bureau of Statistics, Year Book Australia, 1994, 1301.0.
3. Expected in September 2007.
4. See *The 1967 Referendum: 40 Years On:* www.jumbunna.uts.edu.au/research.
5. See *Kruger v The Commonwealth* (1997) 190 CLR 1.
6. See *Milirrpum v Nabalco Pty Ltd* (1971) 17 FLR 141.
7. See *Mabo v Queensland [No 1]* (1988)166 CLR 186; *Mabo v Queensland [No 2]* (1992)175 CLR 1.
8. See *Wik Peoples v Queensland* (1996) 187 CLR 1.
9. See *Mabo v Queensland [No 1]* (1988)166 CLR 186; *Mabo v Queensland [No 2]* (1992) 175 CLR 1.
10. See *Wik Peoples v Queensland* (1996) 187 CLR 1.
11. Section 4(1).
12. Section 23(1).

13. See *Northern Territory National Emergency Response Bill 2007* (Cth) clause 132; *Social Security Bill* clause 4; *Families, Community Services and Indigenous Affairs and Other Legislation Amendment (Northern Territory National Emergency Response and Other Measures) Bill 2007* clause 4.
14. Note, however that a law authorising management of property owned by Aboriginal and Torres Strait Islander people without their consent cannot be justified as a special measure under the *Racial Discrimination Act 2007 (Cth)*: See ss 8(1) and 10(3).
15. Sir William Deane, 'Some Signposts from Daguhagu' the First Vincent Lingiari Memorial Lecture, Darwin, 22 August 1996.

The Brennan family gathered for Gerard's swearing in as Chief Justice on 21 April 1995. (Photo: Heide Smith)

At the swearing in, Brennan was accompanied by his sisters Anne and Sr Mary RSCJ and his cousin Fr Grove Johnson. (Photo: Heide Smith)

Patricia assisted Gerard settling into the Chief Justice's chambers

The Brennan court: standing: Justices Gummow, Toohey, McHugh and Deane; seated: Justices Gaudron, Brennan and Dawson. (Photo: Heide Smith)

Gerard commissioned artist Miriam Rose Ungunmerr to paint 'The Pearl Shells and the Rainbow Serpent: Symbols of power' which hung in the Chief Justice's chambers; Sir Gerard Brennan and Sir William Deane – longtime judicial colleagues and friends. Deane delivered the eulogy at Brennan's funeral.

Gerard Brennan swearing in William Deane as Governor General in the presence of Prime Minister Paul Keating, 16 February 1996. (AUSPIC)

The Brennan Court at work

The Brennan Court in conference

Chapter 10

The Republic

10.1 The Republic Australia Forum

Editor's note

At his swearing in as Chief Justice on 21 April 1995, Brennan addressed the contemporary relevance of swearing an oath of commitment of loyalty to Her Majesty the Queen, her heirs and successors according to law. He said, 'It is a commitment to the head of State under the Constitution. It is from the Constitution that the Oath of Allegiance, which has its origins in feudal England, takes it significance in the present day. As the Constitution can now be abrogated or amended only by the Australian people in whom, therefore, the ultimate sovereignty of the nation resides, the Oath of Allegiance and the undertaking to serve the head of State as Chief Justice are a promise of fidelity and service to the Australian people. The duties which the oath imposes sit lightly on a citizen of the nation which the Constitution summoned into being and which it sustains. Allegiance to a young, free and confident nation governed by the rule of law is not a burden but a privilege.

After his retirement from the bench, Brennan became a strong public advocate for an Australian republic. The Constitution Alteration (Establishment of Republic) 1999 ('the Republic Bill') and the Presidential Nominations Committee Bill 1999 ('the Nominations Committee Bill') were introduced into parliament on 10 June 1999. A Joint Select Committee on the Republic Referendum was set up and was required to report by 9 August 1999. The legislation for the referendum passed both houses of parliament on 12 August 1999. On that day, the Commonwealth Attorney-General, the Honourable. Daryl Williams MP and the Special Minister of State, Senator the Honourable Chris Ellison announced that the referendum would be held on 6 November 1999. The race was on. Brennan was invited to address the Republic Australia Forum convened by the Independent Scholars of Australia and the Library Society at the State Library of New South Wales on 14 August 1999. These were his remarks.

Constitutions are not the gift of government; they are the creation of the people governed. Our Constitution was brought into existence following the agreement 'to unite in one indissoluble Federal Commonwealth' by the people of New South Wales, Victoria, South Australia, Queensland and Tasmania joined later by the people of Western Australia. The Constitution is the people's grant of power to their organs of government. It is the right of the people to change their Constitution, not the right of the Government or even of the Parliament. But the Parliament has to formulate the change to be voted on by the people in a referendum. The Parliament has now settled the question to be voted on at the November referendum. It asks whether we are in favour of –

> An Act to alter the *Constitution* to establish the Commonwealth of Australia as a Republic with the Queen and Governor General being replaced by a President appointed by a two thirds majority of the members of the Commonwealth Parliament.

The first part of this question affects those provisions of the *Constitution* which create our national symbols and confer the executive powers of government. The preamble to the *Constitution* now describes the people of Australia as 'united under the Crown of Great Britain and Ireland'. That has been the constitutional provision for nearly a century. It is reflected in the provision (s 61) which says that 'The executive power of the Commonwealth is vested in the Queen and is exercisable by the Governor General as the Queen's representative'.

Now the Australian people must choose whether to take to themselves full constitutional authority. Or are we content to remain symbolically and nominally under 'the Crown of Great Britain and Ireland' and to have our government's executive power vested in the Queen and the Queen's representative? That choice has never been offered before but, because the choice will be made by the Australian people of today, it will determine for the foreseeable future not only how we are seen by others but, more importantly, how we see ourselves. Our future constitutional arrangements will not be attributable to decisions taken a century ago; they will be attributable to the decision we take on the eve of the century to come.

The second part of the question relates to a model for the appointment of the President. The President under the proposed model, like 'the Governor-General as the Queen's representative' under the present *Constitution*, will be vested with 'the executive power of the Commonwealth'. This power is always exercised in accordance with the advice of the Government of the day, except in the case of the 'reserve powers' as they are called. The Governor-General is bound to follow the advice he is given. He can counsel his Ministers in confidence, but he cannot oppose them politically. In a real sense, it is the Prime Minister and the Ministers who exercise executive power by tendering advice to the Governor-General. And since the Prime Minister and the Ministers are in office only because they have the confidence of the Parliament, they are accountable to the people's representatives in Parliament for the exercise of executive power. Under the proposed model, that would remain the position. Responsible government as we know it, would be retained, even though the Prime Minister would lose his sole power of appointing a Governor-General and he would have to get retrospective approval from the House of Representatives to dismiss a President instead of advising the Queen to dismiss a Governor-General. The essential point is that the Government, in its day to day exercise of power, would remain responsible directly to the Parliament. The essence of our system would be unchanged.

The alternative model that has been discussed is the model of direct election. Many people wish to have a vote on the appointment of their head of State, albeit this model would give the President the political authority of a popular mandate. The Presidency would become a political office, achieved by political means. In the exercise of executive power, the President's political authority derived from a national election would be at least coequal with the authority of the Prime Minister. Of course, the President's exercise of executive power could be restrained by a constitutional requirement for him to act on the advice of the Prime Minister but in practice there would be a change in the political balance. The President's electoral mandate might put him or her at odds with the Government or the Parliament. Direct election would see a substantial change in the system of government as we have known it.

Many people who favour a Republic in principle have reservations about the model on which the Australian people are being asked to vote at the referendum. For them, the question arises whether to vote for a Republic now and hope to improve the model if it is found defective in practice or is the model so flawed that we must continue under the present regime?

There can be no realistic expectation of another Republic referendum in the near future. Nor, in any future referendum for a Republic, can it be said that there would be no reservations about the model then offered. So, the stark question for the Australian people is this:

> Do I favour a Republic which maintains the essential character of the system of government we have or should our Federation continue unchanged under the Crown of Great Britain and Ireland?

If the November referendum is carried, those who have reservations about the model can seek to amend the model in a future referendum. If the November referendum is defeated by Republicans who favour direct election or who have reservations about other aspects of the present model, they must place their hopes on the holding of a future referendum which offers a Presidency by direct election or which changes the aspect that now gives concern. Whether such a referendum would be held in the foreseeable future and whether, if held, it would find more support than the present model must be a matter of speculation.

10.2 First Letter by Zelman Cowen, Anthony Mason and Gerard Brennan

Editor's note

In the month leading up to the Republic Referendum, Brennan joined his predecessor Sir Anthony Mason and retired Governor-General Sir Zelman Cowen in publishing three letters aimed at clarifying the legal issues involved in the referendum campaign. The letters were published on 6 October 1999, 22 October 1999, and 3 November 1999.

---

6 October 1999

The Republic debate has focussed on three questions:

(1) whether we should retain the existing arrangements with the Queen as the nominal Head of State;

(2) whether we should adopt, instead of that existing arrangement, the proposed Republic model to be voted on at the Referendum, with a President elected by the Parliament; or

(3) whether a third arrangement with a President directly chosen in an Australia-wide election would be preferable.

The third arrangement, involving direct election by the people, would bring to office a President with a popular mandate from his election by the people at large. Supported by a popular mandate, such a President might be disposed to take or even join issue with the Prime Minister of the day or even with Parliament. Conflict between a President elected by the people and the Prime Minister or Parliament would present a threat to the stability of our system of 'government responsible to Parliament'. For this reason, that arrangement has not been put forward at the Referendum.

On the other hand, the proposed Republic model with a President elected by the Parliament gives no popular mandate to the President which could encourage him to take issue with the Prime Minister or Parliament. The Republic model therefore presents no threat to our established system of government. That model leaves the President simply with the functions of the Queen and the Governor-General and makes no change to the structure of the *Constitution*.

The Referendum is concerned only with the identity and means of choosing a Head of State with functions that, like those of the Queen and the

Governor-General, are largely but by no means entirely formal and symbolic. The symbolic functions are very important however, since through his or her speeches and other community activities, the Head of State would perform the centrally important function of interpreting the nation to itself.

We offer the following comparison between the two models from which the voters must choose at the Referendum.

Under the present *Constitution*, the Queen appoints the Governor-General on the advice of the Prime Minister. As the Queen has no discretion to reject that advice, the Prime Minister effectively exercises the sole power to appoint the Governor-General. The Republic model invites public nominations and requires the President to be nominated by the Prime Minister, seconded by the Leader of the Opposition and approved by at least two-thirds of the Parliament. This process is more open than the existing system where there is no constraint on the Prime Minister choosing the Governor-General and conveying his advice in confidence to the Queen.

Under the present *Constitution*, the Queen can terminate the appointment of the Governor-General on the advice of the Prime Minister. Again, the Queen has no discretion to reject that advice, though Her Majesty can question the advice and offer cautionary counsel. Because the Queen is bound ultimately to act on the advice, the Prime Minister effectively has the sole power to terminate the appointment of the Governor-General, without being under an obligation to explain his decision to Parliament or to secure its support.

Under the Republic model, the Prime Minister has the sole power to terminate the appointment of the President, but must then obtain the approval of a majority of members of the House of Representatives. This new requirement for approval is designed to make the Prime Minister accountable and to ensure that the power of termination will never be exercised irresponsibly.

These provisions of the Republic model will not be seen by everyone as a perfect solution to the issues of appointment and termination but they do provide a reasonable solution and 'a safe, workable proposal for a republic that continues our tradition of stable parliamentary democracy', to repeat the words of the Attorney-General, Daryl Williams QC.

The proposal, to the extent to which it departs from the provisions of the existing system for appointment and termination, by giving a role to members of Parliament in both appointment and termination and by placing constraints on the power of the Prime Minister, reinforces the principle of responsible government which is central to our Constitution. The people's representatives, assembled in the Parliament, would share the power now possessed by the Prime Minister alone. In this way, the Republic model makes the possibility of arbitrary action even less likely than it is under our existing system.

What we have said states the core of our reasons for supporting the Republic model.

10.3 Second Letter by the Three Knights

22 October 1999

In our earlier letter we compared the proposed Republican model for the appointment and dismissal of a President with the existing arrangements for the appointment and termination of appointment of a Governor-General. As the debate now seems to focus on a comparison between the proposed model and a direct election model, we offer the following comments.

Under the proposed model, the appointed President has no political mandate; he or she must act on the advice of the government of the day except in those extraordinary situations in which the 'reserve' powers can properly be exercised to resolve a political impasse. The restriction on presidential power maintains the Westminster system, which has been the central feature of Australia's Parliamentary democracy. That system makes the Prime Minister and the Government of the day responsible to the Parliament for the way in which executive power is exercised. The popularly elected Parliament holds the Government accountable. The Government bears the political responsibility for what an appointed President does on the Government's advice. Except in extraordinary situations of the kind we witnessed in 1975, the Government's term of office would last as long as it commands the confidence of the House of Representatives. That is an important democratic safeguard over a power to make regulations, to enforce the law, to make appointments to offices, to get in the taxes and to spend the money which Parliament approves.

By contrast, a President who has been popularly elected for a fixed term might claim authority to act on a popular mandate inconsistently with the policies of the Government. As the power to dismiss a Government can be exercised against the wishes of that Government, a popularly elected President might dismiss a Government if its policies conflicted with the policies of the President. Without extensive constitutional constraints, an elected Presidency could destroy the Westminster system of responsible government. In Ireland, where an elected Presidency has been combined with a Westminster system, the Irish *Constitution* prohibited the President from acting on her own initiative. She can dismiss a Government only after consultation with a separate Council of State. But we do not have a Council of State. In Australia, the direct election of a President would be strongly contested by the political parties, for no Party would want a President that was not entirely sympathetic to that Party's policies. The Presidency would be a party political office.

The important issue between the supporters of the proposed model and the supporters of a direct election model is not so much the selection of a President but the preservation of the existing system of responsible Government under which Parliament alone checks the exercise of executive power.

There are two other issues. First, no candidate who would be unwilling to incur the costs and to be involved in the controversies of an election could become our President. The likely candidates would be representatives of. or beholden to, the political parties. The President would not be above politics; he or she would be enmeshed. Secondly, local representation has been a feature of the Federation. In a nationwide election, the policies that would be canvassed would be likely to favour the big cities. If so, there would be risks in the direct election model for regional Australia and for the numerically smaller States.

As the proposed model provides a simple method of transition to a Republic consistent with our existing system of parliamentary democracy, we support that model.

10.4 Third Letter of Three Knights

3 November 1999

In two earlier statements on the referendum proposals to be voted on next Saturday, we argued that the proposed system for an Australian head of state would be better for Australia than either the present monarchical system or a directly-elected presidency.

We regret that loose and extravagant statements by some advocates of a 'no' vote have encouraged confusion, uncertainty, and anxiety in the community. We wish to restate the view which we have expressed before that the proposals are safe, and that they do not put the security of our democratic institutions at risk. There is nothing in them for Australians to fear.

It is said that the proposed system makes the prime minister too powerful. He will in fact have less power than at present. At *present,* the Prime Minister alone chooses the Governor-General. Under the proposed republic, the Prime Ministers nomination for President, made following a public nomination process, requires the support of the Opposition Leader and of two-thirds of both houses of Parliament. At present, the Prime Minister could quickly obtain the dismissal of the Governor-General by the Monarch without having to account to Parliament for his actions, and could quickly obtain the appointment of anyone of his own choosing as Governor-General. Under the proposed republican system, the prime minister must account to parliament for dismissal of the President, and is not able to instal his own choice as successor. No Prime Minister has ever sought the dismissal of a Governor-General, and the proposed system makes it even less likely that a President would be dismissed.

We wish to add one point relating to the election of the President. It arises out of consideration of the character of this very important institution of an Australian republic, and we believe that it has not been adequately stated in the debate. It is a central aspect of the office of President that he or she should always be concerned to promote the unity of the nation. He or she is Head of State, and not of government. He or she should possess the capacity, intuition, and skills to promote the unity of the nation. By speech, conduct, and example, the president can help to interpret the nation to itself, and foster that spirit of unity and pride in the country which is central to the well-being of our democratic society. Direct election of a president would involve opposing candidates backed and financed by political parties campaigning against each other on contentious issues, and winning office against the opposition of a significant proportion of the Australian community. This is not the way to choose a President who will effectively unify the nation and represent it to itself and to the world. We believe that the mode of election proposed in this referendum is more likely to achieve this.

We wish to say to our fellow citizens that they should bear in mind, in casting their votes, that the central issue before them is simply stated. It is whether or not they wish to support an Australian republic in which the Monarch and Governor-General will be replaced by a president with the powers and functions presently held by the Governor-General. We believe that a substantial majority of Australians wish to see such an Australian head of state. We fear, however, that confusion has been generated in the course of the debate, and we regret some of the extravagant and, as we believe, wrong statements which have been made. It is important to remember what lies at the heart of this referendum. Australians now have as good an opportunity as we could hope for to achieve an Australian head of state along lines which are sensible, carefully considered, safe and practical.

Finally, we say this: whichever way the vote goes, there will be inevitable disappointment. This is understandable, but we believe that if this opportunity to achieve an Australian head of state is not taken, there is likely to be continuing discomfort and unease, and in particular discomfort for the reigning Monarch who, asking for nothing or seeking nothing, commands our deep respect.

10.5 A Way to a Republic

Editor's note

With the failure of the 1999 referendum on the Republic, Brennan decided to devote considerable energy to formulating detailed proposals as to how the Constitution could be amended making Australia a republic while at the same time maintaining the balance of power between the Parliament and the Executive. He delivered an address at Manning Clark House on 26 September 2006. He addressed this critical question: 'Can a constitutional solution be devised in order to ensure that a President's executive power is exercised as directed by the Government which is accountable to the Parliament?' He suggested: 'If the exercise of a President's power can be as effectively confined by law as the Governor-General's exercise of power is confined by convention, the manner of appointment or dismissal really becomes a second order question.'

In recent years the polls have shown that most Australians would like to have an Australian Head of State. We see ourselves as members of an independent polity, responsible for our own affairs and mature enough to sever our constitutional connection with the British Crown. That connection was essential for the constitutional birth of our nation but it is no longer necessary to its adult status. Yet, when the proposition that we become a republic was put to referendum, it was defeated. The monarchist minority enlisted the support of the republicans who favoured the direct election of a President and together they defeated the republicans favouring a Republic headed by a President elected by the Parliament.

The manner of electing a President was the focus of the referendum debate. On the one side there was insistence on the democratic right of the people themselves to choose their President; on the other there was the necessity to ensure that a President should not be free to exercise power adversely to the policy of the elected government.

To those people – especially constitutional lawyers and politicians – who regard responsible government in the Westminster tradition to be essential to our democratic system, the direct election model raised seemingly insuperable difficulties. A President who is directly elected would have a mandate – a political mandate – arguably superior to any mandate claimed by the parliamentary party forming the government. He or she would come to office only after a costly and hotly contested campaign in which political parties would field candidates for office who would be naturally in sympathy with their respective backers. A directly elected President, confident of his or her political mandate, would have little reason to observe the convention which has hitherto bound the Governor-General to act only upon ministerial advice (except when exercising the reserve powers), especially if the advice was coming from a government of a different political persuasion. Constitutional chaos would result. Moreover, if accession to the office of President had to be preceded by a nationwide political campaign, candidates of the calibre of some of our best Governors-General would never offer themselves for election. Indeed, it could be surmised that none of Australia's former Governors-General who had not previously been politicians would have been prepared to stand for office if the office were directly elected.

On the other hand, parliamentary election of a President was not so constitutionally dangerous. The proposed ability of the Prime Minister to terminate the appointment of a President would have been a strong incentive for the President to abide by the convention and that would be the safeguard of the Westminster system of responsible government. But there was considerable opposition to conferring more power on serving politicians to appoint our head of State.

Irrespective of the method of electing a President, the critical question which must be solved when Australia moves to a republic is how to control the exercise of Presidential power (including the reserve powers) if we are to preserve the system of responsible government – the system which grew out of the struggle for a constitutional monarchy.

When the Bill for the Commonwealth Constitution was debated in the House of Commons the future Lord Haldane said: 'The difference between the Constitution which this bill proposes to set up and the Constitution of the United States is enormous and fundamental. This bill is permeated through and through with the spirit of the greatest institution which exists in the Empire, ... – I mean the institution of responsible government, a government under which the Executive is directly responsible to – nay, is almost the creature of – the Legislature'. [1]

That system now depends chiefly on convention – ong established convention but only convention, not law. Sir Anthony Mason has explained the role of convention in the system of responsible government 'The principle that in general the Governor defers to, or acts upon, the advice of his Ministers .., is a convention, compliance with which enables the doctrine of ministerial responsibility to come into play so that a Minister or Ministers become responsible to Parliament for the decision made by the Governor in Council, thereby contributing to the concept of responsible government.'[2]

Informed by practical experience, former Governor McGarvie observed: 'The basic constitutional convention that binds the Governor-General to exercise powers as advised by Ministers of the elected Government is the essential link between the exercise of those powers and the sovereignty of the people'. [3]

At present, the convention of acting only on ministerial advice is sustained by a number of factors. It is supported by tradition and by contemporary constitutional practice. It is supported also by the Prime Minister's ability to secure the removal of the Governor-General by the Queen if the Governor-General should breach the convention. That is the ultimate pragmatic sanction if a Governor-General should refuse to act on ministerial advice. A sanction in that form would not be available if the Queen's role terminated. If a fixed term President is to be bound to exercise his or her power in accordance with ministerial advice, convention may not always be sufficient to sustain responsible government. Law, constitutional law, will be needed to ensure the orderly working of government.

Can a constitutional solution be devised in order to ensure that a President's executive power is exercised as directed by the government which is accountable to the Parliament? If the exercise of a President's power can be as effectively confined by law as the Governor-General's exercise of power is confined by convention, the manner of appointment or dismissal really becomes a second order question.

The convention to act and to act only on ministerial advice can be translated into a simple constitutional text which would govern the day to day exercise of a President's power. Leaving aside the problem of the reserve powers for a moment, a constitutional provision that the President must exercise the executive power of the Commonwealth in accordance with ministerial advice and only in accordance with that advice would avoid any risk of constitutional chaos, even if the President were directly elected. But the need to provide for an exercise of reserve powers would require some qualification of such a provision. These are powers which must be exercised very sparingly, as 11 November 1975 shows.

The reserve powers

These are powers exercised without or contrary to ministerial advice. The existence of reserve powers is essential to safeguard stable government and, in the last analysis, the rule of law. Reserve powers exist to protect the people and the *Constitution* against the possibility that a government may pursue an unlawful course of conduct, or refuse to enforce court orders or to ensure that the elements of our parliamentary democracy perform their intended function, especially if they show they are unwilling or unable to do so. The *Constitution* would be destroyed if an executive government were to act illegally or were to refuse to observe or enforce court orders. The *Constitution* would be imperilled if, for example, a government which had lost the confidence of the House of Representatives were to refuse to resign or to advise an election. When any such situation arises, it may be necessary for the Governor-General or a President to act without or even contrary to ministerial advice. Clearly, the occasions calling for an exercise of power without ministerial advice are very limited.

Various proposals have been advanced by advocates of a republic who recognise the necessity to control an exercise of the reserve powers by a fixed term President. A majority of the proposals accept the impossibility of defining exhaustively the occasions for the exercise of reserve powers but propose that the existing conventions should govern their exercise. There are two problems with this solution. First, if the *Constitution* were to provide that the existing conventions should have legal force, an exercise of a reserve power would be subject to High Court challenge. There would be an inevitable delay in mounting the challenge and in the delivery of a judgment. That delay could be damaging to the national interest. And there would be difficulty in defining some conventions although the High Court could no doubt develop a body of law as the occasion arises. Secondly, to prescribe the existing conventions as the governing norms would freeze those conventions and preclude the development of constitutional custom in the future. The first of these objections is avoided by another proposed solution, namely, to accept the existing conventions as no more than conventions and deny them the force of law. But that would leave a fixed term President legally free to refuse to follow the conventions – especially if the President had been elected with an individual political mandate. Some other solution must be found.

So extraordinary is the occasion for an exercise of reserve power that it should be exercised only when it is absolutely necessary to do so to preserve the rule of law and to ensure the effective operation of responsible government under the *Constitution*. The test of absolute necessity has been accepted both by Professor Winterton[4] and by former Governor McGarvie.[5] If the *Constitution* were to define the purposes which can legitimately be served by an exercise of the reserve powers and were then to limit the occasions of their exercise by a test of absolute necessity to achieve those purposes, a criterion would be established for governing the exercise of such powers whether the President is directly elected or not. That would safeguard the system of responsible government. But there would be one further problem to be overcome – litigation. How could the delay and uncertainty of any litigation brought to test the validity of an exercise of a reserve power be avoided?

Professor Winterton suggests that there might be a Council of State which the President would be bound to consult before exercising a reserve power. I respectfully agree with the creation of a Council of State, but not simply as a consultative body. To leave a President free to determine conclusively whether an occasion for exercising the reserve powers has arisen is to risk uncorrectable error and to leave the President exposed to criticism without institutional support. Moreover, the fact that the President had consulted the Council of State before exercising a reserve power would not protect the exercise from a High Court challenge to its validity. The delay involved, in litigation and in the delivery of a judgment might be quite damaging to the national interest. It would be preferable to forestall the prospect of a challenge.

There are some powers which can be exercised without ministerial advice and without the likelihood of challenge; for example, the power to dismiss a Prime Minister after the government is defeated in a general election. These can be easily defined. But there are other powers which should be exercised without ministerial advice only when it is absolutely necessary to exercise a power to ensure compliance with the law or the effective operation of responsible government. The reserve powers limited by this condition would cover the constitutionally defined powers to prorogue the Parliament, to dissolve the House of Representatives, to dissolve both Houses after the Senate has twice failed to pass a proposed law and to appoint and dismiss ministers (ss 5, 57, 64). Should the High Court be the arbiter of the absolute necessity to exercise any of those powers without or contrary to ministerial advice? Surely not, except perhaps in the most extreme cases. The delay and uncertainty of litigation might frustrate the very purpose of exercising a reserve power. In such an event, the national interest could be damaged and constitutional chaos might ensue. But if the people (and the President) cannot have the effective protection of a High Court order, some other mechanism must be found. A Council of State can provide it.

It would be for a President to form the opinion that an exercise of any reserve power is absolutely necessary, but a Council of State, immediately available to the President, could be empowered to certify – if it sees fit – that the President's intended exercise of a reserve power is valid. The certificate should itself be immune from question in any court.

Such a certificate would preclude effective curial challenge. Only if the President had acted without first obtaining such a certificate would it be possible to challenge an exercise of one of those reserve powers in the High Court.

But how should a Council of State be constituted? The Council should be small enough to allow speedy consultation in the event of an emergency. The issues with which the Council would have to deal would be highly political though within a legal context. I would suggest a Council of three, one of whom has served as a Governor-General or President or as a Governor of a State; the second of whom has served as a Chief Justice or Justice of the High Court or as a Chief Justice of a Superior Federal Court or the Supreme Court of a State; and the third of whom should have served in one or more of the offices just mentioned. To ensure that there is confidence reposed by the government in the Council of State I would suggest that they should be appointed by the President after consultation with the Prime Minister in the early days of any government – say within three months after the date on which the Parliament is summoned to meet after a general election.

Removal of a President then becomes another question. There is a clear precedent in the provisions of the *Constitution* dealing with the removal of Federal Judges. That could be adopted with appropriate alteration for removal of a President.

All these provisions can be incorporated into the *Constitution*. If incorporated, Australia could move safely to a Republic, whatever method of election of a President is desired, confident that a system of responsible government can be maintained.

That is at the Federal level. But what of the States?

Constitutional arrangements of the States

It is desirable that, if the *Constitution* were amended to achieve an Australian Republic, the States should move to a corresponding form of government in their constitutional arrangements. At present State Governors are appointed by the British Monarch on the nomination of the Premiers of the respective States. Each State could, if it wished, adopt a Constitution reflecting the Constitution proposed for the Commonwealth – that is, a Governor either directly elected or appointed by the Parliament whose powers are controlled by a mechanism similar to that proposed for the control of the President's powers. But as an alternative, each of the States which desired it could maintain its existing arrangements by placing the President in precisely the same situation as the British Monarch vis-a-vis the Government of the State. In other words, State Governors would be appointed by the President on the nomination of the Premier of the State who would have direct access to the President. The Premier would have the same ability to secure the removal of a Governor as the Premiers respectively enjoy under their current arrangements with the Palace.

It may be, of course, that one or two States would prefer to maintain a monarchical system. (If more than two States wished to maintain a monarchical system, any constitutional amendment for the Federation would fail under s 128). But should a minority of States be permitted to maintain a monarchical system when the majority of Federal electors and a majority of the electors in a majority of the States wish to move to a republican form of government? I think not. It would therefore be necessary to provide, that the President should have the same power and authority vis-a-vis the States as the British Monarch has under their existing Constitutions subject to a State's choosing of some other form of government of solely Australian responsibility. That can be effected by constitutional amendment, (including a Commonwealth power to amend the *Australia Act*).

Conclusion

If these arrangements were acceptable, the way would be open to create an Australian Republic, whichever manner of appointment of a President is preferred There is no need so to divide the community that controversy over the manner of appointing a President frustrates the majority's aspiration for an Australian Republic.

---

1. Cited *Amalgamated Society of Engineers v Adelaide Steamship Co Ltd (the Engineers Case)* (1920) 28 CLR 129, 147
2. See *FAI Insurances Ltd v Winneke* (1982) 151 CLR 342, 364
3. Richard E McGarvie, *Democracy — choosing Australia's republic* (Melbourne University Press, 1999) 61.
4. George Winterton, 'Reserve Powers in an Australian Republic' (1993) 12 (2) *University of Tasmania Law Review* 249, 256; 'The Resurrection of the Republic', Law and Policy Paper No 125, Centre for International and Public Law, Australian National University, 2001, 17. Both the majority and the minority of the Executive Government Advisory Committee to the Constitutional Commission endorsed a test similar to that of 'absolute necessity' — their formula was 'that there is no other method available to prevent': Final Report, Volume 1, 326
5. McGarvie (n 3) 61.

10.6 A Detailed Pathway to a Republic

Editor's note

After his retirement from the High Court, Brennan was appointed Scientia professor at the University of New South Wales Law School where he was able to spend considerable time with Professor George Winterton. They conducted seminars together and discussed the Republic idea at length. After Winterton's death in 2008, the University of Sydney instituted the George Winterton Memorial Lecture. The inaugural lecture had been delivered by Chief Justice Robert French. Brennan delivered the second lecture in the Banco Court, Supreme Court of NSW on 17 February 2011. Honouring Winterton, he set out in fine detail the legal requirements for change as first indicated in his 2006 Manning Clark address. He addressed three major issues: 'First, do we wish to retain our Parliamentary system of government with a Prime Minister whose government is responsible to the Parliament and depends on the confidence of a majority of the House of Representatives? Second, what is the preferable mode of selecting a President? And third, will the States be Republican if we have a Republican Commonwealth?'[1]

I acknowledge the Gadigal people of the Eora nation on whose traditional lands we are gathered this evening – a people to whom this City is irredeemably indebted. That acknowledgement is particularly fitting at the commencement of this, the George Winterton Memorial Lecture in succession to the Inaugural Lecture by the Honourable Robert French, Chief Justice of Australia. These two men, friends from their days at the University of Western Australia, were two of the founders of the Aboriginal Legal Service in that State and in later years contributed much in their respective ways to the elimination of the inequalities to which Aborigines have been subject in this country. For those who knew George, or read his work, he was the profound and uncompromising scholar. After I retired, I was privileged by his request to co-teach a class on the High Court, in the course of which I discovered the riches of his research into the institution from which I had recently departed and, as a virtual student, I benefitted from his erudition. He was a convinced Republican and, although our views about some aspects of a Republican *Constitution* were proximate but not co-incident, I am delighted to honour his memory by speaking about a pathway to an Australian Republic.

But why should we trouble? Australia is, as Donald Horne said, the lucky country. We have been born into, or have become citizens of, a free society under the rule of law, enjoying a comparatively relaxed way of life, a good educational system, a stable political democracy, an economy which survived the global financial crisis, a reasonable level of health care and a shared set of values which make for a peaceful and productive life in a rich, wild and beautiful land. With Dorothea Mackellar, most Australians would say 'Her beauty and her terror – The wide brown land for me!'[2] Living in such a peaceful country and enjoying such freedoms, why should we trouble ourselves about changes to our Constitution? Monarchists sum up this view with the aphorism 'If it ain't broke, don't fix it.'

But our *Constitution* – the principal charter of legislative, executive and judicial power whether federal or state – does need fixing. Our *Constitution* was given to us as a Schedule to the *Commonwealth of Australia Constitution Act 1900* (Imp), an Imperial Statute. Appropriately to our status in 1900 when Australia was colonial in sentiment and in law,[3] we were given the British Monarch as our Head of State by Covering Clause 2 which provided that references to the Queen in the Constitution 'shall extend to Her Majesty's heirs and successors *in the sovereignty of the United Kingdom*'. Yet, a century later, the United Kingdom has been found to be a 'foreign power' whose citizens are ineligible to sit in our Parliament.[4] It is both anachronistic and anomalous to maintain the sovereign of the United Kingdom, a foreign country, as our Head of State.

The sovereignty of the United Kingdom is determined by the *Act of Settlement 1701*, which opened the way to the union of England and Scotland three centuries ago. It was enacted in an age of male primogeniture and religious intolerance. Nowadays its provisions sit uneasily with notions of gender equality and with s 116 of our *Constitution*. That section guarantees that Australians may adhere to any religion of their choosing or to none,[5] yet the *Act of Settlement* requires the Australian Head of State to 'join in communion with the Church of England' and would be ineligible to be our Head of State if she or he 'shall profess the popish religion or shall marry a papist'. There are some suggestions that these provisions may be removed by the United Kingdom Parliament. But it is surely anomalous that Australia should have to rely on the legislative will of a foreign power to broaden the criteria for selection of our Head of State.[6] Our *Constitution* should accord with the reality of our political organization.

Proposals for change excite objections, just as there were objections to Federation. Then, free inter-colonial trade was a major objection that had to be resolved. That was an issue of policy but the objection to a Republic is largely political, social and emotional. Tony Abbott has said that '[t]he wellsprings of [the Monarchy's] appeal are instinctual as much as rational: more akin to loyalty to a team, solidarity within a family or faith in a church than they are to support for a policy. Deep down, they are the heart's reasons that reason doesn't know'.[7]

There are many Australians who are monarchists because they are proud of their British origins, of the values which we have inherited from British sources (not least a commitment to the rule of law), and who wish to keep continuing ties with Britain; many are attached to the symbolism of the Union Jack in our flag and are proud to have fought wars under the King's or Queen's colours; many feel a personal warmth towards Her Majesty and respect her lifetime devotion to duty as Monarch, wife and mother. These and similar factors lead many Australians to reject the Republican proposal as antithetical to their tradition and culture.

But there are many Australians who, while they share the same sentiments, view a move to a republic as a natural, perhaps inevitable, development – a Republic which owns its history, its culture and its institutions and gratefully acknowledges their origins, but a nation which should now bring its *Constitution* into conformity with its independent status in the world community and its destiny as a nation completely separate from the United Kingdom. Many of our indigenous citizens, proud of their culture and their historical custodianship of our country, understandably do not share Tony Abbott's affection for the Monarchy.

And, of course, there are many Australians who come from different traditions and cultures and who do not identify with the traditions and cultures of earlier generations of Anglo-Celtic Australians. For many of these Australians, the Monarchy has no significance except as an anachronistic element of our current form of government.

All of these views are deserving of respect but it is not possible, either by argument or the niceties of textual drafting, to reconcile opposing views which owe so much to familial history and sentiment and to differing visions of our national identity and destiny. Yet republicans might well respect the sentiments of the monarchists in choosing the appropriate time for Australia to become a republic.

The next occasion when Covering Clause 2 will remit the selection of our Head of State to the provisions of the *Act of Settlement* will be at the end of the reign of Her Majesty Queen Elizabeth II. Monarchists and many republicans hold Her Majesty in great respect and affection. It might well accord with majority opinion to select the end of the Queen's reign as the time for an Australian Republic. That would mark the affection and respect in which Australian people hold Her Majesty and deny to the *Act of Settlement* any further operation. But Australians will not assent to a Republic without understanding and agreeing to the form of government that would result from the constitutional change.

No simple change of 'Queen' to 'President' in the *Constitution* would allow a stable form of government to survive. To fashion a Republican *Constitution*, we need to understand how the present *Constitution* fashions the form of government we now enjoy. I assume that we would not want to alter the structures of the Parliament or the judiciary[8] but we would introduce an Australian President as the principal repository of executive power and our Head of State. There are three major issues to be addressed. First, do we wish to retain our Parliamentary system of government with a Prime Minister whose government is responsible to the Parliament and depends on the confidence of a majority of the House of Representatives? Second, what is the preferable mode of selecting a President? And, third, will the States be republican if we have a Republican Commonwealth?

To respond to these issues, I see a need for a small Constitutional Council to supervise the exercise of a President's reserve powers, an Electoral College to select a President, an amendment to s 106 to maintain the self-government of the States within a Republican Commonwealth and, finally, a repeal of Imperial laws including the Preamble and Covering Clauses of the *Constitution Act* in favour of a *Constitution* resting on the will and authority of the Australian people. I focus on the maintenance of responsible government, not on the mode of selecting a President, as the primary issue of substance.

The powers and functions of a President

At present, the Government is responsible to the Parliament for executive decisions, even though many of the most important decisions are taken in the name of the Governor-General. The Founding Fathers recognized[9] that responsible government rests on control of executive power by the elected government. This is effected by requiring the Governor-General to exercise executive power only on the advice of the Government in accordance with long established convention. Sir Anthony Mason has explained: 'The principle that in general the Governor defers to, or acts upon, the advice of his Ministers … is a convention, compliance with which enables the doctrine of ministerial responsibility to come into play so that a Minister or Ministers become responsible to Parliament for the decision made by the Governor in Council, thereby contributing to the concept of responsible government.'[10]

Informed by practical experience, former Governor Richard McGarvie observed: 'The basic constitutional convention that binds the Governor-General to exercise powers as advised by Ministers of the elected Government is the essential link between the exercise of those powers and the sovereignty of the people.'[11]

When the Governor-General acts on advice by ministers in the elected Government, the political consequence of such action is borne by the Government which is responsible to the Parliament. The convention is sustained by a long history and by contemporary practice. But convention may not always be sufficient to control a fixed term President – whether directly elected or not. A fixed term President could not be threatened with removal, a constraint on a recalcitrant Governor-General.[12] Although it has been suggested that existing conventions *should* bind a President, I venture to suggest that law is the preferable constraint to ensure that a President acts only on ministerial advice. But the law would have to discriminate among the powers presently exercised by the Governor-General.

These powers fall into three classes: first, the executive power of the Commonwealth which s 61 vests in the Queen to be exercised by the Governor-General;[13] second, powers vested in the Governor-General in Council;[14] and third, powers simply vested in the Governor-General. Convention requires that all these powers are exercised only on the appropriate governmental advice but, exceptionally, the powers vested simply in the Governor-General may be exercised without or even contrary to ministerial advice in particular circumstances and then the powers are known, somewhat loosely, as the reserve powers. Australians became familiar with the term when Prime Minister Whitlam was dismissed by the Governor-General on 11 November 1975. The major constitutional issue to be resolved if Australia should become a Republic is control of the reserve powers, a question addressed below.

The general executive power of the Commonwealth is the power needed by the Executive Government to administer the affairs of the Commonwealth. By vesting the executive power of the Commonwealth in the Queen, it was understood that the Queen's common law prerogative powers[15] supplied many of the powers needed for administration of the Commonwealth just as her prerogative supplied for the Executive Government of the United Kingdom many of the powers needed for the administration of the United Kingdom.[16]

The royal prerogative is of ancient origin. It is a 'special pre-eminence which the King hath over and above all other persons and out of the course of the common law'.[17] It extends 'to all powers, pre-eminences, and privileges, which the law giveth to the Crown'.[18] In *Cadia Holdings Pty Ltd v State of New South Wales,*[19] (where the issue was the classification of a mine producing gold and copper), the plurality judgment noted that the prerogative 'concerns the enjoyment by the executive government of preferences, immunities and exceptions peculiar to it and denied to the citizen[20] or, more specifically, of an exceptional right which partakes of the nature of property.'[21] The outer limits of the prerogative power have never been determined – historically the

King's powers waxed and waned and it is accepted that the full extent of the prerogative cannot be defined.[22]

The executive power conferred by s 61 includes as much of the prerogative powers of the Queen as 'is appropriate to the position of the Commonwealth under the Constitution and to the spheres of responsibility vested in it by the Constitution', to adopt the words of Mason J in *Barton v The Commonwealth.*[23] The plurality majority judgment in *Cadia*[24] said 'The executive power of the Commonwealth of which s 61 of the Constitution speaks enables the Commonwealth to undertake executive action appropriate to its position under the Constitution and to that end includes the prerogative powers accorded the Crown by the common law.'[25]

As the prerogative is vested in the Monarch personally, the introduction of a republic might arguably eliminate the prerogative and all the 'powers, pre-eminences and privileges" carried by the prerogative.[26] If the non-statutory executive power did not extend beyond the powers attributable to the prerogative, as George Winterton and Peter Gerangelos would hold,[27] the introduction of a Republic might arguably eliminate a major content of the executive power of the Commonwealth. However, the executive power contains more than the prerogative. It includes powers conferred by statute and certain non-prerogative capacities. In the *AAP Case*[28] Mason J held that s 61 confers on the Executive Government 'power to engage in enterprises and activities peculiarly adapted to the government of a nation and which cannot otherwise be carried on for the benefit of the nation'. I adopted this criterion in *Davis v The Commonwealth*[29] and, subject to certain qualifications not presently relevant, that was followed by the majority plurality judgment in *Pape.*[30] In the same case, French CJ may have gone further. He said:[31] 'Section 61 is an important element of a written Constitution for the government of an independent nation. While history and the common law inform its content, it is not a locked display cabinet in a constitutional museum. It is not limited to statutory powers and the prerogative. It has to be capable of serving the proper purposes of a national government.'[32]

Whatever be the scope of the executive power conferred by s 61 and whatever be the content derived from the prerogative, it would be desirable to provide that the scope and content of the executive power is unchanged by a transition to a Republic, though it be vested in and be exercisable by the President. A 'no change' provision would confirm that the law affecting the exercise of the executive power developed in the cases over the last century would be applicable to the new provisions. Thus, the common law conditions on the exercise of a prerogative power[33] would inform the law governing the exercise of a corresponding power under a republican successor to s 61.

The Executive Government's control of the general executive power would be maintained by an express provision that the President would act, but act only, on ministerial advice. That provision would extend to the function of the Commander in Chief of the defence forces under s 68.[34]

In a Republican *Constitution*, no change would be needed to the powers now vested in the Governor-General in Council.[35] They are expressly required[36] to be exercised on advice by the Executive Council and would be so exercised by a President. Apart from some obsolete provisions, these powers relate to the issuing of writs for the election of members of the House of Representatives,[37] the establishment of departments of State[38] and the appointment and removal of Justices of the High Court and other Courts created by the Parliament.[39]

Then there are powers vested in the Governor-General personally. Leaving aside some mechanical functions[40] and powers which have become obsolete, they are powers to appoint and to dismiss the Prime Minister and Ministers (ss 62 and 64), to prorogue the Parliament and to dissolve the House of Representatives (ss 5 and 28), and to dissolve both Houses of Parliament when section 57 permits a double dissolution. These are ordinarily exercised only on ministerial advice but, in particular circumstances, a Governor-General may exercise these powers without, or even contrary to, ministerial advice.

On 11 November 1975, Sir John Kerr exercised the reserve power under s 64 to dismiss Mr Whitlam and to appoint Mr Fraser as Prime Minister, then, acting on the advice of Mr Fraser, he dissolved both Houses of Parliament under s 57. The controversy which followed the dismissal demonstrates the importance of prescribing a mechanism for supervising the exercise of the reserve powers, especially if Australia adopts a Republican form of government.

Sir Harry Gibbs, in a paper written for Australians for Constitutional Monarchy, explained the need for reserve powers:

> According to the conventions, there are some powers which the Governor-General may exercise according to his own discretion, and without the advice, or even contrary to the advice, of the Ministry. These powers, which are rather misleadingly called 'reserve powers', are designed to ensure that the powers of the Parliament and the executive are operated in accordance with the principles of responsible government and representative democracy, or in other words, to ensure that the Ministry is responsible to Parliament and that the ultimate supremacy of the electorate will prevail. The reserve powers provide an essential check against abuse of power by

> the executive or by Parliament. In Australia, ... they fill a real need in relation to the executive.[41]

At present, if a Governor-General were minded to exercise a reserve power unjustifiably, the disincentive would be the risk of peremptory removal from office by the Queen on the advice of the Prime Minister. Sir John Kerr had to face that prospect on 11 November 1975 but, with the support of Sir Garfield Barwick, he attributed his authority to dismiss Mr Whitlam to a convention permitting the dismissal of a Prime Minister who could not secure supply. Professor Winterton, however, stated the convention differently, submitting that the reserve power of dismissal depended on the Prime Minister losing the confidence of the House of Representatives.[42]

Despite the uncertainty and controversy that the events of November 1975 created and the conflicting views of eminent constitutionalists about the content of relevant conventions, the 1998 Constitutional Convention proposed that undefined reserve powers and relevant conventions should continue to exist.[43] Accordingly, the 1999 Bill would have authorized the exercise of a reserve power by a President 'in accordance with the constitutional conventions relating to the exercise of that power',[44] accepting at the same time that the conventions should be allowed to evolve.[45] How would that formula have been applied to the Dismissal? In the United Kingdom, the convention is that dismissal is warranted only when the Commons (which controls supply) loses confidence in the Government,[46] but in Australia, where the Senate has ability to block supply, may the Barwick view of the convention be justified as an antipodean evolution of the United Kingdom convention? The question illustrates an objection to the proposition that reserve power can be controlled merely by reference to 'constitutional conventions'. It is too uncertain to be a sufficient control on the exercise of reserve power by a President who has a fixed term in office. Judicial supervision would not be available to enforce conventions unless they were enacted as law but that would fetter their practical utility. To quote Professor E A Forsey: 'To embody them in an ordinary law is to ossify them. To embody them in a *Constitution* is to petrify them.'[47]

A codification of the conventions was suggested by Dr H V Evatt[48] and was considered by the 1993 Republic Advisory Committee,[49] but, as Forsey points out: 'A law covering, with precision, all the possible circumstances which might call for the exercise of even a single reserve power, let alone the lot, is surely beyond the wit of even the most learned and imaginative draftsman.'[50]

If conventions were reduced to constitutional or statutory text, the text would be subject to judicial interpretation and enforcement would require exposure to judicial review involving inevitable delay and uncertainty. Delay and uncertainty are incompatible with the timely and effective exercise of reserve power in exceptional circumstances. Sir Harry Gibbs pointed out the dilemma: 'If the conventions are not enforceable by the courts, the President might ignore them, even though the *Constitution* stated that they continued; all those considerations which obliged a Governor-General as representative of the Monarch to observe the conventions, would not exist in the case of a President. On the other hand, if the courts can enforce observance of the conventions, the resulting delay and uncertainty could be very damaging in a time of crisis.'[51]

An exercise of a reserve power would ordinarily be required in a situation of urgency (and therefore without judicial intervention) in the event of any breach of the rule of law by the Executive Government – say, by withdrawing funds from consolidated revenue without an appropriation – or any breakdown in the operation of representative and responsible government – say, by a Prime Minister who, defeated in a no confidence vote of the House of Representatives, refused to resign or advise an election.

The problem is not to define the powers which a President may exercise, but the circumstances in which a reserve power may be exercised. It is difficult – indeed, impossible – to define in advance every eventuality which may attract an exercise of a particular power. Professor Forsey observed that the circumstances in which the reserve powers need to be exercised 'are not easy to set out in detail, comprehensively and with precision. They have a disconcerting way of popping up in utterly unforeseen, even unforeseeable, guise'.[52] The reason why the content of conventions is uncertain and fluctuating is that '[c]onventions are political, not legal: political in their birth, political in their growth and decay, political in their death, political in their sanctions.'[53] They are valuable indicia of political situations in which the exercise of reserve power may be needed, but they cannot be exhaustive. Codification of some conventions would be acceptable if the conventions are both clearly established and their application would not be reasonably open to factual controversy that might delay and frustrate the exercise of a reserve power.[54] But codification cannot exhaust all the circumstances in which a reserve power might justifiably be exercised.

George Winterton, conscious of the need for extraordinary circumstances to justify an exercise of reserve power, stated a criterion in general terms: is the exercise '*absolutely necessary* to preserve the rule of law and protect the operation of responsible government from abuse by the executive'?[55] Similar terms were used by the Executive Government Advisory Committee[56] to the Constitutional Commission – their formula being 'that there is no other method available to prevent'.

A President must have authority to exercise the reserve powers flexibly and efficiently in the political milieu,[57] but only when an exercise is absolutely necessary. The open textured phrase 'absolutely necessary' itself needs some mechanism for supervising its application to concrete political situations. That is why I suggest the need for a small council – a Constitutional Council to review any proposed exercise of a reserve power. The Council would determine whether the President has reasonable grounds to believe that it is absolutely necessary to exercise the reserve power proposed in order to ensure compliance with the general law or the effective operation of representative and responsible government under the Constitution. The Council must be capable of speedy consultation and be constituted by persons whose competence and impartiality are not open to question. It would be composed of three members who have previously served as Governor-General or President or as Chief Justice or a Justice of the High Court or as Chief Justice of a State or a federal superior Court. Any exercise by a President of a reserve power, if approved by the Constitutional Council, would be conclusively valid and non-justiciable. Decisions by the Constitutional Council would be non-justiciable. Judicial intervention would be eliminated except in the highly unlikely event of an exercise of a reserve power which the Constitutional Council would not approve. A negative response by the Constitutional Council would warrant judicial intervention to consider whether the President had acted beyond power.

If a republican President is to exercise the same powers and functions as the Governor-General now exercises and is constitutionally constrained to exercise those powers and functions in like manner, the method of selecting a President becomes a secondary question.

The Selection of a President

A prime Minister's ability to secure the appointment or removal of a Governor-General disappears with a transition to a Republic. And the defeat of the 1999 Referendum shows that the electorate will not allow a Prime Minister to appoint a President, even with the concurrence of the Leader of the Opposition and a majority of the Parliament[58] or to remove a President, even with the concurrence of a majority of the House of Representatives.[59] A President, as Head of State, vested with the powers we have discussed but constitutionally controlled in their exercise, should have a secure tenure for a fixed term, say, five years. The President should be removed from office only by vote of both Houses of Parliament on the ground of proved misbehaviour or incapacity.[60]

In the public mind, the preferable method of selecting a President is direct election. In 1999, republicans who were opposed to direct election feared that a directly elected President would be a threat to the stability of our representative and responsible system of government. George Winterton explained:[61]

> that a directly elected President will challenge government policy in speeches, perhaps addresses on television, and by meeting foreign and domestic leaders both at home and abroad, leaving both the Australian people and foreign governments confused regarding government policy, destabilising government, and jeopardising the political neutrality of the presidency. Barry Jones graphically described such a system as 'a car with two steering wheels',[62] and John Howard has warned that it 'would alter for all time the nature of our system of government. It would entrench rival centres of political power. ... [A]n Australian president, having a popular mandate, would feel infinitely more powerful in dealing with an incumbent Prime Minister than would any Governor-General, irrespective of the formal powers which might be given to that president.'[63]

These concerns would be diminished by constitutional constraints on the exercise of Presidential powers. Even so, direct election raises some difficult practical issues. How would candidates get to know, and get known by, voters in every part of the Commonwealth? Would voters in the more populous States prefer local candidates to the prejudice of candidates from smaller States? Could any citizen nominate a candidate, or would the power of nomination be limited? Curiously, a preference for direct election over Parliamentary appointment was said to avoid the creation of a 'politicians' President' but an Australia-wide election campaign for the Presidency would inevitably be funded and managed by party political machinery.

Another consequence of direct election would be the virtual impossibility of selecting eminent, non-political citizens as candidates for the Presidency. If we bear in mind recent Governors-General who have served with distinction in that office after achieving eminence in a non-political field – Sir Zelman Cowen, Sir Ninian Stephen, Sir William Deane, for example – we must doubt whether they would have engaged in an electoral campaign for the office. Popular election is designed to secure suitable candidates to implement policies, but that is not the business of an apolitical Head of State.

Although these are some of the disadvantages of direct election, they could be largely eliminated and the strong democratic desire for direct election could be accommodated by an Electoral College system which is a feature of other geographically large democracies: Germany, India and the United States. An Electoral College of modest size, popularly elected, could efficiently nominate and select a President. The College might be composed by two or four members chosen directly by the people of each State and one or two members chosen directly by the people of each mainland Territory. Members of Parliament could be excluded. An Electoral College could be elected in parallel with a general election for the House of Representatives. The Chief Justice of the High Court might be an ex officio member and chairperson of the College, responsible for convening the members and notifying the selection of the President.

Of course, that is not the only Electoral College model. A model suggested by the German and Indian Constitutions[64] would engage the members of both Houses of the Parliament sitting together with nominees of the State and Territory Parliaments. Although that model would be dominated by politicians, they would have been popularly elected to both the Parliament and the Electoral College. The Chief Justice could preside at College meetings.[65] A majority, say, 70% of those present and voting, could be specified to ensure that the government of the day did not control the process. As Parliamentarians generally are knowledgeable about and responsive to the views of their constituents and as the majorities in the two Houses of Parliament are not always, or usually, of the same political party, selections made by an Electoral College so constituted might well accord with popular expectations.

Whatever the composition of an Electoral College, its procedure could be prescribed by law susceptible to amendment in the light of experience. If desired, it could sit in camera. Unless we choose to have a nation-wide contest among public figures, managed and funded by political parties, there seems to be no practical way other than an Electoral College of giving effect to the popular vote.

The Monarchy and the States

There would be some support for the proposition that each State should determine for itself whether it wishes to adopt a Republican form of government.[66] This was proposed by George Winterton[67] and adopted in connection with the 1999 referendum.[68] The Monarchy is entrenched in some State constitutions and the State procedures which might lead to a Republican form of government vary from State to State.[69] In addition, s 7 of the *Australia Act 1986* (Cth) provides for State Governors to be representatives of the Queen. Prior to the 1999 referendum, however, the States laid the foundation for excluding the operation of s 7 by unanimously requesting the Commonwealth[70] to enact a law allowing each State to pass a law having that effect.[71]

It would be a curious constitutional mélange to maintain a republican Commonwealth with monarchical States. Sir Anthony Mason said it would be a 'constitutional monstrosity'.[72] The *Constitution*, as Quick and Garran observed, provided 'one grand scheme … in which the new national elements are blended harmoniously with the old provincial elements, thus producing a national plan of government having a Federal structure.'[73]

The States derive their constitutional status and powers from the Commonwealth *Constitution*[74] and from the *Australia Act 1986* (Cth) which was enacted pursuant to s 51 (xxxviii) of the *Constitution.*[75] The *Australia Act 1986* (Cth) lifted restrictions on the powers of the Parliaments of the States, terminated all responsibility of the United Kingdom government for the States[76] and conferred ultimate authority to assent to State legislation on the State Governor.[77] Section 7 of the *Australia Act* declared State Governors to be the Queen's representatives in the respective States but the only State function left to the Queen is a formal power to appoint and to terminate the appointment of the Governor – a power exercised on the advice of the Premier.[78] That formality can be discharged by a President without affecting the operation of a State constitution or the political authority of a Premier. There is no logical reason to retain a monarchical form of government for a State provided the transition leaves in place every other element of the State *Constitution*. What should be avoided is any attempt either to impose any change of substance on the Constitutions of the States or to affect the capacities which the States respectively enjoy to alter their Constitutions.[79] Section 7 of the *Australia Act* could be repealed and the Queen's formal power of gubernatorial appointment could be transferred to a republican President by a Commonwealth Act passed at the request of all State Parliaments pursuant to s 15(1) of the *Australia Act* and s 51 (xxxviii) of the *Constitution* – the procedure followed by the States in 1999 to exclude the operation of s 7 of the *Australia Act.*[80] If that unanimity is no longer achievable, the same result would follow from an appropriate amendment of s 106.[81] To allow voters, if they wish, to distinguish between the Commonwealth and the State governments, an amendment to s 106 could be submitted to a referendum separate from, but contemporaneously with, the referendum to introduce a Commonwealth republic.

There is a question whether an amendment to allow the repeal of s 7 of the *Australia Act* would attract the operation of paragraph 5 of s 128 which requires, in addition to the referendum majorities, a majority of voters in a

State to approve certain laws relating to the State. Stephen Gageler, supported by Jack Richardson, Gerard Carney and Anne Twomey, does not think that such an amendment would attract the operation of paragraph 5 of s 128.[82] However, McHugh and Gummow JJ in *McGinty v State of Western Australia*[83] made 'passing reference' to that paragraph as applicable to 'provisions of the Constitution in relation to a State'. This broad view of the paragraph might be only tentative. The former view seems preferable.

The Problem of Constitutional Amendment

The *Constitution* proper is a schedule to the Imperial *Constitution Act 1900.* The preamble to the *Constitution Act* recites an agreement to unite 'under the Crown of Great Britain and Ireland' and the Covering Clauses proclaim a monarchical form of government. As Sir Anthony Mason has commented to amend the *Constitution* while leaving those provisions in place would create 'a veritable constitutional camel'.[84] Despite the inelegance, however, an amendment of the *Constitution* introducing a Republic would be effective even if the Preamble and Covering Clauses remained.[85] The removal of monarchical references in the *Constitution* would leave the Preamble and the monarchical provisions of the Covering Clauses ineffectual. The 1999 Referendum Bill simply ignored those provisions. Nevertheless, it would be desirable as well as elegant to repeal the *Constitution Act* other than the Constitution proper. A succession of Imperial Statutes raises some interesting questions about the steps that need to be taken to achieve that repeal. These questions have been addressed in a series of scholarly articles which identify the problems and propose some solutions.[86] I list some of the sources to which I am indebted and, at the end of the written paper, I have appended some draft clauses which might be considered in drafting a Bill for a referendum to amend the *Constitution.*

In 1900, no repeal of the *Constitution Act* would have been possible: it would have been repugnant to a law of the Imperial Parliament and therefore 'absolutely void and inoperative' by force of s 2 of the *Colonial Laws Validity Act* 1865. That provision was repealed in its application to laws of the Commonwealth by s 2 of the *Statute of Westminster 1931*[87] but s 8 of that Statute declared that the repeal did not confer any power to repeal or alter the *Constitution Act*. By s 8 the Imperial Parliament denied Australia's power to repeal or alter the *Constitution Act* either by the referendum procedure under s 128 or by an ordinary law of the Commonwealth.

In 1986 the *Australia Act* was enacted here[88] and in the United Kingdom[89] 'to bring constitutional arrangements affecting the Commonwealth and the

States into conformity with the status of the Commonwealth…as a sovereign, independent and federal nation.' Section 1 provided that thereafter no United Kingdom statute could extend to the Commonwealth or the States or Territories. Section 15 provided for the repeal or amendment of the *Statute of Westminster* and of the *Australia Act* itself by an Act of the Commonwealth Parliament, enacted *either* at the request or with the concurrence of all State Parliaments[90] *or* in exercise of a power conferred on the Parliament by a s 128 amendment to the *Constitution.*[91] Thus, the Commonwealth Parliament acquired the power to remove the last legislative Imperial fetters on Australian legislative power, dependent on either the unanimous approval of State Parliaments or the approval of the necessary majorities of the Australian people to carry a referendum. Once the *Statute of Westminster* or at least s 8 thereof is repealed in either of the ways provided by s 15 of the *Australia Act*, the preamble and the Covering Clauses of the *Constitution Act* can be repealed and any provisions having continuing relevance to our *Constitution* (for example, Covering Clause 5) can be translated into the *Constitution* proper. There seems to be a consensus about the sufficiency of that procedure.[92] Repeal of s 8 also opens the way to empowering the Parliament to repeal any or all Imperial Acts applicable to Australia, consistently with s 2 (2) of the *Statute of Westminster*.

Another view, endorsed by the 1988 Constitutional Commission, is that, once it is recognized that the Commonwealth is a 'a sovereign, independent and federal nation' and that the British Parliament has renounced authority to legislate for Australia, s 8 of the *Statute of Westminster* no longer limits the scope of the amendments which can be effected by the referendum procedure under s 128, that section being sufficient by itself to '[encompass] all matters relating to our mode of governance'.[93] In *Marquet's Case* a majority of the Court observed that constitutional arrangements in Australia have changed in fundamental respects and that 'constitutional norms, whatever be their historical origins, are now to be traced to Australian sources'.[94] But the *Australia Act* is an Australian source and it affirms the operation of the *Statute of Westminster*, including s 8, unless the Statute is amended as s 15 provides. With respect, the view of the Constitutional Commission must be of doubtful validity.

If repeal of s 8 of the *Statute of Westminster* is desirable before a Republican *Constitution* comes into effect, a Referendum Bill should include two provisions in addition to those prescribing the Republican form of government. One provision would authorize the Parliament under s 15(3) of the *Australia Act* to repeal s 8; the other would delay the coming into effect of the republican provisions until the Parliament had repealed s 8.

When s 8 is repealed, the present preamble and Covering Clauses of the *Constitution Act* should be repealed and a new preamble reciting the sovereignty of the Australian people as the source and sustaining force of the Australian *Constitution* should be inserted. This is no novelty. In *Kirmani's Case* Deane J said that 'whatever be the theoretical explanation, ultimate authority in this country lies with the Australian people'[95] and, in *ACTV,* Mason CJ recognized 'that ultimate sovereignty reside[s] in the Australian people'.[96] This assertion of Australian authority is accepted in a number of High Court judgments.[97] It accords with the de facto independence of our polity and the independent, egalitarian ethos of the Australian people. Geoffrey Lindell contends that the will and authority of the Australian people give the *Constitution* its 'legally binding and fundamental character' and it 'coincides with popular understanding'.[98] It is time that we assumed constitutional authority over our own *Constitution*, repealing the *Constitution of Australia Act 1900* (Cth) except for the *Constitution* proper and declaring that we, the Australian people, give to ourselves our *Constitution*. To that end, I would like to see a new beginning in terms like these:

'We, the people of Australia –

- *Recognizing* the dignity, culture and spirituality of our Aboriginal and Torres Strait Islander citizens and their historical occupancy and custodianship of our lands and seas;
- *Conscious* of the contributions to our national life made by Australians of different ethnic origins, nationalities, religions, traditions and cultures;
- *Proud* of our democratic system of government under the rule of law;
- *Respecting* the inherent dignity of every person and
- *Willing* to participate in the building and maintenance of international peace;

Confirm and give to ourselves this Constitution.'

Thus we would affirm our constitutional independence from all Imperial laws, our freedom to mould our Constitution to the exigencies of our future and our reliance on the genius of our people to shape the character of our nation. For me and, I would hope, for many Australians this would reflect our grateful acceptance of our history and of our present multicultural society, our tolerance, our outward vision and our pride in a free and confident nation.

Suggested clauses for consideration in Bills to amend the Constitution:

The Commonwealth Bill

The Parliament of Australia, with the approval of the electors, as required by the Constitution, enacts:

1 Short title

This Act may be cited as the *Constitution Alteration (Establishment of Republic – Commonwealth) 2011*

2 Schedules

The Constitution is altered as set out in the Schedules

3. Commencement:

1) Schedule 1 comes into force when this Act receives Royal assent.

2) Schedule 2 comes into force either –

a) on the repeal of section 8 of the Statute of Westminster, or

b) on the termination of the reign of Her Majesty Queen Elizabeth II whichever is the later.

Schedule 1—Amendment of the Constitution

Section 51

Insert subsection (xxxviiA):

"the repeal of –

i) section 8 of the Statute of Westminster;

ii) the *Commonwealth of Australia Constitution Act* other than the Constitution the repeal to come into force when Schedule 2 of the *Constitution Alteration (Establishment of Republic – Commonwealth) 2011* comes into force;

iii) section 7 of the *Australia Act* 1986 (Commonwealth and United Kingdom) the repeal to come into force when Schedule 2 of the *Constitution Alteration (Establishment of Republic – Commonwealth) 2011* comes into force;"

Schedule 2—Amendment of the Constitution

Short title, Preamble and Governing Clauses

a) Insert after the words "The Constitution" the words "of the Commonwealth of Australia"

b) Delete the words "The Schedule" after the words: "Chapter VIII.- Alteration of the Constitution" and insert in lieu thereof the following:

'We, the people of Australia –

- *Recognizing* the dignity, culture and spirituality of our Aboriginal and Torres Strait Islander citizens and their historical occupancy and custodianship of our lands and seas;
- *Conscious* of the contributions to our national life made by Australians of different ethnic origins, nationalities, religions, traditions and cultures;
- *Proud* of our democratic system of government under the rule of law;
- *Respecting* the inherent dignity of every person and
- *Willing* to participate in the building and maintenance of international peace;

Confirm and give to ourselves this Constitution:

Covering Clauses:

A. This Constitution and all laws made by the Parliament of the Commonwealth under the Constitution, shall be binding on the courts, judges, and people of every State and of every part of the Commonwealth, notwithstanding anything in the laws of any State; and the laws of the Commonwealth shall be in force on all ships whose first port of clearance and whose port of destination are in the Commonwealth.

B. *The Commonwealth* shall mean the Commonwealth of Australia established on 1 January 1901.

C. *The States* shall mean the States of New South Wales, Queensland, Tasmania, Victoria, Western Australia, and South Australia, and such territories as may be admitted into or established by the Commonwealth as States; and each of such parts of the Commonwealth shall be called a *State*.

D. New Offices of State:

The President

1) The President is the Head of the Commonwealth and must be a citizen

of the Commonwealth capable of being chosen as a member of the House of Representatives;

2) The first President shall be the Governor-General in office when this section comes into force and shall hold office for a term of 2 years thereafter.

3) The President shall hold office for a term of 5 years from the date on which he enters upon his or her office but is eligible for re-election once and shall continue in office after the expiration of his or her term until his or her successor enters upon his or her office

4) The President shall hold no other office of profit

5) The President shall not be removed from office except on the certificate of the President of the Senate and the Speaker of the House of Representatives stating that both Houses in the same session have resolved to remove the President on the ground of proved misbehaviour or incapacity

6) The President may resign office by writing addressed to the President of the Senate.

7) In the temporary absence or inability of the President to discharge his or her functions, the senior State Governor shall assume the duties and functions of the President.

The Electoral College

1) The President shall be elected by the members of the Electoral College composed of –

    a. The Chief Justice of the High Court who shall preside at meetings of the Electoral College;

    b. Two members chosen by the people of each State

    c. One member chosen by the people of each mainland Territory

2) If any chosen member shall be unavailable to take part in the proceedings of the Electoral College, the person next most favoured in the ballot which chose the unavailable member shall take that member's place.

3) The Electoral College shall meet to elect a President not less that 60 nor more than 90 days prior to the expiration of the term of a President or at any time in order to fill an occasional vacancy in the office

4) The procedures for choosing members of the Electoral College and the procedures of the Electoral College may be prescribed by law

The Council of State

1) There shall be a Council of State to advise the President in the exercise of power under s 61(3) of the Constitution.

2) The Constitutional Council shall consist of three citizens –

a. one of whom has served as Governor-General or President of the Commonwealth of Australia or as a Governor of a State

b. one of whom has served as Chief Justice or as a Justice of the High Court of Australia or as Chief Justice of a superior federal court or of the Supreme Court of a State; and

c. one of whom has served in one or more of the offices referred to in paragraphs (a) and (b) of this subsection.

3) Subject to subsection (4) members of the Constitutional Council shall remain in office until their successors are appointed in accordance with paragraph (5)(a).

4) A member of the Constitutional Council –

may resign office by writing under her or his hand delivered to the President;

shall not be removed except by the President in Council, on an address from both Houses of the Parliament in the same session, praying for such removal on the ground of proved misbehaviour or incapacity.

(5) (a) The President, after consultation with the Prime Minister, shall appoint members of the Constitutional Council within 3 months after the day on which the House of Representatives is summoned to meet after a general election;

(b) If, at any time prior to the issuing of writs for a general election, there be a casual vacancy in the Constitutional Council, the President, after consultation with the Prime Minister, shall appoint an eligible person to fill that vacancy.

Section 2.

Delete s 2.

3. Section 51.

Insert after subsection (xxxviiA)(iii):

(iv) "the Australia Act 1986 (UK) and the Statute of Westminster 1931, and

(v) any other laws enacted by the Parliament of the United Kingdom in so far as they are part of the law of the Commonwealth, a State or a Territory:"

4. Section 61.

Delete Section 61 and insert in lieu thereof

1) The executive power of the Commonwealth including the prerogative power and all other immunities, powers, privileges and functions which were vested in or exercisable by the Queen or by the Governor-General before the *Constitutional Alteration (Establishment of Republic – Commonwealth) 2011* came into force are vested in and may be exercised by the President.

2) Subject to subsection (3), the President shall exercise or refrain from exercising any power conferred upon him or her by this Constitution only in accordance with advice tendered to the President by the Federal Executive Council, the Prime Minister or, in the case of a power conferred by or under an Act of the Parliament, a Minister of State responsible for the administration of the Act.

3) The President may, without the advice prescribed by subsection (2) –

a) following the death or resignation of a Prime Minister, appoint as Prime Minister the person who, in the opinion of the President, is most likely to form a government which will have the confidence of the House of Representatives;

b) decline to prorogue the Parliament, to dissolve the House of Representatives or to dissolve the Senate and the House of Representatives simultaneously if the President is not satisfied that–

i. there are reasonable grounds to warrant the prorogation or dissolution; or

ii. the Parliament has granted or will grant sufficient funds to enable the administration of the Commonwealth during the period ending when the Parliament might next meet if the President were to prorogue the Parliament, to dissolve the House of Representatives or to dissolve the Senate and the House of Representatives simultaneously on advice tendered in accordance with subsection (2);

(d) exercise or refrain from exercising a power conferred by section 5, 28, 57 or 64 if the President is of the opinion on reasonable grounds that the proposed exercise of power is absolutely necessary to ensure compliance with the general law or the effective operation of representative and responsible government under this Constitution.

4) In the exercise of power and the formation of opinions under this Constitution, the President and the Constitutional Council shall have regard to the conventions affecting those functions when performed by the Governor-General before the Commonwealth of Australia became a Republic and to any conventions subsequently established.

5) A certificate issued by the Constitutional Council that there are reasonable grounds for the President's opinion under paragraph (3)(d) is conclusive evidence of the existence of such grounds and that certificate shall not be called in question in any court.

Section 64

Delete Section 64 and insert in lieu thereof:

The President may appoint a Prime Minister and other Ministers of State for the Commonwealth to administer such departments of State of the Commonwealth as the President in Council may establish.

Subject to this Constitution, the Prime Minister and other Ministers of State holding office when the Republic commenced shall continue in their respective offices.

The Prime Minister holds office until he or she resigns office by notice to the President or is dismissed by the President under this Constitution.

Ministers of State other than the Prime Minister hold their respective offices during the pleasure of the President but no Minister of State shall hold office for a longer period than three months unless the Minister is or becomes a Senator or a member of the House of Representatives.

The Parliament of Australia, with the approval of the electors, as required by the Constitution, enacts:

Short title

This Act may be cited as the *Constitution Alteration (Establishment of Republic- States) 2011*

2. Schedules

The Constitution is altered as set out in the Schedule

3. Commencement:

The Schedule comes into force when Schedule 2 of the *Constitution Alteration (Establishment of Republic – Commonwealth) 2011* comes into force.

The Schedule – Amendment of the Constitution

Section 106

a) Renumber the paragraph as subsection (1)

b) Delete the words: "as at the establishment of the Commonwealth" and insert in lieu thereof: "as at the coming into force of the *Constitution Alteration (Establishment of Republic – State) 2011";*

c) Insert subsection (2) to read: "Notwithstanding the repeal under s 51(xxxviiA)(v) of any law enacted by the Parliament of the United Kingdom, the provisions repealed in so far as they were part of the law of a State immediately prior to the repeal shall be deemed to be a law of the State unless and until the Parliament of the State shall otherwise provide";

d) Insert subsection (3) to read: "A law made by the Parliament of a State under subsection (2) respecting the constitution, powers or procedures of its Parliament shall be of no force or effect –

   i. unless it is made in such manner and form as may be required by a law made by that Parliament;

   ii. insofar as it purports to confer or vest any power, privilege or function in the Sovereign of the United Kingdom or of any other foreign power;

e) Insert subsection (4) to read: "The powers, immunities, privileges and functions which were vested in or exercisable by the Queen or by the Governor immediately prior to the *Constitution Alteration (Establishment of Republic – State) 2011* coming into force are vested in and may be exercised by the Governor";

f) Insert subsection (5) to read: "Notwithstanding section 61(2) the power to appoint and the power to terminate the appointment of a Governor of a State is vested in the President acting on the advice of the Premier of the State.'

---

1. This address was first published in (2011) 13 (1) *Constitutional Law and Policy Review* 2-17.

2. Excerpt from *My Country:* 'I love a sunburnt country, A land of sweeping plains, Of ragged mountain ranges, Of droughts and flooding rains. I love her far horizons, I love her jewel-sea, Her beauty and her terror – The wide brown land for me!'

3. See *China Ocean Shipping Co v South Australia* (1979) 145 CLR 172, 183 (Barwick CJ).

4. See *Sue v Hill* (1999) 199 CLR 462.
5. See *Church of the New Faith v Commissioner of Payroll Tax (Vict)* (1983) 154 CLR 120, 132.
6. Assuming that any amendment to the *Act of Settlement* could affect the selection of an Australian Head of State: See the discussion in the Final Report of the Constitutional Commission (Vol 1, 1988) 80-82.
7. Neville Bonner Memorial Lecture, Australians for Constitutional Monarchy 11th National Conference, 21 November 2010.
8. Any proposed reforms of the Parliament or the judiciary should be considered on their merits, separate from the proposal for a Republic.
9. See, for example, the speeches of Mr Barton on 19 April 1897 (*Official Record of the National Australasian Convention Debates, First Session: Adelaide,* 910-913), and on 20 September 1897 (*Official Record of the National Australasian Convention Debates,* Second Session: Sydney 903-912).
10. See *FAI Insurances Ltd v Winneke* (1982) 151 CLR 342, 364.
11. Richard E McGarvie, *Democracy – choosing Australia's republic* (Melbourne University Press, 1999) 61.
12. The 1999 Referendum proposal maintained governmental control of Presidential powers by conferring the power to terminate the appointment of the President on the Prime Minister, who is presently empowered to effect the termination of a Governor-General's appointment by advising the Queen to do so. Sir Zelman Cowen, Sir Anthony Mason and I publicly acknowledged that the change would be effective to preserve responsible government even if the proposal was not ideal. The rejection in 1999 of the Prime Ministerial power to terminate excludes it from current consideration.
13. Professor Winterton accepted that, at least since 1926, s 61 should be read as 'exercisable only by the Governor-General': see George Winterton, *Parliament, the Executive and the Governor-General: A Constitutional Analysis* (Melbourne University Press, 1983) 51.
14. Section 63. 'These are powers which the framers of the *Constitution* considered to be purely statutory, or which had, by custom or statute, been detached from the prerogatives of the Crown': Final Report of the Constitutional Commission (1988) Volume 1, 342, par 5.147. But cf par 5.148.
15. See *The Commonwealth & the Central Wool Committee v Colonial Combing, Spinning and Weaving Co Ltd ('the Wooltops Case')* (1922) 31 CLR 421, 437, 461; *The King v Hush; Ex parte Devanny* (1932) 48 CLR 487, 511; *Johnson v Kent* (1975) 132 CLR 164, 174.
16. See *Federal Commissioner of Taxation v Official Liquidator of E O Farley Ltd* (1940) 63 CLR 278, 304 (Dixon J); and *Pape v Federal Commissioner of Taxation* (2009) 238 CLR 1, 89 [233] (Gummow, Crennan and Bell JJ).
17. See *Blackstone's Commentaries on the Laws of England* 239 cited by Chitty *A Treatise on The Law of the Prerogatives of the Crown* (Butterworth & Son, 1820) 4.
18. See *Coke on Littleton, 90b.*
19. (2010) 242 CLR 195, 223.
20. See *Pape v Federal Commissioner of Taxation* (2009) 238 CLR 1, 83 [214].
21. See *Federal Commissioner of Taxation v Official Liquidator of E O Farley Ltd* (1940) 63 CLR 278, 320-321*; Attorney-General (NSW) v Butterworth & Co (Aust) Ltd* (1938) SR (NSW) 195, 246-247.
22. In *Burmah Oil Co (Burmah Trading) Ltd v Lord Advocate* [1965] AC 75, 99; Lord Reid

observed '[i]t is not easy to discover and decide the law regarding the royal prerogative and the consequences of its exercise.' And Nourse LJ in the English Court of Appeal *R v Secretary of State for the Home Department; Ex parte Northumbria Police Authority* [1989] QB 26, 56 observed that – 'It has not at any stage in our history been practicable to identify all the prerogative powers of the Crown. It is only by a process of piecemeal decision over a period of centuries that particular powers are seen to exist or not to exist, as the case may be. From time to time a need for more exact definition arises'.

23. (1974) 131 CLR 477, 498.
24. (2010) 242 CLR 195, 226.
25. See *Barton v The Commonwealth* (1974) 131 CLR 477, 498; *Pape v Federal Commissioner of Taxation* (2009) 238 CLR 1, 61-62.
26. See per Dixon J in *Federal Commissioner of Taxation v Official Liquidator of E O Farley Ltd* (1940) 63 CLR 278, 304.
27. 'Parliament, the Executive, the Governor-General and the Republic: The George Winterton Thesis' in H P Lee and Peter Gerangelos (eds) *Constitutional Advancement in a Frozen Continent* (Federation Press, 2009) 189.
28. (1975) 134 CLR 338, 397.
29. (1988) 166 CLR 79, 93.
30. See *Pape v Federal Commissioner of Taxation* Gummow (2009) 238 CLR 1, 87 (Gummow, Crennan and Bell JJ).
31. (2009) 238 CLR 1, 60 [127]
32. Note also that Hayne and Kiefel JJ (2009) 238 CLR 1, 119 held that 'the ambit of the Commonwealth executive power is to be identified having regard to the whole of the constitutional structure'. The wide construction given to s 61 in *Pape* has been criticised: see Anne Twomey, 'Pushing the Boundaries of the Executive Power – *Pape*, the Prerogative and Nationhood Powers" (2010) 34 (1) *Melbourne University Law Review* 313.
33. See, for example, *Attorney General v De Keyser's Royal Hotel Ltd* [1920] AC 508 and *Burma Oil Co (Burma Trading) Ltd v Lord Advocate* [1965] AC 75.
34. See *Lane v Morrison* (2009) 239 CLR 230, 249-250; and see Volume 1, 346, par 5.175 of the Final Report of the Constitutional Commission (1988).
35. Sections 32, 33, 64, 67, 70, 83 and 103.
36. Section 63.
37. Sections 32 and 33.
38. Section 64.
39. Section 72. A power to appoint members of the Inter-State Commission also requires the advice of the Federal Executive Council: s 103.
40. See sections 7, 15, 17, 19, 21, 35, 37, 42.
41. Reserve Powers of the Governor-General and the Provisions For Dismissal', 21 August 1995.
42. George Winterton, '1975: The Dismissal of the Whitlam Government' in H P Lee and George Winterton (eds) *Australian Constitutional Landmarks* (Cambridge University Press, 2003) 229, 243–245.
43. 'Final Resolutions of the Constitutional Convention, Canberra 2 – 13 February 1998' (1998) 9 (1) *Public Law Review* 55, 56; See comment by Sir Harry Gibbs 'Some thoughts on the Constitutional Convention (1998) 21(3) *University of New South Wales Law Journal* 882, 884.

44. Section 59 as proposed in Schedule 1 to the Constitution to be inserted by Clause 3 of the Bill.
45. Paragraph 8 of proposed Schedule 2 to the Constitution (inserted by Clause 3 of the Bill).
46. See George Winterton, '1975: The Dismissal of the Whitlam Government' in H P Lee and George Winterton (eds), *Australian Constitutional Landmarks* (Cambridge University Press, 2003) 229, 244 and *New South Wales v Bardolph* (1934) 52 CLR 455, 509; See also *Egan v Willis* (1998) 195 CLR 424, 453 and 503.
47. See *Evatt and Forsey on the Reserve Powers* (Legal Books, 1990) xc.
48. H V Evatt, *The King and His Dominion Governors* (Frank Cass and Co, 2nd ed, 1967) 7-9, 285.
49. Report, Volume 1, 95 ff.
50. See *Evatt and Forsey on the Reserve Powers* (Legal Books, 1990) lxxxiii.
51. Sir Harry Gibbs, 'Some Thoughts on the Constitutional Convention' (1998) 21(3) *University of New South Wales Law Journal* 882, 884.
52. See *Evatt and Forsey on the Reserve Powers* (Legal Books, 1990) lxxxiii; Professor Forsey recalled that in 1985 'an Australian Constitutional Convention [in Brisbane] recognized and declared 18 "principles and practices" which "should be observed as Conventions in Australia" governing the exercise of reserve powers "exerciseable through the Governor-General"' but then demonstrated their inadequacy in a number of practical situations.
53. See *Evatt and Forsey on the Reserve Powers* (Legal Books, 1990) p lxxxix.
54. See George Winterton, *The Resurrection of the Republic,* Law and Policy Paper No 15, Centre for International and Public Law (Federation Press, 2001) 17.
55. George Winterton, 'Reserve Powers in an Australian Republic' (1993) 12 *University of Tasmania Law Review* 249, 256; George Winterton, *The Resurrection of the Republic*, Law and Policy Paper No 15, Centre for International and Public Law, (Federation Press, 2001) 17.
56. Final Report of the Constitutional Commission, Volume 1, 26, para 5.66.
57. The Canadians experience of prorogation in 2008-2009 illustrates both the importance of timing in the exercise of reserve power and the difficulty in reaching agreement on the content of relevant conventions. For an Australian example, see George Winterton, 'The Constitutional Position of Australian State Governors' in H P Lee and George Winterton (eds) *Australian Constitutional Perspectives* (Law Book Co, 1992) 274, 304-335.
58. Bill for *Constitution Alteration (Establishment of Republic) 1999*, s 60 in Schedule 1.
59. Bill for *Constitution Alteration (Establishment of Republic) 1999*, s 62 in Schedule 1.
60. Analogously to the procedure for removing Federal judges under s 72(ii).
61. George Winterton, *The Resurrection of the Republic,* Law and Policy Paper No 15, Centre for International and Public Law (Federation Press, 2001) 13.
62. B Jones, '*Framing a New Australian Republic*', paper presented at Australian Academy of the Humanities, 30th Anniversary Symposium, Canberra, 3 November 1999 (unpaginated).
63. J Howard, 'Mr Keating's Mirage on the Hill: How the Republic, Like the Cheshire Cat, Came and Went', in *Upholding the Australian Constitution*, Vol 3: Proceedings of the Third Conference of The Samuel Griffith Society (1994) 115, 130-131.
64. Article 54 of the Constitution of the Federal Republic of Germany; ss 54 and 55 of the Indian Constitution. Both of these Constitutions added votes from the Legislatures of the Lander or the States to the votes of the members of the national Parliament. See also Professor Cheryl Saunders, 'Beyond Minimalism' in Sarah Murray (ed) *Constitutional Perspectives on an Australian Republic* (Federation Press, 2010) 54, 77.

65. It is customary now for the Chief Justice of the High Court to preside over the swearing in of the Members of the House of Representatives after an election.

66. Gerard Carney, *The Constitutional Systems of the Australian States and Territories* (Cambridge University Press, 2006) 339; Anne Twomey, 'One In, All In – The Simultaneous Implication of a Republic at Commonwealth and State Levels' in Sarah Murray (ed) *Constitutional Perspectives on an Australian Republic* (Federation Press, 2010) 20, 38, 40.

67. George Winterton, *Monarchy to Republic: Australian Republican Government* (Oxford University Press, 1986) 103-105.

68. See Janine Pritchard, 'Monarchical States under a Commonwealth Republic' in Sarah Murray (ed) *Constitutional Perspectives on an Australian Republic* (Federation Press, 2010) 106, 107.

69. Anne Twomey, 'One In, All In – The Simultaneous Implication of a Republic at Commonwealth and State Levels' in Sarah Murray (ed) *Constitutional Perspectives on an Australian Republic* (Federation Press, 2010) 20, 24.

70. As provided for in s 15(1) and (2) of the *Australia Act 1986* (Cth).

71. The several Acts were entitled the *Australia Act (Request) Act 1999* (Cth) and were intended to add to s 7 of both the UK and Commonwealth versions of the *Australia Act 1986* (Cth) subsections authorizing the State Legislature to exclude the operation of the earlier subsections of s 7. See, for example, Act No 33 of 1999 (Vic).

72. Sir Anthony Mason, 'Constitutional Issues relating to the Republic as they Affect the States' (1998) 21(3) *University of New South Wales Law Journal* 750, 756; See the collection of descriptions listed by Janine Pritchard in 'Monarchical States under a Republican Commonwealth' in Sarah Murray (ed) *Constitutional Perspectives on an Australian Republic* (Federation Press, 2010) 106.

73. John Quick and Robert Garran, *The Annotated Constitution of the Commonwealth* (1901, 1976 Reprint, Legal Books) 930.

74. See *McGinty v Western Australia* (1996) 186 CLR 140, 171-173, 189, 208-209, 216, 251 and cases there cited: *Victoria v The Commonwealth* (1971) 122 CLR 353, 371; *New South Wales v The Commonwealth* (1975) 135 CCLR 337, 372; *China Ocean Shipping Co v South Australia* (1979) 145 CLR 172, 182; Also see *Yougarla v Western Australia* (2001) 207 CLR 344, 369; John Quick and Robert Garran, *The Annotated Constitution of the Commonwealth* (1901, 1976 Reprint, Legal Books) 930; cf *Western Australia v Wilsmore* [1981] WAR 179.

75. See *Port MacDonnell Professional Fishermen's Association Inc. v South Australia* (1989) 168 CLR 340, 381; *Attorney-General (WA) v Marquet* (2003) 217 CLR 545, 571.

76. Section 10.

77. Section 9.

78. Section 7(3).

79. See Anne Twomey, 'One In, All In – The Simultaneous Implication of a Republic at Commonwealth and State Levels' in Sarah Murray (ed) *Constitutional Perspectives on an Australian Republic* (Federation Press, 2010) 20, 37. They are immune from Commonwealth legislative impairment of their structure or capacity to function: *Melbourne Corporation v The Commonwealth* (1947) 74 CLR 31, 56, 60, 66, 74, 82; *The Commonwealth v Tasmania ('Tasmanian Dam Case')* (1983) 158 CLR 1, 139-140, 213-215, 280-281; *Queensland Electricity Commission v The Commonwealth* (1985) 159 CLR 192, 217-218, 226-227, 231, 232, 248, 260; *Re Australian Education Union; Ex parte Victoria* (1995) 184 CLR 188, 230-232. 248-249; *McGinty v Western Australia* (1996) 186 CLR 140, 173; *Austin v*

The Commonwealth (2003) 215 CLR 185; *Clarke v Commissioner of Taxation* (2009) 83 ALJR 1044.

80. See footnote 70; See also Gerard Carney, *The Constitutional Systems of the States and Territories* (Cambridge University Press, 2006) 331.

81. Section 15(3) of the *Australia Act 1986* (Cth) avoids the possibility that the regime created pursuant to that Act and secured by s 51(xxxviii) of the *Constitution* could not be affected by a constitutional amendment of s 106.

82. Stephen Gageler, 'Amending the Constitution through s 128' in Sarah Murray (ed) *Constitutional Perspectives on an Australian Republic* (Federation Press, 2010) 19; Richardson *Opinion in the matter of s 128 of the Constitution* reprinted in Appendix A of Report of Standing Committee B to Executive Committee, 18 in Proceedings of the Australian Constitutional Convention and Standing Committee Reports (Melbourne 1975) ; Gerard Carney, *The Constitutional System of the Australian States and Territories* (Cambridge University Press, 2006); Anne Twomey *The Constitution of New South Wales* (Federation Press, 2004) 788-791; Quick and Garran *The Annotated Constitution of the Australian Commonwealth* (1976 Reprint, Legal Books) 991.

83. (1996) 186 CLR 140, 237, 275.

84. Sir Anthony Mason, 'Constitutional Issues relating to the Republic as they affect the States' (1998) 21(3) *University of NSW Law Journal* 750, 753.

85. See Opinion of Dennis Rose QC, reprinted in the Republic Advisory Committee, *An Australian Republic – The Options* (1993) Volume 2, Appendix 8; Stephen Gageler, 'Amending the Commonwealth Constitution through Section 128 – A Journey through its Scope and Limitations' in Sarah Murray (ed) *Constitutional Perspectives on an Australian Republic* (Federation Press, 2010) 6, 16-17.

86. John Quick and Robert Garran, *The Annotated Constitution of the Commonwealth* (1901, 1976 Reprint, Legal Books) 989-990; George Winterton, *Monarchy to Republic – Australian Republican Government* (Oxford University Press, 1994 and 1986); Anne Twomey, *The Constitution of New South Wales* (Federation Press, 2004) 788-791; Opinion of Dennis Rose QC, reprinted in the Republic Advisory Committee, *An Australian Republic – The Options* (1993) Vol 2, Appendix 8; Stephen Gageler and Mark Leeming, 'An Australian Republic; Is a Referendum Enough?' (1996) 7 (3) *Public Law Review* 143; Geoffrey Lindell and Dennis Rose, 'A Response to Gageler and Leeming: "An Australian Republic: Is a Referendum Enough?"' (1996) 7 (3) *Public Law Review* 155; Sir Anthony Mason 'Constitutional Issues relating to the Republic as they affect the States' (1998) 21(3) *University of New South Wales Law Journal* 750, 755; Stephen Gageler, 'Amending the Commonwealth Constitution through Section 128 – A Journey through its Scope and Limitations" in Sarah Murray (ed) *Constitutional Perspectives on an Australian Republic* (Federation Press, 2010) 6, 16.

87. Adopted by the Commonwealth in 1942.

88. Pursuant to the States' request under s 51(xxxviii).

89. In accordance with the Commonwealth's request and s 4 of the *Statute of Westminster*.

90. Section 15(1) and (2). No such law has been proposed, but note the unanimous request Acts in 1999, fn 72. supra.

91. Section 15(3). This subsection may merely confirm the power already available under s 128: see Leslie Zines, *The High Court and the Constitution* (Federation Press, 5th ed, 2008) 421- 423.

92. See Sir Anthony Mason, 'Constitutional Issues relating to the Republic as they affect the States' (1998) 21(3) *University of New South Wales Law Journal* 750, 754; Geoffrey

Lindell, 'Why is Australia's Constitution Binding?' (1986) 16 (1) *Federal Law Review* 29, 40; Stephen Gageler and Mark Leeming, 'An Australian Republic: Is a Referendum Enough?' (1996) 7 (3) *Public Law Review* 143; Geoff Lindell and Dennis Rose 'A Response to Gageler and Leeming: "An Australian Republic: is a Referendum enough?"' (1996) 7(3) *Public Law Review* 155; Stephen Gageler, 'Amending the Commonwealth Constitution through Section 128 – A Journey through its Scope and Limitations' in *Constitutional Perspectives on an Australian Republic* in Sarah Murray (ed) (The Federation Press, 2010) 6,16; Appendix 8 to The Report of the Republic Advisory Committee (AGPS, 1993), Advice by Dennis Rose QC as Acting Solicitor General, paras 1-29; Anne Twomey *The Constitution of New South Wales* (Federation Press, 2004), 781-782; Anne Twomey *The Australia Acts 1986* (Federation Press, 2010) 339-341.

93. Volume 1, Final Report of the Constitutional Commission, 122-123, par 3.123.

94. See *Attorney-General (WA) v Marquet* (2003) 217 CLR 545, 570.

95. See *Kirmani v Captain Cook Cruises Pty Ltd (No. 1)* (1985) 159 CLR 351, 442 and see Murphy J, 384.

96. See *Australian Capital Television Pty Ltd v Commonwealth* (1992) 177 CLR 106, 138.

97. See, for example, *Nationwide News Pty Ltd v Wills* (1992) 177 CLR 1, 72 (Deane and Toohey JJ); *Theophanous v Herald & Weekly Times Ltd* (1994) 182 CLR 104, 171 (Deane J); *McGinty v Western Australia* (1996) 186 CLR 140, 230 (McHugh J); and *Grain Pool of Western Australia v Commonwealth* (2000) 202 CLR 479, 523 (Kirby J); *Attorney-General (WA) v Marquet* (2003) 217 CLR 545, 570 (Gleeson CH, Gummow, Hayne and Hayden JJ).

98. See G J Lindell, 'Why is Australia's Constitution Binding?' (1986) 16 (1) *Federal Law Review* 29, 37.

Chapter 11

Law and Religion

11.1 Ecumenical Service for Opening of the Legal Year

Editor's note

Brennan moved to Canberra at the end of 1976, having been appointed President of the Administrative Appeals Tribunal and a Judge of the Australian Industrial Court. At the commencement of the Law Year in Canberra, there was an ecumenical service. Attending his first service on 22 February 1977, Brennan was invited to offer a reflection on the chosen scripture passage, Matthew 8:5-13.

Today we renew a tradition which has marked the life of the Christian church and of the institutions of the Law. The strength of that tradition has changed, and the relationship between the Church and the Law has become more tenuous than before.

No doubt the causes of the change are various.

The community, in framing its laws, now looks increasingly to values and systems of thought which owe little to Christian tradition. And the modern Christian does not see his Faith in quite the same light as did his forefathers.

The lawyer of a century ago found comfort in a conviction that as his knowledge of the law deepened and his practice developed, he acquired a better perception of Christianity. Today his comfort may be envied, but his conviction will not find acceptance.

We cannot, when we administer our laws and when we examine our present appreciation of the Christian faith, assume a concordance in values or in objectives. We may therefore sense a dichotomy between our lives as lawyers and our lives as Christians. We may feel a tension between professional activities and the more essential, personal life of the spirit.

In this, we may be heartened and instructed by the reading this morning from St Matthew's gospel describing the encounter between the centurion and Christ.

The centurion lived under a system of law which owed nothing to Christianity. That system of law, which provided for Roman provincial administration and the power structure of the Roman legions, regulated the centurion's professional life. He was both under authority of that law and empowered to exercise authority by that law. He knew his duty and he discharged it as the law required.

It was his very fidelity to his proper professional standards which led him to make his memorable act of faith in Christ. Understanding the way in which power was lawfully exercised in the society of his time, he came more easily to realize the extent of the power of God.

He was not a Jew; he was not in the theistic tradition. He was a Gentile who stood outside the Messianic promise. In Christ he recognized a prophet who mirrored his own standards of professional conduct: One who was doing the will of the Father and who was empowered to exercise Divine authority.

The centurion's eyes of faith were illumined by the disciplines of his professional life: 'For I am a man under authority with soldiers under me…'

So may it be with us. The life of the lawyer may enrich the life of the Christian. But the enrichment is of a spiritual kind. The material rewards of professional success are immaterial to the life of the spirit, as the centurion clearly perceived.

He stood before Christ, an officer of rank, a representative of the ruling Roman State. He was a man of substance with home and servants. But when Christ, who had no material wealth or power, showed His compassion and generosity, the man of material substance was moved to say: 'Lord, I am not worthy to have you come under my roof'.

Here we find the ultimate reconciliation of our two lives – whatever be the rewards, whether of status or possessions, which our professional lives bring to us, the Christian will not be satisfied. The Christian's satisfaction is derived not from his own success but from the service of others.

By a paradox, it is the duties of our daily lives, the professional discharge of our functions for the good of others, that may enrich our lives as Christians. The material rewards make no contribution to our worth in the sight of God.

This message of St Matthew's gospel may comfort us and encourage us in our concern for the doing of justice, for the proper administration of the law, and for the interests of our clients.

And thus, we pray that we may, in the year to come, fulfil our appointed tasks and secure the Divine benediction: 'Go. Be it done to you as you have believed.'

So may it be.

11.2 The Peace of Sir Thomas More

Editor's note

Brennan had a lifelong devotion to Thomas More. A print of Holbein's portrait used hang in his chambers. In the year of his appointment to the High Court, he returned to Brisbane to deliver the Thomas More Lecture on 30 October 1981. He spoke on 'The Peace of Thomas More'.

Thomas More is an enigma, his life an apparent paradox. He was at once a man of the world, but not of the world; a man of power, yet of humility; the King's good servant, who died as a traitor; one who clung to the processes of the law, though in the end they broke him; who loved his family as few men do, yet let them go to fend for themselves as he rowed down the Thames to the Tower, his trial and the block. He was Lord Chancellor, a knight of the realm – and a saint.

Yet no man of More's stature is so inconsistent in opinion or deed that he changes the centres of his interest, allegiance and affection to achieve distinction first in this world and then in the next. There is a constancy in him which reconciles the apparent paradox and explains the enigma. Life is not lived in separate compartments; a human personality is an entirety which copes with and is informed by the associations and activities of the life in question. More's public life, his trial and execution cannot be understood except as part of a life which found its synthesis in his love of God, of his family and his fellows. Those loves gave him a tranquillity of spirit, an abiding strength, not only to bear the burdens of his public life but to act in his public life so that those burdens, that trial and execution were the inexorable consequences of his spirit.

He was, above all, a man at peace. The crises of the times could not shatter it; it was proof against ambition, power and position; it gave him laughter and the love of friends. The peace of Thomas More suffices to unify his life and to perpetuate his memory – and without it his life would be full of contradiction and the veneration of his memory would be a mockery.

I cannot speak as a scholar of More's life and writings: I have read a little of what he wrote and of what has been written about him. Enough to be caught in the widening web of admirers, who seem thus far to have been attracted by the values he exemplified rather than by adherence to contemporary fashion.

He was born in 1477 or 1478, the son of John More – then an apprentice at law – and his wife Agnes, a daughter of Thomas Granger. He was sent to school at St Anthony's in Threadneedle Street, a school of the highest reputation, and was received into the household of Cardinal Morton, Archbishop of Canterbury and Lord Chancellor under Henry VII. He studied at Oxford, then at New Inn, an Inn of Chancery. At the age of 18, he was admitted to Lincoln's Inn, to read for the degree of barrister.

By that time, his father was a barrister of Lincoln's Inn, with which the family had had a long connection. Thomas More's portrait hangs today on the walls of the dining hall of the Inn. I was shown it by Lord Denning who said 'Sir or Saint Thomas More, whichever you prefer' – and that set me to wondering whether there was a dichotomy in his life reflected in the duality of his titles. I do not think there was.

But I digress, and it is necessary to note the closeness of his connection with his Inn for it was there that he learned the law. His paternal grandfather had been butler and steward and had been admitted as a member of the Society of the Inn.[1] Thereafter he was called to the Bar, became a bencher and on two occasions was appointed a reader. Thomas' father, also John More, succeeded his father as butler, was called to the Bar, became a serjeant at law, a Judge of Common Pleas and a Judge of the King's Bench.

The family was not rich or of noble birth, and their association with Lincoln's Inn must have given to the young Thomas a considerable confidence in undertaking the profession of his father and grandfather. Foss, in his lives of the *Judges of England* eulogizes the system of the Inns at that time:

> This origin, so far from detracting in any degree from the merit either of the chancellor or the judge, must be considered as speaking loudly, not only to their credit, but to the credit of those to whom they owed their elevation; showing that, even in those days, virtue and learning met their due reward, and contradicting the general impression that none but rich men's sons were admitted members of the inns of court. It proves also that, at a time when the barriers between the different grades of society were far more difficult to be passed than in the present day, such a combination of talent with integrity and moral worth as distinguished the progenitors of Sir Thomas could overcome all the prejudices in favour of high descent which were the natural result of the feudal system. [2]

Young Thomas was singularly favoured to begin life at the Bar. He had had a fine classical education and he had taken the eye of Cardinal Morton who opined 'to divers of the nobility who at sundry times dined with him "This child here, waiting at the table, whosoever shall live to see it, will prove a marvellous rare man."'[3] He had shown an acuity of mind which captured the attention of Erasmus who became his life-long friend. When Thomas was 21, Erasmus wrote of him: 'What did nature ever create milder, sweeter or happier than the genius of Thomas More?'[4] Esteemed by the Establishment, admired by the intellectual elite, embraced by the Society of Lincoln's Inn and removed from the threat of poverty, his success seemed assured. The world was before him. He put it aside.

Lord Campbell in his *Lives of the Lord Chancellors* tells what happened next:

> Though called to the degree of barrister, he had not begun to plead in Court; and he was now disposed for ever to renounce the pomp and vanity of the world, and to bury himself in a convent. His modern biographers very improperly shrink from this passage of his life; for if it were discreditable to him (which it really is not), still it ought to be known, that we may justly appreciate his character. He was so transported with the glory of St. Augustine, and so enraptured with the pleasures of piety, and so touched with the peace, regularity, and freedom from care of a monastic life, that he resolved to enter the order of St Francis. But before taking the irrevocable vow of celibacy, shaving his crown, putting on the grey serge garment fastened by a twisted rope, and walking barefoot in quest of alms, he prudently made an experiment how strict monastic discipline would permanently suit him. He began to wear a sharp shirt of hair next his skin. He added also to his austerity a whip every Friday and high fasting days, thinking upon himself. He used also much fasting and watching, lying often upon the bare ground or upon some bench, laying a log under his head, allotting himself but four or five hours in a night at the most for his sleep, imagining, with the holy saints of Christ's church, that his body was to be used as an ass, with strokes and hard fare, lest provender might pride it, and so bring his soul, like a headstrong jade, to the bottomless pit of hell. With this view he took a lodging close by the Carthusian monastery, now the site of the Charterhouse School, and as a lay brother practised all the austerities which prevail in this stern order. [5]

But he was no Jansenist. Nor was his time with the Carthusians a mere retreat from the world. It was a period of growth in scholarship, maturity and the love of God. He was much affected by reading a life of Pico of Mirandola, an Italian scholar of the renaissance renowned for his sanctity. He translated that life into English, and the translation gives us an insight into what More was about:

> Of outward observances he gave no very great force: we speak not of those observances which the Church commandeth to be observed, for in those he was diligent: but we speak of those ceremonies which folk bring up, setting the very service of God aside, which is (as

> Christ saith) to be worshipped in spirit and in truth. But in the inward affections of the mind he cleaved to God with very fervent love and devotion. Sometimes that marvellous alacrity languished and almost fell, and after again with great strength rose up into God. In the love of Whom he so fervently burned that on a time as he walked with John Francis, his nephew, in an orchard at Ferrara, in the talking of the love of Christ, he broke out into these words, 'Nephew,' he said, 'this will I show thee, I warn thee keep it a secret; the substance that I have left, after certain books of mine finished, I intend to give out to poor folk, and fencing myself with the crucifix, barefoot walking about the world in every town and castle I purpose to preach of Christ.' Afterwards, I understand, by the especial commandment of God, he changed that purpose and appointed to profess himself in the order of Friars Preachers.[6]

Thomas himself did not undertake missionary works. He stayed with the Carthusians for a few years, and he deepened his awareness of the love of God. It was a time when life was seen in the perspective of eternity, and his sights were set on the ultimate union with the Divine Lover. He wrote of this love later in the Tower:

> Thus should of God the lover be content,
> Any distress or sorrow to endure,
> Rather than to be from God absent,
> And glad to die, so that he may be sure,
> By his departing hence for to procure
> After this valley dark, the heavenly light,
> And of his love the glorious blessed sight.[7]

That was not a new found vision, but an affirmation of the faith of his lifetime. It reveals the inner peace of Thomas More which explains all that follows. Given the love of God, he had his reason for living and his reason for dying; for loving and laughing; for working and playing. He was a man at peace – with God and eternity, with family and friends, with profession, King and the councils of power.

He left the Charterhouse, taking with him his hair shirt and the regime of rigorous prayer to which he adhered for the whole of his life. Erasmus thought he left because he wished to marry. That may be so, but there is another possible explanation which seems to be more consonant with the rugged self-discipline of More, and his rigorous examination of his own motives. He regarded the Carthusians as men of great spirit, but unless their regular and austere lifestyle was undertaken as a spiritual exercise, there was a risk that the monastic life would be a mere protection from the problems of the real world. That was a risk More was not prepared to run, for he was contemptuous of any who misused the monastic life: 'Under pretext as it seems to them of a humble heart and meakness and of serving God in silence and contemplation, they unconsciously seek their own ease and earthly rest, and with this God is not well content.'[8]

Whatever the explanation, he had a certain nostalgia for the eremitical lifestyle of the Carthusians. He told his daughter Margaret that if it had not been for love of his family, he would have sought the straitened room of a monk's cell.

He began his practice at the Bar, where he acquired a particular reputation as an expert in international law. It is said that he was in all the important cases, and earned a large income. Not long after he commenced practice, he married Jane Colt, the eldest daughter of a country household. His son-in-law, Roper, tells the story of the marriage:

> He resorted to the house of one Master Colt, a gentleman of Essex, that had oft invited him thither, having three daughters, whose honest conversation and virtuous education provoked him there specially to set his affection. And albeit his mind most served him to the second daughter, for that he thought her the fairest and best favoured, yet when he considered that it would be both great grief and some shame also to the eldest to see her younger sister in marriage preferred before her, he then of a certain pity framed his fancy towards her, and soon after married her.[9]

Perhaps it was fitting that he should marry the eldest. He was 26 or 27 at the time, and Jane was 10 years younger. Roper's less than enthusiastic description of the courtship gives no indication of the love which developed between Thomas and Jane. They were married in 1504 or January 1505.

There is no doubt that More's first marriage was a great love affair. Lord Campbell says, 'There never was a happier union. He settled her in a house in Bucklersbury, where they lived in uninterrupted harmony.' But their bliss was not without burden. Thomas had set himself the task of educating Jane, for he had advanced notions about the education of women and he wished to bring her into the circle of Erasmus, Grocyn, Linacre, Colet and the rest, the intellects of the time and Thomas' intimate friends. Their life together in the early years has been described:

> Life was hard in that first year to the girl-bride of seventeen, pent up in narrow streets and courts and pining for green fields and the old home; hard, too, for the young husband, ten years the elder, who, with

> sense enough to shrink from the rough methods of the time, yet tried to play the schoolmaster to his wife before their hearts were open one to another and their desires known. How their spirits must have risen as they rode down into Essex on a summer morning – summer was then the hunting season – past the great church of Waltham; she behind him on a pillion, and straining her eyes over his shoulder to catch the first view of Netherhall, as the road wound round the little hills which were to bring peace. It is good to remember that happiness came before the end. To More, when he wrote his own epitaph, she was 'chara uxorcola', and the years that they spent together were green. [10]

Mr and Mrs More lived in a house called 'The Barge', near where the Mansion House now stands. Mrs More gave birth to Margaret within a year of marriage, to Elizabeth in 1506, to Cecily in 1507, and to John in 1509. These were busy years, not only with the children, but receiving visitors – the fussy Erasmus was a houseguest for a time – and looking after the studious young barrister. Perhaps they were years of some anxiety – for the young Thomas had crossed Henry VII in the year when he and Jane were married, and the monarch did not. But despite the activity, Thomas pursued his life of prayer, and the birth of the children gave him a simple sense of wonder at the power of Providence. For him, a miracle frequently encountered was nonetheless a miracle. He wrote:

> I cannot understand why we should hold it more wonderful to revive a dead man than to witness the breeding, birth and growth of a child into a man. No more marvellous is a cuckoo than a cock, though the one be seen only in the summer and the other the whole year round. And I am sure that if you saw dead men as commonly recalled to life by miracle as you see men brought forth by nature, you would reckon it less wonderful to bring the soul back into the body which still has its shape and is not much perished, than from a little seed to make all the gear anew and make anew soul thereto. [11]

In 1511 Jane died. The love affair was over, and he had four young children on his hands, the eldest only five. He immediately remarried the redoubtable Dame Alice, a widow who would preside over the household and help to bring up the children and, to an extent, share the extraordinary public life which stretched before him. More was a practical man, and once he saw the need for a wife to discharge the duties which Jane's death left unfulfilled, he offered marriage to Dame Alice. It was of course a marriage of convenience, but it was not devoid of affection and respect.

More prepared an inscription for the grave intended to receive the two wives and himself. He wrote:

> Within this tomb Jane, wife of More reclines; This for himself and Alice More designs. The first – dear object of my youthful vow, Gave me three daughters and a son to know. The next – ah virtue in a step-dame rare, Nursed my sweet infants with a mother's care. With both my years so happily have passed, Which the more dear, I know not – first or last. [12]

His family was the centre of his concern – his children, and in later years their spouses and his grandchildren, and his assorted relations. His school for the family was a remarkable feature of the new home at Chelsea, then in the country, which he built as his fortunes improved and his status was enhanced. At the school there were lessons in Latin, Greek, Arithmetic, Astronomy and some elementary science. The Dialectic method was encouraged to open the mind to controversy.

Learning was not only to be valued for its own sake, but because it 'prepares the mind for virtue'. There seems to have been nothing which More undertook that did not tend to the love of God, the advancement of virtue, or the service of the King. Learning was an aid to virtue – as More was to show by his brilliant and lawyerly arguments at his trial – and it was to be pursued for altruistic motives. It was not to be regarded as a passport to prosperity. He wrote to Gonnell, the tutor of his school:

> Though I prefer learning joined to virtue to all the treasures of Kings, yet renown for learning when it is not united with a good life, is nothing else than manifest and notorious infamy . . . among all the outstanding benefits that learning bestows on men, none is more excellent than this, that, by the study of books, we are taught in that very study, to seek not praise but usefulness. Such has been the teaching of the most learned men, especially the philosophers, who are the guides of human life, although some may have abused learning, like other good things, simply to court empty glory and popular renown. [13]

He wished to transmit the strength which his philosophy gave him to his children, and though he was familiar with the trappings of power and the adulation of the masses for those in high places, he would have none of it. Virtue was not to be practised to earn praise. He regretted that those who taught what is good frequently awakened 'the expectation of praise as the proper reward of virtue', and he added:

> Thus we grow accustomed to make so much of praise, that while we study how to please the majority, who will always be the worst, we grow ashamed of being good with the minority. So that this plague of vainglory may be banished far from my children, I do desire you, my dear Gonnell, and their mother and all their friends to harp on the theme, to reiterate it and pound away at it, that vainglory is a vile thing and to be treated with contempt and that there is nothing more sublime than that humble modesty so often praised by Christ and this your prudent charity will so enforce as to teach virtue rather than reprove vice and make them love good advice instead of hating it.[14]

Virtue, or goodness, are attractive to More. He found no joy in the condemnation of vice or evil. But the attraction of goodness for the mind and will is not dependent upon the approbation of others. Goodness is to be pursued irrespective of its impact on others. Thus, More asserted a moral independence which both manifested his inner peace, and left him to do what was right as he saw it. Virtue is to be practised though it be unpopular, and the individual conscience is not to be bent by popular acclaim, nor by popular condemnation. The practice of virtue is supported by the practice of solitary prayer, for which More provided in the design of the Chelsea home. His advice was: 'Let him also choose himself some secret, solitary place in his own house, as far from noise and company as he conveniently can and thither let him sometimes secretly resort alone, imagining himself as one going out of the world even straight unto the giving up of his reckoning unto God of his sinful living.'[15]

Why does the gregarious More insist on the solitary strength of virtue and the need for solitary prayer? It is surely because he sees that it is in the quietness of the spirit that man finds his unity with God and puts the associations and activities of his life into their true perspective. To the busy man, engaged in the great transactions of the time, searching for criteria by which to mould not only his own conduct but the affairs of England, there was a simple but lonely course to follow:

> If you love your own health, if you desire to be safe from the snares of the devil, from the storms of this world, from the await of thy enemies; if you long to be acceptable to God; if you covet to be happy at the last – let no day pass you but you once at leastwise present yourself to God in prayer and falling down before Him flat to the ground with an humble affection of devout mind, not from the extremity of your lips but out of the inwardness of your heart, cry these words of the prophet: 'The offences of my youth and my ignorance remember not, good Lord; but after thy mercy, Lord, for Thy goodness remember me.'[16]

The time for prayer and the time for study were snatched from the night, for he was not willing to make default in the performance either of his public or his familial duties. They were very time-consuming. As Chancellor he worked at a prodigious rate, and he cleared the list of cases – an ambition which few judges realize and none without extraordinary effort. His large extended family made their own demands, so there was little time for More's private affairs. He wrote to a friend in Antwerp, Peter Giles:

> For while in pleading, in hearing, in deciding causes, or composing disputes as an arbitrator, in waiting on some men about business, and on others out of respect, the greatest part of the day is spent on other men's affairs, the remainder of it must be given to my family at home; so that I can reserve no part to myself, that is, to study. I must gossip with my wife and chat with my children, and find something to say to my servants; for all these things I reckon a part of my business, unless I were to become a stranger in my own house; for with whomsoever either nature or choice or chance has engaged a man in any relation of life, he must endeavour to make himself as acceptable to them as he possibly can. In such occupations as these, days, months, and years slip away. Indeed all the time which I can gain to myself is that which I steal from my sleep and my meals, and because that is not much I have made but a slow progress. [17]

His life at the bar, as Under Sheriff of London, a member of Parliament, Ambassador, Privy Councillor, Chancellor of the Duchy of Lancaster and Lord Chancellor must have been extraordinarily busy. Yet study and prayer, alone and away from the public eye, were integral to his life and account for the most notable features of his public career, a career marked by independence in every view he expressed, and informed by much consideration.

His public career began shortly after he left the Charterhouse and before he married Jane. More had become a member of the House of Commons, and a Bill to grant Henry VII a large sum of money was being debated. But young More made 'such arguments and reasons there against, that the King's demands thereby were clean overthrown.'[18] The King was told that 'a beardless boy had disappointed all his purpose', and the King took revenge by exacting an unjustified fine from his father. He was advised to confess the error of his ways and to seek His Majesty's favour. He did not take that advice. It is perhaps the more surprising that he took the stand which he did within a few months of some offices being conferred upon Thomas Granger, his grandfather on his mother's side, and upon his father. In 1503, Granger had been elected Sheriff of London and, after taking his Oath before the Barons of the Exchequer, he attended a feast at the Palace of the Archbishop of Canterbury which was graced by the King's presence. Thomas' father, John More, a new Serjeant at Law, attended the Royal banquet.[19]

But neither gratitude for past favours nor expectation of favours to come, nor fear of reprisal prevented the beardless boy from taking his stand. It was a brave political act, undertaken by one who set no store by the losses he might incur or the advantages he might otherwise acquire.

His career at the bar was affected for the next five years, but thereafter his fortunes changed with Henry VIII's accession to the throne in 1509. He had studied profoundly especially during the five years of Royal disfavour and he was appointed Reader at Furnival's Inn, an Inn under the supervision of Lincoln's Inn. The appointment, twice renewed, was prestigious. He was in all the important cases. He was a master of the common law.

He became an Under Sheriff of London, the legal adviser to the Sheriff's Court. He retained the office for many years. Erasmus tells us:[20] 'No one has settled more cases than has More, and no one has acted with greater integrity. He usually remits the fees due from the litigants – three shillings from the plaintiff and as much from the defendant; no more may be exacted. He has made himself very popular in the City by this.'

In 1514, he gave up his practice at the bar. He was made Master of the Requests, knighted and later sworn of the Privy Council. For the next nine years he was engaged in embassies to the Continent, frequently away from his home and family. He was engaged dutifully in the King's service, but he kept a low profile politically. He had no taste for the battles of power.

In 1523, Parliament was summoned, principally to vote some funds to the King. More became Speaker not merely by popular choice but by the patronage of the Royal Court. That did not sap the independence of his stance. He sought freedom of speech for the Commons. He told the King that the members of the House might be put to silence 'to the great hindrance of your common affairs, unless every one of your Commons were utterly discharged of all doubt and fear how anything should happen of your Highness to be taken.'

The Commons did not wish to grant supply in the amount sought by Wolsey, though More did not find Wolsey's proposals objectionable. In exercise of his great power, Wolsey came into the House – to be met with a frosty silence. Roper records what followed:

> And thereupon he required answers of Master Speaker; who first reverently upon his knees excusing the silence of the House, abashed at the presence of so noble a personage, able to amaze the wisest and best learned in a realm, and after by many probable arguments

> proving that for them to make answer was it neither expedient nor agreeable with the ancient liberty of the House; in conclusion for himself showed that though they had all with their voices trusted him, yet except every one of them could put into his one head all their several wits, he alone in so weighty a matter was unmeet to make his Grace answer. [21]

His response was couched in respectful terms, but the message was clear. More might owe his speakership to the Executive, but his office owed its loyalty to the House. Later, when they met, Wolsey said to More: 'Would to God you had been at Rome, Master More, when I made you Speaker.' [22]

To which More responded honestly, but with that self-deprecating humour which turned wrath aside 'Your Grace not offended, so would I too, my Lord.'

Mr Speaker Cameron thought that More had sown some of the most productive seeds of the freedom and independence of Parliament.[23] Nevertheless, he retained the favour of the King who appointed him Chancellor of the Duchy of Lancaster in 1525.

The King consulted More on the lawfulness of his marriage to Catherine of Aragon, for it had been suggested to Henry that it was not lawful for him to marry his brother's wife. More, who was rightly regarded as competent in these matters as in the common law, showed the King the authorities he had gathered together 'which, although the King (as disagreeable with his desire) did not very well like of, yet were they by Sir Thomas More, who in all his communication with the King in that matter had always most discreetly behaved himself, so wisely tempered, that he both presently took them in good part, and ofttimes had thereof conference with him again.' [24]

To be a royal confidante gave More no special pride. He knew that the King favoured him 'as singularly as any subject within this realm', but he knew also, as he told Roper 'if my head would win him a castle in France, it should not fail to go.'

The good relationship between them survived for a time, and in 1529 More was sent on an embassy to Cambrai. By that time, however, the matter of the King's marriage reached a crisis. Wolsey, failing to secure an annulment, failed the King. He fell from power while More was in Cambrai. The King had the great seal in his hands by 20th October, but there was a fierce debate as to who should be the new Chancellor.

John Guy in his *Public Career of Sir Thomas More* tells us that –

> by 25 October More had indeed emerged as the compromise solution between Suffolk and Tunstall. Henry VIII was enthusiastic. Not only was More uniquely qualified for the chancellor's duties, his

> former political obscurity was now a positive asset. No one could possibly have associated him with Wolsey's discredited clientage. More's personal position was, of course, already tortuous. The chancellorship, the highest office in the realm, was the consummation of the career begun when he entered the Council in 1517. On the other hand, Thomas was a declared opponent of the king's divorce, the greatest future political issue. More hesitated; he perhaps even refused, until the king angrily told him to accept.[25]

More held the office until 16 May 1532. In the legal history of England, More's appointment marks a turning point. Professor Holdsworth states the significance:

> It marks the transition from the administration of equity by ecclesiastics and canonists to its administration by laymen and common lawyers. In the earlier period the ecclesiastical training of the chancellors had led to the infiltration of ideas of the canon law. But now the legal training of the chancellors was to lead to the infiltration of ideas of the common law. The occasion for the transition was political; and both political and religious causes made it permanent.[26]

More was a distinguished common lawyer, to be trusted by common lawyers at a time when the injunction was seen by many as an instrument of equity's avidity for new jurisdictions And the gentleness of his character had made him popular both at home and abroad. Holdsworth says that:

> More's beautiful character would have made him an ideal chancellor at any time. It was exactly fitted to the difficult position which he was then called upon to fill. He was scrupulously pure, and strictly impartial, to the disappointment, on two occasions, of his relations. He is said to have quickly cleared off all arrears of business. He was easy of access, and made it a habit never to grant a subpoena till he was satisfied that the plaintiff had some real ground of complaint.[27]

When the common law judges complained of his use of injunctions, More did not cling to the Chancellor's power. He invited them to reform the rigour of the law themselves, and only when they refused did he warn them that as 'yourselves drive me to award injunctions to relieve the people's injury, you cannot hereafter any more justly blame me.'[28]

His strict impartiality was a by-word. He told Roper his son-in-law – 'I assure thee on my faith, that if the parties will at my hands call for justice, then, all were it my father stood on the one side, and the Devil on the other, his cause being good, the Devil should have right.'[29]

Lord Campbell recites a lovely story of administering public justice in a case involving Dame Alice herself:

> It happened on a time that a beggar-woman's little dog, which she had lost, was presented for a jewel to Lady More, and she had kept it some se'nnight very carefully; but at last the beggar had notice where the dog was, and presently she came to complain to Sir Thomas, as he was sitting in his hall, that his lady withheld her dog from her. Presently my Lady was sent for, and the dog brought with her; which Sir Thomas, taking in his hands caused his wife, because she was the worthier person, to stand at the upper end of the hall, and the beggar at the lower end, and saying that he sat there to do every one justice, he bade each of them call the dog; which, when they did, the dog went presently to the beggar, forsaking my Lady. When he saw this, he bade my Lady be contented, for it was none of hers; yet she, repining at the sentence of my Lord Chancellor, agreed with the beggar, and gave her a piece of gold, which would well have bought three dogs, and so all parties were agreed; every one smiling to see his manner of inquiring out the truth.[30]

The sensitivity of More shown by the respectful treatment of Dame Alice did not impair the impartial justice of the trial. His kindness to her was not bought at another's expense: it flowed from the confidence he had in his familial affections and in the justice of the law he dispensed. There was no conflict between justice and love: there was no ground for withholding either to advance the other. He was a judge at peace.

But the clouds of the King's great question were gathering. The King, manipulated it seems by the schemes of Thomas Cromwell, at first repelled the attempt of the Commons to bring the clerical Convocation into submission on matters seemingly distinct from the King's divorce. Articles of Submission had been sent to the Convocation of the Clergy by the King, stripping the Convocation of their legislative power to enact canons without the King's consent. There followed a political upheaval in the Parliament in the week before 14 May 1532, and it was prorogued on that day. It seems that Thomas More led the pro-Aragonese faction which opposed Henry's plans. On 15th May, the Convocation was told that it must not assemble without royal writ. On 16th, the Convocation submitted, and the Articles of Submission were signed.

At 3.00pm on that day, More surrendered the great seal in the garden at York Place, Westminster.[31] He had been politically defeated. He left office, but there was no sense of personal loss. He told his large family that he had 'little left above a hundred pounds by the year: so that now, if we wish to live together you must be content to be contributaries together' and he proposed that, if they were reduced to penury, 'then may we after, with bag and wallet, go a begging together, hoping that for pity some good folks will give us their charity, and at every man's door to sing a Salve Regina, whereby we shall still keep company, and be merry together.'[32]

This was in keeping with his rejection of affluence. Years before, when some barns had burnt down he had written to Dame Alice counselling a resignation to the will of Providence:

> Let us never grudge thereat, but take it in good worth, and hartely thank him, as well for adversitie, as for prosperitie. And par adventure we have more cause to thank him for our losse, than for our winning. For his wisedom better seeth what is good for us than we do ourselves. Therefore I pray you be of good cheere, and take all the howsold with you to church, and there thank God both for that he hath given us, and for that he hath left us, which if it please hym, he can increase when he will. [33]

Though he would have been content to live privately, not seeking to foment controversy, much less disaffection, the sheer integrity of the man and his presence at a time when expediency knew no bounds ensured his destruction. In concluding his writing on More's public career Guy observes:

> Armed with both humanist technique and secure faith, More combined a clear vision and direct insight to truth with a prominent public reputation. As such, he was an intolerable threat to the new regime, irrespective of Thomas Cromwell's genuine affection and respect for his former opponent. As expressed in his Dialogue of Comfort against Tribulation, written during the fifteen months of his imprisonment in the Tower, More aspired to an ideal of spiritual manhood which would transcend the accepted bounds of human capacity. He stood for moral crusade, and Henry VIII was adroitly cast in this work as the Great Turk. More's brilliant career in law and politics, in particular his active role in the events of 1529-1532, meanwhile ensured that his morality would soon become his executioner. Yet by suffering torment for the truth he had discovered, More gave posterity an assurance that it was not an illusion. When the axe finally fell on 6 July 1535, 'the king's good servant' also earned his place among the very few who have enlarged the horizon of the human spirit. [34]

The Tower, the trial and the execution are familiar history. Throughout it all are the statements of a man at peace. Come what may, that peace was indestructible. If it could have been disturbed, it would not have been necessary to condemn More. But as the peace of the man was indestructible, it was necessary to destroy the man himself.

Throughout the whole of the long proceedings, the only concern which More expresses is his ability to follow his conscience to the end. And when he finds that he has the strength, he is joyous at the discovery. When he had done with his interview with the Councillors about being discharged out of the Bill of Attainder, and it was clear that he was set on the course of destruction, he said to Roper[35]'In good faith, I rejoiced, son, that I had given the devil a foul fall, and that with those lords I had gone so far as without great shame I could never go back again.'

Warned of the risk he was running by the Duke of Norfolk who told him that the wrath of the king meant death, he replied: 'Then. . . is there no more difference between your Grace and me, but that I shall die today, and you tomorrow.'[36]

And when he left Chelsea for the last time, he said 'I thank Our Lord that the field is won'.[37]

When Dame Alice asked him to have some sense, to do the King's will and come home from the Tower, he simply asked 'Is not this house as nigh heaven as my own?'[38]

And as the pressure upon him mounted he gave thanks that 'reason with help of faith finally concluded, that for to be put to death wrongfully for doing well . . . it is a case in which a man may lose his head and yet have none harm, but instead of harm inestimable good at the hand of God.'[39]

At the commencement of his trial, he prayed only that he be given 'my good, honest and upright mind to nourish, maintain and uphold in me even to the last hour and extreme moment that ever I shall live.'[40]

After the sentence was passed and he was back in the Tower he wrote his final letter to his beloved daughter Margaret who had thrown her arms around him as he was led back to his cell. He wrote on the eve of the Feast of St Thomas and the Octave of the Feast of St Peter and said '. . . and therefore tomorrow long I to go to God: it were a day very meet and convenient for me. I never liked your manner toward me better than when you kissed me last: for I love when daughterly love and dear charity hath no leisure for worldly courtesy. Farewell my dear child and pray for me, and I shall for you and all your friends, that we may merrily meet in heaven.'[41]

More did not die because he wished to take the side of the Papacy in the political battles of the day. He died because he could not be false to the truth as he saw it, and he died because he longed to go to God. He was executed because his integrity and spirituality could not be tolerated in the political climate of the time. It is an error to think that More is a saint because he was a martyr; rather he became a martyr because he was a saint.

There is no paradox in More. His life is quite simple. It was a life given to the love of God, and that left him impervious to worldly ambition or desire. Putting no store by position, or power, or wealth, demanding no support from family or friends or patrons along the lonely paths of his conscience, he had the strength of one who wants nothing. There are few men who are so independent; few who do not find their wish to be independent sapped by their own perceptions of what is worldly wise.

More not only had the wit to condemn vainglory, he had the faith which saw temporal advantages as the seductive baubles taking the mind and soul from their eternal objective. The paradox is not in More's life but in the lives of most other men who seek to reconcile virtue with what we call reality, principle with the exigencies of practice, a private faith with a public agnosticism. We sense a tension between daily life and the spirit, and we do not find either is at ease.

But More was a man of peace. All the aspects of his life were in their place. The whole man might devote himself to the service of his King and country, to the work of the Court over which he presided, to the service of the law, to the love and education of his family. To the service of his God. His enormous energies were devoted without stint to all of these purposes, to the great benefit of each. His spiritual life did not attenuate his public efforts: his service to the State was enhanced thereby.

It was the State which lost by his death. It rejected the State's good servant, simply because he was God's good servant first, blind to the reality that if More had been retained and trusted as the King's Lord Chancellor, England would have had the services of one who knew and understood the politics of the Continent, the proper bounds of the Papal power, the aspirations of the English people, and the true interests of the King. Had that reality been grasped, what course might history have taken?

England lost him; the world acquired his memory. He speaks today with the eloquence of example. For the modern world he is the paradigm of independence, and that is a virtue prized by the Judiciary above all others. He shows us that an individual cannot be made independent by others who satisfy his wants; independence is secured by the individual who sheds them. Independence is not a worldly attribute; it is an attribute of a man at peace. The strength of such a man flows not from position, possessions or power, but from a concordance between conscience and action.

More was at peace to the end. We may draw some strength from More's benediction of the troubled man who called out to him on his way to the scaffold. More, within minutes of his death, replied 'Go thy ways in peace, and pray for me, and I will not fail to pray for thee.'[42]

Whether we share the vision of the saint or have a vision of our own, none can resist the attraction of this man of strength and independence – this man of peace.

---

1. Raymond W Chambers, *Thomas More* (Cape, 1935) 52.
2. Edward Foss, *A Biographical Dictionary of the Judges of England 1066-1870*, (John Murray, Ablemarle St, London, 1870) 455.
3. John Lord Campbell, *Lives of the Lord Chancellors and Keepers of the Great Seal of England,* vol ii, (John Murray, Ablemarle St, London, 5th ed,1868) 3.
4. 5 December 1499, P S Allen, 'Letters of Erasmus', Vol 1, 118; cited Raymond W Chambers, *Thomas More* (Cape, 1935) 75.
5. Campbell, (n 3) 6-7.
6. Ernest E Reynolds, *Saint Thomas More* (Burns Oates, 1953) 53-54.
7. William E Campbell (ed), *English Works of Sir Thomas More* (Eyre and Spottiswoode, 1931), Volume 1, 390; cited Bernard Basset, *Born for Friendship* (Burns Oates,1965) 61.
8. Thomas More, *Utopia and Dialogue of Comfort*, Dent, Everyman's Library, No 461, Revised edition 1962; cited in Bernard Basset, *Born for Friendship* (Burns Oates, 1965) 75.
9. William Roper, *The Lyfe of Sir Thomas Moore, Knighte,* ed. E V Hitchcock, Early English Text Society, 1935 cited in Ernest E Reynolds *Saint Thomas More* (Burns Oates, 1953) 55.
10. See *Times Literary Supplement*, (26 December 1918), 654; cited in Raymond W Chambers, *Thomas More* (Cape, 1935) 96.
11. See *English Works of Sir Thomas More*, vol 2, W E Campbell (ed) (Eyre & Spottiswoode, 1931) 46-47; cited in Bernard Basset, *Born for Friendship* (Burns Oates, 1965) 51.
12. Cited in Bernard Basset, *Born for Friendship* (Burns Oates, 1965) 94.
13. Ibid 127-128.
14. Ibid 130.
15. Ibid 59.
16. 'Life of Picus', English Works, Introduction, I, 347-348; cited Bernard Basset, *Born for Friendship* (Burns Oates, 1965) 58.
17. William E Campbell (ed), *English Works of Sir Thomas More* (Eyre and Spottiswoode, 1931), Volume 2, 15.
18. William Roper, *The Lyfe of Sir Thomas Moore, Knighte* 7, 8 cited in Raymond W Chambers, *Thomas More* (Cape, 1935) 87.
19. John Stow, *Chronicles of England* (1580) 876 cited in Raymond W Chambers, *Thomas More* (Cape, 1935) 51.
20. Allen, IV, No 999, 20 cited in Raymond W Chambers, *Thomas More* (Cape, 1935)103.
21. William Roper, *The Lyfe of Sir Thomas Moore, Knighte* 18-19 cited in Raymond Chambers, *Thomas More* (Cape, 1935) 204-205.

22. William Roper, *The Lyfe of Sir Thomas Moore, Knighte* 19 cited in Raymond Chambers, *Thomas More* (Cape, 1935) 206.
23. J A Cameron, 'Thomas More as Speaker', *Quadrant*, No 137, Vol XXII, No 12, December 1978, 41-4.
24. William Roper, *The Lyfe of Sir Thomas Moore, Knighte* 32-3 cited in Raymond Chambers, *Thomas More* (Cape, 1935) 228.
25. John A Guy, *The Public Career of Sir Thomas More* (Harvester Press, 1980) 32.
26. William S Holdsworth, *History of English Law*, Volume 5 (Methuen,1924) 222.
27. Holdsworth (n 26) 223.
28. Campbell (n 3) 35.
29. William Roper, *The Lyfe of Sir Thomas Moore, Knighte* 42 – 43 cited in Raymond Chambers, *Thomas More* (Cape, 1935) 268.
30. Campbell (n 3) 37.
31. Guy (n 25) 201.
32. Campbell (n 3) 45.
33. Campbell (n 3) 24.
34. Guy (n 25) 203.
35. William Roper, *The Lyfe of Sir Thomas Moore Knighte* 69 cited in Ernest E Reynolds, *Saint Thomas More* (Burns Oates, 1953) 288.
36. William Roper, *The Lyfe of Sir Thomas Moore Knighte,* 71 cited in Ernest E Reynolds, *Saint Thomas More* (Burns Oates, 1953) 289.
37. William Roper, *The Lyfe of Sir Thomas Moore Knighte,* 73 cited in Ernest E Reynolds, *Saint Thomas More* (Burns Oates, 1953) 291.
38. William Roper, *The Lyfe of Sir Thomas Moore Knighte* , 84 cited in Ernest E Reynolds, *Saint Thomas More* (Burns Oates, 1953) 298.
39. Elizabeth Frances F Rogers (ed) *The Correspondence of Sir Thomas More*, Princeton University Press, 1947, 542; cited in Ernest E Reynolds *Saint Thomas More* (Burns Oates, 1953) 309.
40. Nicholas Harpsfield, *The Life and Death of Sir Thomas More*, ed by E V Hitchcock, with historical notes by R W Chambers, 1932, 1st edition, 183-97; cited in Ernest E Reynolds, *Saint Thomas More,* Reynolds, 341.
41. See *The Workes of Sir Thomas More,* wrytten in the English tonge, London, 1557, 1457; cited in Raymond Chambers *Thomas More* (Cape, 1935) 345.
42. Chambers (n 1) 348.

11.3 The Independence of Sir Thomas More

Editor's note

When on the High Court, Brennan usually attended the Red Mass in St Mary's Cathedral at the commencement of the legal year. The mass was organised by the St Thomas More Society. On 27 May 1983, Brennan addressed the Society in Sydney on 'The Independence of Thomas More'.

The times in which we live bear some resemblances to the age of Thomas More. Ours, too, are times of questioning. Indeed, ours is an age of iconoclasm. Our household Gods no longer command fidelity; their very existence is in doubt. Our revered saints are alleged to have feet of clay. Our respected institutions are challenged in point of utility and legitimacy.

Christianity is thought to be an outmoded way of life, and many would hold it to be incompatible with human freedom of thought and of action. The law is regarded by many as a profession which is not merely non-productive, but which is directed to the preservation of the privileges of an earlier time. These are criticisms which can be repelled, in a fashion, by saying 'It is not so' and pointing to examples of great intellectual or pastoral activity in some Christian people or by rejoicing in the fairness of the procedures of the judicial process or in the niceties of the legal principle which adjust competing interests. But the criticisms have elements of validity, and they challenge us to consider anew the values that are common to faith and profession, and to identify what the practice of faith and profession offers to ourselves, to our fellow man and to God. It is a salutary development that the unquestioning admiration of Thomas More should give way to more critical analyses.

In recent years – though I pretend to no scholarship on the subject – some historical contributions on More, challenge the traditional views of the protagonists such as Roper and Campbell, and the veritable army of hagiographers. Professor Elton of Cambridge,[1] Dr Guy of Bristol[2] and Dr Alistair Fox of the University of Otago,[3] founding their scholarship upon source documents, have depicted More not as a figure remote in his sanctity but as a man of affairs moved by considerations of a practical kind. Professor Elton holds that More was not so other worldly as to be an unwilling conscript to the King's service as a member of the Council; he was not so careless of his fortune as to be unattracted by the emoluments of the office of under Treasurer; he was not a lawyer of the same professional skill as his father who sat upon the King's Bench. He suggests that More, in the 1520s was 'a man aware of his powers, anxious to put them to practical use, capable of vanity and not always able to conceal his justified sense of intellectual superiority, ready enough to ride opponents down. …He had office, he had profit, he had the ear and friendship of the King, and his ambitions did sufficiently tend that way to make such things not disagreeable. People respected his standing and envied him Henry's favour.'[4]

Though in disagreement with Wolsey's policies, he was compromised by his political loyalties and the political influence he enjoyed. 'Yet in the end', says Elton,

> one more chance offered, all of a sudden. It, too, was flawed. Wolsey's fall, which led to More's elevation, arose from events in which More took his stand against the King's desires. Wolsey was removed not because he had failed in the sense in which More thought he had failed, but because he had not succeeded in the one thing that More did not want to see successfully accomplished. Once again his position was false. He owed the chancellorship to no previous power in Council but rather, ironically, his very lack of power: the king simply did not associate him with the fallen regime.[5]

This estimate of More may be too hard upon him. At all events, Dr Guy describes his performance in the office of Chancellor as 'magisterial', and states that he 'added practical realism to Wolsey's idealism, and so ensured a smooth transition from the age of clerical to that of common-law chancellors'.[6]

The point of present relevance, however, is the revelation that More shares with us, and experienced to a far greater degree, the tensions that are familiar to all who practise law under a system which yields less than perfect justice or who perform a public function in a society which is flawed by venality and by an awe of power. He laboured under no delusions about the law and the society that he served. When he was still in private practice, he had written that society was in reality nothing better than a conspiracy of rich men (especially lawyers), pursuing their own interests against the rest, and in the Tower he thought that most men lived not for justice but for greed and 'worldly fantasies'.[7]

Yet living in and prospering under an imperfect system, he taught us two lessons of enduring relevance. In the first place, his intellect was bent upon discovery of the means whereby the system of law and government could be improved and his will effected those improvements so far as he was able. His pragmatic good sense no doubt told him that he could not straighten every path and make virtue the unquestioned ideal of every soul but, within the limits of his authority in a succession of offices, he sought to leave the system as he knew it the better for his tenure of each office.

His industry, whether as Under Sheriff of London, a diplomat, a member of the Council, Chancellor of the Duchy of Lancaster, or Lord Chancellor was commonly acknowledged though the story that he had cleared the lists in Chancery seems to be mythical. His availability to litigants and especially to poor suitors, attention to the minutiae of legal procedure, control of the writ of subpoena, and the creative but disciplined use of the common injunction, mark him out as a perceptive and constructive judge. By looking to the state of the defendant's conscience as the determinant of the Chancellor's response, he reduced the likelihood that equitable relief might abet acts of moral dishonesty by plaintiffs.[8] Holdsworth, noting that More's appointment as Chancellor in 1529 marks the transition from the administration of equity by ecclesiastics and canonists to its administration by laymen and common lawyers, pays him handsome tribute: 'More's beautiful character would have made him an ideal chancellor at any time. It was exactly fitted to the difficult position which he was then called upon to fill.'[9]

Though More was opposed to the King's divorce and known to be so, he performed his duties as Chancellor to the maximum extent consistent with his conscience. In 1531, he was charged with the responsibility of presenting to Parliament the opinions garnered from various Universities in favour of Henry's case. His address to the Commons accorded integrity of motive to the King, but in no way committed the Chancellor to support the opinions 'Now you of this Common House may report what you have seen and heard, and then all men shall openly perceive that the King hath not attempted this matter of will or pleasure, as some strangers report, but only for the discharge of his conscience and surety of the succession of his realm. This is the cause of our repair hither to you, and now we will depart.'[10]

Duty and industry and genius were committed by the King's good servant, not because the system was perfect or perfectable, but because the system could be made better by that commitment.

The second lesson of More's life is that the dividing line between the permissible and dutiful performance of a function and the impermissible and dishonourable commitment to a false cause is oftentimes difficult of definition. All of his sophistication and experience had to be added to his perception of principle in determining how far honourable ambition, financial security and professional repute were compatible with his adherence to the God he worshipped.

More maintained his own counsel on the King's great question so long as it was possible to do so. But when Cromwell sought to strip the Convocation of Bishops of their power to enact ecclesiastical canons without royal approval. More decided that opposition was necessary. On 13 May 1532, he and the Aragonese faction gained control of the House of Lords and he waged a political campaign in the open, perhaps in continuation of an earlier surreptitious campaign.[11]

On 16 May 1532, on the authority of a rump of Convocation, three bishops and four abbots subscribed the articles of submission. When the bishops agreed to subject the governance of the church to royal power, the relationship of church and state was disordered. That afternoon More surrendered the great seal. He had employed all his natural talents, all his political skills and influence in the struggle, choosing when to be silent and when to speak, upon what issues to support the King, and upon what issues to oppose him. But in the end, he failed to achieve the object for which he had striven. He reached the point where shrewdness and power could go no further without impairing his integrity. Dr Guy comments:

> 'Practical philosophy' was no use any more. More could no longer 'seek .., to handle matters tactfully', making bad better, even though bad could not be made wholly good. „. 'Practical philosophy' might have helped during the years of Wolsey's ascendancy, but it was impotent amid a cut-throat world of true political crisis, where corruption, vice and evil counsels were measured only by the standard of success. More's public career was over, and the time had come to devote himself to God alone and not to meddle in affairs again, 'but that my whole study should be upon the passion of Christ and mine own passage out of this world'. (Rogers, no 214).

And so,

> When the axe finally fell on 6 July 1535, 'the king's good servant' also earned his place among the very few who have enlarged the horizon of the human spirit. [12]

The lessons of More's life are inspiring, but what a price he paid. The ultimate price he paid was, of course, dramatic and extreme, but the instalments too were heavy. In defining the dividing line between what was permissible and what was impermissible, between the course that was fraught with danger and the course that was congenial, he had neither peer group nor mentor to support or guide him. Professional consensus gave no assurance of right conduct, Henry – the source of power and patronage – sought More's support for error, the majority of the bishops seemingly denied the validity of his opinion, the blandishments of his wife would have gnawed at his resolution, the cry of his beloved Margaret would have torn his heart. Integrity of conscience was a lonely and misunderstood thing to cling to.

Yet in this, we, as lawyers in the various departments of our profession, may find the finest example of the quintessential professional virtue: independence. Independence of popular acclaim, of power or patronage, of wealth, of improper influence by State or Church, by family or friends. It is a lonely virtue. It is a virtue which, if it is not to be transformed into stubborn arrogance, requires humility of mind, devotion to learning, and breadth of experience. It is a virtue that we do well to aspire to, and if we should succeed to any extent, well then, to that extent we have climbed a rung or two on the ladder of More's sanctity.

---

1. Geoffrey R Elton, *Studies in Tudor and Stuart Politics and Government,* volume 1, (Cambridge University Press, 1974)
2. John A Guy, *The Public Career of Sir Thomas More* (Harvester, 1980)
3. Alistair Fox, *Thomas More: History and Providence* (Yale University Press, 1982).
4. Geoffrey R Elton, *Studies in Tudor and Stuart Politics and Government,* volume 1, (Cambridge University Press, 1974), 151.
5. Ibid.
6. Guy (n 2) 93.
7. Ibid..
8. Ibid., 69.
9. See *Holdsworth's History of English Law*, (Methuen, 1924) Volume v, 222, 223.
10. Cited in Geoffrey R Elton, *Studies in Tudor and Stuart Politics and Government,* volume 1, (Cambridge University Press, 1974) 163.
11. See Geoffrey R Elton, *Studies in Tudor and Stuart Politics and Government,* volume 1, (Cambridge University Press, 1974) 165 – 171; John A Guy, *The Public Career of Sir Thomas More* (Harvester, 1980) 186 – 201.
12. John A Guy, *The Public Career of Sir Thomas More* (Harvester, 1980) 202, 203.

11.4 The Vocation of the Christian Lawyer

Editor's note

Brennan was invited to address the Ecumenical Church Service at St Peter's Memorial Church, the Lutheran church in Reid, ACT on 28 January 1992. The readings for the service included Isaiah 42:1–8 and Mark 10:41–45. In later years, there was often speculation as to how Brennan held together the highest legal method, absolute judicial integrity and commitment to his Catholic faith. The answer was neatly summarised in the four points he made in this address. While judgment was reserved in *Mabo*, he told his fellow believers and fellow lawyers: (1) 'Declarations of solidarity with or sympathy for a neighbour who suffers an injustice are no substitute for, or solvent of, the duty to do whatever lies within our power to see that justice is done according to law.' (2) 'We have no divine mandate to administer justice in disregard of human law. To the contrary, the professional duty of the Christian lawyer is to administer the law created by the competent organs of society's government.' (3) 'If the law itself is an obstacle to justice, the duty of a Christian lawyer extends to seeking its reform.' (4) 'To aspire to perform our duties, we need wisdom and knowledge, humility and compassion, courage and strength. These are gifts for which we pray and which we commit ourselves to employ.'[1]

The tradition of holding a Church Service at the beginning of a Law Year is of comparatively recent origin. Derriman's *Pageantry of the Law* dates the Service in Westminster Abbey from 1897 though he notes that 'Roman Catholic members of the profession had had a Mass on this occasion in earlier years, since 1895 at least.'

The tradition has waxed and waned in this country. When I began practice, the several Church Services at the beginning of the year were well attended and, with the advent of an Ecumenical Service, the religious divisions which had sometimes found a regrettable resonance in professional relationships were put behind us and the Service became an expression of commitment by all Christian Lawyers. In recent years, attendance at the traditional Services throughout Australia, whether Ecumenical or Denominational, seems to have fallen to some extent. Nevertheless, the tradition is a substantial one and we are part of it.

And so, when Mr Monro asked me to speak at today's service, I lightly agreed, thinking that tradition would be satisfied by re-affirming in conventional terms our need for Divine assistance in performing the duties of our respective offices. But conventional terms, however dear and familiar they may be in the liturgies which we know and love, ring hollow when spoken from a pulpit by one whose place is in a pew. Better, then, to reflect on the question why a group of lawyers, sharing a common belief in the Divinity of Christ, should assemble year by year in a Service of praise and petition, seeking God's blessing on their professional activities.

There would be little purpose in coming here today merely to continue a ceremonial tradition. Nor are we likely to attend merely to conform with the practice of others. Nor merely to acquire a sense of well-being. Cynics may say that we come for the reason that George Essex Evans scorned in his *Ode to the Philistines*:

> Six days shalt thou swindle and lie;
> On the seventh, though it soundeth odd
> In an odour of sanctity
> Thou shalt worship the Lord thy God –
> With a threepenny bit, a doze, a start
> And an unctuous smile
> And a hurried prayer to prosper in another six days of guile.

But we do not come to pray for prosperity. We come, as our predecessors came, because we each have some special responsibility in the administration of justice.

Justice is a social goal, a guarantee of order and peace in the community, a precondition of human development – and it is therefore of concern to every member of our community. For the Christian, justice has a special and central significance: it is a Divine imperative. St Luke tells us that Jesus castigated the unjust judge and promised that God would see justice done and done speedily to those who cry out for it (*Luke* 18:1–8). The radical Christian command to love my neighbour is broken unless I first do what I can to see that justice is done to that neighbour. And a lawyer has many professional neighbours: clients and those who would be clients, those affected by the advice we give or the instruments we draft, litigants and those whom litigation may affect. Declarations of solidarity with or sympathy for a neighbour who suffers an injustice are no substitute for, or solvent of, the duty to do whatever lies reasonably within our power to see that justice is done according to law.

As a lawyer, each of us has respected and admired the work of other members of our profession – not all of them Christians, by any means – who have taken on the responsibility of seeing an injustice rectified for a person who was unable to protect himself, whether by reason of poverty, disability, ignorance or some other cause. These exemplars of professional virtue – whether they knew it or not, and whether they intended it or not – were acting as Our Lord told His disciples to act as recorded in this morning's reading:

> … whoever
> would be great among you must be your servant,
> and whoever would be first among you must be slave of all.
> For the Son of man also came not to be served but to serve, and to
> give his life as a ransom for many.

It is not easy to be the 'slave of all', in the sense in which that phrase is used in Scripture – especially when we are in a profession which proudly proclaims itself to be the servant of none. Yet there is no conflict between Christian and professional duty. In our profession, as in our faith, leadership depends not on office or reputation but on service.

The Christian command to serve directs the conduct of our professional lives. And so we pray that we may not fail to put enough effort into our work or to look up the books, that we do not refuse assistance that we could reasonably afford to render in a just cause merely in order to maximise our leisure or our profits; that we do not prosecute a cause vexatiously; that we do not fail to listen attentively for the truth; that we do not yield to prejudice or impatience; that we do not suffer the law to be a needless source of injustice; that we do not offend the dignity of any person who is involved in the processes of the law. These are heavy responsibilities, and we need Our Lord's assistance to fulfil them.

Of course, our professional responsibility is for the administration of justice *according to law*: it is the law of our society which gives us our authority and imposes on us our concrete professional responsibilities. We have no divine mandate to administer justice in disregard of human law. To the contrary, the professional duty of the Christian lawyer is to administer the law created by the competent organs of society's government. It is part of God's gift of freedom that men and women should have authority within very broad limits to prescribe for themselves the laws of the society in which they live and the means by which those laws should be administered. If it were otherwise, the only legitimate form of government would be a theocracy in which despotic powers would be asserted by those who proclaimed themselves to be God's oracles.

The Christian lawyer has a profound interest in the justice of the set of laws that he or she is bound to administer. Our legal system was formed, as our culture generally was formed, by the civilising values of Western Christianity. Our legal system accommodates and protects people from different traditions, but its fundamental values are the freedom and individual dignity which, proclaimed in the Old Testament, were brought to perfection in the New.

Or way of doing justice is, and please God will remain, the way in which Isaiah tells us Yahweh's beloved servant brings forth justice to the nations: 'He will not cry or lift up his voice, or make it heard in the street; a bruised reed he will not break, and a dimly burning wick he will not quench ....'

Justice is not brought to the people either by populist clamour or by implementing the will of the powerful. It must be sought by careful reflection upon the interests of the individual and of society as a whole and there must be an especial concern for the powerless, the socially insignificant, the weak minority. The bruised reed may be a drug addict, an unemployed boy or girl, an innocent but discarded spouse. The dimly burning wick may present itself as a refugee, a lonely migrant, an aboriginal group removed from its traditional land, the children of a broken family, the lonely aged.

Of course, human laws and the human application of law are never perfect. But the Christian lawyer, sensitive to the scriptural values that inform our culture and our legal system, is capable of recognising injustice and attributing its cause. If the law itself is an obstacle to justice, the duty of a Christian lawyer extends to seeking its reform. These are duties that we share with others but they have an additional dimension for us. Our relationship with God finds, or ought to find, daily expression in our professional lives. That is a relationship that should so mould our conduct that we neither contribute to an injustice nor unreasonably suffer an injustice to go without remedy. To aspire to perform our duties, we need wisdom and knowledge, humility and compassion, courage and strength. These are gifts for which we pray and which we commit ourselves to employ.

Our duties are onerous but, like all Christian duties, they sustain – they do not crush – the human spirit. The more we assume the tasks of seeing justice done, the closer do we unite our work with God's plan to bring justice to the nations, the greater is our solidarity with the people we serve and the more integrated are the professional and personal aspects of our lives. If the public reputation of our profession needs renewal, if our own sense of satisfaction with professional practice needs to be restored, this morning's readings show us the way. Our profession will be honoured and our professional lives will be fulfilled if, at the heart of professional practice, there is quiet and devoted service not only to the strong and powerful but to the bruised reeds and dimly burning wicks who cry out for justice. The nobility of our profession depends, in the ultimate analysis, upon our fidelity to God.

---

1. The address was published as Sir Gerard Brennan, 'The Christian Lawyer', Address at Ecumenical Church Service, Reid, ACT, 28 January 1992, (1992) 66 *Australian Law Journal* 259, 260-261.

11.5 Australasian Christian Legal Convention

Editor's note

Brennan was invited to deliver the opening address to the Australasian Christian Legal Convention held at Ormond College at the University of Melbourne on 1 February 2001. This was his address.

This Convention is to take as its inspiration the verse in Micah 6:8 which the Revised Standard Version translates in this way:

> He has showed you, O man, what is good;
> And what does the Lord require of you
> But to do justice, and to love kindness,
> And to walk humbly with your God.

Read the verse quickly and the Lord's requirements may be thought to be slight indeed: all we need are the right attitudes. If we are acting, we should do so justly; we should be well disposed to others and not be presumptuous in our relationship with the Almighty. We should simply be nice people. The translation in the *Jerusalem Bible* creates that impression even more: what Yahweh asks of you is 'only this, to act justly, to love tenderly and to walk humbly with your God.' But whichever version we read, a re-reading and a little reflection shows that the Lord's requirements are not to do with how we feel or with our outlook on life. The Lord calls us to action of the most demanding kind. We are required to act and, in acting, to do what we can to achieve justice; we are required to love and, in loving, to be kind and gentle; we are required to be the companions of God Himself, not boastful of our privileged association but conscious of His infinite goodness and responsive to His love. These requirements affect our relationship with our fellow human beings and our relationship with God.

The New Testament reverses the order of the requirements as Micah set them out: the relationship with God is primary; our relationship with our neighbour follows: 'You shall love the Lord your God with all your heart, and with all your soul, and with all your mind .., and love your neighbour as yourself' (Matthew 22:37-39)

Love is not an emotional reaction which simply wells up without consciousness of the person loved. It starts from a recognition of the existence and nature of God as revealed by Christ and of the unique dignity of each person as a child of the Father, made in the Divine image. Love is a response to that recognition; it governs thought and directs action. It demands that the things that we think and do accord with the will of our Divine companion. Yet we do not presently know in full the God with Whom we are required to walk. Being loved is a joy, but to love may be difficult when the object of our love is a God Who is only partially known to and knowable by us and when neighbours may be quite unlovable or overly demanding. Yet the commandment to love is absolute, so the first requirement is to use our hearts, souls and minds to know the God Whom we are to love.

Christians believe that God loves us unconditionally and unceasingly, but each of us realizes that love in his or her unique way. We must define our conception of God and respond to His love in order to discern and articulate what He wants of us. You have assembled here from the different parts of Australasia and from differing Christian denominations to discern and to articulate what God wants of you, individually and collectively. At the end of the Conference, you may find a concurrence on a variety of topics which Christian lawyers should be addressing but, whether that is so or not, each of you will deepen your conception of God and then acknowledge the ways in which your professional lives may help to realise your prayer: 'Thy Kingdom come, Thy will be done on earth as it is in Heaven'. In this you will draw support and comfort from one another as you pray together and, in all humility, walk together on a journey of self-revelation.

I confess to a sense of anomaly in your invitation to open this Conference. The participants in this Convention are actively engaged in active practice but my professional life is largely behind me. So, I have to speak not as a current practitioner of the law, but in retrospect. Retrospect is the prerogative of advancing age. It can be uncomfortable if it reveals failures 'to do justice and to love kindness' but advancing age does have an advantage. It focuses the mind more intensely on the life to come when we shall know truly the God Whom we are to love – and not through a glass darkly. Not a God Whom I have distorted by misconceptions conjured up over the years in response to the experiences and vicissitudes of life.

For me and perhaps for many Christians, faith is a gift that has been received from parents and teachers buttressed, perhaps, by an elementary study of Christian sources and surviving in a culture that is not wholly inimical to Christian belief and practice. It can be a comfortable faith provided we are comfortable. We can believe in the goodness of God provided we are the beneficiaries of temporal blessings. I know that, at the struggling beginning of life at the Bar, when energy and ambition had to be harnessed to meet the demands of family life and professional duty, prayer was often the prayer of petition – perhaps even a process of bargaining with Providence to solve the crises of both familial and professional life. If crises were resolved and professional progress was experienced, there were occasions for thanksgiving. Love of God was, to an extent, a response of gratitude. Christian faith was not hard work; rather, it was a comfort that gave security and order to the life of the time. But our God is not a good time God. His love is most valuable when all else fails: 'Come to me all you who labour and are overburdened and I will give you rest.' (Matthew 11:30).

If we survive the run of the mill crises in our familial and professional lives, our sense of dependence on God may be placed in abeyance until some new crisis sends us back to Him. Faith may be acknowledged merely as the civilizing influence on our society and our Christianity may become simply a badge of admission to the body of right-thinking citizens. 'God, I thank thee that I am not like other men'. (Luke 18:11) The tortured, pain-racked figure on the Cross recedes from consciousness and the Cross itself becomes an ornament, not a challenge. In the so-called post-Christian era, continued adherence to Christianity is not so much challenged as coated over with the values of a society that finds its fulfilment in material wealth and the successful pursuit of pleasure. It is easy to develop an increasing complacency of the spirit and a growing deafness to the cry of those who do not enjoy the same privileges. Poverty and other calamities can become the concern of others and faith may inspire little more than judicious donations from what is surplus. The way of the Cross is not the accepted way of life and, if you insist on reading Micah, then it should be read in a 'feel-good' way. There is no great desire to hear the answer to the question: 'Lord, when did we see thee hungry or thirsty or a stranger or naked or sick or in prison, and did not minister to thee?' (Matthew 25:44) And if we are sometimes pricked by the voice of conscience, it inspires the prayer of the young St Augustine: 'Not yet, 0 Lord, not yet!' But ours is not a God of hedonism or selfish affluence. He commended the widow who gave her mite to the temple treasury and told us that 'If any man would come after me, let him deny himself and take up his cross daily and follow me.' (*Luke* 9:23)

With increasing age, the question of a future life looms larger. What does it mean to believe that we live when the body is dead? No eyes to see, no ears to hear, no hand to touch, no brain to process. Yet man has been assured that 'You will see heaven opened, and the angels of God ascending and descending upon the Son of man." (John 1:51) How can this be? Does the recently revived discussion about science and religion present a real obstacle to belief in a life of eternal happiness when we can see the face of God? One of the arguments against religion in the letters column of the daily papers a month or so ago sought to show the scientific fallacy in believing in the Divine creation of the universe. Space and time are correlative concepts or, at least, one is meaningless without the other. Both commenced with the Big Bang. But – so the argument runs – if God was the Creator of the Universe, He must have existed before the Big Bang and 'before' is a temporal concept that is inconceivable until the moment of the Big Bang when space was created. It is a splendid conundrum but it helped me to some comprehension of the notion of eternity.

Ultimate reality cannot be confined by space, nor can eternity be measured by time. Ultimate reality cannot be a material universe to be apprehended by bodily senses; it does not need to be mediated by the bodily senses in order to be known. The ultimate reality must be spiritual and can be comprehended only by the spirit – the spirit of which each of us is conscious as identifying our uniqueness and our personality; the spirit which alone can recognize the Eternal Spirit who identified Himself as 'I am Who am'. When Christ rose from the dead, He was no longer confined by time or space – He vanished at Emmaus (Luke 24:31), He appeared to His disciples in a locked room (John 20:19) and ascended from the outskirts of Bethany into heaven (Luke 24:50-51). Yet He was recognized by, and brought joy to the hearts of, those who saw Him with the eyes of faith. Our finite minds cannot comprehend the infinite Deity, but our knowledge of Him comes with faith. As we try to make sense of the suffering and the joys of this life and the promise of the next, faith tells us that God must be a God Who has suffered as men and women have suffered, Who loves us unconditionally despite our coldness towards and our rejections of Him, Who has given us the dignity of being His children and Who wants us to walk with Him now and in a life to come. Our God wants us to believe in Him, to love Him, to work for justice, to care for the poor and the marginalized members of our society, not to put our faith in wealth or power but gladly to bear our burdens for His sake. He wants our faith to transform our lives so that we see this life in the context of the next. Perhaps we may come to know this God if we pray with heart and soul and mind: 'I believe; help my unbelief?' (Mark 9:24)

And if we are to walk humbly with Him, we must take seriously what Christ said: 'Whoever would be great among you must be your servant, and whoever would be first among you must be your slave; even as the Son of man came not to be served but to serve, and to give his life as a ransom for many.' (Matthew 20:26-28).

This is the key to what He wants lawyers who are His followers to be and to do. The most immediate duty of service is owed to those to whom we are obliged to render legal services, whether in advising, representing or judging. Of course, that duty of service is owed by lawyers other than Christians. Belief in or a knowledge of God is not the only basis on which to construct a morality of legal practice. The rules of law and the ethical practices of the profession can be explained as manifestations of practical wisdom, the product of reflection on human experience. But for the Christian, the precept of service is backed by a Divine command to emulate Christ's own service to humankind.

The content of the Christian lawyer's duty of service depends on, but is not confined by, the provisions of the law itself. The lawyer's authority is derived from the law, and only from the law. It is not derived from academic achievement or from practical experience. No lawyer can practise, with all the privileges of practice, without the law's authority; no judge can pronounce a judgment backed by the power of the State without the investment of the necessary authority by the laws of the State. The authority which lawyers have is to participate, in their respective ways, in the administration of justice according to law. It would be a mistake to construe Micah's admonition to act justly as setting the Christian lawyer on a course of action designed to achieve a better, or different, form of justice than justice according to law. We are concerned here with the exercise of an authority conferred by the lawful civil power, an authority that would be abused if it were exercised otherwise than in accordance with the condition on which it has been conferred and accepted. There is no antinomy between the duty to participate in the administration of justice according to law and the duty to act justly of which Micah speaks. On the contrary, the duty to act justly binds the Christian lawyer to act in the exercise of his or her professional authority in accordance with law.

That is no light responsibility. At the most fundamental level, there is a duty not to assume a responsibility to exercise a lawyer's authority unless the task is within the lawyer's competence. The law must be found, so we must look up the sources of law; the facts must be ascertained, so we must listen attentively to find the relevant truth; we cannot refuse to answer a reasonable call for assistance in the administration of justice according to law, so we cannot insist on unreasonable fees or decline to spend the time or to expend the effort needed to represent the client and protect the client's interests or to exercise the jurisdiction of the court; we cannot allow the procedures of the law to produce unnecessary injustice, so we cannot prosecute vexatious suits or subject clients, opponents, criminal defendants, witnesses or the public to any indignity or gratuitous embarrassment. The Christian lawyer's duties accord with and reinforce the highest ethical standards of his or her profession.

There is a further duty resting on the Christian lawyer. The law itself, being an imperfect human instrument, will sometimes be productive of injustice in an absolute sense. Justice according to law may not always be just. In such a case, what is the Christian lawyer's duty? It is not to frustrate the operation of the law, but it may be a duty to seek its amendment. I say 'may be' because no step can be taken to prejudice the legal rights of a client by whose retainer the lawyer is bound. Subject to that qualification, there are two situations in which, I suggest, a lawyer has a duty (and the Christian lawyer has a cogent duty) to work for the amendment of a law that is seen to be unjust. The first is when a common law rule which appears to be applicable to the instant case would produce what is thought to be an unjust result and the rule is open to reconsideration in an appellate court. It is entirely in accordance with the duties of a lawyer to seek, or for an appellate judge to prescribe, an abrogation or amendment of a common law rule when the present rule produces manifest injustice and when the court before which the issue has arisen has jurisdiction to prescribe that abrogation or amendment. As the history of the common law shows, the appearance of injustice – or inefficiency, which is a form of injustice – has been the stimulus for the common law's development.

Secondly, and perhaps more significantly, where the operation of statutes or regulations or government policies is productive of injustice, the duty of the Christian lawyer is to do what he or she reasonably can to secure an amendment of the relevant law or policy. A supine refusal to act when faced with injustice is hardly consistent with a duty to act justly, much less is it consistent with a duty to love kindness towards those who suffer the injustice. That does not set us off on trying to set the world to rights. Equally, it does not allow us always to leave others to reform injustice when it lies within our own power to do something about it. In this respect, lawyers who understand the legal infrastructure of our society and are aware of the legal mechanisms which can remedy particular injustices can make a special contribution to improve our society. This may involve some participation in public affairs, perhaps in the writing of a letter for publication, the making of a public statement, or engaging in a public debate. Participation in public affairs may involve moral issues on which Christians have a particular view about what is just and what is unjust.

Of course, there may be debate about what constitutes injustice in our society. For example, the debate about euthanasia (by which I mean the taking of an active step in order to cause death) shows that some of our fellow citizens would regard the law of homicide as being unjust in its application to the causing of death of some of those who are terminally ill. Is the Christian, and especially the Christian lawyer, entitled to advance religious values for consideration in this debate? Or does the existence of a pluralistic, secular society invalidate arguments based on principles derived from religious faith? Is there some reason why Christians should refrain from public expression of Christian values touching public issues? Surely, we are all citizens in a free democracy and all – Christian and non-Christian – are entitled to advance and advocate principles in which we believe, provided they are not calculated to destroy the social cohesion of our communities. Perhaps we, and those who are not Christians, have over-reacted to the years when the values of the community were assumed to be what the clergy of the more populous denominations declared they ought to be. Perhaps we have become loath to insist that Christian sensitivities be respected and Christian values be admitted for consideration in the formation of public policies. But Christian sensitivities are entitled to respect, just as the sensitivities of other religions or legitimate associations are entitled to respect. And while Christian values cannot demand public acceptance if a majority of the community otherwise determine, their inherent worth to the community has been demonstrated through the centuries by the civilizing influence of the church and by the Christian foundation of our legal system. There is no reason why the Christian's voice should not be heard and, if Christian principles command majority support, they will be accepted.

I venture to suggest that we, as Christians, have sometimes failed our community by not expressing Christian values when their expression would have enhanced the ethos of our society. Perhaps we were silent when we could have spoken, or we mentioned Christian values apologetically or, worst of all, we demanded conformity with Christian values without demonstrating their social utility. Take a very general political example. In Australia we have become accustomed to political opinion polling and demographic studies by our political parties in order to maximize their prospects of electoral success. We have come to accept the primacy of this method in the formation of policy: pragmatism rather than principle. It makes policy captive to those who, with the assistance of their spin doctors, manipulate the public opinion of the moment. Yet the Christian, believing that each of us has a divine spark and destiny, surely believes that respect for that unique dignity must be the informing principle of political activity. That principle mandates that each person should live with freedom of conscience and in the dignity which a fair participation in the community's wealth and opportunities allows, while each is under a duty to contribute to that wealth so far as it is within his or her power. But do we evaluate political policies by reference to that principle or do we accept the validity of the majority's self-interest as ascertained by the pollsters? Democracy without principle, we should remind ourselves, leads to tyranny.

Let me mention two issues which, in my respectful opinion, illustrate the need for Christian lawyers to contribute their views in the formation of public policy. I do not suggest that Christian lawyers should see themselves as a political pressure group but rather that individual Christian lawyers, conscious of the injunction in Micah and obedient to their duty to be witnesses to the Christian message, should contribute to public discussion when their contribution can advance justice and kindness.

Political parties campaign on a law and order policy and the public, often incensed by unbalanced media reports, clamours for heavier sentences. Then let us consider the destructive culture of our gaols. Others will know better than I the extent to which rape and other violence occur and the effect of the drug trade on young first timers. Yet the state seeks to economize on the provision of prison facilities and often farms out the custody of prisoners to those who undertake the task for profit. Yet we must acknowledge that prisoners, no less than the rest of humankind, are entitled to respect of their dignity as children of God. The crimes of His children may warrant a deprivation of their liberty but not the denigration of their humanity. We can, as we too often have, leave the question of prison reform to the appropriate authorities of the state or we may even hope that the corporations which conduct the gaols will provide adequate protection and facilities, physical and cultural, for the inmates. The responsibility of the legal profession has been too often limited to the curial process, ceasing with the closing of the steel doors. There are probably few votes in an enlightened prison policy, and that will remain the position unless the public conscience acknowledges the inherent dignity of every person, even those who have committed grievous crimes. It is one of the failures of my generation of lawyers that we have not raised professional and public consciousness of the need to respect the dignity of offenders and those charged with offences. There has been a failure to act justly and to love kindness.

Or take the diminishing status of marriage and the family. Marriage, as the law knows it, follows the strict Christian definition: the voluntary union for life of one man and one woman to the exclusion of all others.[1] The commitment of the spouses to a lifetime together with all its joys and sorrows, gains and losses, their joint responsibility for the parenting of their children and the social stability – including the minimising of calls on the public purse – which the institution of marriage creates demand protection by laws affecting property, taxation, inheritance and pensions. The social principle which supports these protective laws is the desirability of assisting the parties to maintain their union and the family unit. Where common law marriages exhibit the same incidents (though there is no public ceremony) there is social justification for similar protective laws. In modern times, however, the sexual revolution has diminished the significance of marriage as a central social institution. The Christian ideal, albeit not realized in every case, has been depreciated as an old-fashioned concept.

There has been increasing pressure to equate the forming of sexual relationships, both heterosexual and homosexual, with the status of marriage and to extend to those relationships the benefits of the laws protective of the marriage institution. Rights to sexual relationships rather than the acceptance of responsibilities to spouse and children are advanced as the justification for conferring the benefit of protective laws. But if A can confer rights on B simply by entering into a sexual relationship with him or her, should not X be entitled to confer similar rights on Y simply by agreement between the two for some form of association without sexual relations?

It is not for Christians to stand in judgment on the sexual relations of others, nor to deny the human tragedies and personal insecurity that account for the disruption of many familial and other personal relationships. But when the extension of laws protective of marriage and family is in issue, there is no reason why the Christian should not seek to maintain the special position of marriage and the family – not only to uphold an institution of central significance to Christians but also to enhance the stability of society.

I mention these two issues only as illustrations of questions to which Christian lawyers may usefully contribute their views. Christians may not share the same views on these or other social issues but that is not to deny either the right of individual Christians to speak on a subject or the benefit of considering what they have to say in determining social policy. Christians, respectful of the views of others, acknowledging the unique dignity of every person and moved by a desire to see justice done should be valuable and valued citizens in our pluralistic, multi-cultural society. Participation by Christians in the life of the community should be a social benefit. And participation in the life of the community, including participation by the contemplative Orders who spend their lives in prayer for the community, is of the essence of the Christian life. That is one of the ways in which we demonstrate love of our neighbours as ourselves. One of the purposes of Conventions of this kind is to allow the Holy Spirit in our midst to inspire us to a fuller Christian life. It is a life which can give joy and satisfaction in our professional endeavours, in which we can find comfort and strength in its trials and courage to speak when there is an occasion where speech can be beneficial to our fellows. The requirements that the verse of Micah lays upon us are substantial, but not worrisome. Indeed, they free us from concerns born of a desire for purely human respect and profit and they encourage us in the service of God and our neighbour. For one who, having the greatest part of a professional life behind him, finds himself in the committed and stimulating membership of this Convention, I can only say: 'Let your light so shine before men that they may see your good works and give glory to your Father who is in heaven'. (Matthew 5:16)

---

1. See *Hyde* v *Hyde and Woodmansee* (1866) LR 1 P&D 130,133; *Family Law Act 1975* (Cth), s 43(a); *Calverley* v *Green* (1984) 155 CLR 242, 259-260.

11.6 Address to Christian Lawyers

Editor's note

Brennan was invited to address the Christian Lawyers Society in Brisbane on 30 August 2001. He spoke on 'Law, Values and Charity'.

The three subjects of this topic relate to our identity. Law, which creates our institutions and provides the framework for our relations with Government and with one another; values which are characteristic of the cultural group to which we belong; and charity, the virtue by which Christians are to be known. Perhaps values should have preceded law in the title for laws exist in order to express and protect those values which need expression and protection by the authority of the State.

Values are broad articles of faith. Some of our individual values come from, or are verified by, practical experience; some come from beliefs we have taken from others and, with or without qualifications, have made our own. As the good and the useful can depend on circumstances, no value can be stated in terms that are universal and absolute. Liberty and equality are estimable values, but absolute liberty can be the enemy of equality and absolute equality would demand the curtailing of liberty.

Values are expressed in broad terms, without the qualifications necessary to define the precise moral or legal precepts which they indicate. Although their content is imprecise, they are powerful influences on thought and conduct. We value what we believe to be good or at least useful. Our values influence what we think and do. They continually contribute to the formation of our attitudes to specific issues or problems.[1] We may not always form our attitudes or act in harmony with our values but we assume that they tell us what is good or useful. Values give us our character, affect our conduct, inform our relationships, and mould our future. They define our identities.

It is a truism that social phenomena reflect the values of society, whether for good or ill. We know that the practices of fascism could not have flourished in a society that valued liberty and equality; equally, we know that the financial excesses of the 1980s were possible only because of a pervasive materialism that asserted greed to be good. No human society is value free; each society reveals and gives effect to its prevailing values in its laws and institutions, in its political and economic policies, in its art, literature and architecture and in the manner in which its people relate one to another. A people's values are the substance of their culture. Bernard Lonergan has said that 'A culture is a set of meanings and values informing [that is giving form to] a common way of life, and there are as many cultures as there are distinct sets of such meanings and values.'[2]

Civilisation is impossible without moral values and a community which does not share or accept a basic set of moral values is a community in chaos. Australians enjoy political stability because we share the basic values of liberty, equality and tolerance; we respect integrity, especially in public office, and we insist on the rule of law. Within those very broad parameters, we conduct our public affairs and frame our laws. Of course, the content of these values is not universally agreed. For example, we do not agree on what we find intolerable. Disagreements stimulate our controversies. The content which Christians give to these concepts is the Christian contribution to our social life.

Liberty is essential to the Christian. It is naturally possessed by everyone and without liberty virtue would be impossible. Any infringement or limitation of individual liberty must be justified. Liberty is not to be taken away by laws, pressures or inducements which are not needed to preserve ourselves from unintended harm or to secure and maintain the common good of our fellows. Therefore, the coercion of the law should be kept to a minimum. Liberty is a value to be preserved not only because we like to live in a free society but because it maximises the opportunities for exercising the freedom of thought and action by which we achieve our own dignity and in which we may acknowledge and discharge our moral responsibilities to our fellow men and women. Liberty is the pre-condition of moral (as distinct from conforming) conduct. Fortunately for us, liberty is a value which is firmly protected by the law, as Sir Isaac Isaacs pointed out in *Ex parte Walsh & Johnson; In Re Yates*:

> (1) primarily every free man has an inherent individual right to his life, liberty, property and citizenship; (2) his individual rights must always yield to the necessities of the general welfare at the will of the State; (3) the law of the land is the only mode by which the State can so declare its will. These principles taken together form one united conception for the necessary adjustment of the individual and social rights and duties of the members of the State. For their effective preservation and enforcement the Courts have evolved two great working corollaries in harmony with the main principles and without which these would soon pass into merely pious aspirations. The first corollary is that there is always an initial presumption in favour of liberty, so that whoever claims to imprison or deport another has cast upon him the obligation of justifying his claim by reference to the law. The second corollary is that the Courts themselves see that this

obligation is strictly and completely fulfilled before they hold that liberty is lawfully restrained.[3]

The value of equality is an acknowledgment that, before God, each individual is equally precious and is equally loved. Race or colour, class or creed, physical or mental perfection or defect afford no warrant for attributing varying degrees of worth and dignity to humankind. This consideration is relevant to debates on euthanasia. Every person possesses the same dignity as a child of God[4] and is entitled to the same respect.[5] Of course, there are differences in natural endowments and massive differences in the societies and environments in which people live. These differences account for or contribute to dissimilarity in the position, especially in the economic position, of individuals within society. Disparities between the rich and poor, between the hungry and the fed are constant thorns in the Christian conscience. 'I was hungry and you gave me to eat'. The achieving of economic equality has particular problems, and I shall return to that issue in a minute.

Thirdly, tolerance: tolerance is a virtue, for Scripture forbids us to be judgmental of one another.[6] Tolerance is also an Australian value, characteristic of a people who wish to live in peace and who are both conscious of the religious, ethnic and cultural diversity of the community and willing to celebrate that diversity. Our laws, notably the statutes which prohibit various forms of discrimination, give legal effect to the value of tolerance.

Others in our community attribute a different content to the values which we hold dear. That does not require us to accept their values and forsake our own. No false modesty, no deference to non-Christian or anti-Christian values should deter the charitable exposition of the Gospel message. The Gospel calls us to be an example to others in our mutual love and in our lived and professed commitment to the values we find in Christ's life and teaching: 'love one another as I have loved you.'[7]

Liberty, equality and tolerance are not optional for the Christian. They are Christian values.

Of course, the Christian is bound to accept that others who, in good conscience, hold different views are free to advocate those views. The cultures of the western democracies, including our own, have become increasingly pluralistic. So, we cannot expect that the law and policies of the State will always accord with Christian values. The law must be the product of the common values of society; not vice versa. If law did not reflect common values, we would lose either our freedom or the peace of our society. Either the law would be ignored, and civil unrest would follow or the law would be enforced by physical duress and freedom would be lost.

Law is not universally regarded as the product of values broadly accepted; community values may be regarded as the product of the law. I remember that, during a visit the People's Republic of China in 1983, five years after the end of the Cultural Revolution, a senior Judge explained to me that it was important to get a body of laws enacted by the Supreme People's Congress, not only to create the necessary legal framework but also to instruct the people in socialist morality. In our own society, the influence of the law on values can be seen when conduct is defended on the ground that a QC's opinion that the conduct was lawful.

By contrast, Australia's Aboriginal Peoples do not distinguish between traditional law and the moral values of Aboriginal society. Law, religion, custom and right conduct are fully integrated in Aboriginal life. That culture was suitable for a stable, unchanging society. But Australian society is multicultural and multi-religious and we must live in peaceful community with those whose values differ from our own. Our laws must provide a cohesive framework for our society but they must be respectful of diverse values honestly held by the differing groups in our community.

In a notable speech to the University of Notre Dame, in September 1984, Governor Mario Cuomo, Governor of New York said:

> I protect my right to be a Catholic by preserving your right to believe as a Jew, a Protestant or non-believer, or as anything else you choose.
>
> We know that the price of seeking to force our beliefs on others is that they might some day force theirs on us
>
> This freedom is the fundamental strength of our unique experiment in government. In the complex interplay of forces and considerations that go into the making of our laws and policies, its preservation must be a pervasive and dominant concern.

So, there are two restrictions on what the law should cover. First, it should not unnecessarily trespass upon individual freedom. Secondly, and consequentially, so far as is consistent with the public good, it should not offend the values of any religious or cultural group in the community. These restrictions have a particular significance for our economic laws. Should we leave economic relations free of legal controls and allow market forces to be the untrammelled arbiter of economic activity? If it be right to own private property, it must be right to devote that property to the lawful accumulation of more wealth. That results, of course, in inequality of wealth. Should the State seek to equalise the possession of wealth? Could it do so without eliminating the private right of property? That issue was addressed by Pope John Paul II in his Encyclical *Sollicitudo Rei Socialis*:

> It should be noted that in today's world, among other rights, the right of economic initiative is often suppressed. Yet it is a right which is important not only for the individual but also for the common good. Experience shows us that the denial of this right, or its limitation in the name of an alleged 'equality' of everyone in society, diminishes, or in practice absolutely destroys the spirit of initiative, that is to say the creative subjectivity of the citizen. As a consequence, there arises, not so much a true equality as 'levelling down'. In the place of creative initiative there appears passivity, dependence and submission to the bureaucratic apparatus, which, as the only 'ordering' and 'decision-making' body – if not also the 'owner' – of the entire totality of goods and the means of production, puts everyone in a position of almost absolute dependence, which is similar to the traditional dependence of the worker-proletarian in capitalism. [8]

The liberty to employ initiative carries the right to garner its fruits. We therefore admit the legitimacy of the accumulation of wealth. When wealth is accumulated, there is a surplus beyond what is needed for the bare sustenance of life. The legal right of the owner is to apply the surplus to any lawful purpose including the accumulation of more wealth and the consequent acquisition of economic power. Economic power can be used to oppress others – employees, competitors, creditors – or to operate against the common good. What is the Christian response to the problem of the misuse of economic power when the right to private ownership of property is acknowledged? The answer is not to abolish private property but to regulate the exercise of economic power. That is a legitimate field of legal regulation. But how far should law go in seeking to control economic power? The right balance of legal control is hard to strike and unlikely to be struck without controversy between the parties on either end of the political and industrial spectrum. Poverty will not be eliminated by law but its incidence and severity can be reduced by appropriate legal controls. We know that the poor will be with us always[9] but that is no warrant for denying to the law and policies of the State the function of protecting the entitlement of everyone, especially the poor, to a life of dignity.

In practical terms, that protection requires some control of capital and of the relationship between capital and labour and some provision for social security. Within certain limits, the extent of control and of social security is properly the subject of political debate rather than moral precept. The Christian contributes to that debate by insisting the individual should neither have his or her initiative destroyed nor be treated as a mere economic integer. The law should protect the unique dignity of each individual and maintain social structures which do not alienate men and women from their fellows. Nor should social structures (including industrial laws) impede the essential relationship between the individual and God who is the creator and end of human existence. Each Christian must determine for herself or himself the morality of concrete proposals and the steps which should be taken to protect the life, the dignity, the autonomy and the religious freedom of the individual within his or her society.

The individual is not perceived as a mere economic integer or as the wielder or subject of political power. The unique dignity of each individual must not be diminished and social structures must not alienate men and women from their fellows. Nor must those structures impede the essential relationship between the individual and God who is the creator and end of human existence.

The doctrine acknowledges that each of us lives in a community formed by a particular history and culture and therefore it does not purport to prescribe the means by which its ideals are to be implemented. But it does define principles by which the local Church and each of its members may determine for themselves the morality of concrete proposals and the steps which should be taken to protect the life, the dignity, the autonomy and the religious freedom of the individual within his or her society.

Apart from legal controls, some charitable gifts are needed to alleviate poverty in individual cases. Can corporate funds be resorted to for that purpose?

Nowadays, an individual's surplus is often invested in corporations or funds under the control of managers. By reason of the accumulation of wealth in corporations or funds, director or managers possess considerable economic power.

But the law does not permit the application of corporate or fund assets to *purely* charitable objects.

When investors place their assets and their confidence in corporations under the control of directors or in funds under the control of managers, the primary duty of directors and managers is owed to the shareholders or investors whose assets are under their control. Generally speaking, these shareholders or investors do not control the deployment of the assets in which they have invested. The initiative of the directors or managers is exercised to secure the maximum benefit for the corporation or fund and thereby to secure the maximum benefit for their shareholders or investors. The primary duty of the directors or managers is not owed to the wider community or to nations or peoples elsewhere. For over a century, the general doctrine governing the application of a corporation's assets by directors has been this: 'They can only spend money which is not theirs but the company's, if they are spending it for the purposes which are reasonably incidental to the carrying on of the business of the company … The test must be what is reasonably incidental to, and within the reasonable scope of carrying on, the business of the company.'[10]

The benefit of the company was understood, in the case of a solvent company, as the benefit of the general body of the shareholders.[11] It was said that 'charity has no business to sit at boards of directors *qua* charity'. However, modern legal writers suggest, and corporate practice accords with the suggestion, that it is permissible to donate corporate assets if the donation is likely to redound to the benefit of the corporation, but donations without the prospect of financial return are not authorized.[12] The legal justification explains such expenditure as 'seed corn' sown in the surrounding ground with a long-term view to profit.[13] Perhaps the distinction is between philanthropy, which is justifiable because it improves the profit-making capacity of the corporation, and charity which improves merely the position of the person benefited. Corporate image could not be improved if, when giving alms, the right hand of the corporation could not let the left hand publicity department know what the right hand was doing.[14] The limited authority of directors to donate the corporations assets means that the chief accumulations of wealth are not likely to be the primary source of charity for the alleviation of individual material poverty, although donations to charitable institutions which work for the alleviation of individual material poverty may be permissible as philanthropic 'seed corn'.

There are sound reasons of policy for imposing a limitation on directors' powers to donate corporate assets. Investors, whose charitable inclinations are diverse, do not authorise directors to dispose of corporate assets to charitable objects of the directors' choice. The choice should remain with the individual investor when he or she obtains his or her share of the distributed profits. From the moral viewpoint, there is no virtue in a directors' resolution to dispose of corporate assets to a charitable object. Virtue consists in the giving of what is one's own, not in the giving of assets that belong to another. And so, the kind of beneficence which seeks and yields no return ordinarily finds no place in the structures of capitalism. Individual poverty must be alleviated, if at all, by the State or by the charity of individuals.

The legal right of the individual to accumulate and to dispose of wealth brings with it the moral responsibility of determining what disposition should be made. The moral decision may not be an easy one for the Christian to make. But we start with Genesis, the Book which tells us that, when God created humankind, he said: 'Behold, I have given you every plant yielding seed which is upon the face of all the earth, and every tree with seed in its fruit; you shall have them for food.' So, we know that the goods of this world were intended by God for the benefit of all. The notion that the earth's goods are intended for all presents a radical challenge to the national and international order as well as a massive disturbance to complacency about our own possessions.

As all humankind has an equal right to live unless it is forfeited in order to protect another person, States and individuals are under the basic duty of doing what they can to ensure the supply of goods and services needed to sustain human life in dignity whenever and wherever it is threatened, whether by natural disaster, mismanagement or sheer poverty.

Where gainful employment is not available or where age or infirmity prevent the earning of a livelihood, it is the function of the State to support in cash and kind a life of dignity for those who are unable otherwise to support themselves. Social security is not a mere budgetary item to be adjusted according to political exigencies; it is not reducible merely to secure an economically satisfactory bottom line; it is a mandatory safety net to prevent fellow citizens from suffering a degrading loss of dignity – a loss of dignity that would be a reproach to society and ultimately a threat to its stability. In a society of increasing complexity and technological sophistication, when education to secondary level is the minimum required to open opportunities for employment, I should think the State is under a further duty to provide that education for those who cannot otherwise acquire it. If the State does provide more extensive educational or other benefits to its citizens, they should be provided without discrimination on the basis of race or colour, class or creed, or (except where special services are needed) physical or mental perfection or defect.

The Christian has a political obligation to see that the State performs its proper function in maintaining the dignity of our fellow citizens. And the duty of personal charity must be to give to those in need what remains after providing for what is required to maintain a person and his or her dependants in his or her station in life becomingly and decently. Our conscience is likely to interpret this duty generously, especially in estimating what must be accumulated to preserve our lifestyle for the future. But conscience may be trouble by the words of St Basil the Great: 'The bread which you do not use is the bread of the hungry; the garment hanging in the wardrobe is the garment of the one who is naked; the shoes you do not wear are the shoes of the one who is barefoot; the money you keep locked away is the money of the poor; the acts of charity you do not perform are so many injustices that you commit.'

That is not a cry for legal reform or for public policy improvements. It is a personal challenge to charity, and one which many of us find daunting. But the just God has given due warning of the consequences if we do not heed the cry of the poor:

> Then he will say to those on his left, 'Depart from me, you who are cursed, into the eternal fire prepared for the devil and his angels. For I was hungry and you gave me nothing to eat, I was thirsty and you gave me nothing to drink, I was a stranger and you did not invite me in, I needed clothes and you did not clothe me, I was sick and in prison and you did not look after me.' They also will answer, 'Lord, when did we see you hungry or thirsty or a stranger or needing clothes or sick or in prison, and did not help you?' He will reply, 'Truly I tell you, whatever you did not do for one of the least of these, you did not do for me.' Then they will go away to eternal punishment, but the righteous to eternal life.[15]

These are terrible words and they are unequivocal. Of particular concern to lawyers are the prisoners whom we did not visit. For most of my professional life, lawyers have paid little attention to the state of our prisons although many of us have had a part to play in the incarceration of the prison population. Yet prisoners, no less than the free, are our brothers and sisters and we have been silent too often when their human dignity has been diminished.

Charity is the virtue by which Christ wished his disciples to be known. Lawyers, who understand the mechanisms of society and professionally meet the rich and the poor, the comfortable and the desperate, the secure and the fragile, have opportunities to practise charity that are given to few. To practise that virtue, the skills and knowledge of the expert are needed but they are not in themselves sufficient. Those who need the lawyer's skills and knowledge but are unable to obtain them have a moral claim on the services of the profession. And when that claim is met, professional work becomes a stimulus to living and, please God, the source of riches in the life to come.

---

1. See Milton Rokeach, *Beliefs, Attitudes and Values* (Jossey-Bass, 1968) 159-161.
2. Bernard Lonergan, *Method in Theology* (Darton, Longman and Todd, London, 1972) 301.
3. (1925) 37 CLR 36, 79.
4. Romans 8:15; Galatians 4:6
5. Matthew 6:29-30; Luke 12:7,25,28
6. Matthew 6:15; Luke 6:36,37.

7. John 15:12.
8. Para 15.
9. Mark 14:7
10. See *Hutton v West Cork Railway Co* (1883) 23 Ch D 654, 671 (Bowen LJ).
11. See *Greenhalgh v Arderne Cinemas* Ltd [1951] Ch 286; *Ngurli Ltd v McCann* (1953) 90 CLR 425; *Gambotto v WCP Ltd* (1995) 182 CLR 432, 443-444.
12. See L C Gowers et al, *Gower's Principles of Modern Company Law* (Sweet & Maxwell, 5th ed, 1992) 555, fn 32.
13. Lord Wedderburn of Charlton, 'The Social Responsibility of Companies' (1985) 15(1) *Melbourne University Law Review* 4, 15. I am indebted to Professor Paul Redmond, Dean of Law at the University of New South Wales for this and other references.
14. Matthew 6:3
15. Matthew 25:41-46.

11.7 Address to Catholic Lawyers Association

Editor's note

Brennan addressed the Catholic Lawyers Association in Melbourne on 5 September 2008. He spoke on 'Law, Values and Culture'.

I was honoured to receive your President's invitation to address the Melbourne Catholic Lawyers Association, and I was pleased that he accepted a suggestion that I should speak about Law, Values and Culture. The very raison d'être of the Association must be its commitment to the law and to the values and culture of a Christian society. For the most part, there is a sympathetic relationship between the law and the values and culture of a Christian society, but there are some laws which run counter to those values and tend to alienate the Christian lawyer. But the general body of the law has been moulded in a Christian society and the common law is law which reflects a Christian culture.

Since the *Charter of Human Rights and Responsibilities Act 2006* (Vic) came into operation, there is a reason to consider more closely the relationship between values and the law. What are these human rights which the Act defines or identifies? Are they truly rights, or are they more akin to values? Rights in the strict sense are possessed by an individual or, in some instances, by a specified group of individuals. They are enforceable in law at the suit of the possessor of the right. Thus contractual rights, or rights to compensation in tort, or rights to benefits under a statute may be enforced by the person who possesses such rights, and the law defines the kind and extent of remedies which are available if such a right is breached. The human rights specified in the Charter are not of this sort. Take, for example, the human right set out in s 8(1), the right which opens the statutory list. The Act says that 'Every person has the right to recognition as a person before the law'. If that proposition were intended to confer a 'right' in the familiar sense, it would seem to be either unnecessary or circular – the human right to be recognized as a 'person before the law' is a right vested in 'every person'. Who are the 'persons' in whom this right is vested? They must be either those whom the law already recognizes as persons or those whom the law identifies as persons in order to recognize them as such. But that is not to say that the right has no content. Article 16 of the *International Covenant on Civil and Political Rights*, from which s 8(1) is taken, has been said to preclude the denial to an individual of a legal capacity vested in other individuals in like circumstances.[1] It expresses the value of equality before the law.

Although human rights are not legal rights in the ordinary sense in which we use the term; they articulate the values which inform the laws and institutions of a free and liberal society. They are to be given a meaning derived from a consideration of international law and the judgments of domestic, foreign and international courts and tribunals (s 32(2)). These are sources to be found, as one would expect, in cultures similar to our own, cultures in which similar values prevail. That is not to say that a Victorian court will give a right defined in the Act an operation which accords precisely with the operation attributed by an overseas tribunal to a corresponding right in the *International Covenant*. The Act is to be interpreted in the Victorian context.

These considerations simply bring home the importance of appreciating the interlocking relationship of Law, Values and Culture. When the foundations of the common law were laid in the 12th and 13th centuries, the English judges drew on the customs of the English people, albeit the content was affected by the practices of the judges and lawyers of the time assisted by scholars familiar with Roman Law.[2] English culture was then and, at least until modern times, remained substantially Christian. In the formative years of the common law, the judges drew on the values of contemporary society, giving institutional force to the values of that society. This is the way in which the common law develops. Judge Cardozo observed: 'Law is indeed an historical growth for it is an expression of customary morality which develops silently and unconsciously from one age to another.'[3]

Sir Ninian Stephen's observation in *Onus v Alcoa*[4] that 'Courts necessarily reflect community values and beliefs' was followed by the joint judgment in the *Native Title Case* where the majority said that 'the content of the common law will, in the ordinary course of events, change from time to time according to the changing perception of the courts.'[5] The common law cannot be developed inconsistently with the enduring values of contemporary society. If it were otherwise, the law would lose its authority.

Australians enjoy political stability and a peaceful society because we share basic values. Most importantly we share the values of human freedom, equality and tolerance of others and we respect integrity, especially in public office. As most of our people share these values, we are able to maintain a civilized and peaceful society. Thus, a want of political integrity will be visited with punishment at the ballot box and unjustified discrimination will generate a response, and not only from those who suffer directly from the injustice. Freedom, equality and tolerance are Christian values and, being entrenched in our culture, they underpin our law.

Liberty is naturally possessed by everyone, and it is essential to the

Christian. Liberty is a value to be preserved not only because we like to live in a free society but because it maximises the opportunities for exercising the freedom of thought and action by which we achieve our own dignity and in which we may acknowledge and discharge our moral responsibilities to our fellow men and women. Liberty is the pre-condition of moral (as distinct from conforming) conduct. Without liberty, virtue would be impossible. Liberty is not to be taken away by laws, pressures or inducements which are not needed to preserve ourselves from unintended harm or to secure and maintain the common good of our fellows. Therefore the coercion of the law should be kept to a minimum. Liberty is firmly protected by the law, as Sir Isaac Isaacs pointed out in *Ex parte Walsh & Johnson; In Re Yates*: '...there is always an initial presumption in favour of liberty, so that whoever claims to imprison or deport another has cast upon him the obligation of justifying his claim by reference to the law. The ...Courts themselves see that this obligation is strictly and completely fulfilled before they hold that liberty is lawfully restrained.'[6]

The value of equality is an acknowledgment that, before God, each individual is equally precious and is equally loved. Race or colour, class or creed, physical or mental perfection or defect afford no warrant for attributing varying degrees of worth and dignity to humankind. This consideration is relevant to debates on euthanasia. Every person possesses the same dignity as a child of God[7] and is entitled to the same respect.[8] Of course, there are differences in natural endowments and massive differences in the societies and environments in which people live. These differences account for or contribute to dissimilarity in the position, especially in the economic position, of individuals within society. Disparities between the rich and poor, between the hungry and the fed are constant thorns in the Christian conscience. 'I was hungry and you gave me to eat'. Although economic equality cannot be achieved merely by law, law may restrain excesses in the capitalist system.

The third value is tolerance. Tolerance is a virtue, for Scripture forbids us to be judgmental of one another.[9] Tolerance is also an Ausity and willing to celebrate that diversity. Our laws, notably the statutes which prohibit various forms of discrimination, give legal effect to the value of tolerance.

Values not only influence our law and legal system; they define our culture. Australia's Aboriginal Peoples do not distinguish between traditional law and the moral values of Aboriginal society. Law, religion, custom and right conduct are fully integrated in Aboriginal life. That culture was suitable for a stable, unchanging society. But Australian society is multicultural and multi-religious and we must live in peaceful community with those whose values differ from our own. Our laws must provide a cohesive framework for our society but they must be respectful of diverse values honestly held by the differing groups in our community.

What is culture? Bernard Lonergan defined it in these terms 'A culture is a set of meanings and values informing [that is giving form to] a common way of life, and there are as many cultures as there are distinct sets of such meanings and values.'[10]

This explains the tensions that are felt by some people about others who come from another culture. A different way of life, the product of different meanings and values, creates a difficulty of acceptance, which can be overcome only by a mature tolerance of difference or by a conformity by the minority to the mainstream Australian way of life. We boast of multiculturism in this country, but it must be admitted that there are many who, while strongly insisting on freedom, see difference in culture as a threat to their well-being. Yet, so long as we share the values which support a free and tolerant society, there is no reason for fear. Indeed, the very diversity of meanings and values in other respects gives our culture a strength and richness of which we can be justifiably proud.

While law must reflect the enduring values and culture of a society, its provisions may in turn affect societal values and culture. Take some of the major changes in the law in recent years. While societal values no doubt facilitated the changes in the law relating to abortion and homosexuality, can it be doubted that judicially accepted defences to criminal charges of abortion and statutory repeal of laws incriminating homosexual conduct have affected the level of community acceptance of conduct that was previously prohibited? Conversely, is not the legal recognition of the land rights of Australia's indigenous peoples the product of the moral and legal value of equality? Land rights followed a growing community awareness of inequality in the recognition of indigenous and non-indigenous culture and a consequent inequality in the protection of indigenous and non-indigenous interests in land. In time those values changed and the law ultimately changed to keep in harmony with the enduring values. Law and the underlying community values substantially shape our culture; they define who we are and what we wish to be. They identify the national character – what it means to be Australian. Perhaps the importance we attach to the value of individual freedom and our sense of national maturity is the reason why a majority of Australians would prefer a Republican form of government, instead of our constitutionally-mandated British head of State.

Christian lawyers are fortunate in the profession which they follow. Their daily work consists in the application of legal rules to particular situations in order to advance or protect the interests of their clients or, in the case of the judiciary, to do justice according to law. If the law generally reflected values or a culture alien to the Christian tradition, it would be difficult to devote a professional life to the law's application. It would be a life devoted to the promulgation of an alien culture. But our general law, far from being alien to a Christian culture, is in truth based on Christian values which, in part through the application of the law, inform even our so-called post-Christian society. *Holdsworth's History of English Law* shows that there was a time when Christianity was held to be part of the law of England.[11] And equity, which owes its fundamental concept of unconscionability to the ecclesiastic chancellors of the 15th century,[12] was designed to give effect to the law of God. The respect due in law to each person irrespective of their background is surely a reflection of Christ's reproof to His host when the woman, a sinner, washed Christ's feet with her tears and anointed his feet with oil. It was she, not the host, who was told to go in peace.[13] Equality before the law reflects the dignity of each person as a child of God,[14] entitled to the same respect.[15] Property law, which has its origins in the feudal relationship of lord and tenant, respected the rights of each. Tort and contract were developed in accordance with the exigencies of the time and the values of the contemporary society – at least nominally Christian – were consistent with that development. In modern times, the Christian influence on the law of torts can be seen in Lord Atkin's famous question in *Donoghue v Stevenson*: 'Who is my neighbour?'[16] But the law stops short of demanding conformity with the precepts of Christian charity.

It is one thing for the law to be largely compatible with Christian values; it is another for the law to demand compliance with those values. As Deane J wrote: 'the common law has neither recognized fault in the conduct of the feasting Dives nor embraced the embarrassing moral perception that he who has failed to feed the man dying from hunger has truly killed him.'[17]

There is a good reason for law stopping short of complete correspondence with the demands of a fully Christian life. The reason was brought home to me recently when I attended a legal conference in the United Arab Emirates. In the course of an informative address on Sharia law by the Chief Justice, he pointed out that 'Islamic Sharia is ...comprehensive in the sense that it finds the legal rules that regulate all the aspects of daily life for individuals and societies.' He added:

> The Koran and the Prophet's Traditions are the two main sources of Islamic Sharia; they provide it with overall rules and basic principles suitable for any practical life arrangement required by man. The basic rules of the Koran and the Sunna do not change according to time and place, but their flexibility allows human legislators to derive provisions

> and secondary and detailed legal rules in all the walks of life. Both the Koran and the Sunna could be considered the constitution in other legislation systems, and therefore all other sources should agree with them.

Now I may have misinterpreted what the Chief Justice was saying, but if the strength of Sharia law is its comprehensiveness in the sense of providing legal rules to govern every action and relationship, it goes far beyond the role which is assigned to the law in a Christian society. In our society, the law stops short of enjoining Christian morality. The shortfall of law from morality is the area of our freedom under the law – in that area, we are free of legal constraint. We regard that as an essential quality of a free society. It maximises the opportunities for exercising the freedom of thought and action by which we achieve our own dignity and provides an opportunity for virtuous conduct. We can be virtuous – or, to use a more Catholic term, we can earn grace – only by the exercise of our free will, and there would be little virtue in acting solely in accordance with the law. Liberty is the pre-condition of moral (as distinct from conforming) conduct. We can scarcely hope for an eternal reward simply by abstaining from murder, rape and theft. Rather, with the Prophet Micah, we must – 'act justly, .. love tenderly and walk humbly with your God.'[18]

And no human law can compel obedience to that injunction. Nor should it try to do so. Law and morality are related but distinct. As Christian lawyers we are fortunate that our law, in general, is compatible with our notions of morality. It is only when our social mores depart from the moral principles which we accept that we encounter laws in the application of which we derive no satisfaction. Yet apply them we must.

The Christian lawyer's authority is derived from the law, and only from the law. No lawyer can practise, with all the privileges of practice, without the law's authority; no judge can pronounce a judgment backed by the power of the State without the investment of the necessary authority by the laws of the State. The authority which lawyers have is to participate, in their respective ways, in the administration of justice according to law. It would be a mistake to construe Micah's admonition to act justly as setting the Christian lawyer on a course of action designed to achieve a better, or different, form of justice than justice according to law. The lawyer's authority, conferred by the State, would be abused if it were exercised otherwise than in accordance with the condition on which it has been conferred and accepted. There is no antinomy between the duty to participate in the administration of justice according to law and the duty to act justly of which Micah speaks. On the contrary, the duty to act justly binds the Christian lawyer to act in the exercise of his or her professional authority in accordance with law. Of course, if the law allows the lawyer a discretion not to act in a jurisdiction governed by a law which the lawyer believes to be contrary to morality, the lawyer may decline to act. Thus, some lawyers have declined to accept matters in divorce. And as a lawyer is required to possess and exercise competence and due care in discharging the duty owed to the client, the lawyer is not expected to act in areas in which he or she does not usually practise.

The Christian lawyer has an obligation which accords with and reinforces his or her ethical obligation. The duty owed to the client cannot be breached without breaching the moral obligation of justice. And sometimes there is a duty to accept a client who, in the absence of the lawyer's assistance, cannot be protected against an injustice. That is the sort of obligation that is taught by the parable of the Good Samaritan. In every case, the law must be found, the facts must be ascertained, and there must be listening to find the relevant truth. The procedures of the law should not be allowed to produce unnecessary injustice, vexatious litigation should be avoided and no lawyer and no judge should subject parties to litigation (including the criminal accused), witnesses or the public to any indignity or gratuitous embarrassment. The Christian lawyer's duties accord with and reinforce the highest ethical standards of his or her profession.

There is no conflict between the role of the lawyer and the life of the committed Christian. Rather, the risk is seeing the role of the lawyer as a public role and the role of the Christian as essentially private. Yet, given an understanding of the true relationship between law and faith, between law and Christian values, we may find in our profession a true Christian vocation. We may not be saints, but we can aspire to the sanctity of our model and patron saint, Thomas More. Hans Kűng, writing of More and his freedom in the world, said this:

> Thomas More, in his secular dress, with his secular culture, in the midst of his family, his possessions, and his public life, was a saint. Not because he was without faults and sins; he had them, like every other human being, and he confessed them often before his death. But, with all his sinfulness, he was a saint, because he, as a sinful man, chosen out and embraced by God's grace in Christ made a radical choice of God, kept himself ready for God throughout his whole life in the world, and finally underwent the supreme test of that readiness in his death. Thus he knew the love of God in Christ, from which nothing can separate a man, neither life nor death:
>
> > All things are yours …,
> > whether the world, or life, or death,

or things present, or things to come:
for all are yours;
and you are Christ's:
and Christ is God's. [1 Corinthians.iii.22-23.] [19]

---

1. See Sarah Joseph, Jenny Schultz and Melissa Castan *The International Covenant on Civil and Political Rights – Cases, Materials and Commentary* (Oxford University Press, 2nd ed, 2004) 299 et seqq.
2. A W B Simpson *History of the Common Law* (1987) 376.
3. Benjamin N Cardozo, *The Nature of the Judicial Process* (1921 Yale University Press, 21st Printing 1963) 104-105.
4. (1981) 149 CLR 27, 42.
5. (1995) 183 CLR 373, 486; see McHugh J in *Re Colina, Ex parte Torney* (1999) 200 CLR 386, 400-401.
6. (1925) 37 CLR 36, 79.
7. Romans 8:15; Galatians 4:6.
8. Matthew 6:29-30; Luke 12:7,25,28.
9. Matthew 6:15; Luke 6:36,37.
10. Bernard Lonergan, *Method in Theology* (Darton, Longman & Todd, London, 1972) 301.
11. See *Holdsworth's History of English Law* (Methuen, 1924) Volume 8, 403, 408.
12. See *Holdsworth's History of English Law*, (Methuen, 1924) Volume 4, 276.
13. Luke, 7, 36-50.
14. Romans 8:15; Galatians 4:6,7.
15. Matthew 6:29,30; Luke 12:7, 25,28.
16. [1932] AC 562.
17. See *Jaensch v Coffey* (1984) 155 CLR 549, 578.
18. Micah 6:8.
19. Hans Kung, *Freedom in the World: St Thomas More* (Sheed and Ward, 1965) 39-40.

11.8 The Role of a Catholic Law School

Editor's note

On 2 May 1996, after Brennan had delivered an address to a conference sponsored by the National Catholic Education Commission, Sr Helen Lombard SGS, the Provost of the newly formed University of Notre Dame, Australia, approached him, saying: 'Sir Gerard, I am sure you would be pleased to know that we are establishing Australia's first Catholic Law School.' Brennan replied, 'Must you?' A year later, the other Catholic university (ACU) decided to set up an Institute of Legal Studies instead of a fully fledged law school. Brennan was asked to launch the Institute. These were his remarks on 22 June 2007, the feast of St Thomas More. ACU set up its own law school in 2014.

The tertiary sector has seen a proliferation of Law Schools in recent years. In part, this is attributable to student demand; in part to the profits to be derived from the teaching of undergraduate law. The Institute of Legal Studies is not simply another law school. It will offer education in specialised areas of law affecting particular fields of professional public service: education, migration, welfare, health and ageing. This fits neatly into the mission of the Australian Catholic University. But a University has functions other than the imparting of knowledge which is useful, and the ACU has a particular function of placing knowledge in the context of values which underlie pedagogical propositions. Moreover, like other Universities, it has an obligation to expand the fields of knowledge or, more accurately in the case of the humanities, to deepen appreciation of the ideas which explain, and the principles which synthesise and systematise knowledge. For that reason, I should hope that it might pursue three fields of scholarly inquiry. First, consideration of the relationship between legal rules and moral principles; second, an enquiry into those moral issues which are not governed by existing law but which will evoke the definition of new legal rules in the foreseeable future; and third, the development of practical legal ethics to guide practitioners of goodwill who desire to see justice done in ways which accord with moral principle.

Contemporary legal rules are not an invention of recent textbook writers nor even the recent pronouncements of the courts. No system of jurisprudence can emerge into the sophisticated state with which we are familiar without the test of centuries of experience. Our legal system is different from the legal systems of many other nations because it has been formed in a culture that has been different from other cultures. Our legal rules were developed in an England that was infused with Christian values and, in earlier times, many of the rules were developed by clerics of the Christian Church. There was a time when a judge would say that 'the Christian religion is part of the law of the land'.[1] But Holdsworth in his *History of English Law* places that proposition in the past. He notes that 'The Christianity upon which the law and the state were once founded, though it might at times unduly magnify the authority of the Church, recognized the need for the secular arm of the State, and generally supported its authority.'[2] He feared, however, the loss of religious sentiment in the application of the law, which might lead to a state resembling 'the modified anarchy of mediaeval political society – without the redeeming grace of the spiritual elements in that society, which sprang from the deeply rooted religious faith of the mediaeval men'.

Harold Berman, the Story Professor of Law at Harvard Law School wrote that:

> Law helps to give society the structure . . . it needs to maintain inner cohesion; law fights against anarchy. Religion helps to give society the faith it needs to face the future; religion fights against decadence.... [E]ven in those societies which make a sharp distinction between law and religion, the two need each other – law to give religion its social dimension and religion to give law its spirit and direction as well as the sanctity it needs to command respect. Where they are divorced from each other, law tends to degenerate into legalism and religion into religiosity.[3]

In today's multi-cultural Australia, the relationship between law and religion is of great importance. There seems to be a growing tendency to regard the words in which law is expressed – in statute, regulation or judgment – as a sufficient and definitive source of the law to be applied in any case. The principles which explain the rules and, more importantly, the values which underlie the principles, are oftentimes treated as insignificant, if not irrelevant. Thus, as Berman observed, the 'law tends to degenerate into legalism.' The answer is not to import Canon law, or the Torah, or Sharia law into the common law but men and women who are Christian or Jewish or Muslim are nevertheless entitled to propose legal solutions to our social problems and to be heard respectfully in the councils of the modern State. For their part, lawyers need to understand the law as being informed by the enduring values of our community. Those are the basic values of the common law.

Sir Anthony Mason has said that 'personal liberty, freedom of expression, no imprisonment without trial, procedural fairness are commonly identified by judges as values which inform legal principle and require an unambiguous expression of statutory intention to override them. This emphasis on values protected by the common law is in one sense an instance of institutional values or morality.'[4]

The law has traditionally been concerned to protect the freedom and the dignity of the individual. That is entirely in accordance with Christian values. These concepts are the touchstones by which modern legislation and modern judicial decisions can be evaluated, and in the light of which statutory material and judicial writing are to be interpreted. When the so-called war on terror is raging, these are values which are vulnerable and which stand in need of defence. To borrow a phrase, the modern lawyer should be 'alert but not alarmed'.

It is therefore timely that the Institute should focus on the law and human rights – both for technical professional reasons and in order to equip lawyers to review critically the laws and policies which are affecting our society. Professionally, an understanding of human rights provides an appreciation of the values required for the correct interpretation of the bare text of the law. Educationally, the study of human rights will develop the critical faculty required for the informed evaluation of the society in which we live.

A second field of scholarly research is the new field of law that is being summoned into being by advances in medical technology – a field of law that is only partially governed by legal rules even though the necessity for legal control is accepted. It is the field which has to do with the beginning and end of human life. There are some issues which are resolved by the courts – for example, the difficult judgments in *Airedale Hospital Trustees v Bland*[5] and the cases dealing with abortion; some by the legislature – witness the recent stem cell legislation; and there are many foreseeable issues untouched by either. The beginning and the end of human life are profound issues which are a litmus of society's value of human existence. They are issues which eminent theologians have examined and are examining and many of them are issues on which the Catholic Church has reached a conclusion. Catholics generally believe that the Church's teaching on the sanctity of human life, is conducive to the well-being of society. The Church has much to offer in this field but, regrettable to say, Australian Bishops do not seem to have the understanding, or perhaps it is the ability, to express the wisdom of this teaching in terms convincing to the public, including the Catholic laity. We need to understand the moral argument, the logical force, the divine inspiration for this teaching. That has not been forthcoming. Take the recent controversy stimulated by Cardinal Pell's intervention in the New South Wales stem-cell debate, warning Catholic politicians of the 'consequences' of voting for the Bill. Is the ambiguous threat of 'consequences' an argument that can be weighed by the politician, the public or the Catholic laity?

An Institute of Legal Studies ('ILS') in a Catholic University can provide both the fora and the scholarship for debating the solution to these novel and difficult questions. The ILS can expose the differing strands of thought and provide the foundation for reasoning to a valid conclusion. It can be the instrument for advancing the Divine appeal of truth to the intellect of people of goodwill who, in turn, can be prophets in the community. A University should never underestimate the effect of what Sir Owen Dixon called 'the contagion of ideas'.

Thirdly, I should hope that the ILS will articulate some of the practical ethical precepts that might be observed by lawyers, including Catholic lawyers, who are interested not only in the technical rules of the law but also in the role which the law plays in influencing the culture of our society and the values which it treasures. In recent times, especially in the corporate sphere, the justification put forward for contested conduct has oftentimes been 'Our advice is that it is legal'. A lawyer concerned with morality cannot rest content with advice of that kind.

Of course, a lawyer's authority is derived from the law, and only from the law. But the lawyer's duty of service to the client is not confined by the provisions of the law. The authority which lawyers have is to participate, in their respective ways, in the administration of justice according to law but justice according to law may not always be just.

The law is an imperfect human instrument; sometimes it produces moral injustice. In such a case, what is the moral lawyer to do? His or her duty is not to frustrate the operation of the law, but it may be a duty to point out the injustice of the law's operation and to place before the client the possibility of an alternative course. It may be such a lawyer's duty – subject to preserving the interests of the client – to seek amendment of the law. In any case, the moral lawyer will try to understand whether there is any disparity between the result which the law will produce in the instant case and the result which would follow if the law were completely just in its operation. When any such disparity appears, the lawyer has an ethical problem in the sense that the lawyer must respect the client's legal interests though that troubles the lawyer's conscience by involvement in the moral injustice. Some of these ethical problems are familiar to every law student: the old problem of defending someone who is guilty, for example. But there are more difficult problems today, not only in commercial law. Can the 'cab-rank' rule which obliges a barrister to accept a brief offered for a reasonable fee in a jurisdiction in which the barrister usually practises impose on the barrister a duty to accept a brief requiring advocacy of a particular cause to which the barrister is morally opposed? The interface between law and morality is replete with difficult problems and the modern lawyer, concerned with the morality of professional life, can be aided in the analysis of the problems which arise and in their right conclusion.

Any attempt to isolate law and its practice from moral values and the observance of moral values can result only in the aridity of purposeless legalism. And if moral values are significant to law and its practice, religious truth has a role to play. We are familiar with Lord Atkin's famous question in *Donoghue v Stevenson* 'Who is my neighbour?'[6] and the answer by which he translated the gospel of the Good Samaritan into the common law. Martin Luther King appreciated the significance of that religious text to the development of the law when he spoke on the night before his death. He said that the road referred to in the Gospel was a dangerous road and –

> In the days of Jesus it came to be known as the 'Bloody Pass.' And you know, it's possible that the priest and the Levite looked over that man on the ground and wondered if the robbers were still around. Or it's possible that they felt that the man on the ground was merely faking, and he was acting like he had been robbed and hurt in order to seize them over there, lure them there for quick and easy seizure. And so the first question that the priest asked, the first question that the Levite asked was, 'If I stop to help this man, what will happen to *me*?'
>
> But then the Good Samaritan came by, and he reversed the question: 'If I *do not stop* to help this man, what will happen to *him*?'

The concern for the other, the stranger, the outsider, is a concern that might find a resonance today in the discussions we have about the morality of the laws which are being advanced or supported as laws in the war against terror. We are living at a time when the morality of law is critical to the welfare of a free and confident nation. I hope that the Institute of Legal Studies at the ACU will make a substantial contribution to this question and thus to the welfare of our people.

---

1. Kenyon CJ in *Williams' Case* (1797) How St Tr 654, 703, cited in Keith Mason, *Constancy and Change: Moral and Religious Values in the Australian Legal System* (The Federation Press, 1990) 4.
2. Holdsworth's *History of English Law* (Methuen, 1924) Vol VIII, 420.
3. Harold Berman, *The Interaction of Law and Religion* (Abingdon Press, 1974) 24-25.
4. Sir Anthony Mason, *Rights, Values and Legal Institutions: Reshaping Australian Institutions* (1997) *Australian International Law Journal* 1. Australian National University, Canberra, Public Lecture, 13 August 1996.
5. [1993] AC 789.
6. [1932] AC 562.

Chapter 12

Religion and Life

12.1 National Prayer Breakfast at Parliament House

Editor's note

Brennan was invited to Parliament House, Canberra to provide an opening prayer at the Second National Prayer Breakfast held on 2 November 1987.

Jesus Christ, our Brother and our Saviour, gathered here in your Name we are assured by your word that You are in our midst. Give us, then, your peace as we pray with You and through You to our Father.

Father, Creator of the universe and our Judge, all things are of your making, all times and seasons obey your laws. In the universe of your creation, You chose to make us the stewards.

You made us in your own image. You entrusted to us the peerless gift of freedom without which love would be meaningless and human dignity could not be fully realized. You gave us your law to guide us; not to diminish our freedom, but to show us how to grow in love and to realize our human dignity to the full.

You entrusted to us the ordering of human society. Grant, we pray You, an abiding understanding of your law and of its twin precepts of loving You and loving our neighbour. Let us see that a society which is ordered according to your law is a society of equality, justice and peace.

By your grace, may we pursue these values in our beloved land regardless of colour or creed, of poverty or riches, of gender or age so that each member of our society is free to worship You according to conscience, free to live in dignity and in the security of a family, free to participate equally with others in the life of the community.

Father, we ask You to send your Spirit to guide our leaders in right judgment in all spheres of communal life, especially in the government of Church and State.

May principle never yield to expediency, popular appeal never prevail over the rights of conscience, justice never be forfeited to sectional interest.

May our leaders be men and women of integrity, at one in the pursuit of equality, justice and peace and tolerant of the diversity of ways of achieving those values.

Make us sensitive to the plight of others less privileged than ourselves in Australia and overseas. Make Australia a nation of peace bringing goodwill among the peoples of the world.

Let us not starve ourselves of humanity by hoarding our affluence.

Let us not lose our dignity by stifling our compassion for others.

Let us see the face of your Son in the features of the suffering everywhere.

Let us have the wisdom to distinguish between a nation that is powerful and a nation that is great.

As we approach the bi-centenary of the coming of European settlement in the land of the Aboriginal Australians, may all our people rejoice in our future together and, living in harmony and mutual respect, may we share the land and the bounty You have lavished on it as we hope to share your love for all eternity.

United in your love, Father, we pray together for the coming of your Kingdom in the words our Saviour taught us:

> Our Father who art in Heaven
> Hallowed be thy Name
> Thy Kingdom come
> Thy will be done
> On earth as it is in heaven.
> Give us this day our daily bread
> And forgive us our trespasses
> As we forgive those who trespass against us
> And lead us not into temptation
> But deliver us from evil.
> For thine is the Kingdom the Power and the Glory
> Forever and ever. Amen.

12.2 Faith in Contemporary Society

Editor's note

Two months after his retirement as Chief Justice, Brennan was invited to deliver the After-Dinner address at the annual Cardinal's Dinner in Sydney on 24 July 1998. At the time, Cardinal Edward Clancy was the Archbishop of Sydney. Brennan spoke on 'Faith in Contemporary Society'.

Madam President, Your Eminence, Ladies and Gentlemen:

Thank you for the warm welcome you have given Patricia and me. We are newly arrived residents in Sydney, though we have known the city for many years and our friendships go back to university days. In Brisbane, where we lived until 1976, there was no Cardinal's dinner – perhaps because there was no Cardinal. There was an annual fund-raising Dinner – in those days, for men only – sponsored by the Xavier Society and addressed by speakers having a much higher profile than retired judges. But the spirit which informed the sponsoring organization and the purposes for which the funds were raised find a resonance in your organization and its charitable purposes.

As retirement is an occasion for retrospection, I hope you will forgive me for recalling some of my earliest years. Primary school, for many in our generation of Australian Catholics, was a lesson in the selfless devotion of nuns and brothers who lived in penury or close to it. Their teaching qualifications were not always of the highest level but the efforts they made to keep ahead of the class and to inculcate knowledge of their subjects was, in retrospect, heroic. The catechism was taught not only with rigour but with an unquestioning belief. We probably did not see at the time the preparation that had to be done, the apprehension that must have been experienced, the faith that had to be deepened and the devotion that had to be maintained year after dreary year. But the message of fidelity and service did not have to be preached: it was taught by example, and the example became an inspiration, no less inspiring because it was subconsciously received.

In retrospect, those distant times may appear to be the halcyon days of peace, sure values, a settled and familiar liturgy and an ecclesiastical structure in which clergy and laity had clearly defined rights and duties. But these were the childhood years when childhood security was comforting and confirming. Since our childhood, we have discovered that there are always new challenges to old values, new insights to be expressed in liturgy, new ecclesiastical relationships (if not structures) that have to respond to a changing and complex society. The spiritual comfort blanket of childhood is not sufficient to warm the faith of the adult Christian.

In earlier times, defence of one's faith was sometimes thought to require only stalwart courage. The story was often told at 'Downlands', the Sacred Heart College I attended in Toowoomba, of the farmer who brought his young son to school and gave Father Rector the instruction: 'Teach him the catechism, Father, and how to fight, so he can defend the faith!' In modern times, defence of the faith is not a matter of repelling external attack; it is a matter of personal response to the unique experiences of our lives. The challenge to faith comes not so much from without as from within. It comes from the value systems, not always articulated, of our times. The 'mainstream' of our society beckons us to be assimilated into it, to celebrate its values and to regret, perhaps to deplore, those minorities who cling to a different ethos. But if the values of the mainstream are not the values of the Gospel, the mainstream's invitation to join cannot be accepted. I think Father Rector, later Bishop Doyle, understood this when he delivered his weekly admonition to the school: 'Be different!'

We did not understand him to advocate the difference of the ghetto. Faith is lived in the community, with our brothers and sisters the children of God, some of us being saints, many of us being publicans and sinners. But faith requires a profound assent to Christ's proposition that 'My Kingdom is not of this world.' We are called to believe in a Kingdom of universal love, of an eternal hope fulfilled, or unshakeable peace. It is one thing to give intellectual assent to that proposition; it is another to live by that conviction.

It is not easy to live in a materialist society and maintain a belief that reality is not to be seen or felt or tasted; that real security is not to be found in property or bank accounts; that true personal fulfilment is not to be obtained by a mere achievement of power; that satisfying joy is not assured by indulgence. Yet the modern Christian must live in contemporary society while seeking to live by values that are alien to it. That is both an individual obligation and a social benefit.

The adult faith of the modern Christian is needed to sustain the civilization of our society. If there be a real love of God, there is respect for the dignity and freedom of each individual made in His image; there is respect for the earth and all that is in it – the earth that He gave us to use and not to misuse; if there be a real love of neighbour in our society, we are tolerant of minorities, we reject unjustified discrimination, we alleviate the sufferings of the disadvantaged and we show compassion for refugees and the desolated communities overseas.

Unless love be the reality, altruism is hard to sustain. Unless the possessors of property and power are minded to use them for the benefit and in the service of others, oppression and chaos intrude on freedom and order. If self-indulgence were unbridled, society would corrupt and collapse.

As a community, we need faith in the Gospel values. It underpins the values which inform our laws and which cement our social institutions and relationships. The modern Christian should feel no antipathy between his or her membership of society and faith in Christ and His teaching. But if, or when, that faith is weakened or the influence of believers wanes, what is left to support a tolerant and compassionate society? Only the hangover of an earlier age of faith and the attitudes formed in the light of that faith. Without its sustaining force, the traditional attitudes gradually lose their coherence. Then self interest, fear and avidity for power and wealth tear the social fabric.

Occasions such as this, Madam President, when Christians gather together in affirmation of a common belief in the Gospel values, strengthen each of us in our belief in a risen Redeemer who acquired for us a destiny higher and nobler than materialism and self-satisfaction can offer. It confirms us as a pilgrim people who pray for ourselves and for one another: 'I believe, O Lord. Help Thou my unbelief.'

12.3 Address to Graduates at the Sydney College of Divinity

Editor's note

Brennan delivered the graduation address at the Sydney College of Divinity on 29 May 1999. The College is an ecumenical undertaking with faculty and students from the major Christian denominations.

Reverend President, members of the Council of the Sydney College of Divinity, Graduates, Ladies and Gentlemen,

It is a rare and somewhat daunting experience for one whose place is ordinarily in the pews to be translated to a pulpit in a congregation of a College of Divinity. The reflections of those who occupy a pulpit are subjected, in my experience, to the most acute and often censorious examination by the congregation. I am reminded of the report of a Redemptorist priest who, in the faraway days of my youth, was invited to a parish to refresh the devotion of the parishioners. Choosing, as was the wont of the Redemptorists in those days, the topic of eternal punishment for sin, he was pacing up and down behind the Communion rails threatening the good and simple faithful with brimstone and eternal flame when his oratory was interrupted by the piping voice of a child asking: 'Mummy, what will we do if he gets out?' However, my greatest protection is likely to be the shared characteristic of most graduation addresses – they are not long remembered by any who hear them. So if I be guilty of heresy in what I say, testimony of the crime may be hard to come by.

We are within the week of Pentecost, the feast which focusses the mind each year on our continuing inability to be entirely one in the Church of Our Lord. There is a strange and worrying paradox in that continuing inability: we yearn to be united but unity seems to be beyond our reach. Today, when we celebrate the graduation of scholars from different Christian denominations who have shared texts, classrooms and ideas for months or years, we wonder why it is that we are separated by traditions and loyalties that seemingly destine us to separation.

Of course, we have thankfully moved away from the times when inter-denominational antipathy was overt and rampant. Perhaps we can draw some lessons from the progress that has been made. In my own Church, the turning point was Vatican II. It was a Council that eschewed the anathemas that were so much a feature of some earlier Councils. Instead, Vatican II opened the Church to the world in which its mission was to be fulfilled, a world which was loved for all its sin and waywardness, a world in which the essential goodness of humankind was celebrated irrespective of colour, creed or class. This change in attitude dictated the abandonment of many practices and disciplines which had served to maintain the comfort of the religious ghetto. When they went, and the Church reached out in friendship and understanding to other denominations, the response was both generous and immediate. After Vatican II, the reserve, not to say suspicion, that infected the relationship between the Catholic Church and other denominations was removed. Ecumenism has become an article of faith in practically every denomination.

There are some in every denomination who are chary of such changes. They would cling to the verities as they see them, verities which mark the character of the denomination to which they belong, verities that cannot be traded for some feel-good reaction towards others who do not share the same beliefs and do not follow the same practices. There is a validity in this view, for it is based on a truly conscientious adherence to the truth as it is perceived. If the biblical assurance that the truth will make you free is to be accepted, the truth is not to be sacrificed for some administrative or organizational conglomerate, for the sake of popular support or even for an enhancement in the number or warmth of personal relations. The following of Christ, as we know, can be a lonely journey and the only valid path is the path dictated by conscience.

Truth is a value at the heart of the Christian tradition. 'I am the Way, the Truth and the Life'. It is not open to compromise or sacrifice. But dialogue which begins with a proclamation of the truth as perceived by one denies communication with the mind of another who perceives truth in a different way. If truth should lead us to assert 'I am right and you are wrong', dialogue is impossible. If truth should lead us to say 'I have the truth, you do not but we will unite when you see the error of your ways', truth has become antithetical to unity, inconsistent with the supremacy of conscience and foreign to charity. Such a devotion to truth as perceived is destructive of the spirit of ecumenism. Dialogue is possible only when there is respect for the integrity of the other and a tolerance of the beliefs which the other entertains and the practices he or she follows. Ecumenical reunion will not be advanced by exchanges of doctrine but by tolerance. Tolerance will grow into love and love will lead us all to the uniting truth.

Tolerance is not a negative virtue; it is sharply to be distinguished from attitudes of laissez faire. It is a positive acknowledgment of the dignity and integrity of another and the conscious rejection of prejudice — however traditional and long-standing the prejudice may be — which alienates one from another. Tolerance can be painful for it demands that each should assess his or her own beliefs and practices where they differ from the beliefs and practices of others, re-examine those beliefs and look again at those practices to see whether they contain inessential accretions to, perhaps barnacles upon, essential truth. Where the inessentials are barriers to a growth in unity, they may have to be abandoned in pursuit of the greater good that all will be one. That may not be comfortable.

In Canberra and in Brisbane, the cities in which I spent most of my professional life, it has long been the practice for Christian lawyers to join in an Ecumenical Service either at the commencement of the legal year or at mid-term during the year. In Sydney, the tradition has been different, and lawyers attend Services according to their confessional allegiance. Some judges and others in positions of professional leadership attend these Services in succession. Now I know that my co-religionists value the Red Mass, as I do, but I respectfully raise the question why the ecumenical spirit has not led to the establishment of an Ecumenical Service of worship for Christian lawyers. The holding of such a tangible example of ecumenical goodwill is in no way inconsistent with the celebration of a Red Mass or other Service by lawyers who wish to worship according to the rites of their respective denominations.

Today, we celebrate the graduation of scholars from different Christian denominations who have shared texts, classrooms, ideas and worship for months or years. The graduates and the Sydney College of Divinity have, by precept and example, shown the way forward. There has been no sacrifice of truth but in the time that you, the graduates, have spent together in your studies and discussions, you have gained a respect and affection for your fellows — bonds of respect and affection that will bind you together in the years to come. In your time together, and in your sharing of prayer and insights, you have deepened not only your mutual respect and affection but your perceptions of the truth that, if it be more fully and more broadly perceived in the years to come will lead us to the Unity that accords with the Divine will. The way forward calls for no sacrifice of what each perceives to be the truth at any stage of the individual's pilgrimage of faith; the way forward calls for mutual love within the bonds of which truth will be more clearly perceived and the aspiration to unity will be more easily achieved.

We, your families and your friends, congratulate you on the attainment of your scholastic achievements; we thank you for the example of devotion and fellowship that you offer; and we pray that your love one for another will lead, as love may always lead, to the realisation of our common dignity and destiny as the children of God.

12.4 Launch of the Centre for an Ethical Society

Editor's note

On 21 November 2006, Brennan was invited to launch the Centre for an Ethical Society at the Pitt Street Uniting Church, Sydney. The Centre was set up with a commitment to the rediscovery and the interpretation of the powerful public metaphor 'the common good'. Responding to Brennan's address, Geoffrey Dornan, Director of Ministry and Mission, UnitingCare Ageing, at the Pitt St Uniting Church, said: 'The common good challenges us with a practical insight: its contemporary version suggests that we must look beyond consumerist models solely preoccupied with wealth generation; that we need to seek out alternatives that can be converted into practical, sustainable behaviour for all people across social, cultural, ethnic, economic and political boundaries. The common good brings into the reach of all citizens the possibility of really living. Sir Gerard, the true purpose of public life is the achievement of the common good. God willing "The Centre" will play a part in its re-introduction into Australian public life.' This was Brennan's address.

Today we gather for the launch of a new venture – the Centre for an Ethical Society, a group of Australians inspired by the Christian message. This is a public gathering and a public venture, but it is not a political gathering, nor is the Centre affiliated in any way with any political party. The purpose of the Centre is to offer some views and some values that are fundamental to our national welfare.

Why bother, you may ask. Recently, both Tony Abbott and Kevin Rudd have been speaking about the importance of Christian values. Isn't it sufficient that such influential members of the main political parties are alive to the importance of Christianity and are themselves believers? The answer lies in the nature and purpose of the Christian message.

Christianity is not primarily concerned with politics. It is concerned with the hearts and minds of men and women. When a lawyer, anxious to get Jesus to define His propositions, asked what was the first and the greatest commandment, he received an unequivocal answer. '[L]ove the Lord your God with all your heart, with all your soul and with all your mind.' (Matthew 22:35). To respond to that commandment, however, the spark of faith is needed. Jesus went on to define a second commandment which is like the first: '[L]ove your neighbour as yourself'. One commandment covers our relationship with God; the other covers our human relationships. We are concerned today with the second of those commandments, which is at the heart of the Christian message. We live in a pluralist democracy but we know that the command to love your neighbour as yourself resonates with every man and woman of good will, whether they be Christian or not, religious or not. That commandment has universal appeal, but it is not primarily a political appeal – it is an appeal to the mind and the heart of each of us. It may be suppressed by avarice or self-interest but it lies deep in the mind and heart of every person of good will.

To love your neighbour is a simple admonition. It has both a negative and a positive application. On the one hand, it forbids self-aggrandisement at the expense of others. And, affirmatively, if we must love them as we love ourselves, our concern must be for their welfare equally with our own. That has a profound significance for public policy because, if individuals respond to that appeal, the values of the community change.

Well, that sounds all very well and good. We can accept that, for we live, do we not, in a civilization that is essentially Christian. But do we? If we want to find out what really motivates us Australians, we can look at our media and the advertising they carry. So we see pages of what we 'must have', we are shown delights that we 'deserve', we are advised to take care of 'number one', each of us is asked whether we would like to 'create wealth' for ourselves. Our attention is directed to the world's or the country's wealthiest people, to stars whose extravagant lifestyles are the cynosure of the media's eyes. We have grown so accustomed to this focus on material possessions that we tend to judge people not by what they are but by what they have. We rate our own success not by the humanity we display but by the wealth we possess. We live in our nuclear families, avoiding those who do not belong to our socio-economic group. We know that there are the poor, the marginalised and the disabled but we may not be greatly moved by their plight.

To the extent that that is the public mindset, it will be reflected in our public policy. But it is not the Christian mindset and, for that reason, the Centre for an Ethical Society has been formed with the support of the Anglican, Catholic and Uniting Churches to invite attention to a different set of values. That is why the Centre for an Ethical Society is concerned with the minds and hearts of the Australian people, not directly with the platforms and policies of political parties or the programs of special interest groups. Its purpose is to affect the values that inform our public life. No human society is value free; each society reveals and gives effect to its prevailing values in its laws and institutions, in its political and economic policies, in its art, literature and architecture and in the manner in which its people relate one to another. In a democracy, government looks to the contemporary values of the community in creating, fostering and organizing the social order and politicians embrace and extol these values in advocating their political goals. In a pluralist, democratic society, the social order is not necessarily shaped in accordance with Christian values but Christians are entitled equally with others to contribute to its shaping. No false modesty, no deference to non-Christian or anti-Christian values should deter the charitable exposition of the Christian message. Of course, the Christian must accept that others who, in good conscience, hold different views are equally free to advocate those views. But the Gospel calls us to be an example to others in our mutual love and in our lived and professed commitment to the values we find in Christ's life and teaching. So, the Centre for an Ethical Society is concerned with a discussion of the values that are inherent in the second great commandment to love one's neighbour as oneself.

Why must we love our neighbour as ourself? Because we are all members of the human family, each with a dignity to be treasured by the individual and respected by others. The Christian attributes that dignity to the fact that we are all children of God[1] with an eternal destiny to know, love and be with Him. Before God, each individual is equally precious and is equally loved. Each person is entitled to the same respect.[2] Those who do not share the Christian faith may attribute individual dignity simply to our common humanity. But whatever reasoning may underlie the value of human dignity, the implication for public policy is profound. It dictates that we treat all people equally. Race or colour, class or creed, physical or mental perfection or defect afford no warrant for attributing varying degrees of worth and dignity to humankind.

If I have a genuine (and not narcissistic) love of myself as a person, I am a person of human dignity. If I am to love my neighbour as myself, I must want him or her also to be a person of human dignity – to be able to live in dignity, to be free to form respectful relationships with others, to have an opportunity to develop capacities and to contribute usefully to society. Then I must do what I reasonably can to see that my neighbour, in his or her situation, enjoys in like measure to me those social benefits which are essential to personal dignity. For my neighbours in this country, those benefits include not only monetary and material benefits but equality under the law, freedom of religious belief and practice, freedom from the exercise of arbitrary power, freedom from discrimination on the basis of sex, race or ethnicity, an opportunity to obtain an education and a means of livelihood, an opportunity to found a family and an opportunity to employ gainfully their capacities. If these were the values of our society, social phenomena would change. Public policy would be directed to achieving the common good – a society in which every person would have an opportunity to develop his or her capacities and to live in dignity – freely, peacefully and with the ability to participate in social life.

Of course, there are differences in natural endowments and in the environments in which people live. These differences account for, or contribute to dissimilarity in the position, especially in the economic position, of individuals within society. But the common good does not demand that policies be designed to redistribute wealth equally among all. That would be an unrealistic goal; and it would destroy individual initiative which is the wellspring of developments that promote the welfare of humankind. Such a policy would in fact diminish human dignity. The liberty to employ initiative carries the right to garner its fruits. Thus, wealth can be accumulated and then the owner is free to apply it in the accumulation of more wealth. That use of property is, in a capitalist society, an essential element in the economic progress of the community. But economic power can be used to oppress others – employees, competitors, creditors – or to operate against the common good, so there must be controls on economic action to achieve the common good.

That is why Church leaders sometimes comment on industrial laws or other matters relating to the conditions of employees. They are concerned, and rightly, to ensure that men and women who do not have the same economic power as their employers are sufficiently secure and enjoy sufficiently adequate conditions to maintain themselves and their dependents in dignity. In contemporary Australia, when the economic power of corporations – including international mega-corporations – is immense, industrial laws are important not only for protection of those with less economic power but for the maintenance of the authority of government itself. If laws simply facilitated the maximizing of corporate profits rather than maintaining the common good, government would be abandoning its authority – an authority which is conferred upon it in order to advance the interests of all Australians. In saying this, I do not venture an opinion on whether the current industrial laws strike the right balance between capital and labour. What I do wish to say is that such laws are of great importance in determining the common good and that it is entirely appropriate for their provisions to be subjected to analysis in the light of Christian values.

Where gainful employment is not available or where age or infirmity prevent the earning of a livelihood, it is the function of government to provide the means by which those who are unable to support themselves can live a life of dignity. Social security is not a mere budgetary item to be adjusted according to political exigencies; it is not reducible merely to secure an economically satisfactory bottom line; it is a mandatory safety net to prevent fellow citizens from suffering a degrading loss of dignity – a loss of dignity that would be a reproach to society and ultimately a threat to its stability. Nor should the services of government be limited to providing money that is merely sufficient to keep body and soul together. In particular, health and educational services are essential not only to assure one generation of adequate opportunities to enjoy the benefits of social life but also to cater for their children who, like all other children, are entitled to an opportunity to develop their physical and intellectual capacities in order to participate as equal members of the community.

We cannot boast that, in this country, we have achieved these aims. I have been told that 20% of all Australian households have an income of less than $400 per week and more than 600,000 children live in jobless households. And this while we have a very large budgetary surplus. The members of those households and those 600,000 children are our neighbours and our Christian duty is to love them as we love ourselves –to do what we can to secure their dignity. A society is weakened by fractures along lines of wealth or opportunity. But if wealth were prized only insofar as it is needed to sustain a lifestyle of dignity in reasonable comfort and if genuine opportunities existed for the poor, the marginalized, the disabled and the outcast to participate as fully as they can in the benefits of society, we would have a strong, a prosperous and a united nation.

Material poverty can destroy human dignity; so can social poverty, which strikes the marginalized and the outcast. The social isolation of many Aboriginal people, of many refugees, of many who are poorly educated and many who suffer from a mental illness erodes the sense of self-worth and deprives them of hope. Yet, like the Levite passing on the other side of the road, we oftentimes seem to ignore their plight or, worse, regard them as a threat to our own well-being. Our laws and policies do not reflect the Christian value of the good Samaritan. The outcasts are, by definition, denied their dignity. When have we troubled about the pressures on our jails, the standover prisoners who assault young offenders or pressure them into the drug trade or the problems of rehabilitation on release? And see how we have tolerated, for five years now, the barbarous treatment of the Australian, David Hicks in Guantanamo Bay, still waiting to be charged, it seems, with an offence under a law yet to be specified and tried by a process which mocks the civilized sense of justice. Do not blame governments alone. This could not have happened if our society were infused with Christian values.

What do Christian values have to say about foreign affairs? Quite a lot. The horrific suffering of war and internal violence is the very antithesis of Christian values. Christianity is a force for peace, for peace is essential to human dignity. The command to love one's neighbour cannot be squared with a policy that sees force as the primary or only answer to national and international problems. If peace were the primary aim of our public policy, we would not now be confronted by the tragedy which is Iraq.

The neighbours to be loved as ourselves are not only those closest to home. They include those in developing countries and in countries destroyed by war and internal conflict. If all have an equal right to live, States and individuals are under the basic duty of doing what they can to ensure the supply of goods and services needed to sustain human life whenever and wherever it is threatened, whether by natural disaster, mismanagement or sheer poverty. The equal right to life of all humankind imposes on us the duty to proffer aid to other countries that cannot themselves sustain the lives of their citizens in dignity. When we are reasonably able to do so, we must seek to give dignity to the people of every nation, not as imperialists imposing our culture and our values but recognizing and respecting the culture and traditions of people in the lands and in the circumstances in which they live. Yet we note that the percentage of GDP devoted to Overseas Development Aid has dropped from 0.48% in 1970 to 0.40% in 1980, to 0.32% in 2000, to 0.26% in 2004-2005. And this while six million children die each year from hunger, thirst and preventable diseases and a billion people live on less than $1.30 a day.

Today is the first step in a long march. It is a march into the minds and hearts of the Australian people. It is a patriotic march to build a free and confident nation, for it is a march born of a love of Australia, of a belief that we have a destiny that is more noble, more visionary, more satisfying than the hoarding of wealth or the living of luxury. Perhaps none of us has recognized the truth of the statement attributed to St Basil the Great 'The bread which you do not use is the bread of the hungry; the garment hanging in the wardrobe is the garment of the one who is naked; the shoes you do not wear are the shoes of the one who is barefoot; the money you keep locked away is the money of the poor; the acts of charity you do not perform are so many injustices that you commit.'

But if it is possible to bring into the market place of ideas the notion that the true purpose of public life is the achievement of the common good – a common good which creates benefits for the rich and poor, the powerful and the underprivileged, the strong and the disabled; a common good which recognizes the equal dignity of all people and presents every person with the opportunity to live a truly human existence, the Centre will have achieved its purpose.

Please God it will.

---

1 Romans 8:15; Galatians 4:6

2 Matthew 6:29-30; Luke 12:7,25,28

12.5 Address to the Salvation Army

Editor's note

This was Brennan's address to the Salvation Army Social Justice Conference held in Sydney on 29 March 2008.

On Wednesday last I returned from a legal conference in Abu Dhabi, in the United Arab Emirates, where my wife and I had been during the Easter Season. We attended the Easter Ceremonies in the Cathedral which is the church for many of the expatriates working there, the majority being Indians. We were inspired by the quiet reverence and devotion of an open-air congregation of perhaps 10,000 on Easter night. What faith! Of course, many at the Conference were Muslims and on the way to the Conference meeting hall in the luxurious hotel was a prayer room. Before and after sessions, there was a procession of people entering the prayer room, the rows of shoes in the entrance portico bearing witness to the fidelity of their wearers. Again, what faith! We in Australia are not accustomed to seeing such manifestations of one of the cardinal virtues, yet I venture to suggest that the cardinal virtues of faith, hope and charity are, and indeed must be, at the heart of any movement which takes its inspiration from the life of Christ. So, it is with the Salvation Army.

Why would you bother with the demands of membership if it were not for the belief that you are fulfilling Christ's commands: '[L]ove the Lord your God with all your heart and all your mind and love your neighbour as yourself.' [Matthew 22:35]. Faith is needed to love God, faith is what justifies acceptance of the command to love your neighbour. That commandment has both a negative and a positive application. On the one hand, it forbids self-aggrandisement at the expense of others. And, affirmatively, if we must love them as we love ourselves, our concern must be for their welfare equally with our own. A commandment not only to suppress avarice and greed but to work for the benefit of our neighbour as much as for ourselves is hard to live by in a society that suggests we should always place 'number one' first. The pages of the media tell us what we 'must have', we are shown delights that we 'deserve', each of us is asked whether we would like to 'create wealth' for ourselves. Our attention is directed to the world's or the country's wealthiest people, to stars whose extravagant lifestyles are the cynosure of the media's eyes. We have grown so accustomed to this focus on material possessions that we tend to judge people not by what they are but by what they have. We are encouraged to rate our own success not by the humanity we display but by the wealth we possess. We live in our nuclear families, avoiding those who do not belong to our socio-economic group. But why should it matter to us that some people suffer social injustice? Oftentimes, it is their own fault and, even if it isn't, we are not usually responsible for the conditions of society that produce the injustice. Ours is a materialist society and, in such a society, the Christian needs to find in his or her faith the justification for going against the materialist tide in order to love our neighbour as ourselves.

Why must we love our neighbour as ourselves? Because we are all members of the human family, each with a dignity to be treasured by the individual and respected by others. The Christian attributes that dignity to the fact that we are all children of God[1] with an eternal destiny to know, love and be with Him. Before God, each individual is equally precious and is equally loved. Each person is entitled to the same respect.[2] Those who do not share the Christian faith may attribute individual dignity simply to our common humanity. But whatever reasoning may underlie the value of human dignity, it dictates that we treat all people equally. Race or colour, class or creed, physical or mental perfection or defect, wealth or poverty afford no warrant for attributing varying degrees of worth and dignity to humankind.

By living the commandment to love God and neighbour, we hope for salvation. That was, if I understand correctly, the inspiration of General Booth in founding the Salvation Army. He wrote that 'I have ever felt that true religion consists not only in being holy myself but in assisting my Crucified Lord in His work of saving men and women, making them into His soldiers, keeping them faithful to death, and so getting them into Heaven.'[3]

All Christians are travelling on the path to salvation, conscious of a duty to love God and to love one's neighbour as one's self. We are conscious too that faith is needed to sustain us if we are to discharge that duty.

The second cardinal virtue is hope. We are in a season of rejoicing in the Risen Lord – a season when we see the triumph of love over injustice, a time of thanksgiving and hope. So, when we meet to discuss social justice and the work to be done to assist those who suffer injustice, we are entitled to hope that, if the work to be done is inspired by faith and by love, it will at least diminish the injustice that would otherwise be suffered. There are, of course, many situations where suffering seems to be beyond human relief. Can a home be found for all the families and lonely people who need it? Will the drug barons cease peddling narcotics to the young? Or can the young be dissuaded from trying them? Can our gaols ensure the physical safety of the young offender and protect him from pressure to become complicit in drug smuggling? You are all familiar with these kinds of intractable problems, yet you do not cease your efforts to combat evil when you see it. Hope is needed to sustain these efforts, faith is needed to justify the effort, and love gives some prospect of success.

Charity or, a better term, love – in this case, love of my neighbour. Mrs Catherine Booth spoke of divine love as being 'shed abroad in the heart by the Holy Ghost'.[4] So, when the Christian works for social justice, it is not in order to be hailed as a political hero or revered as a social reformer. For the Christian, political fame or social status cannot be the sole, or major, wellspring of human action. The Christian remembers Christ's criticism of the Pharisees who 'do all their deeds to be seen by men; for they make their phylacteries broad and their fringes long and they love the place of honour at feasts and the best seats in the Synagogue and salutations in the market places and being called rabbi by men. ' (Matthew 23: 5-7).

That does not mean that the Christian should not embrace the efforts of others who work to achieve social justice. Whatever be the motivation of those who work for social justice, the common object of social justice is so great, so varied, so difficult to attain that no contributor should be rejected. But the Christian remembers that he or she is working in conformity with the prayer Christ gave us 'Thy will be done on earth as it is in heaven'.

This has a profound significance for the Christian engaged in social work. It identifies the work that has to be done as the support of the poorest, of the most lonely, most disadvantaged, most alienated of our people. The work is not to cater for those who can return the compliment with their vote at the ballot box or their advocacy for a cause, or their use of a commercial product. Christ asked us 'If you love those who love you, what credit is that to you?... And if you do good to those who do good to you, what credit is that to you? Even sinners do the same. ... But love your enemies and do good, and lend, expecting nothing in return; and your reward will be great....Be merciful, even as your Father is merciful.' [Luke 6:32-36]

The Christian cannot look on the anxious face of the refugee, or see the desperate anguish of the addict, or the desolation of the impoverished family without seeing the face of the suffering Christ. If the Christian is to work in the face of injustice, it must be because of the love of Him and of all men and women who are, like us, children of God.

Justice is a condition relative to an individual, for justice is accorded to, and injustice is experienced by, individuals – by men and women in their daily lives. We live in society, and each society's traditions and ethos and economy affect what social justice demands for its members. If social conditions were conducive to allowing every person to live in dignity, enjoying the ordinary benefits of living in society, we would have social justice, but if social conditions permit or encourage situations in which individual dignity is offended, or the ordinary benefits of social living are denied, there is social injustice. The manifestations of social injustice are various. You are familiar with them. The addict who is chained to the habit; the single mother or deserted wife who cannot raise the bond to obtain accommodation or cannot meet the mortgage payments on the home; the family whose breadwinner has lost his or her job; the woman who is subjected to sexual harassment or domestic violence, the elderly or the disabled who cannot get to the doctor or do the shopping. To those women and men and to myriad others who do not enjoy the benefits of living with dignity in our society, the Salvation Army has given support – sometimes material support, sometimes simply tender loving care.

The soldiers of the Salvation Army are familiar with the human tragedies that are paraded each day through our criminal courts. You have seen the cruelty, the corruption, the stupidity, the intoxication, the negligence that cause suffering to the victims of crime. You have seen the offenders, sometimes shackled, sometimes broken, sometimes bereft of hope. There is one view that says that crime must be suppressed and that sympathy is wasted on the offenders who cause loss to society and inflict suffering on their victims. That is understandable, but there is much to be said for an alternative view which was expressed by a judicial friend of mine, the late Mr Justice John Kelly of the ACT Supreme Court. John had been invited to give a paper at a high-powered conference on Criminal Law in London. He was not an eloquent speaker and his paper did not purport to expound a theory of criminal responsibility or a philosophy of sentencing, but his contribution electrified the Conference. His thesis was very simple. It was this: No person, whether judge, witness, prosecutor or accused should suffer any loss of human dignity in the conduct of a criminal proceeding. Of course, an offender must receive condign punishment for his offence and in passing sentence a judge may make observations about the gravity of the offender's conduct or the circumstances of the offender's life but those comments must be designed to explain the reasons for judgment, not to denigrate the human dignity of the person on whom the sentence is passed. Adopting that approach, the judge not only preserves the dignity of the participants in the proceedings, including her or his own dignity, but shows that sentencing is an aspect of the rule of law. John's thesis, based on a profoundly Christian sense of human dignity, struck a vital chord in the minds and hearts of the eminent lawyers at the Conference. He was immediately asked to say the occasional Grace at the Conference Dinner. So, when you offer your support to the offender whose dignity has been stripped away, you do more than provide a social service.

You minister to one of God's creatures and you witness to Christ's love of them.

But does social injustice demand anything more than the giving of personal support? Should the Christian be concerned about the causes of social injustice? There can be only one answer. God's will is not done on earth if His people make no attempt to diminish the causes of social injustice. When social injustice is attributable to social structures which are beyond the power of an individual to change, it is necessary to consider the steps that can be taken to alter the structures and eliminate the injustices they cause. In a pluralist democracy, that calls for the enlistment of popular sentiment or, to put it another way, it calls for a change in the community's values. Social phenomena reflect the values of society, whether for good or ill. We know that the practices of fascism could not have flourished in a society that valued liberty and equality; equally, we know that the financial excesses of the 1980s were possible only because of a pervasive materialism that asserted greed to be good. No human society is value free; each society reveals and gives effect to its prevailing values in its laws and institutions, in its political and economic policies, in its art, literature and architecture and in the manner in which its people relate one to another. In a democracy, government looks to the contemporary values of the community in creating, fostering and organizing the social order and politicians embrace and extol these values in advocating their political goals.

Values are the stuff of morality without which civilization would be impossible. The civilization of the western world was developed under the influence of Christianity and two of the values which we hold dear in Australia today – liberty and equality – take their content from Christian ideals. The liberty we cherish is a manifestation of the Christian belief that God gave to each of us a freedom to choose between right and wrong and a capacity to form that judgment, a freedom to do good or to do evil and to be responsible for our own conduct and its results. As it is by the exercise of that freedom that we can earn God's favour, we must prize our freedom and the freedom of our fellows. The value of equality is an acknowledgement that, before God, each individual is of equal value. If this is the belief of the Christian, he or she must do what can be done to proclaim these truths to others and to be active advocates of policies which maximize freedom and preserve human dignity.

We have had a healthy debate about working conditions, and it was right that several of the Christian churches should raise the need to give families some security of employment and a reasonable opportunity for family life and religious observance. When social policies have an impact on the freedom and dignity of the individual and families, the Christian concern for that freedom and dignity demands a Christian expression of that concern in the public forum. The public forum is not the sole preserve of the secular, nor is it captive to Christian or any other sectional interest. The values of a community are reflected in the policies developed in the public forum and, in a pluralist democracy, all sections of the community are entitled to express the values which they would wish public policy to reflect. Now we may be facing a new industrial issue with moral implications. It is not so long ago that this country was concerned by the absence of employment opportunities for school leavers and the unskilled. We now have a low level of unemployment – a factor that is said to be contributing to inflation. At the same time, the credit squeeze and the American situation raises the prospect of recession and a possible increase in unemployment. Unemployment is a demoralizing, a dehumanizing phenomenon, for it destroys the individual's own sense of her or his dignity. Social justice requires the allocation of resources for education and the development of skills which provide the means of restoring dignity to the unemployed and which provide a level of protection against unemployment in the future. At the same time, an educated and skilled workforce enhances productivity which strengthens the economy.

Immigration policies have been designed to diminish the skills shortage in Australia and to assist in the maintenance of a strong economy, but social justice requires that the immigration policies also cope with the relief of tragedies in other countries. It is not long since the inhuman – and inefficient – Pacific solution was abandoned. But the time taken to dispose of applications for asylum and the manner of detention of applicants for asylum work continuing injustice. Do we really need to lock up these applicants once they are screened for health if there is no ground for thinking them to be terrorists? The Christian voice, conscious of the equality of all people, cannot accept the notion that we should subject asylum seekers to inhuman treatment as a deterrent to others seeking asylum in this country. If I am to love my neighbour as myself, I must want him or her to be a person of human dignity living in an acceptable environment in the company of spouse and children, not locked away as a wrongdoer to be quietly disposed of after an intolerable period of uncertainty.

Anti-terrorism laws expose members of the community to detention and compulsory questioning without the usual protections offered by the law. We have seen cases of apparent injustice in the operation of these laws, which are in urgent need of amendment not only to restore the rule of law as we know it, but also to ensure that injustice neither is done to, nor hangs over, our community. When national security is in issue, there has to be a balance between security safeguards and the freedom and dignity of individuals. It is unjust to allow an individual to be a hostage, kept in detention in the name of national security, without recourse to the courts which can test the sufficiency of the grounds of the detention. The Christian voice is entitled to insist on procedures which minimize the risk of such injustice.

Then there are the familiar causes of family distress and career destruction – excessive consumption of alcohol, drug-taking and gambling. There is a general community awareness of these social dangers and some signs that they may be addressed. The initiative of governments to do something about binge-drinking by the young may have some effect but, perhaps more importantly, changes in community and family consciousness of the danger to the individual will save some from loss of self-confidence and damage to personality and career. Public programs to heighten awareness about the risks of excessive drinking, such as the 'Don't drink and drive' advertisements, have had some effect. If the risks of binge-drinking, like the risks of smoking, can be brought home to those at risk, it would diminish the injustice which the ethos of consumption currently produces. In the public forum, the Christian is entitled to press for protective mechanisms in the use of casinos and pokies – mechanisms that would at least minimize the disasters that befall the dependants of improvident gamblers who dissipate a family's income and destroy the prospects of their children. Can it be just to give these families no protection in order to maximize a company's profits or to provide revenue for a government's budget?

Another phenomenon of contemporary life is the vesting of economic power in comparatively few hands, some of whom are the owners of wealth, others are the trustees or directors of invested funds. Such power can be used to oppress others – employees, competitors, creditors – or to operate against the common good. It can produce social injustice, and governmental controls are needed to prevent it. The extent of those controls is an important political question and there is no obvious criterion for determining the measure and nature of those controls, but a purpose can be clearly stated. Whether the controls relate to corporate law, financial regulation, industrial laws, or trade practices, at least one of the purposes of control must be securing the reasonable ability of men and women to live and work in peace and dignity. How that is achieved must remain a matter for political discussion, but the Christian sees wealth and economic power as means to improve the lot of humankind, not as the objects having a right to enhancement or protection. On the other hand, the Christian sees poverty when there is a capacity to relieve it as immoral.

Some structures of social injustice were highlighted recently when a Vatican official noted that 'If yesterday sin had a rather individualistic dimension, today it has an impact and resonance that is above all social, because of globalisation…Attention to sin is more urgent today than yesterday because its dimensions are more widespread and destructive.'

Some of the ways in which, it was said, humans can in modern times 'break their covenant with God and with neighbour' were misinterpreted by the sensationalism of some reporters as a new list of the seven deadly sins. It was nothing of the sort, but it was a wake-up call to the social dimension of sins in our time. Leave aside drug-taking, abortion and paedophilia – the moral significance of these actions is well known – and contemplate the effects of obscene riches, pollution and causing social injustice.

We live, of course, in a materialist age when possessions, if not riches, are highly esteemed. If we were to change our outlook and understand that God gave the gifts of the earth for the benefit of all humankind and that each is entitled to a portion of God's gifts, we would not take pleasure in holding possessions to the exclusion of others but we would be ready to share our possessions when there are others in need. That is not to say that we would be bound to give up what we might reasonably need to keep ourselves and our families in reasonable comfort, but it would encourage a willingness to give to those in need what we do not need ourselves. It would mean that obscene riches become a reproach to conscience – an indication of a moral atrophy which produces isolation from the human family.

Once we realize that there are limits to the material benefits available from the expenditure of human genius on the world's resources, and that the separation of rich and poor is vast and growing, the accumulation of obscene riches can be seen as a deprivation of what the world's poor need to maintain their health and dignity and a swelling of the treasury of those who do not need the riches they possess. Had the possession of obscene wealth been listed as a deadly sin, there would be much to be said for the listing. It is deadly not only for the soul of the possessor; it is deadly for those who need some of that wealth to maintain themselves and their families in health and dignity.

That is not a cry for a compulsory redistribution of wealth. In a capitalist society, that would destroy individual initiative which is the wellspring of developments that promote the welfare of humankind. Such a policy would be counter-productive. It would destroy the ability of society to produce the material goods needed to maintain human dignity and, equally importantly, it would lead to the loss of liberty that we saw in the Eastern bloc before the collapse of the Communist regimes. The liberty to employ initiative carries the right to garner its fruits. Thus, wealth can be accumulated and then the moral imperative not to accumulate obscene wealth becomes relevant. But the solution to obscene wealth is two-fold: mechanisms to prevent the acquisition of obscene wealth and its disposition in relief of those in need. Compulsory redistribution is not the solution; rather, we might hope for a combination of reasonable limitation and charitable disposition.

All humankind have an equal right to live unless it is forfeited in order to protect another person. That right imposes an active duty not only on the State in which life-threatening poverty is suffered but on other States and on other individuals. If all have an equal right to live, States and individuals are under the basic duty of doing what they can to ensure the supply of goods and services needed to sustain human life whenever and wherever it is threatened, whether by natural disaster, mismanagement or sheer poverty. The human right to sustenance is not merely a right to the minimum needed to keep a human body alive from day to day. Men and women are more than animals and each is entitled to sufficient food, shelter, clothing and basic care to allow each to live in dignity. What that entails varies according to the environment and the society. But it impairs dignity if the necessities of life are provided solely by charity. For that reason, social justice demands policies of development which would permit individuals and peoples opportunities to sustain themselves.

Now consider pollution. For many of us, we think of pollution in terms of some smog in the air, or algae in the water or something which keeps the fish out of the harbour or the river – not as something which is life-threatening. But when we get our electricity bills and see how many tons of carbon dioxide were released to give our home its light and power, and when we contemplate the exhausts of our cars or the energy consumed to provide us with transport, with heat and cooling, with food and drink and when we become aware of global warming and the contribution our lifestyle makes to it, we need to reflect. We need to reflect not only on the consequences to the planet, its flora and fauna, but more immediately on the rising sea levels and the desolation of the homes of peoples living in low-lying areas, on the violence of the elements that seems to be increasing and destroying the lives and homes of thousands. Tonight, we shall have a reminder of these facts as the lights are switched off at 8 o'clock in participation of Earth Hour. Let us pause at that time to think about the ways in which we might play our own part in caring for the planet which God gave us and in safeguarding the life and health of those at risk of inundation as well as the life and health of our children and our children's children.

Then consider whether it is sinful to cause social injustice. It is not necessary to see only the Scrooges as sinners in this category. When a group is treated harshly and without justification, is that not a causing of social injustice? In a sense, causing social injustice is a catch-all sin. It is a denial of the duty to love one's neighbour as one's self, and it may take many forms. Racism, which inflicts hurt on others and divides a community, is a sin. Similarly, religious intolerance and class divisions. This sin catches up those who, although they may not possess obscene wealth, seek profits in priority to fair treatment for their employees. Men and women are not mere economic integers whose value is to be calculated according to its effect on the bottom line.

Social justice has to do with social organization. It is not synonymous with a socialist agenda, but it does have to do with social organization that respects people for their innate worth and dignity. It was therefore timely, in my respectful opinion, for the Vatican official to highlight the sins of obscene wealth, pollution and causing social injustice. Evil inheres in such conduct which, however lawful it may be in today's free societies, produces social injustice – that is, injustice to those who have not contributed to the harm they suffer and to which they have been unnecessarily subjected. Treating all people justly – that is, social justice – is an ideal to which the Christian is bound to aspire, albeit the ideal will never be fully attainable.

The reason why we must commit ourselves to seek justice is one thing; constructive effort to achieve justice is another. When we commit ourselves to social justice, we must work in the real world, identifying needs that can be remedied by social action, and charting the action to be taken in relief of the need. How should the Christian go about achieving social justice? Sometimes the action required is personal assistance, sometimes it is institutional or even political change. At the individual level, the Christian meets the victim of social injustice and, to the extent that the Christian can, walks with that person, empathising with the suffering, alleviating the problems and respectfully assuring the person of her or his worth and inalienable dignity. At the community level, the Christian meets with others in the public forum, gives voice to the social injustice that exists, co-operates with others in propounding possible solutions and does whatever can reasonably be done to eliminate the causes of the injustice. In the public forum, the Christian acknowledges the equal right of others to participate in the development of policies and in the actions to be taken.

Then, having done what can reasonably be done to love your neighbour as yourself, the Christian places the rest in the hands of God. Even then, however, there may be a niggling concern about the Christian's own efforts to live by the values and the ideals which he or she has espoused. That concern may come from remembering the admonition which, I am told, is attributable to St Basil the Great: 'The bread which you do not use is the bread of the hungry; the garment hanging in the wardrobe is the garment of the one who is naked; the shoes you do not wear are the shoes of the one who is barefoot; the money you keep locked away is the money of the poor; the acts of charity you do not perform are so many injustices that you commit.'

Those are haunting thoughts. Is there more I could do? More I must do, if I am to love my neighbour as myself? Even if conscience tells you that there is, you may, like me, take refuge in the cry of St Augustine when he realized that he had to abandon his wanton lifestyle and live the life of virtue. 'Not yet, O Lord', he cried, *'not yet!'* But then, Augustine knew that he had to yield and say, 'Here I am Lord, I come to do Your will.'

---

1. Romans 8:15; Galatians 4:6.
2. Matthew 6:29-30; Luke 12:7,25,28.
3. George S Railton, *The Authoritative Life of General Booth: founder of the Salvation Army,* (George H Doran Company, 1912) 11.
4. Address at St James Hall, London, in 1881.

12.6 Graduation Address at Charles Sturt University

Editor's note

This was Brennan's graduation address at the Faculty of Theology of the Charles Sturt University on 12 December 2016.

This is an occasion of celebration when family and friends join with the graduates to celebrate the successful conclusion to those long nights of study and the search for truths that are both profound and transcendent. Many of the graduates have previously graduated in other faculties but have gone on to pursue studies in theology. The reasons may be various but theology offers more than professional training or a rounded education or the honing of intellectual capacity; it offers growth in the student's relationship with God. Few modern universities have a Theology Faculty, yet theology was one of the 'superior' faculties on which the reputation of the University of Paris was founded in the 13th century. Theology's influence on western civilisation has been so fundamental that we do not consciously acknowledge its role in the maintenance of our values. That is understandable in a multi-ethnic, multi-cultural society which prides itself on the separation of church and state, but that is not to say that theology has no role to play in contemporary society. I suggest that our society would be stronger and our lives would be richer if Christian theology had a more influential role to play in the public sphere. So, I hope that some of the work of the newly graduated theologians contributes to the improvement of the standards of our public life.

The superficiality of political debate and the consequent disillusionment of voters are matters of wide community concern. Perhaps modern government is so complex that the bystander simply leaves the decisions to the politicians and the bureaucrats, looking only to the results of their policies and insisting that the results be comforting and to our advantage. And governments, being practical and with ambition for power, do what is necessary to achieve the desired policy results. Thus, governments adopt, whether consciously or unwittingly, the attitude of 'whatever it takes'. Efficacy and efficiency in achieving a result become the criteria for choosing the action to be taken, while the morality of taking that action is at best a subsidiary consideration. The end is what justifies the means. We see an instance of the 'whatever it takes' attitude in the policy governing refugee boat people. It is accepted that their treatment on Manus Island and Nauru is an appropriate means of protecting our borders. Again, while prisons are needed to protect our peace and security, we accept some of the prison conditions which destroy the human dignity of the prisoner. A theologian might challenge a 'whatever it takes' attitude, insisting that the primary consideration is the morality of what is to be done in pursuing a policy and that cannot always be ascertained by reference to the result.

A Christian theologian might also enrich our society by espousing the virtue of tolerance, especially at a time when Christian beliefs and values are not so widely held in our society as they were in earlier times. All Australians aspire to a tolerant society, but what does that mean? Does it mean that, in the interests of a secular peace, the proclamation and practice of Christian faith should be muted or even abandoned? That would be a complete misunderstanding of what tolerance means to a Christian, for Christ proclaimed: 'I am the Way, and the Truth and the Life' (John 14:6). If the Christian believes that proclamation, the Christian must believe, proclaim and live the faith as taught by Christ. Truth is not open to compromise or sacrifice. But truth can be perceived in different ways and there are differences, as we know, in the perception of Christ's truth – differences that lead to the separation of Christian faith communities. Acceptance of a faith, however perceived, is a function of conscience and Christians are bound to respect the freedom of conscience in others, just as they are entitled to freedom of conscience for themselves. That is because they believe that every person is a unique object of God's love and that God has given to each the freedom to accept that love and thus enter into an eternal destiny. So, respect is due to every person's divinely conferred dignity and freedom of conscience. It may be that another's conscience is at odds with the Christian's conscience, but that does not diminish the respect due to the other's dignity and freedom of conscience. Tolerance is not a passive virtue. It does not import the slightest diminution in the faith of the Christian; rather, it calls for acceptance of, and respect for, each person's dignity and freedom conferred by divine gift. It calls for an openness to others who may be different in ways that are foreign to us, perhaps disturbing. There must be freedom for all to believe and to practise the truth as he or she perceives it, limited only by the need to ensure the same freedom for others. Tolerance of that kind binds a society together, making freedom not a loose adhesive of convenience but a basic social convention.

Theology is not as prominent a discipline as it was in the Sorbonne of the 13th century but the ways of theological thought are no less valuable to the secular community than they have been to western society in the last eight centuries. The true value of the discipline, however, is not in the sphere of public affairs but in deepening the knowledge, and thus the love, of God in fulfilment of Paul's prayer for the Ephesians (3:17-19, RSV):

> that Christ may dwell in your hearts through faith; that you, being rooted and grounded in love, may have power to comprehend with all the saints what is the breadth and length and height and depth, and to know the love of Christ which surpasses knowledge, that you may be filled with all the fullness of God.

And that is our prayer for the graduates today.

12.7 Faith and Reason

Editor's note

This was Brennan's address at the Australian Catholic University Graduation on 25 May 2017 when Brennan was conferred with an honorary doctorate. He was delighted when the Pro-Chancellor invited him to present the university's first Aboriginal law graduate David Orr with his testamur for Bachelor of Laws/Bachelor of Global Studies.

Mr Julien O'Connell, Pro-Chancellor, Professor Hillel, Chair of Academic Board, Professor Nicholson, Associate Vice-Chancellor Sydney, Members of Senate of Australian Catholic University, Faculty Members, Distinguished guests, Graduates, Families and Friends:

I join in the acknowledgement of the Dharug/Dharruk Peoples, their Elders past and present. We are gathered today on land of which they have been the custodians for centuries past and which gave life and meaning to those peoples in every generation.

Today is a day of celebration for us graduates and for our families and friends. Those long nights of study – and the occasional shortness of temper – have borne fruit. By contrast, I have received an honorary degree, a humbling honour but no testament to academic achievement. Today you and your families are entitled to rejoice in your academic achievements. But today is only the beginning. A lifetime of professional activity opens before you, presenting challenges and satisfactions, burdens and rewards. A tertiary education is the essential qualification for the life ahead and you have been educated in your chosen faculty of the Australia's Catholic University. The curriculum of study at this University is no doubt similar to, if not identical with, the curriculum in corresponding faculties at other Australian Universities. The same knowledge, skills and experience expected of a graduate from a secular University is expected of a graduate in the corresponding faculty of this University. Is there a difference in the overall intellectual experience of a graduate from a Catholic University? What can that difference be? The difference arises from the ethos of a faith-based University. It has to do with the relationship of faith and reason.

The purpose of a tertiary education is not only to communicate employable knowledge and skills; it is to stimulate thinking and the use of reason – reason based on observation and analysis, logic and the absence of preconception and prejudice. As the beneficiaries of a tertiary education, graduates of every University are expected to exercise their capacities for the good of the community. At a Catholic University, that becomes an obligation of conscience. And the field of activity for rational thinking is expanded beyond the understanding and expansion of secular knowledge to the examination and explanation of the spiritual and transcendent truths of human existence.

Some might think that religious faith limits the freedom to think, that there is some tension between faith and reason. That would be inconsistent with the whole purpose of a university education. Far from being opposed to reason, faith welcomes reason as the pathway to truth, both spiritual and temporal. As Pope John Paul II said: 'Faith does not sprout from the ashes of reason.'[1]

Conflict between faith and reason is impossible, for reason exposes truths and truth knows no inconsistency. Faith does not, cannot, deny truths known by human reasoning. The Copernican theory could not be validly denied by assertions of faith; Galileo was misjudged by the Inquisition. Faith is strengthened when faith is rigorously examined by reason. What accounts for the creation of the observable universe and the human capacity for thought? Faith in a Divine Creator acknowledges that everything in the discoverable universe owes its origin to God and whatever can be known by the exercise of secular reasoning is a manifestation of God's goodness and wisdom. The law of gravity, the principles of cellular biology, nuclear fission, climate change – all phenomena owe their origin to the creative power of God.

Although Christian faith never denies the truth of what is revealed by natural reason, faith does import norms which govern what mankind may morally do to acquire and use the knowledge that reason can reveal. Thus faith, by acknowledging God's conferring of a unique dignity on every person, condemns Dr Mengel's hideous experiments on living people whether or not those experiments might yield some medical knowledge. Similarly, when faith attributes that dignity to a human embryo, it condemns the creation of embryos for the sole purpose of harvesting their stem cells, whatever be the intended use of those cells. These are not examples of restriction of thought. The experimental phenomena are not questioned. Faith and reason are invoked in defining the moral norms of conducting experiments. As Pope Benedict said: 'Without the corrective supplied by religion, reason too can fall prey to distortions, as when it is manipulated by ideology, or applied in a partial way that fails to take full account of the dignity of the human person.'[2]

Although Catholic faith proclaims moral principles, it does not assume authority to dictate the law. Speaking on the sources of law, Pope Benedict said 'Unlike other great religions, Christianity has never proposed a revealed law to the State and to society, that is to say a juridical order derived from revelation. Instead, it has pointed to nature and reason as the true sources of law – and to the harmony of objective and subjective reason, which naturally presupposes that both spheres are rooted in the creative reason of God.'[3]

Catholic faith is not unquestioning. The Church knows that human authority may be guilty of arrogance, abuse of power, want of compassion and worldly ambition. The Church does not confuse mere obedience to authority with faith. Thomas More rejected the English Bishops and went to the block; Mary Mackillop was excommunicated by an errant Bishop. Yet both are canonised saints – saints whose anguished reasoning led them to recognition of true holiness.

A Catholic University invites its students to use their reason to test their faith, to verify its source, to examine its doctrines and to justify its moral principles. Reason must govern the thinking not only about the observable universe but also about the spiritual realities, appreciating that spiritual realities are not to be measured in time and space. Eternity, after all, is not a prolongation of time but its absence. And space defies limitation.

Today we celebrate graduates who are committed to serving the common good and who are willing to grapple with the great questions of human destiny. That is the foundation of a challenging and ennobling life. May God guide and bless you.

---

1. Address of Pope John Paul II to University Professors of All Nations, 9 September 2000.
2. Address of Pope Benedict XVI, Westminster Hall – City of Westminster, 17 September 2010.
3. Address of His Holiness Benedict XVI, Reichstag Building, Berlin, 22 September 2011.

12.8 A Public Attestation of Faith and Thanks

Editor's note

On 23 June 2018, twelve football players aged 11 to 16 together with their coach entered Tham Luang Nang Non, a cave system in Chiang Rai province, northern Thailand. Heavy rains precluded their being able to exit the caves. A major international rescue operation was instigated. The world waited on edge. Between 8 and 10 July 2018, everyone was rescued. Brennan was overjoyed and took the rare step of writing this letter to the Editor. It was published in The Australian on 12 July 2018.

The world watched and waited and millions prayed for the safe deliverance of the boys and their rescuers. The prayers were offered in every faith; they strengthened and supported the compassion, the courage and the competence of the rescuers.

Perhaps the universal concern for those in peril, and the brave and selfless devotion of their rescuers, have shown us how to make our world a better place.

Gerard Brennan, Darling Point, NSW

At his retirement as Chief Justice, Brennan was joined by many of his ex-associates and his longtime secretary Nessie Birchley 'who ensured that nothing ever went wrong'.

Family members admitted to the Bar robed for Brennan's retirement: Frank SJ, Justin Gleeson SC, Madeline KC, Tom SC, and Dan O'Gorman SC

Many of the grandchildren flocked to their grandparents at Gerard's retirement.
(Photo: Viki Yemettas, *The Age*)

Gerard and Patricia greet Archbishop Francis Rush of Brisbane and Gerard receives an honorary doctorate from the Australian Catholic University, speaking on 'Faith and Reason'

Gerard and Patricia were in the official welcome party for Pope John Paul II when he arrived at Fairbairn Base, Canberra for an official visit on 24 November 1986

As Chancellor of the University of Technology Sydney (UTS), Brennan welcomed many visionary speakers including William Deane, Marie Bashir, and Malcolm Fraser. (Photo: Sherran Evans)

Brennan with Nelson Mandela at UTS and launching Donald Horne's *An Australian compact?: what are the core values that all Australians might respect?* (Photos: Sherran Evans and Patrick Jones)

In 2005, Gerard and the editor were presented with honorary LLDs by the University of New South Wales. (Photo: Peter Morris, *Sydney Morning Herald*)

Chapter 13

Catholic Social Teaching

13.1 Address to the National Catholic Education Commission

Editor's note

Brennan was invited to deliver the After-Dinner address in the Great Hall at Parliament House Canberra for the 1996 national conference of the National Catholic Education Commission on 2 May 1996. After he had delivered the address, Sr Helen Lombard SGS, the Provost of the newly formed University of Notre Dame, Australia, approached him, saying: 'Sir Gerard, I am sure you would be pleased to know that we are establishing Australia's first Catholic Law School.' Brennan replied, 'Must you?' This was Brennan's address.

Patricia and I are grateful for your invitation to be with you this evening as you gather in celebration of the work of the Catholic Church in education. The pleasure has a number of sources, some personal, some of national importance. Personally, it is a joy to renew an association with those concerned with Catholic education. Over 20 years ago, I was privileged to be a member of the Catholic Education Council of the Brisbane Archdiocese. Alan Druery was there, already acknowledged as a constructive administrator and a congenial colleague. I trust he has been gratified by the changes in the intervening years. He will join me in paying tribute to the memory of Father Barney O'Shea, the Diocesan Director of Education, and the Parish Priest of Dutton Park. His quiet charism and gentle sensitivity were coupled with a devotion to the education of young Australians. He discharged his pastoral duties and yet found the time and energy to inspire teachers and administrators who were endeavouring to expand the systemic schools into areas of new demand. I imagine that tonight we are privileged to have many in our midst who, like Father O'Shea, have inspired teachers and administrators in their noble vocation. Their presence does us honour.

Each of us has a debt to the Catholic educational system. Mine is substantial. In the heat of a Rockhampton summer, I was sent off to the Infants' School at the Range Convent and there entrusted to the care of the starched and gowned Sisters of Mercy. Mystically, they were able to keep their sartorial elegance during sweltering days as they lovingly but sternly took a scruffy group of infants through the pothooks of the copy books – does anyone here remember them? – the two times tables and, as we grew up, through our preparation for first Confession and Holy Communion. Thereafter, the heroic self-sacrifice and discipline of the Christian Brothers. They staffed a school in West Street during the depression years before the War when those who could afford a fee paid a penny a week and the shortfall was made up by gifts of food that did little to alleviate the spartan diet of the Brothers' table. They produced some fine Priests, Bishops and Rugby League footballers. I am obviously not in the clerical category and I have to confess to being a disappointment in the other. Later, in secondary school at Downlands in Toowoomba, the rugged Australian faith and culture of the Missionaries of the Sacred Heart – both Priests and Brothers – were a tremendous inspiration. That was a time when the world was ready to be renewed. Vital and exciting prospects challenged youthful idealism to realize Australia's new and glorious future. The catechism gave way to Sheehan's *Apologetics* and Frank Sheed's *A Map of Life*; the vestiges of ghetto Catholicity were shown to be narrowing fetters on an outward-looking and confident membership of a great Australian community and conformity to peer group pressure and populist opinion was pilloried by the theme of Bishop Doyle's Saturday night homilies, 'Be different!'

The education of girls – as I and many husbands would testify – is a tribute to the female religious orders. Long before feminism in any of its forms won popular support, they fostered and inspired the dignity and equality of Australian women, acknowledging and developing their professional and educational capacity, their participation in public activities and encouraging each woman in her ambitions. The indebtedness of our generation to the men and women who taught and inspired us in Catholic schools is profound, for they gave purpose and direction to our lives and helped us to the knowledge and love of a God Who, for all the great changes of the intervening years, has remained the rock and reference point for the lives of so many of us. For those of us who have been blessed with children and grandchildren, our debt to Catholic education has been compounded with each generation.

Catholic education in Australia has not been without its shortcomings – often the result of limited educational opportunities for the teachers as well as for the students. It has not been without its blemishes, some of which have caused great suffering, have been revealed too late, have been remedied too ineffectively and have blighted the morale of many who have devoted their lives to the education of the young. But the benefits which Catholic educational systems have conferred on generations of students and thus on the Australian nation are immeasurable and the fine traditions and ethos of the system are not diminished by the occasions when shortcomings and blemishes have marred the contribution they have made.

In your Conference, you are addressing the responses which the entire system of Catholic education should make to the conditions of contemporary and future Australian society. That is a timely exercise, for this age of rapid social change, of the questioning of institutions and of scepticism about absolutes demands new and appropriate responses. The past has lessons to teach, but it gives no certain prescription for the present. It would be futile today to plan for educational services as though the religious orders who bore the principal responsibility in the past were available to bear that responsibility today. The challenge has passed to teachers, academics and catechists who, for the most part, are not called to the religious life and who bring a different charism to their vocational labours. But I venture to suggest that the values which underlie and inform the Catholic educational system do not change. The education of each person, child or adult, must acknowledge that person to be made in the image of God and to be a member of the human family; it must acknowledge that each person has not only a social life but also an eternal destiny; it must acknowledge each person to have a unique dignity. These values have a profound influence on the content and purpose of Catholic education.

In the first place, there can be no contradiction between the purpose of Christian formation and the purpose of instruction in secular subjects. Nor can some false priority be accorded to one aspect or another of human development. To those who believe, the human personality is completed, not diminished, by religious faith. No dichotomy is perceived between knowledge of Christ and openness to His love on the one hand and the acquisition of knowledge and skills in secular subjects. To be a Christian member of the human family is to be exposed to the call of others and to have a supernatural reason to respond. And so, the acquisition of knowledge and skills has two objects which are complementary: fulfilment of the individual's potential and service to fellow men and women, especially to those who stand in need of the knowledge and skills acquired.

Next, if the system is to be true to itself, there must be a confident proclamation of the gospel truths. As Father Christopher Gleeson SJ has said: 'Faith in our own values, our own judgment, is the most powerful motivation for telling the truth. ... Parents and teachers have the challenge and responsibility to help young people understand St John's statement that the truth will make them free (John 8:32).'[1]

The proclaiming of the gospel truths is not an exercise in proselytising. If the gospel truths provide a vision of the reality to which all men and women aspire in the depths of their being, they will be proclaimed not so much by precept as by example. If the gospel truths are valid for all times and places, the means by which they are proclaimed – whether by word or deed – will resonate with the circumstances of each time and place. 'Principles,' said Cardinal Newman, 'must be thrown into new shapes according to the form of society which they are to influence.'[2] And so there must be an expectation – indeed a welcoming – of change. But faith must be fostered by believers and it would be wasteful to sustain a Catholic educational system which offered no more than academic, sporting or artistic success. Perhaps we need to remember the Pope's admission that 'For a long time the Church paid more attention to its institutional and hierarchical dimension and neglected somewhat its fundamental dimension of grace and charism, which is proper to the people of God.'[3]

Many years ago, a young Father Jim Bourke, who was later to become the first Secretary of your Commission, wrote an influential article for his fellow Undergraduates at the University of Adelaide. It had some currency in the Newman Societies of other Universities. It was entitled 'Let your light shine!' Its thesis, as I remember it, was not that Christianity was a religion to be trumpeted from the rooftops, but rather it was a way of life which bore witness to the Fatherhood of God, the redemptive love of Christ and the brotherhood of man. It was a thesis that assumed the autonomy of individual conscience.

Freedom to think, to question, even to reject, is of paramount importance. Without that freedom, virtue is impossible. A will constrained by ignorance or sanction cannot respond freely to the love of God or man. But a mind which is free to accept or reject the loving message of faith is enriched by a positive response and finds peace in its warm relationship with God and other people. And, as against the risk of a negative or inadequate response to a proclamation of the love of God, the parable of the seed and the sower is a caution and a comfort to parents and teachers alike.

At one time, the Catholic educational system was seen by some to be a bastion against the sapping of faith by an outside world hostile to Christian values. I trust that that inward-looking orientation has now disappeared. It was, in retrospect, a disorder of the values which ought to have informed the system. The individual cannot be fulfilled if he or she is isolated from the life and dynamism of the community. Nor should the gifts which an individual possesses – whether of faith, skills or possessions – be locked away from others who are in need. Christian education looks outwards because human development requires it and because service and compassion are at the core of all Christian activity. That is the orientation which makes the system an important contributor to Australian society.

The contribution has been made in many ways. Some are matters of history. The work of Blessed Mary MacKillop and the Josephites in South Australia is but one of the examples of the bringing of education to Australian children who would otherwise have been isolated in ignorance. The Catholic education system numbers their students, past and present, in the millions. The educational standards of the nation would be much lower if it were not for the contribution made by the system with which your Conference is concerned. And it has made another, less tangible but nonetheless real contribution to our society.

Australia is, as it always has been since European settlement, a pluralistic society. Unlike some of the American colonies, no single religious group has guided our cultural development. Rather we have struggled as a nation towards mutual tolerance and understanding, respecting different faiths, ethnic diversity and cultural variations. If we are a mature society, we can boast that the contributions made by each of the elements of our society has made us the richer by making us more familiar with and appreciative of the genius of humankind. The Catholic education system has contributed to this cultural strength by insisting on the equal and unique dignity of every person, by espousing the ideal of service to others, by insisting on respect for religious and political freedom and by inspiring effective compassion for the disadvantaged. Catholic education is not, of course, the only contributor of these ideals to Australian society, but the system is entitled to respectful acknowledgment of the substantial contribution it has made.

Of course, the system has embraced values which run counter to modern popular sentiment, especially in matters of social justice and sexual morality. In a democracy, there is no reason why such values should be compromised or their advocacy muted. The freedom of expression which is a hall-mark of our pluralist democracy is maintained in part to ensure that that democracy is owned and respected by all sections of the community. Each philosophic or religious group in our community has some truth to tell and the telling of it gives all of us the opportunity to learn. If the truths which are held in the schools of the Catholic educational system were no longer to be expounded, society would be the poorer for their silence.

Tonight, you celebrate your faith, your work and your aspirations. You celebrate the contribution you and the Catholic education system are making and have made to this free and confident nation. Your guests are privileged to be included in this celebration of labours that are directed ultimately by Samuel's words: 'Speak, Yahweh. Your servant is listening.' (1 Samuel. 3).

---

1. Christopher Gleeson, *Striking a Balance: teaching values and freedom* (Hodder & Stoughton, 1993), 90-91.
2. John Henry Newman, *An Essay on the Development of Christian Doctrine* (J Toovey, 1845) Ch II, Sec 3, 58.
3. Pope John Paul II, *Crossing the Threshold of Hope* (Jonathan Cape, London, 1994) 175.

13.2 Address to the Catholic Commission for Justice, Development and Peace

Editor's note

Brennan was invited to deliver the Rerum Novarum Lecture for the Catholic Commission for Justice, Development and Peace in Melbourne on 4 May 1999.

We are within days of the 108th anniversary of the publication of *Rerum Novarum,* the encyclical of Pope Leo XIII which claimed the authority of the Church to speak on social issues and which, in exercise of that authority, proclaimed the rights and responsibilities of capital and labour. It was published when land was the chief source of wealth, when, in the wake of the industrial revolution, the conditions of labour were oppressive, when *laissez-faire* was a fashionable economic theory and when the division between capital and labour threatened the stability of society. Forty years later, in his memorable encyclical *Quadragesimo Anno*, Pope Pius XI recalled the conditions which had evoked the earlier encyclical, recorded its seminal influence and proclaimed the power and duty of the State to protect the common good against the individual misuse of private property. Then, after a further sixty years, Pope John Paul II commemorated the hundredth anniversary of *Rerum Novarum* in the encyclical *Centesimus Annus.* In this encyclical, and in *Sollicitudo Rei Socialis,* the Pope developed the theology of the Church's social doctrine, expounded its principles in terms applicable to contemporary conditions and noted that '[t]he world today is ever more aware that solving national and international problems is not just a matter of economic production or of juridical or social organization, but also calls for specific ethical and religious values, as well as changes of mentality, behaviour and structures.'[1]

Although these encyclicals are directed primarily to the Bishops, Clergy and Laity of the Church, their message has resonated in the wider community. Papal authority alone did not produce that result; it was the consequence of founding social doctrine upon the essential and universal character of the individual. Because the individual is the focus of the doctrine and is seen to be a social creature with a Divine spark and destiny, the doctrine goes beyond political or economic theory. The individual is not perceived as a mere economic integer or as the wielder or subject of political power. The unique dignity of each individual must not be diminished and social structures must not alienate men and women from their fellows. Nor must those structures impede the essential relationship between the individual and God Who is the Creator and End of human existence.

The doctrine acknowledges that each of us lives in a community formed by a particular history and culture and therefore it does not purport to prescribe the means by which its ideals are to be implemented. But it does define principles by which the local Church and each of its members may determine for themselves the morality of concrete proposals and the steps which should be taken to protect the life, the dignity, the autonomy and the religious freedom of the individual within his or her society.

It is precisely because the focus of the Church's social doctrine is the essential nature of the human person, recognizing all of his or her spiritual as well as temporal capacities and aspirations, that the doctrine is not a political or economic theory or ideology. In *Sollicitudo Rei Socialis,* the Pope declared:

> The Church's social doctrine *is not* a 'third way' between *liberal capitalism* and *Marxist collectivism*, nor even a possible alternative to other solutions less radically opposed to one another: rather, it constitutes a *category of its own*. Nor is it an *ideology*, but rather the *accurate formulation* of the results of a careful reflection on the complex realities of human existence, in society and in the international order, in the light of faith and of the Church's tradition. Its main aim is to *interpret* these realities, determining their conformity with or divergence from the lines of the Gospel teaching on man and his vocation, a vocation which is at once earthly and transcendent; its aim is thus *to guide* Christian behaviour. It therefore belongs to the field, not of *ideology*, but of *theology* and particularly of moral theology.[2]

It would be a mistake, however, to dismiss the doctrine as having relevance only to a private spirituality, wanting in a broad practical effect. As it speaks to the heart of every man and woman, it creates a ferment of ideas and a striving for true freedom that lead to concrete action. The recent collapse of Communism in Eastern Europe is a dramatic demonstration of the power of Christian – not always specifically Catholic – values, and the transformation that those values produce. A more modest example in our own country can be found in the historical judgment in the '*Harvester Case*'. There Mr Justice Higgins set the standard of a basic wage sufficient to provide food and water, shelter and rest for employees and their families 'and a condition of frugal comfort estimated by current human standards.' Higgins' biographer noted that that phrase reflects the influence of *Rerum Novarum* where it is said that a prudent worker will gladly strive to practise thrift if he 'receives a wage sufficiently large to enable him to provide comfortably for himself, his wife and his children'.[3]

In our diverse and pluralistic society, the doctrine of the Encyclicals can be effective to enhance the dignity of the individual and to create a society of social justice only if it be explained in terms that inform the minds and touch the hearts of Australian men and women of good will, irrespective of their religion, politics, race or economic or social standing.

There is a natural, and sometimes justified, reserve in the public mind about the expression by Churches of their views on issues that touch the political or economic arena. The separation of Church and State is seen as a *cordon sanitaire,* protecting each from interference by the other. Within limits, that separation is appropriate and necessary in a free society – necessary to ensure religious freedom and necessary to preserve the democratic control of government. But the separation does not prevent the State from maintaining the public good against a group or a person who would undermine it in the name of religion; conversely, the separation should not suppress the contribution which the Churches may make to moral issues that are relevant to the political or economic life of the community. Morality in this context is not a canon of personal behaviour but an imperative to be observed by the State and by public institutions. A political or economic program that is morally deficient saps the authority of the State and its institutions and provides ground for disaffection and disorder. For this reason, some of the manifestations of economic rationalism are unacceptable, however successful that policy may be politically or economically. A bottom-line fixation that alienates minorities and the underprivileged and fails to ensure that all have a minimum condition of frugal comfort by current standards is both devoid of morality and a pathway to social unrest. So, we should welcome the contribution of the Churches to political debate when they seek to apply moral principle and ethical values.

In the intemperate climate of Australian politics, politicians frequently demean themselves and their offices by superficial and personal attacks on those who speak on behalf of a Church in a debate that has a moral or ethical dimension. Yet the views which are accepted by Church members in virtue of their religious beliefs and views based solely on secular considerations are equally entitled to consideration. Freedom of speech is mocked if personal denigration is the political response to reasoned and temperate debate. In the end, moral values must be heard lest society descend into conflict and disorder.

The excesses of *laissez-faire* capitalism provoked the growth of communism, both theories ignoring the personal dignity and autonomy of workers. Pope Leo XIII, focussing on the moral character of humankind, repelled both theories and set the path to a more civilized social order. He did not purport to define the specific measures that had to be taken in particular countries to achieve social justice but he proclaimed the moral principles which were needed. Those principles included recognition of the institution of personal property. He wrote:

> To own goods privately… is a right natural to man, and to exercise this right, especially in life in society, is not only lawful, but clearly necessary… But if the question be asked: How ought man use his possessions? The Church replies without hesitation: 'As to this point, man ought not regard external goods as his own, but as common so that, in fact, a person should readily share them when he sees others in need…. No one … is obliged to assist others out of what is required for his own necessary use or for that of his family, or even to give to others what he himself needs to maintain his station in life becomingly and decently … But when the demands of necessity and propriety have been sufficiently met, it is a duty to give to the poor out of that which remains …[4]

Although the Encyclicals emphasise the importance of private property in supporting the dignity of labour and sustaining the labourer and his family, in rewards the industrious and the thrifty and in confining the fields in which it is necessary and legitimate for the State to intervene, a clear distinction is drawn between the ownership of property and its use. The principle on which this distinction is based was stated by the Second Vatican Council:

> God intended the earth and all that it contains for the use of every human being and people. Thus, as all men follow justice and unite in charity, created goods should abound for them on a reasonable basis. Whatever the forms of ownership may be, as adapted to the legitimate institutions of people according to diverse and changeable circumstances, attention must always be paid to the universal purpose for which created goods are meant. In using them, therefore, a man should regard his lawful possessions not merely as his own but also as common property in the sense that they should accrue to the benefit of not only himself but of others.[5]

Pope John Paul, citing Genesis 1:28 explains that 'God gave the earth to the whole human race for the sustenance of all its members, without excluding or favouring anyone. This is the foundation of the universal destination of the earth's goods.'[6] Since material wealth must be available for the support of all people, an incident of the institution of property is the duty of charity, sometimes extending to the duty to give 'even out of one's needs in order to provide what is essential for the life of a poor person.'[7]

The Encyclicals approve a society of free work, of enterprise and of participation[8] but the personal freedom of employer and employee to bargain over remuneration is subject to the obligations of natural justice to pay a wage not less 'than enough to support a worker who is thrifty and upright'. Pope Leo warned that 'If, compelled by necessity or moved by fear of a worse evil, a worker accepts a harder condition, which although against his will he must accept because the employer or contractor imposes it, he certainly submits to force against which justice cries out in protest.'[9]

A century further on, the present Pope lamented: 'Would that these words, written at a time when what has been called "unbridled capitalism" was pressing forward, should not have to be repeated today with the same severity.'[10]

As the forces of an uncontrolled market offer no protection to the underprivileged and to those who rely for support solely on their labour, laws are needed to control oppression.[11] The function of law in securing social justice was not always admitted. Forty years after *Rerum Novarum,* Pope Pius XI observed that the spreading of the teaching of *Rerum Novarum* had overthrown 'the tottering tenets of Liberalism which had long hampered effective interference by the government.' But, he wrote, in consequence of the dissemination of *Rerum Novarum* 'there has arisen a new branch of jurisprudence unknown to earlier times, whose aim is the energetic defence of those sacred rights of the workingman which proceed from his dignity as a man and as a Christian.... Even though these regulations do not agree always and in every detail with the recommendations of Pope Leo, it is none the less certain that much which they contain is strongly suggestive of *Rerum Novarum*, to which in large measure must be attributed the improved condition of the workingmen.'[12]

Pope John Paul II reaffirmed the function of law: 'There is certainly a legitimate sphere of autonomy in economic life which the State should not enter. The State, however, has the task of determining the juridical framework within which economic affairs are to be conducted, and thus of safeguarding the prerequisites of a free economy, which presumes a certain equality between the parties, such that one party would not be so powerful as practically to reduce the other to subservience.'[13]

Although the State and its laws must give labour the basic protection of a just wage, that proposition did not exhaust the Church's teaching on the distribution of profits. *Quadragesimo Anno* condemned the unjust claims of capital which invoked a fictitious economic law to assert that accumulation of riches must fall to the share of the wealthy while the workingman remained perpetually in indigence or reduced to the minimum needed for existence. Equally, it condemned the unjust claims of labour which sought all the profits save those required to repair and replace invested capital. The Pope espoused nothing less than the reconstruction of the social order so as to achieve a fair sharing of the profits of the enterprises to which both capital and labour contributed.

The legal systems of the Western world, including our own, recognize the institution of private property. For the most part, those laws do not draw a clear distinction between the right of private property and the right to use private property. Rather the legal notions which inform the law of property treat the right of property as a right in the owner to use and to dispose of the property as the owner chooses. Limits on the use of property include a duty not to injure the legal rights of another, not to be careless in using property so as to cause damage to another and to conform with statutory safeguards for the environment. Significantly, our laws, recognizing the power which accumulations of property creates, provide structures which facilitate accumulation and confer the resultant power on managers other than the original owners. Trusts and corporations are obvious examples.

Modern trade, commerce and, increasingly, government are carried on by managers controlling accumulations of property. The system has fostered great technological development and has increased the wealth of many nations but the power created by these accumulations of property is not governed by considerations that would devote the earth's goods to the support of the world's people. Pius XI saw this clearly in 1931:

> In the first place, then, it is patent that in our days not alone is wealth accumulated, but immense power and despotic economic domination is concentrated in the hands of a few, and that those few are frequently not the owners, but only the trustees and directors of invested funds, who administer them at their good pleasure.
>
> This power becomes particularly irresistible when exercised by those who, because they hold and control money, are able also to govern credit and determine its allotment, for that reason supplying so to speak, the life-blood to the entire economic body, and grasping, as it were, in their hands the very soul of production, so that no one dare breathe against their will.
>
> This accumulation of power the characteristic note of the modern economic order, is a natural result of limitless free competition, which permits the survival of those only who are the strongest, which often means those who fight most relentlessly, who pay least heed to the dictates of conscience.
>
> This concentration of power has led to a threefold struggle for domination. First, there is the struggle for dictatorship in the economic sphere itself; then, the fierce battle to acquire control of the state, so that its resources and authority may be abused in the

> economic struggles; finally, the clash between states themselves. This latter arises from two causes: because the nations apply their power and political influence, regardless of circumstances, to promote the economic advantages of their citizens; and because, vice versa, economic forces and economic domination are used to decide political controversies between peoples.[14]

The system, without controls imposed by the State or, as needful, by the international community, tends to accumulate further wealth and to acquire greater power in the hands of those who already possess wealth and power. This tendency is accentuated by the increasing importance of know-how, technology and skill as property. Pope John Paul, noting that the wealth of industrialized nations is based more on this form of property than on natural resources,[15] points out that -

> many people, perhaps the majority today, do not have the means which would enable them to take their place in an effective and humanly dignified way within a productive system in which work is truly central. They have no possibility of acquiring the basic knowledge which would enable them to express their creativity and develop their potential. They have no way of entering the network of knowledge and intercommunication which would enable them to see their qualities appreciated and utilized. Thus, if not actually exploited, they are to a great extent marginalized; economic development takes place over their heads, so to speak, when it does not actually reduce the already narrow scope of their old subsistence economies. [16]

He adds that '[t]hose who fail to keep up with the times can easily be marginalized, as can the elderly, the young people who are incapable of finding their place in the life of society, and, in general, those who are weakest or part of the so-called Fourth World.'[17] The free market and technological change have failed to bring benefits, or a fair proportion of benefits, to much of the world's population. The gap between the affluent and the world's poor has widened and, in consequence, the poor are alienated and often lose the sense of their own dignity.

Another source of alienation is found in affluent communities where consumerism has ensnared people 'in a web of false and superficial gratifications rather than being helped to experience their personhood in an authentic and concrete way. Alienation is found also in work, when it is organized so as to ensure maximum returns and profits with no concern whether the worker, through his own labour, grows or diminishes as a person, either through increased sharing in a genuinely supportive community or through increased isolation in a maze of relationships marked by destructive competitiveness and estrangement, in which he is considered only a means and not an end.'[18]

Employers and employees alike are affected by mass advertising which offer the products of the new technology as instant gratification of human needs. Here education, culture and openness to the needs and aspirations of our fellows must keep check on the ambition to possess – and to possess now. *Centesimus Annus* says: 'It is not wrong to want to live better; what is wrong is a style of life which is presumed to be better when it is directed towards "having" rather than "being", and which wants to have more, not in order to be more but in order to spend life in enjoyment as an end in itself. It is therefore necessary to create lifestyles in which the quest for truth, beauty, goodness and communion with others for the sake of common growth are the factors which determine consumer choices, savings and investments.'[19]

The message of the Encyclicals speaks to each of us and to the community in which we live. It does not tell us what our laws must be, but it tells us what our laws should guard against. It does not deny the value of a free capitalist economy, but it does show the evils which such a system brings if it be not controlled. It does not prescribe a particular system of government but it rejects any system which excludes the participation of the people or which intrudes unnecessarily into their lives.

The message of the Encyclicals is that each person, by virtue of his or her creation in God's image, has a unique dignity that demands the opportunity to work, to support or to be supported in a family, to participate in society, to be free so long as the exercise of the freedom assists and does not hurt a neighbour and, above all, to be free to know, to love and to worship God. To protect and advance that dignity many practical measures must be taken – in law, in the economy and in government. It is left to us, appreciating the essential nature of humankind as truly as it has been appreciated by the Encyclicals, to ensure that our laws, our economy and our government protect and advance each person's dignity.

There is much to ponder and much to do, for the problems addressed by *Rerum Novarum* seem to have returned, like a mutated virus, to reinfect today's world. But our hope is that social injustice can be remedied, true freedom can be assured and alienation can be eliminated by dissemination and ultimate acceptance of principles drawn from the nature of humankind and inevitably echoing in the hearts of men and women of every age.

---

1. *Centesimus Annus* par 60.
2. *Sollicitudo Rei Socialis* par 41.
3. John Rickard, *H B Higgins, the Rebel as Judge* (Allen & Unwin, 1984) 173-4.

4. *Rerum Novarum* pars 35,36
5. *Gaudium et Spes* par 69
6. *Centesimus Annus* Ch 2 par 31
7. Ibid Ch 2 par 36
8. Ibid Ch 2 par 36
9. *Rerum Novarum* par 63
10. *Centesimus Annus* Ch 1 par 8
11. Ibid par 35
12. *Quadragesimo Anno* Section I(2)
13. *Centesimus Annus* par 15
14. *Quadragesimo Anno* Section
15. *Centesimus Annus* Ch 2 par 32
16. Ibid Ch 2 par 33
17. Ibid Ch 2 par 33
18. Ibid Ch 2 par 40
19. Ibid Ch 2 par 35

13.3 Address to the Society of St Vincent de Paul

Editor's note

Brennan was a lifelong member of the St Vincent de Paul Society. Even as a High Court judge, he would deliver food hampers to families in need. He was delighted to deliver the 1999 Ozanam Lecture in Melbourne Town Hall on 7 September 1999. Frederic Ozanam, a nineteenth century French professor of commercial law was the founder of the Vincent de Paul Society. Brennan spoke on 'Liberty, Equality and Poverty'.

I stand before you tonight in a false light. The honour of delivering the Ozanam Lecture rightly belongs to those who have acquired the necessary knowledge in the way which Ozanam himself prescribed. The spirit of the man shines in what he wrote:

> The knowledge of social well-being and of reform is to be learned, not from books, nor from the public platform, but in climbing the stairs to the poor man's garret, sitting by his bed-side, feeling the same cold that pierces him, sharing the secret of his lonely heart and troubled mind. When the conditions of the poor have been examined, in school, at work, in hospital, in the city, in the country, everywhere that God has placed them, it is then and then only, that we know the elements of that formidable problem, that we begin to grasp it and may hope to solve it.[1]

Sometimes, and too infrequently, I have had the privilege of accompanying a Brother of the St Vincent de Paul Society on a home visit and the joy of participating in Conferences of the Society, but there are others, many others, who year by patient year bear a quiet and powerful witness to Christ's love of the poor and gain an insight and a sanctity that shines in their quiet eyes. You see them in most Catholic parishes – gentle people, with a smile playing on their lips, and a worldly wisdom which seeks to understand but never to condemn. Sometimes deceived, they are proud to be fools for Christ.

I pay them a deep and affectionate respect and I am conscious that what I have to say cannot be said with the knowledge and wisdom that any of them would bring. So, I can but reflect on some of the institutional problems with which Ozanam, himself a sometime Professor of Commercial Law, was concerned. Especially after the uprisings of 1848, he was concerned with the spirit of a people which define the character of their political and social institutions. Today in Australia, we do not speak so much of the spirit of religion as we do of the values of our multi-cultural society.

It is a truism that social phenomena reflect the values of society, whether for good or ill. We know that the practices of fascism could not have flourished in a society that valued liberty and equality; equally, we know that the financial excesses of the 1980s were possible only because of a pervasive materialism that asserted greed to be good. No human society is value free; each society reveals and gives effect to its prevailing values in its laws and institutions, in its political and economic policies, in its art, literature and architecture and in the manner in which its people relate one to another. In a democracy, government looks to the contemporary values of the community in creating, fostering and organizing the social order and politicians embrace and extol these values in advocating their political goals. Values are the stuff of morality and, for Christians, morality is an expression of the relationship of humankind with God and the recognition of the unique dignity of each individual as a person with a divine spark and destiny. In a pluralist, democratic society, the social order is not necessarily shaped in accordance with Christian values but Christians are entitled equally with others to contribute to its shaping. So far as it is possible to discern the contemporary morality of a community, the laws should be consistent with it but the laws should not be, or be taken to be, exhaustive of that morality. If law and morality coincided, there would be little room for virtue and the authority of individual conscience would be reduced to mere obedience to the coercive power of the State. Laws must reflect morality, but they do not define morality. If morality were to be formed solely by the laws, we would be living in a totalitarian state where concepts of right or wrong would be secondary to obedience or disobedience to the State's command.

Civilization is impossible without moral values and a community which does not share or accept a basic set of moral values is a community in chaos. Australians enjoy political stability because we share the basic values of liberty, equality and tolerance; we respect integrity, especially in public office, and we insist on the rule of law. Within those very broad parameters, we conduct our public affairs and frame our laws. Of course, the content of these values are not universally agreed and the disagreements stimulate our controversies. The content which Christians give to these concepts are the Christian contribution to our social life. No false modesty, no deference to non-Christian or anti-Christian values should deter the charitable exposition of the Gospel message. Of course, the Christian is bound to accept that others who, in good conscience, hold different views are equally free to advocate those views. But the Gospel calls us to be an example to others in our mutual love and in our lived and professed commitment to the values we find in Christ's life and teaching. For the Catholic, there is a rich repository of teaching in Papal Encyclicals and in the Documents of the Second Vatican Council. I draw on parts of those sources for what I have to say this evening.

The civilization of the western world was developed under the influence of Christianity and two of the values which we hold dear in Australia today – liberty and equality – take their content from Christian ideals. The liberty we cherish is a manifestation of the Christian belief that God gave to each of us a freedom to choose between right and wrong and a capacity to form that judgment, a freedom to do good or to do evil and to be responsible for our own conduct and its results[2]. The freedom that we possess by virtue of the divine dispensation is inconsistent with any form of totalitarian regime, whether of the right or the left. Nazism and communism are equally antagonistic to the unique dignity and personal responsibility of each man and woman. Any infringement on or limitation of individual freedom must be justified. That freedom is not to be taken away by laws, pressures or inducements which are not needed to preserve ourselves from unintended harm or to secure and maintain the common good of our fellows. Therefore, the coercion of the law should be kept to a minimum. So, liberty is a value to be preserved not only because we like to live in a free society but because it maximises the opportunities for exercising the freedom of thought and action by which we achieve our own dignity and in which we may acknowledge and discharge our moral responsibilities to our fellow men and women.

The value of equality is an acknowledgement that, before God, each individual is equally precious and is equally loved. Race or colour, class or creed, physical or mental perfection or defect afford no warrant for attributing varying degrees of worth and dignity to humankind. Every person possesses the same dignity as a child of God[3] and is entitled to the same respect[4]. Of course, there are differences in natural endowments and massive differences in the societies and environments in which people live. These differences account for or contribute to dissimilarity in the position, especially in the economic position, of individuals within society. Poverty in mind and spirit, poverty in social life, poverty in material possessions may be attributable wholly or partially to differences over which the individual has no, or little, control; or the poverty may be self-induced and the individual may be incapable of self-extrication without the help of others. What then is the significance of liberty to the impoverished in mind and spirit, in social life or in material possessions? How do the impoverished reach a level of equality with those who do not suffer their disadvantage?

Consider first poverty of material possessions. That is a form of poverty which, if it were the only form of poverty being suffered, would be less corrosive of the human personality than the poverty of social isolation or poverty in mind and spirit. But poverty of material possessions frequently induces the poverty of social isolation and the poverty of mind and spirit. Material poverty can be remedied by material things but other forms of poverty can be ameliorated only by the devotion by one person of himself or herself to another. Those forms of poverty cry out for personal charity, whereas material poverty may be remediable by the State or by International Organizations. Their functions must include at least the elimination of that extreme material poverty which destroys or threatens human life.

Whenever and wherever a man or woman does not have sufficient goods and services to sustain his or her life in dignity, he or she is denied a basic human right. Pope John Paul II pointed out in his Encyclical *Centesimus Annus:*

> The original source of all that is good is the very act of God, who created both the earth and man, and who gave the earth to man so that he might have dominion over it by his work and enjoy its fruits (Genesis 1:28). God gave the earth to the whole human race for the sustenance of all its members, without excluding or favouring anyone. This is the foundation of the universal destination of the earth's goods. The earth, by reason of its fruitfulness and its capacity to satisfy human needs, is God's first gift for the sustenance of human life. [5]

The notion of the universal destination of the earth's goods presents a radical challenge to our economic institutions and to the national and international order.

All humankind have an equal right to live unless it is forfeited in order to protect another person. That right imposes an active duty not only on the State in which life-threatening poverty is suffered but on other States and on other individuals. If all have an equal right to live, States and individuals are under the basic duty of doing what they can to ensure the supply of goods and services needed to sustain human life whenever and wherever it is threatened, whether by natural disaster, mismanagement or sheer poverty. The human right to sustenance is not merely a right to the minimum needed to keep a human body alive from day to day. Men and women are more than animals and each is entitled to sufficient food, shelter, clothing and basic care to allow each to live in dignity. What that entails varies according to the environment and the society but it is not sufficient in any place or in any society if those who are not able to support themselves and their families are driven to depend on the discretion or charity of another. For that reason, equality demands policies of development which would permit individuals and peoples opportunities to sustain themselves. The scandal of unemployment in Australia has long troubled economists and politicians. It is a problem which responds to improvements in the economy and we are conscious of the daily proclamation of measures that are taken or are under consideration to improve the economy. But if the principal object of these measures is the enhancement of the return on invested capital rather than the stimulation of employment, improvement of the economy has been misunderstood. Modern technology and proper management should lead to changes in industrial practice and to the development of new industries, not to the shedding of labour that finds no alternative employment. That is an ideal that is easier to state than to implement, but at least it should be the purpose of economic planning.

The duty to ensure the supply of vital goods and services to all who need them carries implications for domestic policies governing social security and health. Where gainful employment is not available or where age or infirmity prevents the earning of a livelihood, it is the function of the State to support in cash and kind a life of dignity for those who are unable otherwise to support themselves. Social security is not a mere budgetary item to be adjusted according to political exigencies; it is not reducible merely to secure an economically satisfactory bottom line; it is a mandatory safety net to prevent fellow citizens from suffering a degrading loss of dignity – a loss of dignity that would be a reproach to society and ultimately a threat to its stability.

The equal right to life of all humankind imposes on the State the duty to proffer international aid to sustain human life in other countries that cannot themselves sustain the lives of their citizens and, domestically, the duty to provide essential social security and basic health services for those would otherwise be unable to support themselves and have access to those services. In a society of increasing complexity and technological sophistication, when education to secondary level is the minimum required to open opportunities for employment, I should think the State is under a further duty to provide that education for those who cannot otherwise acquire it. If the State does provide more extensive educational or other benefits to its citizens, they should be provided without discrimination on the basis of race or colour, class or creed, or (except where special services are needed) physical or mental perfection or defect.

State activity is not directed to bringing all to the same level of financial viability but to ensure that each person has the opportunity to live in dignity. Equality demands State action to that end – that is, action to ensure for each person an opportunity to engage in, and benefit from, the society in which that person lives. Of course, the State may create and confer more extensive benefits on those who live in its territory, but the factor which governs the distribution of those further benefits is justice rather than equality. It is no part of the State's function to create equality in the possession of material things.

Equality in material possessions is not only an unrealistic goal; its achievement would necessarily destroy the liberty of individual initiative. That would deny the fruits, and ultimately the utility, of human initiative; it would destroy the wellspring of developments that are essential to secure the welfare of humankind; it would diminish human dignity and elevate the acquisition of material possessions to primacy in human aspirations. This was clearly seen by Pope John Paul II in his Encyclical '*Sollicitudo Rei Socialis*':

> It should be noted that in today's world, among other rights, the right of economic initiative is often suppressed. Yet it is a right which is important not only for the individual but also for the common good. Experience shows us that the denial of this right, or its limitation in the name of an alleged 'equality' of everyone in society, diminishes, or in practice absolutely destroys the spirit of initiative, that is to say the creative subjectivity of the citizen. As a consequence, there arises, not so much a true equality as 'levelling down'. In the place of creative initiative there appears passivity, dependence and submission to the bureaucratic apparatus, which, as the only 'ordering' and 'decision-making' body – if not also the 'owner' – of the entire totality of goods and the means of production, puts everyone in a position of almost absolute dependence, which is similar to the traditional dependence of the worker-proletarian in capitalism.[6]

The liberty to employ initiative carries the right to garner its fruits. We therefore admit the legitimacy of the accumulation of wealth. When wealth is accumulated, there is a surplus beyond what is needed for the bare sustenance of life. The legal right of the owner is to apply the surplus to any lawful purpose including the accumulation of more wealth. That use of property is, in a capitalist society, an essential element in the employment of individual initiative and in the economic progress of the community. Nowadays, an individual's surplus is often invested in corporations or funds under the control of managers. By reason of the accumulation of wealth in corporations or funds, director or managers possess considerable economic power. As economic power can be used to oppress others – employees, competitors, creditors – or to operate against the common good, their liberty of economic action is limited in the public interest. That is a legitimate field of legal regulation. And legal mechanisms which effect a division of profits between capital and labour are now familiar features of western legal systems, although the movement to deregulation, the freeing of the labour market and the diminished role of unions in our industrial scene highlights the tension that exists between liberty and social justice.

Without legal controls, massive accumulations of wealth and their attendant economic power would be destructive of free competition and equality in bargaining. Without legal controls, economic life would become 'hard, cruel and relentless in a ghastly measure', to quote Pope Pius XI.[7] Unbridled capitalism is not only oppressive to labour. It is destructive of the authority and integrity of government, it imports a crass materialism that offers the false attraction of a better life by 'having' rather than by 'being'; it undermines the development of new enterprises and preserves uneconomic industries. It is no servant of the market, for it distorts the market's ability to reflect economic reality. Unbridled capitalism produces material poverty and saps the spirit of charity which might otherwise alleviate the plight of the materially poor.

On the other hand, capitalism which fosters individual initiative within a legal framework protective of the common good and social justice ensures, as best society can, human dignity supported by private ownership of property and individual liberty consistent with the common good. How far should law go in seeking to control economic power? Regulation and deregulation each carry the risk of poverty. The best balance of legal control is hard to strike and unlikely to be struck without controversy between the parties on either end of the political and industrial spectrum. Poverty will not be eliminated by law but its incidence and severity can be reduced by appropriate legal controls. We know that the poor will be with us always[8] but that is no warrant for denying to the law and policies of the State the function of protecting the entitlement of everyone, especially the poor, to a life of dignity.

When State action and the operation of the law fail to eliminate poverty, its alleviation depends on charity – that is, the use of one's own property not as the law commands but as morality requires. The giving is not compellable by law. In a notable judgment[9], Sir William Deane observed that 'the common law has neither recognized fault in the conduct of the feasting Dives nor embraced the embarrassing moral perception that he who has failed to feed the man dying from hunger has truly killed him.'

The law neither compels individuals to be charitable nor permits the application of corporate or fund assets to *purely* charitable objects.

When investors place their assets and their confidence in corporations under the control of directors or in funds under the control of managers, the primary duty of directors and managers is owed to the shareholders or investors whose assets are under their control. Generally speaking, these shareholders or investors do not control the deployment of the assets in which they have invested. The initiative of the directors or managers is exercised to secure the maximum benefit for the corporation or fund and thereby to secure the maximum benefit for their shareholders or investors. The primary duty of the directors or managers is not owed to the labour employed in the corporation's or fund's enterprise much less to the wider community or to nations or peoples elsewhere. The law ordinarily precludes expenditure of the assets of the enterprise on any object from which no financial benefit will be derived, either mediately or immediately, by the corporation or the managed fund. For over a century, the general doctrine governing the application of a corporation's assets by directors has been this[10] 'They can only spend money which is not theirs but the company's, if they are spending it for the purposes which are reasonably incidental to the carrying on of the business of the company.…The test must be what is reasonably incidental to, and within the reasonable scope of carrying on, the business of the company.'

The benefit of the company was understood, in the case of a solvent company, as the benefit of the general body of the shareholders.[11] It was said that 'charity has no business to sit at boards of directors *qua* charity'. However, it was admitted that there is 'a kind of charitable dealing which is for the interest of those who practise it, and to that extent and in that garb (I admit not a very philanthropic garb) charity may sit at the board, but for no other purpose'.[12]

Modern legal writers suggest, and corporate practice accords with the suggestion, that it is permissible to donate corporate assets if the donation is likely to redound to the benefit of the corporation, but donations without the prospect of financial return are not authorized[13]. The legal justification explains such expenditure as 'seed corn' sown in the surrounding ground with a long-term view to profit.[14] The limited authority of directors to donate the corporations assets means that the chief accumulations of wealth are not likely to be the primary source of charity for the alleviation of individual material poverty, although donations to charitable institutions which work for the alleviation of individual material poverty may be permissible as 'seed corn'. There are, however, sound reasons of policy for imposing a limitation on directors' powers to donate corporate assets. Investors, whose charitable inclinations are diverse, do not authorize directors to dispose of corporate assets to charitable objects of the directors' choice. The choice should remain with the individual investor when he or she obtains his or her share of the distributed profits. From the moral viewpoint, there is no virtue in a directors' resolution to dispose of corporate assets to a charitable object. Virtue consists in the giving of what is one's own, not in the giving of assets that belong to another. And so, the kind of beneficence which seeks and yields no return ordinarily finds no place in the structures of capitalism. Poverty must be alleviated, if at all, by the State or by the charity of individuals.

The legal right of the individual to accumulate and to dispose of wealth brings with it the moral responsibility of determining what disposition should be made. The moral decision may not be an easy one for the Christian to make. That issue was addressed by Pope Leo XIII in *Rerum Novarum:*

> To own goods privately … is a right natural to man, and to exercise this right, especially in life in society, is not only lawful, but clearly necessary… But if the question be asked: How ought man use his possessions? The Church replies without hesitation: 'As to this point, man ought not regard external goods as his own, but as common so that, in fact, a person should readily share them when he sees others in need … No one… is obliged to assist others out of what is required for his own necessary use or for that of his family, or even to give to others what he himself needs to maintain his station in life becomingly and decently ... But when the demands of necessity and propriety have been sufficiently met, it is a duty to give to the poor out of that which remains'.

That was the injunction which Frederic Ozanam and his colleague Le Taillandier obeyed and exceeded on that cold evening 166 years ago when they carried to a poor family the remaining supply of wood which they had for the last months of a Paris winter. They did this because, as Frederic said, 'we must do what our Lord Jesus Christ did when preaching the Gospel. Let us go to the poor.'[15] After the Society of St Vincent de Paul was well established, after the experience of the early years when the fire of charity carried the brothers of the Society into thousands of the poor homes of France, Frederic wrote 'Let us not be too solicitous for the morrow. "What shall we eat and wherewith shall we be clothed?" Be brave, seek first the justice of God, the good of the nation and all else will be added thereunto.'[16]

The Society which Ozanam founded has been true to his impetuous zeal. It has sometimes sought an improvement in laws and policies to protect the poor but its work has been primarily the gathering of men and women in Conferences bound by personal charity. The Society has sought to alleviate not only material poverty but social poverty and the poverty of mind and spirit. The lonely and the sick, prisoners and the homeless are all the subjects of the Society's care and concern. They and the materially poor are not so much the objects of the Society's charity as they are benefactors who admit the Society's members into the privacy of their lives and share with the members their vulnerable humanity. The members of the Society, in giving themselves, are privileged to acquire a rich fulfilment of their own lives.

For those of us outside or on the margins of the Society, our chief concern is to determine when 'the demands of necessity and propriety have been sufficiently met' in order to quantify our duty 'to give to the poor out of that which remains'. That is not a question that many will answer with the same generosity as Frederic Ozanam. He, being a practical man as well as an idealist, noted that Christianity –

> ensured private ownership by placing it under the protection of God's Commandment: 'Thou shalt not steal'. It did not encourage the surrender of wealth as a precept but as a counsel, declaring voluntary poverty to be a perfection: 'If you would be perfect, sell all you have and give the money to the poor'. In the Church, ownership is a common right, like marriage, but the sharing of wealth, like virginity, is practised by a minority.

Ozanam lived the charity which he proclaimed. He expended himself on his duties to his students – he was a distinguished academic in both Law and Literature – and in his service to the poor. He gave practical expression to the incisive truth in the writings of St Basil the Great:

> 'The bread which you do not use is the bread of the hungry; the garment hanging in the wardrobe is the garment of the one who is naked; the shoes you do not wear are the shoes of the one who is barefoot; the money you keep locked away is the money of the poor; the acts of charity you do not perform are so many injustices that you commit.'

That is not a cry for legal reform or for public policy improvements. It is a challenge to personal charity, and one which will leave many of us wrestling with its solution.

---

1. Louis Baunard, *Ozanam in His Correspondence,* (Dublin: Catholic Truth Society of Ireland, 1925) 279.
2. See *Gaudium et Spes* Ch II Art 62; *Lumen Gentium* Ch IV Art 37.
3. Romans 8:15; Galatians 4:6.
4. Matthew 6:29-30; Luke 12:7,25,28.
5. Paragraph 31.
6. Paragraph 15.
7. See *Quadragesimo Anno* Ch III Sec 1, 51.

8. Mark 14:7
9. See *Jaensch v Coffey* (1984) 155 CLR 549
10. See *Hutton v West Cork Railway Co* (1883) 23 Ch D 654, 671 (Bowen LJ)
11. See *Greenhalgh v Arderne Cinemas* Ltd [1951] Ch 286; *Ngurli Ltd v McCann* (1953) 90 CLR 425; *Gambotto v WCP Ltd* (1995) 182 CLR 432, 443-444.
12. See *Hutton (*n 10) 673 (Bowen LJ).
13. See Laurence Gower et al, *Principles of Modern Company Law* (Sweet & Maxwell, 5th ed, 1992) 555 fn 32.
14. Lord Wedderburn of Charlton, 'The Social Responsibility of Companies' (1989) 15 (1) *Melbourne University Law Review* 4, 15. I am indebted to Professor Paul Redmond, Dean of Law at the University of New South Wales for this and other references.
15. Louis Baunard, (n 1), 65-66.
16. Ibid., 262.

13.4 'The Sky is Red': Address to the Thomas More Society

Editor's note

Brennan was invited to address the Society of St Thomas More in Sydney at the annual Patronal Feast Day Dinner on 6 July 2000.[1] Taking as his starting point the text from Matthew's Gospel 'When it is evening, you say, "It will be fair weather; for the sky is red"', Brennan suggested that 'the task of modern conscience is to discern what is good and valid for our times and what is not. For More, conscience was followed by maintaining silence until silence could no longer preserve his life. For us, conscience may require a more active stance in order to bear witness to the values of the Gospel.' Brennan joined issue with Cardinal Pell who had said, 'Catholics should stop talking about the primacy of conscience.' After the address, Pell and Brennan entered into correspondence about the primacy of conscience.

The title of this paper is taken from that part of St Matthew's Gospel[2] where Christ, answering the Pharisees and Sadducees, said to them: *'When it is evening, you say, "It will be fair weather; for the sky is red."* And in the morning, "It will be stormy today, for the sky is red and threatening". You know how to interpret the appearance of the sky, but you cannot interpret the signs of the times.'

Foretelling the weather from the appearance of the sky is a chancy business, but it has a purpose. Shepherds tending their flocks and farmers tending their fields need to know what weather is imminent. Human activity calls for a degree of prophecy as to the future. Those who can foresee the course of human events are wise; those who chart their course according to that foresight are prudent; those who order affairs with that foresight are effective and efficient – provided, of course, that what has been foreseen actually occurs. But in human affairs, the wisest and most prudent among us may prove to be wrong. And even those who prove to be right in human terms gain only a comparative and temporal advantage.

A certain foresight of an eternal future can occur only in the context of a transcendent faith. Men and women seek a transcendent reality, something beyond human experience to whom or to which they can relate, for that vision positions humankind, gives us our true dignity and enables us to glimpse an ultimate destiny. For the Christian, the transcendent reality is the eternal and all-loving triune God, revealed through the mystery of the Incarnation. For those who admit the existence of that God and the salvation of humankind earned by the crucifixion and death of Christ, there are new points of reference for foretelling the future and deciding how to live in order to achieve it. But in our busy world of human affairs in which wealth, power and position seem so important, the eternal reference points are often disregarded. We do not interpret the signs of the times because we do not see or hear more than our senses tell us, nor do we have confidence in a future which cannot be foretold by human foresight alone. Instead, we look to see if the sky is red and chart our course by the uncertain indicia of human affairs.

On my desk a small clear plastic photo frame sits, big enough for two postcards. Each postcard is a reproduction of a famous portrait. The sides are slightly angled, so that the copy portraits on either side gaze at each other continually. Just as the originals do on either side of a fireplace in a room in the Frick Collection in New York. The originals were both painted by Hans Holbein the Younger. One is the portrait of Sir Thomas More; the other the portrait of Thomas Cromwell – contemporaries, one of whom could interpret accurately the signs of the times, the other a masterful reader of the sky in Tudor England. More discerned what was good and valid; Cromwell perceived what was expedient and humanly sensible.

Both More and Cromwell survived and profited from the fall of Cardinal Wolsey; both achieved high office under their beloved King Henry VIII; both made a great contribution to the administration of Tudor England; and both were executed by the King's command. More lost the King's favour, having given the King his opinion on the annulment of his marriage to Catherine of Aragon. Cromwell, the architect of many of Henry's policies, organized the statutory annulment of his marriage to Catherine of Aragon, supported his marrying Anne Boleyn, then was instrumental in securing her trial and execution, continued in the King's favour when the King married Jane Seymour but slipped from favour when he, Cromwell, chose the unattractive Anne of Cleves as her successor. Cromwell secured his power in part by his administrative and political ability and in part by his facilitation of the King's serial nuptials. But in the end, he suffered the same fate as More. He was executed on Tower Green on 28 July 1540, ten days before the King married Catherine Howard, and a mere five years after More's execution.

These were turbulent and perilous times and it could not have been easy to discern what was good and valid as against what was expedient and sensible. We know from his public utterances what More discerned to be good and valid and why he rejected what was merely expedient and sensible. His fall from civil power came when Cromwell sought to strip the Convocation of Bishops of their power to enact ecclesiastical canons without royal approval. On 16 May 1532, on the authority of a rump of Convocation, three bishops and four abbots subscribed the Articles of Submission. When the Bishops agreed to subject the governance of the Church to Royal power, the relationship of Church and State was disordered. That afternoon More surrendered the great seal. The King was gracious to him then. More acknowledged that, 'by the incomparable benefit of his most gentle prince', he had obtained his life's desire 'that he might have some years of his life free, in which gradually withdrawing himself from the business of this life, he might continually remember the immortality of the life to come.'

The ultimate crisis started with the passing by Parliament in 1534 of the *Act of Succession*. The Act not only pronounced the marriage of Henry and Catherine to be 'void and annulled' but denied the authority of the Pope to sanction that marriage. Succession was to be through the children of Queen Anne. The Act required the taking of an oath in conformity with its provisions and More was summoned to appear before Lord Chancellor Audley, Cromwell and others in Lambeth Palace accordingly. The summons was served on him on a Sunday.

He was not unprepared. He spent the Sunday night in prayer and attended Mass in the village church on the Monday morning. As he was being rowed down the Thames to Lambeth Palace, he said to William Roper: 'Son Roper, I thank the Lord the field is won.' He was not so unworldly or foolish as to think that the King or his interlocutors would recant their views; he must have been speaking of his own internal conquest which he would vindicate in what was to follow.

He was prepared to swear the succession but nothing more. Although he was assured that all the Lords and Commons had taken the oath, he refused, saying: 'My purpose is not to put any fault either in the Act or any man that made it, or in the oath or any man that swears it, nor to condemn the conscience of any other man. But as for myself, in good faith my conscience so moves me in the matter, that though I will not deny to swear to the succession, yet unto the oath that here is offered to me I cannot swear without the jeoparding of my soul to perpetual damnation.'

That was enough to have him taken to the Tower. Later, Cromwell came to the Tower and promised More the King's mercy in exchange for his compliance with the *Act of Supremacy*, but More maintained his silence.

That Act recognised the King as 'the only Supreme Head in earth of the Church of England' and the form of oath under the provisions of the Act denied to the Pope any authority other than that of Bishop of Rome.[3] Cromwell left, and the die was cast. Rich's perjury was used to secure More's condemnation though he, by his silence, had committed no offence.

After More was convicted, he addressed his judges – Lord Chancellor Audley, Cromwell, and others. He said:

> Now that I see you are determined to condemn me (God knows how) I will in discharge of my conscience speak my mind plainly and freely touching my Indictment and your Statute withall. Forasmuch as, my Lord, this Indictment is grounded upon an Act of Parliament directly repugnant to the laws of God and his holy Church, the supreme government of which, or of any part whereof, may no temporal prince presume by any law to take upon him, as rightfully belonging to the See of Rome, a spiritual pre-eminence by the mouth of our Saviour himself, personally present upon the earth, only to St Peter and his successors, Bishops of the same See, by special prerogative granted; it is therefore in law amongst Christian men insufficient to charge any Christian man. This realm, being but one member and small part of the Church, might not make a particular law disagreeable with the general law of Christ's universal Catholic Church. No more than the city of London, being but one poor member in respect of the whole realm, might make a law against an Act of Parliament to bind the whole realm. No more might this realm of England refuse obedience to the See of Rome than might a child refuse obedience to his own natural father. [4]

He was sentenced to be hung, drawn and quartered but the King graciously permitted his death to be by beheading, More expressing thanks that he had 'convenient time and space to have remembrance of my end.' Four hundred and sixty five years ago, almost to the hour, More knelt before the block and prayed 'Have mercy upon me, O God, according to thy loving kindness.'

After nearly half a millennium, does More's life have any relevance to us today? Assuredly it does, for the signs of our times have to be interpreted and More's example teaches us how to interpret them. Our times are not the times of More. Heresy is not now a crime; burning at the stake is no longer a penalty; criminal punishment is not dispensed by executive fiat. Today we debate the topics of good and evil and, in our pluralistic and tolerant society, we embrace tolerance and assert the right to dissent from religious or political orthodoxy. More's denial of the Realm's right to 'make a particular law disagreeable with the general law of Christ's universal Catholic Church' would not now be accepted. But the uncompromising integrity of Thomas More provides both an instruction and an example for our age.

The genius of More was his gift of discernment. While Popes and Abbots pursued temporal wealth and power, More respected their spiritual and pastoral authority. When Bishops tailored their words and actions to advance their own interests, he examined more deeply the New Testament and the traditions of the Church. Good servant of his master, the King, he advocated his cause as far as his conscience would permit. He kept a public silence which, in law, ought to have sufficed to save his life, while remaining faithful to his conscience. He rendered to Caesar what was Caesar's without denying anything to God.

The basic lesson that More teaches is that discernment is not achieved without prayer, study and reflection – assisted, in More's case, by the penance of the hair shirt. More lost his office, his assets and his life for the sake of his conscience – a conscience formed and informed by faith. Prayer entrenched his faith, study informed his mind, and reflection led him to the conclusion that Henry, Cromwell and the Bishops were in error in asserting the King's authority over the governance of the Church in diminution of the authority of the Pope. It must have been difficult for More to reach this conclusion. In a letter to Cromwell, More wrote that 'I was myself sometimes not of the mind that the primacy of that See should be begun by the institution of God, until I read in that matter those things that the King's Highness had written in his most famous book against the heresies of Martin Luther'.[5]

He told Cromwell that once he had considered the Papacy to be a historical evolution but had changed his mind through seven years of study – a period that he later amended to ten years.

In the years before 1534, the Papacy had not inspired confidence in its pastoral role. In his Lecture on 'More's Doubts regarding the Papacy', delivered to this Society in 1977, Father Durning SM observed that the 16th Century Papacy 'lost much of its prestige; the character of its personnel was anything but striking.' Pope Leo X had added to the income of the Vatican treasury by the sale of indulgences and offices and had depleted its resources by expenditure on lavish balls and other entertainments.[6] The short reign of Hadrian VI[7] had restored some stringency to Vatican administration but, after Clement VII[8] became Pope in 1523, he engaged in opportunistic diplomacy between Emperor Charles V and the French King François I in order to protect the Papal States and their interests. He had vacillated over Henry's claim to annul his marriage to Catherine, aunt to Charles V, at a time when Henry was still adhering to Catholic practice. In a sense, the Popes themselves had forfeited the allegiance of the thinking faithful.

On the other hand, More had ample inducement to comply with the Royal will. His and his family's welfare depended on it, he had been favoured with land grants and with office; he had been a faithful servant of the King; he knew the machinations of princes and the sources of power; he respected and was respected by Henry. More was more than familiar with, and delighted by, the advantages of Royal favour. In the summer of 1532, after quitting as Lord Chancellor, he composed an epitaph in which he ran through his public offices:

> [he had been]…called into the court, and chosen one of the counsel, and made knight: then made first Under-Treasurer of England, after that Chancellor of the Duchy of Lancaster, and last of all (with great favour of his Prince) Lord Chancellor of England. But in the mean season, he was chosen Speaker of the Parliament, and besides was at different times in different places the King's ambassador, and last of all at Cameray, when the leagues between the chief princes of Christendom were renewed again and peace, so long looked for, was restored to Christendom.

As Lord Chancellor, More had placed before the House of Commons learned opinions on the question of the validity of Henry's marriage to Catherine of Aragon, widow of Henry's late brother. He knew of Henry's reliance on Leviticus 20:21: 'If a man takes his brother's wife, it is impurity; he has uncovered his brother's nakedness, they shall be childless' and Henry's argument that the Pope had no power to dispense from this biblical injunction. In placing before the Commons academic opinions that the marriage to Catherine was invalid, More assured the House that 'the King hath not attempted this matter of will or pleasure, as some strangers report, but only for the discharge of his conscience and surety of the succession of his realm'. More himself held the marriage to Catherine to be valid. He had told the King so privately. But it appeared that, John Fisher apart, the weight of English ecclesiastical opinion on the question of the King's marriage to Catherine of Aragon was with the King.

As the world knows, More died rather than deny his conscience. It was not a conscience that followed the *ipse dixit* of the Bishops of his Church. It was not a conscience that was born out of institutional loyalty. It was a conscience that grew over the years of prayer, study and reflection and the daily penance of the hair shirt. It was a conscience that sought to understand the Divine will and, having understood it, to be obedient to the truth he saw. The claims of the State he had served, of his friends or even of his family, could not prevail against More's obedience to his conscience.

The signs of the times are not always easy to interpret, but they can be interpreted only by the voice of conscience. And the voice of conscience is more imperious, more uncompromising, than any external command. St Thomas Aquinas says 'The binding force of conscience, even mistaken conscience, is the same thing as the binding force of the law of God. For one's conscience does not say that X is to be done or Y avoided unless one believes that Y is contrary to, or X accords with, the law of God.'[9]

Conscience is the most secret core and sanctuary of man or woman. There he or she is alone with God. To follow one's conscience, as More did, is to do what we believe God wants us to do – not what we would want to do if we left God aside. In the formation of conscience, however, each man and woman is affected by his or her life experiences and it is not to be expected that every honestly formed conscience would assent to precisely the same truths or be expressed by precisely the same conduct. The Protestant martyrs of Tudor England may be clothed in the same white robe as Thomas More. Conscience is unique to each person and what is done in obedience to conscience by one may differ from what is done in obedience to conscience by another.

The divine gift of individual freedom denies the spiritual efficacy of regimentation. Truth must be accepted – internalised, if you like – before it can bind a person to obedience. Hence, to discharge Our Lord's commission to Peter to feed my lambs and sheep and His direction to the Apostles to teach all nations, the Church must proclaim the truth intelligently and inspirationally to all. This is primarily the function of the Pope, the Bishops and the clergy, but it is a function incumbent on the laity as well. What will not do is an authoritarian demand for conformity – a demand that carries no conviction to the mind of the faithful and is alienating to those outside the Church. More's life and death show the distinction between an exercise of the Church's pastoral duty to teach and a purported exercise of ecclesiastical authority to procure submission. He reached his own conclusions about Papal authority; he did not accept the views of the English Bishops or the King's demand that he accept those views. Teaching of the truth, of 'those revealed doctrines which are in their nature beyond and independent of [human judgment]' (to quote Newman[10]) must appeal to every mind and heart and, if accepted, will inform conscience and govern conduct. But a conscience that is informed by the teaching depends on the acceptance of the teaching by a free intellect and will, not on a demand for conformity made in purported exercise of ecclesiastical authority.

As Vatican II declared – 'In all his activity a man is bound to follow his conscience faithfully, in order that he may come to God, for whom he was created. It follows that he is not to be forced to act in a manner contrary to his conscience. Nor, on the other hand is he to be restrained from acting in accordance with his conscience, especially in matters religious.'

How sad it is to hear Archbishop Pell declare here in Sydney that –

> Catholics should stop talking about the primacy of conscience. This has never been a Catholic doctrine (although this point generally cuts little ice). Moreover, such language is not conducive to identifying what contributes to human development. It is a short cut, which often leads the uninitiated to feel even more complacent while 'doing their own thing'.[11]

Had Thomas More and John Fisher followed not their consciences but the majority of the English Bishops at the time, we would not have had their example to inspire the human spirit and the history of the Church and of England would have been the poorer.

Thomas More's concerns were the spreading of Protestantism, the schism of the English Church and Papal authority in an age when Church and State performed complementary functions. Our concerns are different and the task of modern conscience is to discern what is good and valid for our times and what is not. For More, conscience was followed by maintaining silence until silence could no longer preserve his life. For us, conscience may require a more active stance in order to bear witness to the values of the Gospel. Take the ordinary issues of politics and the economy and pause to consider how policy and practice accord with the Gospel values – in particular, the equal dignity and worth of every person.

Materialism, economic rationalism and political expediency focus our daily attention on the financial benefits which one political policy or another will lavish on a section of our population. Polling and demography enable political parties so to frame their policies as to target the sections to be benefited and enhance the prospect of electoral success. We have become so accustomed to this phenomenon that we have forgotten that one of the chief purposes for which political power is conferred is to protect and respect the unique and equal dignity of each person. Each of us has a divine spark and destiny; each is entitled to live in the dignity which a fair participation in the community's wealth allows while each is under a duty to contribute to that wealth so far as it is within his or her power. We are familiar with terms such as GNP and GDP and the 'bottom line' but surely the bottom line of socio-economic policies is what I would call the social dividend – the effect of the policy in enhancing the dignity, the engagement and the social cohesion of all the people. If we insisted on conducting the political and economic debate in those terms, our society would be transformed and, over time, the obscenity of extravagant wealth coexisting with abject poverty would be diminished. Ideals are never fully attainable. Implementation of ideals requires leadership of a high order in a democracy. But cynicism, the abandonment of ideals, destroys the very fibre of a society by exposing the common good to depredation at the hands of powerful individuals.

Take another example closer to the practice of the law. Perhaps the greatest problem of criminal justice is the condition of our jails. While the public clamours for harsher sentences and the political parties find advantage in a law and order campaign, the community tolerates the destructive culture of our prisons.

Others will know better than I the extent to which rape and other violence occur and the effect of the drug trade on young first timers. Prisoners, no less than the rest of humankind, are entitled to the respect of their dignity as children of God. The waywardness of His children may warrant a deprivation of their liberty but not the denigration of their humanity. We can, as we too often have, leave the question of prison reform to the appropriate authorities of the State or, even worse, to those corporations to whom the State has delegated its responsibility to care for prisoners. The lawyers' responsibility has closed too often with the clanging of the steel doors. Yet there is no professional group who, having been aware of a prisoner's antecedents and of the circumstances of his offence, has or ought to have a better understanding of the dangers of the prison environment. Shortage of funds is often the reason given for the retention of subhuman conditions but governments – even those of goodwill – cannot be expected fully to remedy the situation unless the public is alerted to the need. The absence of the alerting is arguably an indication of a failure of discernment on the part of our generation of lawyers.

Or take another question that might trouble a modern Christian as the attack on the authority of the Pope troubled More. I speak of the status of marriage and the family. Marriage, as the law knows it, is the voluntary union for life of one man and one woman to the exclusion of all others.[12] The ceremony of marriage is a public declaration of the mutual rights and obligations of the spouses. The lifetime commitment of the spouses, their joint responsibility for the parenting of their children and the social stability – including the minimising of calls on the public purse – which the institution of marriage creates demand protection by laws affecting property, inheritance, maintenance, custody of infants and pensions. The principle which supports these protective laws is the social necessity to safeguard the interests of both spouses (particularly the more dependent spouse) and the children of the union. The same principle supports similar protective laws in the case of what were known as common law marriages, though in those cases there was no ceremony publicly declaring mutual rights and obligations. In modern times, however, the sexual revolution has diminished the significance of marriage as a central social institution. The institution has been undermined by the option to divorce after twelve months separation and a more relaxed response to sexual infidelity. Common law marriages, of course, are more easily terminated. Some children are born in wedlock, an increasing proportion outside wedlock. Fortunate indeed is the child who is reared to adulthood by both natural parents. For children, irrespective of the relationship of which they are born, there must always be protective laws.

In recent times, there has been increasing pressure to equate sexual relationships with marriage and, presumably, to extend to them the benefit of the laws protective of spouses and children. Increasingly those of marriageable age do not marry but form relationships that last at the discretion of the parties. Most of the non-marital relationships are heterosexual, some homosexual. But if a person chooses to enter a sexual relationship of either kind, why should the mere entry into that relationship be taken legally to be the equivalent of marriage? If the principle which justifies the protective laws attaching to the institution of marriage has no application to particular relationships, there is no justification for attaching the protective laws to the relationship. To do so would alter the fundamental purpose and character of the law of personal relationships and would create a new principle, namely, that entry into a sexual relationship is sufficient to create rights and obligations comparable with those appropriate to marriage. And if A can confer rights on B simply by entering into a sexual relationship with him or her, should not X be entitled to confer similar rights on Y simply by agreement between the two without the need for a sexual association? Should any two-party association, whether sexual or not or, if sexual, whether heterosexual or homosexual, and whether children are involved or not, attract the same legal consequences as entry into marriage?

These are but some of the issues that can evoke our consideration 465 years after the death of More. His life is an inspiration and a challenge. An inspiration, because in following his conscience, he found freedom in this life and salvation in the next. A challenge, because his life invites us to live a life in the world yet free from its attractions, a life in which we meet Christ in the depths of our conscience and follow Him as we perceive His will for us. Hans Kűng, writing of More and his freedom in the world, said this:

> Thomas More, in his secular dress, with his secular culture, in the midst of his family, his possessions, and his public life, was a saint. Not because he was without faults and sins; he had them, like every other human being, and he confessed them often before his death. But, with all his sinfulness, he was a saint, because he, as a sinful man, chosen out and embraced by God's grace in Christ made a radical choice of God, kept himself ready for God throughout his whole life in the world, and finally underwent the supreme test of that readiness in his death. Thus, he knew the love of God in Christ, from which nothing can separate a man, neither life nor death:

All things are yours ...,
whether the world, or life, or death,
or things present, or things to come:
for all are yours;
and you are Christ's:
and Christ is God's. [1 Corinthians.iii.22-23.] [13]

---

1. The address was published in (2001) 2 (1) *Utopia: The Journal of the St Thomas More Society*, 3-7.
2. Ch 16 verses 1-3.
3. Sir William Holdsworth, *History of English Law* vol 1 (Methuen, 1924) 591-592.
4. William Safire (ed), *Lend Me Your Ears: Great Speeches in History,* Rev Ed (W W Norton & Co, 1997) 330.
5. Elizabeth Frances Rogers (ed), *The English Correspondence of Sir Thomas More* (Princeton, 1947), Letter [199].
6. 1513-1522.
7. 1522-1523.
8. 1523-1534.
9. See *Commentarium super epistolam ad Romanos, c.14* cited by Dr Samuel Gregg, Morality, Law and Public Policy, St Thomas More Society, Sydney, 2001, 45.
10. John Henry Newman, History *of My Religious Opinions (*Longman, Green, Longman, Roberts, and Green 1865) 288.
11. George Pell, *Catholicism and the Architecture of Freedom*, Centre for Independent Studies, Occasional Paper 70, 1999, 11.
12. See *Hyde v Hyde and Woodmansee* (1866) LR 1 P&D 130,133; Family *Law Act 1975* (Cth), s 43(a); *Calverley v Green* (1984) 155 CLR 242, 259-260.
13. Hans Kung, *Freedom in the World: St Thomas More* (Sheed & Ward, 1965), 39-40.

13.5 Correspondence on Conscience with Cardinal George Pell

Editor's note

After his address to the Thomas More Society in July 2000, Brennan sent George Pell a copy of the address. Pell who was at this time Archbishop of Melbourne wrote to Brennan on 9 January 2001. Two months later, Pell was appointed Archbishop of Sydney. In early 2002, Pell visited Brennan's parish at St Canice's Elizabeth Bay. Prompted by the meeting, Brennan replied to Pell's letter on 29 January 2002. This is the exchange of letters. In 2003, Pope John Paul II named Pell a Cardinal.

Letter of Archbishop Pell to Sir Gerard Brennan

9 January 2001

Dear Sir Gerard,

Early in July last year you very kindly made available to me a copy of your lecture 'The Sky is Red', delivered to the Society of St Thomas More in Sydney on the occasion of the Patronal Feast Day Dinner. Through my secretary I promised you a response and with apologies for the delay I would now like to offer these few thoughts.

Let me begin by saying how much I enjoyed reading your paper, particularly your account of St Thomas More's life and his response to the crisis that would eventually claim his life, among many others. I too remember those two magnificent portraits in New York, either side of Saint Jerome(?). Rarely has an artist captured so well the cynicism and evil of one and the integrity, goodness and self-sacrificing devotion to truth of the other. At another level, your vigorous defence of appropriate legal protection for marriage and the family was inspiring. I also appreciate the gracious way in which you express your disagreement with me – more in the form of regret than direct criticism. In your covering letter you suggest that the difference in our respective approaches may be a matter of emphasis rather than substance. Certainly, your paper encourages me in the hope that the disparity between us may not be quite as insuperable as it sometimes appears, but I am afraid that ultimately our disagreement is much more fundamental than a matter of emphasis and is a matter of considerable moment.

I stand by the words of mine you quote in your paper – 'Catholics should stop talking about the primacy of conscience'. The alternatives are not the 'ipse dixit' of bishops and institutional loyalty on the one hand and conscience on the other. I am well aware that individual bishops are as fallible as judges, perhaps even as fallible as politicians. 'What God wants' has the primacy and I fully recognize and defend the role of individual conscience, as well as authority, in the struggle to identify this correctly. Over a long period, I have consistently argued for the *primacy of truth*, or of the Word of God, to which a conscience must conform if it is to be a reliable instrument; I have said that this is the *ultimate* rule of action and that the Church only speaks of conscience as a *proximate* norm, not some sort of supreme tribunal.

The most thorough and authoritative treatment of these matters to date is Pope John Paul's encyclical *Veritatis Splendor* (1993). No doctrine of 'the primacy of conscience' is to be found in that document. On the contrary, the Holy Father criticizes the view that 'in the sphere of morality a pluralism of opinions and of kinds of behaviour could be tolerated, these being left to the judgement of the individual subjective conscience' (§4). The Pope is surely right when he complains that certain currents of modem thought – both outside and even inside the Church – absolutize 'freedom of conscience' to the extent that:

> the individual conscience is accorded the status of a supreme tribunal of moral judgement which hands down categorical and infallible decisions about good and evil. To the affirmation that one has a duty to follow one's conscience is unduly added the affirmation that one's moral judgement is true merely by the fact that it has its origin in the conscience.
>
> But in this way the inescapable claims of truth disappear, yielding their place to a criterion of sincerity, authenticity and 'being at peace with oneself', so much so that some have come to adopt a radically subjectivistic conception of moral judgement. (§32)

John Paul goes on to criticize the 'tendency to grant to the individual conscience the prerogative of independently determining the criteria of good and evil' and the quasi-idolatry of freedom and sincerity in much contemporary talk of conscience. In accordance with the Catholic tradition, he proposes that it is only because it can mediate and apply the universal and permanent moral law that we take conscience so seriously; it is *truth* which has primacy. (Cf. §§32, 35, 52, 54-64).

Before quoting me, you quote from the Second Vatican Council's Declaration on Religious Liberty (*Dignitatis Humanae*) to support the argument for the primacy of conscience. It is doubtful whether the Declaration can be used in this way. The *peritus* who had most influence in its drafting, John Courtney Murray SJ, observed: 'The Declaration nowhere lends its authority to the theory for which the phrase ["freedom of conscience"] frequently stands, namely, that I have the right to do what my conscience tells me to do, simply because my conscience tells me to do it. This is a perilous theory. Its particular peril is subjectivism – the notion that, in the end, it is my conscience, and not the objective truth, which determines what is right or wrong, true or false.' If you do not wish to take Fr Murray's word for this, consider the passage in §14 of the Declaration on the relationship between conscience and the magisterium.

It is of course true (by definition) that one ought to follow one's best judgement of what is right and wrong; but what constitutes one's 'best judgement' and what kind of formation and application of conscience this requires, is little appreciated by those who use 'the primacy of conscience' slogan to excuse ill informed preferences and arbitrary choices. Hence Vatican II's important distinction between a true or correct and a false or erroneous or blind conscience (*Gaudium et Spes* §16; see also *Veritatis Splendor* §62), and its insistence on the duty to inform conscience well, in accord with Church teaching. In this the Council followed John Henry Newman, too often misunderstood as an advocate of conscience free of truth or authority, who in fact pronounced 'counterfeit' the arbitrary and subjectivist 'conscience' of modernity.

You rightly pay close attention to the care that Thomas More took in forming his conscience. I think you will agree that few of us, either then or now, work as assiduously at this task as More did. But even with a formation as rigorous as that which More imposed upon himself, *conscience can still be mistaken*. Following one's conscience alone does not ensure that one's acts are morally good. At best, a person whose mistake of conscience leads to an objectively wrong act may be guiltless -– depending on how seriously the person sought first to inform their conscience and then to apply it. But where conscience is in error due to our own fault – and in this, we must not underestimate the power of rationalization and self-deception, or, as you point out, of a lazy or self-serving failure to criticize the prejudices of an unreliable culture – then we may very well be guilty *even when following our conscience*. If there is one thing that the twentieth century has taught us, it is that a clear conscience is no guarantee that good will follow (cf. *Veritatis Splendor* §63). Sincerity cannot make an intrinsically evil act good.

It is in this context that the role of the Church and the magisterium must be understood, that is, to teach the truth. 'Regimentation' or 'an authoritarian demand for conformity' have only a limited ancillary function on rare occasions, usually to protect other believers. You are quite mistaken if you think this is the primary object of the Pope or Cardinal Ratzinger or myself. In a profound passage in *Veritatis Splendor,* John Paul II reminds us that when the Church 'pronounces on moral questions, [she] in no way undermines the freedom of conscience of Christians.'

> This is so not only because freedom of conscience is never freedom *from* the truth but always and only freedom in the truth, but also because the Magisterium does not bring to the Christian conscience truths which are extraneous to it; rather it brings to light the truths which it ought already to possess, developing them from the starting point of the primordial act of faith.
>
> The Church puts herself always and only at the service of conscience, helping it to avoid being tossed to and for by every wind of doctrine proposed by human deceit (cf. Ephesians 4:14),and helping it not to swerve from the truth about the good of man, but rather, especially in more difficult questions, to attain the truth with certainty and to abide in it (§64; cf. §§85,110,117).

It is this understanding of the relationship between the magisterium and conscience that I seek to follow in my own life both as a Christian on 'the great journey of conscience' and as a bishop charged with the pastoral care of others on that journey. It is also, I believe, More's understanding of the matter. More was not a martyr for the primacy of conscience. He died for the primacy of truth – and not just the truth as he saw it. As the Holy Father observed in his recent Apostolic Letter proclaiming Thomas the Patron of Politicians, More's 'passion for truth ... enlightened his conscience' and taught him the truths for which he died: that man cannot be sundered from God, and that politics cannot be sundered from morality. His conscience was not formed privately by his self and it was not ultimately answerable to his self. On the contrary. More's life and death demonstrated that 'conscience is *the witness of God himself*, whose voice and judgement penetrate the depths of man's soul' (cf. *Veritatis Splendor* §58). It is not the witness of human autonomy.

There is one aspect of More's life in particular which is impossible to square with enlisting him in a twentieth century position supporting the primacy of individual conscience, ie his active persecution and punishment of Protestants during his time as Chancellor. His hatred of *seditiosa dogmata* is well documented as is his putting into practice his determination to be as active against the *newe men* as lay in his power. The point here is not whether More's conscience was right or wrong on this (although this is of prime importance), but how to square this with the claim he was a lawyer and public officer who upheld the primacy of conscience. As More said to William Roper, 'were it my father stood on the one side and the devil on the other, his cause being good, the devil should have right'. Cf: Peter Ackroyd's *The Life of Thomas More* (1998) 289 sq.

A couple of other details merit comment, primarily because they might not be simply details. In all honesty, even after nearly six months, it still remains strange to me that a judge, after a lifetime properly enforcing the law, should espouse the primacy of conscience, whatever might be said of your objection to 'an authoritarian demand for conformity'. While the world of religion is different (certainly our church penalties are different now), your apparent endorsement of an antinomian position religiously still seems strange. Any church leader has to have sanctions available to deal with those who break or deny boundaries, even, or especially, for those who honestly disagree. Some years ago I had to point out the error, and limit the activity, of a good priest who felt entitled to teach regularly that Christ was not the eternal Son of God. As a church leader vowed to teach and defend the apostolic tradition, it was my duty not to respect the primacy of his conscience, but to oppose him publicly.

Equally disturbing is your assertion of 'the right to dissent from religious or political orthodoxy'. Certainly the state has no right to impose religious views or hinder them, except when they are dangerous to the common good. However, no Catholic has a right to dissent from the teachings of Christ or the solemn and central teachings of the magisterium; rather all Catholics have a responsibility and obligation to accept them in faith. This is part of what it means to become or remain Catholic.

I am sure you are aware that Hans Küng is one of our better known dissidents, who lost the capacity to teach officially as a Catholic theologian, as long ago as 1979. Few priests over the years have been so publicly opposed to the Papacy and so abusive towards the Holy Father. More would have put him in the stocks if he had spoken like this in England.

The primacy of conscience is a virus introduced into the church at the time of the *Humanae Vitae* debate, not simply that conscience might be exercised in times of dispute among authorities, but as a general principle to be exercised everywhere, untrammelled too much even by Scripture (unlike the Protestant endorsement of private judgement). This virus has severely weakened our resistance to the hostile currents in Western life and has destroyed and is destroying religious orders. I feel bound to oppose its baleful influence.

I enclose with this letter for your interest the text of an article on More written by the Pope's American biographer, George Weigel, and a copy of the Apostolic Letter referred to above. Thank you for continuing the discussion of this matter with me.

With prayerful good wishes to you and your family for the New Year,

Yours in the Lord,

+George Pell

Archbishop of Melbourne

Letter of Sir Gerard Brennan to Archbishop George Pell

29 January 2002

Your Grace,

Our recent meeting reminded me that I had not written to acknowledge and reply to your letter of 9 January 2001. And I have been prompted by the recent readings from the letter of St John. However, the year that has passed, your translation from Melbourne to Sydney and the many responsibilities of your See may have dimmed your recall of the letter which I greatly appreciated. So, I enclose a copy of your letter for ease of reference.

The letter is most helpful in defining the points of difference between us. I hope that the points of difference are not 'fundamental' but perhaps arise from attributing a different connotation to the word 'conscience'. We are in complete agreement about the source of moral truth. 'What God wants' defines what is good; 'what God does not want' defines what is bad. Being creatures of God, made in His image and responding to His love, men and women must seek to discover the truth of what He wants and what He does not want. Then, having discovered the truth, each is obliged to act or to refrain from acting in accordance with the truth. Personal belief in what is morally good or evil does not – axiomatically cannot – define objectively what is morally true. It is false to hold (as Veritatis Splendor points out) that 'one's moral judgment is true merely by the fact that it has its origin in the conscience' or to suggest that conscience alone can 'ensure that one's acts are morally good' (as you clearly state). The objective validity of a moral judgment or the objective character of an act or omission can be determined only by reference to an objective standard – and that standard is 'what God wants'. But that argument is pushing at a door that is already open. All of this is both obvious and cannot rationally be doubted.

If you were concerned that I was commending More for following his conscience because conscience is always the sure guide to moral truth, be assured that that was not my intention. Nor, with respect, do I think a fair reading of what I said would lead to that conclusion. To quote the key sentence: 'It was a conscience that sought to understand the Divine will and, having understood it, to be obedient to the truth he saw.' Your concern that I endorse 'an antinomian position religiously' is, I suggest, misplaced.

The problem is not whether conscience can determine authoritatively the objective moral quality of particular acts or omissions; rather, the problem is about the way in which the individual man or woman forms his or her conscience in order to make a moral judgment about an act or omission and the obligation of that man or woman to act or refrain from acting in accordance with that judgment.

If we focus first on the obligation to act or to refrain from acting in accordance with one's moral judgment, we can more clearly understand the problem of forming the conscience which makes the judgment.

The 'primacy of conscience' is a term which I would use to acknowledge the role of conscience which you describe as the 'proximate norm'. The passage you quote from Veritatis Splendor makes it clear that there is a duty – that is, a valid moral duty – 'to follow one's conscience'. In 'The Primacy of Conscience in the Roman Catholic Tradition' (Pacifica 13, October 2000 299, 307) Brian Lewis says that 'the Primacy of Conscience' is the 'traditional expression [that] has formed part of Roman Catholic teaching for many centuries. It cannot be lightly put aside or considered to be mistaken.' He explains that conscience has never been regarded as 'a law unto itself', but he does quote (at 304) 'startling' illustrations from St Thomas Aquinas, followed by St Alphonsus Liguori, showing the moral obligation to follow conscience, even though the conscience be erroneous. The term 'primacy of conscience', properly understood, is far from being 'a virus introduced into the Church' but is at the heart of Catholic moral teaching. It is clearly stated in Dignitatis Humanae (Chapter 1):

> On his part, man perceives and acknowledges the imperatives of the divine law through the mediation of conscience. In all his activity a man is bound to follow his conscience faithfully, in order that he may come to God, for whom he was created. It follows that he is not to be forced to act in a manner contrary to his conscience. Nor, on the other hand, is he to be restrained from acting in accordance with his conscience, especially in matters religious.
>
> For, of its very nature, the exercise of religion consists before all else in those internal, voluntary, and free acts whereby man sets the course of his life directly toward God. No merely human power can either command or prohibit acts of this kind.

In reference to the limitation on the power of the State, the term 'primacy of conscience' is used by the Holy Father himself in the motu proprio proclaiming More to be the patron of statesmen and politicians: 'The defence of the Church's freedom from unwarranted interference by the State is at the same time a defence in the name of the primacy of conscience, of the individual's freedom vis-à-vis political power.'

What I was concerned to show was that More's conscience, though contrary to the view then expressed by both the King's court and the ecclesiastical establishment of England, bound him to the course which he followed and that he would not have been either saint or hero had he submitted to those contrary views. The 'ipse dixit' of Bishops was no sufficient guarantee of moral truth. Again, I see no difference between what I have said and your observation that 'it is of course true (by definition) that one ought to follow one's best judgment of what is right and wrong'.

The next, and more difficult, question is the manner in which the conscience is to be formed and the sources of guidance available to ascertain what God wants. It is in this context that we are inspired by John's First Letter (3:21-24): 'My dear people, if we cannot be condemned by our own conscience, we need not be afraid in God's presence, and whatever we ask him, we shall receive because we keep his commandments and live the kind of life that he wants. His commandments are these: that we believe in the name of his Son Jesus Christ and that we love one another as he told us to.'

So conscience must be formed in faith and faith is a divine gift. It has not been given to all and sometimes the gift of faith is lost or diminished. What then of a person's obligation to act in accordance with conscience, if the conscience be ill-formed? If I understand correctly what St Thomas and St Alphonsus Liguori were saying, the obligation to act in accordance with conscience is unchanged. If that be right, was I in error in saying that 'Conscience is unique to each person and what is done in obedience to conscience by one may differ from what is done in obedience to conscience by another'? In any event, as consciences do differ, the external expression of consciences will – as a matter of fact – be variable. And in a pluralist society, social order demands a degree of tolerance of those variations. That is of the nature of a free society. It does not follow, however, that those whose consciences are formed in accordance with the Divine will must, or even can, approve of actions done contrary to the Divine will. Tolerance of the conduct of others is not to be equated with moral approval. I live in a society in which the law (however strictly interpreted) permits abortion in certain circumstances, though I find abortion a terrible moral evil.

Members of the Church have the guidance of the Church's teaching on moral issues. It is the scope of that authority and the manner of its exercise which concern me and other Catholics in the present day. Again there is no questioning here of the infallibility of Papal or Conciliar teaching when doctrines are defined solemnly as indicated in Ch III par 25 of Lumen Gentium. But when officers of the Church – even the Roman dicasteries – or individual Bishops assert the power to prescribe what individuals or groups must do or refrain from doing, submission must surely depend on whether the individual consciences accept the prescription. As you say, 'individual bishops are as fallible as judges' – a view which ecclesiastical history and the law reports strongly confirm. And a distinction must be drawn between the teaching of universal truths of faith and morals and the promulgation of edicts which are really no more than disciplinary demands.

In past years, we were instructed not to attend ceremonies in non-Catholic churches. As 'good Catholics', we complied. Thereby we offended unjustly and (understandably) lost our relationship with good friends who had invited us to their weddings. The disciplinary edicts of the ghetto did enormous damage to the Church in Australia. So did the policy of some Bishops to enlist Catholics in the Movement and to isolate clergy who opposed that policy.

The teaching of universal moral truths raises other questions. The aweful responsibility of the Magisterium which the Pope describes in Part II of Chapter 2 of Veritatis Splendor demands that the utmost caution be observed and the clearest exposition of the relevant principles be manifested in the exercise of this teaching authority.

First, a clear distinction must be drawn between the teaching of doctrine by the Magisterium and an individual Bishop's declaration of what he believes when that belief is not otherwise binding on the faithful. As you say, individual Bishops are fallible and it is not possible that the Magisterium might teach with different tongues. So a proclamation of the truth with the authority of the Magisterium should demonstrably be not the mere belief of individual Bishops but the expression of tradition or of collegial consensus.

Secondly, to bind the conscience of the faithful, the teaching should warrant its acceptance. 'The faith must always be presented in a rationally coherent way.' (Ecclesia in Oceania par 20) Minds which are accustomed to the evaluation of concepts cannot (perhaps, should not) be asked to suspend their critical capacities when the teaching is proclaimed for interior acceptance (see Gaudium et Spes, Ch II par 62, Ch V par 92). So the foundation of the teaching must be clearly exposed. This does not mean that truth consists only in what can be deductively proven. Clearly the truths of the faith will oftentimes depend on Divine revelation and its interpretation and the faithful must examine the teaching in love and humility. But there can be no conflict between truth and reason, nor should there be any fear of discussion of the truth. I confess that the Pope's prohibition of discussion on his teaching about women's ordination seems to suggest that discussion is the enemy of truth. Far from leading to acceptance of the teaching, the prohibition casts doubt upon what is taught. It is counter-productive. The teaching authority of the Church is one thing; the power to compel belief is another.

Thirdly, proclamation of the truth is an exercise in charity to assist men and women in their search for God and their quest for eternal life. It is not a demand for conformity to be visited with penalties for non-belief. Regrettably, many recent emanations from the Curia have been portrayed, either accurately or otherwise, as demands for conformity. Thus the 'Statement of Conclusions' of the meeting before the Oceania Synod was dismissive of the Australian characteristic of tolerance although 'it has many positive elements'. Note the shift in language adopted by the prelates to make their point: 'tolerance of and openness to all opinions... can lead to indifference ...' What are the Australian faithful to make of this? That tolerance should be suspect as subversive of truth? That a closed mind is needed to sustain faith? The Tablet said the Statement was to guide the Australian Bishops so that they may 'affirm, admonish and correct' their people. The Statement is again in the language of the ghetto, fearful of exposing and expounding the truth in the public forum.

You express some surprise about an ex-Judge's espousal of the primacy of conscience, but that view reflects (with some modifications) the familiar distinction between the definition of crime (the objective norm) and the criminal responsibility of an alleged offender (who must be acquitted unless the criminal act is done with mens rea). So, if I translate that approach, mutatis mutandis, to the case of your good priest who was preaching heresy, I distinguish between his action (which must be opposed) and his conscience which, if formed in good faith, must be respected. You write: 'it was my duty not to respect the primacy of his conscience, but to oppose him publicly.' That, I respectfully suggest, is a false dichotomy. Given that it was your episcopal duty to oppose publicly the proclamation of what was unarguably false doctrine, would it not be right 'to respect the primacy of his conscience' and then to endeavour to lead him away from error?

This long epistle started from my lament about the proposition that 'Catholics should stop talking about the primacy of conscience.' I find some confirmation of my lament in the Pope's New Year message (The Tablet 22/29 December 2001, p 1859): '... even when the truth has been reached – and this can happen only in a limited and imperfect way – it can never be imposed. Respect for a person's conscience, where the image of God himself is reflected (cf. Gen 1:26-27) means that we can only propose the truth to others, who are then responsible for accepting it.'

I respectfully and humbly accept every word in that statement. I suggest that, properly understood, there can be little difference between the views in your letter and what I said in 'The Sky is Red'. The difference, I fear, lies in our understanding of the meaning of teaching authority. For me, the Church has authority to teach what is true and, as she proposes truth for my acceptance, I love and trust her. But that is an authority over religious truth, not an authority to compel belief or action. I fear that the distinction is being missed in the ecclesiastical bureaucracy of today.

Yours sincerely,

Gerard Brennan

13.6 Address to Catholic Schools Principals

Editor's note

On 2 October 2002 at the Gold Coast, Brennan addressed the Association of Principals of Catholic Secondary School in Australia.

Some years ago, my wife and I had the great good fortune to spend a few days in Garmish-Partchenkirchen, a picturesque town deep in the Bavarian countryside adjacent to the towering Zugspitze. It was noted for the gentle tinkling of cowbells as the cows ambled gently in the afternoon light through the main street on their way to be milked. Not far away is Oberammergau, where the Passion Play is performed. And the fairytale castle of Neuschwanstein is reached along the Romantic Road. Our happy memories of those days are marred by the recollection of two experiences. One was a chance attendance at a Requiem Mass when we called in for a visit at a church in the town. The Church was fairly full and we took our places at the back. However, only a few of the congregation went to Communion and when we realized it was time for us to approach the altar rails, it was obvious that we were not welcome visitors. We were only half way up the aisle when the priest was back at the altar. It seems that we were intruding on those who had assembled to pay their respects to the deceased. Strangers were to be excluded from this Eucharist, though all were gathered around the Lord's table.

The second experience was a visit to another, much smaller, church in the countryside nearby. This was clearly a much-loved centre of Eucharistic devotion attended by the families in the district. On the walls of the porch and of the church proper, there were many commemorative plaques of the deceased sons of these families – young men who had died before the end of the Second World War. Practically every one of them was described as a member of the SS or some other element of the Nazi apparatus. The persecution of the Jews and Gypsies and the destruction or sterilization of the disabled were unknown to them or, if known, still left them committed to the political dominance of the Nazi Party.

Bavaria, it is said, is a profoundly Catholic state in the German federation. But these experiences suggested – it can be put no higher than a suggestion, for no mere tourist impression can be taken as a sociological fact, but at all events it then seemed to us – that a professed Catholicism did not inspire a spirit of inclusion, and the German Government's cruel treatment of the unpopular and the disadvantaged had been of little concern to a people who practised a personal piety. Now, you may rightly ask, what is the relevance of these two experiences for Catholic schools on the other side of the globe?

Only this, that they reminded me of what I want to suggest to you are two of the challenges which face our Australian Catholic schools today. The first, I venture to suggest, is the instillation of that sense of inclusiveness which is a mark of the true Christian. The second is the recognition of a responsibility to ensure that political, economic or national interests are not bought by sacrificing the human rights of others, especially the human rights of minorities or the disadvantaged. The two concepts of inclusiveness and human rights are related – indeed respect for human rights is a corollary of inclusiveness.

St John's Gospel tells us that Jews did not associate with Samaritans, but Christ broke out of that isolation at Jacob's well, giving the Samaritan woman and her people the living water that wells up to eternal life.[1] Inclusiveness is the state of mind of a Christian who wants to live out the new commandment to 'love one another; Just as I have loved you, you also must love one another. By this love you have for one another, everyone will know that you are my disciples.'[2]

The Christian does not discriminate among peoples of different races, or different social classes or different cultures. All of us are children of God, with a divine spark and an eternal destiny. Our common humanity imports a mutual concern for and interest in all people. Speaking of human rights, the Pope said recently:'Every person, created in the image and likeness of God and therefore radically oriented towards the Creator, is constantly in relationship with those possessed of the same dignity.'[3]

Inclusiveness and respect for the human rights of all people are not optional for the Christian. They are at the heart of Christian belief and practice. To worship the all-loving God, there must be respect and concern for all whom He loves – all who are possessed of the same dignity as those who worship. Exclusivity has no place when a school community is gathered around the Eucharistic table. Your theme for this Conference is 'A Journey to the Heart; A Journey to the Spirit' and I imagine that you will be discussing the ways in which the heart and the spirit can be reached. The destination of the journey may be clear, but you would know that there are obstacles on the way.

There are obstacles which militate against a spirit of inclusiveness in the school environment. Education is both labour intensive and expensive, and non-government education has to be paid for largely by parents or, in the case of systemic schools, by the funds of the relevant church institution. Sheer poverty, or pride, may exclude some students from the school population. In the case of well established schools, parents and past students seek a continuity of the school's ethos and traditions, and that translates into a desire to ensure that the school population should be the generation begot by the previous generation. Newcomers, those who come from other countries, other States, other social groups, may feel unwelcome in the settled, self-confident atmosphere of the school. So school populations may become exclusive – indeed, the badge of exclusivity is a positive marketing advantage for some schools.

Some families may be intolerant of particular differences and their attitudes will be reflected in the attitudes of the children. Intolerance of certain differences may create a cultural barrier which cannot be penetrated by those outside it, not even by the countervailing values of the school. Moreover, the competitive pressures on students today tend to make them and their parents focus on the prospect of a successful career. Success is measured by academic or sporting achievement in competition with others, and that measure of success is reinforced by school awards. Competition may blunt any disposition to give attention to the needs of others. So there are powerful influences pulling against a spirit of inclusiveness, a spirit of concern for the human rights of other people.

Our society is itself focussed on the individual, whose rights and interests may overshadow the rights and interests of others. The values of our consumerist society are antipathetic to the spirit of inclusiveness and that leads us to ignore the human rights of others. Indeed, the Pope has recently identified the creation of a sense of global solidarity as the great moral issue of our times. The self-centred, materialist society to which we belong erodes the human personality and, you may think, poses a risk to international peace.

We Australians tend to boast about our tolerance of others, and so we should if we really believe it. There was a time, in the not far distant past, when I and many others believed Australia to be a tolerant nation, but the asylum seekers debate has shaken that faith in ourselves and our sense of toleration. The proclamation of tolerance was easy, so long as those who are different were not confronting us with the difference. We have accepted, admittedly with considerable dissent, the horrible denial of the human rights of families, particularly women and children who have been kept in isolation from their husbands and fathers. The wretched isolation of the asylum seekers, in Woomera, in Nauru and in Manus Island, has left this country divided, many Australians accepting the necessity for inhuman treatment as the price to be paid for maintaining our immigration policies and our boundaries. Like the young men of Garmisch, we have allowed political catch cries to suppress our tolerance and subvert our respect for the human rights of others. We find that tolerance wears thin at times when it is most needed.

There is a need for tolerance in order to maintain a cohesive society. Australia has become a multi-ethnic, multi-cultural society. Our society is stratified according to wealth and social class and by divisions between city and country. Our rhetoric boasts that we celebrate our diversity and that we are a tolerant people but we can hardly hide the ugly tensions that sometimes emerge. How ready are we to accept into our community Aborigines and people from other countries, Muslims, the intellectually disadvantaged and the physically disabled, asylum seekers, the poor, the old and the lonely? Differences which lead to exclusions and to the neglect of others' interests can be, and sometimes are, the fracture lines in our society.

Social cohesion is important enough, but the Christian has a more basic reason for tolerating legitimate differences. To acknowledge the dignity of other people is to acknowledge that they have the gift of freedom,[4] without which virtue would be impossible.[5] Differences arise from the exercise of human freedom as well as from natural conditions. So tolerance of legitimate difference is the practical implication of our Christian belief in the dignity of all men and women.

Tolerance is not a negative virtue; it is to be distinguished sharply from attitudes of laissez faire. Laissez faire does not trouble to distinguish between good and evil, between truth and falsity. Tolerance knows the difference but does not seek to vilify others as evil or false. Tolerance has been misunderstood as a mere acceptance that 'anything goes'. Thus the *'Statement of Conclusions'* of the meeting between some Australian Bishops and the Roman Curia before the Oceania Synod expressed the view that: 'The tolerance characteristic of Australian society naturally affects the Church also. While it has many positive elements, tolerance of and openness to all opinions and perspectives on the truth can lead to indifference, to the acceptance of any opinion or activity as long as it does not impact adversely on other people.'[6]

This is not true tolerance – it conflates tolerance of people with tolerance of evil and error. If a difference is the product of sin, the sin is not to be tolerated although the sinner is not to be rejected. But differences which are not the product of sin require an acknowledgement of the dignity and freedom of another and the conscious rejection of prejudice by ourselves – however traditional and long-standing the prejudice may be.

It is one thing to give intellectual assent to tolerance, to respect for human rights, to inclusiveness. It is another to translate that assent into a conviction which governs conduct and which can transform the ethos of a community. The title of your Conference seems to me to address that problem.

You would know better than I how to instil in your students the values of a Christian citizen. I would not presume to offer advice about the pedagogy of modern education. But I may offer some observations about the way in which those values are esteemed in the wider milieu of our society.

Tolerance and respect for human rights can be regarded as mere conventional values, pragmatically esteemed because they allow us to get on with one another in a complex world. But if that be the basis of those values, they can be trumped by other pragmatic considerations. Thus, to take the example which I mentioned before, the treatment of asylum seekers, the denial of their human rights can be justified – if we have no standards but pragmatism – by the deterrent effect their treatment will have on others who might seek asylum from persecution in Australia without having an entry visa. For the Christian, the foundation for tolerance and respect for human rights is to be found in the dignity with which God has endowed His children and their equal preciousness in His eyes. Unless we believe this, we have no reference point for making and adhering to our moral judgments.

This is a very radical doctrine and its implications are not always comfortable. In particular, the social doctrine of the Church based upon the equal preciousness of all God's children has some very tough lessons for us that we tend to gloss over, comforted by a warm inner glow infused by a prudent contribution to the collection plate or the poor box. Compare that with the teaching of Leo XIII in *Rerum Novarum:*

> To own goods privately ... is a right natural to man, and to exercise this right, especially in life in society, is not only lawful, but clearly necessary... But if the question be asked: How ought man use his possessions? The Church replies without hesitation (in the words of Thomas Aquinas): 'As to this point, man ought not regard external goods as his own, but as common so that, in fact, a person should readily share them when he sees others in need ... No one.., is obliged to assist others out of what is required for his own necessary use or for that of his family, or even to give to others what he himself needs to maintain his station in life becomingly and decently ... But when the demands of necessity and propriety have been sufficiently met, it is a duty to give to the poor out of that which remains'.[7]

If the doctrine of human equality has fundamental implications for the utilisation of wealth, it has correspondingly fundamental implications for the way we regard people who are different from ourselves. 'Love your neighbour' is all very well in theory, but we rather tend to identify with the lyric in 'My Fair Lady' which ends 'wiv a little bit o' luck you won't be home'.

To instil in all of us the values of the Christian citizen, we need both instruction and example. Instruction in the reasons for practising the values, example to be inspired to embrace the truth. Perhaps the greatest obstacle to the general adoption of the values of the Christian citizen is our materialism. We seek an ever more elaborate lifestyle — better homes, better cars, and (if the term is meaningful) better schools for our children. That ambition cannot be risked in order to pursue some idealised notion of beneficence to our fellow humans. We do not quite measure up to what the Pope said in *Centesimus Annus*: 'It is not wrong to want to live better; what is wrong is a style of life which is presumed to be better when it is directed towards "having" rather than "being", and which wants to have more, not in order to be more but in order to spend life in enjoyment as an end in itself. It is therefore necessary to create lifestyles in which the quest for truth, beauty, goodness and communion with others for the sake of common growth are the factors which determine consumer choices, savings and investments.'[8]

Before this lesson is learnt, we need to hear it explained and developed. We need to know that there is a divine command underlying the change in thinking that is proposed for adoption. And we shall not accept this challenge to our lifestyle unless the person expounding the doctrine lives by the doctrine propounded.

Of course, we should hope that our Catholic schools will propound the doctrine and infuse our children with an enthusiasm for sharing with their fellows. Whether that hope is a reasonable expectation, I cannot say. So often we see the students and the past students of our Catholic schools adopting a lifestyle or engaging in conduct that is the antithesis of Christian teaching. Those must be the cases that sadden the hearts of the Principals of Catholic Schools. But it is not surprising, having regard to the materialist, instant gratification, consumerist milieu in which we are immersed. Sometimes I wonder whether we take these alien values to be part of the world which we must accept in equipping our children for the future, hoping that the Christian values of the school will at least place a patina of decency on selfish individualism.

You have challenged yourselves to find the journey to the heart and the journey to the spirit – a journey which can touch the heart and spirit of students and fire them with enthusiasm for the values which inspire the school. That is no small endeavour, but I hope that the extent of the enterprise will be matched by your boldness in its execution.

Why should we be hesitant in proclaiming the divine dimension to our lives? Without it, humanity is diminished. Why should we decline to use the language of obligation when it is only by the fulfilment of duty to God and our neighbour that we can achieve both peace and satisfaction? Why should we substitute comforting emotions for theological truths when the one is pap and the other is solid food? Some lessons are hard to learn, at every stage of life. They are lessons which can be taught, however, only by those who have learnt them well – by those whose lives demonstrate inclusiveness, respect for human rights, tolerance and a willingness to share the excess of their possessions. How easy it is for me so to declare, how difficult to live by the lessons which I have been taught. Like St Augustine before his conversion, my prayer is often 'Not yet, O Lord, not yet!'

The pathfinder on the journey to the heart and the spirit of students will ordinarily be the principal of the school. No doubt, you have many and diverse responsibilities. You have to recruit and mentor and retain your staff; you are constantly engaged with parents and their demands; you have to be a financial expert and ensure that the quality of the education provided is the best that financial constraints permit; you have to maintain relationships with Church officials or religious institutions; you have to satisfy your Boards; and, most importantly, you have to devote time and attention to your students. The Principal has to attend to the housekeeping problems of the school. Who else will bear the ultimate responsibility for the housekeeping if not the Principal? It is all very well to speak about ideals and challenges to realize ideals, but does the time and effort needed to give leadership in these fields leave the Principal with enough time – let alone enough energy – to do all the things that are uniquely his or her responsibility?

It is a tribute to your faith and your courage that you have set yourselves this awesome task. But it is of a piece with your courage in accepting appointment as a Principal. In the difficulties of contemporary Catholic education, the functions of a Principal can be undertaken only by those of enormous faith who are committed beyond reason to one of the great causes of our time: imparting to the generations of the future the gift of faith and the ability to live in and contribute constructively to a complex and challenging world.

As you dedicate yourselves to this cause, and pursue the means by which it is to be realised, you have the appreciation of the students and their parents and you place the community in your debt. But most of all, you bring yourselves closer to the Divine Heart who wished only to bring the little children closer to Himself (Matthew 19:14).

---

1. John 4:5-42.
2. John13:34-35.
3. Message for World Peace Day, 1 January 1999, *The Tablet*, (2 January 1999) 32.
4. *Gaudium et Spes* Ch II Art 62; *Lumen Gentium* Ch IV Art 37.
5. *Dignitatis Humanae* Ch I Arts 2,3.
6. Interdicasterial Meeting with a Representation of the Australian Bishops and the Roman Curia.
7. Leo XIII, *Rerum Novarum* #22.
8. *Centesimus Annus* Ch 2 par 35.

13.7 Centenary of the Missionaries of the Sacred Heart

Editor's note

Brennan and his sons had been educated by the Missionaries of the Sacred Heart (MSCs) at Downlands College Toowoomba and at Daramalan College Canberra. Brennan maintained a close relationship with some of these priests after leaving school. When counsel for the Northern Land Council in the Woodward Royal Commission on land rights, he met with many of the MSCs working on missions such as Port Keats, Daly River and Bathurst Island. Bishop John O'Loughlin then the Bishop of Darwin had been one of Brennan's teachers. When the MSCs were celebrating the centenary of the establishment of their province in Australia, they invited Brennan as a distinguished alumnus to deliver an address at their monastery at Kensington, Sydney on 10 December 2005.[1]

Your Excellency and Sir Nicholas Shehadie, Your Eminence Cardinal Clancy, Father Provincial, Brother Superior, Missionaries of the Sacred Heart, Representatives of other Congregations and other Distinguished Guests, Ladies and Gentlemen:

We gather here today to celebrate a centenary – to celebrate 100 years of worship and committed service by the members of the Australian Province of the Missionaries of the Sacred Heart. For centuries past, however, this site has been – as it remains – in the traditional ownership of the Eora People and we acknowledge that ownership today.

Today's celebration recalls the decree of Pope Pius X in 1905 pursuant to which the Australian Province was erected. It recognized the growth of the Society in Australia since the first MSCs arrived in Sydney 20 years earlier. A translation of the decree reads:

> The Society of the Missionaries of the Sacred Heart, with its headquarters in Rome, now has a wonderful ministry in the Sydney Archdiocese, where it has established three houses; it also has a fruitful ministry in Tasmania. The existence of a novitiate and seminary in Sydney gives promise of an even wider and more fruitful ministry.
>
> Therefore the Procurator General of the Society asked the Holy See to establish these houses of the Society into an Australian Province of the Institute. The Cardinal Archbishop of Sydney supported this recommendation, and so in an audience of 14 November with the secretary of [the Society for the Propagation of the Faith], Pope Pius X bestowed on the Superior General of the Missionaries of the Sacred Heart all the powers needed to erect the Australian Province

> of the society, giving it all the rights and privileges of a Province of the Religious Society. ....
>
> On December 8, 1905, Fr Meyer, the Superior General of the Society exercised the powers conferred upon him and declared that 'on this feast of the Immaculate Conception, we establish the Australian Province of our Society.'

December 8, the feast of the Immaculate Conception of Christ's Mother, is the birthday of the Society as well as the birthday of its Australian Province. The General Council appointed Fr Tréand, a priest much loved and respected by his colleagues, as the first Provincial though he was in indifferent health. In response to his appointment, Fr Tréand, who obviously had a fine sense of humour, wrote to the Superior General recalling the comment of the Cure of Ars who, when the Bishop appointed him a Canon and handed him his mozzetta, said: 'Don't do any more Monsignor, your first try has been unfortunate'.

Father Tréand continued:

> As a matter of fact I am only a poor batman of the Society bringing a kind of mortice to the materials of the others who do the building. I hope that the grace of the good Lord will see only in my new charge a motive for a greater devotion to the work of the Society and for personal sanctification. The day chosen for the setting up of the Province was a day filled with joy. It was the 8th December 1895 when the Cardinal surrounded by the Bishops meeting for their Plenary Synod blessed the foundation stone [that is – the foundation stone of the Kensington Monastery] and it was also 8th December 1897 that he blessed the house and it was on the eve of 8th December the first Novices commenced their first retreat. Our Province will be that of the Holy Virgin; she will see to it that we love the Sacred Heart. The Cardinal [has announced] … that ours is the first Province erected by the Religious Societies in Australia.

The Australian nation had been summoned into existence five years earlier on the first day of 1901. In many respects, parallels can be seen in the histories of the Commonwealth and the Province. Both owe their structure to their parent authority. In Australia, we inherited the Westminster system of Government and the British tradition of an independent Judiciary; the Province inherited the traditional hierarchy of Provincial, Council and consultors, Chapters, Superiors and the respective ministers of particular communities, following the template of the Society elsewhere. Although the Commonwealth of Australia was created with all the powers needed for an independent nation, and although the Province was erected to be largely self-governing, both were closely tied to the parent authority. At first our Governors-General were appointed by the British Government and our foreign affairs were, until the 1940's, in the hands of the British Foreign Service. Some of our legislative powers and the final appellate jurisdiction in some of our court cases were not free of Imperial control until 1986. Similarly, the government of the Australian Province remained in many respects under the control of the General Council in Rome.

Thus, while Fr Tréand was an excellent appointment, he was not assisted by the General Council's appointment of at least one member of his Provincial Council and, regrettably, that caused some troubles for the early days of the Province. In time, the situation changed until the stage was reached when Australians – at first Fr Cuskelly and then Fr McCabe – each became the Superior General of the Society. Now both the nation and the province are effectively self-governing, but while the Society in practice has independent authority in its internal government, it rightly values and adheres to the international charism of the Society and cherishes its relationship with both the General Council and other Provinces throughout the world.

Of course, there were bound to be some tensions in the early days. The Superior General and the General Council had some concerns about the development of the Province and the observance of the rules. Indeed, from 1914 to 1920 the Province was virtually under the authority of a Visitator General, Fr Linckens, in whom many of the powers of the Superior General had been vested. Some difficulties had arisen from personality differences but, as I understand it, the source of most of the tensions is to be found in the diverse demography, history and culture of Europe on the one hand and Australia on the other. And whenever an issue productive of tension arose – for example, about the undertaking of financial burdens – distance and the problems of communication compounded the risk of divergent views. I note, in passing, that when in 1931 the Bishop of Toowoomba persuaded Fr Fleming to establish my Alma Mater, Downlands College, the view of the then Superior General was expressed in the word 'impossible'. I thank God for the courage of the Australian Province. Perhaps Rome should have known better than to question the establishment of a major institution in the midst of a depression. After all, this land was bought and this Monastery was built in the 1880s when the Colony was in dire financial straits and Australian Banks were failing. The Province has always placed its trust in Divine Providence and the generosity of the Australian people and has never been averse to taking risks in the expansion of its mission.

Such tensions as there were between the General Council and the fledgling Australian Province were, in retrospect, creative tensions: they were resolved to form and strengthen the charism of the Australian MSCs. Europe, with its long tradition of Christian spirituality, whether Catholic or Protestant, and with its familiarity with authoritarian regimes, probably found it difficult to appreciate a distant, sparsely populated continent, whose indigenous inhabitants embraced a spirituality not then recognized and whose Anglo-Celtic population saw themselves as an independent, frontier people taking whatever initiatives were appropriate to meet the challenges of a developing nation. Europe could contribute both the tradition of deep Christian spirituality and the framework within which the spiritual life might be fostered. Australia could contribute respect for the vigorous independence of individuals, a sense of solidarity that we call 'mateship' and a willingness to 'give it a go'. Tensions there were between the two. The Australian Province was not always punctilious in the observance of the rules and protocols which were then needed in the formation of the novices and scholastics and in the preservation of the members of the Society in their work of spreading devotion to the Sacred Heart. What emerged, however, was a structured Society which lost none of the robust character of the Australian but which was a disciplined force to carry out the arduous duties which had been undertaken.

The work of the Society expanded. In addition to St Mary's Towers at Douglas Park, Croydon in Victoria was acquired to provide a Scholasticate. From the establishment of the Province and the regime of the scholarly Fr Vandel, professors well trained in philosophy and theology had been highly valued. So soon as opportunity presented, Australian students were sent to the Roman Universities to equip them in the intellectual disciplines for priestly training. Nor were the secular subjects neglected. When schools were opened at Downlands in Toowoomba, Chevalier in Bowral, Monivae in Hamilton, Daramalan in Canberra and St John's in Darwin, priests were available to staff many of the teaching posts. Parishes were staffed in every State and mainland Territory and in New Zealand. During both World Wars, Australian MSCs enlisted as chaplains to the armed forces. Assistance was given to the Apostolic Delegate and to Bishops. The media and their audiences and readers were enlightened by the talks and writings of the legendary Dr Rumble and Dr Paddy Ryan made a great contribution to public affairs in the turbulent post-war years. A National Seminary, St Paul's, for the training of mature aged priests was established on the initiative of Fr Fletcher under a regime devised by Fr Cuskelly. It survived for as long as the flow of vocations warranted. A chaplain has been provided to the University of New South Wales. The laity have been intimately and formally involved by the admission of MSC Associates. The *Annals* have been published continually since the earliest days and writings, both erudite and popular – many by Fr Stenhouse – have been published. Some of the most favoured hymns in church liturgies have been written and composed by Fr Anderson. These and other works show that the centenary of the Australian Province of the Missionaries of the Sacred Heart is an occasion of thanksgiving for the enormous service of the Society to the Catholic Church in Australasia and to generations of the Australian people and the people of New Zealand.

No less significantly, the Province has served the Church and the people in the countries to which missionaries went out. To Papua New Guinea, Kiribati, Fiji, Japan, Vietnam and India. So successful have the missionary efforts been that a separate Papua New Guinea Province of the MSCs was erected in 1989. Many of those missionaries are here today and we acknowledge their lives of love and service. Among them is one of my classmates, Fr Bernie McGrane, who has spent a lifetime in the missions in Papua New Guinea and Japan and who is yearning to return to his people in Eastern Papua. I am reminded of a letter I received many years ago from our old headmaster Fr Doyle who became the Bishop of Eastern Papua and had Bernie as his Diocesan liturgist. John Doyle expostulated: 'Fancy Bernie McGrane telling me how to say Mass!'

Having started on a reminiscence, I must ask you to bear with me while I recall some events from my school days. I do so not to indulge myself in nostalgia but to pay my tribute to the MSCs and to spell out something of the charism which has made them so significant an influence on the faith and the lives of generations of Australians. I take you back to 1941, in the dark days of the Second World War, when our class entered Downlands College for the first year of our secondary schooling. Long before Vatican II, we were introduced to the reasons why we believed what we had learnt by rote in the catechisms of primary school. We were invited to question and to think so that faith could find a root in personal conviction. The emphasis was on our spiritual lives and the formation of our consciences, not on obedience to an externally imposed rule. The changes of Vatican II, the opening up of the Church to the world around us, the rejection of a ghetto mentality – these confirmed, they did not deny the ethos which we imbibed as schoolboys.

Downlands was then a boarding school for Catholic boys and it would have been easy to teach dogma to be believed and to re-enforce it by the regular timetable of daily Mass and prayers. But pietism was not the way of the MSCs. Not for the MSCs was the bowed head, the joined hands and the superficially pious demeanour. Faith was not only a rational belief; its practice was a robust, perhaps masculine, virtue. One of the stories told was of a farmer from south western Queensland who delivered his son into the hands of the Rector, saying: 'Teach him his Catechism and how to fight,

Father, so that he can defend his faith!' On Saturday evenings, Fr Doyle, the Rector returned again and again to his invaluable injunction: 'Be different!' We were to think for ourselves, not be swayed by the say so of others. Then we saw that the hands which raised the host and chalice were the hands that wielded the cricket bat or held the football; we knew that the lips which summoned the Divine Presence were the lips of men whom we assessed to be both intelligent and inspirational in their beliefs. And for living proof of the spiritual life and quiet edification, we saw the sheer, shining, humble sanctity of the Brothers. It is a joy to know that the last of the Faculty in my time, Fr Con Jordan, is with us today.

If there had been misgivings in earlier days about the observance by Australians of monastic rules and protocols, the schoolboys of the 1940's saw no evidence of laxity. From the regular rounds of morning Masses, through the ordered day, the MSCs were busy with their appointed tasks. Even consultations were conducted by a formal, brisk perambulation of the consultors back and forth on the pathways of the College. The prayer life of the community permeated and informed the life of the school.

I presume to speak for all the thousands of students of Australian MSC schools when I say: Thank you for your instruction and your example and for your confirmation and strengthening of our faith. May Our Lord keep you close to His Heart now and in the life to come.

Of course, education was but one of the activities of the Society in the last century. There were many other activities which have commended the Society to the community and which have earned the gratitude of those whom they served. The devotion of the MSCs has been extraordinary. Who, knowing the urbane, sociable and social figure of Fr Vin Dwyer, could envisage him as Director of Education in the Gilbert Islands (as Kiribati then was), visiting his far-flung domain in a laketoi? And I remember the advice I received from the Bishop of Darwin, John O'Loughlin, the first member of the Australian Province to be consecrated a Bishop. He had been our Prefect of Studies and I recall his lectures on the painting technique of the Old Masters delivered in an outbuilding of a Dalby Hotel during the evacuation year of 1942. Years later in Darwin, I sought his opinion on an outline of what was advanced as a draft Aboriginal Land Rights Bill. 'It's quite good', he said, 'but whether it is enacted or not, the MSCs will still be here doing what they can to assist the indigenous people of the Territory.'

Of course, the changes brought about by Vatican II in the Church and its relationship with the world had its impact on the MSCs. Some found the changes disturbing and left the Society; most found them affirming of their faith and spiritual life, emphasizing the need for an outgoing love and compassion and the deepening of a sacramental devotion to the Sacred Heart. Fr Cuskelly sought to re-order the traditional approach to the devotion to the Sacred Heart, saying that the first need was to 'unite our adoration with His, to worship God with Him, to unite our offering of love and praise and thanksgiving with His in the sacrifice of the Mass.' Within the MSC communities, the paramount importance of observing the rule became secondary to the living of a more caring life. And that was another way of maintaining one of the old pillars of the Society, namely, the sense of community which gave strength and support to all members of the MSC family.

Many of you here today will have experienced the caring concern of the MSCs and I imagine that all will have memories of the benefits that have been conferred by an MSC during the last 100 years. Your presence evidences the appreciation that each of us has for the contribution that the Society has made to this nation, to New Zealand and to the communities of the mission countries and our gratitude for the inspiration that has touched the hearts and minds of so many of us. But what of the future?

A future of an ageing membership of the Society; a future of falling vocations, yet larger demands; a future of Churches with half-filled pews; a future of a community obsessed by materialism and self-interest. This is a future that may not be very different from the France of 1854 when Jules Chevalier founded the Society of the Missionaries of the Sacred Heart. And the needed response may not be very different from the vision which he had. What can topple a self-interested materialism? Ultimately, a realization that the pot of gold at the end of the rainbow is a bowl of ashes and that self-interest produces a lonely isolation from the rest of humanity. But what will stimulate that realization? Only a demonstration of love and compassion that removes the isolation and displays the richness of human relationships. And what is the surest way to evoke a demonstration of love and compassion? A belief in the brotherhood of man and the fatherhood of God, that each of us has a Divinely created dignity that commands love for, and compassion for the trials of, our neighbour. Love and compassion are the virtues of the heart – they come from the core of our being. They may require an intellectual conversion from our ordinary way of thought and they may call for an understanding of the circumstances in which our neighbour is placed, but the power to show love and compassion comes from a movement of the heart. And when we seek for divine inspiration, we look to the heart of our Saviour. There is to be found the spirit of love and compassion, as David proclaimed when he praised the Lord Who 'crowns you with love and compassion' (Ps 103:4). It is there that we can find the power to sustain a conversion of our own hearts. So the charism of the

Society of the Missionaries of the Sacred Heart is as necessary in Australia today as it was in mid-19th Century France.

Of course, any voice identified as a voice of the Church today may be treated with a certain reserve, if not summarily dismissed. In the minds of many, the Church has become rule-ridden and dictatorial, even diminishing the role and function of conscience. If mere conformity with rules and an unreflective acceptance of dogma were the badge of orthodoxy and fidelity, however, the institutions of the Church would have become like the scribes and Pharisees whom Christ condemned because they 'tie up heavy burdens and lay them on men's shoulders, but [do not] lift a finger to move them' (Matthew 23:4). No, true orthodoxy focusses on the central teaching to 'love the Lord thy God with all your heart, and all your soul and with all your mind' and to 'love your neighbour as yourself' (Matthew 22:37-39). Jesus instructed His disciples to 'love one another as I have loved you' and promised them that if they kept His commandments 'you will remain in my love' (John 15:10, 12). Love and compassion are the most reliable indicia of orthodoxy and fidelity to the Divine Master. Conscience, formed and informed, dictates what we do or avoid doing in order to live, and to show, that love and compassion. And the teaching of the Church is, to the faithful, the primary means of informing our consciences. Then we are confident in our vulnerability as we expose ourselves to the risk of love and compassion.

So what do we pray for the future of the Society of the Australian Province of the Missionaries of the Sacred Heart? I would pray that they may discern the signs of the times and thus discover the places and people in greatest need of love and compassion. I would pray that they invite those not of their Society to join them in serving those people in those places and that they maintain the discipline and intellectual rigour which can make that service effective. I would pray that they will find joy in that service and in the knowledge that their hands are doing the work of the Divine Heart and bringing those whom they serve closer to His encompassing embrace. And then, with them, I would pray:

May the Sacred Heart of Jesus be everywhere loved.

Forever.

---

1. The address was published in (2006) 40 *Compass: A Review of Topical Theology*, 39-42.

13.8 Heart and Mind in Social Justice

Editor's note

Brennan's sister, Mary was a religious sister. She belonged to the congregation of the Sacred Heart (RSCJ). Mary had taught at the RSCJ's Kincoppal-Rose Bay School. She had also been the Provincial Superior of the sisters in Australia. Brennan was invited to speak at Kincoppal-Rose Bay on 16 November 2007. These were his remarks.

Is the heart more effective than the mind in discerning matters of social justice? What do I mean by social justice and how is it discerned? Justice is a condition relative to an individual, for justice is accorded to, and injustice is experienced by, individuals – by men and women in their daily lives. We live in society and the traditions and ethos and economy of society affect what social justice demands for each person. At base – the bottom line, as it were – below which none should fall are the human rights which allow each person to live in freedom, in dignity and in peace. The various declarations of human rights may give some hope to those who are deprived of their human rights, but the real worth of those declarations is to remind others of their duty to ensure that each person in society is entitled to live in freedom, dignity and peace. If this were achieved, we would be a long way towards achieving social justice. But, beyond that minimum, there has to be an opportunity for each to enjoy a fair share of the benefits available in each society.

That can be postulated as an ideal, but we know that the ideal will never be attained. Yet the ideal is not to be discarded because it is difficult, or even impossible, to attain. Nor does that justify failure in trying to attain it. Why should we try? The humanist would say because our common humanity demands it; the Christian would say that we are all children of God, all loved equally by Him and equally entitled to respect on account of the divine spark that is in us and our divine destiny. We cannot look on the anxious face of the refugee, or see the desperate anguish of the addict, or the desolation of the impoverished family without seeing the face of the suffering Christ. Is it the mind or the heart that perceives this truth? Does it matter, so long as our perception is not dimmed by materialism and self-interest. For the Christian, commitment to social justice is not an optional extra, or a peculiar variant of religious piety. It is an obligation flowing from the divine injunction to love one another as Christ has loved us. The source of the obligation can be seen in the writing of Catherine of Siena who interpreted the mind of God in these terms: 'I have given many gifts and graces, both spiritual and temporal, with such diversity that I have not given everything to one single person, so that you may be constrained to practice charity towards one another.... I have willed that one should need another and that all should be my ministers in distributing the graces and gifts they have received from me.'[1]

The reason why we must commit ourselves to seek justice is one thing; constructive effort to achieve justice is another. When we commit ourselves to social justice, we must work in the real world, identifying needs that can be remedied by social action, and charting the action to be taken in relief of the need. *The Tablet's* recent tribute to Pedro Arrupe, the former General of the Jesuits, recalls that he equated the terms 'commitment' with 'devotion': 'devotion or gift of self, but emphasising that we cannot stop at sentiment but we must go on to act. It means that we cannot seek the spiritual solely, but we must embody our commitment in the actual situation – in persons and in real events.'

Heart and mind are both involved in targeting areas of need that excite compassion. Those areas are not hard to identify. They can be discovered by examining instances where there is gross inequality in the opportunities to enjoy the benefits available to other members of the community – whether those benefits be social, educational, cultural or financial – and where individual freedom, or dignity or peacefulness are compromised. The elderly or the disabled who could be taken for an outing but who have nobody to take them; the seeker for asylum from a cruel regime who is incarcerated in a detention centre for an unreasonable period; the addict who is chained to the habit; the Aboriginal child with few prospects of a satisfying career during a limited life span; the single mother who cannot raise the bond to obtain accommodation; the family whose breadwinner has lost his or her job; the woman who is subjected to sexual harassment or domestic violence. Once we perceive these or other areas of need, the heart and the mind combine to compel some action to alleviate the injustice.

We tend, naturally enough, to see these problems only in our immediate environment. But globalization has widened our horizons. The 2007 Social Justice Statement of the Australian Bishops reminded us that the great commandment of love must be extended to all people and pointed to the role of mind and heart: 'When considering our global connectedness,' they wrote, 'we need to move from the head to the heart. We do the thinking but then we need to move to action. We acknowledge and understand our interdependence with others whose social and economic reality is so different from our own. We are then inspired to take action, to do something to correct the injustices and to put right the situation so there might be an increased prospect of peace, security and development for all. In other words, we move from interdependence to solidarity.'

That is the hard part – to move from interdependence to solidarity – to step outside our comfort zone and to remember the challenge of St Basil the Great: 'The bread which you do not use is the bread of the hungry; the garment hanging in the wardrobe is the garment of the one who is naked; the shoes you do not wear are the shoes of the one who is barefoot; the money you keep locked away is the money of the poor; the acts of charity you do not perform are so many injustices that you commit.'

Perhaps you, like me, take refuge in the cry of St Augustine: 'Not yet, O Lord, not yet!' But Augustine knew that he had to yield and say: 'Here I am Lord, I come to do Your will.'

---

1. Dial. I, 7, cited in para. 1938, Part II, *Catechism of the Catholic Church.*

13.9 Testimonial to the Parish Priest

Editor's note

When Gerard and Patricia Brennan moved to Sydney, they became regular parishioners at St Canice's Elizabeth Bay under the care of the Jesuits. Steve Sinn was their Parish Priest for many years. The Parish Council invited Brennan to speak at a celebration of Steve Sinn's retirement as parish priest on 29 November 2011.

Tonight, we give thanks for the myriad gifts that we, the parishioners and friends of St Canice's, have received and enjoy in 2011. Kevin's gentle story of St Canice's up to 1940 has been tellingly portrayed in word and image, in action and song. We have been taken through the earlier years of St Canice's history and tonight we give thanks for the benefactors of the past. May each of them, whether clerical or lay, rich or poor, indigenous or immigrant, great or humble, rest in Our Lord's eternal love. They gave us this land, this church, these buildings but they also left a tradition that has challenged and inspired their successors.

Most of the Parish history occurred before Vatican II. My generation grew up in that age. The Mass was in Latin but we were familiar with its texts and cadences; we learnt the catechism by rote and passed the test before we were confirmed; we had regular times for prayer and regular occasions for Confession; we were members of the Sodalities – Children of Mary, Sacred Heart and Holy Name – assembling for Mass on the prescribed Sundays of the month; we were edified by the sacrifices of the Sisters and Brothers and we were instructed by the Sunday sermons of the pulpit priest. We were a proud but separated religious minority, following the established practices of the families, schools and parishes to which we belonged.

Then came Vatican II and we were challenged to find a deeper meaning to our faith. The scriptures and the two great commandments – to love God and neighbour – were given a new vitality. The Mass in our own language was an enormous challenge – could we take in the reality of a living, loving Christ Who comes among us on the altar in answer to an invitation in English spoken by a priest who is just like ourselves? And what did it mean to love our neighbour as ourselves in the real and contemporary world? How could we work for God's Kingdom in the here and now?

We come to St Canice's to answer these challenges, to be supported by others who are on the same journey and to be encouraged when we fail. We give thanks for one another and for the comfort of being pilgrims together, and especially do we give thanks for our fellow pilgrim who points the way.

Steve, we are not here to eulogize you but simply to thank you for showing us pilgrims how we might respond to God's love and how we might know and love our neighbour.

When you celebrate the Mass, we have not been left passive in the pews but we have joined you as you pray, speaking to the Father, welcoming the Son, thanking the Holy Spirit. Your bare footed idiosyncrasy and your prayerful silences tell us that you and we are in converse with the loving God. You have not allowed the awkward new Order of Mass to dispel the intimacy of our divine communion. We travelled with you through the intricacies of the Easter ceremonies, despite the vagaries of the paschal fire, to celebrate the central mystery of our faith; you made baptisms joyful community celebrations and requiems marked not so much the life that ended as its continuity with the life to come. Your homilies, marked as they are by anguished hesitations and false starts, contain spiritual gems that we can treasure and that we need to sustain us on our way. We have travelled a faith journey together and we hope that we have confirmed your faith as you have confirmed ours.

Meditation and the study of the scriptures have strengthened the spiritual life of the Parish and you have encouraged devotion to the Rosary and the Stations of the Cross. You undertook the huge refurbishing of the church to make it a better place of worship and community activity. We are proud of the church and its surrounds but, more importantly, we are proud of the variety of people who make up the church that we know. St Canice's extends its welcome to all – to the lonely people of the street and to the comfortable middle class, to the transvestites and the fashionistas, to the public figures and the unknown, to the hungry and the well fed, to the devout and the doubtful. You, Steve, have shown equal respect to all, not judging but being a friend to those in need of friendship, especially the people of the street. You have placed on the Parish an indelible mark of openness, welcoming the refugees, feeding the hungry and clothing the naked. You have reminded us that the poor and the marginalised are God's gift to the rest of us, for we can see His face in them. Canice's Kitchen offers both food and hospitality and if the sounds of the assembled guests are wafted through the windows of the church, they are an authentic hymn of praise to Him who ate with Matthew and other tax collectors and sinners. Could a church have a better background or offer a more authentic welcome than the people who sleep on the porch?

St Canice's is a Parish but it is not parochial. One of the benefits that we have received from the Jesuits is an opportunity to participate in the work of Jesuit Missions and the Jesuit Refugee Service. Whether it is the hunger of the people of East Africa, or the victims of the tsunami in Indonesia, or the plight of refugees in the camps of Thailand or Villawood or the amputees wounded by landmines in Cambodia, we have offered our prayers and practical assistance thankful for the benefits of living in a free and peaceful country. And, thanks largely to Steve, parishioners have been closely involved in our sister parish in Railaco, rejoicing in the rebuilding of a community devastated by conflict.

Closer to home, parishioners have happily responded to the warm friendship that you, Steve, have formed with other Christian communities. The ecumenical spirit has grown as you affirmed our common humanity, shared hopes and faith in our divine redemption. Each year on Good Friday you have led Christians of all denominations in a procession of witness through the Cross to the Sacred Heart Hospice, praying on the way that all may be one. On those days, you have given us the hymns, the scripture readings and the prayers that link Christ's wounds and death to the wounds and death of men and women who lived or worked at the stations where we stopped.

Tonight, we reflect on your contributions to our parish, Steve, but we also want to thank you for the compassion and the friendship that you have given personally to so many of us. You have rejoiced when we have rejoiced and wept when we have wept; you have been a staff to lean on and a shoulder to cry on. One of your parishioners described you as 'love on legs'; another as 'an original'. Whatever the description, you will know how deeply we appreciate what you have been and what you have done for us in your years at St Canice's as the good and faithful servant of the Lord. And while you leave for a well-earned sabbatical, we welcome your successor, Chris Jenkins. We promise you that we will give him our support for we are conscious that, as one of your fellow priests observed: 'He will have big sandals to fill!'

13.10 Parish 125th Anniversary

Editor's note

On 4 May 2014, St Canice's Parish celebrated its 125th anniversary. Brennan was invited to reflect on the life of the parish.

Today we give thanks for the 125 years of service, both spiritual and practical, given by the parish of St Canice. We remember in our prayers the generosity and devotion of the founders and those who have maintained the parish since its foundation. Now we must ask ourselves whether the parish of today remains as relevant to the lives of the people as did the parishes of years gone by. Pope Francis responded to that question in *Evangelii Gaudium*. He wrote:

> The parish is not an outdated institution; precisely because it possesses great flexibility, it can assume quite different contours depending on the openness and missionary creativity of the pastor and the community. … [I]f the parish proves capable of self-renewal and constant adaptivity, it continues to be 'the Church living in the midst of the homes of her sons and daughters'. This presumes that it really is in contact with the homes and the lives of its people, and does not become a useless structure out of touch with people or a self-absorbed group made up of a chosen few. The parish is the presence of the Church in a given territory, an environment for hearing God's word, for growth in the Christian life, for dialogue, proclamation, charitable outreach, worship and celebration. … It is a … a centre of constant missionary outreach. We must admit, though, that the call to review and renew our parishes has not yet sufficed to bring them nearer to people, to make them environments of living communion and participation, and to make them completely mission-oriented. [1]

Older Catholics may tend to hear this as a nostalgic call to return to parish life as it was, in earlier and less pressured times, when the Catholic community was identifiable by the regularity of their church attendance, by bountiful priestly and religious vocations, public displays of Catholicity, lay dependence on clerical instruction, commitment to Catholic schools and hospitals and missionary endeavours devoted to the proselytising of non-Catholics. Then the Church was indeed living in the homes of those identified as her sons and daughters. But that is not what Pope Francis was speaking about.

Pope Francis is speaking post Vatican II which opened eyes, minds and hearts to the universality of Divine love and mercy, to the common humanity of every person, to their equal dignity and to their entitlement to a share in the world's riches to sustain that dignity. Now, as in the past, the Church must live in the homes of her sons and daughters, but those homes are not confined to the ghettos of the past. As a parish, St Canice's has been proud to welcome all who have chosen to worship here, but parishioners today are called to know, to respect, to care for – indeed, to love – all people. And that may impose on us, the parishioners of St Canice's, a particular obligation towards all in the local community, the people who live on the streets and those who live in comfort, the people who work in boardrooms, in bars and in brothels, people who staff offices, hospitals and hotels; all who are our neighbours to be loved as ourselves. And then to recognize the world of poverty and need in other places.

It is for us, the parishioners in the pews, to ensure that our minds and hearts respond to Pope Francis' call to make St Canice's an 'environment of living communion and participation and to make [it]completely mission-oriented'. That is our challenge for the years to come.

---

1. Pope Francis, *Evangelii Gaudium, #28.*

Chapter 14

Human Rights Beyond Our Shores

14.1 The Significance of the Beijing Statement

Editor's note

At the Bar, Brennan had been a longtime supporter of LAWASIA which is a regional association of lawyers, judges, jurists and legal organisations advocating for the interests and concerns of the Asia Pacific legal profession. LAWASIA states its mission as being 'a platform to promote the cross-jurisdictional exchange of legal knowledge; as a voice of the legal profession; and as a conduit for encouraging adherence to mutually held principles of the rule of law, professional integrity and the protection of human rights'. Brennan attended his first LAWASIA conference in Jakarta, Indonesia in 1973. As Chief Justice, he was one of 20 Chief Justices who signed the Beijing Statement of Principles of the Independence of the Judiciary in the LAWASIA Region at the 6th Conference of Chief Justices held in Beijing on19 August 1995. He was invited to address the 15th LAWASIA conference in the Philippines in Manila on 30 August 1997. This was his address.

The Beijing Statement of Principles of the Independence of the Judiciary in the LAWASIA Region is remarkable for the extent of the concurrence that it has achieved. Through their respective Chief Justices, 32 Nation States of the Region have assented to the statement of principles which it contains. The concurrence is remarkable because the Statement expresses ideals common to legal systems of very different kinds. Systems which are based on the common law and systems based on the continental (especially the German) legal system have found common ground; societies informed by different value systems esteem the judiciary as 'an institution of the highest value in every society'. States whose governments follow the Westminster model, States based on the American model and states whose governments have developed from earlier socialist forms all acknowledge that the objectives and functions of the judiciary include:

> '(a) [ensuring] that all persons are able to live securely under the rule of law;
>
> (b) [promoting] within the proper limits of the judicial function the observance and attainment of human rights; and
>
> (c) [administering] the law impartially among persons and between persons and the State.'[1]

Of necessity the Beijing Statement is expressed in general terms. Each Nation State which applies the Principles of the Statement achieves the stated objectives of judicial independence in the context of its own legal system. In Australia during the past year the Chief Justices of the Supreme Courts of the States and Territories took the Beijing Statement into account in making a Declaration of Principles relating to judicial appointments. The Chief Justices declared their opposition to the appointment of acting judges instead of permanent judges except for reasons of necessity. And they opposed the appointment of judges to offices or to perform functions where the appointment or the continuation of the appointment is at the discretion of the executive government of the state or territory. The Declaration is a practical example of the way in which the general principle of judicial independence is applied to ensure that public confidence in the manifest impartiality of the judiciary is maintained. That general principle is embodied in Chapter III of the Australian *Constitution* which requires judges appointed to the High Court of Australia or to other Federal courts to be appointed permanently with security of tenure until the age of retirement and with irreducible remuneration. As that provision ensures the independence of the justices of the High Court and of other Federal courts it was unnecessary for me as Chief Justice of the High Court or for the Chief Justices of other Federal Courts to join in the Declaration made by the Chief Justices of States and Territories.

Although the Beijing Statement was taken into account by the Chief Justices, it would be a mistake to think that it was either the inspiration of the Declaration or the catalyst for making it. The Declaration itself described the Beijing Statement as a prescription of 'minimum standards for judicial independence making due allowance for national differences in the LAWASIA region'. Nonetheless the Beijing Statement expresses values which are common throughout the region. The description of the Beijing Statement as a prescription of minimum standards illustrates both its utility and the need for further understanding of national differences.

So far as the Beijing Statement prescribes minimum standards and commands the support of the several judiciaries of the region, it provides the matrix of understanding that allows the judiciary and the legal professions to meet and discuss matters of common concern. It affords a bond of mutual support in repelling attacks on judicial independence and it combines the judges and lawyers of the region in a powerful phalanx devoted to the doing of impartial justice according to law.

But the application of the principles in the Beijing Statement must take place in the context of particular legal systems. The purpose of the Statement is not to protect the judges but to guarantee the rule of law at the hands of an impartial judiciary. The Beijing Statement will not achieve that objective if the hands of the judiciary are tied by restrictions on their jurisdiction. This is recognized by Articles 33 and 34 of the Statement which declare, inter alia, that the judiciary must have jurisdiction over all issues of a justiciable nature. But each legal system prescribes the issues that are justiciable and the issues that are not. In those countries where the courts are accustomed to exercise jurisdiction to review executive action, or even legislative action, in accordance with *Marbury* v *Madison*,[2] the rule of law is made to govern a broad range of State activity. In countries which do not admit the principle of *Marbury* v *Madison*, the rule of law depends in part upon its acceptance by the repositories of State power. The Beijing Statement has a different operation in countries of these two kinds. Thus, it appears that the Beijing Statement does not prescribe a norm adherence to which will produce comparable legal systems throughout the region. It would be a mistake to expect the statement to do more than provide a moral incentive to each country to create and maintain a competent, incorruptible and independent judiciary. Such a judiciary advances and preserves the rule of law by fearlessly applying it in each case independently of external influence, whether by the executive government or by any other source.

The rule of law must be the aim and object of every legal system, else legal power becomes an instrument of oppression and corruption. By extending the jurisdiction of the judiciary, by appointing competent, incorruptible and independent judges, by shielding their independence with proper tenure and remuneration, by isolating the judges from the pleasure or displeasure of the executive branch of government and by providing the courts with the resources needed to exercise their jurisdiction efficiently, the rule of law is advanced and preserved. Diminish any of these safeguards and freedom and the stability of society are placed at risk.

So much can be accepted as axiomatic. But until further study is done to disseminate understanding of the way in which the principles of the Beijing Statement are applied in the respective jurisdictions within the Region, there will be misunderstandings about those principles and the fidelity of particular countries to them. In other words, there is much more to be done to ensure that the same understanding of the rule of law is shared throughout the Region. If justice according to law were commonly understood in every country and were done in every country, we should all be at peace, we should all have our own and our peoples' dignity respected and we should be enabled to share in the prosperity that can come with a predictable and firm trading regime.

This is still some distance off. But the Beijing Statement is a step along the way. If ever we reach the end of that road, LAWASIA will have contributed much to the peace, order and good government of the world.

---

1. See *Beijing Statement of Principles of the Independence of the Judiciary in the LAWASIA Region*, par 10.
2. 5 US 137 (1803).

14.2 Domestic Law in International Relations

Editor's note

Having retired as Chief Justice in May 1998, Brennan was invited to deliver the annual lecture to the Singapore Academy of Law on 2 September 1998.

Municipal courts and municipal law deal chiefly with domestic issues. But judges and practitioners, accustomed to the application of local laws to local issues, find that the pattern of litigation is changing. As our countries move into a world of transnational trade and commerce and agreed international standards touching social, environmental and economic issues, international law has an increasing influence on the content of municipal law. In earlier times, when international law related chiefly to the affairs of sovereign States, it had comparatively little effect on municipal law. The ordinary laws governing relationships between individuals, the powers of government and prohibited conduct were not the concern of the international community.

With increasing frequency, especially in the last twenty years, the international community has sought to contain international tensions and consolidate peaceful relations by treaties setting common standards to be implemented by nation States according to their own legal systems. Municipal courts have been called on to implement a changing international legal order. Municipal courts, more than international tribunals, have become the expositors of international law.

When international law speaks to matters within the domain of municipal law, the question whether and to what extent municipal law responds must be answered by national courts and legal professions. Some legal systems, embracing the monist theory, treat international law and municipal law as parts of a single body of law, administered in accordance with an internal set of rules. Kelsen perceived international law to be the basis of the national legal order in the sense that an international legal norm defines the organs of a legitimate national government and thereby delegates the authority to create a national legal order.[1] Other legal systems, Singapore and Australia among them, regard international law and municipal law as distinct. This is the theory of dualism. It distinguishes between the two systems on these: first, the subjects of municipal law are individuals while the subjects of international law are nation States. Secondly, the juridical origins of the two systems are different.[2] The common law jurisdictions find municipal law in statutes and regulations and in judicial decisions. The sources of international law are the customary law of nations, treaties, binding resolutions of the

United Nations Security Council and the general principles of law recognised by the courts of civilised countries.

Whether a State embraces the monist or the dualist theory, the practical question that has to be addressed by a municipal court is whether and to what extent the provisions of international law are to be applied to the case in hand. That is not to say that municipal courts apply international law: they do not. In the judicatures of common law countries, only municipal law is applied. But the incorporation or transformation of international law into municipal law is often the means by which a State discharges its international legal obligations.

The international community has a legitimate interest in two aspects of the work of municipal courts. The first aspect relates to the implementation of the provisions of international law by the municipal legal system. That depends on the principles of municipal law that govern the adoption of international law. The second aspect relates to the revelation by court decisions of the way in which the rule of law operates in a particular society. I turn first to the principles governing the domestic application of international law.

Australian practice, I must say, in this respect substantially follows English precedent. The citation of English and Australian authority by the Chief Justice in the recent judgment of the Court of Appeal of Singapore in *Public Prosecutor* v *Taw Cheng Kong*[3] leads me to proceed on the footing that no difference will be found in this respect between the law and practice of Singapore and Anglo-Australian law and practice.

The common law and customary international law

Municipal law distinguishes between customary international law, embodying the practice of civilised nations as acknowledged by jurists,[4] and international law derived from treaties. Blackstone's opinion was that the law of nations - that is, the whole of customary international law - is part of the law of the land.[5] That principle of incorporation was adopted in the 18th century[6] and was affirmed at the beginning of this century by Lord Alverstone CJ in 1905[7] who insisted on proof that the proposed norm of customary international law had already been recognised and acted upon in England or was of such a nature that no civilised state would repudiate it. Then Lord Atkin, delivering the opinion of the Privy Council in *Chung Chi Cheung v The King*, said:

> It must be always remembered that, so far, at any rate, as the courts of this country are concerned, international law has no validity save in so far as its principles are accepted and adopted by our own municipal law. The courts acknowledge the existence of

> a body of rules which nations accept amongst themselves. On any judicial issue they seek to ascertain what the relevant rule is, and, having found it, they will treat it as incorporated into the municipal law, so far as it is not inconsistent with rules enacted by statutes or finally declared by their tribunals.[8]

This doctrine of incorporation was affirmed in later cases. In the *Tin Council Case* in the House of Lords, Lord Oliver pointed out that incorporation is limited to the existing rules of international law and municipal courts have no authority 'to legislate a rule into existence for the purposes of domestic law and on the basis of material that is wholly indeterminate.'[9]

Now arguably, the Australian approach to customary international law is different. In *Chow Hung Ching v The King*[10] Dixon J adopted the opinion of Professor Brierly that international law 'is not a part but one of the sources of English law'.[11] This proposition transforms rather than incorporates the international norm into the common law and would accept the authority of the court to develop the transformed international norm to meet the exigencies of each case. Whichever approach is adopted, the court must first determine whether the international norm contended for has been acted upon, or would certainly be acted upon, by the community of nations. Then it must appear that there is no statute or binding court decision inconsistent with the proposed norm.

Treaties and the statutes implementing them

Under the Westminster form of government, the Crown or the executive government has the exclusive power to enter into treaties and thereby bind the State. But the executive government is not the repository of legislative power and it cannot enact new law by the exercise of executive power;[12] new laws must be enacted by the legislature or with the legislature's authority.[13] Therefore, it has been held in Australia[14] as in England[15] 'that the provisions of an international treaty to which Australia is a party do not form part of Australian law unless those provisions have been validly incorporated into our municipal law by statute.'

When the provisions of a treaty are enacted in the terms in which the treaty is drawn, however, the municipal court construes these terms not by reference to the municipal rules of statutory construction but by the international rules applied in the interpretation of treaties. When *The Hague Rules* were incorporated into the *Carriage of Goods by Sea Act 1924* (UK), Lord MacMillan said: 'It is important to remember that the Act of 1924 was the outcome of an International Conference and that the rules in the Schedule have an international currency. As these rules must come under the consideration of foreign courts it is desirable in the interests of uniformity that the interpretation should not be rigidly controlled by domestic precedents of antecedent date, but rather that the language of the rules should be construed on broad principles of general acceptation.'[16]

Now a similar issue arose in Australia when the *Racial Discrimination Act 1975* (Cth) was enacted in substantially the same terms as, and to give effect to, the *International Convention on the Elimination of All Forms of Racial Discrimination*. In *Koowarta* v *Bjelke-Petersen* I observed that '[w] hen Parliament chooses to implement a treaty by a statute which uses the same terms as the treaty, it is reasonable to assume that Parliament intended to import into municipal law a provision having the same effect as the corresponding provision of the treaty.'[17]

The reasons for this approach are 'certainty and uniformity of application'.[18] Therefore, the basic rule of interpretation is to be found in Article 31 of the *Vienna Convention*,[19] the work of the United Nations International Law Commission.[20]

However, the interpretation of some treaty provisions may be affected by the prior history of the rule. If the treaty simply expresses a rule, especially a rule of commercial or maritime law, which has been applied by municipal courts before the treaty was entered into, the true meaning of the treaty rule may be found in judicial precedent. This has been the subject of discussion in Australia.

The effect of treaties on the construction of statutes generally

The proposition that the provisions of treaties are not part of municipal law unless incorporated by statute means that, under municipal law, statute prevails over treaty where there is any inconsistency between the two. Speaking for the Court of Appeal in *Seow Teck Ming* v *Tan Ah Yeo,*[21] Chan Sek Keong J said '[I]t is settled law that the duty of the court is to give effect to national law and not international law if there were a real conflict between them.'[22]

The priority accorded to municipal law can, of course, be ceded by statute so that the provisions of a treaty override an inconsistent municipal law. When Singapore statutorily incorporated the United Nations Convention on Contracts for the International Sale of Goods 1980,[23] the Act (*Sale of Goods (United Nations Convention) Act 1995 (Singapore)* provided that the Convention should prevail over other laws to the extent of any inconsistency.

Although treaties do not become part of municipal law unless incorporated by a valid statute, it is erroneous to think that unincorporated treaty provisions are wholly irrelevant. Such provisions have been held to be relevant to the construction of statutes where the language of a statute is either so general or ambiguous that it can be interpreted to conform with treaty obligations.[24] Australian courts, following English authority,[25] construe ambiguous statutes to accord with treaty obligations[26] 'at least in those cases in which the legislation is enacted after, or in contemplation of, entry into, or ratification of, the relevant international instrument.'[27] The explanation of this approach to the construction of an ambiguous statute is the presumption that 'Parliament, prima facie, intends to give effect to Australia's obligations under international law.'[28] But as Lord Denning reminds us, where a treaty is expressed in terms that are 'so wide as to be incapable of practical application, ... it is much better for us to stick to our own statutes and principles, and only look to the Convention for guidance in case of doubt.'[29]

The effect of international law on the common law

International law generally has now been recognised in Australia as a legitimate source of development of the common law. This approach is similar to the view taken by Dixon J that customary international law is a source of the common law. With the concurrence of two other Justices in *Mabo* v *Queensland [No 2],* I said 'The common law does not necessarily conform with international law, but international law is a legitimate and important influence on the development of the common law, especially when international law declares the existence of universal human rights.'[30]

In *Minister for Immigration and Ethnic Affairs* v *Teoh*, Mason CJ and Deane J, cautioned against too ready an incorporation of international law norms into municipal law. Their Honours said:

> The provisions of an international convention to which Australia is a party, especially one which declares universal fundamental rights, may be used by the courts as a legitimate guide in developing the common law. But the courts should act in this fashion with due circumspection when the Parliament itself has not seen fit to incorporate the provisions of a convention into our municipal law. Judicial development of the common law must not be seen as a backdoor means of importing an unincorporated convention into Australian law.[31]

The adoption by Australia of the First Optional Protocol to the International Covenant on Civil and Political Rights conferred on individuals a direct right of access to the Human Rights Committee sitting in Geneva. It is impossible to suppose that the jurisprudence that the Committee will develop in construing the International Covenant will not be regarded by Australian courts if similar issues arise for determination by those courts. Sir Robin Cooke, as he then was President of the New Zealand Court of Appeal in 1994, expects that New Zealand courts will give effect to the International Covenant.[32] But in England, the common law has reacted more conservatively to the existence of an unincorporated treaty, in that instance the European Convention on Human Rights.[33] Australian sensitivity to a determination of the Human Rights Committee resulted in federal legislation designed to nullify the effect of a State law which the Committee held to be inconsistent with the Covenant.[34]

Treaties and discretionary powers

It would be no great leap of principle to presume that, when Parliament creates a discretionary power, it intends the repository of the power either to exercise the power consistently with treaty obligations or at least to have regard to treaty obligations in exercising the power. That question arose in *Teoh's Case*,[35] a case which stimulated some controversy. The Minister ordered a foreign national, convicted of a drug offence, to be deported. The deportee was married to an Australian with young Australian children. The *United Nations Convention on the Rights of the Child*, to which Australia is a party, directs that the best interests of the child should be a primary consideration in all actions concerning children. That direction had not been taken into account in ordering the deportation. A majority of the High Court held[36] that, although the Convention was not a source of individual rights and obligations,[37] there was nothing in the statute to exclude consideration of the Convention by the Minister. Mason CJ and Deane J said: 'Rather, ratification of a convention is a positive statement by the executive government of this country to the world and to the Australian people that the executive government and its agencies will act in accordance with the Convention. That positive statement is an adequate foundation for a legitimate expectation, absent statutory or executive indications to the contrary, that administrative decision-makers will act in conformity with the Convention and treat the best interests of the children as "a primary consideration".'[38]

The Court quashed the decision to deport, holding that if the Minister did not intend to give effect to the Convention direction, he was bound to give the deportee an opportunity to submit that the Convention direction ought to be followed. The Minister, somewhat concerned by the implications of the *Teoh* decision, subsequently observed that the ratification of a treaty 'is a statement to the *international* community to observe the treaty measures in question; it is not a statement to the *national* community - that is the job of the legislature, not the executive.'[39] Although legislation has been proposed to override the principle of the *Teoh* decision, no legislation has yet been enacted.

In a similar case in New Zealand, the Minister argued that he was entitled to ignore the *International Covenant on Civil and Political Rights* and the *Convention on the Rights of the Child* in ordering a deportation. Sir Robin Cooke said: 'That is an unattractive argument, apparently implying that New Zealand's adherence to the international instruments has been at least partly window-dressing.'[40]

However, a final decision on the argument was not given in that case.

In England, an issue of principle similar to that in *Teoh's* case arose before the House of Lords in *Ex parte Brind*.[41] It was argued that, as the courts presume that Parliament intends to legislate in conformity with treaty obligations, it should be presumed that discretionary powers are to be exercised within limits imposed by treaties. The argument was rejected. Lord Bridge thought that proposition went beyond a mere rule of statutory construction to resolve an ambiguity and would impute to Parliament an intention to enforce conformity with the treaty.[42] Clearly, the thesis that the executive should not blow hot and cold in its international dealings and in exercise of its domestic discretions will be subject to further judicial examination.

The implication of the *Teoh* decision is far reaching. If the existence of a ratified but unincorporated treaty gives rise to a 'legitimate expectation' that its terms will be observed and if a general discretionary power is exercised without observing those terms, the decision is voidable unless the party affected thereby has been given an opportunity to submit that the treaty should be observed. *Teoh* might prove to be a growth point of principle governing the effect of international law on executive power.

Of course, municipal courts will often refer to decisions of international courts and tribunals where such decisions have construed a treaty or defined a proposition of international law.[43] But the modern plethora of treaties and the domestic subject matter of many of them will continue to require expositions of treaties by municipal courts. Australia, for example, is party to more than 900 international instruments. It may not be appreciated that the experience of municipal courts in dealing with domestic issues gives them a special competence to evaluate the operation of treaties or proposed treaties affecting domestic issues. That experience could provide a useful reference point for an executive government invited to conclude a treaty impinging on the commerce or conduct of its people.

I have not canvassed the problems raised by the extraterritorial operation of national laws and the doctrines which restrict the justiciability of claims based on the penal, revenue or other 'public laws' of a foreign State.[44] I have simply footnoted some cases relating to this point. Though these topics are important to international relations, they stand outside a discussion of the effect of international laws. Treaties of the future may standardise and codify the relevant rules and thereby reduce the possibility of international tensions arising from the decisions of municipal courts on issues arising from the laws and sovereign acts of other States.

Apart from the international community's interest in the exposition of international law by municipal courts, the exercise by those courts of their ordinary jurisdiction plays an important, though largely unacknowledged, role in international relations.

However, as we noted earlier, international relations in the modern age are legitimately concerned with many aspects of the municipal legal order. They are concerned with the operation of the laws of trade and commerce, of shipping and the movement of currencies, of criminal law (especially the laws dealing with terrorism, drug trafficking and organised crime), of the laws affecting human rights, official corruption, the environment, intellectual property, resources and energy, health and quarantine. Irrespective of a nation State's adoption of international standards by its municipal law, the way in which municipal courts exercise their respective jurisdictions in dealing with these subjects is material to the relationship of one nation State with another.

The independence of the courts, the decisions they give, the sentences they impose, the procedures they adopt, the efficiency with which they dispose of their business are the product of, and a formative influence upon, the society in which they exercise their jurisdiction.

The decisions of municipal courts reveal the extent to which a society is governed by the rule of law, the competence and independence of the judiciary, the efficiency of judicial remedies and the restraints on discretionary power. A true appreciation of the dynamics of a society cannot be had unless the actual working of its municipal courts is understood. The bare text of constitutions or laws must be clothed with the decisions of the courts before the true shape of the legal system can be seen.

The nation States of Asia and the Pacific contain a variety of cultures, laws and systems of government. Each of those legal systems has evolved to meet the challenges of the particular society and finds its legitimacy in local conditions. But the diversity of cultures, laws and systems of government is pregnant with the possibility of international misunderstanding. When international misunderstandings have arisen with respect to the exercise of jurisdiction by municipal courts, the cause has often times been an insufficient appreciation of differences in culture, in laws, in systems of government or in the relationship that exists between the judicial and the political branches of government.

In this, the fiftieth Anniversary of the signing of the *Universal Declaration of Human Rights*, an example may be found in the definition and protection of human rights. In 1995, at and subsequent to a meeting of the Chief Justices of the nations of Asia and the Pacific, the Beijing Statement was adopted, setting out the objectives and functions of our respective judiciaries to be as follows:

> (a) to ensure that all persons are able to live securely under the Rule of Law;
>
> (b) to promote, within the proper limits of the judicial function, the observance and the attainment of human rights; and
>
> (c) to administer the law impartially among persons and between persons and the State.

It is one thing to assert a judicial function to promote the observance and attainment of human rights; it is another thing to agree on their practical content and the 'proper limits of the judicial function'. The culture and system of government of each nation State affects that State's concept of human rights and the part they play in the municipal legal order. Diplomatic tensions on issues of human rights could be moderated by a better understanding of the municipal legal order.

It is anomalous, I suggest, to confine diplomacy to exchanges between the Executive branches of governments if the point of the exchanges is the practical working of the municipal legal system. Judicial exchanges, explaining the legal, cultural and social factors that contribute to municipal decisions, can dispel misunderstandings that might otherwise go unexplained. And such exchanges would assist in providing practical answers to problems that arise in the course of international dealings.

The trader may want to know if judicial relief is available when excessive customs duty is levied or administrative powers are misused. The investor may need to discover the judicial remedies available to protect an investment or to enforce a security. The inventor, local or foreign, will be interested to find out if there is effective protection of intellectual property. Environmentalists and other nation States wish to discover whether there are legal remedies to enforce compliance with environmental standards or obligations prescribed by treaty. Families are anxious to ensure that there is legal protection for expatriate workers. A custodial parent seeks assurance that wrongfully abducted children will be returned. Law enforcement agencies want to be confident that no country should be a haven for drug dealers, organised crime figures or terrorists.

The factors which are relevant to the assessment of a State's commitment to the rule of law are not ascertained merely by reference to the laws of a State. The predictability and normative effect of the law depends on the actual practices and traditions of each nation State. It is surprising, perhaps, that so little attention has been given internationally to the significance of the work of municipal courts. A better assessment of their work would do much to dispel international misunderstandings and to focus attention more precisely on some of the sticking points of international diplomacy. A real understanding of the way in which the rule of law operates in each State and of the way in which the law of the State works to protect legal interests that are the concern of other States can be built gradually by free discussions between the judges of the respective States. Such discussions are an untapped source of international understanding and a valuable means of diminishing tensions that arise from a failure to appreciate accurately the institutional differences that reflect the differing cultures and systems of government in our region. Judicial resources could be harnessed to enhance regional understanding. But how is this to be achieved?

Not by brief and fortuitous meetings among lawyers attending a conference, valuable though such contacts may be. Rather, the experience, intellect and authority of the senior judiciary of the Region should be drawn upon in a Forum in which they would focus, each from his or her national standpoint, on the great issues of international concern falling within their respective jurisdictions. In such a Forum, mutual confidence and understanding of different viewpoints could be built and, if there be substantial issues in controversy, they could be defined more precisely and addressed with a real prospect of resolution. It is surely in the interests of the Region to create a framework in which differences can be explained and the legal infrastructures necessary for peaceful co-existence and international trade, commerce and intercourse can be improved.

An Asian-Pacific Judicial Forum of this kind, constituted chiefly by senior judiciary, would require the support and encouragement of the executive governments of participating nation States. The judiciary must meet with the clear understanding that their exchanges will be seen to be beneficial to their own States and to the Region. The Forum would have a serious diplomatic purpose: the development in time of a clearing house of ideas that are relevant to international relations. It would become a valuable adjunct to the diplomatic and political exchanges that are already an established feature of Regional activity.

No nation State should seek to exercise a controlling influence on the organisation of the Forum. Its secretariat, small and relatively inexpensive, should be funded by the participating States. Desirably, the headquarters should be in one of the ASEAN capitals. The membership should consist of the ASEAN nations, their regional dialogue partners and those Pacific nations who would wish to join - probably the larger Pacific nations whose breadth of international legal interests would approximate those of the smaller ASEAN nations. The People's Republic of China, Japan and the Republic of Korea would be valuable contributors to the Forum.

Its future development and its agenda must be left until its membership is established. Many lessons would be learnt in the exchanges. For example, the highly developed system of judicial training in Japan would no doubt be of interest to many regional judiciaries. Similarly, the judicial orientation courses for newly appointed judges in Australia may provide a model for other common law countries. The technological experiences of the Singapore Courts, of which the Integrated Criminal Justice System is a notable example, would offer a valuable resource for court organisation and case management. And the meetings themselves would create a climate of mutual judicial support that would strengthen the legal infrastructure of the Region.

Initially, seminars of a few senior judges either from each partici-pating nation or from each nation in a sub-regional cluster would be convened with an agenda devised by the secretariat. Investment and taxation regimes, the definition and protection of human rights, environmental protection and international criminal law are topics that would command early attention. The discussions would be led by invited authors of papers, whether judges or academic lawyers, drawn from different jurisdictions. The Forum would grow according to its utility in enhancing mutual respect and understanding, in providing mutual assistance and in developing a sense of regional identity of interest.

This proposal should not duplicate any existing arrangements. In particular, although the Chief Justices of the participating States would be invited to approve the existence of the Forum, to support attendance by their judges and to constitute a Board to supervise the secretariat, there would be no duplication of the biennial meetings of Chief Justices held in conjunction with the meetings of Lawasia. Those meetings not only include many more Chief Justices than could be accommodated in a working Forum; the purpose of their meeting is largely to address common organisational problems rather than to discuss the way in which the decisions of their courts are reached and the laws that are applied.

It has been for me a great satisfaction to learn that the Australian Government, conscious of the need to ensure that the future of the Forum should be in the hands of participating nations, has authorised the provision of an interim secretariat if the notion of a Regional Judicial Forum should prove acceptable to other nations. The Centre for Democratic Institutions of the Australian National University in Canberra, a Centre funded by the Australian Government, would undertake the organisation of an opening seminar.

Therefore, Chief Justice, I venture to suggest that the time has passed when the work of municipal judiciaries is immaterial to international relations and when the voices of municipal judiciaries are silent on issues which concern other nations. An Asian-Pacific Judicial Forum would provide a framework for strengthening the rule of law and thereby contributing to the peace, the order and the good government of our Region.

---

1. Hans Kelsen, *Principles of International Law* (Holt, Rinehart and Winston, 2nd ed, 1966) 562.
2. See Joseph Gabriel Starke, *Introduction to International Law* (Butterworths, 10th ed, 1989) 72, 73.
3. [1998] 2 SLR 410.
4. Michael Akehurst, 'Custom as a Source of International Law' (1975) 47 (1) *British Yearbook of International Law* 1, 53.
5. See *Blackstone's Commentaries on the Laws of England,* (Oxford, Clarendon Press, 1769) Volume 4, 55.
6. See *Bavot* v *Barbuit* (1737) Cases t Talb 281; *Triquet* v *Bath* (1764) 3 Burr 1478; 97 ER 936.
7. See *West Rand Central Gold Mining Co* v *R* [1905] 2 KB 391, 406-407. *Chow Hung Ching* v *The King* (1949) 77 CLR 449, 462.
8. [1939] AC 160,167 168.
9. Ibid 512, 513.
10. (1948) 77 CLR 449, 477.
11. (1935) 51 LQR 24, 31.
12. See *J H Rayner* v *Dept of Trade* [1990] 2 AC 418, 476-477, 499, 500.
13. See *Simsek* v *McPhee* (1982) 148 CLR 636, 641-2; *Commonwealth* v *Tasmania* (*'Tasmanian Dam Case'*) (1983) 158 CLR 1, 224, 225, 231 232.
14. See *Minister for Immigration and Ethnic Affairs* v *Teoh* (1995) 183 CLR 273, 286, 287 (Mason CJ and Deane J).
15. See *Attorney-General for Canada* v *Attorney- General for Ontario* [1937] AC 326, 347; *Rayner (J H) (Mincing Lane) Ltd.* v *Dept of Trade and Industry*; [1990] 2 AC 418, 500; *Reg* v *Home Secretary; Ex parte Brind* [1991] 1 AC 696, 747,760.

16. See *Stag Line, Ltd* v *Foscolo, Mango & Co* [1932] AC 328, 350; and see *James Buchanan & Co Ltd* v *Babco Forwarding and Shipping (UK) Ltd* [1978] AC 141, 152; *Fothergill* v *Monarch Airlines Ltd* [1981] AC 251; *Sidhu* v *British Airways* [1977] AC 430.

17. (1982) 153 CLR 168, 265.

18. See *Shipping Corporation of India Ltd.* v *Gamlen Chemical Co. A/Asia Pty Ltd* (1980) 147 CLR 142, 159.

19. See *Koowarta* v *Bjelke-Petersen* (1982) 153 CLR 168, 265; *Commonwealth v Tasmania (Tasmanian Dam Case)* (1982) 158 CLR 1, 93, 177; *Applicant "A"* v *Minister for Immigration and Ethnic Affairs* (1997) 142 ALR 331.

20. '(1) A treaty shall be interpreted in good faith in accordance with the ordinary meaning to be given to the terms of the treaty in their context and in the light of its object and purpose;

(2) The context for the purpose of the interpretation of a treaty shall comprise, in addition to the text, including its preamble and annexes:

(a) any agreement relating to the treaty which was made between all the parties in connection with the conclusion of the treaty;

(b) any instrument which was made by one or more parties in connection with the conclusion of the treaty and accepted by the other parties as an instrument related to the treaty;

(3) There shall be taken into account, together with the context:

(a) any subsequent agreement between the parties regarding the interpretation of the treaty or the application of its provisions;

(b) any subsequent practice in the application of the treaty which establishes the agreement of the parties regarding its interpretation;

(c) any relevant rules of international law applicable to the relations between the parties;

(4) A special meaning shall be given to a term if it is established that the parties so intended.'

21. [1991] SLR 169; see also *Polites* v *The Commonwealth* (1945) 70 CLR 60.

22. See also *Reg* v *Home Secretary Ex parte. Brind* [1991] 1 AC 696, 747, 748, 760, 761.

23. See *The Sale of Goods (United Nations Convention) Act*, No 14 of 1995. Reported in (1995) 15 *Asian Yearbook of International Law* 267. The Convention has been incorporated into Australian law by State and Territory legislation.

24. See *Polites* v *Commonwealth* (1945) 70 CLR 60, 77.

25. See *Quazi* v *Quazi* 1980 AC 744, 808; *Garland* v *British Rail Engineering Ltd* [1983] 2 AC 751, 771; *Attorney- General* v *Guardian Newspapers* [No 2] [1990] 1 AC 109, 283; cf *Duke* v *Reliance Systems Ltd* [1988] 1 AC 618, 639-640.

26. See *Chu Kheng Lim* v *Minister for Immigration* (1992) 176 CLR 1, 38; *Dietrich* v *The Queen* (1992) 177 CLR 292, 306, 360

27. See *Minister for Immigration and Ethnic Affairs* v *Teoh* (1995) 183 CLR 273, 287.

28. Ibid 287.

29. See *Reg* v *Chief Immigration Officer: Ex p. Bibi* [1976] 1 WLR 979, 984.

30. (1992) 175 CLR 1, 42; see also *Dietrich* v *R* (1992) 177 CLR 292, 306, 321, 360.

31. (1995) 183 CLR 273, 288, 301 302, 304; cf McHugh J, 315.

32. See *Tavita* v *Minister of Immigration* (1994) 2 NZLR 257, 266.

33. See *Reg* v *Ministry of Defence; Ex parte Smith* [1996] QB 517, 558, 564.

34. In the *Toonen Case*, see Ivan Shearer, Únited Nations and Human Rights Committee: *The Toonen Case* (1995) (1995) 69 *Australian Law Journal* 600.

35. (1995) 183 CLR 273.

36. (1995) 183 CLR 273, 287-288, 301 302, 304; Cf McHugh J, 315.

37. Following *Reg* v *Home Secretary; Ex parte Brind* [1991] 1 AC 696, 748.

38. (1995) 183 CLR 273, 291.

39. Senate G Evans, 'The Impact of Internationalisation on Australian Law: a Commentary', The Mason Court and Beyond Seminar, Melbourne, 10 September 1995, 4, quoted by Sir Anthony Mason, 'The influence of international and transnational law on Australian municipal law' (1996) 7 *Public Law Review* 20, 23.

40. See *Tavita* v *Minister of Immigration* [1994] 2 NZLR 257, 266.

41. [1991] 1 AC 696

42. [1991] 1 AC 696, 748.

43. In recent years in the High Court of Australia, in cases relating to Commonwealth power in respect of fisheries and territory below the low water mark (*Bonser* v *La Macchia* (1969) 122 CLR 177, 186, 190, 201, 214; and see 215 216; *New South Wales* v *The Commonwealth ('Seas and Submerged Lands Case')* (1975) 135 CLR 337, 451-452, 454, 466, 475, 500-501; and *Raptis (A) & Son* v *South Australia* (1977) 138 CLR 346, 387) the reasons for judgment of Justices of this Court drew on the opinions of the Judges of the International Court in the *North Sea Continental Shelf Cases* [1969] ICJ Reports 3 and the '*Fisheries Case', United Kingdom* v *Norway* [1951] ICJ Reports 116; [1952] 1 TLR 181. In cases relating to racial discrimination and Aboriginal land rights (*Koowarta* v *Bjelke -Petersen* (1982) 153 CLR 168, 205, 219; *Mabo* v *Queensland [No 2]* (1992) 175 CLR 1, 40-41,181 182 and *Gerhardy* v *Brown* (1985) 159 CLR 70, 128, 129, 135 136) reference was made to the judgments in *South West Africa Cases* [1966] ICJ Reports 3; the *Advisory Opinion on Minority Schools in Albania* (1935) Ser A/B No 64; *Namibia (SW Africa) Advisory Opinion* [1971] ICJ Reports 16; *Advisory Opinion on Western Sahara* [1975] ICJ Reports 12 and *Barcelona Traction, Light and Power Company Limited* [1970] ICJ Reports 3. In dealing with the sources and nature of international law, judgments in *Commonwealth* v *Tasmania ('Tasmanian Dam Case')* (1983) 158 CLR 1, 222 and *Polyukhovich* v *Commonwealth* (1991) 172 CLR 501, 559-560 drew on *Barcelona Traction, the North Sea Continental Shelf Cases* and *Nicaragua* v *United States of America* [1986] ICJ Reports 14. Nationality - a question that fell for consideration in *Sykes* v *Cleary* (1992) 176 CLR 77, 106-107, 109, 111, 131 evoked references to the *Nottebohm Case, Liechtenstein* v *Guatemala* [1955] ICJ Reports 4.

44. See the discussions in *Attorney- General of New Zealand* v *Ortiz* [1984] 1 AC 1, 20-24 and in *Attorney-General (United Kingdom)* v *Heinemann Publishers Pty Ltd* (1988) 165 CLR 30, 40-44, 48.

14.3 Australia and the Rule of Law

Editor's note

On 4 December 2003, Brennan addressed the International Law Association (Australian Branch). This was his address.

International Law has been much in the news in recent years. And rightly so. The legitimacy of the use of force in Afghanistan and Iraq has been the subject of both professional and popular concern. I am not alone, I think, in the belief that our nation has been led into an unlawful and immoral war in Iraq but this is not the occasion to debate the validity of that view. Rather I raise for your consideration whether Australia can maintain with undiminished commitment the rhetoric of the Rule of Law. That is a question which is at the heart of the debate about the response to terrorism; it is question which concerns the powers of executive government and trust in the judicial process.

In a lecture delivered on 25 November 2003 Lord Steyn observed:

> Even in modern times terrible injustices have been perpetrated in the name of security on thousands who had no effective recourse to law. Too often courts of law have denied the writ of the rule of law with only the most perfunctory examination. In the context of a war on terrorism without any end in prospect this is a sombre scene for human rights. But there is the caution that unchecked abuse of power begets ever greater abuse of power. And judges do have the duty, even in times of crisis, to guard against an unprincipled and exorbitant executive response.[1]

His Lordship focused on Guantanamo Bay. He drew attention to the provisions of Article 75(4) of the First Protocol additional to the Geneva Conventions which provides 'No sentence may be passed and no penalty may be executed on a person found guilty of a penal offence relating to the armed conflict except pursuant to a conviction pronounced by an impartial and regularly constituted court respecting the generally recognised principles of regular judicial procedure . . .'[2]

Although the United States has not ratified the Protocol, Lord Steyn asserts that it is generally accepted that Article 75 reflects customary international Law. Our Attorney-General on the other hand, is willing to distinguish the legal obligations of the United States from those of Australia because Australia has, and the United States has not, become a party to the Protocol.[3] That is evidently one of the bases on which the Australian Government seeks to justify the detention of Australian citizens in Guantanamo Bay.

The United States evidently contends that the prisoners at Guantanamo Bay are unlawful enemy combatants liable to be tried and punished by military commission. What has made them enemies in a relevantly legal sense? There was no declaration of war against Afghanistan. If the United States was not at war with Afghanistan what was its authority to deploy troops in that country, to take prisoners and to transport them to Guantanamo Bay? Reliance is placed on a Presidential Order authorizing the indeterminate detention of the prisoners. The Order makes the President's state of mind conclusive of the liability of a person to detention. It defines the persons subject to the Order as -

> . . . any individual who is not a United States citizen with respect to whom I determine from time to time in writing that:
>
> (1) there is reason to believe that such individual, at the relevant times,
>
> (i) is or was a member of the organization known as al Qaida;
>
> (ii) has engaged in, aided or abetted, or conspired to commit, acts of international terrorism, or acts in preparation therefor, that have caused, threaten to cause, or have as their aim to cause, injury to or adverse effects on the United States, its citizens, national security, foreign policy, or economy; or
>
> (iii) has knowingly harbored one or more individuals described in subparagraphs (i) or (ii) of subsection 2(a)(1) of this order;
>
> and
>
> (2) it is in the interest of the United States that such individual be subject to this order.

To make assurance doubly sure no individual subject to the Order is 'privileged to seek any remedy or maintain any proceeding, directly or indirectly, or to have any such remedy or proceeding sought on the individual's behalf, in (i) any court of the United States, or any State thereof, (ii) any court of any foreign nation, or (iii) any international tribunal'. An American Court has held that it has no jurisdiction to entertain claims for Habeas Corpus. [4] The English Court of Appeal has commented 'On the face of it we find surprising the proposition that the writ of the United States courts does not run in respect of individuals held by the government on territory that the United States holds as lessee under a long term treaty.'[5]

Their Lordships noted that the case may go the Supreme Court but went on to say 'What appears to us to be objectionable is that Mr Abbasi should be subject to indefinite detention in territory over which the United States has exclusive control with no opportunity to challenge the legitimacy of his detention before any court or tribunal. It is important to record that the position may change when the appellate courts in the United States consider the matter.'[6]

Two Australians – Messrs Hicks and Habib – are being held under the Order.

Lord Steyn notes 'that the military will act as interrogators, prosecutors, defence counsel, judges, and when death sentences are imposed, as executioners. The trials will be held in secret. None of the basic guarantees for a fair trial need be observed'.[7] Everything is 'subject to decisions of the President as Commander-in-Chief even in respect of guilt and innocence in individual cases as well as appropriate sentences'.[8]

But it seems that Australia has brokered a deal about the way in which Australian prisoners will be treated. The United States will not seek a death penalty in the case of the Australian prisoners; an Australian lawyer with appropriate security clearances may be retained as a consultant (but not as a representative); conversations with lawyers will not be monitored and 'subject to any necessary security restrictions' the trial will be open. [9]

These arrangements do not follow from any Rule of Law. They are simply executive arrangements brokered between the executive governments of the two countries. No doubt they place the Australian prisoners in a privileged position comparable with some of their fellow prisoners. Lord Steyn notes that the British prisoners have similarly been excluded from the death penalty and comments 'This gives a new dimension to the concept of "most favoured nation" treatment in international law. How could it be morally defensible to discriminate in this way between individual prisoners? It lifts the curtain a little on the arbitrariness of what is happening at Guantanamo Bay and in the corridors of power on both sides of the Atlantic.'[10]

Australia has accepted that two of its citizens should be kept in prison, incommunicado, without charge, without consular intervention, without the ordinary access to law and lawyers, with no legal authority recognisable by International Law. Australia has accepted the jurisdiction of a drumhead tribunal which will determine the guilt of these citizens under no law which any court administers, not even an ordinary military court, unable to be defended by any lawyer save one assigned to him by his prosecutors on evidence not governed by any of the ordinary rules.

This failure to condemn the breakdown of the Rule of Law, this 'monstrous failure of justice'[11] as Lord Steyn calls it, is not the only notable example of Australia's ambivalence to the Rule of Law. The other instance, closer to home, relates to the executive steps taken with respect to the arrival of 'boat people'. I would not wish to enter into a discussion about the desirability of mandatory detention – we shall hear a lot about that, no doubt, in the months ahead. But the steps which are taken to repel boat people have demonstrated a fear of the Rule of Law. And that is a fear which has found a resonance in a large – perhaps a majority – proportion of the Australian electorate. The rule of law protects the personal liberty of every citizen and of every alien who is within the jurisdiction of the court. Well established authority was quoted by the English Court of Appeal in *Abassi's* case.[12] Their Lordships recalled Lord Scarman's citation of Lord Atkin's judgment in *Liversidge v Anderson,* pointing out that '...no member of the executive can interfere with the liberty... of a British subject except on the condition that he can support the legality of his action before a court of justice'. [13]

Their Lordships held that 'This principle applies to every person, British citizen or not, who finds himself within the jurisdiction of the court: He who is subject to English law is entitled to its protection.'[14] It applies in war as in peace; in Lord Atkin's words (written in one of the darkest periods of the last war):'In this country, amid the clash of arms, the laws are not silent. They may be changed, but they speak the same language in war as in peace.'[15]

If international law entitles refugees to claim asylum in other countries and our *Migration Act 1958* (Cth) recognizes that entitlement, why were the *Tampa* refugees sent to Nauru and why was the 'Pacific solution' devised? Why were the islands to the north of Australia excluded from the migration zone by Executive Order until that Order was disallowed by the Senate? Not because Australian law was inadequate to deal either with applicants for asylum or those who arrive in Australia unlawfully and without an asylum claim. It was to prevent the boat people – a mere fraction of those who are in Australia without valid visas - from invoking the application of Australian law. It was to forestall the possibility that the law, administered by the courts of this country, might be invoked. The Kurds and their boat were towed out to sea; the *Tampa* refugees were taken by Australian transport to Nauru. This was the kind of conduct which, 350 years ago, was the basis of the accusation against the Earl of Clarendon that he sent persons to 'remote islands, garrisons, and other places, thereby to prevent them from the benefit of the law, and to produce precedents for the imprisoning of any other of His Majesty's subjects in like manner'. That gap in the law of Habeas Corpus was remedied in 1679 to allow the writ to run outside England until, in deference to the emerging authority of colonial courts, it was enacted in 1862 that no writ of Habeas Corpus should be issued out of England by any English judge or court into any colony or foreign dominion where there existed a court having authority to issue and enforce obedience to the writ.[16]

In England, the Court of Appeal has noted a movement 'founded on modern international human rights norms, which is infused by the principle that any measures that are restrictive of liberty, whether they relate to nationals or non-nationals, must be such as are prescribed by law and necessary in a democratic society. The state's power to detain must be related to a recognised object and purpose, and there must be a reasonable relationship of proportionality between the end and the means.'[17] Reasonable restrictions on the liberty of asylum seekers may be justified in order to process applications – a 'recognized object and purpose' – provided the period of restriction bears 'a reasonable relationship of proportionality between the end and the means', but executive detention for other purposes finds no support in the history of our law. As Justice Deane said in *Re Bolton; Ex parte Beane*: 'The common law of Australia knows no lettre de cachet or executive warrant pursuant to which either citizen or alien can be deprived of his freedom by mere administrative decision or action'.[18]

And so three of the Justices in our High Court in *Chu Kheng Lim v Minister for Immigration* said that 'the involuntary detention of a citizen in custody by the State is penal or punitive in character and, under our system of government, exists only as an incident of the exclusively judicial function of adjudging and punishing criminal guilt.'[19]

But what is the purpose of Australia's mammoth efforts to repel the boat people by mandatorily transporting them to Pacific Islands and by excluding parts of Australia from the statutory migration zone by executive action? The Prime Minister has given the answer: 'The point of our policy is to deter people from arriving here illegally….'[20]

When asked 'Why is it more appropriate to tow these 14 [Kurdish] people back to Indonesia than process them here?' the Prime Minister replied 'Because it sends a message that people should not expect to be able to arrive willy nilly in Australia and gain access to our legal system. That's why it's important.'

Is it important that those who arrive in Australia to claim the status of refugee under international law and under the law of this country should be prevented from gaining access to our legal system? The problem is not with the law – for that can be amended – but with Australia's respect for the legal process. I can only hope that this Association will maintain not only its interest in international law but in its insistence that the provisions of international law, which are the product of so much human endeavour and wisdom over so long a time, are respected, observed and enforced by the spirit as well as the curial institutions of this nation.

1. Lord Johan Steyn, 'Guantanamo Bay: The Legal Black Hole' (2004) 53 (1) *International and Comparative Law Quarterly* 1, 2.
2. Steyn, 'Guantanamo Bay: The Legal Black Hole' (n 1) 6.
3. Philip Ruddock, 'A Response from the Commonwealth Attorney-General, the Hon Philip Ruddock, MP' (2003 Summer) *Journal of the NSW Bar Association* 26.
4. See *Rasul v Bush* 321 F 3d 1134. Subsequently, on 28 June 2004, the Supreme Court reversed the decision, holding that the United States courts have jurisdiction to consider challenges to the legality of the detention of foreign nationals captured abroad in connection with hostilities and incarcerated at Guantanamo Bay.
5. See *Abassi v Secretary of State for Foreign and Commonwealth Affairs* [2002] EWCA Civ 1598, par 15.
6. See *Rasul v Bush* 321 F 3d 1134 par 66.
7. Steyn, 'Guantanamo Bay: The Legal Black Hole' (n 1) 9.
8. Ibid.
9. Philip Ruddock, 'A Response from the Commonwealth Attorney-General, the Hon Philip Ruddock, MP' (n 3) 26.
10. Steyn, 'Guantanamo Bay: The Legal Black Hole' (n 1) 9.
11. Ibid., 11.
12. See *Abassi* (n 5) par 60.
13. See *R v Home Secretary; Ex parte Khawaja* [1984] 1 AC 74, 110 (Lord Scarman); citing the classic dissenting judgment of Lord Atkin in *Liversidge v Anderson* [1942] AC 206, 245 and *Eshugbayi Eleko v Government of Nigeria* [1931] AC 662, 670).
14. Ibid.
15. See *Liversidge v Anderson* [1942] AC 206, 244.
16. Holdsworth's, A *History of English Law*, Vol IX, 120-125.
17. See *A, X and Y and Others v Secretary of State for the Home Department* [2002] EWCA Civ 1502.
18. (1987) 162 CLR 514, 528; affirmed in *Chu Kheng Lim v Minister for Immigration* (1992) 176 CLR 1, 19
19. (1992) 176 CLR 1, 27-28 (Brennan, Deane and Dawson JJ).
20. ABC radio *AM program,* 14 November 2003.

14.4 Judge Weeramantry's Quest Towards One World

Editor's note

Christopher Weeramantry was a Sri Lankan lawyer who held the Sir Hayden Starke Chair of Law in the Monash Law School from 1972 to 1991. He was then appointed a Judge of the International Court of Justice in The Hague. He retired as Vice-President of the Court in 2000. Weeramantry and Brennan knew each other well. They shared a strong commitment to the rule of law but also a strong Christian faith. Weeramantry shared with Brennan the draft of his 1998 book 'The Lord's Prayer: Bridge to a Better World'. In 2010, Weeramantry published the first volume of his memoirs dealing with his years in Sri Lanka – 'Towards One World: The Sri Lankan Years'. In 2011, he published his second volume 'Towards One World: The Australian Years'. He asked Brennan to write the Foreword.

In this memoir of his years in Australia, Judge Weeramantry shares with us the growth and flowering of his interest in what he has described as 'the harmonization of cultures and the multiple advantages flowing from this central concept on which so much of the human future depends'. His earlier memoir of the Sri Lankan years describes his stellar career as student, practitioner and Supreme Court Judge and the earlier years of marriage and family. They were fulfilling years, yet administrative and economic restrictions in Sri Lanka precluded his active participation in international fora. In 1972 a new and liberating opportunity was presented – appointment to a Professorship at Monash University in Melbourne.

It must have taken considerable courage to leave behind the friendships, the security, the status and the familiar social milieu of life in Sri Lanka and to venture a new life for a close-knit family in a new country, a different culture and an unknown social milieu in Australia. The risks were manifest but, fortunately, the risks were minimised by a welcoming reception from Australian relatives and friends, from fellow parishioners and from professional colleagues in the University.

Professor Weeramantry had already established a high academic reputation in 1967 with the publication of *The Law of Contracts*. That book, which was a comparative study of the Roman-Dutch, English and Customary laws relating to contract, had earned the author A Doctor of Laws from the University of London. It was favourably reviewed by distinguished scholars and by scholarly journals. So he entered on his academic career with an acknowledged expertise in fields wider than the common law. He found Monash to be a happy and stimulating place; it hosted some distinguished visitors whose interests corresponded with his own: Lord Denning, Professor

Julius Stone, the Dalai Lama and various judges and practitioners with whom Professor Weeramantry enjoyed the exchange of ideas.

The Monash years gave him opportunities to develop his vision of the law as a normative influence in society not by philosophical reflection alone but by observing, sensitively and insightfully, social phenomena which illustrated the informing values of law. He saw a decline in social standards and social harmony, an alienation of youth, religious apathy and an increasing profile of terrorism at a time when law, which should be 'a prime instrument' to reverse these trends was in crisis. He attributed the crisis to various causes, not least of which was the profession's loss of idealism and its elitism as it served the privileged rather than the marginalized. Drawing on his understanding of different legal systems and a wide range of legal texts, in 1975 he wrote *The Law in Crisis: Bridges of Understanding*. It inspired the establishing of the annual Law Week, first in Victoria and later throughout Australia.

His international standing as a lawyer and sociologist of the law led to a steady flow of invitations to contribute to international conferences and other fora. Governments were able to engage his scholarship and wisdom in the solution of several international problems. This memoir recalls these experiences, not simply as a personal chronicle but as occasions when new insights were gained into law, the values underlying the law and the practical operation of law. What is truly remarkable is Professor Weeramantry's avidity for these insights, the acuity of his observations, their scholarly and humane evaluation and the practicality of the lessons to be derived. The chapters of this memoir are the journal of a vigorous mind addressing issues of fundamental importance to humankind.

In 1976, he was invited to make a presentation to a Conference of the World Association for the Philosophy of Law and Social Philosophy held in St Louis, Missouri. The Conference was part of the celebrations of the bicentenary of the American Declaration of Independence and it was attended by some of the world's foremost legal philosophers. The theme was Equality and Freedom. There were three presentations relating to Equality and Freedom from the perspectives of the Western World, the Communist World and – the Weeramantry presentation – the Third World. Extensive research was called for in the preparation of such an important presentation. The juristic problems of the Third World flowing from centuries of colonialism and empire building became an abiding interest of Professor Weeramantry while his revelation of the Third World's rich tradition and philosophy of equality and freedom broke new ground. He drew attention to Hindu, Buddhist and Islamic thought which the western mindset had not fully appreciated. Professor Weeramantry expanded his presentation into a monograph titled

Equality and Freedom: Some Third World Perspectives. One commentary in *Asiaweek* described the monograph as 'a Magna Carta for the Third World.' The Conference was a seminal event in Professor Weeramantry's career; it identified him as a scholarly authority on the Third World and a jurist of international significance.

Then, in 1979, Professor Weeramantry accepted an invitation to visit Stellenbosch University in South Africa. South Africa and Sri Lanka shared the Roman-Dutch legal system discussed by Professor Weeramantry in his treatise on Contracts. It was the system in which he had practised and which he administered as a Judge of the Sri Lankan Supreme Court. He was a Visiting Professor for a time at Stellenbosch, but he travelled outside Johannesburg and he observed acutely the cruel obscenities of apartheid. To the credit of Stellenbosch, the University raised no objection when Professor Weeramantry spoke against apartheid in the lecture room and, on his return to Australia, he published a book *Apartheid: The Closing Phases?* in which he not only foretold the imminent demise of apartheid but proposed a number of programs to assist in its dismantling. South Africa banned the book but it was twice secretly reprinted there. Its production was hailed for its research and insights.

Professor Weeramantry's belief in the unity of the human family was strengthened by a growing recognition of human rights, on which his brother Lucian had worked in the International Commission of Jurists. Professor Weeramantry succeeded in establishing the study of human rights at Monash – not as a mere construct of legal philosophy but as a subject relevant to the content of law. In 1979, when he had a fellowship for research at the University of Tokyo he was impressed by the availability of Civil Liberties Commissioners in every city, town and village who achieve informal resolution of disputes and are able to give practical effect to human rights in a society that is oriented more to community obligation than to individual rights. In 1983, he wrote The *Slumbering Sentinels: Law and Human Rights in the Wake of Technology.* This examination of the relationship between technological advances and the protection of human rights was referred to by United Nations Secretary General, Boutros Boutros Ghali to support his recommendation that science, technology and human rights should be included in the agenda of the World Conference on Human Rights. *Slumbering Sentinels* was followed by Professor Weeramantry's co-ordination of a group of experts based at the United Nations University in Tokyo who produced extensive studies on technology and human rights. Then, addressing the role of scientists in the development of nuclear weapons, he proposed an ethical code for scientists in *Nuclear Weapons and Scientific Responsibility.*

The multi-cultural legal system of Sri Lanka was a natural foundation of Professor Weeramantry's interest in comparative law. He was familiar with Roman, Roman-Dutch, English and Islamic law and with the customary laws of Sri Lanka. He acquired an interest in the laws of Australia's indigenous peoples. As he visited Papua New Guinea, New Zealand, Nauru, Fiji and Lesotho in the course of a busy round of professional engagements, he took the opportunity to study the customary laws of those nations. Appreciating the wisdom that inheres in different legal systems, he laments the monocultural framework of much legal education.

Having written on Islamic jurisprudence, he was challenged to write on the values of Christianity, his own religion. He found in the Lord's Prayer 'the basic principles of human conduct appropriate for the new millennium about to dawn... a complete code of social conduct.' The universality of God's fatherhood proclaimed the unity of all humanity and the values expressed in Jesus' prayer showed us how we all might live in peace and friendship. Professor Weeramantry's multicultural background encouraged him to examine the values which other religions might contribute to legal thinking. The examination revealed a rich lode of wisdom in Hinduism, Buddhism, Judaism, Confucianism, Zoroastrianism, Jainism and the Baha'i Faith. Amongst other values, there is a powerful consensus of caring for the environment.

His broad legal interests led not only to academic invitations but also to advisory roles for overseas governments. In 1984, he joined a group of jurists to advise the King of Lesotho to retain the system of Roman-Dutch law in force in the Kingdom. In 1987, he was invited to chair the *Commission of Inquiry into the Worked Out Phosphate Lands of Nauru* – a task which involved considerations of international affairs and international law. His expertise in comparative law, human rights and international law made him eminently suited to the task. The work of the Commission was a precursor to his later work on the International Court.

Professor Weeramantry's Australian years did not diminish his interest in, and affection for, Sri Lanka. He published *A Call for National Reawakening* in 2005 and he ends this part of his memoir with an impassioned plea for peace and national unity in that nation, based on human rights. The Australian years end with Professor Weeramantry's election as a Judge of the International Court of Justice in 1991 and his subsequent election as Vice President of that Court. The memoir traces in part the experiences and the research which endowed him with the ability to discharge his judicial functions as an outstanding jurist. The next part of his memoir will cover the author's transition from Professor to Judge of the International Court of Justice. Judge

Weeramantry served his terms of office on that Court with such distinction that the City of The Hague named him as the person representing the City's pre-eminence in the field of international justice.

This volume is an attractive memoir, not only because it charts the formative experiences of a fine judge. Some memoirs are attractive because they are felicitously written, some because the author is a figure of note or notoriety, some because the reader has had a similar experience. But in this memoir, the reader is allowed to share a distinguished author's participation in the development of concepts that affect the future of humankind. Judge Weeramantry's faith in the normative influence of law is founded on a thesis that law gives expression to the deepest aspirations shared by peoples of every race and age, aspirations that are common to all the world's great religions and cultures, aspirations that invest each individual with dignity and demand respect for the world in which we live. The memoir not only describes Judge Weeramantry's part in identifying these aspirations and the role they should play in the formation of the law but also describes social institutions and forces that might be features of civilisation in the Third Millenium.

Australia is not Judge Weeramantry's country of origin but it has been honoured by his adoption of it as an alternative home. He was appointed as a member of the Order of Australia for his services to the law but his service is truly to the whole human family.

14.5 A Reflection on The Tokyo War Crimes Trials

Editor's note

Brennan's father died on 6 August 1949. Brennan was 21 years old. He was a university student at the time but he needed to find employment. He became associate to Mr Justice Kenneth Townley on the Supreme Court of Queensland. In 1950, Townley was appointed to conduct the Australian War Crimes Trials of Japanese soldiers held on Los Negros Island in Papua New Guinea. Spending six months as clerk to Townley in PNG, Brennan was in court one day when the death penalty was imposed on one of the five Japanese sentenced to death. This event had a profound influence on Brennan. He remained a strong opponent of the death penalty. A precondition of his sitting on foreign courts after his retirement from the High Court of Australia was that he would not sit on death penalty cases. It was only late in life that Brennan spoke about his experience at the War Crimes Trials. He participated in a conference with Australian and Japanese participants convened by Professors Yuki Tanaka, Tim McCormack and Jerry Simpson who then invited him to write the Foreword to their 2011 book 'Beyond Victors Justice? The Tokyo War Crimes Trial Revisited'.[1]

This book submits the Tokyo War Crimes trial, an historic and emotionally charged event, to the dispassionate analysis of scholars drawn from nations engaged on either side of the war in the Pacific. It demonstrates the capacity of the human intellect, cultured in an academic environment, to surmount the barriers of historical antipathies, to shed light on some issues hitherto darkened by preconceptions and to kindle friendship and respect for former adversaries.

The international community now generally accepts that trials for crimes alleged to have been committed in armed conflict between nations should be held before tribunals created by international resolution, not by edict of the victor nations. But that was not the established view at the end of the Second World War. However, the trials then held by the victor nations, seeking to demonstrate an international legitimacy, played a significant role in developing the substantive law and the procedures of contemporary international law and practice. The Tokyo trial has not had the same influence as the Nuremberg trial but this book provides a critical analysis which will allow a more informed assessment of its significance.

Although I knew some of the Australian personnel taking part in the Tokyo trial, I was too young to be present at any of its sessions. But I had a minor role to play in a series of trials conducted by Australians under Australian legislation.

In 1950, at the age of 22, I spent six months as the Clerk of Court during the last of the Australian War Crimes Trials conducted on Los Negros Island, a small island separated from the larger Manus Island by a narrow strip of water. It was then an Australian Territory, two degrees south of the equator. I went to Los Negros as Associate to Mr Justice Townley, an outstanding judge of the Supreme Court of Queensland. Americans would say that I was the Judge's Clerk. Townley had been appointed to preside over the trials and, as they were to follow the form of a military Field General Court Martial, he was elevated to the rank of Brigadier. Most of the other members of the Court had the rank of Major. None, so far as I know, had legal qualifications. The Chief Prosecutor was Mr C V Rooney, KC, Chief Crown Prosecutor in New South Wales. He was a colourful Irish expatriate, who wore a monocle which would drop from his eye as he affected surprise at any answer which did not appeal to him. Micky, as he was affectionately known, developed asthma for the first time in his life shortly after arriving on Los Negros and had to be repatriated to Sydney early in the proceedings. The other prosecutors were Army Officers whose abilities were variable.

The accused persons, all of whom were kept in custody in a compound near the naval station on Manus Island, were represented by four Japanese counsel – Messrs Nakayama Choji, Kamimura Yunosuki, Takano Junigiro and Sakai Yusuke. But these counsel were not familiar with the law and procedure of a criminal trial in a common law jurisdiction.[2] To assist them in their difficult task, a Sydney barrister, Major George Dickenson, was assigned as their consultant.

The Court was constituted under the *War Crimes Act 1945* (Cth) to try charges of violation of the laws and usages of war and 'war crimes' as defined by a wartime instrument which had appointed a Board (including Sir William Webb) to investigate such crimes. No challenge to the jurisdiction or the constitution of the Court was permissible under the Act. The Court assembled each day in a large Quonset hut, open on either side to allow ventilation in the tropical climate, constructed on a concrete base without floorboards. Behind the bench, was a retiring room for the members of the Court. Facing the bench, the defence table was immediately in front of the dock in which the accused sat, guarded by a member of the Papua New Guinea constabulary armed with a submachine gun. Occasionally, during the hot afternoons, a policeman would nod off to sleep and the gun would clatter on the concrete floor to the consternation of everyone, but the safety catch must have been firmly on as no bullets were ever discharged.

I found some aspects of the Los Negros trials disturbing. I was familiar with the Queensland practice that a judge who was presiding at a criminal trial would not meet with counsel for either the prosecution or the defence in the absence of counsel for the other side. But in Los Negros, all members of the First Australian War Crimes Section – both members of the Court and the prosecutors – were members of the same Army mess. I was the secretary who had to keep the accounts! The Japanese counsel, their interpreters and their support staff were accommodated in a compound nearby and there was no social communication between them and the members of the Army mess.

Of course, George Dickenson, who was a member of the Army mess, had unrestricted access to the Japanese compound. He followed the best traditions of the Australian Bar. He was continually researching points that might be of assistance, even going so far as to enquire of me, a mere undergraduate, whether I had any text with me that might be relevant to his research. He accompanied the defence counsel as they interviewed their respective clients and was always available when called upon. I admired him enormously and, in later years, when he became a somewhat idiosyncratic solicitor for the Darwin City Council, we would meet and reminisce on the Los Negros trials. George visited Japan in later years, being feted by the counsel he had assisted. George and, I believe, counsel for the defence, had a high regard for the President, Townley. George commented in an article published in the *Australian Quarterly* in 1952: 'It was a good thing for Australia that the War Crimes Court at Manus had as its president an able and experienced lawyer and Supreme Court Judge, and it was indeed fortunate that he was assisted by a bench of fair-minded officers, all with battle experience in the Second World War. However, a great mass of evidence had to be sifted by the President and the real evidence and facts put in their proper order before the lay members of the Court, despite s 9 (1) of the *War Crimes Act*.'[3]

Section 9(1) was a radical departure from the ordinary rules of evidence. It provided:

> At any hearing before a military court the court may take into consideration any oral statement or any document appearing on the face of it to be authentic, provided the statement or document appears to the court to be of assistance in proving or disproving the charge, notwithstanding that the statement or document would not be admissible in evidence before a field general court martial.

Thus, it was unnecessary for any eye witness of an event to give oral testimony or to be cross-examined. In practice, the prosecution case consisted of affidavits that had been obtained either from witnesses to the events charged or from investigators deposing to confessional statements made by an accused. These documents were in English. If the witness or an accused spoke Japanese, his statement had been translated into English, recorded and retranslated back to him before the document was signed. There was little that the defence could do to challenge affidavits or statements tendered by the prosecution.

If the prosecution documents established a case calling for an answer, the accused person usually – it may have been invariably – entered the witness box. Frequently, superior orders were raised as a defence rather than a denial of the crime alleged. Dickenson observed that the defence could prevail only if the order was not 'obviously unlawful', but that criterion was 'a difficult matter for a Japanese fisherman or peasant trained to obedience by the Imperial Rescript.' When 'superior orders' were raised, General Imamura Hitoshi, former General Officer Commanding 21 Army Group, a short, stocky but extremely impressive officer, was summoned from his gaol on Manus Island to give evidence of the strict penalties that awaited any Japanese soldier who did not immediately carry out the instructions of a superior officer. General Imamura had been commandant of the Japanese Staff College and had served with the North Lancashire Regiment in the First World War. He bore himself with great dignity and his authority was not diminished in the least by the orange fatigues which were prison issue.

The Los Negros trials lasted nearly a year – from 1 June 1950 to May 1951. They followed one another in an orderly manner, interrupted sometimes by the rain squalls that hammered the roof of the Quonset hut in the early afternoon. There was another interruption on the first Tuesday in November. My Judge instructed me to approach Mr Nakayama to enquire whether he would be agreeable to an early adjournment that day so that the Australians could listen to a shortwave broadcast of a notable Australian sporting event. 'What is it?' enquired Mr Nakayama. 'The running of the Melbourne Cup' I replied. 'Of course,' said Mr Nakayama, 'what is the favourite? Can I get a bet?' Sadly, the tentacles of the off-course bookmakers which had spread everywhere in Australia, had not reached the tropic islands.

During the Court's sittings, 92 accused persons were charged in 26 trials. 36 were acquitted, some of whom had been charged with more than one offence. Five were condemned to death.[4] There was one dramatic trial which later featured in three books,[5] one of which[6] was reported as alleging that the trial was rigged and vengeful. It was the trial of Lieutenant General Nishimura, Commander of the Konoye Division of the Imperial Guards charged with ordering the execution of 140 Australian and Indian prisoners of war many of whom were wounded. They had been captured after a fierce battle at Parit Sulong as the Japanese forces advanced down the Malayan Peninsula. They were bound, shot and burnt with gasoline. One of the prisoners escaped to tell of the massacre. The General had given the order 'shobun seyo'. The affidavits by three of General Nishimura's staff officers produced by the prosecution and a confessional statement by his co-accused, Lieutenant Nonaka, said Nishimura had thereby ordered the execution of the POWs. The staff officers confirmed Nishimura's order in further affidavits produced by the defence. These documents had been translated from Japanese into English. Nishimura said that 'shobun seyo' was intended to mean, and meant, that the POWs should be 'disposed of' by being taken to a camp at General Yamashita's headquarters, a 'long distance' in the rear of the advancing troops.

After General Nishimura's examination by Mr Nakayama and cross-examination by Mr Rooney, the Court asked whether there was any transport available to take the prisoners to General Yamashita's headquarters. Neither the unit guarding the prisoners nor divisional headquarters had transport available. General Nishimura gave an explanation as to how transport might have been found but the Court had ample evidence to reject that explanation as fallacious. So it is not surprising that the Court rejected the innocent meaning of the order 'shobun seyo'.

General Nishimura was convicted and sentenced to hang. This was the first time that I had heard the passing of a death sentence. It was appalling, and I sensed that the members of the Court, who were conscientious and experienced soldiers, were distressed by the duty they believed they were bound to perform.

There are, no doubt, many lessons that can be drawn from War Crimes Trials. They do answer the deep-seated cry for retribution that moves victims of war crimes and their loved ones to demand condign punishment for the perpetrators of the crimes. They can affirm the continuing validity and operation of the international laws of war – laws that are not suspended by the outbreak of hostilities. Properly conducted, war crimes trials can be powerful examples of judicial impartiality and the rule of law. But they should not be the revenge of the victors. If international law is to be universally applied, if condign punishment is to be justly imposed on offenders irrespective of their national allegiance and if the rule of law is to be truly vindicated and judicial impartiality practised, the jurisdiction to try a prisoner for a crime against the laws of war should be exercised by an International Tribunal rather than by a national tribunal. In that way the International Criminal Tribunals for the former Yugoslavia and Rwanda, dealing with serious crimes committed in the course of armed conflict, have acquired the moral authority to exercise their awesome jurisdiction. The post-war Tribunals conducted by individual victor nations did not, I fear, acquire the same moral authority in the international community.

Looking back after 60 years, I am saddened to think that I did not have an opportunity of closer social contact with the younger members of the Japanese team at Los Negros. Sitting opposite me during those months was a young Japanese interpreter – one of six interpreters whose names I had forgotten until I saw them listed recently.[7] What I have not forgotten was his unfailing courtesy. Suwabe Michiomi (I think that was his name) and I became friends and, as young people did in the post-war years, we talked about our beliefs and ambitions and the world of the future. Had we been able to socialize together, we might have gone fishing together in Seeadler Harbour, taking care to avoid the crocodiles and the fishermen from the Naval base who caught their fish with a stick of dynamite; we might have gone together over the mountain to the markets at Lorengau accompanying the local missioner, Father Patrick, who charged his jeep with 100 octane petrol from the fuel dumps left behind by the US Airforce in the jungle of Manus; we might have practised our Pidgin English, each with his accent of origin. Each of us would have been left with a sad appreciation of the high emotions generated in the cauldron of battle which have driven soldiers to commit terrible deeds. But we might also have understood better the cultures of our countries, the old and the young, the Oriental and the Occidental, the communal orientation and the radically individualistic, the formal and the informal. Nevertheless, the experience I had was sufficient to ensure that I would never believe the racial antipathy that had been a feature of wartime propaganda, but rather acknowledge that we are all members of the human family – the human family with its capacity for good and for evil, certainly for violence and cruelty, but also for loyalty and devotion, for honour and respect, for the love of family and of friends and for the joy of laughter. That is the grandeur of the human soul. And we are all blessed to possess it.

---

1 Yuki Tanaka, Tim McCormack and Jerry Simpson (eds) *Beyond Victors Justice? The Tokyo War Crimes Trial Revisited* (Martinus Nijhoff, 2011). Brennan's foreword is at xi-xv.

2 Section 10 of the 1945 Act adopted with qualifications the Imperial Army Act and the Rules of Procedure made thereunder.

3 George Dickenson, 'Japanese War Trials (1952) 24 (2) *Australian Quarterly*, 69.

4 Particulars can be found in Dickenson's article 'Manus Island War Crimes Trials' (1952) 38 (2) *Journal of the Royal Australian Historical Society* 66-77.

5 Ian Ward, *Snaring the Tiger* (Media Masters, 1996); Gilbert Mant, *Massacre at Parit Sulong* (Kangaroo Press, 1995); Lynette Ramsay Silver "*Bridge at Parit Sulong*" (Watermark Press, 2004).

6 Ibid.

7 See George Dickenson 'Manus Island War Crimes Trials' (1952) 38 (2) *Journal of the Royal Australian Historical Society* 66-77.

Chapter 15

Tributes to Gerard Brennan

15.1 Eulogy - Sir William Deane AC KBE KC

Editor's Note

Brennan died on 1 June 2022, two days prior to the 30th anniversary of the Mabo decision. At his funeral at St Mary's Church, North Sydney, on 17 June 2022, Sir William Deane, his long-time friend and colleague from their days on the Federal Court and on the High Court, delivered the eulogy after William Barton played the didgeridoo. Brennan's daughter, Madeline KC, delivered a family tribute (see [15.3]), and the Editor delivered the homily ([15.2]).

I always hate speaking after William Barton. William says it all. Thank you.

By any measure, Francis Gerard Brennan – 'Sir Gerard', 'Gerry', 'Ged'- was and remains one of the truly pre-eminent Australians of his or any generation: a leading Queen's Counsel at both national and international levels; President of the Australian Bar Association; an inaugural member of the Federal Court of Australia; the first President of the Australian Administrative Appeals Tribunal; Chair of the Council of the Order of Australia; a Justice and then the Chief Justice of the High Court of Australia; and, after his retirement from the High Court, a Judge of Hong Kong's Court of Final Appeal and of Fiji's highest Court, Chancellor of the Sydney University of Technology and the Foundation Scientia Professor of Law of the University of New South Wales.

Many public honours and decorations appropriately acknowledged those achievements: Knight of the British Empire; Companion of the Order Of Australia; Honorary Doctor of Laws, Doctor of the University or Doctor of Letters from an extraordinary number of Universities, including the University of Dublin; and, to add a touch of the exotic, the very high award of Gold Bauhinia Star in the Honours System of Hong Kong.

Those achievements and honours are important in themselves. They also reflect Sir Gerard's great abilities, qualities and character. Each of us who knew him well has his or her personal memories, impressions and assessments. All I can do today is share some of mine as one who was privileged not only to know him as an admired colleague on the Federal and High Courts but to call him a very close friend for upwards of 45 years.

On two things at least, those who knew him well will be agreed.

The first is that the citadel of his life was his family. In the forefront, of course, his late wife Pat - Dr Patricia - who subordinated her own career as a medical practitioner to be the mother of their seven children and Ged's counsellor, supporter and beloved companion throughout the more than 65 years of their wonderful partnership.

The second thing, which I specifically mention in this setting, was the importance to him of his religion. While advancing years and events have led many of us to falter, he remained steadfast in his core beliefs, particularly in his love of the Mass. At the same time, his natural humility and generosity ensured that he was always deeply respectful, indeed protective, of the beliefs and convictions of others.

Putting to one side the strength and scope of his intellect and knowledge and his irrepressible sense of the ridiculous, for me the most important of Ged's qualities was that he cared so profoundly. Not only about Pat, their family and many friends. But about people and things generally, particularly injustice and those in need.

Tracing back at least to his work at the Bar as Senior Counsel for the Northern Land Council, he had a deep knowledge and awareness of Australia's Indigenous peoples, their past treatment and their continuing disadvantage. It is truly fitting that, in recent days, so much has been written about how his judgment in *Mabo* effectively became the judgment of the Full High Court of Australia and will always represent a major step along the road to true reconciliation.

The last period of Ged's life, with serious health challenges and under the necessary constraints of Covid in an aged care facility, was a difficult one. But even in those days of personal difficulty, he retained his sense of humour. And his deep concern for those suffering injustice or disadvantage seemed to me to be even more strongly in the forefront of his being.

Thus, as is well known, his last real intervention in public affairs was twelve months ago to protest about the plight of a family of asylum seekers. But the impact of what he said is not, and was not intended by him to be, confined to that one family. His love of country, his decency, his convictions and his sheer goodness shine through his words and I can do no better than conclude these inadequate comments by quoting some of them. 'How can Australia', he wrote in a letter to major newspapers, 'proud of our freedoms, respectful of all our peoples, and insistent on human dignity, inflict cruelty on Australian children as a means of achieving a goal of government policy?' '(P)roud of our freedoms', 'respectful of all our peoples', 'insistent on human dignity' … that is the voice of Sir Gerard Brennan; add 'love of family and friends' and 'concern for the vulnerable and disadvantaged' and you have the man himself.

Ged has left us. But his spirit and his influence remain. Through his judgments, his writings, his achievements and his example. In his children, his grandchildren and great grandchildren. And with all of us who were privileged to know him … for as long as we remember.

May he rest in peace.

15.2 Homily – Frank Brennan SJ

Gerard Brennan was humble, unfailingly courteous, generous and charitable. He was also ambitious for the higher gifts, with a relentless ethic of work and duty garnished with an Irish sense of humour.

He once offered me a lift in his Commonwealth car to the annual reception at the papal nunciature in Canberra. On arrival, we alighted at the main entrance. The nuncio greeted us with the words: 'You two. You are related. I did not know.' Dad responded courteously in the affirmative. We made our way down the red carpet. Dad turned to me with a glint in his eye and said, 'I think we both just went down in his estimation.'

Gerard and Patricia lived in a very quiet *cul de sac* on the edge of Canberra. Each work day, the Commonwealth car would be there to take him to the High Court with a wonderful view of the Brindabella mountains *en route*. One weekend, Dad was working in the garden. A little girl approached and asked, 'This is the judge's house, isn't it?' Dad answered, 'Yes'. She further inquired, 'Are you the judge's gardener?' He answered, 'Yes.' The little girl went off, well satisfied at having met the judge's gardener. Dad was even more content, being taken to be the judge's gardener, for indeed he was.

I was at home one Christmas Eve. He returned from delivering the Vinnies Christmas hampers to families in need. On one call, he was given the wrong address. A very smartly dressed woman in party mode came to the door and said, 'Hello darling. What are you doing? Selling mushrooms?' I told Dad he should have answered that he was a High Court judge doing his Vincent de Paul rounds. But he would never do that.

One day, at the High Court, he was escorting me in the lift up to his chambers. A new attendant having no idea who he was said, 'You can't go up there. This area is prohibited to members of the public.' A little nonplussed, Dad simply answered, 'But I work here.'

After his retirement, his daughter, Bernadette took him to the Gama festival in Arnhem Land. He was chuffed to enter a tent which had on display various judicial quotes including from his *Mabo* judgment. He stood there feeling quite pleased with himself. For once he let down his humble public reserve. He turned to the young people beside him and said, 'I wrote that.' They looked on in utter disbelief.

Fifty years ago, way back in 1971, he was Vice President of the Queensland Bar during troubling times with a state of emergency being declared by the Bjelke-Petersen government during the all-white Springbok Rugby tour. He published this letter in the national newspaper:

> The contemporary discussion of law and order has been overlaid with other issues: apartheid and football (as to which there is little disagreement), politics and protest (as to which there will always be disagreement).
>
> The fact remains that law and order are essential to a civilised community.
>
> Law binds both the ruler and the ruled. The ruler who contemns the law can scarcely insist upon its observance by the ruled.
>
> Each must obey the law in the appropriate way – the ruler, by exercising no more power than the law gives him, and by exercising that power honestly and fairly and with statesmanship; the ruled, by refraining from deliberate infringements of the laws properly enforced by the rulers.
>
> Law and order are bilateral – if either side rejects law and order the other side is encouraged to do the same. The moral obligation of obedience is diminished.
>
> When legitimate protest degenerates into unlawful disruption, governments are invited to assume powers of doubtful legality, and to condone unlawful actions by police. When governments do not exercise their powers honestly and fairly and with statesmanship, they invite disruptive expressions of protest.
>
> In either case both the rulers and the ruled attack the concept of law and order. Is it not time for both to examine their consciences?[1]

That night he came home and told Mum and me that he had been confronted by one of the doyens of the Queensland Bar at lunch who told him: 'That's it, Brennan. Now you'll never be a judge.' He matter of factly said to us: 'Well so be it.' But that wasn't it at all. Within a decade he was a Justice of the High Court of Australia.

You don't get to be President of the National Union of Australian University Students, President of the Australian Bar Association, and Chief Justice of Australia just by being in the right place at the right time, causing offence to none, being unfailingly courteous and humble. When he became a High Court judge, his beloved clerical cousin, Grove Johnson presented him with a bible inscribed: '*Salus animorum suprema lex* (The salvation of the soul is the supreme law) – when the lawyer perceives this truth with perfect clarity, embraces it with total surrender and applies it with impeccable professional skill, holiness and genius have met. I can wish you no greater success, Grove.'

Gerard Brennan brought true justice to the nation without crying out or shouting aloud, and without breaking the crushed reed, nor quenching the wavering flame. When taking his Oath of Allegiance and Office as Chief Justice he said, 'Allegiance to a young, free and confident nation, governed by the rule of law, is not a burden but a privilege'.[2] Reflecting on the promise to 'do right to all manner of people according to law without fear or favour, affection of ill-will', he said, 'In appellate courts, the law may authorise a tension between abstract justice and a rule of law to be resolved by an alteration of the rule….If the right is to be done according to law, right will be done only if the law be just.'

Famously in his *Mabo* judgment, he observed that 'no case can command unquestioning adherence if the rule it expresses seriously offends the values of justice and human rights (especially equality before the law) which are aspirations of the contemporary Australian legal system.'[3] And in his dissent in *Marion's case*, he said: 'The law will protect equally the dignity of the hale and hearty and the dignity of the weak and lame; of the frail baby and of the frail aged; of the intellectually able and of the intellectually disabled. …Our law admits of no discrimination against the weak and disadvantaged in their human dignity.'[4]

The law, family, and the nation were Dad's abiding concerns as a person of resolute Christian faith in the Catholic tradition. He constantly prayed 'before the Father, from whom every family, whether spiritual or natural, takes its name that each of us would be planted in love and built on love, being filled with the utter fulness of God.' Since Mum's death, he spent much of his time in the St Vincent's nursing home at Bronte enduring Covid lockdowns, not knowing whether family could be present in his final days. Mercifully the lockdowns passed. Dad took the opportunity during the lockdowns, with his very identifiable copper plate script, to pen a letter to his family speaking of the 'fundamental love that we have all had one for another' which was 'due chiefly to the unselfish love that Mum gave each of us.' He confessed, 'Sometimes I was too preoccupied with professional ambition and I ask your forgiveness. I hope that some of the things I achieved were of value to you.' He concluded with this benediction: 'God bless you all, give you a faith that informs your hope and inspires your love. May you have good health, the support of family and friends and the satisfaction of contributing to a free and confident nation.' His entire public life was dedicated to that free and confident nation – a phrase which he took from the great Justice Reg Smithers when Dad first became a judge.

As death approached, Dad's simple faith sustained him. On the morning of the day he died, I asked him what words he had for the congregation at mass in the nursing home. He smiled and repeated: 'Happy days are here again. Happy days are here again.' The congregation loved the message. After mass he received the smallest particle of the communion wafer with great delight. I told him quite firmly: 'Go in peace'. He smiled. I then bid farewell and as I reached the door, he called out 'Goodbye'. That was the last word he ever uttered. For him, Jesus always was the way, the truth and the life.

The family joke was that he wanted to spend his birthday with us on May 22 and his wedding anniversary with his darling Patricia on May 26. He lingered another five days. We had visions of the two lovers meeting at the pearly gates and Mum declaring, 'Ged, once again you're late for our anniversary.' May they enjoy eternal peace and rest together in Our Father's house of many rooms where holiness and genius always meet. May he rest in peace. Amen.

---

1. Letter to the editor, *The Australian* (2 August 1971).
2. Brennan CJ, reply, at swearing in as Chief Justice, (1994-5) 183 CLR x.
3. See *Mabo* v *Queensland (No 2) (Mabo Case)* (1992) 175 CLR 1, 30.
4. See *Department of Health and Community services* v *JWB and SMB (Marion's Case)* (1992) 175 CLR 218, 266.

\

15.3 A Family Tribute – Madeline Brennan KC

On behalf of our family, Tom has welcomed all of you present here today in person and by live stream. We have all shared in Dad's life in various way. I now have the privilege of offering a family tribute to our loyal and loving father.

Thank you, Senator Dodson, for your acknowledgement of country and tribute to a 'true boss'. Dad cherished the lessons and honours afforded him by indigenous elders who demonstrated to him the long-lived experience of the coherence of place, body and spirit.

Senator Dodson, our gratitude for your acknowledgment takes on a further personal dimension. Dad's great grandmother, on the Brennan side, as a widowed mother with five children, migrated from Ireland in 1863 on the second of the imperial boats to arrive off the shores of Maryborough. It anchored off the coast, not knowing where to disembark. Two of the crew rowed to shore. They found two members of the Butchelor nation who walked 40 km to Maryborough to raise the alert, whereupon a pilot boat was dispatched and, two days later, the *David McIvor* and her 414 passengers were brought to safety. We remain indebted for that early and critical welcome of our ancestral offshore arrival.

Dad was a man of quiet dignity. He lived a reflective life, true to his values. His values were Gospel values. In Dad's life, the imperatives that, *seemed to me*, to have most informed his being were: to act justly, to love tenderly and to walk humbly with his God in the service of others. He expressed these values in his public life of service, and in his private life as a family man.

To Act Justly

Justice was at the core of Dad's being. It was not law, but the imperatives of justice that guided his reflection. As Senator Dodson has told us he committed his professional life to working the tension between law and justice. In his private life, it was manifest in his interest in, and civility to all, and in his commitment to the more vulnerable, particularly through active participation in the St Vincent de Paul Society.

Dad valued independence of thought. He preferred a lonely road with freedom, lived according to principle, to the pursuit of success or accolades that required any sacrifice of independence. Our parents encouraged each of us to find our own pathways, to be independent, and to live with integrity and purpose. They gave us a strong framework for discerning the meaning of our own lives and relationships, always knowing there was a safe harbour of home.

Dad was committed to the pursuit of excellence. He spoke of the 'artisan judges' who developed the common law. He knew that the daily workings of a lawyer may not be glamorous and that a rigorous attendance to the law, mindful of one's underlying purpose, played a pivotal role in creating and preserving fair and good ways of life in our society. Our most treasured moments were in the day to day of family life: Dad's waiting on the curb for your tram to leave; meeting and becoming friends with his colleagues; waving to tell him you were the child he could not account for in the surf; the quiet hour on the Noosa River, Lake Conjola or the Forster lakes. But he also encouraged each of us to be artisans of the trade of our choosing. And he was so proud when, in that calling, we faced the challenges of life with reflection, purpose and resilience.

At an early age, Dad was introduced to the law by his father, the Central judge of the Supreme Court of Queensland, on whose shoulders he came to stand with great love and confidence.

Dad loved his time at the bar, his professional home. He considered himself fortunate indeed to work with so many colleagues of remarkable character and humanity.

Sir William Deane, thank you for the honour you have afforded Dad and all of us today with the sheer beauty of your eulogy and tributes to him. We are truly grateful.

Dad had such fond recollections of his days and relationships on the High Court, such stories invariably ending with: 'Oh it was such fun. I enjoyed every minute of it.' On his valedictory, he expressed his gratitude:

> It has been a privilege to be engaged with and stimulated by colleagues, past and present. It is a privilege impossible to convey in words for it is based in the acknowledged integrity and industry of colleagues whose work is done in the privacy of their chambers and in the isolation of each judicial conscience…

Dad's commitment to his judicial oath and to the need for independence was resolute. Privately, it meant that he was diligently restrained in conversations that could potentially encroach on judicial decision making and cautious in expressing views on public matters. He remained so even in retirement. Frank tells the story of when he attended St Vincent's Bronte, the aged care home where Dad lived since the end of 2019. Another resident pressed Dad to express a view on ICAC's treatment of the former premier.

Frank jokes that no conversation could have been more off the record than this one. Ever resolute, Dad offered no view.

There were some reasoned exceptions. We have heard from Sir William of Dad's public expressions on our country's treatment of the 'Biloela' family. Another was crafting, as recently as January 2022, the forward to the book, *"Keeping them Honest"*, by Stephen Charles and Catherine Williams. On 22 May 2022, our father celebrated his 94th birthday with his family. His physical energy was depleted, but in his waking moments he spoke with elation of the news that the Nadesalingam family would be returning to Biloela and that there would be a Federal integrity body. His innate sense of justice remained acute, even when his body was failing him.

To Walk Humbly

Dad travelled life with humility. His approach to judicial respons-ibilities reflected that character. Bret Walker SC described Dad's Court:

> There was a firmness which is valued by everyone, particularly in the course of the contest. But, there was a humility, a courtesy, a gentleness, a sparing of those who needed help.

On the night before Dad's valedictory in 1998, the family and some close friends gathered for a mass of thanksgiving and celebratory dinner. Retirement, with the health and opportunity for international travel seemed, to many of us, a wonderful alternative to the unrelenting workload of the High Court and its associated isolation for Mum. At the mass, the grandchildren were asked to express prayers of the faithful. Grandson Michael at the age of seven, concerned that grandad had lost his job, prayed that he could find a new one.

How prescient he was. Dad had a long, active and productive life after retirement. One 'new job' was as a non-permanent judge on the Court of Final Appeal in Hong Kong. At the Court, there was a gentleman whose job was to deliver tea to the judges. He spoke no English and Dad spoke no Mandarin or Cantonese; but Dad, ever eloquent, did not need language to communicate respect for his fellow traveller. Dad was in Hong Kong in 2008 when he received news that beloved grandson, Michael had been tragically killed. On that day, the gentleman brought the tea cart into Dad's chambers. Seeing Dad, he did not say a word but simply held him in a long embrace. Dad gifted, but also received so many more gifts in return from his life of commitment and humility.

And he Loved Tenderly

A Rockhampton boy, dad had a glorious childhood. The second, but first surviving, son of the Honourable Frank Tenison and Gertrude Brennan, he was the eldest of three children. Dad's was a close and loving family, each member showing a profound concern for the welfare of the others.

His beloved sister, Anne, was a nurse and social worker. His sister, Mary, with whom he shared a love of literature, theology and philosophy, became an RSCJ sister, Provincial of the order and principal of Sancta Sophia College at the University of Sydney.

Another member of Dad's birth family was Cousin, Grove. He came to live with the family as the Great Depression took hold of regional Queensland. He was more an older brother. He trained for the priesthood in Rome during Mussolini's reign, and brought back to the young Gerard, an exuberant view of a bigger world, a mastery of the romantic languages, and a knowledge of European art and opera.

Dad heeded well the example of his father and Grove in travelling 'to meet new faces'. Happy memories of travels shared with him abound, often with an evening glass of red with a fine meal and good conversation.

Dad was educated by the Christian Brothers in Rockhampton; and infused with the charism of the MSCs of Downlands, Toowoomba. One of Dad's classmates at Downlands was a Frank O'Hara. It was known that he had a very good looking and very bright sister, Patricia O'Hara.

Mum

In 1946, Gerard and Patricia met at Queensland University in the throng of the Newman society and student politics. All who knew Dad, know of his unyielding devotion to his wife and to his family.

As our sister, Anne beautifully stated in her eulogy for Mum, Mum 'was the wind beneath my father's wings and his career.'

Dad was her rock and companion. They shared a deep faith and joint purposes in life.

Dad deferred to Mum, and was in awe of her in managing, as truly wonderful and considered parents do, the various needs and wants of the family.

Dad had a keen awareness that his combined professional success and the demands of family life came at the cost of limiting Mum's opportunities to develop her gifts as an accomplished doctor. He carried a responsibility to make the most of the opportunities that Mum gifted him. Theirs was a vibrant exchange on the finer points of morality, including medico legal principles and bioethical issues which arose through various committees, in which one or the other had an interest. Dad recounted that it was only after deep conversations with Mum that he could get right his thinking on the principles invoked, though not their application, in *Marion's Case*, one of his proudest judgments. Sir Anthony Mason, though of a different view from my father as to the outcome of that case has observed that the Brennan judgment 'contains the best exposition in Australian law of the common law right to integrity of the person.'

In a love letter in 2003, Dad wrote Mum:

> You bore our children and bestowed on them not only intelligence but the values to guide their use of it. That was because of your deep and simple faith. We have been wonderfully blessed, nowhere more clearly than when Frank celebrated the Eucharist today.

How right he was then. And how grateful and proud he would be of you, Frank, today. Frank, thank you for the abundant blessings you have bestowed on family. Thank you for the blessings bestowed on all of us today through your careful and reflective preparation of today's liturgy in celebration of Dad's love and his life; and in such difficult circumstances for you.

Our parents' tender love for each other was the cradle of a vibrant family life whose flame has carried through the generations.

The current O'Hara-Brennan family includes 21 grandchildren and 22 and three quarters great grandchildren.

As a granddad or DiDi, as he is known to some, Dad knew how to be engaged in the moment, asking: 'so tell me, what is your news?' With love, he might challenge the grandkids, like he challenged their parents, in a Socratic dialogue. In the last weeks, the procedural rules were abridged: 'tell me in five minutes, what is your news?' And there was no challenge; just gratitude and joy as you will hear from Bernadette's and Margaret's children, Madeline and Cameron.

Dad was a happy and loving great-grandfather. He delighted in remembering every great-grandchild's birthday. As great-grandson, Patrick noted on the receipt of something called cash, Didi made him rich.

In fact he did, because he passed on to Patrick, and to all of us the greatest of legacies: the challenge to live an active and reflective life, inspired by matters of the common good, marked by generosity and open to new possibilities; all deepened by the sharing of a loyal and tender love.

As Frank has told us, on 26 May this year, Dad celebrated his deepest and abiding love for his beloved Patricia, on the occasion of their 69th wedding anniversary. After she returned to their Lord in September 2019, he missed her every day.

And so now, Dad, we celebrate your extraordinary life lived true to your Gospel values.

In grand-daughter Patricia's copy of the *Mabo* decision, Dad inscribed: 'May you run the good race in all your life – with courage and endurance to bring loving kindness and hope to the lives of others.' We celebrate that you, Dad, ran- maybe walked- that good and courageous race in all your life and you showed so many of us how we could do the same. We will always be grateful that we were companions on your journey, and you had the love and wisdom to be the wit and mentor in ours. We miss you dearly. We are comforted knowing that Mum gives you a late anniversary embrace.

15.4 Brennan's Constrained Compassion – Patrick Keane AC KC

Editor's Note

Patrick Keane had been Solicitor-General of Queensland in the Wik Case. He then served as a Justice of the High Court of Australia from 2013 - 2023. After his retirement from the bench, he chaired the Expert Advisory Group set up by the Australian Government to guide reforms to the Administrative Appeals Tribunal. On 14 November 2024, he delivered the Selden Society Lecture in the Supreme Court of Queensland entitled 'Sir Gerard Brennan: Constrained Compassion'. This is a substantive extract of the lecture.

It is a great honour to have been asked to give this evening's lecture in memory of Sir Gerard Brennan. His professional life as a barrister and a judge was encompassed by the five decades after the end of World War II. During that time, Sir Gerard was without peer, save for Sir Anthony Mason, in the contribution he made to the administration of justice in Australia. In the roughly three decades since Sir Gerard's retirement as Chief Justice of the High Court of Australia, the work of Australia's highest court can be seen to consist, in large part, of the working out and consolidating the landmark developments in the law in Australia wrought by the Courts in which Sir Anthony and Sir Gerard participated and over which they respectively presided. Developments in relation to the requirements of a fair trial in the criminal law and procedural fairness in governmental decision-making, the constitutional guarantee of freedom of political speech and native title are the most obvious examples.

Many of the judgments by which Sir Gerard's historic contributions to the law in Australia were made are worthy of a lecture - or indeed a book - in their own right. But it is important to remember also that Sir Gerard's legacy also includes his work as the foundation President of the Administrative Appeals Tribunal (AAT) from his appointment in 1976. He established the AAT, a world-leading innovation, as a guarantor of the integrity and quality of decisionmaking by the Executive Government of the Commonwealth. The success of this institution which he did so much to establish would, in the decades that followed, inspire the Australian States to emulate the Commonwealth's initiative.

The barrister

F G Brennan QC was President of the Australian Bar Association when he was appointed to the Federal Court of Australia. Any discussion of his contributions to the legal life of our nation must include reference to his work as a barrister, both as an advocate for his clients, and, as leader of the Australian Bar, as an advocate for the Bar itself as an institution whose work he saw as integral to the due administration of justice.

Both as a barrister and a judge, he believed that good advocacy was essential to the doing of justice. And so believed deeply in the importance of the Bar as an institution dedicated to ensuring the quality of advocacy in our courts. He was a firm adherent to the view of Sir Owen Dixon that 'the honourable practice of the profession of advocacy affords the greatest opportunity of contributing to the administration of justice according to law' and that 'there is no work in the law that admits of a greater contribution.'[1]

May I take a moment, then, to say to those who did not see Brennan QC in action that he was a truly mighty advocate. He and his great rival, P D Connolly, stood at the pinnacle of a sequence of brilliant Queensland barristers. They were the leaders of a tradition of highly skilled advocacy in which the Queensland Bar evolved a culture of excellence, especially in the administration of criminal law, equal to any Bar in the country.

May I also say to those who never saw Brennan QC argue a case that he was not only a formidable advocate: he was a passionate one. That assertion may come as a surprise to those who saw only his Olympian serenity as a judge, or who know of his advocacy only from the summaries of his beautifully articulated arguments in the *Commonwealth Law Reports*. I remember, as an articled clerk, watching him present an argument in the Supreme Court of Queensland. My firm was on the other side, but I thought that his argument was utterly compelling, truly a thing of beauty, as aesthetically pleasing as it was legally persuasive. The Court thought otherwise; and summarily rejected his argument on the spot. The lawyers for both sides left the courtroom together. It was only as all of us got into the lift to leave the building that, unable to restrain himself any longer, he exploded with genuine indignation slamming his brief and saying 'That decision is as wrong as hell!'

In 1996, the year before he retired as Chief Justice of Australia, he made a memorable speech to the Australian Bar Association. In a few lines he gave a characteristically eloquent insight into the passion that informed his own work at the Bar:

> The Bar captures the mind and governs the life of those who join it. Its rewards are sometimes financially parsimonious. It is a profession to be entered only by those who have a passionate desire to be a barrister. But that is the best of all reasons. For those, the experience of practice does not disappoint.[2]

Some idea of his passion for the work of the Bar – and for the life of a barrister – can be obtained from the oral history held by the Supreme Court of Queensland in the record of a conversation between Sir Gerard and Mr John Gallagher (in 2002). This conversation is well worth reading as well as an enduring example of Sir Gerard's genuine enthusiasm for the life at the Bar. In this regard, I speak of 'conversation' advisedly because John Gallagher asked a question which Sir Gerard stopped answering after thirty-six closely typed pages. I exaggerate only slightly.

The judge

As much as Sir Gerard loved the work of the Bar, he loved his work on the Court even more. As I have said, his time on the Court was a time of landmark changes in the outlook of the High Court. In relation to some of those landmark changes, he was an important ally to Sir Anthony Mason who was the leading spirit. The radical reunderstanding in *Cole v Whitfield*[3] of s 92's constitutional guarantee of freedom of interstate trade, commerce and intercourse is the most momentous example. In that case, the High Court resolved much of the vexation and uncertainty that had attended the operation of s 92 since federation. The decision in *Ha v New South Wales*[4] had much the same effect in relation to s 90 of the *Constitution* which confers exclusive power on the Commonwealth Parliament over the levying of duties of customs and excise.

In other areas of the law, Sir Gerard was the more dynamic influence. His great decision in *Mabo,*[5] with which Mason CJ and McHugh J agreed, is the most famous example. A somewhat less celebrated example is the judgment in *Lange v Australian Broadcasting Corporation.*[6] The unanimous judgment of the High Court in that case ensured that the freedom of political communication said to be implicit in the *Constitution* survived challenges based largely on the uncertainty generated by diverse attempts to articulate its metes and bounds. The judgment of the High Court, speaking with one voice, ensured that the idea of a freedom of political communication implied as a matter of indispensable necessity to the realisation of the representative democracy established by the *Constitution* would not be consigned to the historical scrapheap of failed judicial experiments.

A further, less well-known example of his practical leadership was manifest in the High Court's willingness to devote a greater part of its time to the development of the criminal law and to ensuring the due administration of criminal justice.

In the area of tort law, his principled and steadfast – and for some time, rather lonely – opposition to the idea of proximity as a controlling concept in the law of negligence was ultimately vindicated although this could not be seen to be clearly the case until after he had left the Court.[7] The High Court's jurisprudential flirtation with the proximity heresy reached its nadir in its decision in *Bryan v Maloney*.[8] The dissenting judgement of Brennan J in that case would ultimately be vindicated: but what is particularly remarkable about that judgment for my purposes is the respectful manner in which he stated his position. In explaining the errors in the majority position, he was as always, moderate in his language, refraining from the kind of personal attack and vituperation that are apt to diminish public confidence in the courts. To that topic I will return.

His term of leadership of the High Court as Chief Justice of Australia was, of course, quite brief: only three years. Paul Keating told me that when the decision to appoint Sir Gerard as Chief Justice was made by Keating's government, there were some within the government who argued that the appointee as Chief Justice should have a longer term in office than three years. Keating silenced those doubters by insisting, no doubt in his characteristically emphatic way, that the period of time in office was of less importance than the clarity of the appointee's moral compass while in office. It was his firm view that, in this respect, Sir Gerard was the outstanding candidate for the office. Time would confirm the wisdom of Keating's assessment.

Keating, the political hardman, greatly admired Brennan, the compassionate intellectual, for the integrity with which Brennan exercised his power as a judge. Keating's assessment of the stability of Brennan's moral compass was an insightful appreciation that Brennan was above petty or partisan considerations, including the tribalism that has sometimes been a problem for Irish Australians, and for our fellow citizens as well. Brennan remained faithful to the compassion that is the best element of the Catholic faith so dear to him and so central to his view of the world.

When one considers Sir Gerard's jurisprudence as a whole, the injunction in Matthew 7.1, 'Judge not, that you be not judged' comes to mind. St Matthew's exhortation was not a denial of the legitimacy of the judicial function. In truth, it is a direction to recognise the limits of one's authority over others. The first duty of any tribunal is to be satisfied of his jurisdiction over the matter before it. It is a direction in favour of judicial modesty, to refrain from arrogating to one's self the authority reposed by law in others. Sir Gerard's great example to those who came after was to temper compassion, the greatest of the human emotions, in the desire to do justice with modesty, that rather rare judicial virtue.

All of which leads me to the title of my remarks this evening, and to what some might see as a tension in his significant judgments between his personal views, his deeply felt compassion for others, and his adherence to the legal rules he was obliged to give effect as a judge. The most poignant example of this tension is provided by his judgment in the *Wik Case*[9] in which he adhered to the legal analysis which was the foundation of the landmark decision in *Mabo.*

There would be little doubt, I think that among Brennan's many significant contributions to Australian law, the most famous was his leading judgment in the High Court's decision in *Mabo* in 1992. In that decision it was held that the common law of Australia recognised that the rights of occupation of Australia's indigenous people of their ancestral lands survived British settlement under the Crown. Five years later in the *Wik Case*, Brennan CJ, as he had become, dissented from the majority view that these rights had not been extinguished by historical grant by the Crown of pastoral leases under colonial and State legislation prior to the enactment of the *Racial Discrimination Act* (Cth) in 1975. I suggest that the key to understanding the consistency of his judgments in these two cases lies in an appreciation of Brennan's fidelity to the constraints upon judicial decision-making required by the constitutional separation of legislative and judicial power.

Before turning to discuss these cases, I want to say something about another case in which he explained the constitutional underpinning of his view of the limited scope of legitimate judicial law making. I will then go on to suggest that Brennan's understanding remains the orthodox view of the separation of powers enshrined in our constitutional arrangements. That orthodoxy may now be subject to challenge, but a very different constitutional order would emerge if it were to be displaced.

Dietrich v R

Brennan J's understanding of the relationship between legislative and judicial power is crisply stated in his judgment in *Dietrich v R.*[10] In that case, the argument put for Mr Dietrich was that 'an accused person charged with a serious crime punishable by imprisonment, who cannot afford counsel, has a right to be provided with counsel at public expense'.[11] The High Court held that no such right existed under the common law; but the majority were nevertheless able to reason to a conclusion that vindicated Mr Dietrich's claim that he should not have been tried without the benefit of legal representation. Brennan J dissented.

The position in Australia stands, of course, in stark contrast to that in the United States where the Sixth Amendment to the US *Constitution* expressly provides: 'In all criminal prosecutions, the accused shall enjoy the right ... to have the Assistance of Counsel for his defence.' And so, in *Johnson v Zerbst,*[12] the US Supreme Court held that in all federal cases, a court must appoint counsel to represent defendants who are unable to afford their own. The Supreme Court said:

> Since the Sixth Amendment constitutionally entitles one charged with crime to the assistance of counsel, compliance with this constitutional mandate is an essential jurisdictional prerequisite to a federal court's authority to deprive an accused of his life or liberty. [13]

If one thing is clear in this field of discourse, it is that neither our Federal *Constitution* nor any of our State *Constitutions* contains a provision remotely resembling the Sixth Amendment.

The argument that an individual accused enjoys a right to be provided with Counsel at state expense could not stand with the settled view of the constitutional role of the judiciary. As Brennan J explained:

> The courts can point out that the administration of justice is an inalienable function of the State and that the very security of the State depends on the fair and efficient administration of justice, but the courts cannot compel the legislature and the executive government to provide legal representation. Nor can this Court declare the existence of a common law entitlement to legal aid when the satisfaction of that entitlement depends on the actions of the political branches of government. In my opinion, to declare such an entitlement without power to compel its satisfaction amounts to an unwarranted intrusion into legislative and executive functions. [14]

In *Dietrich*, the majority of the judges held that the power of the courts to ensure a fair trial of a criminal charge extended to granting a stay or adjournment of the trial where representation of the accused is essential to a fair trial, as it is in most cases where an accused is charged with a serious offence. That view was based on the proposition that the judicial power should not permit itself to be deployed unjustly.

Brennan J explained his rejection of the reasoning of the majority:

> Although the desirability of according an entitlement to legal aid is manifest, the critical legal question in this appeal is whether this Court can and should translate that desirability into a rule of law or, if there be any difference, into a rule of practice governing the conduct of criminal proceedings. In my respectful opinion, this Court cannot properly create such a rule. [15]

He noted first that 'the common law has never recognised such a rule'.[16] He then observed the difference between our constitutional law and the constitutional law of countries which have empowered their courts to 'construe broadly expressed guarantees to include a right to counsel.'[17] Next, he noted that there is no 'valid analogy between cases of unfairness which result in a miscarriage of justice and cases in which an indigent person charged with a serious offence goes unrepresented' for the reason that 'many trials of unrepresented persons do not result in a miscarriage of justice.'[18] Brennan J concluded with this observation:

> The courts do not control the public purse strings; nor can they conscript the legal profession to compel the rendering of professional services without reward. The provision of adequate legal representation for persons charged with the commission of serious offences is a function which only the legislature and executive can perform. No doubt, demands on the public purse other than legal aid limit the funds available.[19]

For Brennan J, within the legal tradition of the common law as it has evolved, and under our *Constitution* predicated upon that evolution, it was only the institution of Parliament that can create the positive rights that give practical meaning to the great political idea of fraternity without injustice to those of the citizenry who must pay for them even they themselves may derive to benefit from the allocation of society's resources. To declare and enforce such rights against all the people of a community who have not agreed to pay the price of doing so puts one in mind of St Augustine's description of a State without justice as nothing more than a great band of robbers.[20]

In Australia the great political principle of fraternity has, as a matter of historical fact, thrived to an extent that is the envy of the world. That success has been dependent upon an engaged citizenry rather than upon the wisdom or generosity of judges. Those of us who know something of our history have ample reason to have faith in our parliaments to create positive rights for our citizens. The Hon E G Whitlam said:

> Parliament has been our great liberating force … There is no freedom without equality. To redistribute and equalise liberty has been one of the principal functions of Parliament. Parliament alone can give equality of opportunity and thereby increase liberty for all. If we are to have economic equality of opportunity, which is the next stage in the advance of liberty, we must have effective parliamentary government and, accordingly, dispense with fetters on Parliament rather than contrive them.[21]

Sir Gerard found Gough Whitlam, a most interesting politician, though his admiration was not unqualified. I am reasonably confident that Sir Gerard did not agree with everything that Gough Whitlam ever said or did. But there can be no doubt that Sir Gerard's understanding of the relationship between legislative and judicial power was profoundly in accord with the notion that the parliaments elected by our people are the exclusive source of the positive rights that we Australians enjoy in such abundance.

Brennan had no truck with arguments that the *Constitution* enshrined some deep unspoken limitations on the legislative power of Parliament of the kind spoken of by Sir Edward Coke in *Dr Bonham's Case*: I am speaking here of the Blue Eyed Babies style of argument, by which I refer to the rhetorical device deployed by advocates, and sometimes by judges, to deny the validity or effect of legislation on the basis that 'the exercise of legislative power is limited by the inviolability of fundamental legal rights.'[22] The idea is that a law requiring the murder at birth of blue eyed babies is not a law. This rhetorical strategy invokes the approach famously adopted by Sir Edward Coke in *Dr Bonham's Case*:

> [I]n many cases, the common law will … controul Acts of Parliament, and sometimes adjudge them to be utterly void: for when an Act of Parliament is against common right and reason, or repugnant, or impossible to be performed, the common law will controul it, and adjudge such Act to be voided.[23]

More recently, in *Fraser v State Services Commission* Lord Cook of Thornton spoke of '… some common law rights may go so deep that even Parliament cannot be accepted by the Courts to have destroyed them.'[24]

To the extent that this rhetorical device involves an appeal to a strain of natural law thinking or to personal intuitions of what is right, it is tempting to dismiss it out of hand as 'fundamentally undemocratic'.[25] The Blue Eyed Babies argument postulates a community gone mad and so is not a reasonable test of the validity of a law. But it represents a persistent argument that has come in and out of fashion over the years.[26] It is a hardy perennial, being a favourite of those who take an expansive view of judicial power.[27]

It is a kind of argument that Brennan never encouraged: he certainly never deployed it himself. I venture to suggest that, in point of authority, he would have regarded it as contrary to the *Engineers' Case*[28] and, in point of principle, he would have regarded it as contrary to the dignity of the people of the Commonwealth to approach the interpretation of legislation on the basis that the members of the judiciary were possessed of wisdom and goodness beyond that shared by the people of the Commonwealth and their elected representatives.

Mabo

So, coming to the decision in *Mabo*, Sir Gerard's understanding of the limits of legislative power that underpinned his reasoning in *Mabo* was not sourced in natural law notions that some things are not permitted to the legislature, but in the compelling constitutional consideration that the federal system, and particularly s 109 of the *Constitution*, subordinates the statute laws of the State Parliaments to the laws of the Commonwealth in cases of inconsistency. It was strictly on this basis that he was to hold in *Mabo* that the *Racial Discrimination Act 1975* of the Commonwealth ensured the continuing enjoyment of indigenous occupation of land recognised by the common law that had not previously been extinguished by State legislation. While it was well within the province of the judges to recognise and give effect to the common law rule that acknowledges the peaceful occupation and enjoyment of land as a matter of indigenous custom, that common law position was inherently vulnerable to alteration by legislation.

That was Brennan J's understanding of the common law rights of indigenous people in peaceful occupation of their traditional lands, in harmony with the deepest values of the common law. From the earliest moments of the common law's self consciousness in the 12th Century, the causes of action developed by the courts of common law were astute to vindicate the rights of those in peaceful occupation of land against any intruder who could not show a legal title that trumped their peaceful possession. When the common law travelled over the seas that is how it saw things when it was not blinkered by the fiction of terra nullius. But that position could be displaced by the exercise of sovereign power. And within the web of sovereign authority exercised by the officers of the executive and judiciary bound to the Imperial Crown by oaths of office and allegiance, the only sovereign authority was that of the Crown in Parliament. As a matter of the very nature of sovereign authority, there can only be one.

The *Wik Case*

I come now to the *Wik Case*. I should begin by recalling that in the course of the hearing the argument put for Queensland was that, because of the vulnerability of native title to extinguishment by the exercise of sovereign power, the grant to pastoralists of exclusive possession of land by Crown leasehold extinguished any right that might have been asserted by the Wik People. In the course of that argument, Brennan CJ responded with what was nothing less than a cri de coeur, that in this way, Aboriginal communities had been destroyed. This was one of those extraordinarily dramatic moments that occasionally happen in courts. The power of such a moment is not captured in the transcript, much less in the Law Reports. The Chief Justice's observation was followed by what seemed like a very long moment of silence in the courtroom. I can attest that it certainly seemed like a long time to the wretched barrister who was appearing for Queensland. The Chief Justice's real and genuine anguish was palpable. Counsel for the State of Queensland could say nothing useful in response. In hindsight, the moral delinquency of what had happened was indefensible. Quite a few people observing the proceeding considered that the Chief Justice's likely disposition of the case was clear.

In his judgment in *Wik,* Brennan CJ held that if it be right to hold that the mere grant of pastoral leases 'extinguished the native title of the traditional Aboriginal inhabitants, the law will be held to destroy the legal entitlement of the inhabitants to possess and enjoy the land on which they have lived since time immemorial. That would be a significant moral shortcoming'.[29] He held that the shortcoming cannot be remedied by denying the 'true effect' of the Queensland statute and the pastoral leases granted thereunder. The 'true effect' of the Queensland statute was to be ascertained by application of the general law as to the interpretation of the statutes. Much as it galled him personally, he recognised that he was obliged to accept that, in the end, the morality of legislation was a matter for the legislature as the elected representatives of the people.

The issue on which the decision in *Wik* turned was whether the statutory provisions under which pastoral leases were granted provided for the conferral of a right of exclusive possession on the lessee from the Crown; that is to say whether the lessee was granted the right to exclude indigenous people from the land the subject of a grant. Such a grant would be inconsistent with, and would therefore extinguish, rights of occupation and enjoyment of land recognised by the common law. Brennan CJ was unable to regard the grant of a lease under the *Land Act* (Qld), being the relevant Queensland legislation as doing other than conferring the right to exclude all others from the land. Underlying the contrary view, the view that prevailed, was the notion that the legislation that authorised the grant of a pastoral lease should be read down so as to deny pastoralists the right to exclude native title holders from their ancestral lands.

It might be said that the approach of the majority, in reading the Queensland *Land Act* as if it exempted native title – unknown and unacknowledged at the time of its enactment – from its provisions in favour of pastoralists attributed to the legislation a distinctly ahistorical solicitude for indigenous occupants of the land. That is especially so given the evident legislative intention to encourage the opening up of what were explicitly regarded as 'the waste lands of the Crown' to exploitation by the settlers. The question was not whether pastoralists had purported to exercise their right to exclude others from the leased lands as against native title holders, but whether they were entitled to do so under the terms of their grant. And the entitlement to exclude all others from leased land is the characteristic legal entitlement of any lessee.

In order to avoid that critical obstacle, the reasoning of the majority had to confront substantial legal authority. Some might think that the majority attempt to do so was compelling. But, Brennan CJ was unable to see his way clear to ignoring the settled understanding recently reaffirmed by the decision of the High Court in *American Dairy Queen v Blue Rio*[30] in 1981 that, when the Queensland legislation spoke of a lease it was necessarily speaking of a lease, the incidents of which are those of a lease at common law. Those incidents include the right to exclude all others from the leased land. To ignore that well-settled understanding by a strained reading of the legislation would, in his view, have been impermissibly to second guess the legislature.

Conclusion

Whatever one's view about the majority's interpretation of the particular legislation in the *Wik Case* experience elsewhere demonstrates the practical wisdom of Brennan's constrained understanding of the scope of judicial power.

To reflect on the experience of the United States is to see the abiding importance of recognising the constitutional constraints upon the personal moral values of the judges as a dynamic in judicial decision-making. In the United States, issues about judicial appointments divide political parties and the nation in a way that is, happily, quite foreign to our experience. In Australia, the appointment of judges to the High Court almost never generates political controversy. In the United States, the appointment of judges to federal courts, and especially the Supreme Court, is an issue of fundamental political importance in which all politically engaged citizens have a vital interest.

Recent experience in the United States reflects the response of the community to the work of a judiciary – itself now ideologically polarised – that has shown itself to be willing – and indeed anxious – to shoulder what it sees as the necessary burden of making the great political and moral decisions that the other branches of government seem to be unable to make or to make in a way that is satisfactory to sections of the populace. The judiciary has been punished by a political backlash that reflects a loss of confidence in the institution as an independent arbiter of the people's disputes.

In this regard, CNN's exit polling at the 2016 US Presidential election disclosed that, for 56% of those who voted for the Republican candidate, the issue of Supreme Court appointments was the **most** important factor in their vote, with only 37% saying that this issue was not important to them at all.[31] The Republican candidate well understood the state of affairs reflected in these figures. Indeed, his appreciation of the point was a major part of his political strategy. He told a rally in July 2016 that even if conservative voters didn't like him, they would have to vote for him anyway. 'You know why?' he asked; 'Supreme Court Judges', he answered.[32] And in this regard, as events have shown, he proved as good as his word, appointing Supreme and Federal Court judges to resounding applause from his political base and to the dismay of almost half the population.

For several decades now, there have been on the Supreme court of the United States judges who find the prospect of what they see as 'a significant moral shortcoming' in the outcome proposed by other members of the Court, not only, as a reason to set at nought the decisions of the legislature, but also as an occasion to engage in direct and personal attacks on their fellow judges in the case, because they have a different moral and political viewpoint. These attacks serve to delegitimise the judicial function.

A strong, but not atypical, example of this latter problem can be found in the observations of the late Scalia J in *Obergefell v Hodges.*[33] His Honour attacked the majority opinion which favoured constitutional recognition of gay marriage in the following terms: 'The opinion is couched in a style that is as pretentious as its content is egotistic .... (T)he opinions showy profundities are profoundly incoherent'. In famous footnote 22, Scalia J went on to say:

> If, even as the price to be paid for a fifth vote, I ever joined an opinion for the Court that began: 'the Constitution promises liberty to all within its reach, a liberty that includes certain specific rights that allow persons, within a lawful realm, to define and express their identity': I would hide my head in a bag. The Supreme Court of the United States has descended from the disciplined reasoning of John Marshall and Joseph Story to the mystical aphorisms of the fortune cookie.

This vigorous vituperation may be amusing to some; it may perhaps not be out of place in an academic law journal. But it has no place in a judgment of a court. As a purely practical matter, once the members of a court begin to attack each other as traitors to their judicial oath, the public has little reason to retain confidence in the institution, that is especially so, where the Court is concerned to resolve great political and moral questions contrary to the will of the people's elected representatives in their legislatures. These practical considerations aside, in principle, it is necessary to recognise that these great questions are very difficult to resolve. Honest and reasonable minds may differ. As St Augustine said: 'On great questions unanimity of opinion is the privilege only of angels.' No judge is wise enough or good enough to make adverse judgments about the morality of, or of the wisdom of that judge's fellow judges to resolve the controversies that confront them. Making such judgments is no part of the role of any judge. Just as it is no part of the role of the judge to judge the morality and wisdom of legislation.

The United States experience offers a salutary warning of what can happen when judges fail to heed Matthew's advice 'to judge not, lest ye be judged.'

The modest restraint that informs the great judgments of Sir Gerard Brennan remains an essential part of the legacy that continues to inspire and guide our lawyers and judges of my generation. I commend it to the lawyers and judges, and the people of the next generation.

---

1. Sir Owen Dixon, 'Address when first sitting as Chief Justice of the High Court of Australia in Melbourne', 7 May 1952, see Sir Owen Dixon, *Jesting Pilate* (Law Book Co, 1965) 250.
2. 'Profession or Service Industry: The Choice', Opening Address, Australian Bar Association Conference, San Francisco, 18 August 1996.
3. (1988) 165 CLR 360.
4. (1997) 189 CLR 365.
5. See *Mabo* v *Queensland (No 2) (Mabo Case)* (1992) 175 CLR 1, 30.
6. (1997) 189 CLR 520.
7. See *Brookfield Multiple Ltd v Owners Corporation Strata Plan 61288* (2014) 254 CLR 185.
8. (1995) 182 CLR 609.
9. See *Wik Peoples v Queensland* (1996) 187 CLR 1.
10. (1992) 177 CLR 292.
11. Ibid., 293.
12. 304 US 458 (1938).
13. 304 US 458 (1938), 467, 468.
14. (1992) 177 CLR 292, 317-323.
15. Ibid., 317.
16. Ibid.
17. Ibid.
18. Ibid., 322.
19. Ibid., 292, 323
20. Augustine, *The City of God Book IV*, Ed G P Goold. The Loeb Classical Library 1963, vol II at 17. "Remota itaque iustitia quid sunt regna nisi magna latrocinio?".

21. Cited in Andrew Moore, 'A mace to swat two blowflies: interpreting the *Fitzpatrick and Browne* privilege case', (2009) 55 (1) *Australian Journal of Politics and History* 32, 33.
22. See *Durham Holdings Pty Ltd v New South Wales* (2001) 205 CLR 399, 401.
23. (1610) 8 Co Rep 113b, 118a, 77 ER 646, 652.
24. [1984] 1 NZLR 116, 121.
25. See *Durham Holdings Pty Ltd v New South Wales* [2001] HCA Trans 512, 32-33 lines 1355-1365.
26. See, for example, *Re Patterson Ex parte Taylor* [2000] HCA Trans 737, 161-163; *Durham Holdings Pty Ltd v New South Wales* (2001) 205 CLR 399, 401, *Alexander v Minister for Home Affairs* [2022] 78 ALD 432 at 468 [182], 471472 [197].
27. See *Alexander v Minister for Home Affairs* (2022) 78 ALD 432 [182], 471-472 [197].
28. See *Amalgamated Society of Engineers v Adelaide Steamship Co Ltd* (1920) CLR 129.
29. (1996) 187 CLR 1, 8788.
30. (1981) 147 CLR 677, 683-684; 686.
31. Compare Bump 'A quarter of Republicans voted for Trump to get Supreme Court picks – and it paid off.' *The Washington Post* (June 26, 2018).
32. See *The Economist*, (September 15, 2018).
33. (2015) 576 US (The Gay Marriage Case).

15.5 The Legacy of Sir Gerard Brennan to Australian Public Law – Justice Stephen Gageler AC

Editor's note

A year before his appointment as Chief Justice, Justice Stephen Gageler delivered this address at the University of Melbourne Centre for Comparative Constitutional Studies Global Public Law Seminar on Monday 15 August 2022. Gageler knew Brennan well, having been Associate to Chief Justice Mason and having appeared often before Brennan in the High Court.[1]

'Law', as Sir Maurice Byers once said, is 'an expression of the whole personality'.[2] For those who have immersed themselves for a professional lifetime in the administration of the law, that is true. To them, law is not readily compartmentalised. Who they are cannot readily be separated from what they do. Of judges 'trained within a system of judicial functioning' Sir Gerard Brennan himself said that 'their minds are cast in the mould of the system, they develop personal qualities which are compatible with the system' and that '[t]hey both determine and are formed by the functions which they discharge'.[3] Their personalities have been shaped by their professional experiences and by the legacies of those who have gone before them. Their own legacies will inevitably be expressions of their personalities as so shaped.

An examination of the legacy of Sir Gerard Brennan to Australian law, or to so much of Australian law as might be classified as 'public' law, can therefore start with a reflection on the personality of Sir Gerard Brennan. Nowhere is that personality better depicted than in the official portrait of him as Chief Justice of the High Court. The portrait hangs in Court Room No 3 of the High Court building in Canberra. There it hangs in a line of succession with portraits of past Chief Justices who worked in that building before him and after him, beginning with Sir Garfield Barwick and currently ending with Robert French. The portrait was painted by Robert Hannaford in 1996 during the first of Sir Gerard's three years as Chief Justice.

Portrayed is a man 67 years of age in evident good health and good humour. He is seated casually. Yet tellingly, in his casualness, he is still dressed in judicial robes. He is evidently comfortable occupying the ultimate judicial office to which he has been appointed. For that office he is impeccably qualified. He has been a judge for two decades: most recently a Justice of the High Court and before that an inaugural member of the Federal Court. Overlapping with his time on the Federal Court, he has been the first

President of the Administrative Appeals Tribunal. Before becoming a judge, he has been a barrister for a quarter of a century. A decade of that, he has spent as a Senior Counsel.

He looks directly and calmly at the viewer. The light falling from behind and to his right highlights his face in repose. There is a glint in his glasses. Or is it a twinkle in his eye? His demeanour is one of composure. Some might describe it as tranquility. He exudes a wisdom which surpasses mere accumulation of knowledge. He exudes intellectual humility borne of life experience. He exudes compassion.

Held in his two hands and resting lightly on one knee is a copy of what is evidently volume 175 of the *Commonwealth Law Reports*. The volume covers the period 1991–1992. It includes the report of the judgment in *Mabo v Queensland (No 2)* (*Mabo*),[4] which commences at the very beginning of the volume. Inserted into the volume is a bookmark. What is marked by the bookmark is unclear. It might be a passage in his own celebrated reasons as the pivotal member of the majority in *Mabo*. It might equally be the commencement of the report of the judgment in *Secretary, Department of Health & Community Services v JWB* (*Marion's Case*),[5] decided a month before *Mabo* and reported immediately after *Mabo*, in which he delivered a powerful dissent. In an interview he much later gave as part of the National Library's Oral History Project, he described it as the hardest judgment he had ever written.[6]

Marion's Case and *Mabo* might or might not qualify as 'public' law. That depends on the taxonomy adopted. Howsoever, the category of 'public' law might be defined within any given taxonomy, Sir Gerard Brennan's enduring contribution to the category of 'public' law can only be fully appreciated taking account of his reasons for judgment in those two cases. Together they manifest the deep humanity which was at the heart of who he was, and which in turn was central to the entirety of his legal philosophy and his judicial technique.

Famously on display in Sir Gerard's reasons for judgment in *Mabo* was his embracing of moral responsibility for what he described as the 'organic development' of legal doctrine in order to 'accord with contemporary notions of justice and human rights' while respecting and maintaining what he described as 'the skeleton of principle which gives the body of our law its shape and internal consistency'.[7] In *Mabo*, he exercised that moral responsibility with unsurpassed technical skill to reappraise feudal notions of land tenure and to restate the common law of Australia with reference to land title in order to redress an historic injustice by which the rights and interests of Australia's indigenous inhabitants had been treated as non-existent.

Spelt out in *Marion's Case* was a fundamental animating consideration, which can be seen to have informed the moral choice starkly made in *Mabo* and to have pervaded Sir Gerard's jurisprudence more generally. The central question in *Marion's Case* was as to the power of another, be that other a parent or a guardian or a court, to authorise the sterilisation of an intellectually impaired child. The majority view was that a court had power to authorise sterilisation by reference to the 'best interests' of the child.

Sir Gerard disagreed. Absent community consensus on the ethical principles to be applied, the 'best interests' approach appeared to him to depend so much on the 'value system of the decision-maker' as to give rise to an 'unexaminable discretion in the repository of the power'.[8] The 'best interests' approach for that reason provided an insubstantial protection of 'human dignity'.[9] 'Human dignity' he explained to be a value 'common to our municipal law and to international instruments relating to human rights' which required 'that the whole personality be respected'[10] and which was required to be afforded equally to all.[11]

Sir Gerard's namesake and onetime associate, Gerard Carney, has pointed out that a concern for human dignity, equally afforded to all, was at the core of Sir Gerard's approach to the judicial administration of the whole of the law.[12] In a lecture at Bond University shortly after his retirement, Sir Gerard took on the herculean task of mapping out the respective roles and immunities of the Parliament, the Executive and the Courts under the *Australian Constitution*. True to that core concern, he commenced not with reference to the constitutional structure or constitutional text, nor to constitutional history. He commenced instead with the observation that '[c]onstitutions are made for a people and a time'. Inevitably times will change, he went on to say, but 'humankind will remain the same – with the same mystical spark that gives each a unique dignity and, as those who believe would hold, an eternal destiny; with the same basic concerns for life, liberty, property and human relationships that can be satisfied only in a society governed by law'.[13]

Essential to the preservation of human dignity in a society governed by law, as Sir Gerard saw it, was the imposition of legal limits on the capacity of any one person or body of persons to exercise power to affect the interests of any other person. The unique and essential function of courts in such a society was to declare and enforce those legal limits on power. Indispensable to the capacity of courts to perform that unique and essential function was maintenance of public confidence in those courts as faithful guardians and neutral arbiters of disputes about those legal limits on power. And indispensable to the maintenance of that public confidence was the appearance, and much more so the actuality, of competence, fairness, and impartiality on the part of the judiciary.

With customary elegance, Sir Gerard explained that '[t]he rule of law depends on and is perhaps synonymous with confidence in the courts', that 'it must rest on the common acceptance by all who are subject to the jurisdiction of the courts of the authority of the courts to determine cases and controversies' and that to destroy public confidence in the courts is to destroy the foundation of the rule of law'.[14] He said that:

> Public confidence depends both on the reality and the perception of a judiciary that is competent, of unshakeable integrity and isolated from influences that might improperly affect the administration of justice according to law. Its awesome powers must be exercised always in the service of others. It must always respond to any application duly made to it. And it must account publicly and to the parties for the reasons for its decisions. It is a judiciary for a society living under the rule of law. Its standards must be, and be seen to be, unimpeachable.[15]

Practising what he preached, Sir Gerard personified those essential judicial attributes.

Judicial review is a topic that must lie within the heartland of 'public' law on any taxonomy. Sir Gerard's enduring contribution to our collective understanding of judicial review followed directly from that broader conception of the essentiality of the judicial function to the preservation of human dignity in a society living under the rule of law.

Judicial review of administrative action, he told us, 'is neither more nor less than the enforcement of the rule of law over executive action; it is the means by which executive action is prevented from exceeding the powers and functions assigned to the executive by law and the interests of the individual are protected accordingly'.[16] Moreover, he told us, there is an essential unity in the role of a court engaged in judicial review of administrative action and the role of a court engaged in judicial review of legislative action. In each case, as he famously put it in *Attorney-General (NSW) v Quin*,[17] in language destined to become canonical, '[t]he essential warrant for judicial intervention is the declaration and enforcing of the law affecting the extent and exercise of power' and 'the duty and jurisdiction of the court … do not go beyond the declaration and enforcing of the law which determines the limits and governs the exercise of [the relevant] power'.

With those words, he articulated a pure conception of judicial review: untied to the jurisdiction or powers of any particular court, uncomplicated by obscure nomenclature, and uncluttered by notions of grounds of review or concerns about the availability of particular judicial remedies. In its simplicity lay its strength. By strictly confining a court engaged in judicial review to the declaration and enforcement of law, it ensured that the judiciary remained within its peculiar field of institutional competence. In so doing, it enhanced the public confidence in the judiciary on which the continuing ability of courts to engage in judicial review ultimately depended.[18]

In due course, that pure conception would come to inform our understanding of the express constitutionally entrenched jurisdiction of the High Court to engage in judicial review of the exercise of power by Commonwealth executive and judicial officers as well our understanding of the implied constitutionally entrenched jurisdiction of the State Supreme Courts to engage in judicial review of the exercise of power by State executive and judicial officers.[19]

As to the judicial discernment of the content of the law which determines the limits and governs the exercise of power, Sir Gerard saw plenty of scope for the *Constitution* to be interpreted to keep pace with long-term changes in Australian society,[20] just as he saw plenty of scope for common law principles of statutory interpretation to be developed to ensure that the exercise of powers conferred by statute kept pace with contemporary conceptions of justice.[21] What he insisted upon was that any constitutional implication be firmly anchored in the text and structure of the *Constitution*[22] and that any principle of law to be judicially developed be capable of being stated with precision and preferably in the form of a syllogism.[23]

A conference was held at the Australian National University to honour Sir Gerard's contribution to administrative law not long after his retirement. There, Sir Anthony Mason delivered a paper on Sir Gerard's contribution to judicial review. Sir Anthony perceptively said of Sir Gerard that '[r]ule-based rather than discretionary justice was central to his jurisprudence'.[24]

Commenting on that paper at that conference, I suggested that an analysis by Sir Anthony of the contribution of Sir Gerard to administrative law was like an analysis by Picasso of the contribution of Matisse to modern art.[25] Sir Gerard was not especially pleased with the analogy. He saw himself as a Rembrandt or a Vermeer. Over 20 years later, I am still convinced that on this point, he was wrong. They were masters of an earlier age. He, like Matisse, was a master of the modern age. And he, like Matisse, had a distinctive style characterised by distinct forms and harmonious composition.

More than once in his extra-curial writings,[26] Sir Gerard referred to Learned Hand's posthumous tribute to Benjamin Cardozo published in the

Harvard Law Review in 1939.[27] Hand referred to the 'customary law of English-speaking peoples' as 'a structure indubitably made by the hands of generations of judges, each professing to be a pupil, yet each in fact a builder who has contributed his few bricks and his little water, often indeed under the illusion that he has added nothing'. Sir Gerard Brennan was a judge who should not have been under any such illusion. To the question of what he added to Australian public law, the answer can be given with a precision which would have pleased him. I give that answer now. He added its essential unity. He added its guiding principle. He added its moral compass.

---

1. The address was first published: Stephen Gageler, 'The Legacy of Sir Gerard Brennan to Australian Public Law' (2023) 33 *Public Law Review* 303.
2. Sir Maurice Byers, "From the Other Side of the Bar Table: An Advocate's View of the Judiciary" (1987) 10 *University of New South Wales Law Journal* 179, 182; James Allsop, "The Law as an Expression of the Whole Personality" [2017] *Bar News* 25.
3. Gerard Brennan, 'Limits on the Use of Judges' (1978) 9 *Federal Law Review* 1, 2.
4. See *Mabo v Queensland (No 2)* (1992) 175 CLR 1.
5. See *Secretary, Department of Health & Community Services v JWB (Marion's Case*) (1992) 175 CLR 218.
6. Sir Gerard Brennan interviewed by Fiona Wheeler and Michael Coper in the History of the High Court of Australia Oral History Project (25 October 2007).
7. See *Mabo v Queensland (No 2)* (1992) 175 CLR 1, 29.
8. See *Secretary, Department of Health & Community Services v JWB 'Marion's Case'* (1992) 175 CLR 218, 271.
9. Ibid., 272.
10. Ibid., 267.
11. Ibid., 266.
12. Gerard Carney, 'Sir Gerard Brennan – The Principled Judge' in Michael White and Aladin Rahemtula (eds), *Queensland Judges on the High Court* (Supreme Court of Queensland Library, 2003) 85, 88
13. Gerard Brennan, 'The Parliament, the Executive and the Courts: Roles and Immunities' (1997) 9 (2) *Bond Law Review* 136, 136–137.
14. Sir Gerard Brennan, 'Courts for the People – not People's Courts' (1995) 2 *Deakin Law Review* 1, 3. See also Sir Gerard Brennan, 'Courts, Democracy and the Law' (1991) 65 *Australian Law Journal* 32, 39–42; Sir Gerard Brennan, 'Why Be a Judge?' (1996) 14 *Australian Bar Review* 89, 94–96; Sir Gerard Brennan, 'The State of the Judicature' (1998) 72 *Australian Law Journal* 33, 33–34.
15. Sir Gerard Brennan, 'Courts for the People - Not People's Courts', (1995) 2 *Deakin Law Review* 1, 12.
16. See *Church of Scientology Inc v Woodward* (1982) 154 CLR 25, 70.
17. See *Attorney-General (NSW) v Quin* (1990) 170 CLR 1, 35–36.

18. See Sir Gerard Brennan, 'The Purpose and Scope of Judicial Review' (1986) 2 *Australian Bar Review* 93; Gerard Brennan, 'Principle and Independence: The Guardians of Freedom' (2000) 74 *Australian Law Journal* 749.
19. See Stephen Gageler, 'The Constitutional Dimension' in Matthew Groves (ed), *Modern Administrative Law in Australia* (Cambridge University Press, 2014) 165–179, discussing *Plaintiff S157/2002 v Commonwealth* (2003) 211 CLR 476; [2003] HCA 2 and *Kirk v Industrial Court (NSW)*(2010) 239 CLR 531; [2010] HCA 1.
20. See *McGinty v Western Australia* (1996) 186 CLR 140, 168.
21. For example, *Attorney-General (NSW) v Quin* (1990) 170 CLR 1, 36.
22. For example Sir Gerard Brennan, 'Foreword' in HP Lee and Peter Gerangelos (eds), *Constitutional Advancement in a Frozen Continent : Essays in honour of George Winterton* (Federation Press, 2009) vi; Sir Gerard Brennan, 'Foreword' in Gabrielle Appleby, Nicholas Aroney and Thomas John (eds), *The Future of Australian Federalism: Comparative and Disciplinary Perspectives* (Cambridge University Press, 2012) xvi.
23. For example, *Dietrich v R* (1992) 177 CLR 292, 320–323. See Sir Gerard Brennan, 'A Critique of Criticism' (1993) 19 (2) *Monash University Law Review* 213.
24. Sir Anthony Mason, 'Judicial Review: The Contribution of Sir Gerard Brennan' in Robin Creyke and Patrick Keyzer (eds), *The Brennan Legacy* (Federation Press, 2002) 38, 38.
25. Stephen Gageler, 'Sir Gerard Brennan and Some Themes in Judicial Review' in Robin Creyke and Patrick Keyzer (eds), *The Brennan Legacy* (Federation Press, 2002) 62, 62.
26. Gerard Brennan, 'Judging the Judges' (1979) 53 *Australian Law Journal* 767, 770; Gerard Brennan, 'New Growth in the Law – The Judicial Contribution' (1979) 6 (1) *Monash University Law Review* 1, 10.
27. Learned Hand, 'Mr Justice Cardozo' (1939) 52 *Harvard Law Review* 361, 361.

15.6 High Court Special Sitting of Remembrance

KIEFEL CJ:

This ceremonial sitting is held to mark the death on 1 June 2022 of Sir Francis Gerard Brennan, or Sir Gerard, as he was known.[1] Sir Gerard was a Justice of the Court from 1981 to 1995 and served as its tenth Chief Justice from 1995 to 1998. He was the third Chief Justice to hail from Queensland.

Justice Steward regrets that he is unable to sit with us today. Present in the Court this morning is Sir William Deane, who served with Sir Gerard on this Court. The Honourable Murray Gleeson is present in the courtroom in Sydney. Sir Anthony Mason, who preceded Sir Gerard as Chief Justice and Sir Daryl Dawson, who also served with Sir Gerard, regret that they are unable to attend.

There are many apologies, including from the Prime Minister; the Chief Justice of New Zealand; and former members of this Court, the Honourable Robert French, the Honourable Mary Gaudron, the Honourable Michael McHugh, the Honourable Michael Kirby, the Honourable Ian Callinan, the Honourable Susan Crennan, the Honourable Virginia Bell, and the Honourable Geoffrey Nettle; the Chief Justices of Tasmania, the Northern Territory, Victoria, Western Australia, New South Wales and the Australian Capital Territory; and the Solicitors General for the Commonwealth, New South Wales and Tasmania.

Also present at this morning's proceedings are the Honourable Mark Dreyfus, the Attorney-General for the Commonwealth; members of Sir Gerard's family, some of whom are seated at the Bar Table; the Honourable Paul Keating, a former Prime Minister; the Chief Justice of the Federal Court of Australia; the Chief Justices of South Australia and Queensland; the Chief Justice of the Federal Circuit and Family Court; the President of the New South Wales Court of Appeal; the Shadow AttorneyGeneral; former Justices of this Court, the Honourable William Gummow and the Honourable Kenneth Hayne; 15 former associates of Sir Gerard; the Solicitors General of the Australian Capital Territory, Western Australia, South Australia, the Northern Territory, Victoria and Queensland; the President of the Australian Bar Association; the Presidents or representatives of the Bar Associations of Queensland, Victoria, New South Wales, Western

Australia, the Australian Capital Territory and the Northern Territory; the President of the Law Council of Australia, and the President of the Australian Capital Territory Law Society.

Sir Gerard was born on 22 May 1928 in Rockhampton. He was educated at the Range Convent and High School and the Christian Brothers College in Rockhampton, and later Downlands College in Toowoomba. His father, Frank Brennan, was the Supreme Court judge resident in Rockhampton. Sir Gerard described his father as a 'person who had a profound understanding of human nature and a passion . . . for the dignity of people.' The same might be said of Sir Gerard.

Sir Gerard explained in 2007 when he was interviewed for the oral history project, conducted by the Australian National University in partnership with the National Library of Australia, that from his earliest days he wanted to be a lawyer, and described himself as having a feverish ambition to become a barrister. He commenced studies in a combined degree of law and arts in 1946 at the University of Queensland, where Bill Gibbs, as he was known to the students (later to become Sir Harry Gibbs) taught him evidence. He was President of the National Union of Australian University Students. It was his engagement in student politics which resulted in his meeting his future wife, Patricia O'Hara, one of the few women studying medicine, and with whom he would have seven children, 21 grandchildren and 23 greatgrandchildren. Lady Brennan died in 2019.

Following his graduation, and after a short period as his father's associate, Sir Gerard became the associate to Justice Townley of the Supreme Court of Queensland. It was in that position that he had the memorable experience of working with the judge who had been commissioned to preside over a military court established under the *War Crimes Act 1945* (Cth) on the socalled 'Manus Island war crimes trial', proceedings which, in later life, he would recall as 'quite disturbing' and as fortifying his opposition to the death penalty. Sir Gerard was admitted as a barrister in 1951. His early practice consisted of crime and what he called 'nisi prius' work, before embarking on major civil litigation, mostly in the area of torts law. A notable appearance was for the Fijian sugar farmers' Alliance Party in Lord Denning's arbitration concerning the Fiji sugar industry. The farmers sought a better deal from the Australian-owned Colonial Sugar Refining Company, which owned the local mills. The farmers were so successful in the arbitration that CSR sold its interests to the Fijian government. Perhaps on the strength of Sir Gerard's advocacy for the farmers, he was offered the office of Chief Justice of Fiji, which he declined. He was counsel for the Northern Land Council before the Aboriginal Land Rights Royal Commission conducted by Justice Woodward.

Sir Gerard later said that this experience gave him some appreciation of the complexities of land title arising under the common law when he came to write the lead judgment in *Mabo (No 2)*.

Sir Gerard took silk in 1965 in Queensland and was subsequently appointed Queen's Counsel in New South Wales, the Northern Territory, Papua New Guinea and Fiji. His High Court practice was extensive. He first appeared as junior counsel for the appellant in *Harris v Wagner*, which concerned s 92 of the *Constitution*. His first appearance as lead counsel was in 1962, in a matter concerning procedure. He had his first success appearing for the appellant in *Porter v Latec Finance (Qld) Pty Ltd*. Thereafter, he regularly appeared in the High Court in a diverse range of matters, including banking, defamation, contracts, damages, bankruptcy, constitutional law, criminal law, negligence, local government, restraint of trade, industrial law, companies, trademarks and mining.

Sir Gerard was an active member of the profession. He was a member of the Executive of the Law Council of Australia from 1974 to 1976; the President of the Queensland Bar Association from 1974 to 1976 and President of the Australian Bar Association from 1975 to 1976. He was a parttime member of the Australian Law Reform Commission from 1975 to 1977.

Sir Gerard might properly be described as a giant of the new administrative law which emerged in the mid1970s. After being appointed to the Australian Industrial Court and the Supreme Court of the Australian Capital Territory in 1976 he was made the inaugural President of the Australian Administrative Appeals Tribunal, and the first President of the Administrative Review Council, the cornerstones of this new area of law. At Sir Gerard's swearing in to this Court in 1981, the Attorney General, Mr Peter Durack, acknowledged that the effectiveness of the administrative reforms of the time was 'due in no small way to the fact that [Sir Gerard] identified the major theoretical problems and contributed substantially to their solution'. Sir Gerard regarded the field of administrative law as vitally concerned with the balance between the interests of the citizen and the government, which he regarded as critical to a free society.

He was one of the founding members of the new Federal Court in 1977, and became the first member of that court to be appointed to the High Court. His ascension to the High Court in 1981 was met with universal acclaim. The same applied to his elevation to Chief Justice.

His early years on the Court saw the final abolition of appeals to Privy Council, with the consequence that this Court became the 'sole arbiter of the content of Australian common law and . . . the sole arbiter of the construction of Australian statutes', a matter which he regarded as demanding a 'mindshift' and the end of what he delicately described as 'a period of judicial embarrassment', a reference to the unusual situation where a litigant from a State court could appeal either to the High Court or to the Privy Council.

Sir Gerard's judgments in so many areas of the law reveal a depth of intellect and prescience. I am spared the difficulty of having to identify the most important or memorable of the judgments of Sir Gerard because he referred to them himself in his interview for the oral history project, with the usual caveat that each case that comes before the Court is important. He singled out as being particularly memorable, *The Tasmanian Dam Case, Waltons Stores v Maher*, *Street v Queensland Bar Association*, *Todorovic v Waller*, *Marion's Case* (which he described as the hardest judgment he ever wrote) and, of course, *Mabo (No 2)*. His judgments appear in 48 volumes of the *Commonwealth Law Reports.*

The qualities of the man necessarily informed his judgments. The idea of egalitarianism infused his thinking; he said that '[p]eople are entitled to equal treatment in equal circumstances'. He often referred to the inherent dignity of the individual, to independence and to autonomy. He regarded 'the absence of unjustified discrimination, the peaceful possession of one's property, the benefit of natural justice, and immunity from retrospective and unreasonable operation of laws' as of critical importance. His recourse to these fundamental values was not, as he put it, an invitation to 'unstructured idiosyncrasy'; rather, he saw them as values which served to explicate and illuminate the common law, tempered by the need for the law to develop incrementally and in accordance with precedent, the judicial method and the separation of powers. Unprincipled judicial discretion was anathema to him. What was necessary was consistency and predictability.

As to his conception of this Court and its place in our society, I can do no better than to cite Sir Gerard himself:

> I think its role is vital. It's vital to the rule of law in every sense, that is, in maintaining the law in a coherent and relevant state, in ensuring the independence and impartiality of the judiciary, and in applying our *Constitution* and the settled law of the Commonwealth in a way that gives people their assurance of continuity with the necessary amount of change to deal with changing social conditions.

He observed at the ceremonial sitting on the occasion of his retirement that:

> it is for the service of the people that the courts are created and perform their functions. The courts sit in public, think and write

> in private, then publish to all the world their decisions and their reasons. No other branch of government responds so unfailingly to every application within its jurisdiction nor gives so adequate an explanation of the reasons for its decisions. The courts must be available to serve the litigants by quelling their disputes, else raw power prevails untrammelled by the rule of law.

He later spoke of his enjoyment of life on the Court, referring to the variety of the work and the intellectual stimulation it provided. He derived a real sense of satisfaction from producing judgments. In the days before his death, reflecting on his 17 years at the Court with his son, Father Frank Brennan, he said, 'I loved every minute of it.'

His energies were not devoted solely to the judicial task: his extracurial writings and speeches were legion and continued to be so after his departure from the Court. Sir Gerard remained active in the law after his retirement, sitting on the Hong Kong Court of Final Appeal from 2000 to 2012 and the Supreme Court of Fiji from 1999 to 2000.

His achievements were recognised by his being made a Knight Commander of the British Empire and a Companion of the Order of Australia. He was conferred with Honorary Doctorates of Law, an Honorary Doctorate of Letters, and Honorary Doctorates of the University from a number of universities including Trinity College Dublin, the Universities of Queensland and Melbourne, the Australian National University, the University of New South Wales and the University of Technology Sydney. He was Foundation Scientia Professor of Law of the University of New South Wales and served as Chancellor of the University of Technology Sydney from 1999 to 2005.

In addition to these accolades, Sir Gerard was held in the highest esteem by the legal profession, and he was respected by his colleagues. He valued collegiality and enjoyed the company of and discussions with his colleagues. Sir William Deane says of Sir Gerard that:

> he was the truly ideal member of a collegiate Bench. He was always conscious of the importance of the proper and effective functioning of our courts in the community and nation which they exist to serve. In addition to the scope of his own intelligence, knowledge and insight, he was invariably respectful of the views of others, and extraordinarily generous in his desire and willingness to share, to communicate, to listen and to confer.

Sir Gerard was a model of judicial patience and courtesy. His achievements and his qualities as a judge would influence many lawyers, including Queensland lawyers of my and Justice Keane's generation. Sir

Gerard made an enduring contribution to Australian law and thus to the Australian community, its peace, order and good government. He will be remembered as an exemplary judge. The Court extends its sympathies to his children Frank, Madeline, Anne, Tom, Margaret, Paul and Bernadette, and to his grandchildren and greatgrandchildren.

---

1. This sitting took place in the High Court in Canberra on 18 August 2022.

INDEX

References in italics indicate photographs

www.ingramcontent.com/pod-product-compliance
Ingram Content Group UK Ltd.
Pitfield, Milton Keynes, MK11 3LW, UK
UKHW020259051026
15470UKWH00024B/1842/J

9 781923 224704